The Grammar of Good Intentions

The Grammar of Good Intentions

Race and the Antebellum Culture of Benevolence

SUSAN M. RYAN

CORNELL UNIVERSITY PRESS

Ithaca & London

A version of chapter 2 first appeared as "Misgivings: Melville, Race, and the Ambiguities of Benevolence," *American Literary History* 12, no. 4 (2000): 685–712. Reprinted by permission of Oxford University Press.

A version of chapter 5 and portions of the epilogue first appeared as "Charity Begins at Home: Stowe's Antislavery Novels and the Forms of Benevolent Citizenship," *American Literature* 72, no. 4 (2000): 751–82. Reprinted by permission of Duke University Press.

First published 2003 by Cornell University Press

Printed in the United States of America

Library of Congress Cataloging-in-Publication Data

Ryan, Susan M.
    The grammar of good intentions : race and the antebellum culture of benevolence / Susan M. Ryan.
        p. cm.
Includes bibliographical references and index.
    ISBN 0-8014-3955-8 (cloth : alk. paper)
1. American literature—19th century—History and criticism.   2. Race relations—United States—History—19th century.   3. Benevolence—Social aspects—United States.   4. Race relations in literature.
5. Benevolence in literature.   6. Racism in literature.   7. Race in literature.   I. Title.
    PS217.R28R93 2003
    810.9'355—dc21

                                2003002041

Cornell University Press strives to use environmentally responsible suppliers and materials to the fullest extent possible in the publishing of its books. Such materials include vegetable-based, low-VOC inks and acid-free papers that are recycled, totally chlorine-free, or partly composed of nonwood fibers. For further information, visit our website at www.cornellpress.cornell.edu.

Cloth printing   10 9 8 7 6 5 4 3 2 1

*To Mary Josephine Ryan,
who gives benevolence
a good name*

Contents

Illustrations

Acknowledgments

It would be impossible to complete a book on the complications of benevolence without becoming wary of my own good intentions. That said, these investigations haven't made me equivalently suspicious of my gratitude for the assistance and intellectual companionship that my mentors, colleagues, and students have provided. Philip Gura, who supported this project from its inception, deserves my warmest thanks. His patience in the early stages and faith in the work overall were invaluable, as is his ongoing friendship. My debt to Bob Levine's scholarship is made clear throughout the book; I also thank him for his kind encouragement, for astute revision suggestions, and for his willingness to answer my most arcane questions. Over the years, dozens of people provided research leads and critical insights or commented on work in progress. I especially wish to thank William Andrews, Matthew Biberman, Marc Bousquet, Bob Cantwell, Charles Capper, Patricia Crain, Elizabeth Dillon, Leigh Edwards, Susan Griffin, Glenn Hendler, Robert Johnstone, Heather Julien, Joy Kasson, Laurie Maffly-Kipp, Laura Mielke, James Peterson, Sarah Robbins, Jim Ryan, Jill Swiencicki, and Etsuko Taketani. Tony Mick's expert research assistance late in the process preserved my sanity. Sheri Englund, my editor at Cornell, was unfailingly helpful, not to mention efficient, while anonymous readers for the Press and for various journals helped me to refine the project and saved me from any number of missteps. I'm grateful for their careful and challenging readings.

My involvement with two writing groups has made this process more collaborative and less lonely than I could have imagined. My thanks to Alleen Barber, Karen Chandler, Anne Eckman, Jessica Fields, Ben Hufbauer, Nancy Jesser, Carol Mattingly, and Michelle Mouton. Their critiques and suggestions, not to mention the richness of the work they've shared with me, have shaped my writing at every stage.

For financial assistance and timely votes of confidence, I thank the Charlotte Newcombe Foundation, the Graduate School of the University of North Carolina at Chapel Hill, the American Antiquarian Society, the Library Company of Philadelphia, and the Office of the Vice President for Research at the University of Louisville. My department chairs, Debra Journet and Dennis Hall, have been most supportive. I was fortunate, too, in being able to draw on the expertise of many librarians. In particular, I wish to thank Phillip Lapsansky, Jim Green, and Cornelia King at the Library Company of Philadelphia; Caroline Sloat, Laura Wasowicz, Joanne Chaison, Marie Lamoureux, Georgia Barnhill, and Tom Knoles at the American Antiquarian Society; and Delinda Buie at the University of Louisville. Thanks also to the editors of *American Literature* and *American Literary History,* Houston Baker and Gordon Hutner, for the opportunity to publish early versions of chapters 2 and 5. Duke University Press and Oxford University Press have kindly granted permission to reprint.

The generosity of my friends and family has been overwhelming. Drew Curtis, Beth Schultz, and Teresa Roberts housed and entertained me while I did research in New England, helping to remind me that there's life outside of academe. Old and new friends in Louisville, especially Dana Todd, Leigh Viner, and Beth Willey, provided excellent company and badly needed diversion. Angela Ryan gave much encouragement and thousands of frequent flyer miles to the cause, sending me to a number of conferences and libraries. Marty Ryan identified some of the personal investments animating the book. For that, and for his ongoing support, I'm grateful. Bill Ryan, retired engineer and remodeling hobbyist, improved my house while I read and wrote. And the younger Bill Ryan helped me to think about need and responsibility in ways that extend beyond academic inquiry.

My most significant debts are also the most personal. Brian Gallup's presence has sustained me throughout this process. His patience, intelligence, and love have proven inexhaustible. Sara Gallup, who lived with us at a crucial juncture, helped more than she knew. Finally, I want to thank my mother, Mary Ryan, to whom this book is dedicated. My love and respect for her mark every page.

SUSAN M. RYAN

Louisville, Kentucky

The Grammar of Good Intentions

Toward a Cultural History
of Good Intentions

It is probable that there is no point of duty, where conscientious persons
differ more in opinion, or where they find it more difficult to form discrimi-
nating and decided views, than on the matter of charity.

CATHARINE BEECHER,
A Treatise on Domestic Economy (1841)

To say that antebellum Americans were preoccupied with their moral
identities hardly distinguishes them from individuals of other countries and eras. Indeed, Catharine Beecher's assertion that "the matter
of charity" inspires both contention and indecision seems in no way limited to
her contemporaries. But this apparent universality—what we might call the
banality of goodness—disguises the fact that such identities and the language
that frames them are historically contingent. The competing rhetorics of
benevolence that circulated among mid-nineteenth-century Americans demonstrate this premise with particular force: not only did these conversations draw
on and, in turn, shape the era's social crises, but they also overlapped with and
helped to construct its ideologies of race and nation.

In a period of heated public debate over such issues as slavery, Indian removal, and Irish Catholic immigration, the categories of blackness, Indianness,
and Irishness (or, at times, a generic "foreignness") came to signify, for many
whites, need itself. Blackness in particular seemed to haunt earnest white activists, as the following example attests. In 1863, New Yorker J. D. McKenzie
chaired a "Committee of Merchants" organized for "the relief of colored people" harmed during the city's violent draft riots. In the committee's published
report, he asserted whites' keen interest in the "condition" and "future" of
black Americans; he called this, in fact, "the great question of the age," one
that he believed engaged whites even more than it did the black community
leaders to whom he addressed some of his remarks.[1] In a moment of strange
intensity, he added: "Go where we may[,] the black man does not escape us,
when we sit at our tables surrounded by our families—although you are not
personally present in bodily shape still you are there—when we retire to our

I

chambers you follow us—and even in the sanctuary of the most High God the question will come without bidding to every heart, what shall be done with the negro."[2] For McKenzie, the black man is an absent presence, ghostly and inescapable. He follows the benevolent white speaker into spaces where actual African Americans would typically have been present as servants, not as lurking questioners. This image suggests that, for the charitable merchant, needy black Americans imposed an inappropriate and unwanted degree of intimacy, breaking down the always tenuous boundary between the benevolent and the oppressed. Social problems that invade the domestic realm, as McKenzie's invention does, belie attempts to keep things neatly subdivided, to live out the ideal that sufficient public charity could guarantee the safety, privacy, and moral self-satisfaction of the privileged home.

With a similar fervor, Lydia Maria Child wrote in 1862 of her ongoing efforts on behalf of enslaved Americans: "I *want* to do other things, but *always* there is kneeling before me that everlasting slave, with his hands clasped in supplication."[3] For Child, at this point a veteran of three decades of abolitionist activism, the antislavery movement's emblem of the pleading slave all but comes to life, riveting her attention and circumventing her desire to move on to other causes. The longevity of need produces a certain exasperation here— "that everlasting slave"—even as it positions Child as a figure of authority or intercession, she to whom the supplicant kneels. Her ambivalence, at the same time wanting and not wanting to be begged from, suffuses every word.

McKenzie and Child shared a vision of white benevolence as a compulsion, one arising from and understood by means of a collective racial guilt. I cite them not as outliers—a merchant and an author unaccountably fixated on the inconveniences of conscience—but instead as anxious representatives. Anglo-American reformers and charity workers in the mid-nineteenth century meditated at length on the implications of race, casting slaves and free blacks, for example, as both quintessentially dependent and insidiously threatening.[4] Moreover, injustices toward racial others impeded reformers' attempts to fashion the United States into a benevolent nation. The frequent pronouncements that American poverty was minimal when compared to that of Europe and the praise, both domestic and foreign, of Americans' reformist institutions and organizations were inevitably undercut by the realities of slavery, Indian removal and extermination, and urban race riots. McKenzie's "black man" metaphorically entered thousands of chambers and sanctuaries, insisting that reform-minded Americans notice the gap between their ideals and the national reality.

But if blackness haunted white benevolence at midcentury, then surely benevolence haunted African Americans and other marginalized people as they attempted to assert and define themselves, as individuals and as communities. Most obviously, the figures of the slave and the fugitive troubled northern free blacks, reminding them of their responsibility to those still in bondage as well as of their own precarious freedom, given the frequency with which members of their communities were kidnapped and sold into or returned to slavery. A kind of survivor's guilt inflected antebellum debates among African Americans over emigration and a range of activist and charitable projects. But whites' officiousness proved unsettling as well. The black community leaders to whom McKenzie would address his remarks expressed their gratitude for the relief efforts of the Merchants' Committee, but their comments also betrayed a distinct discomfort with Anglo-Americans' benevolent interventions. These leaders offered the following suggestions, should whites ask themselves "what is the best thing we can do for the colored people?": "Suffer no one to hinder us in any department of well directed industry, give us a fair and open field and let us work out our own destiny, and we ask no more."[5] This invocation of a liberal discourse of equal rights and equal access suggests that McKenzie's model of almsgiving was less than welcome. Harriet Jacobs's conclusion to *Incidents in the Life of a Slave Girl* (1861) illustrates the burden of white benevolence more personally. When the fugitive Linda Brent's northern employer, Mrs. Bruce, buys the former's freedom, she does so in spite of Linda's claim that "being sold from one owner to another seemed too much like slavery" and that "such a great obligation could not be easily cancelled." Linda, once bought, no longer has to fear the machinations of her former owners, but she also finds herself bound to Mrs. Bruce by "gratitude" for a service not of her choosing.[6] The good intentions of her white patron prove as coercive as they are genuine.

Twenty-first-century readers, however much they sympathize with the frustration of Jacobs's narrator, nevertheless tend to find Mrs. Bruce's actions comprehensible—she does not want Linda to suffer further under the threat of reenslavement. But antebellum Americans also used the language of benevolence to argue for a range of interventions that today strike us as pernicious and self-serving. Antislavery activism was figured as a means of doing good unto the "unfortunate" African race, but in the rhetoric of the other side, so was ongoing enslavement. Proslavery forces argued that their actions were benevolent not only because American slavery had brought about the Christianization of Africans but also because members of this "naturally" dependent race fared better under the tutelage of their white owners. Proponents of African colonization, for their part, claimed a transatlantic benevolence: sending former slaves to Liberia would grant those emigrants access to positions of leadership, even as it led to the redemption of native Africans and the peaceful homogenization of the United States. Similarly, some advocates of Indian removal argued that their course of action would bring about the civilization and preservation of native tribes.

Interracial benevolent projects were not the only avenues activists sought. Many white-run charitable organizations, in fact, served only Americans of European descent, while much of the conversation about benevolence overtly addressed differences of class rather than race.[7] Authors of charity texts wondered how the poor might be made to reform their improvident habits or how orphans might best be educated for self-sufficiency. Free African Americans devoted their benevolent energies to intraracial projects as well, focusing on the material needs of their own communities and on the moral reform of their least "respectable" neighbors.[8] Nevertheless, the beliefs and investments that undergirded Americans' interracial efforts suffused benevolent discourse at midcentury even when helper and helped were of the same race or were racially unmarked. All-white schools and orphanages, for example, operated on the assumption that racial mixing might harm the institutions' already disadvantaged charges, while the sufferings of poor Euro-Americans were likened—or, in the case of proslavery rhetoric, opposed—to the condition of slaves. By the antebellum period, slavery loomed so large in the national imagination that it became a key referent in discussions of a range of injustices, from the law's disregard for the rights of married women to the plight of underpaid seamstresses and Irish day laborers.[9] Moreover, the language of degradation and rescue had a distinctly hierarchical and color-coded quality: the ignorant and the destitute required "elevation" out of darkness; "fallen" women benefited from the interventions of the respectable; and the new urban slums were dark spaces into which the light of reform must shine.[10] These habits of speech dovetailed with widely held beliefs about a hierarchy of the races, such that elevation and degradation, privilege and lack, inclusion and exclusion could easily be mapped onto the designations "Anglo-Saxon" and "negro" (or "Indian" or "Celt").

That this rhetoric coexisted with and enabled violent and exploitative acts has left its users vulnerable to accusations of hypocrisy. But such accusations, when made at a significant temporal remove, often entail an unacknowledged presentism, in that they seek to preserve the purity of good intentions as we conceive them—that is, the only intentions that count as good are those that twenty-first-century readers and scholars can endorse. Further, hypocrisy as an object of inquiry inevitably comes up against the inaccessibility of historical actors' private thoughts and self-conceptions. What this introduction's title promises, a history of good intentions, is paradoxical: we cannot know with certainty what these figures *truly* believed they were up to. All we can recover is their words and images, and words and images about them—which is why this book is not so much about good intentions themselves as about the cultural practice of articulating them. Some of the figures I cite likely used benevolent language disingenuously, but the more intriguing possibility is that antebellum Americans' benevolent claims were genuine, that the best of intentions, combined with a particular set of beliefs about race, class, and nation, produced the outcomes we see.[11] Self-interest, in this formulation, is not the opposite of genuine benevolence but rather its complement. The relevant question, then, is how the desire to do good and the language used to describe such desires came to correspond so neatly with self-interest.

The road to hell, it is often said, is paved with good intentions. As this adage suggests, the term has become ironic, standing in for a notion of activism gone awry or for charity as subterfuge. Taking seriously the good intentions of antebellum Americans, by contrast, reconstitutes moral earnestness as a problematic rather than an object of derision. In pursuing that goal, I employ a strategic credulity, one that does not preclude judgment of these figures, but that aims for a more nuanced understanding of them. Such a method allows us to move beyond the question of whether benevolence was progressive or retrograde, in order to consider how authors as disparate as Ralph Waldo Emerson and William Wells Brown and the recording secretaries of the era's many charitable organizations used, shaped, and lived within its rhetorics.

Needy Subjects, Benevolent Citizens

Linking the terms *race* and *nation* has become commonplace in recent years: the formation of the United States as a cultural and political entity now seems inextricable from its history of racial ideologies and injustices. Toni Morrison's oft-cited call to study the Africanist presence in our national culture, one of many late-twentieth-century challenges to the monocultural perspectives of much prior scholarship, has been taken up energetically in literary and cultural studies.[12] The antebellum culture of benevolence, however, has had no such currency. It has sometimes been subsumed (and obscured) within the more familiar category of sentimentalism, a matter to which I will return, but more often it has simply been dismissed as cloying, dull, or hypocritical— a discourse that reflective and astute individuals are assumed to have critiqued from a distance. The field changes considerably, though, if benevolence is understood as a central paradigm in antebellum culture, one that provided Americans with ways of understanding, describing, and constructing their racial and national identities.

Americans' benevolent projects bore the marks of their racial ideologies, as the period's novels, charity society reports, and other texts abundantly demonstrate. But the culture of benevolence also shaped Americans' beliefs about race, just as, in David Roediger's landmark study of white working-class formation, workers' fears of dependence and their adjustment to new work rhythms and modes of discipline contributed to their constructions of white racial identity.[13] What we might call benevolent whiteness emerges here as less self-assured and less admirable than its antebellum proponents claimed. Its champions appropriated the qualities of efficiency, rationality, and circumspection that were becoming central to the era's investments in commerce and professionalization, but they also betrayed their fears of excessive emotion and foolish dispensation of aid. White commentators attributed similarly mixed qualities to the racial others they purported to help, representing them as dangerously dependent at one moment and all too autonomous the next. And while Anglo-Americans figured the nation's nonwhite populations as its most dangerous elements, they also characterized intervention into such lives as whites' greatest opportunity for redemption. Through benevolence, they could claim a caretaking quality that might counterbalance the aggressiveness and expansionism for which they were becoming known.[14]

Racially marginalized groups, on the other hand, worked to revise whites' pronouncements, though they often addressed intraracial concerns as well. Both Native American and African American writers identified, for example, an arrogance and intrusiveness among benevolent whites that they found impossible to overlook. And when the Cherokees critiqued the benevolent claims of Andrew Jackson's proremoval allies or when free African Americans insisted on their ability to make their own way, once whites removed unjust barriers to their success, they were disputing whites' attributions of weakness. Further, for many black authors, intraracial benevolence became integral to community building and to arguments for or against emigration. Their assertions that African Americans were capable of caring for their own people countered widespread (and, increasingly, pseudoscientific) theories of natural black dependence, lassitude, or immaturity. Whether they were pressing for full inclusion within the United States or for the creation of a separate black nation, African Americans' conceptions of benevolence informed how they articulated their collective readiness for civic participation. Thus black commentators participated in a broader national conversation about the shape, character, and composition of the United States, as well as of the nations that might emerge from it. Should benevolent Americans attempt to make this a peacefully multiracial republic? If so, on what terms? Or ought they work toward racial homogeneity by means of (purportedly) benevolent acts?

The mapping of moral onto national identities was a feature of various appeals and controversies, as commentators emphasized that the United States was, in effect, on stage, with God, the rest of the world, Americans themselves, or some combination of the three arrayed to judge its performance. Sometimes this discourse of national morality was overtly self-congratulatory. In arguing for benevolence toward Jewish Americans, for example, the Reverend Reuben Smith proudly asserted that "our own country is the only one that does not labour under the curse of having persecuted the Jews."[15] In other cases, admonition and recrimination took precedence. At the height of the Cherokee removal debates, the antiremoval activist Jeremiah Evarts promised that an "indelible stigma" would be "fixed upon us" if injustices against the Indians were allowed, while George B. Cheever, who would later become a prominent advocate of temperance and abolition, warned readers of the *American Monthly Magazine* that injustice toward Indians might devastate the nation. "We know there is an eternal, indissoluble connection," he wrote, "between national virtue and national prosperity; as there is a connection, equally indissoluble, and terribly certain, between national crime and national misery."[16] In other words, we must do right for our own good. The slavery debates occasioned similarly pointed remarks. Frederick Douglass, in his 1852 speech "What to the Slave Is the Fourth of July?" meditated on the contrast between white Americans' celebration of their own freedom and "the mournful wail of millions! whose chains . . . are . . . rendered more intolerable by the jubilee shouts that reach them." Even the nation's monument to its first president, he insisted, "is built up by the price of human blood." The white antislavery poet Elizabeth Margaret Chandler, years earlier, offered a comparable lament: "Think of our country's glory, / All dimm'd with Afric's tears— / Her broad flag stain'd and gory / With the hoarded guilt of years!"[17]

Race, nation, and benevolence came together with particular force in the construction of U.S. citizenship. Conventionally, benevolence was invoked as one of many responsibilities devolving on those who, by virtue of their sex, race, nativity, and (for a time) ownership of property, enjoyed unquestioned access to civic and political participation. As Linda Kerber has argued, academic analyses of citizenship tend to privilege rights at the expense of responsibilities. I follow her in emphasizing that citizenship places demands on individuals even as it offers them certain protections and privileges, although the nineteenth-century citizen's responsibility to be benevolent was not legally enforceable, as were the more discrete obligations Kerber treats (e.g., military service or jury duty).[18] For white male citizens, the primary addressees of the admonitions quoted above, shoring up the moral authority of the nation was considered a matter of civic duty, one closely aligned, not incidentally, with the prevention of class and race warfare.[19] While their status as citizens was presumed, their benevolence apparently had to be coaxed, advertised, and sometimes redirected. Such "full" citizens, however, as the political scientist Rogers Smith explains, formed but a subset of the "intellectually puzzling, legally confused, and politically charged and contested status" represented by the term *citizen* more broadly conceived.[20] Native-born white women, for example, were generally acknowledged to be U.S. citizens in the antebellum period, even though they were excluded from any number of the rights and duties of their male counterparts. Benevolence offered them a means of participating in civic life without challenging the era's strictures against their more overt involvement in the political sphere (by voting, holding office, or speaking in public to mixed audiences).[21] For these women, benevolent activism was the very substance of their citizenship.

For those excluded to varying degrees from the civic life of the nation, benevolent citizenship took on an aspirational quality. As Matthew Frye Jacobson has written, U.S. conceptions of citizenship were predicated on a "racially recognized 'fitness for self-government,'" one that identified the supposedly natural dependence of African Americans as just cause for their exclusion.[22] Within the logic of the era, then, benevolent agency, which entailed both freedom from dependence and the capacity to aid others, became available as an argument for citizenship. A gendered version of this move surfaced in the appeals of post–Civil War woman's rights activists, who claimed that women's participation in such benevolent projects as abolition qualified them for suffrage.[23] For African Americans and their advocates, blacks' achievement of benevolent agency shored up arguments against various forms of exclusion, from the civic effacement of slavery to the literal deportation of African colonization. In the process, they shifted the burden of proof for citizenship from the conventional question of who one is to the more fluid register of what one does.

This dynamic model posits an intersubjective or relational citizenship, a designation understood by means of lines of responsibility among variously positioned Americans and, crucially, affirmed through others' acknowledgment of those ties. As such, it works against the abstracted individualism on which most traditional conceptions of U.S. citizenship have relied.[24] A model of citizenship based on benevolent activism suggests at least the possibility of greater inclusiveness, of structures that bind individual political subjects to one another rather than each primarily to the state. Such a reconfiguration is not necessarily egalitarian, as my analysis of Harriet Beecher Stowe's version will show, nor does it unseat secure white citizens as judges of others' legitimacy, but it does challenge dominant antebellum notions of political personhood.

My emphasis on citizenship and national identity should not be taken to suggest that benevolence was somehow divorced from religion, its more widely acknowledged foundation. Religious beliefs and prejudices were intertwined with questions of national formation throughout the period, turning up, for example, in the widespread suspicion of Roman Catholics' divided loyalties and in the inclusion of Bible literacy as a cornerstone of civic education.[25] Beyond such overt national concerns, the U.S. culture of benevolence had strong ties to religious doctrines, practices, and organizations. Specific sectarian differences, however, were of limited concern within this culture. By the antebellum period, Protestant leaders, especially those who ran urban benevolent organizations, tended to play down such distinctions in order to create, in Charles Foster's terms, a "united evangelical front." Paul Boyer explains this development as an attempt to combat the perceived threat of Roman Catholicism, especially as practiced by recent immigrants.[26] In keeping with this interdenominational strategy, by the mid-1830s the officers and governing board of the American Tract Society (ATS), the era's foremost publisher of didactic literature, included members of "thirteen different denominations."[27] In this book I adopt the pan-Protestantism of mainstream antebellum benevolence in order to foreground the ways in which the language of benevolence suffused public discourse beyond the boundaries of any particular sect—and, indeed, beyond the boundaries of formal charitable organizations.

Defining Benevolence

The term *benevolence* is rarely used these days. When it does appear, particularly in scholarly contexts, it is handled with the same suspicion accorded to *good intentions*. The postcolonial theorist Gayatri Spivak, for example, has used *benevolence* as a synonym for a well-intentioned misapprehension, a blind spot that its possessor must be prodded to recognize.[28] Historians, too, have often defined the term narrowly and disparagingly. Anne Boylan, in her study of early nineteenth-century women's organizations, associates benevolence with conservative, quietistic efforts to spread Christianity or to alleviate suffering on a small scale, without altering broader social structures. She categorizes as either reformist or feminist groups and individuals with more progressive or disruptive agendas. Thus Boylan remarks that "one was either a benevolent lady or a reformer, seldom both."[29] These distinctions would have made little sense to nineteenth-century Americans. Certainly they perceived significant differences in scope and political orientation among organizations and individuals, but benevolence, for them, was a much broader concept—one that activists across the political spectrum engaged, applauded, and argued over. Frederick Douglass, for instance, hardly an advocate of the existing social order, used the term *benevolence* approvingly in an 1852 speech, associating it with a principled activism in which American churches had failed to engage; more effusively, in the long dedication to *My Bondage and My Freedom,* he praised Gerrit Smith for "his genius and benevolence."[30]

I have used in this book the broader notion of benevolence common among antebellum authors, conceiving of it as a contested paradigm rather than a delimited and conservative set of beliefs and practices. And, like those authors, I sometimes substitute related terms, including *philanthropy, humanity,* and, most often, *charity.* In the mid-nineteenth century, *benevolence* was what Raymond Williams has called a "keyword," a term that defies brief or singular definition, engaging instead a complex field of "ideas and values."[31] The term and its variants were everywhere, appearing not only where one might expect, in sermons, tract literature, domestic fiction, and the titles and publications of myriad charitable organizations, but also in political pamphlets, secular periodicals, and the writings of now-canonical literary authors. Antebellum Americans themselves commented on this ubiquity. South Carolina Congressman Henry L. Pinckney, for example, asserted in his 1835 address to Charleston's Methodist Benevolent Society that "the theme of Benevolence . . . is destitute of novelty." But, he added, "it is not, therefore, deficient in importance or in interest."[32] If, for Pinckney, the topic's familiarity presented no barrier to his earnest disquisition, for others the conventionality of benevolence made it an object of parody. In 1839, a Boston publisher issued a pamphlet titled *Constitution of the Anti-Bell-Ringing Society,* which claimed that its members "have the same right to unite and form an Anti-Bell-Ringing Society, as others of our fellow citizens have to unite together and form Anti-Slavery, Anti-Swearing, Anti-Smoking, Anti-Tea-and-Coffee-Drinking . . . and other Moral and Benevolent Societies already in existence." The rest of the document lampoons the cumbersome, self-important rules that benevolent organizations adopted. The September 1853 issue of *Harper's* offered a less jovial spin on the era's abundance of benevolent rhetoric, comparing the realities of crime and corruption to "that flood of noble sentiment which is daily issuing in so many streams from the press, the newspaper, the public lecture, and the literary discourse."[33] While the suggestion of collective failure or hypocrisy was commonplace among commentators on benevolence, this opposition between language and "real" problems undercuts a central premise of much of the era's rhetoric—that words and social effects are intimately linked.

At midcentury, then, Americans agreed that benevolence was widely invoked but reached no consensus as to what the term meant or how credibly it could be applied to particular projects. The historian Conrad Edick Wright has claimed that, for New Englanders of the eighteenth and early nineteenth centuries, *benevolence* meant "wishing good," while the active manifestations of those good feelings were called *beneficence.* Some employed this distinction as late as the 1850s, though they often added a third term, *active benevolence,* in place of *beneficence,* which came more and more to mean simply almsgiving.[34] But others blurred the distinctions earlier, imbuing *benevolence* with both contemplative and active elements. Webster's 1828 *American Dictionary* offered "good will"—the literal translation of the word's Latin roots—as its primary meaning but included the active element in its second definition.[35] The term took on gendered connotations as well. Bruce Dorsey has argued that in the antebellum period benevolence was increasingly associated with a natural feminine compassion. Nevertheless, masculine investment in the culture of benevolence persisted, as the many men quoted in this study demonstrate.[36] And antebellum authors described both men and women as having a benevolent appearance, insisting that goodwill left its mark on the body, especially the face.

More pressing than these variations in usage, however, were the disagreements over what forms "goodwill" and "good actions" ought to take. The ubiquity of benevolent rhetoric signaled its instability; that is, antebellum Americans so often wrote about benevolence because they were engaged in ongoing and at times vitriolic conflicts over its meaning. For the era's most conservative commentators, social inequality was a divinely ordained and permanent state, the purpose of which was to spark industry and ambition, and to provide opportunities "of doing good to others by acts of encouragement, beneficence and charity." Benevolent individuals, according to this view, should work to soften the effects of poverty but should not attempt to eradicate inequality itself, for in doing so they would eliminate their own *"means of moral improvement."*[37] Benevolence here is a spiritual heuristic, one whose importance lies in its effects on the agent rather than the recipient. Others resisted such complacency, conceiving of benevolence instead as a means of bringing about more thoroughgoing social and economic transformations.

At issue as well were the specific forms that benevolent activism might take. The Unitarian minister Andrew P. Peabody, frustrated by his peers' dissensus on the question, called such conflicts "excuses for the neglect of benevolent efforts" and elaborated on the most common of them: "Says one: 'individual effort is worse than useless. The principle of association lies at the foundation of all effective charity. . . . ' Says another: 'trust not the judgment of large bodies of men. The funds of benevolent societies are always either squandered or misapplied. If you would do good, seek out your own objects.' " The era's broader tensions between association and autonomous action, not surprisingly, infused these debates. But the choice of charity's "objects," as Peabody recognized, was at least as controversial:

> Would you aid in the general diffusion of knowledge? You may be raising men of humble powers above their proper rank and callings. . . . Would you forward the plan of African colonization? You may be riveting the chains and augmenting the sufferings of the slaves left in the country. Would you join the ranks of those who aim at the immediate abolition of slavery? You are perhaps preparing rapine and slaughter for the whole slave-holding population. . . . Would you give your money or goods to feed the poor? They may expend your gifts in the means of dissipation, and be made more wretched, not more comfortable, by your charity.[38]

No well-intended act, it seems, was utterly free from harmful consequences. But this confusion, according to Peabody and most of his contemporaries, did not remove the moral obligation to do good; one still had to find a sphere of action that seemed, if not blameless, at least defensible. The anonymous author of an 1837 pamphlet titled *The Friend* also noted the ambiguity of benevolence, asserting that any effort to do good could result in some collateral harm: "To be misapprehended . . . , by some, is the inevitable lot of all who address their fellow-men on any subject of interest. In this essay I would do only *good*. But that cannot be. Man has no such power nor privilege."[39] Here it is not only the complications of charitable acts but the slipperiness of language that hinders or renders impure the work of benevolence.

These conflicts pervaded antebellum print culture. Contributors to antislavery newspapers mocked the benevolent claims of slaveholders; ministers, in their printed sermons, exhorted readers to accept certain definitions of benevolence over others; charity society officers used their annual reports to assert proper means of expressing benevolence and to warn against those means they deemed dangerous; and novelists created fictions in which the values of charity were realized, betrayed, or reconceived. A final example attests to the contentiousness, and to the textuality, of benevolence. An 1836 pamphlet addressed "To the Christian Public" praises the charitable efforts of a German immigrant named Frederica Misca and encourages the donations that will enable her to continue her work. However, Misca's trustworthiness was not universally accepted. Not only does the text incorporate a number of testimonials asserting, a bit too energetically, her probity and defending her against "calumny and misrepresentation," but the American Antiquarian Society's copy also includes a handwritten note at the bottom of the first page referring to Misca as "a gross Impostor and vagrant Beggar."[40] This reader was sufficiently outraged by Misca's benevolent practices to add his or her own vehement commentary, evidence of the extent to which antebellum Americans waged their war over meanings on the printed page.

Benevolence in Print

According to historians of the book, antebellum Americans witnessed a rapid expansion in the range, volume, and availability of printed materials, in large part owing to cheaper printing technologies and to improved distribution networks.[41] Not only did a tremendous amount of commentary on benevolence appear in print, but benevolent societies, especially Bible and tract societies, also helped to bring about print's expansion by adopting new technologies and devising new ways to inundate Americans with morally elevating reading material, much of it accompanied by instructive illustrations.[42] As testimony to this faith in the power of word and image, the ATS used symbols that explicitly conjoined textual production and notions of divine sanction and moral enlightenment. The main image from the society's certificate of membership features an angel extending a scroll toward a young printer, who leans across his press, hands outstretched. The printer thus takes his place with Moses and the authors of the gospels as a direct recipient and transmitter of sacred text. Inset images of a man distributing tracts door-to-door and of a young girl reading complete the cycle, from production through distribution and consumption.

As the ATS's illustrations suggest, producing, distributing, and reading the right kinds of printed matter were, for many Americans, interlocking forms of benevolence. Families and individuals read moral books in their homes; Sunday-school students received books and tracts as rewards for high achievement or good behavior; and young people were admonished to make books available to the unfortunate. As Lydia Sigourney's popular *Girl's Reading-Book* asserted, "to distribute useful and pious books among those who are able to read, is an excellent form of bounty."[43] With a similar self-assurance, the antislavery movement pursued its mission of moral suasion through print, producing and disseminating gift books, newspapers, and tracts, many of them replete with graphic descriptions and images of violence against enslaved people calculated to engender outraged activism. Abolitionist children's literature especially foregrounded the benevolent possibilities of print. To cite but one example, Hannah Townsend's *Anti-Slavery Alphabet* combined literacy instruction with such moral lessons. "A is an Abolitionist," Townsend wrote, "A man who wants to free / The wretched slave—and give to all / An equal liberty." "B," the text continued,

is a Brother with a skin
Of somewhat darker hue,
But in our heavenly Father's sight,
He is as dear as you.[44]

Learning to read, for Townsend and her allies, involved learning benevolence.

Works we typically categorize as literary, such as Melville's "Benito Cereno," Stowe's *Uncle Tom's Cabin*, Emerson's "Self-Reliance," and Douglass's *My Bondage and My Freedom*, are best understood when placed in con-

1. From the American Tract Society's certificate of membership. Courtesy, American Antiquarian Society.

versation with this expansive print culture. As a result, it becomes clear that Melville's attention to the epistemologies of blackness and need is not his singular obsession but instead gives literary form to questions that his contemporaries also considered pressing. Emerson's insistence that autonomous manhood depends on rejecting the dictates of mainstream benevolence stands in contrast to the antebellum men I cite who embraced benevolent identities. At the same time, his often-quoted question, "Are they *my* poor," comes to seem quite conventional in light of contemporary debates over the limits of benevolent responsibility. And Douglass's struggles with the Garrisonians emerge as part of a network of interracial benevolent relations, in which the "helped" resisted in various ways the authority and the attributions of their benefactors. Most important, this reconstruction shows that the ambivalent representations we find in the work of our now-canonical authors were not distanced reactions to a monolithic cult of benevolence. Rather, literary authors took part in rhetorically complex debates within the broader culture over how good intentions ought to be expressed and enacted.

Continuities and Boundaries

This book is bounded chronologically by the Indian removal debates of the late 1820s and the Civil War, both conflicts over the literal shape and membership of the nation. As such, they provide apt temporal limits for a consideration of the relationships among benevolent discourse, racial ideologies, and national identities. But the culture of benevolence did not suddenly emerge in the Jacksonian period. On the contrary, the related projects of defining social responsibility and articulating particular moral identities have a long history in American culture. An originary, though perhaps overly mythologized, moment is John Winthrop's claim in "A Modell of Christian Charitie" that the Puritans' new colony would be "as a Citty upon a Hill." Winthrop's image is both a promise and a threat: the emigrants he addressed would form a better society for all to see and emulate, or their iniquity would be equally broadcast, "made a story and a by-word through the world."[45] As a number of historians have argued, the Puritans did not conceive of themselves as establishing a separate American identity; instead, they set out to construct a better Englishness, one that the unregenerate English across the Atlantic would be forced to recognize.[46] But their sense of a collective moral identity subject to evaluation by a judgmental world would be reinvoked by antebellum Americans, many of whom saw, especially in the institution of slavery, the nation's failure to live up to its ideals. While Tocqueville remarked that "the American's heart easily inclines toward benevolence" and Dickens (though he elsewhere criticized American cruelty) asserted that Boston's "public institutions and charities" were "as nearly perfect as the most considerate wisdom, benevolence, and humanity can make them," English abolitionists and other international critics made sure that Americans did not forget their moral failings.[47] The American city upon a hill was threatened not so much by unbelievers or outsiders as by the suffering of its own residents.

Eighteenth-century intellectual and theological currents had a more immediate bearing on antebellum benevolence. According to Joseph Conforti, nineteenth-century reformers and missionaries were strongly influenced by the notion, developed most influentially through the writings of Jonathan Edwards and Samuel Hopkins, of a disinterested benevolence—that is, a benevolence to "Being in general," as Edwards phrased it, that seeks no individual recompense.[48] *An Account of the Life of the Late Reverend Mr. David Brainerd . . .* (better known as the *Life of Brainerd*), a text Edwards constructed from the diary of an especially devout, self-sacrificing, and short-lived missionary, became a touchstone for nineteenth-century Americans invested in the work of benevolence, serving to revivify and disseminate eighteenth-century notions of doing good.[49] Critical, too, was a shift in dominant conceptions of God. Eschewing older Puritan views of a vengeful deity, Hopkins and others in the New Divinity movement conceived of God as fundamentally benevolent toward human beings, who would in turn be responsible for extending that benevolence to others.[50] As Lemuel Haynes, a black minister who embraced and advanced New Divinity theology, remarked in an 1805 sermon, "the people of God consider themselves as active instruments to bring about his holy designs."[51] Although most nineteenth-century Protestants would reject the strict Calvinism of Hopkins and his cohort, they embraced this view of a kinder, gentler God whose will would be carried out on earth by the benevolent faithful.

Antebellum benevolence had a more secular genealogy as well, in what is often called the history of affect. As Karen Halttunen has shown, nineteenth-century reform culture emerged from a broader humanitarianism that had developed during the previous century, a new set of attitudes toward suffering that was negotiated largely through the emerging culture of sensibility, whose hero, " 'the man of feeling,' . . . [possessed a] tender-hearted susceptibility to the torments of others."[52] As suffering came to seem less inevitable and acceptable, its prevention grew ever more urgent and, Halttunen claims, its infliction more taboo and therefore more erotic, a matter to which I attend at various points in the book. These changes owe much to the writings of David Hume, Francis Hutcheson, and especially Adam Smith, who developed a notion of spectatorial sympathy, an imaginative self-extension prompted most readily by seeing another in pain or, as readers of sentimental literature would find, by creating a mental image based on elaborate description. Antebellum proponents of benevolence endlessly pondered those extensions and, like their eighteenth-century counterparts, worried over the implications: Would they undermine a healthy (and prosperous) individualism? Did they promote too much social leveling? And were they ultimately just opportunities for a voyeuristic self-indulgence?[53]

Clearly the discourse of benevolence transcends conventional periodization.[54] Mid-nineteenth-century commentators engaged in many of the same debates as their eighteenth-century predecessors and invested in similar ideologies of responsibility and moral identity. Further, some historians have cited the 1810s and 1820s, rather than the decades immediately prior to the Civil War, as the heyday of Anglo-American religious benevolence, pointing out that benevolent societies were most frequently founded during those years.[55] African Americans, for their part, began in the late eighteenth century to form mutual aid and fraternal societies that were structured by benevolent and communitarian ideals.[56] Nor do such continuities end with the Civil War. Postbellum phenomena, from the efforts of the Freedmen's Bureau to the writings of reformers like Frances E. W. Harper, Jane Addams, and Jacob Riis, relied on the intersecting rhetorics of benevolence and race or ethnicity. Nevertheless, the distinctiveness of the antebellum period bears exploring. In the decades before the Civil War, Americans' beliefs about and representations of doing good became intertwined to an unprecedented extent with considerations of racial difference, racial injustice, and the terms of national inclusion.

Again, such linkages were not born in the antebellum period. John Saillant has shown that earlier commentators, including the white theologian Timothy Dwight and the black minister Richard Allen, brought together considerations of benevolence and racial injustice, while the period between 1790 and 1820 saw the development of an antislavery discourse that eroticized black male bodies and "represented intimacy between a black man and a white man with the sentimentalist vocabulary of benevolence." Julie Ellison has noted that, by the turn of the nineteenth century, the concept of sensibility, closely related to benevolence, was firmly associated with antislavery positions. Christopher Castiglia has argued that, in the early republic, "defining the interests of white America (in fact, defining 'whiteness' as the grounds of American interest) became a subtle but significant duty of benevolent organizations."[57] But the increasing salience of racially charged social and political issues from the late 1820s onward—including slavery, Indian removal, immigration, and urbanization—energized the language of benevolence in new ways, even as the period's pronounced attention to social problems informed the ways in which Americans talked about race. And while racial injustice clearly continued after the Civil War, the eradication of chattel slavery and the legal declaration, if not the reality, of black (male) citizenship significantly altered the terms of benevolent discourse.[58] The antebellum period invites discrete attention because it saw the construction of a particular kind of benevolent racism, a set of beliefs about racial difference and racial policy that gained strength and widespread attention in the context of the era's reform projects—and that have reverberated in U.S. social policy ever since.

Benevolence and Sentimentalism

As their common roots in eighteenth-century notions of sympathy and sensibility suggest, the cultures of benevolence and sentimentalism overlapped significantly. Most obviously, many who deployed the language of benevolence also used sentimental strategies. According to these authors and activists, benevolence—both as a state of mind and a set of practices—was most effectively prompted by means of sentimental identification, often across lines of race, class, and region. Stowe's *Uncle Tom's Cabin,* to cite an obvious example, recounts the sufferings of slave mothers whose children have been taken from them. By meditating on the loss or potential loss of his or her own children and by imaginatively occupying the slave mother's anguished position, a reader would experience a bond with slavery's victims and would, theoretically at least, be spurred to antislavery action. This paradigmatic example shows how sentimentalism's "allusions to loss," as Marianne Noble has written, "function as a unifying mechanism."[59] Benevolent discourse shared with sentimentalism an emphasis on such familial bonds of responsibility and affection, through which other kinds of social responsibility might be understood. But the culture of benevolence also accommodated a distinctly and deliberately antisentimental strain that emphasized bureaucratic and rationalized processes for determining whom to aid and to what extent. These elements, early instances of a professionalizing social work, rejected sympathetic identification altogether as untrustworthy, espousing instead a set of investigative strategies fueled more by suspicion than by sentiment. Charity society reports, children's stories, and newspaper articles warned readers that sympathetic identification led to unwise giving, as unscrupulous and deceptive supplicants manipulated the emotions of unwary donors.

In the 1999 article "What Is Sentimentality?" June Howard urged scholars to rethink the conflation of sentimentalism and domesticity, claiming that "to fail to distinguish the two categories is to become unable to examine the complex historical process that weaves them together."[60] This book argues for an analogous reconsideration of sentimentalism and benevolence. For much of the twentieth century, the terms were similarly devalued. Both were associated with inauthenticity, manipulativeness, and laziness; taken together, they represented for many a convergence of bad art and bad activism. But the marked attention to sentimentalism in the past twenty years or so has not prompted a recuperation of benevolence. If anything, the prominence of sentimentalism in academic discourse has led to its more thorough dismissal.[61] For many, the power differentials and hierarchies that characterize so many of the era's benevolent practices make it tempting to cordon off benevolence as "what's wrong with sentimentalism," naming it as the site of sentimentalism's most egregious appropriations and inequities. More neutrally, because benevolence has been so thoroughly subsumed within sentimentalism, we tend to think we understand how the former operates and fail to give it more specific attention. I am claiming, on the contrary, that a thorough analysis of the language of benevolence can help us to understand the effects of a key tension within sentimentalism, and so within antebellum culture as a whole: the inevitable incompleteness of sympathetic identification. Moreover, benevolence and sentimentalism locate trust and credibility very differently, a divergence crucial to the investigation of nineteenth-century social activism and its textual representations.

To think through sentimentalism's common ground with benevolence, it makes sense to turn, briefly, to their shared eighteenth-century genealogy. According to Adam Smith's model of sympathetic identification, expounded in his *Theory of Moral Sentiments* (1759), the imagination enables us to conceive of the tortures of "our brother . . . upon the rack," to think of "ourselves enduring all the same torments." Consequently, "we enter as it were into his body, and become in some measure the same person with him, and thence form some idea of his sensations, and even feel something which, though weaker in degree, is not altogether unlike them." This imaginative occupation of the other undergirds sentimentalism's extensions of feeling as well as the acts of benevolence that follow from them. But Smith's text is a problematic point of departure, insofar as its digressions and self-qualifying statements adumbrate the conflicts that made sentimentalism so troubling for antebellum Americans. Smith claims that we erase distinction through acts of imagination—"enter[ing] into" the sufferer's "body" and "becom[ing] in some measure the same person with him"—but he then backs away from this melding, suggesting only that we "form *some idea* of his sensations," something "not *altogether unlike* them."[62] This tension between the erasure of difference and its stubborn resurgence animates much scholarly work on sentimentalism and sympathy. As Glenn Hendler has noted,

> To critics from a variety of perspectives . . . the politics of sympathy is fatally flawed by its drive to turn all differences into equivalences, all analogies into coincidences. The limits of such a politics of affect become apparent when it comes up against any significant cultural or experiential difference between the subject and object of its paradigmatic act of sympathetic identification: if I have to *be* like you and *feel* like you in order for you to feel *for* me, sympathy reaches its limits at the moment you are reminded that I am not quite like you.

"Still worse," Hendler adds, "sentimentalism can respond to difference by attempting to negate or suppress it," a gesture that critics of sentimentalism's politics, in the nineteenth century and today, have rigorously interrogated.[63]

Examining how sentimental identification works in the context of antebellum benevolence provides one way of thinking through this tension between imagined—or enforced—sameness and irrepressible difference. Most antebellum commentators agreed that some sort of common ground between helper and helped was critical to the practice of benevolence: "charity begins at home" and "love thy neighbor" were among their favorite catchphrases. One problem, of course, lay in determining how that connection ought to be defined and which commonalities ought to be privileged. But such emphasis on connectedness, and on the extensions of sympathy it would seem to impel, was also at odds with the hierarchical structures and distancing rhetorics of benevolent activism. Within benevolent relations, this conflict had a certain utility. For example, a middle-class woman may have been especially touched by the sufferings of a poor mother who sewed all day in dim light to provide for hungry children, because she could imagine her own horror at seeing her much-loved children go hungry. And yet it is the seamstress's difference, her abjection, that prompts a donation.[64]

The play of identification and difference is foundational to antebellum benevolence in at least two ways. In an immediate sense, the person in a position to help must perceive the desperation of the supplicant in order to be willing to give. Whatever degree of sympathetic identification may be at work—and to read nineteenth-century accounts, such extensions could become quite intense—there had to be a concomitant recognition of difference, something that made one social actor the helper and the other a proper recipient of that help. If the identification worked too well, the would-be helper might herself come to feel more desperate than generous. In the realm of "active benevolence," identification could only go so far before it risked dismantling the larger project.

This conflict resonates beyond the immediate charitable encounter. The explicit purpose of much antebellum benevolence is the elevation of the helped, their reformation (not surprisingly) in the image of their benefactors: missionaries sought to bring the unchurched into Christian communion, while home visitors urged the poor to adopt middle-class standards of cleanliness and domestic management. But a too-thorough identification between helper and helped risked a degree of social leveling that most donors would have resisted, as well as the loss of the destitute other against whom the benevolent defined themselves. The impossibility of complete sympathetic identification, then, is a phenomenon integral to what sentimental benevolence is and how it works. The simultaneous erasure and persistence of difference facilitates both the sentimental bond that creates the desire to give and the maintenance of hierarchy that suggests that such giving is safe, that it does not threaten the identity or the status of the giver, that it does not, ultimately, make helper and helped the same.

The antisentimental strain of antebellum benevolence wishes to question precisely this perception of safety. Instead of encouraging a measured identification, a significant number of commentators, especially those who addressed the problem of urban poverty, highlighted instead the risks of emotional investment and proposed elaborate, decidedly unsentimental methods for discerning which supplicants were worthy of aid On the one hand, a prominent critique holds that literary sentimentalism is cheap, that it produces its effects too easily. Antebellum writers on charity, on the other hand, suggested that sentimentalism might be too expensive—that it resulted in giving too much, giving to the wrong people, giving unreservedly in a culture that in many ways valued reserve. These concerns spurred a bureaucratizing movement within charity organizations, designed to undermine any advantage that the anonymity of newly urbanized spaces might confer. One poverty relief organization in New York City, for example, urged citizens to carry with them a tiny (2" by 2") directory of agents, each of whom was responsible for dispensing aid to needy residents of a small geographical area. Instead of feeling sympathy for and giving alms to "apparently" suffering beggars, then, individual New Yorkers would refer them to experts, who, the agency claimed, were better able to distinguish the worthy from the vicious and who would provide the consistency and accountability needed to foil dissemblers. Here the dyad of personalistic benevolence gives way to a network or, in keeping with the layout of newer parts of the city, a grid, a revisioning of urban space that maximizes opportunities for surveillance and rationalizes the act of giving.[65] In issuing these prescriptions, antisentimental commentators privileged investigation over the mobilization of sympathy. Why risk identifying, they implicitly asked, with the sensations and emotions of a supplicant whose authenticity has not been, and perhaps cannot be, verified? But antisentimental benevolence was hardly a realm free from emotion. The discourse is characterized by suspicion and fear on the one hand and by pride and satisfaction on the other—pride in deceptions uncovered or in aid carefully dispensed. Despite an occasionally snide tone, these texts are not typically dismissive of sentiment. Instead, they represent it as all too powerful, capable of undermining the faculties of judgment and circumspection that these commentators considered essential to successful benevolent projects.

This emphasis on suspicion obscures the fact that both sentimentalism and antisentimental benevolence operated within economies of trust. The moment of sympathetic self-extension on which sentimentalism depends requires that the reader or spectator believe in the authenticity of the suffering at hand. Whether this moment is face to face or mediated textually, the "object" of the sentimental gaze must be credible for such identification to occur. So the readers who claimed that Stowe's Uncle Tom was impossibly saintly or unrealistically abused were marking their resistance to her sentimental project as a failure of trust. And it is not only the sufferer whom readers are invited to trust; often a figure emerges within the text whose extensions of feeling and whose benevolent acts the narrative endorses. Stowe's readers are encouraged to believe that Mrs. Bird, who meditates on her child's recent death as she assists the runaway slave Eliza, knows best and that her husband, a senator who initially resists identifying with the fugitive, must be converted.

Doubt does sometimes intrude in sentimental texts. Lydia Maria Child, for example, in *Letters from New-York* (1843), questions the wisdom of giving alms to a poor woman she encounters on the street. Child acknowledges that "political economy reprove[s]" the donation and goes on to claim that the "pence" she gives "can but appease the hunger of the body; they cannot soothe the hunger of [this woman's] heart." Finally, she concedes that her donation may not make the world any better—it may even make it "some iota the worse"—but adds that she is nevertheless compelled to follow her benevolent impulse.[66] Doubt here threatens to overwhelm the speaker: Does almsgiving somehow exacerbate urban poverty? Is it a pointless indulgence of her sympathetic impulses, one that cannot aid the sufferer in any meaningful way? Child poses these questions but does not doubt the destitution of the woman she encounters or the foundational rightness of her own feelings. Suffering, for her, is thoroughly credible.

The antisentimental strain of benevolent discourse, by contrast, invites readers, listeners, and potential donors to locate trust outside of the representation of suffering. To an extent, this trust is to be placed in the benevolent agent, who solicits and disburses funds according to an elaborate set of rules. But such investments were rarely stable, to judge from the frequency with which benevolent agents came under suspicion during this period. Perhaps in response to these scandals, the published reports and appeals of benevolent organizations went to great lengths to encourage the public to credit their agents and their policies. But the texts of these organizations and a number of other disquisitions on charity ultimately sought to reassign trust from persons to practices. The would-be giver is invited to place his or her confidence in an organization's system of assigning agents, its curriculum for training destitute youth, or its rules for vetting requests. The inadequacy, dishonesty, and gullibility of individuals grow less and less important within this subgenre, as charity becomes a network of guidelines and safeguards. The identities of the individual charity agents listed in a pocket-sized directory matter little. What matters is that everyone follows the rules, which delineate how to proceed when trusting the supplicant seems out of the question.

Looking at the discourse of benevolence through and in conflict with sentimentalism informs our understanding of both. For one thing, such an analysis complements recent work on sentimentalism and gender, which has shattered the notion of rigidly separate men's and women's spheres in nineteenth-century America.[67] While the culture of benevolence was gendered in all sorts of ways—women supplicants had considerably more latitude in claiming legitimate destitution, for example—I find no thorough divergence of benevolent women and callous men or of sentimental benevolent women and protobureaucratic benevolent men.[68] The language of benevolence may also yield a fuller understanding of antisentimentalism, too often associated with highbrow aestheticism and intellectualism. Jane Tompkins and others have undermined that association by showing the extent to which "old canon" authors like Hawthorne were embedded in the culture of sentiment and by arguing for the value of sentimental literature.[69] My analyses reconstruct an antisentimental discourse that was at times quite formulaic and certainly not conventionally literary or intellectual. In short, the antebellum culture of benevolence, rather than recapitulating what we already know or think we know about the history of affect, is instead an important site of contestation over the value, the utility, and the risks of feeling.

Contentious Conversations

Thoreau wrote in the "Economy" chapter of *Walden* that "there is no odor so bad as that which arises from goodness tainted."[70] It would seem that his contemporaries agreed, if we take as proof the vehemence of their attacks on what one author termed "the mad zeal of misguided philanthropy."[71] Nevertheless, attacks on the culture of benevolence were most often launched from within, as critics of benevolence took issue with its forms rather than with what they perceived to be its essence.[72] Thoreau himself provides a pointed example. He asserts early in *Walden* his distaste for active benevolence, claiming that "if I knew for a certainty that a man was coming to my house with the conscious design of doing me good, I should run for my life." And yet, several chapters later, he writes of trying to "help" the Irish laborer John Field "with [his] experience," advising him on how to build a better house and how to disengage from the cycle of poverty in passages that, as Paul Lewis has argued, recall the conventions of the charitable home visit.[73] Thoreau may have considered philanthropy to be "greatly overrated," but he nevertheless spends several pages, in addition to his remarks on John Field, articulating ways in which charitable impulses might be better expressed and enacted.[74]

The works I foreground in this book evidence a similar play of critique and engagement. Melville's *Confidence-Man* calls into question the credibility of all need and the selflessness of all donation, but its enchained scenes of charity tainted bespeak an unwillingness to abandon benevolence in pursuit of some other organizing principle that might produce more humane or more honest results. Stowe's investment is conflicted as well. While her novels dissect and dramatize the inconsistencies of benevolent slaveholding, they also work to create in the fictional aftermath of slavery a utopia (or utopias) built on benevolent relations. Perhaps most poignant is the example of Elias Boudinot's journalism, when read against his subsequent actions. Writing in the *Cherokee Phoenix* several years before the Trail of Tears, he rejected with great sophistication the proremoval bureaucrat Thomas McKenney's proffered friendship. Yet Boudinot later demonstrated a benevolent paternalism that McKenney would well have recognized when he signed the long-resisted removal treaty—for his people's good but against their will.

My choice of authors and texts, in some cases, will seem obvious. Stowe, widely read in her own time and in ours, was a key figure in disseminating an ethos of benevolent activism through print. Melville's mid-1850s texts, though not especially influential at the time, are now acknowledged to be among the era's most sustained and astute meditations on the vagaries of charity. Other works are included because they embody or dramatize key tensions within the discourse of benevolence. William Wells Brown's European travel narratives, for example, limn the complications of benevolent hierarchies in a transnational context, while juvenile fiction by Jacob Abbott, T. S. Arthur, and others provides glimpses of the values that antebellum Americans wanted to inculcate in their children, as well as the conflicts and inconsistencies they could never quite keep at bay. My attention to the northern black press, most evident in chapter 6, moves beyond the canonized genres of nineteenth-century African American writing—the slave narrative and the autobiography—to engage a broader range of authors and rhetorical styles. Throughout, I emphasize published writings over journals and personal letters in order to analyze the language of benevolence as a public discourse, one that shaped social life and social policy in the antebellum years.[75]

This varied and contentious culture of benevolence defies the imposition of a single diachronic argument. Instead, the chapters that follow tell multiple—at times even contradictory—stories about Americans and their good intentions. Taking up the Indian removal debates of the late 1820s and 1830s, chapter 1 examines the intersections and antagonisms among benevolence, expansionism, and racialized violence. Chapter 2 then analyzes how Americans' fears of duplicity, most dramatically expressed in their anxieties over urban begging and racial masquerade, became intertwined with their notions of effective charity. Integral to the debates over begging was the notion of self-reliance, one of nineteenth-century Americans' shibboleths. Chapter 3 considers how Americans figured self-reliance as a social good, even as such independence among African Americans and other outsiders came to signify a threat to white supremacy. Building on this ambivalent cultural response to the prospect of black autonomy, chapters 4 and 5 take up emancipation, actual and projected, as a focus of benevolent activism, with attention to interracial literacy instruction, schools for the recently freed, and fictional renderings of the utopias that might emerge in slavery's wake. African Americans' debates over benevolence, threaded throughout the book, are foregrounded in chapter 6. Despite limitations on their access to publication, the racial others who peopled white Americans' benevolent imaginations made it clear, in print, that they were not the silent and unquestioning recipients some authors conjured.

My attention to discord, to the fissures within antebellum benevolence, serves to critique two opposed positions. The first insists that the culture of benevolence was both misguided and unself-conscious, something that the era's more trenchant intellects sought to dismantle, while the second figures nineteenth-century charity as a prelapsarian state, with the next century's initiation of government-sponsored welfare standing in for the Fall.[76] Against these views, *The Grammar of Good Intentions* offers a messy middle ground. The culture of benevolence it reconstructs is neither a series of cloying (or disingenuous) missteps nor the voluntaristic utopia that some contemporary critics of the welfare state seek.

The cultural sites under scrutiny here also call to mind recent debates in the United States over the causes of poverty and the dangers of immigration, as well as the many representations in contemporary culture of manipulative beggars and irredeemably violent urban youths. Racialized rhetorics of benevolence are far from consistent or transcendent, as my efforts to historicize their antebellum expressions show. Nevertheless, in our own time Americans recur to these familiar modes of representation, retelling stories (though with new inflections) about the desirability and the risks of self-reliance, about the threat of being duped, by either charitable collector or supplicant, and about the moral authority of the benevolent speaker. Within literary studies, this afterlife is most apparent in the notion that our canonized authors ought to have been good people, however defined, and in the defensiveness that erupts whenever someone suggests that they were not. The discourse that this book takes up, then, resonates well beyond its temporal boundaries, reminding us of our ongoing implication in the national ritual of laying claim to good intentions.

CHAPTER ONE

Benevolent Violence
Indian Removal and the Contest of National Character

The time seems to have arrived . . . when some new effort must be made to meliorate the condition of the Indians, if we would not be left without a living monument of their misfortunes, or a living evidence of our desire to repair them.

LEWIS CASS, *North American Review* (January 1830)

Robert Montgomery Bird's 1837 novel *Nick of the Woods,* set in late-eighteenth-century Kentucky, features a Quaker named Nathan Slaughter who is ridiculed by his fellow Anglo frontiersmen for his pacifism—in particular, for his (initial) refusal to fight the area's Indians, whom Bird represents as brutal in the extreme. Nathan's benevolence toward Indians, the narrator eventually discloses, has brought about the destruction of his own family: the "Shawnee chief" to whom he once handed over his weapons in a gesture of peacemaking used them to murder Nathan's wife, mother, and five children.[1] Within the logic of Bird's narrative, a white man's benevolence toward native people signals his complicity in the destruction of his "true" dependents, the women and children of his own family and race, who rely on him to fight off, even to terrorize, dangerous outsiders. The novel's linking of benevolence and violence proves more complex, however, as it becomes clear that Nathan has a dual identity. The hapless pacifist is also an Indian-killer (the titular "Nick of the Woods") who carves crosses into the chests of his victims with "a malice and lust of blood which even death could not satisfy," a fact that the novel's white characters never discern despite rather obvious hints, including Nathan's increasingly violent behavior.[2] If *Nick of the Woods* is about the failure, even the idiocy, of benevolence toward Indians, it might also be read—admittedly, against the grain—as a story about Anglo-Americans' resistance to seeing the violence undergirding the benevolent claims of their contemporaries.

Bird's murderous Quaker, whether read as a figure of hypocrisy or of unsuccessful repression, embodies the intertwining of benevolence and violence in U.S. culture. This conjunction was extensively elaborated in the Indian removal debates of the late 1820s and 1830s, in which participants on all sides used the language of benevolence to shore up their arguments. Some claimed that removal, however disruptive, was the only means of saving the Indians from certain extermination, suggesting that those who moved westward would, as Lewis Cass phrased it, serve as "living evidence" of whites' goodwill. Others argued, in a vein that now seems self-evident, that this was a false benevolence and that forestalling removal was the only morally defensible course of action. Jeremiah Evarts, one of removal's most ardent opponents, wrote that "the oppression" occasioned by such a plan would not "be less odious on account of its being accompanied by professions of great benevolence."[3]

This chapter foregrounds such "professions," the arguments and self-justifications of those who favored removal, in large part because it is so difficult for twenty-first-century readers and critics to conceive of those interventions as credibly benevolent.[4] In other words, because the pronouncements of these self-styled benevolent removalists do not sound benevolent to us, we must be especially careful to reconstruct the belief systems within which they made sense, swayed opinion, or accrued moral authority, at least among certain readers. Finally, these removalist texts—and the Cherokee counter-rhetorics with which the chapter concludes—presage other forms of benevolent violence that would proliferate in the decades leading up to the Civil War, from the punitive almsgiving analyzed in chapter 2, to the twinning of African American militancy and social responsibility addressed in chapter 6.

Thomas McKenney, head of the Office of Indian Affairs under Jackson and, like Bird's Nathan Slaughter, raised a Quaker, was among the most outspoken proponents of benevolent removal.[5] In keeping with the claims of many contemporaries, McKenney emphasized removal's national significance. "Our country is deeply concerned," he wrote, "in the question of saving our Indians, or permitting their destruction. I believe it has the power to accomplish the one, and avert the other. Dreadful will be the responsibility if it shall not act!"[6] The exhortation that "our country" must not "permit" the Indians' destruction suggests some outside threat that could either be confronted or allowed to work its harm. But Anglo-Americans themselves embodied that threat, most directly in the form of settlers invading Indian land and state legislators enacting laws calculated to harass members of native tribes.[7] McKenney's rhetoric fractured Anglo-American identity, pitting benevolent eastern bureaucrats against Georgia's violent white settlers. But because that splitting threatened the health and cohesion of the nation as he conceived of it, McKenney's removal project also sought to repair whiteness through the construction of separate American utopias: a peaceful, Anglo-American core, made possible by the presence of a permanent Indian shelter in the West. In the process, he participated in one of the nineteenth century's crucial enterprises, the articulation of what Susan Scheckel has called "compelling narratives of the nation as a stable, consensual union of virtuous citizens."[8]

McKenney's writings demonstrate the extent to which the rhetoric of benevolence penetrated political and bureaucratic circles. But such language appeared more predictably in the writings of missionaries, whose positions on removal ranged from vehement opposition to cautious support.[9] Prominent among the advocates of removal was Isaac McCoy, a Baptist missionary, surveyor, and lobbyist, who saw the plan as an opportunity to "elevate" native peoples, though he deplored the greed that animated much proremoval activism.[10] Whereas McKenney focused on the sites of intergroup conflict from which Indians were to be evacuated—a "burning building" model, if you will—McCoy trained his attention on the western territory to which Indians would relocate, an orientation evident in his tendency to call the project "colonization" rather than "removal." McCoy's writings promoted the ideal of a new and gradually self-governing Indian territory west of the Mississippi—one that would emerge out of white benevolence and replicate its hierarchies but that would eventually install as its benevolent elite the Cherokees and other eastern tribes. For McCoy, these groups' superiority to western Indians was an article of faith.

McKenney and McCoy argued for removal at a time when Americans' dominant racial ideologies were in flux. Born in the mid-1780s, both men came of age when environmentalist theories still held sway, though as William Stanton has argued, they were never universally accepted.[11] Such theories attributed the visible distinctions among various groups largely to climactic forces, allowing for the possibility of further alteration over time, and focused on religio-cultural rather than biological difference. As Matthew Frye Jacobson, among others, has pointed out, through the early 1800s European Americans' prejudicial treatment of other groups "relied on a logic of 'civilization' versus 'barbarism' or 'savagery,' or of 'Christianity' versus 'heathendom.'"[12]

By the time McCoy published his *History of the Baptist Indian Missions* in 1840, however, notions of innate and immutable racial difference had taken hold.[13] Writing against the views of "some of our most scientific countrymen," he spent several pages disabusing readers of any notion of inherent racial traits among the Indians. "There is naturally no difference," he remarked, "between the natural propensities of the white and the red man."[14] McCoy's use of "white" and "red" here was conventional; "the white man," "the red man," and the Indians' "white brothers" were common locutions at the time. But these usages suggest that while McCoy and his allies clung to certain environmentalist tenets, especially the notion that Anglo-American identity was founded on "civilized" Christianity, their color-coding of difference reinforced the kinds of physical, visually perceived distinctions that clashed with such cultural axes. And whatever their views on the origins of difference, their rhetoric betrayed a curious and mutually supporting mix of determinism and meliorism, as their investment in the immutability of Anglo-Indian animosity and mutual harm was made to serve the idea that moving Indians away from contact zones in the East would initiate native peoples' improvement.

The Cherokees, for their part, were far less malleable than either McKenney or McCoy imagined, as is evidenced by the responses to benevolent removal that appeared in the *Cherokee Phoenix,* a newspaper published by the Cherokee Nation in the late 1820s and early 1830s. While the paper cannot be taken to speak for all Cherokees—its editor, Elias Boudinot, would prove to be a highly controversial figure among his own people—it nevertheless provides clues to native perspectives on and responses to removalist rhetoric.[15] These published interventions did not prevent the Cherokees' forced removal, but they do record an artful practice, on the part of these supposed objects of rescue, of "talking back" to white benevolence.[16]

Thomas McKenney and the New York Indian Board

McKenney is best known as the coauthor, with Judge James Hall, of the three-volume *History of the Indian Tribes of North America* (1836–44), a work that memorialized the vanishing Indian. In 1829 and 1830, however, he was more directly involved in effecting native disappearance, taking a prominent role in the Jackson administration's attempts to achieve a measure of moral credibility for its removal plan.[17] The benevolent rhetoric McKenney used in these efforts depended on the claims of other administration representatives—notably, that removal was the only available means of saving the Indians and that no force would be used in the process. Although Jackson and his associates often asserted that Georgia was justified in extending its sovereignty over Cherokee territory, at times they used a less imperious tone, suggesting that the state's actions were perhaps unfortunate, but insisting that the federal government could not defend the Cherokees' claims without grave threat to the Union.[18] Native tribes, then, were figured as the unfortunate victims of the higher principle of states' rights; they were told that they could enjoy the protection of the federal government only if they moved to territories west of the Mississippi, which fell outside the jurisdiction of any particular state. In this way, the administration could assign responsibility to Georgia and its white citizens for the difficulties the Cherokees faced, while simultaneously condoning and enabling that aggression. These declarations of regrettable last resorts set the stage for McKenney's elaborate language of benevolence, through which he sought to mediate between the exterminationist rhetoric of hard-line Indian-haters and what he characterized as the dangerous idealism of removal's opponents.

In the summer of 1829, McKenney formed the Indian Board for the Emigration, Preservation, and Improvement of the Aborigines of America, a loose affiliation of New York clergymen and laymen, primarily of the Dutch Reformed Church.[19] McKenney's involvement with this group marked the culmination of his efforts to use the language of benevolence to support removal. Thus, the documents relating to the board's formation and activities, most of which were published at federal government expense in an 1829 pamphlet, are useful for investigating the strategies and implications of that rhetoric.[20] The board never became the powerful voice of moral removalism that McKenney had hoped it would be and collapsed after his dismissal from the Jackson administration in 1830. Nevertheless, its core publication was reviewed and invoked in such periodicals as the *North American Review* and the *American Monthly Magazine,* suggesting that the positions represented there were considered crucial to the larger debate.[21]

This pamphlet emphasized that, for McKenney and the Indian Board, the physical proximity of whites and Indians was acutely undesirable. As McKenney put it, *"a near connexion with a white population"* had *"perishing consequences to the Indian."*[22] He sometimes, conventionally, attributed this harm to Indians' tendency to adopt whites' bad habits, claiming that Native Americans, once numerous, had either "retired," presumably to areas remote from Anglo settlements, or had "perished under the influence of those vices which accompany the march of civilization."[23] But McKenney's more intriguing appeals focused instead on the dangers that white strength posed. In a letter to Jeremiah Evarts, reprinted in the board's *Documents and Proceedings,* he asserted that whites' assumption of superiority was itself harmful to the Indians: "Who does not see the effect of intellectual superiority, even among our own citizens? And where we see one absolutely superior, and another absolutely inferior, does not the consciousness of that inferiority in the person feeling it depress his energies, and paralyze [*sic*] his efforts?" The Indian, he continued, "finds himself *always* the victim of that intellectual superiority, and feels that he *must* always remain so."[24] Whiteness, in this formulation, is a sort of toxic mirror, showing Indians their "inferiority" and dampening their initiative or, as a twenty-first-century speaker might put it, their self-esteem.

McKenney occasionally portrayed a less innocent white superiority, evident in his remark that natives suffered great harm by their exclusion "from all that is honourable" in a white-controlled state.[25] Nevertheless, he focused on the Indians' internalization of their inadequacy, which acted on them as "the worm within, eating out [their] vitals."[26] McKenney urged Indians to pursue "improvement" in a racially segregated and, therefore, in his view a less competitive setting. Once settled in the West, away from the bulk of the white population, they would "attain an elevation, to which in their present relations, they can never aspire. And thus would new influences be created, ennobling in their tendencies, and animating in their effects."[27] For McKenney, it was the *"intellectual, moral, political,* and *social* relations which exist between them and us"—rather than "destiny" or some "physical or moral malformation"—that threatened the Indians' destruction.[28]

White superiority, however, did more than simply depress the spirits of supposed inferiors. It also damaged white Americans themselves, just as, according to abolitionists, the fact of holding power over slaves corrupted and imbruted the master class. In McKenney's view, the recognition of another person's inferiority sparked violent impulses. "Unfortunately for man . . . ," he claimed, "there is the disposition in his nature to exercise upon such [beings] cruelty, injustice, and revenge."[29] Anyone living near "inferior" persons was likely to give in to this "disposition," so aggressive white Georgians were not particularly blameworthy because they were only acceding to a natural inclination. This belief led to some strange erasures of agency; for example, McKenney argued that once settled west of the Mississippi, native tribes "would be at once relieved from the direct action of those elements, which as I have shown, beat so destructively upon them in the States."[30] In a letter to removal supporter Heman Lincoln, written shortly after the publication of the Indian Board documents, he made this atmospheric metaphor more explicit: the board's members, he wrote, have come forward to "counsel the Indians [on] how to save themselves from the fury of the storm."[31] McKenney's rhetoric suggests that violent human actions are, like the weather, uncontrollable, much as many Anglo-Americans considered westward expansion to be natural, that is, divinely ordained and unstoppable. Accordingly, he focused his efforts not on prevention but on warning the imperiled away from impending danger.

McKenney set up an opposition, then, between natural violence and volitional benevolence. Benevolent action, in his view, could mitigate the effects of violence but could not stop that violence from occurring or change the hierarchical relationships that he claimed engendered it in the first place. And while violence was the hard fact that McKenney's benevolence purported to confront, his formulations evaded the more complicated questions surrounding benevolent whites' relationship to it.[32] Had the benevolent managed to squelch what he described as a natural tendency toward superiority-bred cruelty, or had they merely been shielded from their baser impulses by their distance from the catalyst of Anglo-Indian encounters? To what extent did the benevolent depend on the existence of violence to give their appeals meaning and urgency? And in what ways did they gain from acts of violence for which they could simultaneously disclaim responsibility? The Indian Board project was predicated on such evasions. McKenney's address to the board in August 1829 assured members that, contrary to widespread accusations, the Jackson administration had no intention of using force to effect the removal of the Cherokees.[33] The board's support for removal was contingent on these assurances, yet its claims that removal would stave off threatened violence depended on the credibility of those threats for their effectiveness and legitimacy. Board members' ideological reliance on anti-Indian aggression was echoed in the language of their appeals. Their February 1830 memorial to Congress, for example, declared that the Indians "appear to us as if standing on the very verge of ruin" and insisted that "if they remain where they are, they must inevitably perish." The memorial's language also warned of material decomposition, describing the natives to be removed as "the scattered remains of the Indian tribes"—remaining members, but also soon-to-be remains if the proposed emigration were not undertaken. The board's insistence on "the final and speedy removal" of these "scattered remains" elided the distinction between moving the living westward and dealing with the bodies of the massacred dead.[34]

However painful and disruptive removal might be, it was made to seem benign in contrast with such depredations. Thus McKenney and his allies worked to salvage an admirable white identity in the face of abundant criticism of removal, but their claims and arguments were meaningful only in light of the white violence that they both conjured and obscured.

McKenney and the Indian Board registered significant discomfort with more overt discussions of violence. They often spoke of the threats that Indians faced in vague, general terms, as when, in a discussion of Indian sovereignty and states' rights, McKenney warned of the "fatal consequences" to the Indian of coming "into collision" with our "system [of government]." The "friends of the Indian," he wrote, must not, in a "misguided philanthropy[,] . . . give accelerated force to those causes which have been so long warring upon the happiness and lives of this people," and he described the western territory as a place where no "perishing influences will be permitted to exist."[35] Logic dictated, however, that there must be some agent here (beyond the "system," "causes," and "influences" he invoked), some expediter of this perishing and extermination. Such a figure appeared only occasionally in McKenney's rhetoric, as in his discussion of the cruelly superior white population, whose "action . . . upon" the Indian he quickly depersonalized by comparing it to inclement weather.[36]

Despite such evasions, the white settlers who demanded Cherokee lands and harassed Cherokee farmers lurked in the Indian Board texts as dangerous others, the antitheses—but also the allies—of benevolent easterners. The distinction McKenney wished to draw between himself and violent settlers emerged in one of his more ambiguous images, a rare instance in these documents in which he personified the danger to which he so often alluded. In one of many urgent calls to action, he asked, "is it not plain that while we are reasoning in the forum, the enemy, having scaled the walls, is within the city, devastating and whelming it in ruins?"[37] McKenney's "we" referred to himself and other well-meaning, rational holders of social and political power, associated here with citizens of the ancient Roman republic. But the identity of their "enemy" is unclear. Broadly, it could be a personification of the threat to the Indians generally, or it could refer to the destroyed Indian himself, who would end up destroying the city—a metaphor for the nation—by ruining its (wished-for) reputation for humanitarianism and fair dealing. The enemy crawling over the walls seems most aligned, though, with the violent white settlers to whom McKenney referred elsewhere so indirectly, a menace whose origins lay outside McKenney's imagined community of well-intentioned whites.[38]

The personal and political advantages of this dissociation were significant. The violent settler was a foil for easterners who favored removal—he (I use the masculine pronoun advisedly) could be counted on to force the Indians out, to serve as a proxy for those who would not soil themselves with literal acts of aggression but who nevertheless wanted a nation without Indians.[39] But the division soon collapsed, insofar as McKenney and his Indian Board associates were indissolubly linked to and dependent on the white settler. Not only did this settler make their humanitarian arguments credible, but as an agent of white westward expansion, he made possible life in the East as they knew it. In providing a place to which the restless and the economically marginal could migrate, expansion not only facilitated the "removal" of certain potentially disruptive individuals from eastern cities and towns, but it also held out the hope—or the myth—of infinite mobility, a chance to remake oneself socially and economically. Expansionism in the Jacksonian period was often figured as the self-assertion of the democratic masses, increasing the domain of Christianity and civilization. But the masses were objects of profound ambivalence as well, at least for elite Americans. As a result, western settlers were portrayed, alternately, as uncouth ruffians the East was better off without and as the courageous forerunners of an advancing civilization.[40]

Such attempts at splitting East from West were further complicated by the fact that Georgia, the focus of the debates, was no longer unequivocally the frontier.[41] European Americans were settling lands much farther west in the late 1820s, and the natives whom white Georgians encountered were hardly the "savages" of popular fiction and frontier legend. The Cherokees, whom supporters hailed as the most civilized of the native tribes, had to some extent adopted the language, religious beliefs, and farming practices of Anglo-Americans. Nevertheless, Georgia was still a frontier in the most literal sense—a site where disparate nations or cultures meet—and removalists sought to alter precisely that status. Within the logic of McKenney's theory that proximity to the inferior other bred cruelty, removal became a means of exorcising the violence of white Georgians by removing its "cause," thus healing the rift in removalist rhetoric between frontier settlers and reasonable easterners. Of course, these conflicts would recur among other settlers and at other frontiers farther west, as removal's opponents were quick to point out. But McKenney and his cohort chose to focus instead on the Indians' salvation from their immediate environment and, less explicitly, on the conversion of threatening white Georgians that such evacuations would make possible.[42] After having argued so strenuously for the violence inherent in proximity, McKenney found himself having to invent a racial geography miraculously devoid of conflict-prone borderlands.

Remapping the West

Isaac McCoy, who began his missionary career among the native tribes of the old Northwest, was by the late 1820s one of the nation's most energetic advocates of Indian removal, with ties to both western missions and Washington political circles.[43] In an 1832 report to Lewis Cass, published under the title *Country for Indians West of the Mississippi,* he related his recent government-sponsored exploring and surveying expedition, describing the width and water quality of various rivers, the incidence of woodlands, salt springs, and coal beds, and even the distance between markers along the line that divided

Cherokee and Creek lands.[44] This Indian territory was no remote site of already accomplished rescue, as McKenney would have it, but rather a complex network of geographical features and disparate peoples that were to be converted into a unified and elevating entity.

Despite their differences in geographical orientation and emphasis, McCoy was, like McKenney, convinced of the dangers inherent in Indians' proximity to the white population. In *Remarks on the Practicability of Indian Reform* (1827), he wrote that "the condition of the Indians becomes more and more deplorable, as the whites approach nearer to them," a phenomenon he blamed primarily on whites having habitually *"fixed upon them"* a *"mark of infamy."*[45] By claiming that whites had assigned to Indians their low status, McCoy was suggesting that Indians' "degradation" was not natural but had developed through contact with a hostile dominant culture. Thus he laid the ideological groundwork both for the feasibility of Indian improvement and for the necessity of racial segregation. McCoy claimed, moreover, that even benevolent whites could not usually overcome their prejudice against Indians and so failed to compensate for the negative influence and damaging attributions of their unsavory brethren:

> The society which Indians generally find among the whites, is that of the most degraded and worthless kind; and those who are pent up by the whites [i.e., placed on small, isolated reservations], feel the effect of this principle most sensibly. Even the good men, who surround and pity them, do not take them into their society as they would so many whites, under similar circumstances. Doomed, therefore, to mingle with their own corrupt selves, and the very filth of civilized society, . . . they grow worse and worse.[46]

According to McCoy, the "filth of civilized society" encouraged among Indians the two habits for which they were most often excoriated: intemperance and war-making. His *History of the Baptist Indian Missions* was replete with tales of alcohol-induced violence and degradation, which could only be forestalled, he claimed, by removing Indians from the influence of the "whiskey sellers" who "dragged [them] into the vortex of ruin."[47]

The figure of the drunken Indian as the pawn and victim of white greed was commonly invoked in the discourses surrounding the "Indian question." More unusual was McCoy's claim that the Indians' proclivity toward war owed more to their interactions with whites than to their "natural" tendencies. "Many tribes," he wrote, "have become more and more warlike, by the example and the repeated aggressions of white men," although he had remarked elsewhere that war had the advantage of enforcing a separation of the races: "On this account the cankerous evils which result to them from coming into direct contact with us, are avoided."[48] In an effort, perhaps, to prove the tractability and peacefulness of the Indian in (relative) isolation, McCoy remarked in his *History* that members of the western Osage tribe, reputed to be "an uncommonly fierce, courageous, warlike nation of Indians," were not, in fact, intimidating. He claimed that he "had never before seen Indians so obedient to their chiefs and principal men, so subservient to traders, and so easily managed by the United States' Indian agent."[49]

Not all white influence was to be eschewed, of course. Both McCoy and McKenney considered white missionaries to be a desirable presence in the Indian territory—not only would they acculturate and educate the natives, but their numbers would be relatively small, since few would seek such arduous and poorly compensated work. McCoy worried, however, that whites intent on harm would also follow the Indians westward and he argued for proper legal and bureaucratic regulations to avert violence and exploitation. White settlers, in McCoy's view, were a land-hungry and rapidly reproducing population who imperiled the well-being and stability of Indian settlements. A general "ingress of a white population into the Indian territory," he insisted, due to improper management of land claims and a lack of vigilance on the part of government administrators, would in all likelihood cause the eventual removal of the Indians farther westward (525). Undesirable whites also interfered more immediately in McCoy's benevolent projects. He wrote that "little difficulty would attend the transaction of business with Indians [specifically, the reaching of agreements], when it is designed to do them justice, were it not for mischievous white men who are always found hovering around them, so that it may properly be said that it is the management of those white men that occasions difficulty in Indian negotiations" (528).

Among the most influential of these "mischievous white men" who were "opposed to the plan of organizing an Indian territory, and of rendering the Indians secure in their possessions" were certain missionaries and activists who, through what McCoy considered a misguided benevolence, advised the Indians to resist removal (529). According to McCoy, they were partly responsible for delaying the establishment of a permanent Indian territory in the West and, more seriously, for allowing the carnage of the Second Seminole War and other armed conflicts. Such wars would never have happened, the argument goes, if Indians had accepted removal peacefully. "I fully believed," McCoy wrote, "that not a little of the distresses of these wars were justly attributable to the misdirected zeal and indiscretion of missionaries, and the societies which patronised them, though among them there were honorable exceptions" (502). Closer still to the Indians were "white men married to Indian women, who identify themselves with the Indians as much as possible, and are permitted to remain in the Indian country." Because they preferred "savage to civilized society," McCoy noted, they "do not desire the improvement of the former." Also included under this rubric were government agents, who "easily perceive, that by the improvement of the condition of the Indians they will become capable of managing their own matters, and that the necessity for agents will vanish," and traders, who "can make more profitable speculations on poor, ignorant, suffering Indians, oppressed beneath their wants and woes, than upon a people in more comfortable circumstances" (529). Traders were particularly insidious in their ability to undermine benevolent projects. Unlike McCoy, who struggled to learn Indian languages, many traders conversed fluently and were "in habits of daily intercourse with [the Indians], often allied by marriage, and otherwise by blood."[50]

Such amalgamators, advantage-takers, and feeders at the government trough, McCoy asserted, worked to maintain Indian degradation because they themselves had unaccountably developed a taste for that way of life—proof of their deviance—or because they stood to profit from it, or both. McCoy's menacing whites bore the taint of market values and sexual license, trading in dangerous fluids—whiskey, literally, but also the intermingled fluids of Anglo-Indian sexual relations and the "mixed blood" of interracial offspring. White government agents, whom McCoy saw as perpetuating and profiting from a pattern of Indian dependency, involved themselves in these impure activities by "feeding on" the Indians' social problems, while less specifically identified whites, whom McCoy called a "merciless crew," were known to "hover about Indians who have money coming to them, like buzzards about a carcass, . . . [and] pick them bare."[51] It is difficult to tell what bothered McCoy more: the fact that "mischievous whites" were making money to the Indians' detriment or the fact that many of them expressed an affinity for Indian culture. Their patterns of affiliation and exploitation (or, to use Eric Lott's phrase, "love and theft") marked these troublesome whites as distinct from McCoy's benevolent class, who had not lost sight of the superiority of Anglo civilization, had resisted the allure of easy profit, and, crucially, had not grown to "love" the Indians carnally.[52] White missionaries—those who went along with removal, at any rate—and others who passed McCoy's benevolence test would serve, then, as a sort of vaccination, a salubrious dose of whiteness that might stave off a broader, more harmful invasion.

Though he paid a great deal of attention to the fracturing and categorizing of whiteness in these writings, McCoy expressed little interest in recuperating white identities (other than, perhaps, his own). Unlike McKenney, who sought to rescue white Georgians from their own violence, McCoy focused on the Indians' disparate identities and animosities. He acknowledged the differences among various tribes and pointed out their particular customs, circumstances, and difficulties, but he also organized this superabundance of detail into two main categories: the more or less anglicized eastern tribes, whom he sometimes called "our Indians," who would move or had moved to the West; and the "indigenous" western tribes, who were largely unconverted to Christianity and, McCoy argued, were very much in need of civilizing influences. The challenge for McCoy in laying out a plan for the western territory, as a surveyor and a would-be policymaker, was to devise some way of melding into a single community the many distinct groups and two overarching classes of Indians, whose previous interactions had been, as he wrote in 1832, "a series of mutual intrigues, and acts of injury upon each other's property and persons."[53] That

McCoy took up this challenge speaks to his relative optimism about the Indians' future, given that many removalists believed it was only a matter of time before the tribes would die out. Their destruction, he argued, could be averted and eventual unity achieved if the Indian territory were made permanent and inviolable.

Under McCoy's plan, each tribe would send delegates to a general council. Although he proposed that a white superintendent (for which role he offered himself) should oversee things for a time, ultimately self-government was to prevail. In the 1830s, he wrote extensively on the merits of this arrangement and lobbied Congress in favor of bills that would institute some of these policies. One such bill was passed in the Senate in 1838, but it was never brought up for a vote in the House and so never became law.[54] Few of McCoy's specific plans came to pass, in fact, and the western haven he envisioned never materialized. Still, McCoy's proposals merit consideration as a case study in American utopianism, as he sought to organize what he saw as chaotic difference into a rational, unified hierarchy based on Anglo-American ideals of social organization and benevolent exchange.

In arguing for a unified Indian territory in the West, McCoy sought to bring the various tribes together on the basis of their common experience as a marked and exploited group, yet he realized that they would not automatically recognize this commonality as meaningful or determining. McCoy was outraged, in fact, when the U.S. government used Native Americans as part of a combat force against the Seminoles in Florida, thereby setting the stage for intertribal animosities. Once the Seminoles migrated to the western territory, those combatants would "be compelled to live in the same neighbourhood," he lamented, "immediately after they had been shooting at each other."[55] McCoy's proposed unification, however, seems not to have been based on some natural affinity that merely had to be uncovered. He tended to discount the essentialist beliefs about Indians in circulation at the time, remarking for instance that whites had grossly overrated Indians' so-called natural abilities as trackers: "We admit that, by habit, an Indian is better qualified to trace the footmarks of a man or of a beast than a man who has been educated in the City of New-York. But his skill in this respect is not superior to that of thousands of white men in new countries." Perhaps to prove his point, McCoy portrayed Mograin, his Osage tracker on an 1828 expedition, as a hapless and unobservant fellow—a corrective to the almost supernaturally talented Indians of Fenimore Cooper's novels and popular legends.[56] Reinforcing the primacy of "habit" and "circumstance" over natural characteristics, McCoy wrote: "If the habits are formed by circumstances surrounding him [the Indian], as they are formed by those which surround us, then the point can be established that a change in circumstances would be followed by a change of habits. Let this change be favorable to civilization and religion."[57]

McCoy presented the unification of the Indians as the result of such a reengineering of circumstances, achievable through proper organization of geographical and social space. Once the Indians' territory has been established and mapped,

> United States' troops may be necessary to prevent impositions upon them by lawless persons from among ourselves, and to defend their frontiers against occasional injuries by war parties from remote tribes; but not to preserve peace among those who are . . . located within the territory. *Here* it will be their interest to be at peace among themselves. *United in one community,* war among themselves would be as unnatural as war between so many counties of one of our States.[58]

War among themselves would become "unnatural," then, not because of some deeply felt kinship but because it would be against their "interest" to create conflict within this structured and interdependent polity. (McCoy was assuming, of course, that people naturally act in their best interest.) Unification, he believed, was a politically expedient compact premised on common interests and a shared history of oppression.

Other circumstances would come into play as well. Under conditions of numerical strength—that is, freedom from the burdens and stresses of being outnumbered by whites—and by the fact of permanent residence, the Indians would "naturally feel something of national character, and would aspire to an equality with their white neighbours."[59] In keeping with this faith that external factors could alter people's affective relations and investments, McCoy proposed that the new Indian territory should include a literal common ground, a centrally located "tract of 30 or 40 miles square . . . on which individuals of any tribe might settle; and within which, would eventually be located their seat of government."[60] This experimental settlement, he suggested, would promote a unity that could then be exported to the rest of the territory.

Acculturating Indians

Significantly, McCoy did not propose a union of disparate equals but a social body held together by the same patterns that structured Anglo-American society: superiority/inferiority, teacher/taught, and benevolent/helped. He wished to replicate, specifically, an Anglo ideal of a meritocratic and benevolent social hierarchy, with eastern, anglicized Indians as the governing elite who would work to improve, Christianize, and educate the western tribes. Benevolent whites, through removal, missionary work, and administration of the territory, would make possible the Indians' geographical proximity to one another and would begin to educate them, but the elite Indians would eventually take over such responsibility themselves.[61] The Cherokees occupied a prominent place in this argument. Opponents of removal had long claimed that because the Cherokees were so "improved" and "civilized," they should be allowed to stay in the East, but McCoy countered that these same qualities would make the Cherokees and other southeastern tribes particularly apt agents of benevolence in the West. Indeed, their acquiescence to removal would itself constitute a benevolent act:

> The spirit of christian benevolence which they have imbibed, must have great influence upon their choice in favour of removal. A people who can form among themselves charitable associations for the relief of those of another nation [as the Cherokees had], must feel great solicitude for their perishing countrymen, and could not refuse so favourable an opportunity of doing them good as would be offered in the territory. There they could afford the less improved, the influence of precept and example in whatever relates to time and to eternity.[62]

McCoy put a great deal of faith in the power of anglicized Indians as agents of acculturation, arguing that "in both civil and religious matters, Indians with suitable qualifications could be more useful than white men among their countrymen. Indian language being their mother tongue, and being by kindred identified with Indians, their opportunities of usefulness would surpass those of strangers."[63] These Indians, many of whom were of mixed Anglo and Indian parentage, functioned as boundary-crossers, though their "in-betweenness" was complicated by the fact that no monolithic native culture—or white culture, for that matter—preexisted their mixed status. Even without white intervention, the eastern tribes would have differed significantly from those in the West, and from one another.

Proponents of removal did not always look favorably on such figures. Some argued, for example, that the majority of Cherokees wanted to move west of the Mississippi but were prevented from doing so by "half-breed chiefs" (apparently, elite and influential Cherokees with significant Anglo ancestry) who opposed the plan.[64] And McCoy himself emphasized the hazards posed by another cultural hybrid, the Indianized white man. But in his figuring of the anglicized Indian as the agent of successful colonization, the saved savior, McCoy channeled the disruptive potential of the hybrid—the very quality that some postcolonial theorists would later celebrate—into a mode he considered safe and useful.[65] Most significantly, he sought to accomplish this cooptation by emphasizing the social dominance that the Cherokees and other anglicized tribes would enjoy in the new pan-Indian society. "They know," he wrote, "that in the Indian territory, their superior acquirements will give them the ascendancy among their brethren, and that situations of honour, trust, and profit, will be occupied chiefly by themselves."[66]

McCoy's strategic use of these figures is hardly unique in the history of American race relations. The most obvious contemporary parallel was the positioning of African Americans within the white-sponsored African colonization movement. Proponents of colonization argued that a central purpose in sending these Americanized and Christianized people "back" to Africa, a place the vast majority of them had never been, was to make them agents of civilization and conversion among native Africans. They were declared the superior acculturators of "heathen" Africans because of a common racial identity and because they were thought naturally suited to the African climate, while white missionaries were dying there with a frequency that alarmed their potential replacements. The other strain in whites' colonizationist writings was that free blacks had to be expelled for the safety of the white republic. Having imbibed freedom, they were thought likely to foment rebellion among the enslaved or, if they resided in the North, to pose a threat to the job security of the white working class. White America's poison, proponents of colonization suggested, would be Africa's salvation.

But the scheme was also promoted as a boon to the emigrants. Like McCoy, colonizationists stressed that the experience of being the socially elite colonizer would allow ex-American blacks to replicate the Anglo-American model of self-improvement. McCoy, himself an advocate of African colonization, echoed these sentiments when he wrote that Indian colonization "proposes to place the Aborigines on the same footing as ourselves; to place before them the same opportunities of improvement that we enjoy. . . . The result, therefore, cannot be doubtful. The colony would commence and improve, much after the manner of all new settlements of whites, which have been begun and carried forward, under favourable circumstances."[67] Although neither free blacks nor Indians were thought capable of handling the rigorous competition of the white-dominated American marketplace, both groups, it was argued, would flourish in less competitive environments.

A critical difference, however, between whites' plans for African colonization and McCoy's proposed Indian territory lay in the relationship between the colony and the United States. Advocates of African colonization argued, however speciously, that their project would return emigrants to a site to which they had some ancestral tie; further, the Liberian colony operated under the jurisdiction of the American Colonization Society rather than the U.S. government and became an independent nation in the 1840s.[68] McCoy, by contrast, made no claim that the projected Indian territory was the eastern Indians' ancestral homeland. What was more important, the colony he proposed would continue to exist in a curious inside/outside relation with the United States: it would be a self-governing but constituent part of the nation, lying beyond the borders of the states, yet within the nation's purchased lands and within its eventual range of settlement. McCoy wrote in his *Address to Philanthropists in the United States* that

> all Indian tribes which now reside or ever have resided east of the Mississippi, are, or have been, within the claims of some State or Territory of the United States. *Here* [in the western Indian territory] no such claim exists. Hitherto the several tribes have not been united to one another, nor to the United States;—*Here* they are to be united in one common bond of civil community, and constituted an integral part of the United States.[69]

In McCoy's view, it was clearly hazardous for Indians to reside within existing states, but moving outside the United States' protective grasp was equally unwise. The paradoxical siting he devised was necessary to save the nation as he understood it. To honor Indian land claims in the East, however just such an act might seem, would destroy the United States. "The very existence of our Government," he wrote, "was predicated upon the supposition that the Indian had no landed rights on the east of the Mississippi."[70] But silencing Indian dissent through direct or indirect extermination would contradict his notion (or desire) that his was a benevolent nation. Benevolence, then, allowed McCoy simultaneously to preserve the white nation and to reproduce its most vital elements in a parallel though still subordinate form.

Benevolent Whiteness

McCoy's *History of the Baptist Indian Missions* recorded his commitment to benevolent action despite almost comically adverse circumstances. He explored the western territory with inadequate supplies and amateurish guides, established missions in desolate regions, and was compelled to absent himself from an alarming number of family members' deathbeds so that he could, after weeks of arduous travel, lobby for Indian reform in "Washington City." All this he did for the sake of the Indians, or so the story goes. But as historians have noted, McCoy profited from government surveying contracts related to removal and he campaigned (unsuccessfully) for the superintendency of the western territory, a position that would have provided him with a comfortable income.[71] Thomas McKenney, too, emphasized his concern for the Indians, although many have suggested that the zeal with which he pursued the Indian Board project indicated how badly he wanted to keep his post in the Jackson administration. Some degree of duplicity in these figures, then, is likely. Of greater interest, however, is the possibility that McKenney and McCoy had, at least some of the time, genuinely good intentions, and that those intentions could coexist with such destructive outcomes as the Trail of Tears.[72] The question is not how did good intentions go awry—or how did violence overpower benevolence—but rather how were their ideas of "the good" constructed so as to facilitate what we (and many of their contemporaries) view as injustice? McKenney's good intentions, if we are willing to grant him such, were contingent on the ideal of racial homogeneity, the desirability of white expansion, and the belief that certain levels of coercion were not only acceptable but salubrious. Similarly, McCoy's rested on a belief in the intractability of whites' prejudice and on the notion that white models of social organization could and ought to be emulated. In short, both men's good intentions were contingent on what it meant to them to be white Americans.

The version of whiteness that emerged in McKenney's rhetoric depended on a homogenization of nonfrontier white Americans in the construction of a benevolent "we," splitting off from other, less savory versions of whiteness when convenient but also reabsorbing and sanitizing them whenever possible.

Ultimately, McKenney and his allies on the Indian Board claimed for this reconstructed whiteness a benevolence toward racial others, without sacrificing the ideology of Anglo-American superiority or the prospect of white dominion over desired lands. The very terms of benevolent discourse enabled the simultaneity of these claims. Taking on the subject position of the helper in an interracial benevolent dyad was tantamount to asserting higher status, so when McKenney and the New York Indian Board offered to save the Indians from white aggression, their rhetoric affirmed whites' superiority far more than it conceded their culpability.

McCoy, in contrast, suggested that there need not be a hierarchy with whites at the top and Indians at or near the bottom. He emphasized Indians' potential for (a limited) independence and capacity to take on subjectivities that very much resembled those available within the dominant Anglo culture. Indianness, for McCoy, was a malleable, even effaceable, set of identities that could be made to *resemble* whiteness if the proper steps were taken. If mimicry in colonial contexts entails, as Homi Bhabha has argued, both "resemblance and menace," McCoy counted on geographical separation to neutralize the latter, that is, to establish among the Indians a near-whiteness and a subnationhood in the West, where the imitativeness he urged on them would pose no affront to Anglo-Americans' self-conceptions. Crucially, neither would such imitation cross over into complete identity with Anglo-Americans, which might allow for renewed cohabitation.[73] Thus McCoy differentiated his schema from the Cherokees' earlier mimicry of the U.S. Constitution, an attempt to prove their "civilization" and retain their eastern lands that, in Priscilla Wald's formulation, "recontextualized the logic of United States nationalism" and so "posed an important symbolic threat to the Union."[74]

The casting of acculturation as a condition of near-equality is hardly unique in U.S. history. What matters about McCoy's version is his figuring of benevolence as the very cornerstone of whiteness, as well as the means by which others might gain access to its advantages. For Anglo-Americans, the implications of this notion were both deflating and aggrandizing: benevolence was not the special property of whites but could be taken up by the Indians themselves. Yet something remained for McCoy of the power of what we might call *original whiteness*. It could be exported to other groups and made to take hold, but those transplantations could never be confused with their source; the still-visible distinctions between whites and others would inevitably engender discord and exploitation. Therefore, for McCoy, the boundary around the Indian territory must remain inviolable, and the Indians themselves must remain both outside and within the white nation.

Friday on the Mississippi?

In her introductory essay to a collection on the Anita Hill–Clarence Thomas hearings, titled "Friday on the Potomac," Toni Morrison used the relationship between Friday and Crusoe in Defoe's novel to examine the position of the rescued other:

> Unlike the problems of survivors who may be lucky, fated, etc., the rescued
> have the problem of debt. If the rescuer gives you back your life, he shares
> in that life. But, as in Friday's case, if the rescuer saves your life by taking
> you away from the dangers, the complications, the confusion of home, he
> may very well expect the debt to be paid in full. Not "Go your own way
> and sin no more." Not "Here, take this boat and find your own adventure,
> in or out of your own tribe." But full payment, forever.[75]

Benevolent removalists described what they were doing as rescue and, as payment, seemed to expect that their "Fridays" would adopt what Morrison calls "the master's tongue," that is, their worldview and their values.[76] But the objects of such efforts did not apparently perceive themselves as having been saved and refused to accept the identities that removalists tried so diligently to assign them.

Some of the most arresting illustrations of that resistance appeared in the pages of the *Cherokee Phoenix,* which served as both a community paper—with articles in the Cherokee language, accounts of recent intratribal conflicts and resolutions, and news of U.S. political developments that would affect the tribe—and an example of what Mary Louise Pratt has called *autoethnography,* a text in which "colonized subjects undertake to represent themselves in ways that *engage with* the colonizer's own terms."[77] The paper's English-language editorials and articles appropriated and redeployed elements of Anglo-American discourse, including the discourse of benevolence, in an attempt to represent the Cherokee nation as an entity to be listened to rather than simply removed or rescued. Like other autoethnographic texts, the paper addressed both the "literate sectors of the speaker's own social group" and members of the dominant culture, the white readers occasionally referred to in the text and taken into account as one of the paper's important audiences.[78] The double-voicedness of the *Cherokee Phoenix* is striking: while it worked to apprise the Cherokee people of the debates and events that menaced them, it also functioned as a public relations vehicle, a means of proving to whites that Indians (at least the Cherokees) had become "civilized," sophisticated users of rhetoric. The paper itself became an argument against removal, evidence that proximity to white Americans had not, in fact, hindered Indians' quest for "improvement."

At times, contributors to the newspaper employed the strategy of acknowledging white benevolence while simultaneously asserting something other than what removalists wished to hear. In June 1828, for example, the paper reprinted correspondence exchanged five years earlier between U.S. commissioners, who urged the Cherokees to leave their lands in Georgia, and the Cherokee General Council, whose members refused to accede to such a plan.[79] In addressing the Indians, the commissioners reminded them of the "kind protection" of their "earthly fathers" (the U.S. presidents) and asserted that "if the President practices towards you the kind treatment of father, it becomes your duty to return the obedience and gratitude of children." Here, the price of benevolent treatment was, as Morrison put it, "full payment, forever." The members of the General Council began their response with a long, appreciative paragraph assuring U.S. officials that "the many favors which have been bestowed on us by the fostering hands of our father the President, are always fresh in our recollections, and we are ever ready to acknowledge our gratitude." They went on to state, however, that "it is the fixed and unalterable determination of this nation, never again to cede *one foot* of land."[80] Benevolence, they suggested, merited gratitude and fond recollections but not utter subservience.

The *Cherokee Phoenix* also ran articles in which native authors focused on whites' benevolent language, in an attempt to hold the latter accountable to their claims. When confronted with a series of not-so-veiled threats should they persist in their refusal to remove, the Cherokee General Council replied with pointed questions: "Brothers, do you wish to impair the high confidence which we entertain of the magnanimity of your Government? . . . Have you not told us that the President has the same *love* towards *us* as his white children?" The following October, editor Elias Boudinot responded to Secretary of War Eaton's claim that removal would not involve the use of force. The Cherokees, Boudinot wrote, "never thought that the United States in her Federal capacity would come out against the Indians in military array & say, you must remove. She dare not do such a thing in the face of an enlightened world." In staking this claim, he tapped into Anglo-Americans' desire that the nation be perceived as benevolent and gambled on the notion that the federal government might be susceptible to moral embarrassment. He went on to discuss, though, the "unjust measures" (short of military force) that the government had employed and appealed "to an enlightened, generous and Christian public to say, whether such prevaricating conduct is worthy of a great and magnanimous nation, and whether such proceedings as are now employed to remove the poor Indians can be called *peaceful measures*?" One of the Cherokee Nation's memorials to Congress, reprinted in the *Phoenix,* made a similar appeal to national pride and moral authority, reminding lawmakers that they represented "a virtuous, intelligent and christian nation."[81] In adopting the rhetoric of benevolent nationhood, Cherokee writers attempted to write those claims into being, to make them reflect reality by asserting that they already did.

Appropriately, the *Cherokee Phoenix* engaged in its most direct contestations over benevolence in a series of exchanges with Thomas McKenney. After the paper had published some sharp critiques of his arguments and methods, McKenney wrote in to demand that the Cherokees refrain from such commentary and acknowledge him instead as their warm and devoted friend. Boudinot published this letter, replete with dire warnings of what would happen to the Indians if they continued to oppose removal, and responded with a direct attack on McKenney's benevolent claims. As usual, however, he took care not to impugn the latter's motives: "With the motives of Col. M'Kenney we have nothing to do—they may be good—he may be a 'real friend'—he may be a 'wise counsellor;' but after all we must beg leave to judge for ourselves, and choose our own friends. . . . Let us have the privilege of judging and acting for ourselves—of saying *what is best under all circumstances for us to do.*"[82] Boudinot and the Cherokees did not feel, as this editorial makes clear, the gratitude McKenney so transparently sought.

These excerpts suggest the range and sophistication of the Cherokees' attempts to use benevolent rhetoric to their advantage while reserving the right to repudiate its implications when they threatened Indian self-determination. What is less apparent in these texts is the degree to which the Cherokees also struggled to counter the force of such rhetoric within their own communities. Boudinot, who had spoken so eloquently against a presumptuous white benevolence in his editorials, eventually imitated its structures when he signed the New Echota Treaty in 1835. As Mary Young has argued, Boudinot and the other members of the "Treaty Party" adopted the model of a paternalistic benevolent elite when they took it upon themselves to save their people from what they eventually saw as a doomed resistance effort. They came to believe, Young writes, as their "missionary mentors" had taught, that "the virtuous and the enlightened have a duty to do what they can for the good of the people, even when the people fail to understand what is good for them."[83] Other Cherokees responded with violence rather than editorials, murdering Boudinot in 1839.

The Cherokees' deployment of and protest against the benevolent paradigm obviously did not change the government's course of action. Anglo-American policymakers, including those who voted for the Indian Removal Act of 1830, paid a great deal more attention to the *North American Review* than to the *Cherokee Phoenix* and were disposed to credit the statements of Andrew Jackson, Lewis Cass, Thomas McKenney, and Isaac McCoy more than those of Elias Boudinot or the members of the Cherokee General Council. Nevertheless, the Cherokees, like many putative objects of benevolence, posed a threat to the social order, which the authors of benevolent texts sought in myriad ways to contain. The core issue was not that the Cherokees were spectacularly destitute, a drain on local (white) charity, but that they controlled resources that whites wanted for themselves. So benevolent arguments in favor of removal were not simply about circumventing violence and defusing the symbolic power of murdered Cherokees, which would undermine white Americans' claims to a national benevolence. They were also attempts to reposition as abject a people who seemed to be, if anything, insufficiently needy. McCoy's representation of the Cherokees as a benevolent elite in the making, when considered in this light, seems close to an admission of how poorly the label of benevolent object fit them.

Although it is tempting to think of rhetorics of benevolence as means of justifying the use of power, of claiming to do for a good reason what one wants to do anyway, the act of defining what is good at a particular historical moment—of asserting what will contribute to the well-being of another and what will not—is best understood as an exercise of power in itself. As the case of Indian removal demonstrates, these definitions and assertions are neither transparent nor benign. In chapter 2 I continue to explore such uses of power and the forms of resistance they engendered, focusing on the ways in which beggars and slaves, the antebellum era's most striking figures of need, threatened to undermine the social and rhetorical structures that the self-appointed benevolent classes so diligently constructed.

In the years between 1830 and the Civil War, the period that the remaining chapters engage, benevolent Americans' categories and definitions—for example, their notions of cultural difference, of social hierarchy, and of susceptibility to improvement—would incorporate "hardened" notions of racial distinctions and racial character inflected by the increasing prominence of scientific racism. Though a benevolent meliorism would persist, it would do battle with these concepts of immutability and, more interestingly, with their disavowed counterpart—the suspicion that while identity and difference perhaps could not be truly altered, they could certainly be obscured. Such conflicts suffused even what we would identify as the more progressive quarters of benevolent activism. As social justice movements, most obviously abolition, intensified their calls for the elimination of certain forms of racial oppression, the racialized hierarchies of benevolent relations would remain to be challenged and reasserted.

CHAPTER TWO

Misgivings
Duplicity and Need in
Melville's Late Fiction

Pence I will give thee, though political economy reprove the deed. They can but appease the hunger of the body; they cannot soothe the hunger of thy heart; that I obey the kindly impulse may make the world none the better— perchance some iota the worse; yet I must needs follow it—I cannot otherwise.

LYDIA MARIA CHILD, *Letters from New-York* (1843)

There's a sucker born every minute.

Commonly attributed to P. T. BARNUM

As these epigraphs suggest, antebellum Americans struggled to balance social responsibility and suspicion. The desire to help the suffering that Child expresses so fervently was at odds with myriad cultural warnings that to follow such impulses might do more harm than good. At the same time, the "sucker" remark points to the pervasiveness—and the appeal— of trickery, despite all efforts to circumvent or expose it. In the kinds of public amusements that P. T. Barnum and his competitors presented, the suspicion of duplicity could be a source of fun, if we take as proof the popularity of their enterprises despite widespread knowledge of their many deceptions.[1] The stakes seemed higher, however, when artifice entered other realms. In particular, Americans saw the intrusion of duplicity into their acts of benevolence as troubling, even malignant. The possibility that one might be tricked into aiding the unworthy occasioned anxious interrogations of the practices of charity.

In this chapter I explore how antebellum Anglo-Americans represented duplicity's threat to benevolence. Their voluminous writings on charity often functioned as an anatomy of suspicion, promoting elaborate rituals of authentication and constructing the ideal donor as a rational, well-trained investigator rather than the emotion-driven caretaker of Child's self-presentation. Commentators worried over the risks of unregulated sentiment, the feelings of identification with and sympathy toward the poor that might circumvent good sense and discernment. In particular, they expressed a deep concern that the bodies of the disadvantaged could never be the legible indices of need that sentimental authors conjured. Such antisentimental charity experts returned to the body endlessly in their descriptions of worthy and unworthy supplicants, noting, for example, the physical disabilities and maladies that warranted dependency. But they also warned of the body's many deceptions—disability, after all, could be faked, as could illness, hunger pains, and a host of other sympathy-eliciting elements. The bodies of the poor, they argued, had to be both observed and discounted.

To judge from a range of antebellum publications on charity, these concerns emerged most vividly in the context of urban begging. Contrary to the cherished myth that beggars only rarely populated/polluted American cities, antebellum observers documented their abundance. This crisis of national identity, insofar as economic opportunity in the United States had long been opposed to European destitution, was also a crisis of credibility, as anonymous beggars on city streets laid claim to worthy poverty. In *The Confidence-Man* and "Benito Cereno," Melville inscribes these concerns onto black (or apparently black) bodies, thus intertwining the epistemology of doing good with the question of "knowing" blackness. Here Melville exploits white Americans' tendency to associate black people with need, an association that both abolitionist and proslavery rhetoric reinforced, though for different ends. But his texts also call up the era's widespread pairing of blackness and threat, expressed through images of deceit and insurrection. Such representations distill broader concerns about the presence of the needy in a society whose increasingly stratified and market-driven economy coexisted uneasily with its much-vaunted benevolence. More pointedly, they speak to the specifics of black and white racial formation in the antebellum United States and to the role of benevolent rhetoric in that vexed process. The anxious moments of exchange and withholding explored here reveal the ways in which benevolent hierarchies and racial hierarchies were mutually constitutive in U.S. culture. As Melville's texts suggest, duplicity in the form of racial masquerade threatened to disrupt those codes and, in the process, to trouble the era's conjunction of whiteness and benevolent authority.

Identities

The charity society publications, advice manuals, juvenile fiction, and cartoons cited in this chapter demonstrate some of the ways in which antebellum white Americans with access to publication talked about benevolence and its risks. Like Melville, these authors drew on what had already appeared—in print and in other cultural forms such as lectures, jokes, and oral narratives—and in turn contributed to the available modes of representation. Undeniably, nonwhites also used and contested the language of benevolence, often explicitly revealing their racial identities in the process and referring to whites' more voluminous and more widely distributed interventions. African Americans in the urban North, to cite the most prolific of these commentators, at times identified worthy and unworthy supplicants according to the same criteria whites used, but they also offered theoretical and practical critiques of whites' benevolent projects and took free blacks to task for their supposed overreliance on white aid. Native American writers, as I argued in chapter 1, attempted to hold Anglo-American leaders to their promises of benevolence, even as they insisted on their people's right to choose their own "friends." And Jewish Americans, who were not generally accorded the privileges of whiteness in the nineteenth century, worked to establish a reputation as benevolent people who took care of their "own."[2] Anglo-American authors of charity texts, in contrast, rarely mentioned their own racial identities, though they discussed at length the racial characteristics of the immigrants, slaves, and other outsiders whose social positioning they charted. Instead, these authors relied on the fact that most American readers presumed a white default in public discourse. By drawing attention to their identities and by considering the racial constructions inherent in their texts, I seek to undermine the implied universality of antebellum white benevolence and analyze it instead as a raced discourse.

The men and women who ran mainstream charity organizations and wrote their reports, who published advice manuals and juvenile literature, and who fashioned themselves as charity experts, tended to be Protestant, of Anglo or northern European descent, and relatively well-off economically, though economic security grew tenuous in the early and mid-nineteenth century.[3] These authors took various positions on the era's pressing social and political issues, most notably slavery and immigration, but they generally shared the view that people of means bore some responsibility for alleviating the suffering of others. And they typically wrote for an implied audience much like themselves, sometimes constructed broadly as "concerned and benevolent citizens," sometimes as fellow charity workers or potential donors. When they addressed audiences more distant from themselves—impressionable young people in need of guidance or ideological opponents in need of convincing—they usually did so with a tone of racial and class solidarity.[4]

To label these speakers *white* is to use a convenient, and perhaps indispensable, but nevertheless imperfect shorthand. As recent scholarship has shown, the membership and putative character of nineteenth-century whiteness were fluid, contested, and often contradictory constructions, shifting both diachronically and situationally.[5] Antebellum discourses of benevolence were among the many social and linguistic forces working to constitute the category. That is, access to a white racial designation and its privileges depended to some extent on whether one needed help or was in a position to help others. This claim warrants qualification: the level of one's participation in benevolent exchange could not single-handedly grant the privileges of whiteness or push one unequivocally outside its boundaries. And nonwhite Americans practiced benevolence, most often within what they defined as their own communities, such that the designations "white" and "benevolent" were not neatly coextensive. But a group's perceived status within benevolent hierarchies affected the degree to which its members were considered "absorbable" into whiteness. That Irish immigrants, for example, were widely believed to make up a high percentage of urban beggars delayed the group's acceptance into the white mainstream.[6] Building on the logic of such exclusions, James Rees, editor of the Philadelphia-based monthly *The Philanthropist, or Sketches of City Life,* went so far as to claim in 1855 that "professional beggars" were "all of foreign birth," implying that the very act of begging proved an individual's alien status.[7]

The language of benevolence also informed what it meant to be white. Americans of Anglo-Saxon descent, as whites somewhat erroneously defined themselves, asserted that they possessed a natural aggressiveness in commerce and combat but also insisted on their suitability for the task of caring for and improving society's "weaker" members.[8] In their many accounts of benevolent projects, and especially in their narratives of deceptions discovered or discouraged, Anglo-Americans arrogated to themselves the rationality and circumspection that they claimed made for successful social uplift. But these qualities—and the managerial and investigative practices they facilitated—existed in tension with other possible and much-feared identities as dupes or wasters of resources. So while the fear of being tricked impelled charity workers' repeated inquiries into the credibility of need, their representations of such inquiries had contradictory effects, figuring the white benevolent establishment as both exceptionally discerning and essentially trickable—else why the vigilance?

Pretenses

Alongside their deep suspicion of supplicants, antebellum writers who addressed the issue of poor relief expressed a more general conviction that benevolence, if mismanaged, could be hazardous.[9] To cite one of many debates over the proper means of social reform, Charles Loring Brace, founder of the Children's Aid Society, argued vehemently that placing poor and recalcitrant children in asylums, a common practice at midcentury, would undermine their potential for self-reliance. Better, he thought, to remove "street urchins" from the urban scene entirely, where their concentration presented a risk, and allow them to flourish in small towns and rural communities.[10] Benevolent projects attracted the most criticism, however, when they dispensed direct material aid, especially in the form of money. Almsgiving was considered dangerous because it afforded the poor at least temporary autonomy, insofar as they could choose whether to purchase necessities or spend the money on alcohol or gambling or some other vice. Charity experts feared that such freedom might prove all too seductive, tempting the poor to shun permanently the world of work and its array of consequences.

Acknowledging this concern, the Baltimore Association for Improving the

Condition of the Poor (AICP) admitted in 1851 that "the alms of benevolent societies, and of private liberality, are often misapplied, and as often abused by those who receive them." Four pages of caveats followed, all calculated to help charity workers circumvent the designs of the dishonest; chief among these was the injunction *"to withhold all relief from unknown persons."*[11] A suppliant's seemingly honest face, on its own, was not to be trusted. Similarly, the children's story "Benevolence" (1850) portrays a boy who gives alms to an apparently needy man, only to discover later that he is a drunkard who mistreats his "wife and half starved, half clothed children"; the boy is horrified to find that his donation has enabled the man to drink himself into a stupor.[12] Even when it did not lead to these dramatic abuses, such "indiscriminate giving," a popular conduct book aimed at young women claimed, might nevertheless "encourage idleness and dissipation" among the needy.[13] As these texts suggest, the wrong kind of giving or even too much of the right kind encouraged in the recipient an exaggerated sense of entitlement that could result in "pauperism" and related social ills, including vice, indolence, improvidence, and the crime that some might turn to "whenever they have become so well-known that begging ceases to be profitable."[14]

Donors were scrutinized as well. The Boston Society for the Prevention of Pauperism went so far as to suggest that what often passed for a benevolent impulse was, in fact, a combination of laziness and squeamishness. "Many are too busy" to make appropriate inquiries regarding beggars, the group's 1859 report asserted, while "others give charity in order to get rid of them; being careless whether the stories which they hear are true or not."[15] Such irresponsible figures resisted the role of the assertive, investigative caregiver, preferring instead the passivity of an isolated, reactive donation. In other cases, the honesty of benevolent agents—who, as fundraisers, were supplicants as well as donors—was called into question. Stories abounded of charitable collectors who fleeced well-meaning citizens. The *Colonization Herald* of July 1853, for example, warned Philadelphians of a "heartless man" disguised "in a Friend's garb" who had "been robbing Africa" by pretending to collect donations for the Pennsylvania Colonization Society.[16] Those identified as the objects or would-be objects of benevolent efforts had their own doubts about charity agents' probity. The white-administered Association for the Care of Coloured Orphans, based in Philadelphia, found that "various excuses were urged by coloured people against trusting us with their young dependants [*sic*], although their real objections evidently arose from a want of confidence in the Association—they could not rely on the sincerity of our professions." The report continued, "it will require time and experience to remove those fears and apprehensions, which have originated in that system of cruelty and deception, to which the coloured people have been subject for so many generations."[17] These agents saw in their role the potential to undo years of racism, even as they found themselves silently accused of it by those they wished to aid.

The suspicions confronting donors and charity workers derived not only from concerns that they might be lazy, dishonest, or racist, but also from the ever-present danger that they might do good incorrectly and so contribute, however unintentionally, to the moral and social decay of the populace. Thus charity experts worked to present themselves as trustworthy donors, largely by elaborating in their fundraising appeals and annual reports on the widespread notion that the poor could be divided into the worthy and the "vicious" and by outlining their exacting methods for determining where an individual supplicant belonged in that taxonomy. Karen Halttunen has argued that middle-class Americans responded to the threat of duplicity by creating an elaborate social etiquette that would verify their class status. Such rules were needed, however, not only for settings in which middle-class Americans performed gentility for their supposed social peers but also for points of contact between the well-off and the destitute. In addition to their codes of manners, then, antebellum Americans developed an etiquette of charity, one that identified the duplicitous beggar as its enemy.

The Baltimore AICP, one of many groups that elaborated such an etiquette, subdivided the less-than-worthy poor, differentiating those "who have become mendicants through their own improvidence and vices" from "professional paupers," those who avoided work in calculated and at times highly sophisticated ways. The improvident, the association's publications claimed, were salvageable; they should be granted minimal aid, always less than they could get by laboring, and should be instructed in better habits and the avoidance of vice. Those identified as "professionals," however, should be turned away outright, lest the association "become a willing accessory in perpetuating the evils of vagrancy and pauperism."[18] Well-executed plans to avoid work merited more disapproval than bad habits and weakness of will, in that the former represented a willful avoidance of responsibility, while the latter suggested powerlessness, even victimization (e.g., individuals were often described as "falling under the influence" of intemperance or "succumbing" to sloth). "Professional" beggars, by contrast, had all too much agency. In defiance of the cliché, these beggars were in fact choosers: they threatened to overturn benevolent hierarchies by selecting an appropriate dupe, rather than being chosen by the charity agent as a worthy recipient.

With these distinctions in mind, commentators attended closely to a supplicant's self-presentation. The third edition of *The Young Lady's Guide to the Harmonious Developement [sic] of Christian Character* (1841), for example, expressed a commonplace sentiment when it warned charity-minded readers that "as a general principle, it is not best to give to *beggars*. . . . The more deserving poor are retiring, and unwilling to make known their wants. It is better to seek out such, as the objects of your charity, than to give indiscriminately to those that ask for it."[19] This approbation of silent sufferers, whose destitution must be discovered by an investigative philanthropy, existed in tension with a pervasive suspicion of those who begged in public and complained of their troubles. The latter group, according to many commentators, lacked appropriate Christian forbearance in the face of suffering and shame in the face of middle-class standards of respectability, and were perhaps out to mislead potential donors with exaggerated or invented tales of hardship. The very fact of a public appeal, then, damaged a supplicant's credibility.

A common argument against street begging, in the twenty-first century as well as in the nineteenth, is that it undermines other residents' quality of life. As a spectacle—indeed, a performance—of desperation, begging elicits uncomfortable emotions (guilt, pity, fear, disgust), reminding passersby that all is not well in the social and economic life of the republic. For antebellum Americans, the violation of gender expectations contributed to these disruptions. A woman begging in public announced her departure from or failure to internalize the norms of appropriate female behavior—including demure resignation and an aversion to hailing strangers—and thus her similarity to prostitutes and other transgressors. Moreover, her presence as a street beggar suggested (to those invested in patriarchal social and economic structures, which would have included most observers) some man's failure to prevent her destitution.[20] For men, too, public begging marked a departure from a socially approved gender identity, in that the beggar obviously had not achieved the self-sufficiency of which industrious and able-bodied men were said to be capable in the United States.[21]

The central issue, however, for those who railed against public begging was the difficulty of verifying supplicants' claims.[22] Nineteenth-century Americans perceived urban poverty to be an ever-worsening crisis, marked both by an increase in the numbers of people requesting aid and by their greater opportunities for deception. According to David Rothman, colonial Americans' primary concern in determining whom to aid was jurisdiction rather than the character of the applicant: they asked, was he or she truly this town's responsibility?[23] But by the antebellum period, major cities had grown to the point that beggars could take advantage of their anonymity, moving to different neighborhoods as passersby began to recognize them. Urban deracination, however much it has been cited as a source of loneliness and discontentment, also represented an opportunity to remake oneself. Just as conduct books warned that some on the urban scene might adopt the trappings of a higher class status in order to gain access to certain kinds of employment, or social events, or marriage partners, charity literature cautioned against individuals who took the opposite tack, pretending to a level of destitution that might win them alms. Such figures accepted the accompanying loss of dignity, charity experts suggested, in exchange for freedom from labor and the satisfaction of a successful ruse.

When begging worked, it did so largely because the beggar managed to elicit the donor's sympathy. But as Glenn Hendler observes in the context of sentimental fiction, sympathy poses "a potential threat to the sympathizer's identity," a too-thorough identification resulting in the loss of oneself.[24] A donor's identification with a beggar, as described in charity texts, was typically less protracted and intense than those experienced by Hendler's protagonists. Nevertheless, individuals who identified too closely with street beggars risked damaging the larger charitable project, in that their resulting selflessness was thought to undermine cautious assessment. Authors of charity texts considered sympathy less risky if it were not so vigorously courted, if donors themselves selected the recipients. Under these circumstances charity workers retained the power to identify and investigate the needy, most notably by means of home visits, which came to be seen as the best available guarantors of an applicant's legitimacy. In 1847, for example, a visitor reported to the New York AICP his discovery that a black woman who had been begging on the street was not so poor as she claimed: after following her home he made "some inquiries" and discovered "that her husband drove a cart, owned some property, and was un-usually well off, for a person of his class." Nevertheless, the woman "pursued begging about as regularly as the husband his work, and had continued this course for years."[25] By locating and, typically, entering the ostensibly needy person's home, charity workers could take account of his or her environ-ment—the material markers of suffering or comfort and the other human be-ings who might betray the influence of vice or provide information that would unmask a deceiver. A hovel full of sick children and sewing projects, after all, signified very differently from one occupied by a drunken spouse and littered with incongruously luxurious goods.

The beggars whom these strategies were meant to foil engaged in a variety of passing. They faked destitution or illness, pretended to be blind, or bor-rowed hungry-looking children to make their appeals seem more urgent, all because they preferred such deceptions to working for a living, or so the story goes. As Harryette Mullen has argued, "passing is a kind of theft" within the nineteenth century's cultural logic; those who passed as needy, according to antebellum writers on charity, cheated not only the individual who gave them aid but also the "truly" impoverished, who went unaided as a result.[26] The trickster-beggar, according to Rees's *Philanthropist* editorial, "tells his sad (made up) story with a broken voice, and a tearful eye—his acting is so natu-ral—his grief so poignant, that the spectator falls into the snare, and is of course robbed on the instant."[27] That charity writers so dwelled on these mo-ments of deception suggests that they recognized them as challenges to their own authority, even as they drew attention to the deceiver's indirect victims, the worthy poor.

The methods by which professional beggars passed were salient topics in the discourse on charity. Eliza Farrar's *Adventures of Congo, in Search of His Master,* an English children's story republished in the United States in the 1840s, presents a gang of beggars in Cork, Ireland, whose leader dresses in rags and filth to elicit sympathy. He attempts—without success—to trap Congo, the African American protagonist, into a life of deception and de-bauchery by paying for his food and lodging, then demanding that he beg for the money to discharge his debt.[28] Professional beggars not only manipulated the better-off into unwise giving, Farrar was suggesting, but might also work to corrupt destitute innocents. Rees envisioned broader conspiracies. Street beggars, he claimed, are organized strategists who form "troops" and hold an "annual meeting" at which they "compare notes, and plan out ways and means for another year's campaign." Switching from martial to municipal metaphors, he went on to remark that "not unfrequently [*sic*] sums are paid by parties for the sole privilege of begging in certain streets; and a perfect system of . . . tax collectors, as they call themselves, is thus organized."[29] Here the beggar is a master of bureaucratic organization, administering a subterranean city government grown prosperous from the foolish offerings of unsuspecting members of the "legitimate" classes.

While Rees's imaginings hit a paranoiac high-water mark, other authors and illustrators cautioned against only slightly less intricate deceptions. Because the common injunction that one ought to be able to earn a living in the United States presumed able-bodiedness, a particularly good way to pass as needy, authors claimed, was to affect some sort of physical disability.[30] Such ruses were thought to be so common that the crutch served as an emblem of duplicitous begging. A cartoon, for example, that appeared in the June 1856 issue of the humor magazine *Yankee Notions* shows several alarmed citizens looking at what is labeled a "Characteristic Portrait of a Street Beggar, with two borrowed children and a sick husband." The portrait is festooned with wooden crutches, which frame the image of a woman in madonna-like garb who thumbs her nose at an apparently respectable group of onlookers. A *Vanity Fair* cartoon, also concerned with implements of deception, depicts a young crossing-sweeper who approaches an adult beggar as he is removing his wooden leg. To the boy's question, "Are you going to knock off already?" the beggar replies that he is only stopping to attach the prosthesis to the other knee and adds: "You don't suppose a fellow can beg all day on the same leg, do you?" In another issue of *Yankee Notions,* the representation of affected disability, this time of the "invisible" variety, features a woman with stereotypically Irish rhythms of speech whose ruse of affecting blindness is discovered by the man she tries to deceive.[31]

Each of these representations plays with the notion of disrupting established social hierarchies and patterns of deference. Although the woman who pretends to be blind does not succeed in duping the "gentleman" the first time, she has the audacity to try again with a different and equally incredible claim. Similarly, the nose-thumbing portrait betrays the woman's blatant disrespect toward her patrons and the vindictive pleasure she takes in the success of her charade. And the "one-legged man" who presumably tricks passersby into sympathizing with his condition attempts to elevate himself to the level of industrial workers by appropriating their increasingly vocal concerns regarding working conditions, comfort, and safety—though the image also implies that workers who raise such concerns are tantamount to beggars.

Characteristic Portrait of a Street Beggar, with two borrowed children and a sick husband.

2. Cartoon from *Yankee Notions*, June 1856. Courtesy, American Antiquarian Society.

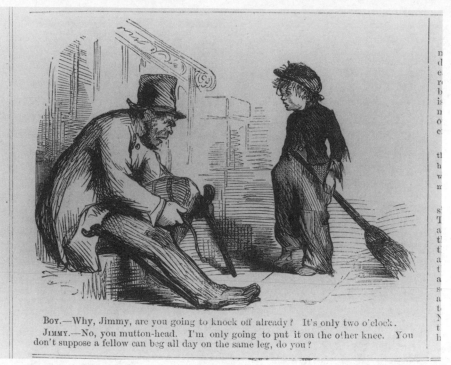

Boy.—Why, Jimmy, are you going to knock off already? It's only two o'clock.
Jimmy.—No, you mutton-head. I'm only going to put it on the other knee. You don't suppose a fellow can beg all day on the same leg, do you?

3. Cartoon from *Vanity Fair*, 11 February 1860. Courtesy, American Antiquarian Society.

These narratives and images suggest that, within the era's benevolent exchanges, power was more diffuse than it sometimes appeared. Those who considered themselves arbiters of need had to be circumspect lest they be made into or revealed to be fools. The problem was not so much that deceptive supplicants formed a "crafty aristocracy"—Melville's term in *Israel Potter* for begging Londoners who claimed to be war veterans—but rather that they made a mockery of the newly emerging middle class.[32] The professionalization of begging that charity texts invoked was both a perversion and a parody of Americans' growing investment in the worth of occupational expertise, the "culture of professionalism" that Burton Bledstein has identified as a dominant force in U.S. culture after 1840. The new American professional, Bledstein writes, "penetrated beyond the rich confusion of ordinary experience, as he isolated and controlled the factors, hidden to the untrained eye, which made an elaborate system workable or impracticable, successful or unattainable."[33] So, too, did professional beggars, whose understanding of human gullibility and sympathy allowed them to develop effective systems of deception. In antebellum discourse the beggar became the professional's dangerous other, one who rejected the constraints and expectations of conventional social and occupational advancement but who nevertheless discerned opportuni-

YANKEE NOTIONS.

Beggar.—"Young gentleman, plaize give a poor blind woman a penny."
Gent.—"How did you know that I am a man if you are blind?"
Beggar.—"O, I forgot, it's deaf and dumb I am, sure!"

4. Cartoon from *Yankee Notions*, November 1864. Courtesy, American Antiquarian Society.

ties and profited from study and calculation, all the while seeking a mode of achievement—a career—divorced from middle-class respectability.

From the donor's perspective, then, the professionalization of begging had to be matched by the professionalization of donors.[34] Charity writers promoted this change by creating an authoritative literature on benevolent practices, by championing rationality over emotion and rule-following over impulsivity, and by publicizing the work of increasingly bureaucratic charitable organizations. These efforts accorded with ideas about Anglo-Americans that were forming at other sites in the culture—that they possessed the managerial skills that immigrants and slaves supposedly lacked and that their positions of authority were both natural and beneficial to others. While the professionalization of social work would become thoroughly established only after the Civil War, its theoretical foundations and its earliest practical incarnations occurred earlier and owed much to the perception among the "charitable classes" that duplicity represented a pressing, if remediable, threat.

Some, of course, resisted this emphasis on ferreting out trickster-beggars. In keeping with sentimentalism's investment in the credibility of need, a number of antebellum authors, especially of sentimental poems and stories aimed at children, represented beggars' uninvestigated claims as entirely credible and urged readers to be generous.[35] But resistance to suspicion emerged in other kinds of texts as well—including some aligned more with reason than emotion. Along these lines, a few commentators argued against the strict categorization of the poor into the worthy and the unworthy. William Logan Fisher proposed in an 1831 treatise that pauperism owed more to structural inequities within the economy (specifically, the excessive accumulation of wealth by a few individuals) than to misguided benevolence toward the morally suspect.[36] Others turned to religious doctrine, claiming that God was a more appropriate judge than human beings of who merited assistance and who did not, while a small minority acknowledged the possibility of deception but advocated a willingness to give in spite of doubts. Henry L. Pinckney, a South Carolinian, gave voice to the latter position, declaring that it was better "a little charity should be thrown away, than that the waters should cease to flow. . . . Let it fall, like the gentle rain, upon the evil and the good."[37] The Universalist clergyman Edwin Hubbell Chapin most directly countered antebellum charity's ethos of suspicion: "If there were no alternative between the cleverness that suspects everybody, and the credulity that trusts everybody, I think I had rather be one of the dupes than one of the oracles. For, really, there is less misery in being cheated than in that kind of wisdom which perceives, or thinks it perceives, that all mankind are cheats."[38]

Such alternative views demonstrate the complexity of this cultural conversation, but even those who argued against suspicion typically acknowledged its prevalence. The rhetoric of suspicion appeared not only in the texts I have cited but also in sermons, novels, and periodical literature.[39] Donors and potential donors who shared that mistrust focused much of their attention on reading the body—reading hunger, disability, and, as the remainder of the chapter shows, race—as an indicator of character and "potential," the potential to achieve self-sufficiency as well as to deceive. But because the body offered such unreliable testimony, donors looked to other means of authentication, from "respectable" references to home visits. The illegible—or worse, the theatrical—supplicant was constantly changing tactics, remaking himself or herself in response to those who attempted to establish rules and safeguards. Dissatisfied with the assurance that, whatever the beggar's true circumstances, their alms met some sort of need, the benevolent sought a guarantee that, by their standards, they were doing well at doing good.

Duplicitous Others

Given the intensity of antebellum concerns over immigration and slavery—and given white Americans' growing attention to pseudoscientific theories of Anglo-Saxon superiority—it makes sense that race, ethnicity, and nationality would figure prominently in the era's discourses on benevolence. In some cases, Irish immigrants and African Americans were presented as especially deserving of aid because of their extreme poverty and histories of oppression. Such representations typically served arguments over slavery, in which, not incidentally, the interests of the two groups were pitted against each other: proslavery authors took northerners to task for their hypocritical mistreatment of Irish laborers, while abolitionists emphasized kindness toward black people, in contradistinction to southern injustices.[40] More often, though, whites who sought to establish themselves as arbiters of need portrayed racial, ethnic, and national outsiders as especially warranting suspicion. James Rees's editorial, cited above, suggested that Swiss and German farmers, less despised than the Celts but "foreigners" nevertheless, often hired out their land so that they could "emigrate to . . . [the United States], put on the dress of beggars, and actually make quarterly remittances home."[41] These invidious representations did not go uncontested. The Irish American author Mrs. Mary Sadlier, for example, presents in her novel *Willy Burke* a family of poverty-stricken Irish Catholic immigrants who are models of industry, piety, and independence. The title character's mother attends Mass each morning, "after which she commenced her daily toil with cheerful alacrity, for she had offered it to God, and did all for His sake."[42] But the more numerous charges of outsiders' laziness and dishonesty drowned out such counterclaims, however energetically they were put forth.

Anglo-Americans reacted with particular intensity to the prospect of blacks' duplicity, fearing that it might lead to "amalgamation" and other forms of social mixing. The supposed dishonesty of African Americans was a prominent theme well beyond charity discourse, as evidenced by the frequent representations of slaves who dissembled, stole, plotted rebellion, or ran away, and of those, both enslaved and free, who attempted to pass as white. The fugitive slave notices Harriet Beecher Stowe published in *A Key to Uncle Tom's Cabin,* with their descriptions of light-skinned slaves who were thought likely to try to pass, attest to the prominence of such deceptions in slaveholders' imaginations as well as in the practices of actual runaways.[43] But even an admitted fugitive could not necessarily be trusted. In a case that prefigured Harriet Wilson's portrayal of a fake fugitive slave in *Our Nig* (1859), a Worcester, Massachusetts, newspaper article from 1850, titled "Beware of Imposition," warned of a man named Charles W. Swift who claimed to be a runaway slave but who, the piece's antiabolitionist author declared, "finally exposed himself" as a fraud.[44] Allegedly false sufferers like Swift were said to gull abolitionists into helping them materially, publicizing their dubious stories, and launching their careers as public speakers, all the while stirring up political passions along with "misplaced" sympathy. In such cases, misguided benevolence was figured as a threat to the Union itself.

With the passage of the Fugitive Slave Act, especially acrimonious debate erupted in the 1850s over what precisely it meant to do good unto the United States' black populations. Proslavery, antislavery, and colonizationist factions had articulated and were promoting with renewed vigor plans for saving both the African race and the American republic. That African Americans might practice some sort of deception within those paradigms pointed to the possibility that the hierarchies on which they depended were more fluid than was readily apparent. What if emancipated slaves affected gratitude and docility for a while but then "turned" angry, demanding reparations or retribution? Or, less dramatically, what if the African American stranger collecting donations to redeem his children from slavery was in fact childless and used this ill-gotten money to eat better than his patrons? While the power of duping one's benefactors was in no way equivalent to the overt political, economic, and military power that many whites held, it nevertheless had the potential to disrupt things on a local level, to affect whose judgments proved accurate and whose definitions held sway. Saidiya Hartman's description of slaves' resistance pertains to these deceptions as well. Their "local assaults and pedestrian challenges," though "provisional and short-lived," nevertheless managed to "exploit the cleavages of the social order."[45]

Performing Need

Melville attends to these reversals and diffusions of power in his mid-1850s fictions of benevolence gone awry. Like his contemporaries, he locates the disarming, even threatening, quality of "the helped" in their illegibility, their resistance to the scrutiny of those characters who offer them aid, though his texts, unlike the charity literature on which they draw, provide no blueprints for a better practice of benevolence. In "Bartleby the Scrivener" (1853), for example, the narrator initially pursues a benevolent course toward his recalcitrant employee as a means of "cheaply purchas[ing] a delicious self-approval" but finds that he is not the charitable man-in-charge of his fantasies.[46] A well-executed managerial benevolence would never permit the "wondrous ascendancy" that Bartleby achieves over him, yet the narrator's attempts to follow the etiquette of charity fail miserably. He questions Bartleby closely to discover his origins and searches his belongings in imitation of charity agents' home visits but gleans nothing that might quell his discomfort or make his efforts more successful. Bartleby's recalcitrance, too, disrupts the geographies of urban charity, in that he moves his home into the lawyer's office. But this dwelling, in defiance of charity texts' claims that the homes of the poor served as reliable evidence, proves an inscrutable and at times literally inaccessible testament. As Bartleby more and more often "prefer[s]" not to do the work the narrator assigns him and yet "prefer[s]" not to "quit" him, the workplace/home becomes a site of work refusal—for charity experts, a clear sign that benevolence has failed.[47]

Despite its portrayal of the narrator's self-absorption and Bartleby's stubbornness, the story evokes in many readers a deep sympathy for both figures. *The Confidence-Man,* by contrast, though it more fully represents Americans' preoccupation with the vagaries of charity, maintains a greater affective distance from the needy and those to whom they appeal. The riverboat *Fidèle,* which serves as the novel's setting, stands in for, among other things, the anonymous city—one of many elements of nineteenth-century life that, according to charity writers, fostered unwise benevolence. But in its meditations and debates on the nature of charity, greed, and good intentions, Melville's novel eschews the self-assured didacticism of many charity texts, which posited an innocent donor whose benevolence must only be channeled appropriately and protected from the wiles of dishonest supplicants. Instead, *The Confidence-Man* problematizes both the donor's intentions and the very notion of benevolence, presenting a series of exchanges in which neither donor nor supplicant looks particularly blameless. That is, the title character assumes various guises in the course of this April Fools' Day voyage, but over and over he plays on the venality, cruelty, or dishonesty of his donors and dupes. Rather than invest in supposedly more reliable sources of information once the supplicant's body and self-presentation have proven untrustworthy, as charity experts advised, Melville explored the broader implications and hazards of that unreliability as well as the moral and social instabilities of donors.[48]

Such interrogations are especially pointed in one of the novel's early episodes, where "Black Guinea," a "grotesque negro cripple," catches in his mouth the coins a crowd of white passengers pitch to him.[49] This ostensibly black beggar moving among what Melville calls the "white flock" (*CM,* 11) recalls the figure of the masterless slave, whom proslavery forces used to represent the cruelties of wage labor and the likely results of emancipation, and whom antislavery forces used to indict slave owners who claimed to care for elderly and disabled slaves but often merely turned them out. Melville, however, does not situate Black Guinea securely in either discourse, using him instead to dramatize the challenges to white benevolence that black emancipation posed. Ultimately, the episode's attention to the racial identity of the beggar stages an epistemological quandary, one that exposes the intimate relationship in antebellum America between knowing race and knowing benevolence, even as it establishes the questions of identity and trust that dominate the rest of the novel.

Integral to the episode is Melville's unflattering portrayal of whites engaged in public acts of donation. While the narrator calls the exchange between passengers and beggar a "game of charity" and refers to the coin-tossers' acts as "frolic benignities" (*CM*, 12), it becomes clear that not everyone is having fun: Black Guinea, as he bobs back and forth catching coins, struggles to keep them "this side [of] the oesophagus" and winces when some come "inconveniently nigh to his teeth" (*CM*, 11). This dehumanizing game—the narrator remarks that "as in appearance [the beggar] seemed a dog, so now, in a merry way, like a dog he began to be treated" (*CM*, 11)—also conjures up unsavory images of sexual exploitation, in that the beggar, whose face is at the level of the other passengers' upper thighs, takes into his mouth the excesses of the economically better off.

The representation of charitable giving as purchased entertainment, as public humiliation, and indirectly as hired fellatio was atypical, to say the least, for the era.[50] Melville's portrayal intersects with more conventional modes of discourse on benevolence in its insistence that charity is "a singular temptation" (*CM*, 11) that can entrap unsuspecting individuals, but it is unusual in its attention to charity's more unsettling pleasures. It was one thing to enjoy reading or writing about successfully executed benevolent plans or to derive satisfaction from the timely discovery of a supplicant's trickery, but quite another to take pleasure in the act of tossing coins into someone's mouth. While those more frequently acknowledged pleasures constructed benevolent Americans as morally upstanding and admirably astute, Melville's representation highlights the donors' unseemliness, their cruelty, and their quasi-erotic enjoyment of another's humiliation.

As the episode exposes these pleasures, however, it also manifests the threat that the beggar's suspected duplicity presents. Like many of his contemporaries, Melville makes much of donors' attempts at detection. One onlooker, a "wooden-legged" and "sour-faced" man whom the narrator presumes to be a "discharged custom-house officer," insists that benevolence and wisdom are mutually exclusive qualities. Before others voice their suspicions, the onlooker asserts that the beggar's "deformity" is "a sham, got up for financial purposes," and that he is "some white operator, betwisted and painted up for a decoy" (*CM*, 12, 14).[51] In the latter statement the specifics of the beggar's ruse (that he is "betwisted" and "painted up") are subordinated syntactically to a declaration of his foundational whiteness and dishonesty. If "looks are one thing, and facts are another," as the doubter insists, then racial identity belongs to the latter category, regardless of appearances (*CM*, 14). The choice of the word *decoy* is pertinent as well. As something used to draw an animal or person out of hiding, it marks the white passengers as imperiled, drawn into firing range, so to speak, by the beggar's antics, but it also suggests that qualities they might prefer to hide—pettiness, cruelty—are being drawn out for scrutiny. The wooden-legged man reverses the terms of his own metaphor by treating Black Guinea as his quarry and works to turn the crowd against the beggar despite their apparent affinities. The narrator, after all, describes the beggar and his accuser as "fellow-limper[s]" and suggests that the latter, himself a victim of suddenly halted patronage, might have cause to identify with the beggar's dependence (*CM*, 12). But limping is, strictly speaking, a volitional act, not proof of incapacity, just as, for this observer, one's apparent skin color can be achieved through paint and therefore has no bearing on the "facts."

Located at this intersection of appearances and facts is the beggar's body, that which might verify or disprove his claims to legitimate destitution and that through which the wooden-legged man might know himself as astute doubter or as ill-tempered tormentor. In his zeal "to prove [the beggar's] alleged imposture on the spot," the investigator "would . . . have stripped him and then driven him away" had he not been prevented from doing so by the crowd, who were temporarily "taking part with the poor fellow" (*CM*, 12). The proposed but never-enacted stripping reinforces the sexual titillation of the beggar's submissive penny-catching and gestures toward other means of shaming him through physical assault and exposure. The white passengers shrink from this openly aggressive method, but they, too, doubt Black Guinea's honesty and pursue their own, more decorous guarantees. The "young Episcopal clergyman" whom the narrator introduces, with "innocence, tenderness, and good sense triumvirate in his air," stands in for the charity establishment's genteel investigators, going off "with kind haste" to find a respectable white man who can "speak a good word for" the beggar (*CM*, 13, 14). White speech, his actions suggest, is less alarming and perhaps more trustworthy than black flesh.

Beggars and Slaves

The clergyman's search for a white man to verify Black Guinea's story echoes the tactics of abolitionist editors, who certified African Americans' slave narratives through white-authored prefaces and appended letters. The episode as a whole, however, recalls the iconography of the antislavery movement more than its editorial practices. That the beggar's "deformity," real or affected, cuts him "down to the stature of a Newfoundland dog" (*CM*, 10) invites comparison to the movement's widely distributed emblems, which featured a kneeling African American slave and the words "Am I not a man and a brother?" or "a woman and a sister?"[52] Because the emblem's message was formulated as a question rather than a direct statement, its creators placed the activist weight—the power to alter the slaves' status—on the (implied) white viewer's affirmative response, implying that African American "elevation" was contingent on white benevolence. The white citizen, though not represented within the image, was nevertheless its addressee and the instrument through which its work would be performed.

ANTI-SLAVERY EVENTS

DURING THE YEAR ENDING 5TH MARCH

1863.

AM I NOT A MAN AND A BROTHER

AM I NOT A WOMAN AND A SISTER

" Can we behold, unheeding,
    Life's holiest feelings crush'd ;—
While *Woman's* heart is bleeding,
    Shall *Woman's* voice be hush'd ?"

5. *Am I Not a Man and a Brother, Am I Not a Woman and a Sister.* This image combines the male and female versions of the emblem. Courtesy of the Boston Athenaeum.

These antislavery emblems created a disturbing slippage between the figure of the oppressed slave and that of the conniving beggar. Although the emblem's public supplicant was legitimized and distributed by white-run antislavery organizations and contained within a white-authored representation, he or she nevertheless posed a challenge to culturally dominant beliefs about appropriate modes of appeal. The image's effectiveness depended on its hyperpublicity, in the sense of both its mass circulation and its exposure of the violence and injustice of slavery. In pursuing this publicity, however, the image and its disseminators risked mobilizing the hostility and mistrust that Americans and, in particular, middle and upper-class urban northerners felt toward beggars. The transgression of privacy codes was crucial to antislavery political work: undermining the privacy and inviolability of the patriarchal southern household, after all, weakened the institution of slavery, just as publicizing the tortures and privations experienced by slaves and runaways proved, for some audiences, the urgency of the cause. But the antislavery emblem nevertheless worked to relocate this particular "race problem" within urban centers rather than on faraway plantations, insofar as its visual and verbal association of blackness with supplication and need may have heightened northerners' fears that emancipation without colonization would result in all too many pleading African Americans in "their" cities.[53]

Melville's grotesque portrayal of an importunate black man plays on the anxieties that this image conjured, but it negotiates the relationship between race and benevolence quite differently. Within the nineteenth century's racist logic, color had to be deemphasized if kinship were to be convincingly asserted on any large scale, given that most Americans, including most white abolitionists, were still acutely uncomfortable with what they termed *amalgamation,* the incorporation of racial others into one's "blood" family. So the antislavery emblem asked for inclusion, an acknowledgment of siblinghood, despite the supplicant's race and enslaved status. Melville's beggar, on the other hand, asks for alms on the basis of his putative racial identity and disability, which offer an explanation—other than vice or indolence—for his poverty. And because he asks for alms, which would only reinforce his low status, rather than for "elevation" to a familial relation with whites, his blackness, it would seem, need not be overlooked for the request to be granted. Nevertheless, precisely at the moment when black racial identity becomes the basis of an appeal to benevolence, it is called into question, becoming analogous, though not identical, to an unnecessary crutch or a borrowed sick child. In other words, Black Guinea is unproblematically black until he attempts to trade on his blackness.[54]

The text never resolves the mystery of the beggar's blackness, nor does it assure readers that the confidence man's subsequent personas are reliably white. Carolyn Karcher, in *Shadow over the Promised Land,* calls into question the racial identities of these later incarnations: "Is the Black Rapids man [for example] a white man who earlier masqueraded as a black, or a black man now masquerading as a white? There is no way of knowing, and that is precisely the point. Nothing could more radically discredit the concept of race."[55] I would take Karcher's point further. If, as Michael Rogin has written, "beneath the masquerade of *The Confidence-Man,* there is nothing at all," then perhaps all of the confidence man's racial identities, like his other identity markers, are masquerades.[56] He has no "real" race, just as he has no genuine place of origin, or profession, or habitual dress; he is a series of projections with no underlying substance, at least none that the novel allows us to discern. At issue for many contemporary readers, then, is his intelligibility, to borrow Amy Robinson's formulation, rather than his essence.[57]

Melville, however, lived in a world in which racial identity, however illegible or susceptible to masquerade, was widely thought to have ontological significance. Antebellum Americans generally believed that their racial attributions recurred to some natural and unalterable truth, which racial passing momentarily obscured. To the majority of whites, the most alarming prospect, as nineteenth-century fiction and polemical writings attest, was the possibility that someone designated black might pass for white and thus escape from slavery, or eat in the dining room of a northern hotel, or, most shockingly, marry someone who was "really" white and produce mixed-race children. Black Guinea, however, is accused of faking blackness rather than whiteness—not a clearly advantageous move, though his apparent disability minimizes one danger of faking blackness convincingly in 1850s America, that of being sold into slavery. Antebellum readers would have been familiar with the mimicking of blackness in minstrel shows, whether or not they attended such shows themselves, and the black beggar's performance, replete with tambourine and exaggerated dialect, certainly recalls the minstrel mode. But as Eric Lott points out, while some audience members mistook "blackface performers for blacks," for the most part the faked blackness was a joke that the audience was in on. "Minstrel sheet music . . . ," Lott notes, often "pictur[ed] blackface performers out of costume as well as in" or, more precisely, pictured them both in the costume of black performers and in the costume of white gentlemen, to discourage the public from falling for the ruse.[58] The *Fidèle*'s white passengers, although they are paying for a performance just as minstrel show audiences did, encounter no equivalent gesture of inclusion. Blackface, then, comes to represent for the passengers the embarrassed position of public uncertainty.[59]

For the white donors and onlookers, the most obvious problem with blackface begging is that it disrupts the prescribed hierarchies of benevolence in which donors are supposed to hold more social power than supplicants. If the supplicant is, as some of the passengers suspect, a trickster rather than (or in addition to) the destitute figure he claims to be, then his would-be patrons are in fact his dupes and can no longer think of themselves as astute judges of who merits help. In keeping with charity writers' warnings about the ostensibly weak figure's hidden power, the passengers must entertain the possibility that the beggar is in fact controlling the game, eliciting their sympathy and their donations under false pretenses. The implications of such a reversal extend beyond the immediate exchange. For one thing, the suspicion that the beggar is faking his blackness in an attempt to win the passengers' sympathy suggests that blackness, like disability, constituted a legitimate excuse for dependency, to the extent that it signified a lack of economic opportunity. But if a white person could affect blackness for a begging advantage, then what would stop "real" black people who were not actually poor—like the New Yorker who begged despite her husband's relative wealth—from using it as well? And what would happen to dark skin as a marker of social marginality if, in certain contexts, it became profitable?

Although blacks' destitution had the potential to elicit whites' sympathy, it also fulfilled whites' expectations, proving the degradation of the race (caused, many believed, by an inborn lack of motivation and industry) and the wisdom, even the necessity, of excluding its members from full citizenship. In this regard, racialized poverty is distinct from poverty that results from disability. Though some disabilities were congenital, and though there was still in U.S. culture a tendency to see physical deformity as a mark of the individual's or the parents' moral failings, it was also clear that disability could happen to anyone. A socially prominent family might include a disabled son or sister, while a previously successful worker might find himself, following an accident, suddenly unemployable. So disability was acknowledged to be a more porous category, one whose members might maintain ties of kinship, residence, or inheritance with the nondisabled. Race, meanwhile, occasioned more rigid policing of social boundaries.

Benevolent hierarchies and racial hierarchies were mutually reinforcing in antebellum culture, such that the black person as supplicant came to seem commonsensical. In this sense, the image of a black beggar would be comforting to some because it would reaffirm whites' belief in black incapacity and in their own superiority. Therefore, the possibility that Melville's black beggar is not actually black alarms the donors because it undermines their self-congratulatory associations and unsettles the ingrained tendency to associate need with other reified forms of marginality. A more pressing anxiety in Melville's text, however—one that has the white passengers feeling "a little qualmish about the darkie," as one of them puts it (*CM,* 16)—is the implication that, by participating in this pitch-penny game with one whose racial identity is in doubt, they may be degrading the wrong kind of person. Black Guinea's humiliation, after all, is extreme. His body is not only treated as untrustworthy evidence, like the bodies of other supplicants, but it also becomes a repository for the donors' spare change. So if the beggar is not black but is nevertheless humiliated in the ways Melville's narrator describes, then the donors are degrading or dehumanizing someone who, according to their culture's dominant logic, does not deserve it. As Karcher puts it, Black Guinea's performance leaves the passengers "no way of being sure that the treatment American society has reserved for him as a black may not have been 'mistakenly' inflicted on a white."[60] The status, by which I mean the minimal guaranteed dignity, of all nonblack people is thereby called into question. A white trickster who would initiate such a ruse is a sort of race traitor, manipulating other whites into degrading a member of their own race. And if the performance is not exclusively a trick—if destitution and trickery coexist in this figure and a white man needs money so badly that he would go to these lengths to get it—then in the process he mobilizes the white passengers' fear of falling, of ending up so desperate themselves that they, too, might take up begging, in blackface or otherwise. Only if it goes undiscovered can the ruse of blackface begging leave intact the myth of white able-bodied self-sufficiency.

My reading of this episode has focused on the passengers' perspectives and on their analogous relationship to white antebellum readers of the novel, who would likely have felt similar discomfort with beggars and who would have situated African Americans similarly in their notions of benevolent exchange. In some sense, the novel encourages this emphasis. Textual evidence strongly suggests that the beggar is one incarnation of the confidence man, who is marked by that epithet as one not to be trusted: Black Guinea names as his references and authenticators some of those who, later in the novel, appear more obviously as confidence men, including the man with the weed, the herb doctor, and the man with the brass plate. And, near the end of the episode, the beggar conceals a country merchant's dropped business card, which the confidence man's next avatar uses in order to pretend an acquaintanceship with him. So the beggar is in some sense cheating (and in this instance, investigating) his patrons, although from another perspective they are getting precisely what they pay for—a game or performance. This exchange exemplifies what Wai Chee Dimock has termed the "folly of contract," the choice that complicates their identities as victims.[61] The role that self-interest and volition play in the behavior of Black Guinea's donors prepares readers for the novel's subsequent confidence games, which explicitly take advantage of the dupes' greed.

However complicit the donors/dupes may be, though, they are the characters whose subject positions Melville most clearly invites readers to consider: he represents their voices, their musings, and their doubts throughout the chapter. At times, the narrative attends more closely to the conflicts and exchanges between white men that Black Guinea's presence prompts than to the beggar himself.[62] A prominent interpretive strain within twentieth-century scholarship pushes readers further in this direction by associating Black Guinea and the confidence man with the devil or with abstract evil, thereby suggesting, if not insisting, that readers identify with and trust Melville's white donors rather than his beggar.[63] Nevertheless, the novel's representations encourage a disgust with the passengers' behavior and a sympathy for the beggar that does not allow readers' identification with the former group to persist comfortably. The narrator's attention to the unpleasantness of penny-catching gives way to a fuller consideration of the beggar's position: "To be the subject of alms-giving is trying, and to feel in duty bound to appear cheerfully grateful under the trial, must be still more so" (*CM*, 11). He goes on to note the beggar's labored grins and his swallowing of "secret emotions" (*CM*, 11). These remarks are phrased as conjecture rather than as direct representations of the beggar's experience—he remains essentially unknown and, within the logic of the narrative, unknowable—but they nevertheless draw attention to his perspective. In doing so, they destabilize the reader's sympathies, identifications, and pleasures, all the while undermining any simplistic or comfortable assessments of what Melville has to say about charity. Perhaps, then, one reason *The Confidence-Man* was received so unenthusiastically in its time is that it left white readers feeling "a little qualmish" about their own ostensibly benevolent acts.

The Unwise Donor

"Benito Cereno," published serially in the fall of 1855, also features an intersection between white benevolence and racial masquerade.[64] The deception here, however, involves individuals whose black racial identity is never called into question but who adopt a posture of subservience in order to pass as slaves, a performance that obscures the fact of their recent rebellion. At issue is not their racial designation per se but its social and political significance; Amasa Delano, the New England-born ship's captain who serves as their audience and dupe, considers them appropriate objects of benevolence only so long as they adhere to his racist expectations. In its examination of the racial contingencies of white benevolence, "Benito Cereno" dramatizes what *The Confidence-Man* only hints at: far more than pennies and pride are at stake when benevolent actors misread the objects of their aid.[65]

Like all effective confidence men, Babo and his co-conspirators devise their ruse according to the ideologies and expectations that condition not only what their dupe wants to see but what he is able to see. They rely on the fact that Delano finds a way to interpret all that he encounters, including profoundly incongruous events, in accordance with a foundational equation of blackness with enslavement. Early in his visit on board the *San Dominick*, Delano focuses on its captain, Benito Cereno—his apparent ill health, his nervous tics, and his inadequacies as a leader—all in an effort to discern how he and his ship have arrived at this state of (apparent) destitution and whether his intentions are benign or "piratical" (*BC*, 68). That Delano discerns the ship's distress and chooses to approach it—a benevolent method that charity authorities considered superior to answering direct appeals for aid—gives him little comfort. But for all the suspicion he directs toward Cereno, the American captain presumes the ship's black inhabitants to be utterly transparent. When Delano does pay attention to Babo, the leader of the revolt, he reads him as the quintessence of what he believes all black men to be: loyal, affectionate, and adept personal servants, naturally cheerful, with "the docility arising from the unaspiring contentment of a limited mind" (*BC*, 84).[66] (Atufal, the "slave" who appears before Cereno in chains every two hours, is something of an exception, a point to which I will return.) The solution to the puzzle—that the small, deferential black man is actually in charge—is the one possibility Delano cannot entertain.

Once it becomes clear that Babo and the other purported slaves have murdered a number of whites, including their owner, and taken over the ship, Cereno's strange behavior can be reconceived as the result of his terrorized position as mock-captain and Delano's shuttling between good-natured officiousness and misplaced suspicion can be reinterpreted as monumental obtuseness. This revelation has often been read as an assault on the logic of slavery, suggesting that Africans are not naturally servile, as the antebellum era's scientific racism would have it, but must learn subservience in the course of their captivity and, in the case of the *San Dominick* rebels, must explicitly and self-consciously perform it.[67]

Just as "Benito Cereno" undermines the ideologies of slavery (though the effectiveness and consistency of that critique are a matter of debate), the text also destabilizes the theory and practice of white benevolence. Benevolence, the narrator informs us, is Delano's most salient characteristic. He possesses "a singularly undistrustful good nature," is reluctant to acknowledge "malign evil in man," and is at times "oblivious of any but benevolent thoughts" (*BC*, 47, 80). This element of his temperament finds expression not only in his irrepressible need to attribute to others good intentions but also in the alacrity with which he comes to the aid of the distressed ship, providing its inhabitants with water, cider, and pumpkins, among other supplies and services. He is the quintessential unwise donor—eager, impulsive, and ready to commit resources well before his investigation of the needy is complete. The narrator's remark early on that benevolence might be incompatible with great intelligence further suggests that Delano is a fool. Had he been less blindly good-natured, he would have had the rebels "safely" back in chains a good deal sooner.[68] But there is also the assertion, voiced by Delano himself and supported to some extent by the story's outcome, that his benevolence—the interweaving, Delano claims, of his "good nature, compassion, and charity"—saves him from being murdered by the rebels (*BC*, 115). More negatively, Delano can be taken to represent an obtuse brand of northern humanitarianism, one whose proponents have drained sympathy for the oppressed of its critical content. He provides the "slaves" with food and water but cannot fathom giving them their freedom or altering their circumstances in any other way.

The cultural work of Delano's benevolence is best understood in the context of the antebellum discourse on slavery. The assertion of a caring, familial relationship between master and slave, long a staple of proslavery rhetoric, became a central preoccupation of slaveholders and their allies after the publication of *Uncle Tom's Cabin* (1851–52). In direct response to Stowe's portrait of that ideology's failures, novels such as Mary Eastman's *Aunt Phillis's Cabin* (1852) and John W. Page's *Uncle Robin, in His Cabin in Virginia, and Tom without One in Boston* (1853) depicted loyal, affectionate slaves who either lived only to serve "massa" and "missus" or were tempted away by scheming abolitionists, only to find that northern wage labor, like northern weather, was far from congenial. Babo's performance of loyalty, subservience, and loving care toward Cereno, particularly in the oft-cited shaving scene, parodies such idealized representations, while Delano's credulous response to that performance suggests the extent to which proslavery representations conditioned nonslaveholders' beliefs about interracial benevolence. In fact, Delano so admires

Babo's and Cereno's embodiment of this ideal that he wishes to acquire it for himself by purchasing Babo. Delano's encounter on the *San Dominick* becomes a fantasy of benevolent white supremacy. He wishes to rescue the ship's desperately needy black inhabitants, to provide them with the sustenance that, in the absence of effective white leadership (or so he imagines), they have been unable to procure for themselves, and to enjoy, in return, the ministrations of this most devoted servant.

Delano's thoughts of replacing Cereno with himself address what the American captain sees as a pressing problem: Cereno's inability to fulfill his responsibilities as benevolent patriarch. Delano notes what he perceives as lapses of discipline on board the *San Dominick,* including black sailors who show inadequate deference to whites. Cereno fails to take charge at the expected moments, yet he seems inordinately harsh, even tyrannical, in his behavior toward certain slaves, (apparently) keeping Atufal in chains and cutting Babo's face with a razor to punish him, or so Babo claims, for inflicting a small cut while shaving his master. Melville's use of the word *friend* bears on this question of Cereno's inadequacy. Delano says to Cereno, after hearing of Babo's great devotion, "I envy you such a friend; slave I cannot call him" (*BC,* 57). On one level, this remark works to sustain the story's irony: Babo, the reader eventually discovers, is neither Cereno's friend nor his slave. But *friend* signifies in other ways as well, suggesting a mutuality or peer status that works against the usual hierarchical structures of benevolent exchange. In fact, the exercise of benevolence within a friendship might ultimately prove destructive rather than helpful, as dependency and superiority work to unsettle a previously equitable relationship. Despite these considerations, the word *friend* was often used to signify an agent of benevolence. Within the logic of paternalism, the slave owner occupies this agent's role, sheltering his slaves from the inhumanity of wage labor and enjoying, in return, their loyal service but not *their* benevolence. If Cereno has made a slave his friend, in the sense of either peer or benefactor, then something has gone wrong.

Given Delano's belief that "nothing more relaxes good order than misery" (*BC,* 51–52), an obvious component of his benevolent project on the *San Dominick* is the reimposition of sociopolitical hierarchy. But as Delano's dealings with Cereno indicate, not just any white patriarch will do. There are divisions and gradations within whiteness and within masculinity that bear on the successful maintenance of the hierarchies Melville invokes. Cereno is a slender, sickly captain with "small, yellow hands" and little apparent managerial or sailing skill, whose Spanish and Catholic origins seem to Delano to foster cruel and capricious behavior (*BC,* 58). To an extent, however, Delano attempts to "repair" Cereno through a carefully configured benevolence. While much of this effort takes the form of advice on how Cereno might restore his eroded authority, Delano also structures his material aid so that Cereno can reclaim an appropriately high status. He demands from Cereno eventual repayment, so that his "donations" can be reconceived as a loan from one peer to another.

Benevolence toward the ship's black inhabitants, however, is explicitly contingent on and calculated to maintain their subservience, insofar as racial identity determines, for Delano, what kinds of suffering merit his intervention. In the end, Babo and the other conspirators must be punished not only because they have killed a number of whites but also because they have attempted to finesse these distinctions. By accepting white benevolence under false pretenses, they have made a mockery of Delano's paternalist fantasies.

Delano's particularly strong benevolent feelings toward Atufal, the "slave" in chains, complicate this schema, suggesting that his perceptions and responses have been shaped, albeit obliquely, by antislavery as well as proslavery discourses. By the 1850s, a white northerner's sympathy for a chained slave would have been informed by an abundance of visual images and verbal descriptions of slaves' mistreatment. As Elizabeth Clark has written, "in the 1830s . . . the gruesome tribulations of the body became a staple of antislavery literature." Prominent examples of the genre include Lydia Maria Child's *Appeal in Favor of That Class of Americans Called Africans* (1833), which featured, among other proofs of cruelty, drawings of various horrific implements of torture, and Theodore Dwight Weld's *American Slavery as It Is* (1839), which Clark calls a "catalog of atrocities."[69] This emphasis on bodily punishment persisted throughout the antebellum period, especially in slave narratives and antislavery newspapers, with the oft-stated goal of teaching sympathy and inspiring abolitionist activism. Although Delano does not see Atufal being whipped or otherwise tortured, the latter's confinement in chains and his regimented appearances before his "master" recall this elaborate discourse and iconography of the suffering slave (*BC*, 62). But Delano's sympathy extends only to his advising Cereno to unchain the man. Antislavery discourse might stimulate certain kinds of sympathy, concern, or outrage, but in contrast to the hopes of authors like Child and Weld, the next step—action toward emancipation—was not necessarily forthcoming.

On one level, Delano's reaction to Atufal's treatment accords with his hierarchical view of benevolence—specifically, his requirement that black candidates for aid be as destitute and "degraded" as possible. Atufal appears as the most subjugated of the apparent slaves on board—he is the only one in chains, after all—and therefore seems the most deserving of aid. But this correspondence is complicated by Delano's outrage at Atufal's treatment, which rests on the incongruity between Atufal's subjugation and his physical stature, apparent strength, and reputed status as kidnapped African royalty. He is someone who would perhaps have held slaves himself, someone who, to Delano's way of thinking, was not always like this.[70] Delano's investment in Atufal's supposedly diminished status and power works against his attributions at other points in the text of an essential black subservience. Moreover, his impulse to help Atufal implies a desire to restore some portion of the latter's former dignity, which recurs to a belief in his natural elevation above the other Africans.

Delano's contemplation of Atufal's suffering carries a significant erotic charge as well. As Karen Halttunen has argued, by the antebellum period tales of cruelty toward slaves (and toward prisoners, sailors, the insane, and others) participated in a "pornography of pain." Despite their apologies and disclaimers, "reformers were caught up in the same cultural linkages of revulsion with desire that fueled a wide range of popular literary explorations of pain"—sensationalist murder tales, gothic horror, and sexually explicit material that we would now call sadomasochistic. And although reformers tried to educate their readers in appropriate responses to "spectacles of suffering," they could not control how their representations would be used or interpreted.[71] While many of these images involved female victims and presumed heterosexual desire, Delano's "surveying" of Atufal's "colossal"—and chained—"form" also operates within this well-established system of desiring gazes and subjugated bodies (*BC,* 62). Images of chained and whipped slaves, whether male or female, conjured more than chaste humanitarian outrage. But the sexualizing of benevolence also found expression in other aspects of the culture, in representations of beautiful, vulnerable seamstresses and orphans ever on the verge of sexual defilement, as well as in the suggested fellatio of Black Guinea's coin-catching game. And the phenomenon continues to extend well beyond the fantasy life of the reader/viewer/benevolent actor. The sexual exploitation of "helped" populations has proven all too common within asylums, families, and other social institutions structured by benevolent ideals. Though some would argue that such exploitation has more to do with opportunity—with the coexistence of more and less powerful individuals within a privatized space—than with the infusion of benevolent discourse, I maintain that the two are inseparable, that the language of benevolence works to construct both the inequality and the social space within which it occurs.

The erotic elements of Delano's experience on the *San Dominick* operate very much within this paradigm. In addition to his meditation on Atufal's subjection, Delano indulges in a long look at a bare-breasted "slumbering negress . . . lying, with youthful limbs carelessly disposed . . . like a doe in the shade of a woodland rock" (*BC,* 73) and an extended observation of Cereno and Babo's physical intimacy, which calls up Delano's "old weakness for negroes" (*BC,* 84).[72] The black people on whom he rests his gaze are, he presumes, the passive, unthreatening objects of his desire as well as the grateful recipients of his benevolence. The overturning of the ship's social and racial hierarchies, then, also suggests that the objects of one's sexual desire or fantasy-level gratification may not be what one thinks they are, though that intimation may prove erotic as well. In Delano's case, the docile "doe" of a slave woman, the sight of whom "somehow insensibly deepened his confidence and ease" (*BC,* 73), was one of those who would have tortured Aranda to death had the others not restrained them, while Babo, the white man's body servant, is actually holding a blade to his throat.

Perhaps most disturbing for Delano and for Melville's white readers is the transferal of the subjugated position within this pornographic scene of pain from a captive African to his European adversaries, Cereno and Aranda. What was previously a mildly titillating spectatorship, complete with Delano's (and perhaps the white reader's) safe identification with—and mild disapproval of—Cereno as the inflictor of pain, is transformed upon the revelation of the slaves' rebellion into an identification with Cereno and Aranda as victims, if we extend the narrative's alignment of Delano's subjectivity with Cereno's.[73] The Spanish captain's experience of the shaving scene must then be reread as a moment of subjugation rather than servicing, and Aranda's death and burial at sea must be reimagined as a scene of murder and dismemberment so horrible that Cereno cannot relate it.[74] The text's implied substitution of European for African bodies represents a change in what Marianne Noble calls its "grammar of domination," such that different beings come to occupy the positions of torturer and tortured.[75] Delano's previously comfortable desires, then, metamorphose into something nightmarish and unpredictable. In response, the eroticism of pain that initially focused on the imagined subjugation of black bodies must instead become explicitly masochistic, be made somehow nonsexual, or be thoroughly repressed.

Peter Stallybrass and Allon White, in their analysis of the sexualization of hierarchy, write that "the 'top' attempts to reject and eliminate the 'bottom' for reasons of prestige and status, only to discover, not only that it is in some way frequently dependent upon that low-Other . . . but also that the top *includes* that low symbolically, as a primary eroticized constituent of its own fantasy life."[76] This characterization accords with Delano's objectification of "the low" prior to the disclosure of Babo's ruse, in that his descriptions evince a mixture of desire and disgust. But the story's outcome suggests that his experience is less about some ongoing incorporation or fusing than about a reversal and its correction, a process that ultimately kills Cereno but leaves Delano, the more skilled at repression, unchanged. Like the "bright sun," "the blue sea, and the blue sky" he cites, Delano has "forgotten it all" (*BC*, 116).

Sustainable Benevolence

Captain Delano's encounter with this threat of sexualized domination is only one of many stagings in *The Confidence-Man* and "Benito Cereno" of white panic and recontainment in the face of unstable benevolent and racial hierarchies. Delano and the *Fidele*'s penny-pitchers, serving as proxies for Melville's benevolent readers, experience the precariousness of their positions and the manipulable nature of their charitable gestures and judgments even as they work, with varying degrees of success, to reestablish what Robert Levine has called their "captaincy."[77] In these texts, benevolent projects and their accompanying rhetorics speak more reliably about the helpers than the helped. We never really know Babo or Black Guinea or, perhaps most poignantly, Bartleby the Scrivener, whose relationship with his employer engages the hierarchies and complications of social class. What motivates these figures, how they conceive of their actions and their positions within the scenes of benevolence Melville creates, remains undisclosed or, in the case of Bartleby, unintelligible. Readers' final impressions of them are enigmatic and exteriorized—Black Guinea "forlornly stump[ing] out of sight" (*CM*, 17), Bartleby huddled dead against a wall, and Babo's decapitated head, that "hive of subtlety, fixed on a pole" (*BC*, 116).

Melville's erasures are not consistently borne out elsewhere in antebellum culture, however. Not only were the voices of the helped ventriloquized in any number of texts, fictional and otherwise, but individual recipients (or seekers) of aid sometimes found their own way into print. Authors of slave narratives, for example, recounted instances of white benevolence, in the process betraying their ambivalence as well as their gratitude. Less widely read now are the beggars' narratives that Ann Fabian analyzes in *The Unvarnished Truth* (2000), texts through which destitute authors sought to turn their misfortune into "a little authority and a little cash."[78] Slaves, beggars, blind girls, one-armed men, orphans, and widows: figures of need pervaded antebellum print culture, whether they appeared as ciphers, as voiced subjects, or, most often, as overt projections of a (relatively) privileged author's ideologies and concerns. Such figures signified in varied, even contradictory, ways, marking at some moments the limits of national inclusion and at others the promise of a transformed social order.

For benevolent Anglo-Americans, representations of the needy crucially informed their articulations of their own identities and their attempts to inculcate certain values and perspectives in subsequent generations. An article from *The Slave's Friend,* an antislavery periodical for children, makes this reproduction explicit. The anonymous author of a piece titled "The Boys We Want" remarks that "little abolitionists must be noble-minded, generous, hardy, self-denying, courageous. If they are not, how can they manage the affairs of the Anti-Slavery society when they are grown up?"[79] A relationship with a needy black population, mediated through an established organization, emerges here as a constitutive element in the character formation of white boys, who are encouraged to develop the qualities that will make them good managers of benevolence. Certainly abolitionists hoped for a speedier end to slavery than this quotation suggests, but inherent in the language of the antislavery movement and in the charity discourses with which it overlapped was the notion that white benevolence—its narratives, practices, and institutions—would produce better white people in the present and coming generations. And those improved citizens required the ongoing presence of the needy (slaves, the destitute, the ignorant) to continue their work. As much as abolitionists and others who sought to aid the oppressed worked for change, they simultaneously registered the wish that those unfortunates might serve as stable referents, the ever-in-need and ever-suffering beings with respect to whom they could shore up their identities as good people. In the absence of destitute others, claims of salvific whiteness would make little sense.

However complex and contradictory, benevolent white Americans' self-fashioning through alterity was far from idiosyncratic. More intriguing is the fact that those who used benevolence as a mode of identity construction, dependent as they would seem to be on the stability and knowability of the helped, repeatedly acknowledged the impossibility of such certitude. The preoccupation with duplicity that we see in antebellum charity discourse marks its participants' awareness that the helped were not always as they appeared. Within the range of available deceptions, including faked disability and undisclosed resources, racial masquerade took on particular significance: in the context of the antebellum period's increasingly rigid notions of racial differentiation, its investment in the power of science to define the characteristics, capacities, and prospects of the various races, racial masquerade was especially revealing of white donors' lapses of judgment. Whites who expected debility and inferiority among those of African descent, who, in effect, expected black beggars, were particularly susceptible to such a figure's faked destitution. And if a black person could convincingly fake whiteness or a white person could fake blackness, then those supposedly immutable qualities of the races and, by extension, the racial coding of benevolent projects proved unreliable or illegitimate after all.

It makes sense, then, that so many charity experts invested themselves in structured, vigilant investigative practices, even as others made their peace with uncertainty. Coupled with charity texts' articulations of an idealized, saving whiteness, there emerged an anxious and always possibly foolish whiteness, one exposed and indeed structured by duplicitous need. All this is not to dismiss the genuine desire to alleviate suffering that many antebellum authors expressed. But such earnestness could not cancel out the workings of power within what Peggy Pascoe has called "relations of rescue."[80] Benevolent projects are always in some sense about power and its pleasures—the power to give or to withhold, to identify the needy and the deserving, to alter the patterns of comfort and suffering within a society. Antebellum writers on charity represented this as a troubling endeavor, ever threatening to slip out of their control, to allow a redistribution of resources, of voice, and of authority that might work against their interests or what they perceived to be the interests of society as a whole. The possibility of duplicity ensured that, at any given moment, this exercise of power could produce results other than those the helper anticipated or intended. Such were the foundations of whites' much-represented misgivings.

CHAPTER THREE

The Racial Politics of Self-Reliance

I am for doing good to the world once for all and having done with it.

HERMAN MELVILLE, *The Confidence-Man: His Masquerade* (1857)

In Melville's *Confidence-Man*, Frank Goodman, the last of the title character's many avatars, engages in an extended conversation over a bottle of port with a fellow passenger named Charlie Noble. After trading observations on the nature of charity and geniality, Frank announces to his companion that he is "in want, urgent want, of money" and adds that, while he needs fifty dollars, he "could almost wish" he needed more so that Charlie might prove the "noble kindliness" implied by the latter's prior remarks. Charlie, however, responds with a most ungenial "go to the devil, sir!" Calling Frank an "impostor," he asserts that he was "never so deceived in a man" in all his life.[1] The immediate joke is that Charlie Noble, himself a confidence man or "Mississippi operator," as he is later called, has chosen for his dupe a fellow trickster whose manipulative skills exceed his own (*CM*, 196). But rather than acknowledge his thwarted designs, Charlie adopts a representative bourgeois outrage, excoriating Frank for turning out to be just another "beggar" (*CM*, 179).

Dressed as a well-off eccentric and commenting self-assuredly on human nature, Frank Goodman, up to the point of his request for money, pretends to possess what beggars purportedly lack: self-reliance. Writers of charity literature deplored beggars' dependence, their failure to prosper or, barring that, to achieve a meek subsistence. And yet, as I argued in chapter 2, the trickster-beggars whom antebellum authors so often represented and vilified were objectionable precisely because they were far *less* dependent than they claimed. Their transgression consisted of obscuring the qualities and resources that might render them self-sufficient after all. As Melville's episode and the larger cultural conversation on beggars make clear, questions of dependence and independence permeated antebellum representations of benevolence: Which forms of each were morally and socially acceptable? Who was thought capable of achieving independence and, by extension, who was eligible for membership in a nation that increasingly conceived of itself—or, at least, of its white male population—as a collection of independent, self-asserting, and self-supporting individuals? And how might charity agents bring about those desired transformations? Integral to these questions was a nexus of terms—*self-reliance, self-support, self-exertion, self-dependence,* and *self-elevation*—that were almost as overused and overdetermined in the antebellum years as *benevolence.* The terms were not interchangeable: self-elevation, for example, implied a preexistent degradation that the individual needed to remedy, while self-support might have been in place all along. But whatever their nuances, all posited an ameliorative liberalism, an individual human agency that could overcome hardships, social boundaries, and restrictions. In doing so, they drew on a conception of ideal personhood that was developing not just within liberalism but within the antebellum discourse of benevolence as well. The desirable social actor in this context was fundamentally unburdensome. He or she demanded nothing of benevolent organizations or individual donors and did not tax the loyalty and goodwill of family or friends, at least no more so than was thought age- and gender-appropriate.

Emersonian self-reliance, with which this chapter begins, is one of many antebellum attempts to represent and evaluate dependence and its opposites. While some commentators presented self-reliance as a desirable and achievable goal, if facilitated by the strategies of charity experts, others expressed great unease about such transformations, especially when the (initially) dependent population was of African descent. The era's debates over how to help the nonwhite population of the United States focused with particular intensity on the issue of independence—how to encourage its development or how to accommodate a group's "natural" lack of it. But such controversies included an anxious subtext: How would the nation's social and political structures be altered if once-needy black people became self-reliant? Or, how would those structures have to change in order to bring about or allow such an outcome? Among the strategies that writers on charity developed vis-à-vis these questions was to emphasize mutual aid, already well established among free African Americans in the North, rather than the model of self-reliance that they endlessly recommended for needy whites. Through such intraracial benevolent organizations, some suggested, black communities would take responsibility for "their own" without raising the specter of *individual* black independence. Frederick Douglass was among those who questioned this insistence on a collective black identity, though in doing so he struggled to balance independence and self-assertion with a responsibility to community that was structured by benevolent ideals.

By beginning with Emerson and ending with Douglass, I risk reproducing the terms of much twentieth-century scholarship, which narrates the triumph of American possessive individualism and self-making from Benjamin Franklin forward. One of many problems with that trajectory is that Douglass was too conscious of the risks and compromises of individualism and too invested, albeit ambivalently, in African American communities to fit neatly into it. The more complicated story told in this chapter puts Emerson and Douglass into conversation with their era's voluminous writings on benevolence. These authors and their more obscure contemporaries, through their representations of dependence and independence, were negotiating and in some sense defining both masculinity and the racial and moral identities crucial to its expression. Self-reliance was not simply a matter of earning one's keep—it was a means of asserting, for oneself and for one's race, a social and moral maturity that antebellum Americans strongly associated with manhood.

The Nonchalance of Boys

In a famously cranky passage near the beginning of "Self-Reliance" (1841), Emerson writes:

> Do not tell me, as a good man did to-day, of my obligation to put all poor men in good situations. Are they *my* poor? I tell thee, thou foolish philanthropist, that I grudge the dollar, the dime, the cent I give to such men as do not belong to me and to whom I do not belong. There is a class of persons to whom by all spiritual affinity I am bought and sold; for them I will go to prison, if need be; but your miscellaneous popular charities; the education at college of fools; the building of meeting-houses to the vain end to which many now stand; alms to sots; and the thousandfold Relief Societies;— though I confess with shame I sometimes succumb and give the dollar, it is a wicked dollar which by and by I shall have the manhood to withhold.[2]

Though his phrasing is extreme, Emerson is expressing widely held views. Many of his contemporaries shared his annoyance at being harassed or cajoled into charitable giving. Further, his disdain for supplicants ("fools" and "sots") and for the act of donation itself accords with the era's pervasive suspicion of direct charitable aid. Antebellum writers, especially those who formed what we might call the benevolent establishment, often figured the strategic withholding of charity as an integral step in inculcating self-reliance among the needy. Misguided almsgiving was thought to breed indolence and an inappropriate sense of entitlement on the part of recipients—the very antithesis of the unburdensome personhood that this literature enshrined. And like those in the broader culture who "characterized softness toward pauperism as an unmanly trait," Emerson suggests that giving, especially when one would prefer not to (to echo Melville's enigmatic supplicant, Bartleby the Scrivener), compromises one's identity as a self-reliant man.[3] Self-sacrificial or ill-conceived benevolence, Emerson implies, is the province of women and weak men, those who succumb to a well-phrased appeal, allowing the pressure to give to override their own judgment.

But Emerson takes the matter further, linking the manly withholding of alms to a more general and highly idealized resistance to expectations from whatever quarter. Throwing off all externally imposed standards—"nothing is at last sacred," he writes, "but the integrity of your own mind"—the nonconformist adheres to a radical self-trust, "carry[ing] himself in the presence of all opposition as if every thing were titular and ephemeral but he."[4] This intellectual and spiritual independence, the core of Emerson's notion of self-reliance, extends to the matter of social and even familial responsibility. In these contexts, benevolence emerges as a dangerous distraction from the self-involvement that genius requires. Emerson writes, "I shun father and mother and wife and brother, when my genius calls me. . . . Expect me not to show cause why I seek or why I exclude company" (30). And above all, as the quotation with which I began this section asserts, do not ask me to help those outside my narrowly defined affiliations. Emerson did aid certain individuals whom he apparently felt "belong[ed]" to him; he gave money quietly to Bronson Alcott's family and allowed Thoreau to build a cabin on his land near Walden Pond. But for the public Emerson of "Self-Reliance," the era's many calls for benevolence were interruptions rather than, as some commentators claimed, opportunities for moral redemption and social engineering.

In "Self-Reliance" and elsewhere, however, Emerson betrays a more fundamental mistrust of benevolence. In addition to lampooning the practices of conventional charity societies and naming benevolence as one of many barriers to a self-reliant life of the mind, Emerson takes issue with benevolent relations more broadly and theoretically conceived. Benevolent exchange itself, a model of relationships structured by need and gratitude, elicits his suspicion. This foundational aversion is most obvious in his appropriation of the language of supplication to signify a failed intellectual independence. "Most natures are insolvent," he writes in "Self-Reliance." They "cannot satisfy their own wants, . . . and do lean and beg day and night continually." Emerson refers not to the poor but to a timid bourgeoisie, the "parlor soldiers" whose intellectual and spiritual "housekeeping" he describes as "mendicant" (43). Similarly, he implies that a man who fails to "know his worth"—that is, who fails at nonconformity because he does not sufficiently trust himself—"skulk[s] up and down with the air of a charity-boy" and "feels poor" when he looks on towers or marble statues because he "find[s] no [corresponding] worth in himself" (36). The most "affecting lesson" of "great works of art," Emerson avers, is that "they teach us to abide by our spontaneous impression with good-humored inflexibility." Should we fail to achieve this tenacity, "to-morrow a stranger will say with masterly good sense precisely what we have thought and felt all the time, and we shall be forced *to take with shame* our own opinion from another" (italics added) (27). Invoking his culture's attention to the ignominy of begging, Emerson presents intellectual borrowing or influence as a species of supplication (to Europeans, to the past, to books), a hierarchical relationship inflected by shame, regret, and resentment of the magnanimous thinker-donor. "In the hour of vision," he writes, "there is nothing that can be called gratitude" (39). The American Scholar he conjures elsewhere is a self-reliant and self-determining Man Thinking, a counterpoint to the beggars, both intellectual and material, who surround him.

As these declarations suggest, Emerson resists the role of supplicant as thoroughly as that of donor. In "Gifts," from *Essays: Second Series* (1844), he writes that "we do not quite forgive a giver. The hand that feeds us is in some danger of being bitten. We can receive anything from love, for that is a way of receiving it from ourselves; but not from any one who assumes to bestow."[5] In addition, Emerson's writings sometimes dismiss benevolence altogether, as in the address "Emancipation in the British West Indies," delivered in Concord in 1844. Through much of the text Emerson engages with rhetorics of benevolence. Reversing proslavery claims of blacks' grateful dependence, he calls slaves "our benefactors" because they produce the goods that whites consume and suggests that slaves are the patient, caretaking adults whose owners, like spoiled children, thrive on "irritating and tormenting" them.[6] And he relates at length the efforts of English abolitionists to emancipate West Indian slaves and to inaugurate "a new element into modern politics, namely, the civilization of the negro"—efforts that fit neatly within established patterns of interracial benevolence. But then, near the end, he repudiates these structures, declaring that "you must save yourself, black or white, man or woman; other help is none."[7] This passage is intriguing not so much because it calls for self-reliance—such appeals were common in Emerson's speeches and writings and in contemporaneous texts, many by African American activists—but because this declaration of the irrelevance of external aid appears immediately after a prolonged discussion of the successful, if delimited, benevolent project of West Indian emancipation. While Emerson felt no compulsion to consistency, as he memorably asserts in "Self-Reliance," this is a startling contradiction nevertheless.

Emerson disavows benevolent relations more subtly in a passage from "Self-Reliance," exposing in the process his gendering of independence. "The nonchalance of boys who are sure of a dinner," he writes, "and would disdain as much as a lord to do or say aught to conciliate one, is the healthy attitude of human nature."[8] These irresponsible and independent boys, however, *are* embedded within relationships of dependence, whether or not Emerson acknowledges them to be so, in that they receive aid—in the form of daily appearing dinners—from their mothers, or their families' domestic servants or slaves, or other (usually female) caretakers. What Emerson presumes but does not state, what makes this embeddedness permissible, and what allows the boys' nonchalance to survive their positioning among "the helped," is that each boy's relationship to whoever does the cooking is a socially sanctioned form of dependence, one that does not degrade him or limit his access to self-reliance.[9] Mothers who could not afford servants were supposed to cook for their sons and in the cultural myths surrounding domestic servitude, paid and chattel, cooks were supposed to relish their opportunities to please the young man of the house. The boy awaiting dinner violated no cultural expectation that he ought to prepare it himself. This enshrined dependent relationship between boy and cook, in fact, works to produce the boy's ingratitude, the very arrogance and self-absorption on which Emerson's ideal of self-reliance depends. The cook, meanwhile, goes unrepresented, marked only through the dinners and, indirectly, the self-assurance she so reliably produces. While Emerson declares women's equal obligation to "save" themselves in the passage from "Emancipation" quoted above, implying that they, too, can achieve self-reliance, he also structures self-reliance in ways that inscribe women's interconnectedness, reminding them that they do not have the luxury of "exclud[ing] company."

Self-Helping Men

These erasures, however incomplete, of dependence underscore Emerson's rejection of benevolent relations, in contrast to many of his contemporaries, for whom achieving self-reliance also involved attaining the position of benevolent agent. In place of the benevolent dyad, Emerson championed another pairing: friendship between peers who are explicitly *not* in need. Where the needy evoke aversive reactions, the "self-helping man," Emerson declares in "Self-Reliance," is "welcome evermore to gods and men. . . . For him all doors are flung wide: him all tongues greet, all honors crown, all eyes follow with desire. Our love goes out to him and embraces him, because he *did not need it*" (italics added).[10] This ideal love is free of the burden of responsibility. While the terms *self-help* and *self-reliance* imply that need itself is foundational, they also insist that it can be channeled back into the self, allowing interactions between individuals to take place on some axis other than that of need. So the "self-helping man" is needless insofar as he does not need others.

Bound up in this all-important needlessness is the notion of self-possession, which Emerson repeatedly claims, in the 1841 essay "Friendship," is essential to the interpersonal bonds he idealizes:

Let [the friend] not cease an instant to be himself.

There must be very two, before there can be very one [united in friendship]. Let it be an alliance of two large formidable natures, mutually beheld, mutually feared, before yet they recognize the deep identity which beneath these disparities unites them.

We must be our own, before we can be another's. . . . the least defect of self-possession vitiates . . . the entire relation. There can never be deep peace between two spirits, never mutual respect until, in their dialogue, each stands for the whole world.[11]

Emerson's is an agonistic model of friendship, one that valorizes self-assurance and force of will over concession and compromise. "Deep peace" between individual "spirits" is a product of the expansive, unyielding discourse of each; friends must be "large, formidable natures," negotiating their alliance through a fearful, wary gaze ("mutually beheld, mutually feared"); and neither party can conciliate the other in any way that might make him not "himself" for "an instant." Moreover, the mutual possession arising out of self-possession ("we must be our own before we can be another's") that Emerson describes requires that both parties be free from debt, from gratitude, from the skulking and smallness of need. But needlessness, however crucial, is not sufficient to achieve the ideal: the individuals coming together should also be extraordinary, each "stand[ing] for the whole world." In an especially fanciful formulation, Emerson writes in "Character" (1844) that "when men shall meet as they ought, each a benefactor, a shower of stars, clothed with thoughts, with deeds, with accomplishments, it should be the festival of nature which all things announce."[12] He describes each party in this image as a benefactor, but the union he imagines occurs between benefactors in the absence of the needy.

Emerson is not always so sanguine about the prospects for a pure union of self-possessing men, admitting that "in the golden hour of friendship, we are surprised with shades of suspicion and unbelief."[13] At certain moments, he acknowledges the impossibility of perpetual strength and self-possession, adopting a more conventional acceptance of a friend's occasional neediness: "[friendship] is fit for serene days, and graceful gifts, and country rambles, but also for rough roads and hard fare, shipwreck, poverty, and persecution."[14] Moreover, some of Emerson's essays temper the exuberance and insouciance of the self-reliant ideal on which his notion of agonistic friendship depends. "Experience" (1844), poignant in its simultaneous disavowal and demonstration of grief, acknowledges that circumstances impinge on those attempting to make their own worlds, while the later essay "Fate," from *The Conduct of Life* (1860), avers that "a man's power is hooped in by a necessity, which, by many experiments, he touches on every side, until he learns its arc."[15] But these more balanced, even chastened, interventions do not entirely undercut Emerson's notion of self-reliance. We may indeed "live amid surfaces," as he asserts in "Experience," but there remains this business of "skat[ing] well on them." Similarly, while "a man" must learn the "arc" of his existence, he is nevertheless compelled to use his intellect to convert "every jet of chaos which threatens to exterminate [him] . . . into wholesome force. . . . The water drowns ship and sailor, like a grain of dust. But learn to swim, trim your bark, and the wave which drowned it, will be cloven by it, and carry it, like its own foam, a plume and a power."[16] Only those capable of exerting power and intellect against fate make worthy friends and competitors.

Emerson's emphasis on friendship between self-possessed and self-reliant peers would seem to argue for a species of equality among men. But his thought is not antihierarchical in any sustained way; indeed, according to some recent critics, Emerson is as much an apostle of hierarchy as of culture or anything else.[17] Passages from a number of his essays support this line of interpretation. In "Character," for example, Emerson posits an essential hierarchy of personal power: "[Character] is a natural power, like light and heat, and all nature coöperates with it. The reason why we feel one man's presence, and do not feel another's, is as simple as gravity. . . . All individual natures stand in a scale, according to the purity of this element in them. The will of the pure runs down from them into other natures, as water runs down from a higher into a lower vessel."[18] Here he shifts from a perceptual economy—"we feel one man's presence, and do not feel another's"—to a conventionally spatial one, with individuals arranged vertically on a Great Chain of Consciousness. Superiority is like gravity, Emerson claims—inexorable and above all "simple." The image's final movement, from discrete gradation to inevitable influence, is strangely physical: the "will of the pure" that "runs down . . . into other natures" conjures thoughts of rain or sweat or urine flowing from the select onto the inferior, degrading even as it improves them.

The essay "Manners," which immediately follows "Character" in *Essays: Second Series,* includes a less quiescent notion of hierarchy. Here Emerson invokes the specter of class warfare in his declaration of aristocracy's inevitability:

> If [aristocracy and fashion] provoke anger in the least favored class, and the excluded majority revenge themselves on the excluding minority, by the strong hand, and kill them, at once a new class finds itself at the top, as certainly as cream rises in a bowl of milk: and if the people should destroy class after class, until two men only were left, one of these would be the leader, and would be involuntarily served and copied by the other.[19]

Emerson once again compares the ascendancy of the superior to a physical process, in this case to cream rising in milk. But more relevant is the final imagined scene: here, the meeting between civilization's last two men is about mastery and involuntary imitation. Serving and copying, for Emerson, are allied and mutually reinforcing activities.

These inequalities, like those among Melville's characters, involve a certain eroticism. Julie Ellison and Christopher Newfield, in their work on Emerson's relationships with other men, both emphasize that, in Ellison's words, "the crucial point about Emersonian intimacy is that hierarchy is the medium of desire."[20] Newfield argues that for Emerson, the "male couple is most divine when it means relations between unequals." In keeping with his argument that Emerson espouses "a submissive kind of individualism," Newfield adds that Emerson "cherishes private friendship for its rewarding subjections." Ellison, for her part, is more interested in the range of possible positions within Emerson's homosocial hierarchies, arguing that he "found a way to stage masculine intimacy as a sentimental drama of differentiation, installing power at the heart of tenderness."[21]

Such explorations are more compatible than they might seem with my portrayal of Emersonian friendship as free of benevolent dependencies and responsibilities. The perfect mutual needlessness I have described is not identical to equality, in that the absence of a hierarchy structured by and articulated through benevolence does not guarantee, or even suggest, that there is no ascendancy, no submission, no power, no fear. Hierarchy, and the self-positioning and competition it engenders, inheres in even the most apparently equal relations. At one point in "Friendship" Emerson goes so far as to assert that "in strictness, the soul does not respect men as it respects itself," implying that the kind of union he champions elsewhere is never free from competitive assessments. This unending competition is brought out more forcefully a few paragraphs later: "I ought to be equal to every relation. It makes no difference how many friends I have, and what content I can find in conversing with each, if there be one to whom I am not equal. If I have shrunk unequal from one contest, the joy I find in all the rest becomes mean and cowardly."[22] The burden here is on contest rather than equality. The "two large, formidable natures, mutually beheld, mutually feared" that unite in Emerson's imagination do so because they achieve a precarious balance in which neither can overpower the other. It is a fantasy about a moment of stasis, of tentative and tenuous equality in the midst of a continuing struggle for mastery or, as Newfield would have it, for a satisfying submission. The hierarchies within which these struggles take place appeal to Emerson—where benevolent hierarchies do not—because they lack the scripted roles he associates with charitable pairings. Although the exercise of power within benevolent relations was far more complicated than appearances would suggest, Emerson seems to have preferred the open contests available to (ostensibly) needless men.

This model of an eroticized power struggle between men inflects some of Emerson's more explicit statements on benevolence, including one of the few instances in which he expresses a desire to involve himself in benevolent or reformist projects:

> Do you ask my aid? I also wish to be a benefactor. . . . Surely the greatest
> good fortune that could befall me, is precisely to be so moved by you that I
> should say, "Take me and all mine, and use me and mine freely to your
> ends!" . . . We desire to be made great, we desire to be touched with that
> fire which shall command this ice to stream, and make our existence a bene-
> fit. If therefore we start objections to your project, O friend of the slave, or
> friend of the poor, or of the race, understand well, that it is because we
> wish to drive you to drive us into your measures. We wish to hear ourselves
> confuted.[23]

The reluctant reformer admits that he wants to be overmastered, taken, freely used—that he wants to occupy, simultaneously, disparate positions within a benevolent hierarchy: "we wish to drive you to drive us." We wish, Emerson claims, to be proven wrong, to be compelled into action, to be *made* to do good, and so to be transformed or improved ourselves. In effect, Emerson wants the position of benefactor to be less securely powerful, more like the contest of wills between powerful men that so attracts him. That, finally, would make benevolence an absorbing enterprise, one worthy of a self-reliant man.

Boon Companions

Julie Ellison writes that Emerson is "not only the saint of self-reliance but the artist of its embarrassments."[24] In Melville's *Confidence-Man,* one of the principal embarrassments of Emersonian self-reliance is its aversion to others' admissions of need. But Melville's treatment of the morally questionable implications of self-reliance is not so much an analysis of Emerson's thought, which he oversimplifies, but a consideration of widespread cultural attitudes that uses Emerson as a point of entry. In other words, Emerson—who critics generally agree is the model for Mark Winsome, Melville's Transcendental philosopher of withholding—is not the only referent here. At issue are the hierarchies that antebellum discourses of benevolence described and produced, and that Emerson's prose reinforced. But even as Melville proposes, through the pronouncements of Frank Goodman, that Emersonian self-reliance is a pseudophilosophical excuse for selfishness, he also presents as inevitable the social inequalities engendered by need on the one hand and the luxury of choice, of donation or dismissal, on the other.

The pairings in chapters 28 through 41 of *The Confidence-Man*—between Frank Goodman and, in succession, Charlie Noble, Winsome, and Egbert—recall Emerson's sparring couples: in each encounter, two apparently needless men engage in dialogue and competitive mutual observation. But Melville upsets this delicate balance by introducing Frank's appeal to Charlie's benevolence, with which this chapter began. As far as Charlie is concerned—and as far as Egbert, who reprises Charlie's role in the debate, is concerned—their friendship is predicated on Frank's independence, financial and otherwise. Echoing Emerson's praise of the self-helping man, Melville invokes the proposition that only those who do not need a friend deserve one. Charlie's violent reaction to Frank's need, soothed only by Frank's subsequent claim that his request had been a joke, begins an extended meditation on the incompatibility of benevolence and friendship. The core of this conflict, for Winsome and for Egbert, his mouthpiece, is that needing help reveals an inherent flaw. Egbert remarks that "there is something wrong about the man who wants help. There is somewhere a defect, a want, in brief, a need, a crying need, somewhere about that man." When Frank continues to beseech him, Egbert/Charlie responds that such requests are foolish "when to implore help, is itself the proof of undesert of it" (*CM*, 206). These statements recall the writings of conventional charity experts, who looked with suspicion on anyone asking directly for help and who maintained that able-bodied men should never need alms. But where those authors praised the silent, uncomplaining poor, Winsome and

Egbert leave no room for respectable or worthy poverty. For them, need itself is a defect.

To extend his dissection of the social structures of need and relief, Melville has Egbert give voice to another of antebellum charity's commonplaces—that benevolence degrades the recipient. Whereas many writers on benevolence cited methods for circumventing such degradation, usually by insisting that the helped must also help themselves, Egbert sees the acceptance of benevolence as inevitably lowering an individual within social hierarchies. "The man who calls himself my friend," Egbert states, "is above receiving alms" (*CM*, 202); he admits, in fact, that one of his criteria for choosing friends in the first place is their apparent economic security. According to Egbert's logic, any man who accepts alms is beneath his friendship, while any friend who asks for alms—and in doing so belies his prior reputation for needlessness—is no longer a friend. The moment of benevolent exchange both proves and produces the recipient's inferiority.

Frank, for his part, resists this loss of status, referring to the money he seeks as a loan rather than alms. Here the text echoes Frances Trollope's notorious *Domestic Manners of the Americans* (1832), which ridiculed Americans' apparent aversion to expressing gratitude and their habit of asking to *borrow* items they have no intention of returning or paying for.[25] Like Trollope's acquaintances, Frank attempts to retain for himself and for the exchange some measure of dignity through the pretense that he will eventually repay the money. Egbert, however, forestalls this attempt, arguing that lending money is no friendly act because it involves interest and security and the threat of foreclosure, putting the debtor's "heart up at public auction" (*CM*, 203). As an illustration, Egbert tells the story of China Aster, a candlemaker whose life is ruined by "a friendly loan" (*CM*, 220).[26] But improving the terms of the loan is, for Egbert, no solution. To Frank's hopeful claim that an interest-free loan would also be cruelty free, he responds that a loan without interest or the threat of foreclosure is no loan at all, but alms.

Egbert's insistence that alms be called such compels those in need to give up any pretense to dignity. In so doing, these more honest, because accurately named, beggars make their donors feel both superior and generous. Egbert's final reply to Frank makes literal these considerations: "Take off your hat, bow over to the ground, and supplicate an alms of me in the way of London streets, and you shall not be a sturdy beggar in vain. But no man drops pennies into the hat of a friend, let me tell you. If you turn beggar, then, for the honor of noble friendship, I turn stranger" (*CM*, 223). Through this exchange, Melville parodies those who want benevolent hierarchies to be as obvious as possible, who want tableaus of suffering and magnanimity, of degradation and superiority. And above all, he parodies those who wish to maintain or even expand the social distance between beggars and donors rather than experience the disturbing proximity of a friend in need. The ideology of self-reliance,

Melville's text implies, underlies these differentiations, in that the supplicant's request invalidates his status as Emersonian peer, whereas the donor's insistence that giving involve no emotional attachment maintains the latter's separation, his access to the isolation of genius.

Melville suggests, then, that Winsome and Egbert (and, by extension, Emerson), despite their self-fashioning as Transcendental nonconformists, are all too representative of middle-class Americans, who look for a way to feel morally comfortable with their selfishness and, when they engage in benevolent projects, seek out those among the needy who are willing to play clearly demarcated inferior roles. But the text is more critical than activist. For all Frank Goodman's counterarguments and chastisements, Melville's representation of the exchange with Egbert conveys a marked resignation. It suggests that the hierarchies and degradations Egbert wants laid bare are integral to benevolent relations and that the crucial matter is whether one tries to obscure them. After all, as much as Frank decries the attitudes that Egbert and Winsome express, his dealings and those of the confidence man's other incarnations offer no egalitarian counterexample, no model of benevolence that does not degrade and no request that does not dupe. In contrast to Emerson's fantasies of leaving benevolent relations altogether, *The Confidence-Man* reinscribes, even as it laments, their ugliness.

Correcting Dependence

Scholars have made much of *The Confidence-Man*'s intertextuality, its parodies and appropriations of sources such as Emerson's essays or Judge James Hall's *Sketches of History, Life, and Manners, in the West* (1835), which informs the novel's account of Indian-hating.[27] Similarly, Emerson's debts to European, especially German and English, thinkers have been well documented.[28] I wish now to trace a different web of influence, turning to a broader print culture in which questions of charity and dependence were constantly negotiated. Regardless of whether Emerson and Melville read or responded to a particular pamphlet, sermon, or didactic tale, they were exposed to the arguments and points of view represented in the texts under discussion here. When Emerson complains in "Self-Reliance" of the importunities of charity agents, he demonstrates his familiarity and his impatience with a well-established culture of benevolent societies, their agents, and their publications. And when Melville elaborates on the indignities of need, he is drawing not only on Emerson (and possibly on his own financial embarrassments) but also on an abundance of verbal and visual representations of shameful supplication. My discussion, then, recontextualizes these canonical authors, examining in the process the various ways antebellum Americans defined and attempted to inculcate self-reliance.

Although Emerson and Melville echoed certain conventional views of benevolence, in other respects their work lay outside the mainstream. For example, antebellum writers on charity largely rejected the Emersonian notion that self-reliance depended on a radical self-trust and a commitment to whatever nonconformities might ensue from it. Perhaps in response to Emerson, H. (probably Henry) Clapp, the author of an 1845 antislavery piece called "Self-Reliance," wrote that he did not advocate "that intense egotism which discovers no wisdom beyond the narrow walls of its own mind, and which is therefore as superficial as it is supercilious, and as intolerable as it is intolerant."[29] Though Clapp counseled Americans to prove their independence by opposing slavery and the social conventions and organizations that upheld it, he argued that unconventionality had its limits. In keeping with this moderate stance, most who wished to encourage self-reliance among the needy recommended a careful emulation of the better off, especially in terms of their attitudes toward work, temperance, and cleanliness. Nor was Melville's critique of self-reliance as selfishness widely endorsed. On the contrary, most commentators took it as an article of faith that the kinds of independence they prescribed improved the individual morally as well as socially. To illustrate this point, writers often set up stark contrasts between commendably self-reliant persons and their "degraded," willfully dependent counterparts: the "improving" poor versus paupers; yeoman farmers versus slaveholders; and responsible, task-oriented children versus self-indulgent whiners.

Children were often the targeted audience for as well as the subjects of authors' pronouncements on self-reliance. To an extent, Americans conceived of childhood as a time of acceptable dependence on parents, servants, and other adults. The nineteenth century saw the development of a cult of childhood in England and the United States, manifested in contradictory images of innocent carelessness and salvific but terminal saintliness, of which Stowe's Eva is among the best-known examples. But adults also worried over how to inculcate proper values, and especially the value of independence, in the nation's children, who were not, like Eva, already perfect. Helen Knight's *Saw Up and Saw Down; or, the Fruits of Industry and Self-Reliance* (1852), one of countless stories that demonstrated to children the folly of laziness, depicts a mother and her three sons, long accustomed to material comfort, who are left bankrupt after the (conventionally) sudden death of their spendthrift husband and father. The oldest son, Madison, has spent too long in the home of his father's wealthy, indolent cousin and at first resists his mother's insistence that he join her and his brothers on the "higher and more responsible ground" of self-support. When Madison has a difficult time cutting wood, his mother advises him to "saw up and saw down, patiently and courageously. Now do it—conquer it—or you are not fit to be a man." Madison eventually reforms himself, becoming the self-reliant man his mother wants him to be, but the wealthy cousin dies a "poor, and a broken-hearted, desolate old man" whose "sons have ruined him," presumably because he has never taught them the value of hard work.[30] "Uncorrected" children, the story suggests, carry in their dependence the seeds of future ruin, while children whose parents teach them the value of self-help are the family's and the nation's best hope.

The anonymous *Gertrude Lee; or, the Northern Cousin* (1856), published by the American Reform Tract and Book Society, features a girl who has already achieved a gender-appropriate self-reliance, in that she performs domestic duties competently, cheerfully, and without the aid of servants. In the course of the narrative, she improves her lethargic southern relatives, convincing them to end their dependence on slave labor and to adopt the (supposedly) northern value of industry. In this case, learning self-reliance entails a degree of nonconformity: family members end up defying their neighbors' standards of behavior, but they do so only within what the text defines as an aberrant southern culture. Antislavery authors figured slaveholding as the antithesis of self-reliant adulthood and portrayed northern characters who spend time in the South as either succumbing to its slothful atmosphere or working to reform their misguided hosts. While Stowe's Miss Ophelia is a comic and only partly successful representative of the latter category, Gertrude Lee is unequivocally victorious. She astonishes her cousins' slaves by rising early and refusing the assistance of a "waiting-maid," asserting that "I want no waiter at all. I would sooner sacrifice my life than my personal independence." Grace, one of Gertrude's cousins, "was about a year younger . . . and, had she been trained in the same school of industry, order, and perseverance, she might have been her equal in many respects." But the "lax discipline of that house, where labor is held dishonorable," has made her inferior, a young example of the enervated and pampered southern white woman whom abolitionists deplored. In the course of her stay, Gertrude inspires her relatives to greater physical and mental activity, eventually converting them all to the (here paired) doctrines of self-reliance and abolition. They decide to educate their slaves in preparation for freedom and to move to the North themselves, where they believe whites will not be ridiculed for doing their own work. The family's slaves, too, are susceptible to Gertrude's improving influence. Once they are assured of their freedom and the responsibilities it implies, they have a "strong incentive to labor" and attain "rapid proficiency in every department of knowledge."[31]

Gertrude's easy triumph over indolence, however, bears little resemblance to antebellum Americans' conceptions of the intractability of the habitually dependent. As Nancy Fraser and Linda Gordon have argued, the term *dependency*, prior to the rise of industrial capitalism, was a "general-purpose term for all social relations of subordination" and was conceived of as a natural and therefore unremarkable situation within rigid and ubiquitous hierarchies. But by the mid-nineteenth century, as white workingmen gained civil and political rights in the United States, the term's economic meaning "shifted from gaining one's livelihood by working for someone else to relying for support on charity."[32] Dependence, in other words, became deviant, with the poor standing out as the most obvious offenders.

Among the strategies developed to minimize such dependence was the House of Correction, a workhouse for vagrants, street beggars, the intemperate, and the improvident. As one tract put it, such institutions were needed where the dependent could be "confined in a place where they would be compelled to work and earn their support, and not live upon the honest and industrious portion of our citizens." The Baltimore Association for Improving the Condition of the Poor (AICP) expressed a similar faith in compulsion, though by means of neglect rather than institutionalization. "The idle and indolent," the organization's 1851 report stated, "must be compelled to work or left to suffer, and taught that wholesome doctrine, that if they do not work they cannot eat."[33] Members of charity organizations generally shared the belief that institutions like the House of Correction would become unnecessary as the needy became truly self-reliant, internalizing the values of hard work and prudent spending. Ideally, through their action or inaction, charity agents would help to bring about this alteration. The Baltimore AICP, addressing its charitable home visitors, expressed widely held sentiments regarding the potential influence of the benevolent:

> You will become an important instrument of good to your suffering fellow-creatures, when you aid them to obtain this good from resources within themselves. To effect this, show them the true origin of their sufferings, when these sufferings are the result of imprudence, extravagance, idleness, intemperance, or other moral causes which are within their own control; and endeavor . . . to awaken their self-respect, to direct their exertions, and to strengthen their capacities for self-support.[34]

Even those "who have been reduced to indigence by unavoidable causes" and who show "a preference for self-denial to dependence upon alms" must be aided cautiously, lest they be "degrade[d] . . . to habitual dependence." In all circumstances, the aid distributed "should never be of a kind, or to a degree, that will *make this dependence preferable to a life of labor.*"[35] Antebellum charity experts did not consider self-reliance to be sufficiently attractive to the poor as an abstract value, nor did they believe its inculcation through print to be a potent enough strategy alone. The poor, in their view, required the credible threat of unpleasant alternatives.

Not all the supplemental strategies employed were negative, however. Charitable citizens were instructed to encourage independence among the needy by such practical means as providing education and vocational training and recommending the use of savings banks. Lydia Sigourney, in *The Girl's Reading-Book,* counsels benevolent young ladies to give the poor work to do "and pay them promptly and liberally" for it, a strategy that "saves that self-abasement which minds of sensibility suffer, at receiving charity."[36] The best kind of material aid to the poor, authors often asserted, was that which enabled them to earn their own money. An 1842 children's story, which set out to show "the advantage of discrimination in charitable distribution," contrasted the efforts of two sisters. The older gives her supply of alms to the first person who asks her for it, who turns out to be a liar and a habitual beggar. The younger, though she has less money to give, bestows it more wisely: she buys a new knife for a poor basket maker who has lost his old one, so that he can continue to be self-sufficient.[37]

Writers on charity reserved some of their most effusive praise for individuals who overcame hardships in order to achieve, or regain, financial independence. One report mentioned a laborer, injured in a fall from a scaffold, who "before the completion of a slow recovery—[was] patiently sitting beside his patient wife, training his rough hands to ply the needle, that even in his maimed and broken state he might live without charitable aid." Predictably, the most vitriolic criticism was heaped on those who refused such opportunities. An especially vindictive story published by the American Tract Society features a blind beggar who has rejected a surgeon's offer of cataract surgery. The narrator, who regrets having given the beggar alms, suggests that he has refused treatment out of laziness and self-indulgence: "Instead of sitting begging, and living in idleness on the labor of others, he [if cured] must have worked for his bread: he was an idle man, and did not like the idea of this trouble." In addition, "the operation . . . is painful, and he would not bear a few minutes' pain to gain a good which might have lasted him all his life."[38] Anyone so lacking in personal energy and toughness, the erstwhile donor suggests, does not her deserve help.

The kind of transformative benevolence this beggar refuses was the stated goal of most charity agents, who wished to make the poor self-sufficient. T. S. Arthur's story "Uncle Ben's New-Year's Gift" dramatizes this ideal. Peter and Hannah Miller, the title character's struggling relations, are hard-working—an essential ingredient in their eventual self-reliance—but "it was work without wisdom" and, as Uncle Ben asserts, "such work never turns out well."[39] The Millers do not take a newspaper or pursue any form of self-culture, and as a result they make ill-informed, costly decisions. They find their situation increasingly desperate and hope that Ben will rescue them financially, but he does not. Instead, he offers Peter advice and buys the family a newspaper subscription. This paper, standing in for a range of educational offerings within the era's expanding print culture, changes the Millers' lives: Peter learns new farming techniques and acquires the information he needs to negotiate better prices for his crops, while his previously ignorant children become interested in intellectual and cultural matters. By the end of the year, Hannah is once again singing as she works because the family is out of debt and can afford to hire help so that the children can attend school. All of this they achieve without accepting any donation other than Ben's initial gift.

Arthur and the other writers cited here chart a middle course between the ideology of Melville's Frank Goodman, who advocates "confident" and indiscriminate giving, and that of Egbert, who is willing to give only impersonally and only when the supplicant accepts complete degradation. The benevolent figures whom these tales applaud devise ways of convincing or forcing the needy to help themselves. They are out to reform, not to rescue. But the means of encouraging self-reliance were more controversial and their outcomes more ambiguous than these stories implied, especially when the needy population was of African descent.

Black Self-Reliance

Although charity literature, including didactic tales like Arthur's, assured readers that a benevolent project was successful to the extent that it brought about the self-reliance of the helped, such elevation nevertheless hinted at a range of social disruptions. While it was widely believed that perpetual benevolence produced pauperism, that most dreaded of social ills, transformative benevolence resulted in a measure of social mobility among groups against whom the better-off had grown accustomed to defining themselves. These disruptions were especially alarming to whites when they involved a newfound independence among African Americans. What if benevolent activism encouraged this population's violent domination over their former helpers, as antiabolitionists warned? What if the outcome were power sharing and social mixing between the races? The fear of such reversals and blendings was evident in the era's vicious parodies of "uppity blacks" who dressed in finery or pursued intellectual achievement; in violent reprisals against African Americans who attempted to improve their socioeconomic status; and in white authors' frequent references to the horrors of San Domingo, antebellum shorthand for the potentially murderous outcomes if slaves attained their freedom. Whereas helping destitute European Americans—except perhaps the Irish and other particularly despised groups—meant enabling them to slip into a self-sufficient mainstream where their presence would likely go unremarked, assisting African Americans was another matter, as those who altered their social positions were figured as harbingers of coming upheavals.[40]

In an 1837 treatise, the African American minister Hosea Easton described the monstrous quality that self-reliant black men acquired in whites' imaginations:

Having been instructed from youth to look upon a black man in no other light than a slave, . . . [whites] cannot look upon him in any other light. If he should chance to be found in any other sphere of action than that of a slave, he magnifies to a monster of wonderful dimensions, so large that they cannot be made to believe that he is a man and a brother. Neither can they be made to believe it would be safe to admit him into stages, steam-boat cabins, and tavern dining-rooms. . . . Mechanical shops, stores, and school rooms, are all too small for his entrance as a man; if he be a slave, his corporeality becomes so diminished as to admit him into ladies' parlors, and into small private carriages. . . . Thus prejudice seems to possess a magical power, by which it makes a being appear . . . at one moment too large to be on board a steam-boat, the next, so small as to be convenient almost any where.[41]

Easton's account of the transformations wrought by freedom illustrates what many of his contemporaries felt quite keenly—that there was no "convenient" place in the nation for an independent African American. Sarah M. Douglass, a black educator who experienced racial discrimination among Philadelphia's Quakers, put the matter more concisely: "In proportion as we become intellectual and respectable, so in proportion does their disgust and prejudice increase."[42]

A significant number of antebellum whites answered the threat of black self-reliance by denying that such a thing were possible. Their rhetoric replaced the "monstrous" body of Easton's free black man with the image of a perpetual child who was better off under the care of a master, whether he or she knew it or not. The antiabolitionist Theophilus Fiske, for example, challenged his antislavery opponents to "look for one moment at the squalid, miserable, degraded condition of the free blacks in the Northern cities, . . . utterly incapable of providing for themselves, living or rather starving, in brutal ignorance and sloth." William Gilmore Simms, in his novel *Woodcraft,* portrayed this "miserable" being's happily enslaved counterpart, who rejects his master's offer of freedom on the grounds that a "free nigger" has no one who will provide him with food.[43] Juvenile fiction dramatized this ideology of perpetual dependence as well, presenting black characters who fulfill their destinies in the service of benevolent whites. Jacob Abbott's *Congo; or, Jasper's Experience in Command* (1857) relates how a young white boy, the Jasper of the title, learns through his relationship with Congo, a hardworking but essentially dependent black youth, how to be a benevolent leader. At every turn, Jasper discovers the truth of his grandfather's claim, that "it is one of the characteristics of the colored people to like to be employed by other people, rather than to take responsibility and care upon themselves." Congo accepts literacy instruction amiably enough but loses interest when it comes to learning to write more than his own name. He also enforces a rigid division of labor: because Jasper "had all the responsibility of determining what was to be done, without any assistance from Congo in respect to those burdens, it was right Congo should do his own [physical] work in full without asking any assistance."[44]

Abbott insists on the appropriateness of Jasper's leadership in the book's last episode, in which the boys are trapped by a hotel fire: "Congo was so frightened that he was almost beside himself, though the composure and courage which Jasper manifested somewhat sustained him." When help arrives, Jasper insists that Congo be rescued first, claiming that it was his "duty" to protect the life of his dependent.[45] Jasper is prepared to go down with his ship, so to speak, in a dramatic illustration of heroic white paternalism. But in this case the controlling and protecting figure is a child, a patriarch in training, who must learn—through his grandfather's admonishments and Congo's demonstrations—the intersections among whiteness, masculinity, and "command." Congo's submissive role, meanwhile, comes to him quite naturally.

Such attributions of black dependence—and the pseudoscientific and proto-sociological theories on which they were based—did not go uncontested. Slaves who ran away announced unequivocally their preference for the hardships of freedom over the supposed security of enslavement. The speeches and writings of free black Americans, too, testified to their distaste for dependence. Some, in their attempts to prove blacks' resistance to relying on whites, mirrored the white charity establishment's growing investment in statistics. An 1852 report from New York's State Convention of Coloured Citizens, for example, insisted that "the colored population" of New York City was "27 per cent. less burdensome" to "the poor fund" than the white population and asserted that "this happy state of things had arisen, in part, from the fact that the former class have mutual benefit societies, with a cash capital of $30,000, from which they take care of their sick and bury their dead."[46]

Among those whites less overtly fearful of black autonomy, the question of how black Americans might achieve self-reliance was a central preoccupation. Some commentators minimized racial differences, seeking to apply to those of African descent the same strategies and influences, including the withholding of alms, that were thought to work well among needy and dependent whites. William D. Kelley, in an 1850 address delivered at Philadelphia's Colored Department of the House of Refuge, asserted that "the colored man is depressed by the causes that depress the white man; and the agencies which strengthen and develop the Anglo-Saxon child would, if fairly applied, give him a sturdy competitor in his darker neighbor." The American Union for the Relief and Improvement of the Colored Race, after detailing the particular degradation of urban free blacks and the "many embarrassments and impositions" under which they suffered, recommended strategies that had become conventional for all needy persons: religious, academic, and vocational instruction, along with specific training in "the habit of saving" and in the "self-denial" on which that habit depended. The Unitarian minister James Freeman Clarke, recognizing the problem of prejudice but not its impact on African Americans' earning power, gave this blunt advice: "Colored people ought to make money. . . . No race in this country will be despised which makes money."[47] Not only should black Americans, in Clarke's view, pursue independence by the same means as whites, but they should also pursue the variety of independence that whites seemed to respect the most.

Counterbalancing these homogenizing gestures were proposals for eliminating or recasting black dependence that relied on and in some cases further developed notions of racial difference. One such intervention, a charitable organization's benevolent appeal on behalf of needy black New Yorkers, figured the latter as substantially more mild-mannered and trustworthy than the city's rowdy and unpredictable immigrant workers. Immediately following New York City's 1863 draft riots, in which black residents had been killed, beaten, and forced from their homes in alarming numbers, a committee of white merchants collected and disbursed more than forty thousand dollars for "the relief of colored people" whom the rioters had harmed.[48] The committee's lengthy report also suggested the ways in which black Americans ought (and ought not) to be independent. The version of self-reliance it proposed for free blacks was a steady nondestitution: they were not to be the newly rich equalizers James Freeman Clarke conjured but rather dutiful workers who posed no challenge to the racial and class hierarchies of New York City's market economy. In the wake of the riots, this state was to be brought about through strategic charity, which would enable black families to return to the city, reestablish their households, and get back to work.

To garner support for its projects, the Committee of Merchants sought to construct in its published document a black population that merited help but that constituted a grave threat if left unaided. Black New Yorkers, this report asserted, were "a peaceable, industrious people" who "seldom depend upon charity" and who had successfully run "their own churches, Sunday-schools and charitable Societies." Victims of the riots were described as "quiet" and "inoffensive," "industrious and sober," "harmless and law abiding."[49] But those desirable qualities, the report as a whole suggests, could not be presumed immutable. At one point, the merchants warned that if whites acceded to the rioters' threats and refused to hire (or rehire) blacks, "the colored population[,] . . . deprived of their just rights to earn an honest living[,] . . . [would] become a dependent, pauper race." It was the "duty" of white employers, a member of the committee claimed, "to see that [black workers were] protected in their lawful labors, . . . [so that they might] save themselves from becoming dependent on the charity of the city."[50] Given how frequently the terms *pauperism* and *crime* were paired at midcentury, the underlying threat of violence and social decay is easy to discern.

In keeping with the larger nineteenth-century conversation on charity, this committee presented work as the unassailable solution to social problems. Black New Yorkers would achieve or regain independence following the riots in the sense that they would once again be wage earners rather than recipients of alms. But this version of black self-reliance strategically posed no threat to the white merchants' superior social position and access to profit. If New York City's black population could be bound, through fear and gratitude, to low-status occupations and to a deferential manner of relating within the city's social and economic structures, then all the better for business. In this instance, the language of benevolence did the cultural work of stabilizing class relations, enabling white elites to define themselves against the rioters, generally identified with the city's immigrant working class, and to claim the moral high ground in the process. The merchants' rhetoric served two interrelated purposes: it asserted that their class played no role in perpetuating the racial antipathy that fueled the riots, and it defined tractable, native-born black workers as separate from and preferable to a nonnative working class perceived as all too independent in its violation of the law and of established patterns of social deference.[51]

By insisting that free blacks could be reabsorbed peacefully into the city's work force, the Merchants' Committee implicitly rejected the embattled project of African colonization, whose white proponents had, for decades, articulated a limited theory of black independence: they sought to convince potential donors and emigrants that freeborn blacks and emancipated slaves were too weak to compete in a permanently hostile, white-dominated society but, at the same time, were sufficiently competent to found their own colony.[52] Colonizationists' writings were replete with assertions that settling in Africa would enable blacks to achieve self-reliance, a state marked by their ownership of land and establishment of economically self-sufficient, privatized domestic spaces. In effect, colonizationists offered black Americans access to a mainstream white model of self-reliance, which involved the right to self-assertion, freedom from a visually encoded, structural inferiority to another group, and the opportunity to instruct, employ, and govern persons of lower status (in this case, native Africans)—but they insisted that such achievements could happen only across the Atlantic. Further, they pursued this argument in highly gendered terms. As Bruce Dorsey has written, the movement's spokesmen "depicted colonizing as a masculine endeavor," even as they called into question the self-reliant manhood of those they encouraged to emigrate.[53]

While some who favored colonization theorized that the emigrants' transformation from dependence to self-reliance would occur within the United States, prior to their departure, the majority maintained that the requisite changes in the "character" and circumstances of black Americans could occur only through the process of emigration. White prejudice, they argued, compounded by blacks' perception of their own inferiority, made such alterations impossible within the United States. The author and editor Sarah Josepha Hale, whose 1853 text *Liberia* distills and (to an extent) novelizes mainstream colonizationist arguments, writes that freed slaves become "a drain" on American society "whenever the conduct of their life is given in their own hands." But the conventional representations of burdensome blackness that dominate the first half of the book give way to a narrative of improvement in which a few "noble exceptions" to the rule of black dependence achieve self-reliance in Africa. According to Hale and other colonizationists, the ex-slave's transformation from social burden to independent citizen occurs because, once free of whites' insults and socioeconomic superiority, the colonist has an incentive to achieve, a chance at the self-improvement that Anglo-American culture has foreclosed. Hale's proposal sends manumitted slaves and free blacks to a place where, according to her standards of judgment, everything is so backward, so uncompetitive, that the emigrants cannot help but seem superior. One black character asserts that in Liberia, "the natives look up to us as something wonderful." According to Hale, this perceived superiority solidifies over time into reality, as the colonists learn to live up to the natives' admiration and learn to lead for the simple reason that there is no one on the scene whom they can reasonably follow.[54]

For Hale, as for many of her peers, self-reliance was intimately related to citizenship: one could be truly independent and self-directing only when one had access to the political and economic power that the rights of citizenship supposedly guaranteed. But Hale's narrative maintains that eligibility for citizenship depends on whether an individual can claim to be a founder of the nation in question (or a descendent of founders). Regardless of how early their ancestors had arrived in America, black people were denied access to the activities and rewards of nation building or found that their contributions had been disqualified, and so, according to Hale's logic, they could not stake such a claim within the United States. Her advocacy of Liberian colonization, then, offers people of African descent access to the Anglo-American model of nation building: they must find a country to call their own, force its inhabitants to bend to their will, and establish for themselves and their progeny the status of founders.[55]

Black emigrationists also linked racial separation, citizenship, and independence, though on terms quite different from Hale's. The black-run African Civilization Society, of which Martin Delany and Henry Highland Garnet were members, included in its constitution the statement that "the basis of the Society, and ulterior objects in encouraging emigration, shall be—Self-Reliance and Self-Government, on the principle of an African Nationality, the African race being the ruling element of the nation, controlling and directing their own affairs."[56] "African nationality," an imprecise but evocative term, stood in for a commitment to racial affiliation while it implicitly rejected the "Americanness" and literal U.S. citizenship that anti-emigrationists sought. A nationality predicated on blackness, the society suggested, would produce the independence, both personal and governmental, that African Americans had been denied in the United States—though it would also, as Delany elsewhere makes clear, maintain a hierarchical structure, with native Africans living and working under the direction of African American emigrants.[57] But one did not have to be an emigrationist to perceive the interdependence of self-reliance and citizenship. For the staunchest white supremacists, the innate dependence of blacks precluded their eligibility for citizenship, while for black Americans and their allies, the barriers to black citizenship within the United States were conceived of as barriers to black self-reliance in the fullest sense.

Mutual Aid versus Self-Reliance

Citizenship as theorized in the West posits the social and political significance of the individual, who enjoys certain rights and on whom certain responsibilities devolve. So, too, did the antebellum era's thorny and much-elaborated questions of individualism inform the relationships among benevolence, self-reliance, and racial difference. Self-reliance, as nineteenth-century Americans articulated it, relied on a belief in a discrete self on whom one could or could not learn to depend. That idealized, if illusory, self was conceived of, at least momentarily, apart from his (and sometimes her) attachments, responsibilities, and dependencies. The drama of so many representations of self-reliance, in fact, consisted of a person's achievement of such advantageous individuation. The successfully self-reliant being might very well (and according to some commentators, was obliged to) reconstruct those interconnections, but he—and in some cases she—was expected to occupy a helping rather than dependent role. The problem of black self-reliance, then, was not only a problem of citizenship but, more foundationally, of individualism.

Commentators on slavery took up these questions with a marked ambivalence. Black and white abolitionists worked to humanize and individuate black persons for their white audiences by relating the stories of specific, named slaves who escaped or were killed in bondage and by introducing black speakers and autobiographers who insisted on themselves as beings with particular histories. Nevertheless, aspects of antislavery rhetoric undercut these goals. Abolitionist leaders, as Frederick Douglass's famous complaints about Garrison and his cohort reveal, wanted slave narrators to fulfill certain generic expectations, especially the repetition of tales of abuse and degradation, that made the fugitive seem as representative as possible of the enslaved masses. Moreover, the extensive third-person descriptions of slaves' suffering that appeared in antislavery newspapers and pamphlets from the 1830s onward presented a blur of violated black bodies, often undifferentiated in their representation. Even Douglass, the era's foremost promulgator of black (male) individualism, created in his 1845 *Narrative* what Deborah McDowell has called "a bloody mass of naked backs"—the women, often not "identified by name," who occupy his scenes of the white master's cruelty.[58]

Proslavery forces, for their part, more pointedly resisted blacks' individuality. Slave catchers were known to seize any unprotected dark-skinned person on the streets of a northern city in order to sell him or her as a runaway. It mattered little whether the captured being fit any *particular* fugitive slave's description. Slave owners, meanwhile, could sell, exchange, or rename slaves at will and often insisted that a slave accept a replacement spouse if the original died or were sold. The irrelevance of individual slave identities to the decisions of many owners was countered by contemporaneous representations in plantation literature of adored "uncles" and "aunts," slaves who, the narrators insisted, were "like family." But however much authors insisted on whites' affection for these figures, the stereotypes through which the characters were drawn only reinforced in the imaginations of many white readers the belief that black Americans were first and foremost members of a group rather than individuals or, for that matter, representatives of a universal humanity.

Despite these prejudicial uses of black collectivity, a tradition of mutual aid and communal benevolence had long flourished among free African Americans. In the last decades of the eighteenth century, black residents of northern cities began forming mutual aid associations, which, among other activities, used members' initiation fees and dues as emergency funds that would ensure the proper burial of deceased members and aid those in difficult economic straits.

While many of these societies were short-lived, mutual aid as an organizing principle had great staying power among both men and women. Elizabeth McHenry points out that "by 1849, Philadelphia had 106 mutual aid societies, to which more than half of the African American population belonged," and Anne M. Boylan notes that "by the 1820s . . . separate women's groups had begun to multiply."[59] In addition to providing an economic safety net, mutual aid associations facilitated the emergence of community leaders and the enforcement of behavioral standards. Philadelphia's Free African Society, for example, "expelled a member for abandoning his wife and child to live with another woman," while the African Society of Boston specified that "any member who brought a disability on himself because of intemperance was not eligible for benefits."[60] Certainly, the latter restriction indicates that African Americans, like their white counterparts, divided the poor into the deserving and the culpable. But the structure of these organizations indicated a substantially different conception of the relationship between the benevolent and the needy. Mutual aid societies, unlike most organizations run by whites, depended on the deeply held belief that any member, no matter how comfortable at the moment, could become desperate. Given the precariousness of African Americans' livelihoods in a racist and unstable market culture, such an awareness was critical to survival.[61]

Anglo-American commentators on charity put the tradition of African American mutual aid to different uses, however. In the context of discourses and practices that undermined blacks' individuality, those who wrote about the social problems of African Americans often relied on a rhetoric of mutual aid rather than on the language of individual self-reliance that otherwise so dominated conversations on charity. These authors focused on instances in which black Americans helped or might be encouraged to help one another. Becoming unburdensome, then, meant ceasing to rely on the assistance of whites. This ideal of mutual aid, in addition to canceling whites' benevolent obligations toward African Americans, both reflected and reinforced the perceived interchangeability of racial others evident elsewhere in the dominant culture. One black person, these representations implied, was indistinguishable from another, so intraracial helping became the equivalent of self-help, one of the charity establishment's most cherished goals. African Americans who promoted a mutual aid model had other objectives in mind, primarily mitigating the suffering of their people, clearing "the race" of charges of excessive dependence on whites, and proving their collective capacity and strength of character. But such practices also shored up the broader culture's insistence on the collective identity of racial others.

The rhetoric of mutual benefit was perhaps most prominent in the writings of white colonizationists, who globalized black collective benevolence by insisting that persons of African descent should be the ones to Christianize and civilize Africa, all the while achieving economic security and social prominence as colonists.[62] It was even thought that black emigrants from the United States should be the ones to halt the illegal but ongoing trans-Atlantic slave trade.

Black mutual aid in this context meant "unburdensomeness" to whites, even as it entailed correcting whites' sins. The 1865 pamphlet *Christian Education for the South* mobilized a similar logic, though in an exclusively American context. It began with the assertion that the "sudden" emancipation of slaves "who have been kept in utter ignorance and in subjection, but who now are expected to maintain themselves among a population hostile to their advancement" represented a signal opportunity for benevolent whites, the implied audience of the piece. But, the pamphlet insisted, such benevolent agents ought to bring about their own obsolescence by educating *"a class of colored men and women who can become in turn the teachers of their race."* These black teachers would then work to "elevate those of their own color, both by stimulating them to a like culture, and by showing to the whole world the abilities and possibilities of the colored race."[63]

This pamphlet suggested that the degree to which African Americans enacted these models of intraracial aid marked the relative success or failure of the group. To an extent, African Americans themselves adopted this view. An unsigned article in the September 1859 issue of the *Anglo-African Magazine* took black Americans to task for the inadequacy of their benevolence: "We [Americans of African descent] do not manifest any remarkable force of character in the love we bear each other." The author claims that "our benevolent Associations . . . [are] but health insurance companies in fact—our Mutual Relief, Wilberforce, Daughters of Zion . . . and a hundred others of equally pious nomenclature" are less benevolent than self-serving, satisfying an "instinct of preservation against the force of circumstances which tend to crush us" and assisting only "those who are active, PAYING members." The truly destitute, the children and the aged of the community, are provided for instead "almost entirely" by white-run organizations.[64] Dependence on whites, this author insisted, shames black Americans in their own eyes and in the eyes of whites, while dependence on one another, were it cemented by true benevolence, would be a source of pride.

More sanguine commentators, black and white, praised black communities for their efforts at intraracial benevolence. James Freeman Clarke, for instance, despite his insistence on the curative effects of individual economic advancement, also commended black people for their mutual caretaking. "In Boston, and in other cities," Clarke wrote, "it is quite unusual to see a colored beggar, for, in general, the colored people take care of their own poor." Unlike Irish and German beggars who, Clarke claimed, were "common" in American cities, "the only colored beggars seen in New York are those who ask for money to help buy their wives, their sons, or their daughters."[65] The few black beggars one saw, in other words, were engaged in a form of intraracial helping. When the English author Mary Howitt took the United States as her subject in *Our Cousins in Ohio* (1849), she contrasted the deceptions of Irish and German beggars with the nobility of African Americans' benevolence. A black-run and-supported orphan asylum, which the white protagonists visit, clothes and educates needy black children, though it struggles to stay afloat, while an elderly black widow, whose husband has worked to purchase her freedom and his own, survives after his death by inviting a younger black family to live with her and help her manage the household and land. Whites in Howitt's story sympathize with and attempt to aid the black characters they encounter because the latter are constantly helping one another. Howitt and many of her contemporaries insisted that the mutually helping race, like Emerson's self-helping man, was vastly more appealing than one that looked to members of the "dominant" race for rescue. In some sense, mutual aid among African Americans was considered analogous to intrafamilial aid, an appropriate reliance on those who were thought to bear a primary responsibility for the needy person's welfare.

The practices of intraracial benevolence and mutual aid surely contributed to social cohesion and overall quality of life within black communities, whose members faced a judgmental and hostile white society. Nevertheless, the ideology of mutual aid had less salubrious effects as well. For one thing, it worked to render black need less visible. The relative absence of African American beggars in Boston, for example, in addition to garnering Clarke's praise, allowed whites to ignore widespread poverty among the city's black residents and, by extension, the racial exclusions that exacerbated it. If white commentators, through their praise of intraracial benevolence, could enlist the aid of black residents in producing that invisibility, then all the better for easing whites' consciences. This emphasis on interdependence and on quiet, behind-the-scenes mutual aid also worked to defuse the symbolic power of the self-reliant, free black individual, the "monster" who, according to Hosea Easton, haunted white Americans at least as much as did images of African American destitution.

Individuals and Communities

An anecdote reported by Philadelphia's Association of Friends for the Free Instruction of Adult Colored Persons illustrates this tension between an individualistic model of self-elevation and a communitarian model of mutual aid. At a ceremony closing the instructional year, the association's 1858 *Annual Report* claims,

> the older pupils entreated the younger to . . . be true to their best interests. They counselled them to read the lives of great men; of those who have risen out of obscurity into distinction; doubtless desiring to inculcate the idea, that an acquaintance with such examples might stimulate to that self-exertion and self-reliance, which the colored man especially needs, if, in the face of many obstacles, he would elevate his rank in the scale of society.[66]

The older, more experienced students in this account encourage the others to model themselves after self-made individualists, "great men" whose rise "out of obscurity" marks a personal transformation rather than the alteration of any group's circumstances. The "best interests" invoked here would seem to refer to individual advancement, without regard to the improvement of the race as a whole. And yet this advice-giving is itself a kind of mutual aid insofar as the older students assist the younger, whose improvement would eventually work to "elevate" the race as a whole. Moreover, the report posits a collective experience of racial injustice, evident here in the "obstacles" that the self-improving black individual encounters.

For many antebellum black Americans, as for these student advisers, notions of possessive individualism and self-reliance were in conversation and sometimes in uneasy cooperation with models of mutual aid and collective advancement. That phenomenon emerges with particular force in the writings of Frederick Douglass, the self-made "great man" who nevertheless wished to represent, and so form a part of, his community. The New York *Tribune,* perhaps unwittingly, invoked these tensions when it described Douglass as "the representative man of his race in America by virtue of self-help."[67] Self-containment, it seems, ultimately produced connection.

Douglass has been positioned, in American literature curricula and in much scholarship, as an exemplar of black self-reliance. His acquisition of literacy, escape from slavery, success as an author, and eventual break with Garrison, a controlling and paternalistic mentor, have all been used to mark his exceptionalism, his movement away from, or above, the communities of his youth and early adulthood. This positioning is not simply an artifact of twentieth-century scholarship and canon formation. Douglass himself, particularly in his 1845 *Narrative,* foregrounded his isolation and personal agency, de-emphasizing and in some cases erasing altogether the communities and individuals who had enabled his success.[68] And in *My Bondage and My Freedom,* he confronted benevolent whites' fears of black self-reliance, insisting on himself as a self-directing peer (to white abolitionists and his former masters, among others) rather than the mouthpiece and witness his sponsors wanted him to be. But Douglass's gestures toward individualist self-making and the scholarship that reproduces those gestures have not gone unchallenged. Valerie Smith and Deborah McDowell, among others, have looked at Douglass and the Douglass industry from feminist perspectives, examining the ways in which Douglass's narratives of acquiring manly self-reliance marginalize particular women in his life (especially his mother and his wife, Anna Murray) as well as the feminine more broadly conceived.[69] Smith argues as well that Douglass, "by telling the story of one man's rise from slavery to the station of esteemed orator, writer, and statesman, . . . confirms the myth shared by generations of American men that inner resources alone can lead to success." Douglass's "story of his own success," she continues, "actually provides counterevidence for his platform of radical change." Along similar lines, Waldo Martin suggests that Douglass's investment in individual success through hard work, which reflected his "deeprooted commitment to both capitalism and the Protestant work ethic," ignored the dehumanization of workers as well as the fact that "there was no assurance that work, along with good character, high morals, and lofty goals, would produce success."[70]

Nevertheless, scholars have also asserted Douglass's investment in community. Martin, for example, claims that Douglass's speech on "Self-Made Men" demonstrates that "the supreme irony of the self-made man concept . . . was the inevitability and necessity of human interdependence." For William Andrews, *My Bondage and My Freedom* is "the story of a black man's circuitous route toward black community." Robert Levine, too, has noted the ways in which black community comes to play an important role in *My Bondage,* but he emphasizes that Douglass joins, rhetorically, the individual and the group, "mak[ing] his representative identity as temperate revolutionary synonymous with African Americans' 'group identity.' "[71] As this well-known and extraordinary individual works to represent the race, he must fashion himself as both transcendent and embedded, elite and populist, self-reliant and interconnected.

Douglass's ongoing engagement with "the politics of representative identity," to borrow from Levine, had much to do with the discourses of benevolence and self-reliance outlined in this chapter. His insistent rhetoric of individual and self-directed advancement countered many whites' assertions that interracial benevolence and black mutual aid were the only means by which African Americans might attain "elevation." But Douglass was unwilling to abandon the goal of a black community that improved collectively as well as individually. His varied and often contradictory engagements with the discourses of black improvement conjoined an individualistic self-reliance with a program of mutual aid. In other words, he wanted it both ways—a collective, mutually helping elevation among black Americans but with the explicit visibility and publicity of his own self-reliant leadership. This commitment to communally oriented elevation was not always apparent, however. In 1853, Douglass lamented the failure of Gerrit Smith's attempt to encourage agrarianism among northern free blacks by means of extensive land grants. "Colored people," he claimed, "will congregate in the large towns and cities; and they will endure any amount of hardship and privation, rather than separate, and go into the country." This resistance to independent farming indicated to Douglass that American blacks were "wanting in self-reliance—too fond of society—too eager for immediate results—and too little skilled in mechanics or husbandry to attempt to overcome the wilderness."[72] "Overcom[ing] the wilderness" and, Douglass suggested, overcoming racial prejudice and economic deprivation, required patience, skill, and above all separation from what he implied were communities of failure. These remarks dovetailed with Douglass's most extreme rhetoric of self-reliance, which invoked a discourse of rights and possessive individualism as the means of elevating Americans of African descent. In speeches like "We Ask Only for Our Rights," delivered at a New York state convention of free blacks in 1855, Douglass demanded that blacks be granted the "responsibilities" of citizenship. Turning the language of benevolence against its white users, Douglass decried the supposedly philanthropic efforts of the Colonization Society and asked that whites perform only the "magnanimous" act of allowing "their disfranchised colored brethren" to vote.[73] Douglass shared the colonizationists' premise that citizenship was essential to self-reliance but insisted that such citizenship be American rather than Liberian.

In making his case for equal rights before the law, Douglass sometimes argued explicitly against benevolent intervention: "If [the black man] lives, well. If he dies, equally well. If he cannot stand up, let him fall down."[74] At such moments, Douglass placed justice and benevolence in opposition, insisting that if black Americans were granted the former, they would not need the latter. More often, however, he balanced the two, claiming that the elevation of African Americans would require the guarantee of equal rights as well as philanthropic efforts to undo the economic and spiritual damage of enslavement.[75] This dual investment is obvious in Douglass's attempts to negotiate and define his own identity as a benevolent agent. Near the end of "The Trials and Triumphs of Self-Made Men," he asserted that self-culture and self-making, however successful, must be "joined to some truly unselfish and noble purpose" if they are to "amount to much in this world." "Patriotism, religion, philanthropy," he continued, "some grand motive power other than the simple hope of personal reward must be present." Thus the link to community and, in many cases, to some sort of benevolent (philanthropic, religious) agenda within that community was crucial.[76]

For Douglass, this benevolent imperative took its most dramatic form in his return to the United States from England in 1847, a move that he characterizes in *My Bondage and My Freedom* as involving both personal sacrifice and benevolent vision. Remaining in England was impossible, Douglass asserted in a letter to Henry C. Wright, because his "sphere of usefulness" was in the United States and there it seemed his "duty to go."[77] He felt, in other words, a moral obligation to return to his native country in order to work toward his people's emancipation and elevation. But after having enjoyed comparative freedom from racial prejudice in England, Douglass found on embarking for home that his first-class berth had been given to someone else and that he was forbidden from entering the ship's "saloon." His voyage, "cooped up in the stern of the Cambria," symbolized and foretold the discrimination he would soon experience on his return to the United States. Suddenly he was no longer Frederick Douglass, the great man, but was instead a socially unacceptable being, one whose "dark presence" was "an offense" to his white fellow passengers.[78]

Douglass reestablishes his individualism and great-man status at the beginning of the next chapter, when he introduces his plan to pursue social change by means of editing a newspaper: "My friends in England had resolved to raise a given sum to purchase for me a press and printing materials; and I already saw myself wielding my pen, as well as my voice, in the great work of renovating the public mind, and building up a public sentiment which should, at least, send slavery and oppression to the grave, and restore to 'liberty and the pursuit of happiness' the people with whom I had suffered, both as a slave and as a freeman."[79] Douglass's language here seems purposefully self-aggrandizing, conveying his once-inflated hopes and setting up readers for the disillusionment he relates next—the Garrisonians' resistance to his plans. Nevertheless, the passage illuminates a critical element of Douglass's self-positioning. The "renovating" pen and voice are extensions of Douglass the editor, who represents even as he saves "the people" with whom he "had suffered." Here he articulates his own exceptionalism, his ability to represent the race because he exceeds the race. Embedded within an account of Douglass's return to America as a self-sacrificial benevolent project, the establishment of the paper emerges as an insistently public mode of intraracial mutual aid, one that combines a desire to improve the situation of black Americans *as a group* with an audacious individualism. (Douglass admits, after all, that it might have seemed "ambitious and presumptuous" for a man only nine years out of slavery to begin a newspaper.) This audacity, later reinforced when he renames his publication *Frederick Douglass's Paper,* works to undo the invisibility of the racialized benevolent actor that was written into whites' praise of black mutual aid.

Girls and Men

"Fie! you're a girl" (*CM,* 206). So says Egbert to Frank Goodman in *The Confidence-Man,* when confronting the latter's incessant appeals for aid and his sentimental responses to Egbert's equally tireless refusals. From Emerson's self-helping men, to charity literature's veneration of the hard-working head of household, to Douglass's equation of self-assertion and manhood in his accounts of the fight with Mr. Covey, representations of self-reliant Americans were overwhelmingly masculine. This is not to say that women were utterly denied access to the cultural value of self-reliance. Exemplars of (white) female self-reliance in antebellum texts sometimes depended financially on male relatives, which was acceptable for women whose husbands, sons, and fathers could bear such burdens, but they managed their households efficiently, without relying unduly on servants or complaining of their trials. Those heroines who could not depend on male support were praised for their ability to weather downward mobility cheerfully or were applauded for their skill in training the next generation of men for wage-earning roles. Some texts challenged these narrow definitions: Fanny Fern's *Ruth Hall* (1855), for example, presents a woman who achieves a degree of independence usually thought available only to men, including financial self-sufficiency, and expresses no desire to return to a state of "feminine" dependence. But in general, the kinds of independence thought appropriate for women were more limited than those prescribed for white men. Tellingly, a failure of self-reliance did not make a woman less womanly, but it did compromise her male counterpart's masculinity.

Adulthood, as it was variously defined, was also critical to the achievement of self-reliance. Egbert, after all, calls his needy companion a girl, not a woman, while didactic fiction that encouraged self-reliance among children did so as part of the child's training for and movement toward adulthood. But adulthood and masculinity were not neatly differentiated concepts in a society that denied women the right to vote, among other markers of legal competence, and that had long conceived of women as covered, legally, by the rights of their fathers or husbands. As testimony to the imbrication of the concepts of adulthood, manhood, and self-reliance, antebellum print culture's many representations of black male dependence—from tales of happy, well-cared-for slaves to images of kneeling black beggars—involved equal doses of infantilization and emasculation. African Americans countered those images through a rhetoric of self-reliant black manhood, usually figured as the endpoint of an arduous conversion, though they disagreed vehemently as to what that transformation might entail.[80] Black emigrants to Liberia, for example, credited leaving the United States with effecting their transformation into men. Jacob Harris, who left for Liberia in 1848 at the age of twenty-four, asked the recipient of his letter to "tell [his "Colored friends"] that we are all well Satisfied [with Liberia] and we have grown to the full stature of men," an impossibility, he suggests, within the United States.[81] A piece that appeared in the *Liberator* in 1853 turned this rhetoric against the emigrants, describing them as "utterly lost to every sense of manhood."[82] For these "Anti-Colonization Believers," as they called themselves, remaining in the United States to fight slavery and oppression was the true mark of manhood. To cite a more familiar example, in the passage from his 1845 *Narrative* to which I alluded above, Douglass promises to show readers "how a slave was made a man" by his refusal to allow another man to dominate him. He elaborates on this theme in *My Bondage and My Freedom*: "I was a changed being after that fight [with Mr. Covey]. I was *nothing* before; I WAS A MAN NOW. It recalled to life my crushed self-respect and my self-confidence, and inspired me with a renewed determination to be A FREEMAN." Sounding eerily like Emerson, he adds that "a man, without force, is without the essential dignity of humanity. Human nature is so constituted, that it cannot *honor* a helpless man, although it can *pity* him; and even this it cannot do long, if the signs of power do not arise."[83]

Such equations of black manhood with moral power and social elevation raise a critical question: To what extent was "manhood" a synonym for the dignified humanity that antiracist activists sought for all black Americans, male and female, and to what extent did it signify opportunities or ways of being reserved specifically for men? Those who spoke of black manhood in their calls for civil rights sought the elevation of the race as a whole, but the means in which they placed their faith—especially black male suffrage; access to permanent, legal marriage; and property ownership by a male head of household—suggested that the success of the group was contingent on the elevation of black men over black women.[84] The gender inequities inscribed within rhetorics of racial progress continued well beyond the period under study here. Kevin Gaines points out, for example, that activists such as Pauline Hopkins, Ida B. Wells, and Anna Julia Cooper found their connections to the black intelligentsia at the turn of the twentieth century "eroded by the patriarchal trappings of black intellectual endeavor, racial uplift ideology, and black leadership." Such structures have extended to the dominant culture's conceptions of African American communities, as Phillip Brian Harper argues in *Are We Not Men?* Contemporary U.S. culture, he writes, sees "African-American society in terms of a perennial 'crisis' of black masculinity whose imagined solution is a proper affirmation of black male authority."[85] The language of self-reliant black manhood lives on.

In the antebellum period, this rhetoric was never far removed from the discourse of benevolence. Whether advocating Liberian colonization or African American suffrage, commentators participated in ongoing discussions about black need and "degradation," on the one hand, and black elevation on the other. The language Americans used to explore both benevolence and self-reliance worked to establish the kinds of gender identities and gender relations thought possible or desirable, just as they informed the relations between selves and communities thought possible or desirable. If dependence was figured as emasculation and if African Americans were widely held to be especially, even constitutionally, dependent, then the assertion of masculinity was crucial to the assertion of black independence. Such a claim does not excuse the gender inequities that some advocates of black elevation fostered—inequities that Hazel Carby, in another context, labels "a conceptual and political failure of imagination"—nor does it imply that these inequities were imposed on black Americans by the dominant white culture without their participation or agency.[86] Rather, the advocacy of certain kinds of gender inequality among African Americans became culturally and socially useful in the mid-nineteenth century, a usefulness whose foundation was the language of benevolence that both black and white Americans were speaking and creating.[87]

CHAPTER FOUR

Pedagogies of Emancipation

The sudden emancipation of three or four millions of human beings, who have been kept in utter ignorance and in subjection, but who now are expected to maintain themselves among a population hostile to their advancement . . . provides a field for benevolent action unparalleled in extent and importance.

Christian Education for the South (1865)

The end of slavery was a crucial moment in the American culture of benevolence, though its import was interpreted in radically different ways. Proslavery paternalists argued that emancipation would mark the end of interracial benevolence; in their view, feckless slaves, once freed, would be exposed to the cruelties of the free market and denied the protections their masters once offered. For colonizationists, domestic emancipation inaugurated the former slaves' failure, owing, they insisted, to the intractability of white racism and the accretion of blacks' learned inferiority (vis-à-vis a "superior" race)—that is, unless benevolent whites succeeded in encouraging and expediting blacks' emigration to Africa. Antislavery forces, for their part, fell into two main camps. Gradualists endorsed the notion of educating and "improving" enslaved people in preparation for their eventual independence, while advocates of immediate abolition tended to see emancipation as the endpoint of one phase of benevolence and the initiation of another, geared toward ameliorating slavery's legacies.

In all but the proslavery view, pedagogy—and especially literacy instruction—was critical to the project of emancipation and, for many, to the larger project of making slaves into citizens, whether of the United States or Liberia.[1] Conversely, this proliteracy rhetoric figured the illiterate as social contaminants. For the anonymous author of *Christian Education for the South,* for example, freed slaves represented both threat and opportunity, chaos and healing: "If kept in ignorance and degradation they will contaminate all with whom they come in contact, and being free to come and go at will, they would soon become a *pest* to both the North and the South, whereas, if educated and Christianized, they would be a source of wealth and strength to the whole country, welcomed in every part of the land."[2] Benevolent pedagogy, this author insisted, was white America's best means of defense. Almost a decade earlier, a fundraising circular published by the Washington Association for the Education of Free Colored Youth made a similar argument, that "free people of color" must be "elevate[d] by religion and education," lest they become "a permanent and increasing weight on our prosperity."[3] The conspicuously white community invoked here was invited to link benevolence with economic self-interest.

Across a range of ideological investments, activists celebrated the word made legible, as literacy came to represent both Christianization—though clearly religious training could also take place orally—and induction into the "productive" portion of the community. These pedagogical gestures, as Christopher Castiglia has pointed out in an earlier context, implicate the agent of benevolence as much as its object. If "the effective teacher . . . is also the exemplary citizen," as Castiglia's subjects and mine suggest, this "citizen comes into being . . . in the pedagogical moment." Such citizenship "is always relational" and, Castiglia emphasizes, always hierarchical.[4] A recurring title-page illustration from the children's antislavery periodical *The Slave's Friend* reinforces the point. This image of a young white man towering over a group of eager black boys, whose attention is dutifully trained on their open books, presents to the implied audience of white children a familiar scene of classroom instruction. By representing African American children as students, the image invites readers to make room for racial others in their conceptions of schooling and perhaps to identify with those who, within the illustration's frame, occupy the readers' accustomed positions. But the caption, "The lips of the wise disperse knowledge," interrupts these identifications, redirecting attention to the white teacher and inviting viewers to emulate him, to ascend the pedagogical hierarchy by achieving wisdom and "dispers[ing]" knowledge to needy and ignorant others. The quiescence of the black students figured here suggests the naturalness of this ascent, reinforcing both the students' fitness for instruction and their white teacher's fitness for leadership.

In the first sections of this chapter I examine such racialized representations in a range of texts written by Anglo-Americans in the 1850s and 1860s, including the reports of Washington, D.C.'s Normal School for Colored Girls, Lydia Maria Child's *Freedmen's Book,* and Harriet Beecher Stowe's *Uncle Tom's Cabin,* whose twinned pedagogues, Miss Ophelia and Eva St. Clare, were among the era's most widely disseminated figures of white benevolence. The mid-nineteenth century was a time of active public conversation over the question of emancipation and black education, so active that numerous texts addressed similar themes. I have chosen these examples because their authors approach benevolent pedagogy from disparate ideological positions, claim different regional affiliations, and articulate an intriguing range of moral identities for the white pedagogues they represent. Most of the commentators are women, a fact that is in some degree coincidental, though it also reflects women's historically prominent role in literacy instruction and their increasing

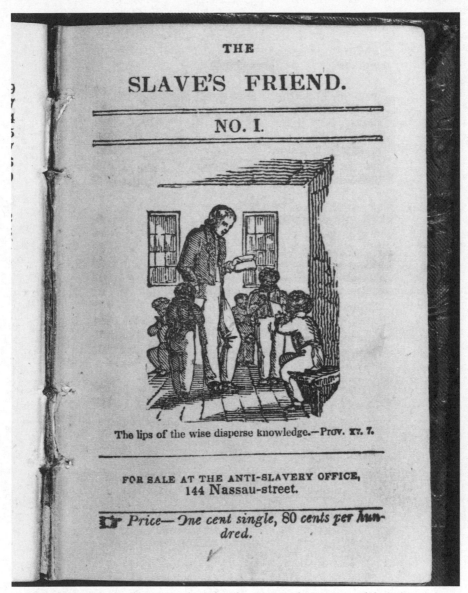

THE

SLAVE'S FRIEND.

NO. I.

The lips of the wise disperse knowledge.—Prov. xv. 7.

FOR SALE AT THE ANTI-SLAVERY OFFICE,
144 Nassau-street.

☞ Price— One cent single, 80 cents per hundred.

6. Woodcut wrapper illustration for *The Slave's Friend*. Courtesy of the Library Company of Philadelphia.

participation in U.S. education overall in the nineteenth century.[5] In their representations of interracial pedagogy, Anglo-Americans—male and female—staked out positions on black Americans' prospects for "elevation" and, ultimately, for membership in the nation. But the pedagogical relations figured here worked to constitute the identities of teachers as well as students, creating and justifying versions of white authority that accorded with the national and moral identities already in anxious circulation.

The mid-nineteenth century's powerful cultural images of white teachers and their black pupils tell only part of the story, however, given that much literacy instruction took place within African American communities. Literate slaves taught others to read in secret, while free blacks in the North, as Elizabeth McHenry and Julie Winch have shown, formed literary societies that acculturated their members into investment in literacy and the literary.[6] In keeping with this countertradition of intraracial pedagogy, then, I examine the Civil War–era writings of Charlotte Forten, a light-skinned and free-born African American who traveled to Union-occupied South Carolina in order to teach newly freed slaves. Forten's writings demonstrate the complexity of racial identification and the tenuousness of racial solidarity at midcentury, especially in the context of teaching and learning. In the process, they insist that we look at identity interstitially—at the ways in which Forten's gender, class, level of education, and regional affiliation, in concert with her race, inform her representations. Her subtle, elusive prose defies any presumption of commonality between freeborn African Americans and their newly emancipated "brethren," even as her journeys southward invoke a symbolic reknitting of the fractured republic. Forten's South is a site of cultural mediation through benevolence, where her uneasy alliances with white fellow reformers and black pupils lay claim to a better, though still imperfect, union.

"If You Are Not a Teacher Cannot You Become One?"

Not only did myriad conversations over the meaning of benevolence take place in print, but print was itself conceived of as a primary medium for the dissemination of benevolent principles. Books, newspapers, and pamphlets were thought critical to the projects of evangelizing, improving, and in some cases politicizing individual readers, which in turn guaranteed that the creation and distribution of appropriate reading material and the appropriate teaching of literacy were widely held to be benevolent acts.[7] Defining what was appropriate, of course, proved contentious, and the selection of texts, though less politically charged than the question of the proper recipients of instruction, was considered a challenging task. Lydia Sigourney's *Girl's Reading-Book,* for example, encouraged the distribution of reading material as part of a broader program of benevolence, though it also cautioned readers against books that may appear "useful and pious" but that in fact contain harmful elements: "Read the books that you intend to distribute, attentively, before you buy them. Be sure that there is nothing in their contents, but what is intended to benefit the reader."[8] The proliferation of printed materials in the antebellum period was thought to expand access to moral and social elevation, but as Isabelle Lehuu has pointed out, that breadth of options "made reading potentially as transgressive an entertainment as other public amusements such as the theater . . . or the saloon."[9]

Despite these cautions, antebellum Americans invested enormous resources in the creation and distribution of reading material on benevolence. Tract literature, children's literature, and other didactic texts promoted the values of temperance, kindness toward animals and siblings, and proper treatment of the poor and the abused. The author of an 1856 tract emphasized the catalytic potential of such texts, admonishing readers not to "cast . . . aside these pages with the presumption that an idle breath of fancy gave them birth. Should they create within you sighs of pity for the lowly and oppressed, or arouse you to a sense of your own long forgotten duty, the highest wish of the Author will have been gained."[10] Sunday-school pupils received such improving books as rewards for good behavior or outstanding performance, while reform-minded agents distributed the Bible and temperance tracts among "heathen" adults (e.g., immigrants and the urban poor) whose behavior seemed to warrant intervention. As Thomas Allen, a charitable Philadelphian, wrote in 1830, "the circulation of moral and religious truth through the medium of Bibles and Tracts, I consider among the most important means placed in my hands of doing good."[11] The vast print output of organizations like the American Tract Society and the American Sunday-School Union suggests that Allen's belief was widely shared.

The linked themes of reading and benevolence figured prominently within these improving texts as well as in the conditions of their distribution. For example, the burgeoning genre of fiction about and, often, explicitly for children frequently depicted reading as central to moral development. In some stories recalcitrant youngsters receive and benefit from improving books, while in others already pious children use the Bible or other good books to help them through hardships. In Susan Warner's *The Wide, Wide World* (1850), Ellen Montgomery and her mother, soon to be parted, engage in an elaborate ritual of purchasing the trappings of literacy, a Bible and a fully stocked writing desk; the latter will be the child's means of communicating with distant loved ones, while the former, a portable source of authority and guidance, must substitute for the nurturing, monitory parent.[12] This guiding-book trope also appears in Louisa May Alcott's *Little Women* (1868–69). Mrs. March gives her daughters copies of Bunyan's *Pilgrim's Progress* as Christmas presents so that they might see how far they can proceed, with the help of this famously didactic text, along the path of moral and spiritual self-improvement. Notably, this project is to be pursued in the time "before father comes home" from the Civil War, suggesting again that the moral book mitigates the loss or absence of a parent.[13]

The Sign of the Cross; or, Edah Champlin (1856), a little-known narrative by Lucy Ellen Guernsey, illustrates the extent to which literacy instruction and the encouragement of reading were thought to be crucial expressions of benevolent impulses. This book, as a material artifact, played a role in the circulation of improving texts within benevolent institutions: the copy held at the American Antiquarian Society includes the inscription "Presented to Jane B Denby at the Festival of the Sunday School of All Saints Church, Worcester, Mass. Christmas-Day, 1857." For Jane Denby, the book served as a reward or a token of the institution's regard for her, even as its content was calculated to propel her along a particular path toward social responsibility and engagement with benevolent literacies—the forms of literacy that the narrative itself champions. Guernsey's protagonist, the Edah Champlin of her title, is a wealthy young woman who learns to sacrifice worldly pleasure in order to serve her initially ungrateful stepmother and half-siblings, whom her father has left destitute. Edah goes to live in their modest home, located in a dull, unfashionable town, and begins to transform the community through pedagogy, both formal and informal. To pay off her father's drinking debts, she takes a job as a schoolteacher, in which role she manages to redeem an especially recalcitrant adolescent boy through love and understanding, and she begins a Sunday-school class for the children of the town, whose religious training has been shamefully neglected. Finally, she continues her course of edifying reading, borrowing books from the area's only wealthy, cultured family, whose visiting son she convinces to return permanently as the town's minister.

The book's mapping of benevolence onto pedagogical relations is clearest in the final chapter, when the narrator addresses readers directly on their options for doing good: "Is there a Sunday School in your parish, and if there is, what have you done for it? If you are a pupil, do you set an example of regular attendance and good lessons? . . . If you are a teacher, are you doing all you can . . . for the good of your class? If you are not a teacher cannot you become one?"[14] Readers—especially, though not exclusively, female readers—are invited to take their places, like the self-sacrificing Edah, within a matrix of pedagogical relations. Antebellum Americans repeated this message, though sometimes with more subtlety, in story after story, tract after tract, building up in the process a thorough interdependence of benevolent texts and benevolent acts.

Interracial Pedagogies

One of the great inconsistencies of mid-nineteenth-century culture is that these endorsements of benevolent pedagogy coexisted with a marked resistance on the part of many Anglo-Americans to literacy education for enslaved and free African Americans. To most slaveholders, the risks of such endeavors far outweighed the benefits that so many didactic texts proclaimed. Black literacy was thought to undermine white security, not only because slaves who could read and write might use those skills to launch rebellions or write passes that would facilitate their escape but also because literacy allowed access to proscribed knowledge—to the many biblical passages incompatible with slave-holding, to abolitionist arguments and strategies, and to information about places where slavery was illegal. The preamble to an antiliteracy act passed by the North Carolina General Assembly in the early 1830s put the matter bluntly: "The teaching of slaves to read and write, has a tendency to excite dis-satisfaction in their minds, and to produce insurrection and rebellion, to the manifest injury of the citizens of this State."[15] As Janet Cornelius has pointed out, slaveholders used various means to undermine slaves' access to literacy. Some southern states passed proscriptive laws, like the one cited above, and in-dividual owners inflicted brutal punishments, such as whippings or dismem-berment, on those caught reading or teaching. Some owners discouraged liter-acy in more subtle ways, by limiting access to the printed word or by keeping their slaves too exhausted to expend the energy that learning to read required. Such obstacles to literacy were not universal—Cornelius presents evidence of slaveholders who taught slaves to read, arranged for such teaching to take place, or chose to ignore evidence that literacy was being taught surrepti-tiously—but were sufficiently widespread that U.S. slavery has rightly been as-sociated with enforced illiteracy.[16]

Resistance to black education extended well beyond the South, however. Anglo-Americans in the free states thwarted the cause of black education in various ways, ranging from dismissal of its importance and withholding of fi-nancial and political support to outright obstructionist and violent acts.[17] Not surprisingly, the prospect of integrated classrooms met with vehement disap-proval, though contention over integration should not be taken to suggest that all-black schools enjoyed widespread support. When Prudence Crandall, for example, attempted to conduct a school for African American girls in Canter-bury, Connecticut, in 1833, white townspeople responded by refusing to sell her supplies, harassing her students, and threatening members of her family. After a series of legal maneuvers failed to close the school, area whites at-tacked the building directly, once setting it on fire and later vandalizing it, forcing Crandall to shut down in 1834.[18] In a slightly earlier Connecticut case, white residents of New Haven blocked the establishment there of a "college for colored youth." They claimed not only that such a project would be tanta-mount to condoning abolition but also that "the establishment of a College in the same place to educate the colored population is incompatible with the prosperity, if not the existence of the present institutions of learning [in New Haven], and will be destructive of the best interests of the city."[19] An example of what George Lipsitz has called the "possessive investment in whiteness," the premise of these activists was that the very fact of a school for African Ameri-cans lowered the value of Anglo-Americans' property-in-education.[20]

Inadequate funding of black education was common as well. The Pennsyl-vania Society for Promoting the Abolition of Slavery, reporting on the condi-tion of Philadelphia's schools for African Americans, indicated that, although some schools flourished, others were barely functioning. One school in West Philadelphia, visiting agent Benjamin C. Bacon wrote in 1853, "is so much crowded at times that some scholars are obliged to crawl under, and others over the writing desks, to get to and from their places." On one February afternoon, he noted, there were "twelve broken panes of glass, besides many other large apertures to let in cold. Good order, under all the circumstances, is out of the question."[21] While the following year's report cited improvements— this school was eventually moved "from the hovel in which it was so long kept, to the basement of the Colored Baptist Church"—free black education remained a low priority for most policymakers in the North.[22]

Such disregard notwithstanding, some whites championed the cause of black education, despite the personal cost of doing so. A sampling of midcentury texts—Margaret Douglass's 1854 narrative of her trial and imprisonment for teaching free black children, two pamphlets issued by Washington, D.C.'s Normal School for Colored Girls (1854 and 1856), and Lydia Maria Child's *Freedmen's Book* (1865)—demonstrates the variation and complexity within representations of white-to-black pedagogy. Margaret Douglass's text disrupts the era's usual alignments by advocating literacy instruction for free black children while continuing to support slavery and to argue for blacks' inherent and permanent inferiority. Myrtilla Miner, founder of the Normal School, posits instead the improvability of African American girls, whose susceptibility to elevating white influence proves the value of gradual emancipation. White pedagogy, she suggests, provides a necessary foundation for such transformations, circumventing the potential harm of a presumptuous or premature black agency. Child's *Freedmen's Book,* the most progressive of the three by twenty-first-century standards, sets up a more collaborative model, one that invites African Americans to participate as both teachers and students, even as it retains some inequalities of status and authority. With emancipation as its originary moment, Child's text balances exhortation to improvement against celebration of African Americans' already considerable accomplishments. Taken together, these three pedagogical interventions demonstrate the extent to which black literacy had become, by midcentury, the grounds for theorizing— or for disallowing—black citizenship.

Margaret Douglass's proslavery sentiments and southern regional identification are made clear from the beginning of her narrative. *Educational Laws of Virginia* insists on its author's positioning as "a Southern woman" speaking to fellow southerners, despite the fact that Douglass and her daughter, Rosa, moved to Philadelphia after her release from jail and that her account was published by John P. Jewett and Company of Boston, which had brought out *Uncle Tom's Cabin* two years earlier. This association with antislavery publishing notwithstanding, Douglass's self-presentation as a southerner rests on her disavowal of emancipationist sentiment. She insists early on that she wishes "to do away with any impression that I was or am an *Abolitionist,* as that term is usually understood at the South" and describes herself instead as a former slave owner who, "if circumstances rendered it necessary or practicable, . . . might be such again."[23] Figuring slavery as an "abstract question" with which she has "nothing to do in this book," Douglass focuses instead on the "particular" law prohibiting the instruction of free blacks, a law, she claims, against which "a large portion of even the inhabitants of Virginia are beginning to rebel, as contrary, not only to good morals, but to the spirit of our country's institutions."[24]

Douglass's narrative, an intriguing counterpoint to the more famous Douglass's narrative published almost a decade earlier, sets up a conventional homology between literacy instruction and moral formation. Where she differs from most of her contemporaries is in her attempt to separate black literacy from the question of emancipation—a disarticulation that neither southern authorities nor abolitionists accepted, apparently. Virginia's judicial system, in choosing to punish Douglass, implicitly rejected her claim that free black literacy need not threaten the institution of slavery, while her publisher worked to elide her proslavery sentiments in advertisements for the book, which ran in such antislavery periodicals as the *National Era* and *Frederick Douglass's Paper*. These notices focused on the injustice of her imprisonment ("for the Crime of Teaching Free Colored Children to Read!!!") but omitted any mention of her attitude toward slavery, allowing her in some sense to pass as an abolitionist.[25] That erasure—along with the assertion of her identity as "a Southern woman" and the promise of "ASTOUNDING DISCLOSURES!"—was calculated to heighten the book's appeal, marketing it to northern abolitionists as both a curiosity and an affirmation of their views.

Despite this reductive representation of Douglass as generic victim and foe of injustice, her narrative is much more immediately and elaborately about herself than about the children whom she has taught. For Douglass, benevolent pedagogy allows her to lay claim to a higher class status than her occupation or lifestyle would seem to endorse. While she writes that she supports herself "with [her] needle" and suggests that economic necessity has compelled her to live among neighbors who "were not of the most refined class," she rejects the class status to which these facts would seem to assign her.[26] Dismissing the nineteenth-century stereotype of the seamstress as object of benevolence, Douglass constructs herself instead as the quintessential, if aggrieved, benevolent citizen, a woman for whom charitable acts are her primary means of interacting with the outside world. Referring to herself and her daughter, she writes: "Our only association with society was that into which we were led by the exercise of our feelings of humanity" (6), which extends not only to instructing African American children but also to "practicing mercy and charity to all who came in our way, both black and white" (7). While she shrinks from any interaction with her neighbors that would position them as peers (they "would prove no associates for us"), she asserts that she has "endeavored to be kind and obliging to all who stood in need of [her] sympathies" (9). Invoking a noblesse oblige incommensurate with her relative poverty and social isolation, Douglass figures benevolence as both sign and effect of her superiority.

Douglass's self-positioning is more variable when her narrative focuses on her legal difficulties. In some passages she presents herself as "a weak and helpless woman"—specifically, a woman unfamiliar with state law. That teaching free black children was illegal, she claims, "was the most profound news to me" (1). But Douglass also sets herself up as a courageous dissenter, asserting that instruction of both slaves and free blacks ought to proceed and even comparing herself to Jesus Christ. "I remembered," she writes, in reference to the moment of her arrest, "that our Saviour was persecuted for doing good, and why should not I be"(15). To the roles of innocent and martyr she adds amateur lawyer and protofeminist, speaking in her own defense in the courtroom and insisting that the Virginia statute's use of a masculine pronoun calls into question whether the law would necessarily apply to her and, by extension, whether the masculine can be universalized at all (62).

Ultimately, Douglass's protest against the "educational laws of Virginia," in terms of her courtroom statements and her personal narrative, is specifically not transformative, however forceful her staging of principled dissent. On the contrary, her narrative asserts the fundamental rigidity of social and racial hierarchies, a stability that interracial pedagogy, in her view, can in no way disrupt—just as her own downward economic mobility cannot undermine her superiority, as expressed here through her status as benevolent pedagogue. Douglass's remarks emphasize her students' worthiness as objects of benevolence: "Punctual in their attendance, and under good discipline," they "made rapid progress in their studies," while the larger black community "showered upon [Douglass and her daughter] their grateful blessings" (20). But while she foregrounds free blacks' compliance and gratitude, she also emphasizes their limitations: "Our slaves and servants, whether bond or free, . . . can be nothing else in our community" (33). Douglass's prosecution, then, is a violation of "common charity," which "would have attributed to [her] only a feeling of sympathy for a lower order of society" rather than the charge of undermining social stability (53). Invoking common charity as common sense, Douglass installs herself as its arbiter, insisting that interracial pedagogy does not threaten the social transformations that so many whites feared. The text's ostensible protest thus becomes a statement of faith in the stability of racial hierarchies and in the benevolent relations with which those hierarchies were intertwined. Not to worry, Douglass insists—literacy instruction is not so powerful after all.

In contrast to Margaret Douglass's regionalism, the fundraising circulars published on behalf of the Normal School for Colored Girls posit African American education as a national concern. The 1856 circular (written by William H. Beecher, a less-famous brother of Catharine Beecher, Henry Ward Beecher, and Harriet Beecher Stowe and, for a time, the school's fundraiser) asserted that the school was founded in Washington "because it is National ground, and the Nation is responsible for the well-being of its population."[27] Myrtilla Miner, a New York–born educator and gradual abolitionist who began the school in 1851, despite having no personal tie to the city, claimed in a letter to Senator William H. Seward that "if any influence can be felt in behalf of the colored people any where—it can be most felt in the city of Washington."[28] Assertions of benevolent responsibility on a national scale were commonplace in the antebellum years, but the circumstances of this intervention are especially intriguing. In a decade of increasing interregional conflict, Miner chose to establish a school for free African American girls within the nation's capital, still a slaveholding district and thus an especially potent symbol of collective guilt and responsibility.

Unlike Douglass, Miner sought to use education to advance the cause of (eventual) black emancipation. Although the school would accept no enslaved or fugitive girls for fear of attack from proslavery elements of the community, Miner clearly associated free black education and "elevation" with the cause of emancipation. In a letter to the novelist Mrs. E.D.E.N. Southworth, for example, she writes of her conviction that "the time has come [when] the merciful should stretch forth the hand of sympathy and love & employ every just & lawful means to bring them [African Americans] up from the prison house of bondage, & what can I better do than faithfully instruct them?"[29] Some of her emancipatory rhetoric edged further into the drama of self-sacrifice; in a letter to the abolitionist Gerrit Smith, she refers to her plan of opening the school as an "offering" of herself "upon the antislavery altar of my country."[30]

The Normal School's publications fit neatly into the antebellum genre of the charity society report/fundraising appeal, whose hallmark is a delicate balance between hope and threat. On the side of hope, the school provided evidence for the claim that African Americans could be "elevated" via pedagogy. As the Unitarian minister and social reformer William H. Channing claimed, Miner's school was "the place to demonstrate by culture, [free black girls'] intellectual and moral power, and thus justify their aspirations for refinement and usefulness."[31] The acquisition of culture under the tutelage of a northern white woman here becomes, in a kind of circular logic, a justification for aspiration itself. The students' attainments, in other words, legitimate their desire for advancement by proving to an audience of white observers, donors, and citizens that young African Americans had "intellectual and moral power" commensurate with the education so many would deny them. These texts also deployed a negative logic, emphasizing the social crises that threatened should Channing's projected demonstration be thwarted. Miner pleaded that African Americans "*may be saved from crime or insanity* by the removal of those fearful maladies—ignorance and want."[32] The threat that black ignorance poses to whites' well-being is made clear on the following page. "These hard-handed workers," Miner continued, "will in time become physically strong—and, if left in *ignorance,* no wise counsel can stay the tide, should they rise in their might and desperation, to roll back the flood of power that deprives them of privileges, which, ignorant as they are, they know to be the 'inalienable right' of every honest person who treads American soil."[33] Beecher claimed, with a similar urgency, that the free black population "as a class, through ignorance and neglect, . . . are fast becoming a heathen people, in the bosom of a Christian nation."[34] If illiteracy and ignorance cause crime, insanity, rebellion, and irreligion, then pedagogy becomes a means of inoculating the social body against these ills.

A salient feature of the Normal School circulars is their ambivalence toward the possibility of African American ascent within pedagogical hierarchies. On the one hand, Miner's very project would seem to endorse such an ascent. In speaking of her current students, she writes that "many of them will become teachers, and by their refinement and good morals exert such an influence upon their associates, as shall relieve the world of much degradation and consequent misery."[35] The girls are expected eventually to assume superior positions within benevolent hierarchies, effecting the moral and social reclamation of their charges as well as announcing and reifying their own elevated status. On the other hand, both the 1854 and 1856 texts undermine that endorsement. Beecher's circular asserts that the main reason for training African American teachers is that "white teachers cannot be found in sufficient numbers, nor would they be permitted to enter, to any adequate extent, those Southern States where this population [i.e., black children] most abounds."[36] Black teachers, in this schema, are only substitutes (pun intended) for their superior but currently unavailable white counterparts.

More bracing is Miner's angry account of the inadequate education she claims some of her older pupils (ages fifteen to seventeen) have received in black-run schools: "There were previously five or six private schools in the District taught by colored men, from which some of these girls professed to have graduated, *i.e.*[,] learned all their instructors could teach them. But they were unable to apply the knowledge they had acquired to any practical use. While professing to be able to read well, they had no proper understanding of what they read; while professing to understand grammar, they rarely spoke or wrote good English."[37] For Miner, this is a false literacy, productive of arrogance rather than elevation. The girls' high self-opinion, it seems, troubles her more than their specific deficiencies. When "thrown into classes with *children* who were acquiring first principles," she claims, their "pride was so shocked . . . that every one, the good as well as the bad, *left school* after six months or a year."[38] Ultimately, they defy the institution's mission, returning "to their various avocations, quite unwilling to assume the responsibility of teaching, though they had entered the school with the full understanding, that it was established to educate a class of girls particularly for that profession." A "younger and more morally healthful class," to use Miner's descriptors, fares better at the school, where its members engage in "various studies calculated to enlighten their minds, refine their tastes, cultivate proper habits, and develop all their powers for usefulness and happiness." These "earnest seekers after knowledge," Miner suggests, are successful in large part because they have come to her early, before they could be corrupted by poorly run schools.[39] To be fair, Miner does not denigrate all black-run schools but neither does she offer competent counterexamples. While she asserts that she "find[s] no difference of native talent, where similar advantages are enjoyed, between Anglo-Saxons and Africo-Americans," it becomes clear that, programmatically at least, white pedagogy constructs African Americans' achievement and, by extension, their access to positions of benevolent agency.[40] As Miner writes elsewhere, her project is predicated on the belief that "the colored people will never rise *alone* & without aid."[41]

Margaret Douglass's narrative and the Normal School documents address themselves primarily to white audiences. Child's *Freedmen's Book,* in contrast, directly addresses African Americans, enacting a project of interracial pedagogy while arguing for its value in the abstract. Child allows for white participation, as her authorship of the text attests, but she foregrounds the perceptions and experiences of African Americans throughout, in part by including texts by and about black people (entries by black authors are marked in the table of contents with asterisks), and she registers considerable respect for blacks' intelligence and autonomy. Combining biographies of admirable African Americans (such as Benjamin Banneker and Phillis Wheatley), retellings of successful escapes from slavery, proemancipation speeches and poetry, and exhortations to good hygiene and good horticulture, Child's text is both celebratory and didactic. It applauds black achievement, on the one hand, and white goodwill on the other—both embattled notions in the 1860s, to be sure—but it also works in a heavy dose of the rhetoric of elevation, a process inextricable, for Child, from the achievement of benevolent agency.

The Freedmen's Book marks a society in transition from a troubled acceptance of slavery to an ambivalent eradication of it. Some selections record the deeds and sufferings of enslaved people, while others focus on emancipation and its aftermath. Not surprisingly, the author struggles with a slippery set of categories: the term *freedmen* suggests relatively recent enslavement, figuring the individual as the object of an outside agent's emancipatory efforts, and yet she exhorts those individuals—the book's target audience—to embrace self-determination and self-improvement. Child also discusses and includes writings by admirable representatives of the race who have never been enslaved (or who escaped from slavery long ago), presenting them as both like and unlike the book's newly freed implied readers. Her broader term, *colored,* seems meant to bridge that divide, to allow crossings from the category of the recently freed slave to that of the literate exemplar. The act of reading this book is conceived as a means of bringing about such a transition but so are the many acts of benevolence, largely intraracial, represented within its pages. Readers are urged to invest themselves in the education of black children, to serve as examples of self-sufficiency and moral probity in order to hasten "the emancipation of poor weary slaves in other parts of the world," and, most immediately, to read this book "aloud to others" who cannot read it for themselves.[42]

Benevolent transformation is the subject of the essay "Kindness to Animals," one of Child's contributions to the collection. "The fact that [animals] cannot speak to tell of what they suffer," Child writes, "makes the sad expression of their great patient eyes the more touching to any compassionate heart" (97). Operating within the discourse of sentimentalism, Child here foregrounds vision, one of the primary means by which the "compassionate heart" comes to know the suffering of others. She next establishes a homology between beasts and slaves: "Fugitive slaves, looking out mournfully and wearily upon a cold, unsympathizing world, have often reminded me of overworked and abused oxen; for though slaves were endowed by their Creator with the gift of speech, their oppressors have made them afraid to use it to complain of their wrongs" (97). Again, the gaze of the sympathizer is mediated by the eyes of the sufferer—the "sad expression" of the animal's "great patient eyes," the mournful and weary look of the fugitive—as looking is made to stand in for and is intensified by the absence of speech. Child then extends the comparison, describing a horse that refuses to budge after being forced to pull heavy loads: "He has apparently come to the conclusion that it is better to be killed at once than to die daily. Slaves, who are under cruel taskmasters, also sometimes sink down in utter discouragement, and do not seem to care for being whipped to death" (98). If the despair is the same, then so is the remedy. "The best way to cure the disheartened and obstinate laborer," she writes, "is to give him just wages and kind treatment; and the best way to deal with the discouraged and stubborn horse is to give him light loads and humane usage" (98). Child's reversal of the order of the comparison only reinforces the interchangeability of the two categories of abused beings.

The alignment of slaves with animals had a complicated history within debates over slavery. Proslavery commentators used such comparisons in order to justify their inhumane treatment of slaves, claiming that the latter, like animals, had little family feeling or were relatively insensitive to pain. Authors of slave narratives, meanwhile, typically identified such comparisons and the resulting similarity of treatment as products of whites' prejudice, as when Harriet Jacobs claimed that southern women considered their husbands' illegitimate slave children to be "as marketable as the pigs on the plantation."[43] Child's comparison of suffering slaves to suffering beasts is a strange hybrid, sympathetic to the plight of the slave but suggesting a similarity that owes more to genuine commonality than to whites' prejudicial perceptions. Although Child presents this as a commonality of experience rather than essence and embeds it within a text that otherwise celebrates black agency, her comparison nevertheless suggests a certain passivity and predictability on the part of slaves. But Child also undercuts that suggestion, inviting former slaves (who, she claims, "know how to sympathize with the dumb creatures of God") to develop a particularly strong compassion toward animals.[44] Further, the second half of the essay, devoted to anecdotes illustrating the success of gentle persuasion in controlling the behavior of animals, positions the freedman-reader as the trainer and user of animal labor, rather than as the animal's analogue. "Reasonable and kind treatment," Child concludes, "will generally produce a great and beneficial change in vicious animals as well as in vicious men."[45] The once-enslaved reader here occupies two positions—that of the abused fellow sufferer and that of the newly enlightened, gentle master. Ex-slaves are invited to elevate themselves from one category to the other through benevolence, to take on the qualities of Child's exemplars, not by designing a city as Banneker did or leading a revolution like Toussaint L'Ouverture (another of the book's biographical subjects), but simply by choosing not to beat an animal—or, when given the opportunity, another human being.

Alongside Child's benevolent instruction, there emerges a deep defensiveness, a fear of being perceived as insensitive or self-serving. Her brief preface insists that she has received no payment in exchange for her work on this book and that the book itself is sold "at the cost of paper, printing, and binding." Addressing her African American readers directly, she claims that "whatever money you pay for any of the volumes will be immediately invested in other volumes to be sent to freedmen in various parts of the country . . . and whatever money remains in my hands, when the book ceases to sell, will be given to the Freedmen's Aid Association, to be expended in schools for you and your children."[46] Child's fear that she will be perceived as an agent of false benevolence is very much in evidence here, as is a desire to remind readers of her long service as an antislavery activist by signing the preface "your old friend."[47]

This keen sense of accountability to the population Child seeks to aid, the fact that she worries about offending or being misunderstood by her African American readers, is unusual in the era's discourse on benevolence. Authors often expressed anxiety that potential donors or the public at large might misapprehend their efforts but worried far less often that "the helped" might do so. This rhetoric of accountability suggests that, for Child, benevolent exchange is not unidirectional, that reception and recursion are inevitably a part of any benevolent project, and that "true" benevolence, however defined, requires not just the consent of the helped but their active participation. While the forms of pedagogy she represents here are certainly racialized, her text allows for teaching to proceed along multiple axes and insists on the benevolent agency of black Americans, not just in some idealized future but in the chaotic present as well. As conventional as many of Child's pronouncements are—her final contribution to the volume, for instance, advises readers on everything from timely mending of clothing to graceful acceptance of freedom's disappointments—the text as a whole is more respectful of the helped and more collaborative in orientation than what most of her contemporaries were producing. For Child, African Americans were already part of the nation, the benevolence of which would be tested through its handling of slavery's aftermath.

Sentimental Education

The ideological projects of interracial pedagogy proceed perhaps most famously in Stowe's *Uncle Tom's Cabin,* a text that, like *The Freedmen's Book,* endeavored to prove white benevolence and black potential. Toward this end, Stowe creates multiple scenes of instruction: the reader's first glimpse into Tom and Chloe's cabin reveals thirteen-year-old George Shelby teaching Tom to write the alphabet, while in later chapters Miss Ophelia teaches Topsy to read, and Eva St. Clare instructs her family's slaves in matters of faith and mourning. The nonfictional texts foregrounded elsewhere in this chapter emerged in a cultural context already suffused with Stowe's characters and representations, which Americans encountered through direct experience of the novel and through its aftershocks: the conversations and arguments it sparked, as well as the illustrations, songsheets, children's books, and stage versions it inspired. A closer look, then, at Stowe's representations of benevolent pedagogy—and at some of the texts that reconstituted them—illuminates the tropes and expectations that structured interracial teaching at midcentury.

Stowe's reiterated moments of instruction in *Uncle Tom's Cabin* serve as explicitly political and ethical interventions, in that they assert literacy's power to bring slaves into the moral community of the free. The era's two dominant celebratory narratives of African American literacy acquisition—one charting a movement toward freedom-seeking and possessive individualism, à la Frederick Douglass's *Narrative,* and the other toward a deepening investment in Christianity—are, for Stowe, complementary rather than antagonistic. Though she acknowledges that literacy can exacerbate a slave's discontentment—George Harris's level of education, for example, makes it difficult for him to submit to the mindless work his master assigns—she nevertheless posits the acquisition of literacy as a movement toward a kind of Christian self-possession. Topsy must be free in order to spread Christianity in Africa, and George can only embrace the faith once he fully possesses himself and his wife Eliza.[48] Insofar as literacy promotes both the will and the means to self-possession, it also enhances the individual's ability to internalize and disseminate Christian teaching.

In keeping with these interrelated agendas, the novel's scenes of instruction stand in for a range of transformative projects, including the teaching and learning of benevolence itself. Such engagements mirror Stowe's relationship with her implied readership—those Americans who might be susceptible to moral suasion but who have not yet committed themselves to the work of ending slavery. Self-consciously establishing this agenda, she positions the novel as one of many similarly activist works of art. "Every influence of literature, of poetry and of art, in our times," she claims in the preface, "is becoming more and more in unison with the great master chord of Christianity, 'good will to man.' "[49] In the final chapter, Stowe exhorts readers to stop conceiving of slavery as something to be "apologized for" or "passed over in silence" and rebukes northern mothers for failing to instruct their children in benevolence: "If the mothers of the free states had all felt as they should, in times past, the sons of the free states would not have . . . connived at the extension of slavery" and would not "trade the souls and bodies of men as an equivalent to money" (*UTC*, 384–85). In a final comment, which appeared only in the *National Era*'s serialization of the novel, Stowe addresses in particular "the dear little children who have followed her story":

> You will one day be men and women; and [the author] hopes that you will learn from this story always to remember and pity the poor and oppressed, and, when you grow up, show your pity by doing all you can for them. Never, if you can help it, let a colored child be kept out of school, or treated with neglect and contempt, because of his color. Remember the sweet example of little Eva, and try to feel the same regard for all that she did.[50]

Here Stowe generalizes her benevolent project, exhorting children to show benevolence toward "the poor and oppressed"—not just slaves but all who stand in need of aid.

Stowe's attention to Eva in this appeal accords with her use of the benevolent white child as an icon of transformative instruction, one whose resonance extended well beyond the boundaries of the narrative, to judge by the degree to which allied texts, especially children's books, dwelled on her. Eva's kinswoman Miss Ophelia, a deeply flawed figure who must herself be transformed by the child's exemplary life and death, is an equally powerful emblem of white pedagogy, of its failures and means of redemption. The novel, then, highlights two complementary visions of white benevolence: Eva conjures images of luminous perfection, a salvific whiteness that cannot fail to instruct, whereas Ophelia embodies the white female pedagogue as object of ridicule, ineffectual until she absorbs some of the other's valence. So while Stowe's representations of Eva and the many related representations that followed work to reify the figure of the white female as benevolent instructor, the depiction of Ophelia provides a useful corrective, an emblem of officious northern pedagogy. The hard-won lessons of that pedagogy align with the relative modesty and defensiveness of Lydia Maria Child and with the eventual reeducation of Stowe herself, whose novel *Dred* reflects her growing regard for African Americans' social and political views.

Within *Uncle Tom's Cabin*, Eva's pedagogical apotheosis occurs in chapter twenty-six (titled "Death"), when she takes leave of her family's slaves. Initially, the power of the scene is visual, as Eva becomes the focal point of a sentimental tableau: she "lay back on her pillows; her hair hanging loosely about her face, her crimson cheeks contrasting painfully with the intense whiteness of her complexion . . . and her large, soul-like eyes fixed earnestly on every one" (*UTC*, 250). On seeing her, the slaves "were struck with a sudden emotion" and maintained "a deep silence, like that of a funeral." Eva's impending death, here briefly imagined as having already occurred, heightens her instructive power, as the slaves' eager reception of her subsequent speech attests. Beginning with a declaration of love for her audience, which produces in them "bursts of groans, sobs, and lamentations," Eva then adopts an overtly pedagogical tone. "If you love me, you must not interrupt me so," she scolds. "Listen to what I say. I want to speak to you about your souls" (*UTC,* 251). Chastising the slaves for "thinking only about this world," the child reminds them of heaven, "a beautiful world, where Jesus is," to which she invites them to follow her (*UTC,* 251). Eva then offers the slaves specific prescriptions. To achieve salvation, she tells them, "you must pray to [Jesus]; you must read—"; but before completing the admonition (presumably to read the Bible), Eva stops herself, looks "piteously at them," and says " 'O, dear! You *can't* read,—poor souls!' " (*UTC,* 251). Her adept blending of the rhetorics of mourning, evangelism, and literacy comes up against what Harryette Mullen has called slavery's "compulsory illiteracy," an interruption that allows Stowe to highlight the importance of reading and the mistreatment of slaves, even those working under the comparatively good conditions the St. Clare family provides.[51] But she cannot allow Eva's pedagogy to fail on this point. Like a classroom teacher discovering her students' limitations, Eva reassesses her auditors and offers them another avenue to success: " 'Never mind,' . . . 'I have prayed for you; and I know Jesus will help you, even if you can't read. Try all to do the best you can . . . get the Bible read to you whenever you can; and I think I shall see you all in heaven' " (*UTC,* 251). She ends the lecture by giving each slave a lock of her hair, a gesture that accords with the widespread antebellum practice of keeping such locks as tokens of love or as memorials. But the severed curl also serves as a religious relic, a devotional mnemonic calculated to remind the slaves of Eva herself and, by extension, of her faith and benevolent instruction.[52] "When you look at [the curl]," she tells the slaves, " 'think that I loved you and am gone to heaven, and that I want to see you all there' " (*UTC,* 251).

While Stowe's narrative initiated Eva's positioning as a pedagogical icon, the illustrators and children's authors who abstracted and recreated her did much to advance that process.[53] One of the most widely disseminated visual images associated with the novel presents Eva engaging in what appears to be a pedagogical exchange with Tom. The version included in the first edition of the novel is captioned "Little Eva reading the Bible to Uncle Tom in the arbor." With the Bible on her lap, one hand on Tom's hand and the other pointing toward a lake, Eva appears to be making a point of vital importance. This is not, strictly speaking, a moment of literacy instruction; Tom already knows how to read, though he enjoys no great fluency, and neither he nor Eva is actually looking at the book in any of the several versions I have encountered. But the image, like the narration of Eva's deathbed lecture, links literacy (reinforced by the open book in her lap) and benevolent instruction, in keeping with the era's emphasis on literacy as a social practice in which conversations about books were as important as direct encounters with print.[54] Tom's attentive gaze and forward lean mark him as a dutifully attentive student, absorbing the child's revelations and interpretations. The image is so striking and was so widely reproduced in the nineteenth century that it is easy to overlook the fact that it invokes benevolent pedagogy far more than does the accompanying narrative, which positions Tom as confidant rather than pupil. There Eva compares Lake Pontchartrain to the "sea of glass, mingled with fire" that she has read about in the Book of Revelations and declares that she will soon be going to heaven.[55]

Some of the children's texts that capitalized on Eva's popularity also expanded and elaborated on her pedagogical presence, sometimes in quite literal ways. For example, an English imprint called *Little Eva's First Book for Good Children* features an illustration inside the front cover captioned "Little Eva teaching Topsy to read." The two girls, against an opulent, orientalist backdrop, sit with a large book between them, which rests on the white child's lap. While Topsy's hand extends to the printed page, her gaze appears fixed on Eva, whose patient, mild expression signals her benevolence. The rest of the text consists of upper-and lower-case alphabets, numbers, vocabulary words with syllabic divisions, and simple reading passages, among them an abbrevi-

LITTLE EVA READING THE BIBLE TO UNCLE TOM IN THE ARBOR. Page 68.

7. From the first edition of *Uncle Tom's Cabin; or, Life among the Lowly*. Courtesy of the Library Company of Philadelphia.

ated version of Stowe's story (so abbreviated, in fact, that it omits Eva's death), which emphasizes moments of interracial benevolence.[56] The New York-published *Little Eva: The Flower of the South* expands Eva's pedagogical presence even further. An illustration titled "EVA, TEACHING THE ALPHABET" presents the child as a schoolmistress, who points to a large capital *A* affixed to the wall while several slave children look on. The accompanying text focuses on the "pleasure" Eva takes in teaching "the little colored boys and girls" and "making them happy." A second illustration from the same work features Eva "reading the Bible to the colored people," who halt their labor and bow their heads as they listen.[57] Echoing the relations in Stowe's novel, the narrator adds that, while the child has "learned" some of the slaves to read, "they would rather hear Eva read than read themselves, for they say her voice is so sweet; and she always explains all the questions they ask her so pleasantly, that it is a greater pleasure to hear her."[58] Both texts' images and commentary present benevolent pedagogy as entirely personalistic: the charismatic teacher mediates between the slave and the printed word, reinforcing the necessity and moral authority of white intervention.

Within Stowe's narrative, Eva's role as a literacy instructor is far more limited. She reads to Tom, asks her mother why they do not instruct the slaves more generally and systematically, and gives reading lessons to Mammy, a slave whose separation from her husband is made all the more painful by the couple's inability to communicate in writing. But Stowe's Eva does not engage in formal literacy instruction with Topsy or with groups of slaves, as these subsequent texts would have it. More pertinent, though, than this exaggeration is the fact that antebellum authors and publishers chose to make Eva the thematic focus of alphabet and vocabulary books and simple readers. These usages transformed her from an evangelist for whom literacy is one of many emphases into an emblem of evangelical literacy, as Eva instructs not only the slaves within these texts and illustrations, but also the books' more privileged readers.

The images that accompanied or appropriated Stowe's narrative reduced the complexity of its pedagogical relations, ignoring in particular the novel's occasional positioning of black characters in teaching roles. For example, Tom initially explains to Eva the biblical passages that she reads aloud but does not fully understand and works to refamiliarize her father, Augustine St. Clare, with the scripture that the latter has forsaken. But the novel, at crucial moments, also privileges white benevolence and white reading. Tom, after all, would rather listen to Eva than read for himself, a preference that perhaps reassured some white readers that granting literacy to slaves would not mean severing ties of affectionate dependence. Thus, although Stowe champions here a kind of subaltern pedagogy, she simultaneously works to contain and temper its results.[59] The figure of Eva is critical to that containment. She is so engaging, so young, and, ultimately, so near death that the hierarchical and co-

EVA, TEACHING THE ALPHABET.

Here you see, is little Eva teaching the little colored boys and girls the alphabet. See how pleased they are, for they all love Eva, and would do anything to please her; and Eva takes a great deal of pleasure in teaching them and making them happy. She is teaching them the letters one by one, which she marks on the black-board.

8. From *Little Eva: The Flower of the South*. Courtesy, American Antiquarian Society.

ercive elements of the interracial pedagogies she enacts can be underplayed, nearly effaced, in a haze of pleasure and mourning.

Miss Ophelia's pedagogical style, meanwhile, is distinctly unpleasurable, so much so that it becomes an object of comic ridicule within the novel. Whereas Eva elevates those around her through affectionate and, some have argued, erotic bonds, Ophelia's initial bearing is cold, rigid, even antierotic.[60] The narrator describes her as "tall, square-formed, and angular. Her face was thin, and rather sharp in its outlines; the lips compressed, like those of a person who is in the habit of making up her mind defiantly on all subjects; while the keen, dark eyes had a peculiarly searching, advised movement, and traveled over everything, as if they were looking for something to take care of" (*UTC*, 137). That "something" is likely to be disorder, whether domestic, social, or spiritual. As an "absolute bond-slave of the '*ought*,'" she is appalled by indolence and moral failure, especially the failure of slaveholding (*UTC*, 138). But Ophelia's sympathy for slaves is largely an abstraction; as she herself admits, she has "always had a prejudice against [actual, individual] negroes" (*UTC*, 246). As Stowe writes in *A Key to Uncle Tom's Cabin,* Ophelia's shortcomings are calculated to call attention to the fact that, while New Englanders had emancipated their slaves, they nevertheless retained "the most baneful feature of the system [of slavery] . . . —the prejudice of caste and color."[61]

Ophelia's cousin St. Clare, simultaneously amused and awed by her energetic conscience, purchases Topsy, the most intransigent and wily of slave children, and hands her over to Ophelia for elevation and instruction. This project Ophelia pursues tirelessly, teaching the child reading and Christian doctrine as well as the more mundane skills of needlework and chamber-cleaning, but she withholds from her all affection, all personal contact. Topsy's obvious intelligence notwithstanding, the experiment is a miserable failure, as the child refuses to obey her elders in any consistent way and, more disturbingly, refuses to care whether or not she does wrong. For Ophelia, the project of instructing Topsy becomes, for a time, "a kind of chronic plague, to whose inflictions she became . . . as accustomed, as persons sometimes do to the neuralgia or sick head-ache" (*UTC*, 218). But if Topsy is, as Elizabeth Young has argued, "a constitutive feature of white fantasy," the fantasy at work here is the transformation of failed benevolence into triumphant moral suasion, as the slave child finally proves susceptible to loving reformation.[62] Ophelia learns from her "warmer" southern relatives, especially Eva, how to incorporate the feelings that will give her beliefs some force in the world, accepting, ultimately, that efficiency without sentiment is doomed.

Richard Brodhead, in his influential essay "Sparing the Rod: Discipline and Fiction in Antebellum America," uses Ophelia's conversion as a paradigmatic representation of the cultural ascendancy of what he, following Foucault, terms "disciplinary intimacy." This theory of childrearing and character formation, whose most obvious tenet was a rejection of corporal punishment, featured "a strategic relocation of authority relations in the realm of emotion, and a conscious intensification of the emotional bond between the authority-figure and its charge." Horace Bushnell, one of the era's best-known proponents of such a bond, argued that "the well-nurtured child is not surrounded with rules but bathed in 'genial warmth and love.' " Brodhead puts it in somewhat more sinister terms: "This ideally intensified *love*-power has the effect of holding—indeed of virtually enclosing—the disciplinary subject in a field of projected feeling."[63] Ophelia's interminable prescriptions, lectures, and (mostly threatened) whippings, by contrast, stand in for old-fashioned educational theories, which held that adherence to an abstract set of principles could be taught and enforced through impersonal repetition and, if necessary, through violence. Stowe's narrative, as Brodhead demonstrates, comes down on the side of a gentler pedagogy. Only when Topsy feels herself enclosed in that "field of projected feeling"—first through Eva's love and later through Ophelia's—can she replace her drives toward amusement and self-gratification with what Brodhead calls an *"inwardly* regulating moral consciousness," an internalized version of the benevolent whiteness her teacher works to exemplify.[64]

But Stowe does not simply reproduce, without modification, the model of disciplinary intimacy so prominent in antebellum domestic advice manuals and educational theories. Before Topsy can internalize the standards, desires, and judgments of her adult teacher, that adult must herself be "intimately disciplined" by another child, the naturally benevolent Eva. So Stowe's version of disciplinary intimacy works in two directions, with absorption and internalization occurring in both adults and children. True, as Brodhead argues, Ophelia's "influence" over Topsy becomes "something not wholly unlike slavery," and Topsy's later missionary efforts can indeed be read as a departure from the subversive exuberance of her childhood.[65] But if this process constitutes a new enslavement, then Ophelia is also enslaved, although Stowe presents it as interconnectedness, a responsibility toward others that can only be enacted by apprehending and internalizing the values of one's teachers, be they dying children or duty-minded adults. Stowe's representation of Ophelia's struggle, then, amounts to more than comic relief. Whatever the limitations of antebellum benevolence generally and of Stowe's versions in particular, the novel constructs through Ophelia a benevolent whiteness that must learn from and with the racial (and regional) others it purports to serve.

Charlotte Forten's Civil War

Despite the cultural dominance of interracial models like Stowe's, some representations of African American literacy instead emphasized intraracial teaching or autodidacticism. Frederick Douglass's *Narrative* (1845), to cite the best-known example, replaces white benevolence (in the form of his mistress Sophia Auld's short-lived pedagogical efforts) with the narrator's acts of self-assertion and opposition—acts that, from the perspective of the master class, amount to a theft of literacy. Harriet Jacobs's *Incidents in the Life of a Slave Girl* dwells less on the acquisition of literacy than on its effects. The skill that leaves Linda Brent open to her master's advances in the form of his lascivious notes also allows her to trick him after her escape, when she taunts him with letters supposedly sent from the North. Not surprisingly, given the eloquence and power of such accounts, a great deal of the scholarly attention devoted to literacy among mid-nineteenth-century African Americans has been trained on its representation within slave narratives. In these readings, the slave's trajectory from South to North and from enslavement to freedom is often mapped—too neatly, some have argued—onto a move into literacy.[66]

I wish now to examine a geographically opposite move, in which Charlotte Forten, free born and formally educated in the North, goes south to teach recently freed slaves. Her relationship to literacy is vastly different from those described by authors of slave narratives—she has enjoyed a high level of access to books and literary conversation, evident in the many references in her journal to specific titles and exchanges—and her efforts to educate former slaves involve very different extensions across lines of region, class, and color (which, for her, is far from identical to race) from those the era's white teachers articulated. Forten's story, then, allows us to complicate both dominant narratives of black literacy—that of the rebellious slave acquiring it and the white woman bestowing it. The persona Forten presents in her early 1860s writings has much in common structurally with the northern white women whose pedagogical ventures were, and remain, more fully recognized. In choosing her project, Forten in some sense aligns herself with Stowe's Miss Ophelia and her analogues, fictional and actual, who sought to bring enlightenment to the ignorant South. She shares their distaste for (supposed) southern indolence, their exoticization of and discomfort with (current or former) slaves, and their veneration of efficiency, forthrightness, and hard work. But Forten is not quite Ophelia's twin. For one thing, her narrative persona is rarely comic, nor has she Ophelia's blustery self-righteousness. More significantly, her African ancestry complicates how she represents her relationship to her students and how others respond to her, while the threat of violence under which she lives in the South, however played down in her published writings, separates her from her fictional counterpart, whose racial privilege and association with a prominent southern family lend her protection despite her antislavery views.

The Port Royal experiment, as this early effort by Forten and others was termed, was a much-publicized test case for the improvability of "degraded" former slaves and, by extension, for the social and economic prospects of African Americans overall. In this context, Forten's racial identity mattered to those who endorsed the project as well as to those who hoped to see it fail. If the venture were deemed successful, the participation of an African American woman would have advanced its authors' larger goals; if unsuccessful, Forten's inclusion among the teachers might be read as further evidence of the inadequacy of the race. But Forten's published writings treat her racial identity with more complexity and ambiguity than such partisan agendas would suggest. These texts demonstrate little of the racial solidarity her white contemporaries and twenty-first-century readers might expect her to feel with her students. Instead, she seems to identify most often, though never seamlessly, with her white coworkers.[67] At key moments in her accounts, we see that her "race"— specifically, whites' perception that she is not white—places her in particular danger, but these experiences do not lead to any epiphany of commonality with the former slaves. Even Forten's most earnest affirmations of the Port Royal project register a deep ambivalence about the possibility of an interclass and interregional racial affiliation. These instabilities are intertwined with and to some extent constitutive of the mixed feelings Forten expresses about her role as teacher. Instead of the clear path from discouragement to triumph that Stowe writes for Miss Ophelia, Forten represents her experiences as far more variable, recounting periods of great frustration punctuated by moments of satisfaction.

Forten's most widely distributed commentaries on her efforts at Port Royal appear in letters published in the *Liberator* and in a two-part *Atlantic Monthly* essay titled "Life on the Sea Islands" (1864). The *Atlantic* essay, which incorporates material from the *Liberator* letters and from Forten's journals, announces itself through its title and much of its rhetorical style as belonging more to the related genres of travel writing and ethnography than to that of reformist literature, although involvement in the Port Royal effort would have been widely perceived to be an abolitionist statement.[68] The inclusion of a few antislavery remarks (e.g., Forten notes how happily the children play "now that the evil shadow of Slavery no longer hangs over them") does little to alter the tone, given that the more difficult questions of postemancipation policy are not raised.[69] Thus the essay begins not with an explicit argument in favor of black education, but with a description of the northern group's arrival at Hilton Head, which Forten, sounding much like the Puritan William Bradford, describes as "desolate . . . —a long, low, sandy point, stretching out into the sea, with no visible dwellings upon it, except the rows of small white-roofed houses which have lately been built for the freed people" (587). This is a foreign and forbidding land in Forten's account, without appropriate accommodations, her phrasing suggests, for people like herself and her fellow travelers. Although her later descriptions present the islands in a more favorable light, botanically if not climactically, she reiterates the strangeness of the place throughout.

Also striking in this introduction is Forten's way of racially marking and exoticizing those she encounters in South Carolina. In describing the "motley assemblage" waiting on the wharf that first day, she notes that "black was . . . the prevailing color" (587). She revisits matters of complexion several times in the essay, describing one man's face as "nearly black" and referring to the "dark, eager faces" of those gathered for a "shout," a traditional mode of performance whose exuberance captures Forten's imagination (590, 672).[70] A crowd gathered for a New Year's Day celebration, at which the Emancipation Proclamation is read, includes faces "of every complexion," a descriptor that asserts the lively heterogeneity of the scene even as it suggests, in keeping with decades of abolitionist rhetoric, the sexual coerciveness of the now-absent white masters (668). Forten emphasizes her own distance, literal and metaphorical, from these figures. She notes, for example, in her description of the Independence Day gathering, that she and the other northern activists "looked down on the crowd" from an elevated stage (668). And, like other travel writers, she pays attention to the unfamiliar dress of the Sea Islanders. The women's "bright-colored head-handkerchiefs" meet with her approval, much more so than the "straw hats with gay feathers" some wear, while a more unusual outfit is described to comic effect: one man shows up at a local store wearing "a complete suit of brilliant Brussels carpeting," taken, she assumes, "from his master's house" (589, 594). Scarlett O'Hara's sartorial inventiveness, it seems, had historical analogues.

Amid these racialized descriptions, "Life on the Sea Islands" largely obscures Forten's identity as an African American, which helps to reinforce the essay's similarity to conventional nineteenth-century travel writing, in which the narrator's complexion, style of dress, and accent typically go unremarked, the trappings of a dominant culture that need not define itself. Most often, Forten's narrator uses the first-person plural, referring to herself and the other northern activists and teachers. She never explicitly describes herself as a "colored" woman, the term she typically uses in her journals, and until the final paragraph, she asserts no racial connection to the freed people or to the African American soldiers she encounters. Her teaching efforts reinforce this disaffiliation. She mentions, for example, having told her students "about Toussaint, thinking it well they should know what one of *their* own color had done for *his* race" (591; italics added). Even the "colored population" of the North, when mentioned at all, appears with the designation *they* rather than *we* (591). As Carla Peterson and Lisa Long have noted, such linguistic self-distancing occurs in Forten's Port Royal journal entries as well, in contrast to prior entries, written when she lived in the North.[71]

In "Life on the Sea Islands," Forten aligns herself instead with her northern white coworkers and, by extension, with a conventionally unmarked—and so, for the *Atlantic*'s readers, presumably Anglo-American—narrative voice. Further, Forten expresses throughout the essay a typical northern disdain for southern culture. A wharf built by Union forces in Beaufort, for example, becomes an opportunity "to marvel," by contrast, at the "utter shiftlessness" of southerners (587). This statement is inflected by the abolitionist argument that slavery destroys the industriousness of whites and by Forten's distaste for slaveholders in general, but it also smacks of a general sense of northern superiority. Forten shares many of her comrades' stereotypes about southern African Americans as well, noting with surprise that they "had much better taste in selecting materials for dresses than we had supposed." Instead of the expected "gaudy colors," they "prefer neat, quiet patterns" (592). A love of jewelry among the women and girls, however, does not escape her disapproving notice. Striking, too, is Forten's assumption, along with her northern coworkers, of class privilege and an attendant division of labor.[72] Having taken over a house abandoned by white slave owners, the narrator and her companions give the "freed people" a few "directions for cleaning the house," while they drive over to investigate the Baptist Church that will soon become their schoolhouse (588). Perhaps most noticeably, Forten's frequent representations of the Sea Islanders' distinctive dialect mark not only her difference from them but also her adoption of a touristic perspective, one closely associated with the dominant Anglo culture, though not, as I will argue, of a piece with it.

These identifications and alignments do not go unchallenged. In the last paragraph of the essay's second installment, Forten includes two statements that raise the very questions much of the essay has worked to obscure. In the first, describing her return to South Carolina after a hiatus in the North, Forten remarks that "I shall dwell again among 'mine own people'" (676). The phrase references the Book of Kings, in which a woman uses the claim "I dwell among mine own people" to signify her social and material well-being.[73] Forten's allusion associates the Sea Islands with home and comfort, invoking a self-sufficiency born of connection, of cultural or ancestral solidarity—sentiments not much in evidence elsewhere in her essay or journal entries. But apart from the gap between the biblical citation and the sense of displacement Forten registers in her Port Royal writings, the use of quotation marks here is jarring. Certainly, they signal a reference to another text, but they also work to ironize or undermine her assertion of racial affiliation, given how thoroughly those connections are elided in the body of the essay.[74] Are these *really* her own people, or has she, as a devoted teacher, adopted them, in the way that, earlier in the essay, she refers to the students as "our" or "my" children? Forten's final sentence also gestures toward but does not explicitly proclaim her racial identity. "My heart sings a song of thanksgiving," she writes, "at the thought that *even I am permitted* to do something for a long-abused race" (676; italics added). Again, the statement is ambiguous. Is it a conventionally self-deprecating tag, the kind of assertion of unworthiness that nineteenth-century Christianity encouraged? Or is Forten referring to her second-class status as an African American, someone who could not presume access to this or any setting? And whose permission has been granted—that of the divine, of the organizations that sponsored efforts in Port Royal, or of those who could have done her bodily harm during her earlier sojourn but did not? These remarks complicate Forten's earlier self-presentation, calling into question the distance she asserts there between teacher and taught.

Another counterpoint to Forten's incomplete elision of her racial identity comes at the beginning of the essay. Inserted just below the title is a headnote signed "J. G. W." (the poet and abolitionist John Greenleaf Whittier, a friend of Forten) and addressed "To the Editor of the 'Atlantic Monthly.'" Here Whittier writes that "the following graceful and picturesque description of the new condition of things on the Sea Islands of South Carolina, originally written for private perusal, seems to me worthy of a place in the 'Atlantic.' Its young author—herself akin to the long-suffering race whose Exodus she so pleasantly describes—is still engaged in her labor of love on St. Helena Island" (587). Despite Whittier's mention of the "private" nature of the piece, Forten likely understood all of her missives northward to be (potentially) public utterances, given that she was engaged in a widely publicized and politicized effort and given how eager Civil War-era northerners were for any news from battle zones or occupied areas.[75] More to my point, however, is Whittier's assertion of the author's racial identity, subordinated within an assurance of the grace and pleasantness of her prose. But the claim itself is tricky: here Forten is only *akin* to the "long-suffering race" she describes, not *of* it, which suggests, on the one hand, that she is of mixed racial ancestry and, on the other, that the "colored people" of the North and the recently freed slaves of the coastal South were not quite of the same race. Whittier here allows for a certain fluidity of racial categories, a kinship without explicit membership, which reinforces the (anonymous) author's dual positioning as credible witness and exemplar of African American achievement.

This frame—Whittier's headnote and Forten's final paragraph—complicates the erasure of African American identity evident elsewhere in Forten's essay. Most directly, it inflects how one reads the three "alarms" Forten describes. One night, while sleeping in a room with another of the northern women, the narrator is awakened by "what seemed to us loud and most distressing shrieks, proceeding from the direction of the negro-houses." Thinking that the "Rebels . . . were trying to carry off some of the people [i.e., the former slaves]," the two women sit terrified, expecting "to hear them at our doors." "Knowing," she continues, "that they had sworn vengeance against all the superintendents and teachers, we prepared ourselves for the worst," an eventuality that, in keeping with nineteenth-century decorum, Forten leaves undefined (595). Her terror turns to chagrin when, the next day, the mystery is explained. The "shrieks," one of the freed slaves tells her, were simply the sound of a whistle that black soldiers had used to communicate with "'der folks'" across a local creek (595). The second incident presents greater extremes, both of terror and ridiculousness. One night, Forten awakens to the sound of someone repeatedly attempting to open her locked door from the outside. She rouses the woman in the adjoining room, and the two of them sit side by side on the bed in their nightclothes, waiting with revolvers pointed doorward for a group of "Rebels" to burst in. Panic soon changes to boredom, however, as the noise ceases and the two women, growing sleepy, go back to bed. While this mystery goes unexplained, Forten states that "the people" would certainly not have entered the house, so it must have been burglars. "There is nobody to be feared" on the islands, she writes, "but the Rebels"

(595), a claim that stirs wartime animosities while counteracting proslavery paranoia about the murderousness of freed slaves.

The last in this series of false alarms has Forten hearing footsteps on the stairs one night and, as before, picking up her revolver and awakening "the other ladies" (596). Although the intruder turns out to be harmless—the husband of one of the women in the house, a lieutenant in a regiment encamped nearby—Forten forgoes the comic postscript this time. She ends the essay's May installment with the following account: "I shall never forget the delightful sensation of relief that came over me when the whole matter was explained. It was almost overpowering; for, although I had made up my mind to bear the worst, and bear it bravely, the thought of falling into the hands of the Rebels was horrible in the extreme. A year of intense mental suffering seemed to have been compressed into those few moments" (596). What goes unstated in this passage is the fact that, as an African American woman, Forten was especially imperiled. Certainly, all the northern women risked violence at the hands of Confederate soldiers, who, Forten insists, had sworn "vengeance" on them all. But Forten's risk was greater: not only was she a more likely target of immediate attack than the white women around her, given southern ideology and precedent, but she was also vulnerable to enslavement, a circumstance that might prove permanent should the Union lose the war. This gap in the text—what gives these alarms force—is filled in advance by Whittier's initial note, his "outing" of the author as racial other, and in retrospect by Forten's own closing remarks. The woman perched on the edge of the bed in her nightgown, holding a revolver against possible rape, assault, or murder, is reinscribed as African American, even as the narrative persona presents herself, simply, as one of "the ladies."

Forten's journals, unpublished until well after her death, are more candid about race—about her own positioning as a "colored" woman, to use her descriptor, and about the discrimination she experiences and witnesses. For example, in a May 1863 entry she responds to rumors that a white friend, a Mr. Thorpe, has romantic feelings for her: "I *know* it is not so. . . . Although he is very good and liberal he is still an American, and w'ld of course never be so insane as to love one of the prescribed [sic] race."[76] Her identification with benevolent northerners is more problematic in the journals, too. Remarking on a kindness done her by the abolitionist senator Charles Sumner before she goes to South Carolina, she quips, "I suppose I have to thank my color for it."[77] Not only does Forten's comment reveal her discomfort with what she perceives as the tokenism and condescension of Sumner's act, but it also reinforces her consciousness of occupying a category separate from his, with boundaries not easily bridged by common goals or sentiments. And in reference to her living situation in South Carolina, among white coworkers, she writes that "[a] yearning for congenial companionship will sometimes come over me in the few leisure moments I have. . . . Kindness, most invariable,—for which I am most grateful—I meet with constantly, but congeniality I find not at all in this house."[78] Rather than the "we" of the *Atlantic* essay, the journal entries suggest a subtle division, one that seems to preclude real friendship. In this entry, not surprisingly, Forten next rededicates herself to the benevolent motives that brought her to South Carolina in the first place: "Let the work to which I have solemnly pledged myself fill up my whole existence to the exclusion of all vain longings."[79]

Historical records also suggest that, at least initially, the former slaves perceived Forten to be different from and inferior to her white companions, a sentiment of which she was likely aware. Laura Towne, a white northerner central to the Port Royal project, wrote in her diary that "the people on our place are inclined to question a good deal about 'dat brown gal,' as they call Miss Forten. Aunt Becky required some coaxing to wait upon her and do her room. . . . I hope they will respect her."[80] Without the obvious status granted by whiteness, Forten must assert her class positioning through other means. As T. W. Higginson reported in an 1863 letter to his wife, hearing Forten play the piano, a traditional marker of education and refinement for women, "quite put them [the former slaves] down, and soon all grew fond of her."[81] In contrast to the easy assumption of class privilege that Forten portrays in the *Atlantic* essay, these accounts suggest that "the people" did not at first perceive her to be among those they had to serve.

My point is not that Forten represents herself disingenuously in "Life on the Sea Islands" and authentically in the journals but rather that the published essay adheres to codes of silence about racial difference that she seems not to follow, or to follow differently, in her private writings. It is not clear why Forten chose to de-emphasize her racial identity in the *Atlantic* essay, nor am I certain that it was her decision rather than the result of editorial intervention, though the editor's inclusion of Whittier's clarifying headnote argues against the latter possibility. It is also difficult to say how typical or atypical Forten's strategy was. Certainly, many authors self-identified as African American in this era, but we cannot determine how many others, playing along with readers' presumptions, passed as white. Forten's *Liberator* letters are similarly cagey about the author's racial identity (though, again, editorial interventions identify her more or less clearly as African American).[82] In one letter, Forten refers to a student as "one of my people," but the phrase is ambiguous. Is it meant to assert racial affiliation or simply a teacher's proprietary feelings toward her charge?[83] It may be that Forten's reticence was an element of her public voice, a habit of nondisclosure that she used with the wider world and especially with white audiences. Given broad cultural assumptions about whiteness and pedagogy, Forten may have believed that her self-representation as a teacher of freed slaves would be most powerful if her racial identity were submerged.

Forten's role as teacher had much to do with her ambiguous identifications. The position itself, one of nineteenth-century America's most widely represented forms of benevolent superiority, worked to reify Forten's difference from her pupils. Common African ancestry was further overshadowed by other axes of identity that accentuate Forten's separateness, most notably her regional affiliation, level of education, and free-born status. As a bearer of civilization, to use the lexicon of the era, Forten did not come to feel less "colored"—her journals argue against such a claim—but she seems to have been acutely aware of herself as a *differently* racialized being, one whose refinement and benevolent agency separated her from those she wished to aid, yet whose positioning outside of whiteness belied any neat alignment with the other northern teachers and activists. While in the journals Forten's occupation of this third category is invoked fairly directly, in the *Atlantic* essay it is recoverable only through a relayed reading of the essay's frame against its center.

The pedagogical relations that complicate Forten's self-presentation suffuse "Life on the Sea Islands" and the *Liberator* letters more thoroughly than is initially apparent. The Port Royal effort as a whole was sufficiently well publicized in the North as a teaching project that, for Forten's readers, the texts reference benevolent pedagogy even when the prose treats matters not immediately related to students, classrooms, or literacy. Forten also addresses her teaching efforts directly, though these accounts, like the rest of her prose, leave gaps that the reader must attempt to fill. In the *Atlantic* essay, for example, Forten expresses considerable admiration for her students. "We noted with pleasure," she writes, "how bright and eager to learn many of them seemed" (589)—more eager, she claims, than the students she encountered in New England schools. "Coming to school is a constant delight and recreation to them," she declares. "They come here as other children go to play," while "many of the grown people are desirous of learning to read" (591). Making clear the larger social purpose of the Port Royal schools, Forten goes on to say that "it is wonderful how a people who have been so long crushed to the earth, so imbruted as these have been,—and they are said to be among the most degraded negroes of the South,—can have so great a desire for knowledge, and such a capability for attaining it" (591). If these people can learn, the not-so-buried subtext reads, any freed slave can.

The rhetoric of benevolent pedagogy demanded tales of success, of eager and adept students, and Forten delivers here, but her prose suggests deeper struggles. For one thing, her praise of the students in the *Atlantic* essay is guarded—"many of them" seem bright; "the majority learn with wonderful rapidity"—which leaves open the possibility that some pupils were low achievers, incapable or defiant (591). Occasionally, Forten acknowledges these counterexamples, as when she remarks that "of course there are some stupid ones" (591). (In the journals she is even more derisive, claiming at one point that "most of the children are crude little specimens.")[84] But more often she attributes the students' academic difficulties to their personal histories or to their youth. Confessing her difficulty, for example, in holding their attention, she writes that this is "not strange, as they have been so entirely unused to intellectual concentration" (591–92). And in reference to her students' restlessness,

Forten notes that most of them were "very small"—"too young," she claims, even "to learn the alphabet" (591).

Forten's letter to Garrison states that "every day" she enjoys her teaching "more and more." This claim allows for a negative reading—that every day her misery abates somewhat—but the overt meaning is that her teaching is going well. The *Atlantic* essay, however, expresses more obvious ambivalence.[85] For all her gestures of admiration and understanding of her students, the essay betrays an undercurrent of discontentment, even despair. For one thing, Forten's material circumstances were far from comfortable. In the winter months, the building "was particularly damp and cold" with "no chimney," and an attempt late in the season to install a stove proves fruitless—it will not "draw" and fills the room with smoke (670). "We got so thoroughly chilled and benumbed within," she writes, "that for several days we had school out-of-doors, where it was much warmer" (670). Even in fair weather, Forten experiences significant frustration. "The first day at school was rather trying," she admits, relating how the very young children in her class—the siblings of other students, too young to be left at home alone—"seemed to have discovered the secret of perpetual motion, and tried one's patience sadly" (591). (One wonders whether Forten got these particular students by chance or was assigned to them by individuals higher up in the reformist hierarchy.) Though she soon learns to manage and quiet "the tiniest and most restless spirits" (591), it remains the case that the school is seriously overcrowded, without separate rooms for the different groups. Consequently, "to make one's self heard, when there were often as many as a hundred and forty reciting at once, it was necessary to tax the lungs very severely" (592). In contrast to the figures of effortless pedagogical authority presented in so many of the era's narratives and visual images, Forten finds herself struggling, literally and metaphorically, to find her voice.

Unlike Stowe's Ophelia, who succeeds once she learns to love the object of her aid, Forten's efforts come up against circumstances and obstacles that have little to do with her affective states or her pedagogical vision. Indeed, although she uses sentimental strategies at certain points in "Life on the Sea Islands," most obviously to recount slaves' daring escapes and reunions with family or their past suffering at the hands of cruel masters, her representations of her teaching are relatively unsentimental. In particular, she relates no tearful reclamations of Topsy-like "lost" children. Instead of adopting Stowe's vision of a northern pedagogue warmed by southern sentiment, Forten presents herself as a figure chilled to the point of despair in the South Carolina winter, driven more by duty than by love, shouting to be heard over a roomful of restless children. Still, despite her trials, Forten conveys a belief in the value of the project and a deep investment in its outcome. This buoyancy is most apparent in the final paragraphs of "Life on the Sea Islands," where she assures readers that "daily the long-oppressed people of these islands are demonstrating their capacity for improvement in learning and labor. What they have accomplished in one short year exceeds our utmost expectations" (676). Forten's testament accompanies her own rededication to the project after a period of rest in the North: "While writing these pages I am once more nearing Port Royal. The Fortunate Isles of Freedom are before me" (676). Erasing, for the moment, the hardships of her earlier teaching efforts, Forten here comes closest to articulating a pedagogy shaped by affect: "I shall gather my scholars about me, and see smiles of greeting break over their dusk faces" (676). She returns to the site of struggle and, within this invocation of the affectionate bonds between teacher and students, calls attention once again to the difference ("their dusk faces") undergirding her benevolent extensions.[86]

Forten's texts expose the slipperiness of affiliation in the context of benevolent projects. Writing within a discourse that struggled for, though it never achieved, a neat division of benevolent agent from object, Forten's ambiguous positioning—"dat brown gal," as the Sea Islanders supposedly called her, "akin" to a "long-suffering race," in Whittier's terms—complicates the categories. But if, as Carla Peterson writes, she represents "a lonely middle term" between the "two extremes" of freed slave and white abolitionist, it is a productive loneliness, one that allows her to mediate among seemingly intractable differences of race, region, and class.[87] Forten is uneasy in South Carolina, for good reason, but her very presence there stages an argument for African American participation in the ongoing project of bringing former slaves into the category of the literate and, ultimately, into the category of the citizen. Within the worldview of Port Royal's northern activists, Forten included, this was a project of reclaiming the South and reunifying the nation through benevolence.

Literacy instruction in general and the education of African Americans in particular, as the foregoing readings attest, were important touchstones for mid-nineteenth-century commentators on benevolence. That slaves and former slaves sought literacy so energetically, and that proslavery forces worked so hard to proscribe it, speaks to a widely shared belief in its potency. But as Charlotte Forten's writings suggest, this nexus was complicated indeed, a site through which affiliations and identities might become more rather than less ambiguous. Disparate figures claimed the role of benevolent pedagogue, but none could control its varied significations or effects.

Representations of race and pedagogy almost inevitably engaged questions of national membership, whether the author's project was to harden the category or to broaden it. For Margaret Douglass, interracial pedagogy only reaffirmed the common sense of white supremacy, ensuring the usefulness and piety of the black noncitizen. Stowe, at the end of *Uncle Tom's Cabin,* creates in Topsy a hard-won transformation from monstrous child to missionary but then exports both her citizenship and her pedagogical agency to Liberia. And Forten, writing in the midst of the Civil War, figures her pedagogy as a means of defying the power (military, terroristic) of the Confederacy and troubling the ideologies equating free blacks and slaves, even as such efforts advance the two groups' interdependent claims to national inclusion. Chapters 5 and 6 continue these conversations, taking up questions of benevolence, race, and citizenship from both Anglo-American and African American perspectives. The ensuing conflicts reveal the extent to which mid-nineteenth-century Americans' arguments over benevolent strategies and priorities were, at every level, arguments over the terms of U.S. citizenship.

CHAPTER FIVE

Charity Begins at Home
Stowe's Antislavery Novels and the Forms of Benevolent Citizenship

Never has there been a crisis in the history of this nation so momentous as the present. If ever a nation was raised up by Divine Providence, and led forth upon a conspicuous stage, as if for the express purpose of solving a great moral problem in the sight of all mankind, it is this nation.

> HARRIET BEECHER STOWE,
> Preface to *Dred:*
> *A Tale of the Great Dismal Swamp* (1856)

The United States, for Stowe and for many of her contemporaries, was a proving ground for benevolence, where good intentions, "momentous" wrongs, and international scrutiny converged. Stowe's two antislavery novels, *Uncle Tom's Cabin* (1851–52) and *Dred* (1856), stage that convergence as a confrontation with the "great moral problem" of slavery and a reimagining of the nation in its aftermath.[1] In doing so, the novels dramatize two distinct versions of benevolent citizenship: the conventional model, in which those who already enjoy the status of citizen are called on to prove the nation's moral fitness through benevolent acts, and a less commonly invoked aspirational model, in which benevolent agency becomes, for the socially marginalized, a means of achieving or inhabiting citizenship.

As I have argued in prior chapters, the benevolence of the secure citizen was an ideal to which a broad range of Americans subscribed, but they reached no corresponding consensus as to the forms such benevolence might take. Instead, they engaged in a series of debates over how to prioritize social responsibility and how to define affiliation. To whom does one owe benevolence? Should activist allegiance be organized by regional, racial, or national affiliation, to name a few of the many options? If charity begins at home, as Americans endlessly reminded one another, then how might the boundaries around home and family be drawn? Amy Kaplan and Lora Romero, among other scholars, have contended that the home and the nation were intimately linked for antebellum Americans, such that defining each in relation to the other ranked among the principal ideological projects of the day.[2] In that sense, the configuration of the family and the home within benevolent discourse bore a strong relationship, metaphorical and analogical, to the configuration of the United States.

When read against contributions to this discourse, Stowe's shifting representations of family, nation, and benevolent allegiance take on new resonances. Both *Uncle Tom's Cabin* and *Dred* are meditations on the ideological construction of the homes where charity might begin. And both to some degree undermine proslavery belief structures, in particular the tenets that loyalty to one's region should supersede other considerations and that people of African descent would always need white aid. But the novels diverge significantly in their resettlement of fugitive slaves and in their utopic visions. *Uncle Tom's Cabin* ends with a movement toward racially separate utopias, with the characters who survive slavery leaving North America to do the work of benevolence among their "own" people in Africa, whereas *Dred* ends with the establishment of permanent interracial communities in the northern United States and Canada. Colonizationists asserted that African Americans' benevolent activity in Liberia, especially the work of Christianizing the African natives, would be the catalyst that transformed them from slaves and outcasts into citizens of a new nation. Stowe implies a similar transformation at the end of *Uncle Tom's Cabin,* though she uses a somewhat different tone. But as her writings and statements after the novel's publication suggest, Stowe ultimately comes down on the side of an interracial affiliation that, played out in the context of maternal or pseudomaternal domesticity, prefigures—indeed makes possible—a harmoniously interracial United States. This vision emerges most clearly in *Dred*'s conclusion, which grants at least some former slaves access to citizenship through their role in the repair and reproduction of the family-as-nation. Thus benevolent agency becomes, for Stowe, both the mark of their inclusion and the price of the ticket.

Scholars have explained Stowe's shift—from advocating African colonization to representing domestic emancipation—as deriving from her initiation in the mid-1850s into abolitionist orthodoxies. Her encounters and correspondence with black and white abolitionists, among whom Liberian emigration had long been discredited, surely played a central role in her rejection of colonization.[3] But Stowe also engaged a much broader discourse on benevolent affiliation and agency that included sermons, tracts from across the political spectrum, and proslavery novels written in response to *Uncle Tom's Cabin.* By the time Stowe wrote *Dred,* she was a veteran of these debates; she had weathered criticism from both abolitionists and proslavery ideologues and had experienced, along with great celebrity, great derision. By restoring elements of this conversation that have faded from view, my inquiry makes available a more nuanced understanding of Stowe's racial and national politics, illuminating in the process the ways in which her representations and utopian imaginings worked to extend and energize the confluence of benevolence and U.S. citizenship.

Families, Neighbors, and Nations

Disagreements over benevolent priorities have a long history in American culture. As Evan Radcliffe has shown, eighteenth-century Anglo-Americans vigorously debated how far benevolence could or should extend. Were human beings, as Jonathan Edwards claimed, obliged to enact a "general benevolence" that ignored community, party, and nation? Or was some ranking of responsibilities inevitably in effect?[4] By the antebellum period, these debates had been extensively elaborated. While some clung to the notion that one owed benevolence to anyone, anywhere in need, more often commentators resorted to variations on local themes, arguing that individuals ought first to care for their own families and neighbors (however defined). Most presumed that sympathetic identification, seen by many as foundational to benevolent action, could only go so far. The abolitionist lawyer Lysander Spooner, for example, in an 1846 tract titled *Poverty,* asserted that doing good to others "depends almost entirely upon sympathy—upon one's susceptibility of being affected by the feelings of others." Such a circumstance, he continued, "is mostly . . . the result of having had, in some measure, a similar experience with others, or of . . . having had social relations with them. Thus those who have been sick, sympathize with the sick; the sorrowful sympathize with the sorrowful; the rich sympathize with the rich; . . . and all men more or less with their immediate personal acquaintances." A more just society, Spooner went on to argue, far less conventionally, would therefore necessitate minimizing experiential differences among citizens, especially those arising from economic disparities.[5] The antislavery play *The Kidnapped Clergyman* (1839) introduced a similar identity of experience as the key to benevolent acts. Its protagonist, a self-serving minister who preaches against abolition, is converted to the antislavery cause only after a long and vivid dream in which he and his family are enslaved.[6]

The play's attention to imperiled family members tapped into a broader discourse on familial love, loyalty, and responsibility. Not only did antebellum Americans describe benevolent relations in familial terms (note, for example, the proslavery camp's frequent insistence that caretaking masters and loyal slaves formed a family), but they also presented benevolence toward one's blood relations as a primary and unavoidable responsibility. The "Visitor's Manual" published by the Baltimore Association for Improving the Condition of the Poor (AICP) drew on this widespread notion of family duty, claiming that *"where there are relatives of the indigent who are able to provide for them, alms should never be given when relief can possibly be procured from such relatives."* Alms, if given in spite of this warning, "offend against a higher law" in that "their tendency or result is to cancel just claims on kindred or consanguinity." Charity workers were thus charged with enforcing appropriate gradations of responsibility by awakening the "natural sympathy of relatives."[7]

In the antebellum United States, the concept of familial bonds slid easily into that of racial bonds. Racial mixing was figured as a threat to the purity and safety of the family, and both kinds of relationships were described in terms of "blood." At times, *family* was used as a metaphor for race, as when the New Jersey senator Frederick Frelinghuysen remarked that "colored" men's "swarthy complexion ever marks them as members of a family different from ours."[8] Oliver Wendell Holmes, in an 1855 discussion of slavery, linked race, family, and benevolent responsibility more directly. *"Our sympathies,"* he argued, *"will go with our own color first. . . .* No abstract principle of benevolence can reverse the great family instinct that settles the question for us" (italics added).[9] For Holmes, allegiance to one's own race was simply an expression of "family instinct," one that overrode abstract benevolence. Perhaps the strongest articulation of these sentiments, though from a black nationalist perspective, appeared in the writings of Alexander Crummell. "Races," he asserted, "like families, are the organisms and the ordinance of God; and race feeling, like the family feeling, is of divine origin. . . . Indeed, a race *is* a family."[10]

Anglo-American proponents of African colonization invoked similar notions of racial allegiance. An 1851 article in the *Colonization Herald,* titled "Africa to Be Christianized by Africans," declared that "God in his all-wise providence has reserved this great and important work (the civilizing and evangelizing of Africa,) for her own sons and daughters" and noted that white missionaries "have all either died, or been driven to their native homes" without effecting the conversion of Africans.[11] Many colonizationists claimed that black visitors to Africa enjoyed a relative resistance to the "fever" we now identify as malaria and cited their survival rates as proof that God had ordained a program of intraracial benevolence.[12] Others used social rather than medical justifications for sending black missionaries to Africa, asserting that "permanent results" "must come from men whose race is similar to the people among whom they dwell, and with whom it can mingle freely and advantageously."[13]

While free blacks deplored the white supremacy that underlay much colonizationist rhetoric, not to mention its goal of black deportation, some insisted on a primary benevolent responsibility to one's own race. Samuel Cornish, a well-known advocate of such racial allegiance, based his appeal on circumstantial rather than essential commonalities. Though he remarked that he did not "love one class of men more than another," he asserted that, because of their common oppression, African Americans ought to "labor *especially* for [their own] people, until *all their disabilities are removed.*"[14] The constitution of a black-run charitable organization also made intraracial benevolence a high priority, relating its commitment "to do good unto all men" but "especially those of *our race*" (italics added).[15] Members of this group surely recognized that intraracial efforts might prove less burdensome to black communities than the acceptance of whites' benevolence, but the remark also suggests a more general belief in racial affiliation as a determinant of charitable priorities. Other free African Americans resisted this emphasis on racial or, as one *National Reformer* article put it, "complexional considerations," arguing instead that benevolence should be color blind.[16]

The question of national allegiance figured prominently as well. Despite free blacks' widespread interest in a range of emigrationist plans, some argued for loyalty to and benevolent action within the nation of one's nativity. "We have been born and reared in America," one author wrote: "Here are all our general and local interests implanted—here let us cherish and sustain them . . . until they bud, blossom, and bring forth fruit that will make our country renowned in the eyes of civilized nations."[17] Drawing on a similar sentiment, the white abolitionist Gerrit Smith argued for national allegiance and interracial responsibility in an 1847 broadside in which he chastised his neighbors for sending food to "the starving Irish" but forgetting their "infinitely greater debt" to their "enslaved countrymen."[18] Others, usually antiabolitionists, invoked region rather than nation as the relevant grounds of affiliation, claiming that benevolent slaveholders should take care of southern African Americans while northerners of conscience should devote their efforts to the poor within their own communities.

Although assertions of benevolent priority usually employed a language of primacy rather than exclusion—insisting that Americans deal first (rather than only) with whatever circumstance the speaker privileged—the intransigence of most social problems and the limits on resources suggested strongly that one's first project would consume all one's energy into the foreseeable future. Moreover, the flexibility that this rhetoric of primacy promised belied the vitriol many speakers reserved for those who defied their proposed rankings. Such violations elicited the charges of hypocrisy that suffused the culture of benevolence. Practitioners of this "misguided" benevolence were asked why they did not "remove the beam from [their] own eyes" before concerning themselves with "motes in the eyes of [their] neighbors." One outraged citizen described thousands of homeless in New York City and wondered why the "sham philanthropists" who supported abolition did not utter "a solitary 'shriek' in behalf of these perishing classes," while antiabolitionist cartoons and lithographs opposed plump, happy, dancing slaves to cold, emaciated white seamstresses or overworked English factory workers.[19] The popular author Emerson Bennett, whose 1855 novel *Ellen Norbury* featured the sweetest and most hapless fictional orphan since Oliver Twist, asked in his preface why northerners supported missionary and antislavery efforts when "hundreds of human beings, both white and black, were annually perishing of cold, starvation, and neglect" in their own cities.[20] Similarly, David Brown's proslavery text *The Planter; or, Thirteen Years in the South* (1853) excoriated the "Quakers of Philadelphia" for allowing the most desperate poverty to exist in their city, all the while expending their "benevolence" and "philanthropy" in the service of "the negroes of the South, who need none of their sympathy."[21] This mode of recrimination was flexible enough to serve opposed political ends. The anonymous author of "Missionary Hymn, for the South," for example, derided slaveholders who concerned themselves with faraway "heathen," but barred slaves from reading the scripture:

> Send Bibles to the heathen,
> Their famish'd spirits feed!
> Oh! haste, and join your efforts,
> The priceless gift to speed!
> *Then flog the trembling bondman,*
> *If he shall learn to read!*[22]

Slaveholders, the poet argued, perverted benevolence by seeing to it that reading the Bible resulted in abuse rather than comfort and salvation.

As these examples attest, disagreements over the questions of benevolent citizenship in general and racial allegiance in particular produced especially bitter accusations as the nation moved toward disunion, an escalation made clear in the lithograph reproduced here.[23] This image critiques abolitionists' commitment to interracial benevolence by portraying a well-dressed white man (who bears a striking resemblance to the abolitionist senator Charles Sumner) giving alms to a ragged, barefoot black girl while her equally ragged and far thinner white counterpart goes empty-handed. The white girl, with her outstretched arm pointing toward the coins dropping from white hand to black, protests her exclusion by asserting "I'm not to blame for being white, sir!" The man, however, rejects her attempt to put charity literature's rhetoric of blame in the ser-vice of a claim to racial innocence, telling her instead that "charity ought to begin where it is most needed, and you, certainly, are the better off, having more friends and less oppressors." Here, the donor serves as an emblem of selfishness and sophistry. In his right hand is a cane positioned for decoration rather than support, suggesting his relative prosperity and reinforcing his heartless refusal to aid more than one supplicant, however deserving.[24] In this image the "unnatural" act of turning away a needy child blends with the supposed unnaturalness of helping a member of another race rather than a member of one's own. This donor's abstract hierarchy of need, which privileges African Americans at the expense of whites, is represented as a violation of good sense and human sympathy.

Segregating Benevolence

As the conversation outlined here demonstrates, no consensus emerged in the antebellum United States as to how benevolent responsibility ought to be defined and structured. While some of these volleys seem plainly calculated to justify the speaker's exploitative practices, the debates taken as a whole betray deep conflicts within notions of social justice and social authority—conflicts that undergirded the era's most divisive political issues. In particular, such debates exposed a disjunction within the larger discourse of benevolence. The

9. *I'm Not to Blame for Being White, Sir!* Courtesy, American Antiquarian Society.

notion on which these disparate claims depended—that benevolence required some preexisting similarity or proximity—would seem incongruent with the fact that much benevolent rhetoric and most actual charitable practices instead foregrounded the social and spiritual distance between helper and helped. In other words, the "neighbors" whom this prioritizing discourse championed existed in tension with the abject and fearsome supplicants whom so much charity literature conjured. So while gradations of responsibility were often articulated in terms of affiliation—helping members of one's own family, neighborhood, race, region, or nation—this language of benevolence also asserted the superiority (racial, regional, moral) of the helper and the degradation of the helped.

The complicated and shifting logic of benevolent responsibility in *Uncle Tom's Cabin* provides a means of exploring this contradiction. In order to achieve its mission of generating antislavery sentiment and action, particularly in the North, the novel asks readers to identify with suffering people across racial and regional divides. Stowe uses the psychology of benevolent affiliation (a sense of immediacy, proximity, even empathy) to create a feeling of responsibility where literal proximity and similarity may not obtain; for example, she asks readers to imagine or relive the loss of their own children, in sympathy with the slaves whose actual or threatened losses she represents. Mrs. Bird, the senator's wife who takes pity on the runaway slave Eliza and her son, enacts within the text the very process of benevolence via identification that Stowe encourages among readers: she weeps over her dead child's folded garments as she prepares a care package for the fugitives. As Philip Fisher has pointed out, *Uncle Tom's Cabin,* like other sentimental novels, creates an "extension of feeling . . . by means of equations between the deep common feelings of the reader and the exotic but analogous situations of the characters." Elizabeth Barnes puts the matter more directly, claiming that, within Stowe's novel, "sympathy is made contingent upon similarity."[25]

The terms of that similarity shift, however, in the course of the novel. Initially, like her antislavery peers, Stowe invokes a national benevolent responsibility that supersedes loyalty to region or race. Northern readers are invited to concern themselves with the condition of southern slaves, while characters within the narrative are applauded for their willingness to rise above racial and regional loyalties. But Stowe's conclusion removes most of the novel's surviving black characters from the United States and, in doing so, fundamentally alters the construction of the nation whose cohesion she advocates elsewhere in the text. Even though the success of its overall argument depends on creating a sense of responsibility that crosses racial lines, the novel ends with a resegregation of benevolent relations and a reinscription of racial allegiance. Stowe relies, then, on an imagined affiliation that renders itself superfluous, making possible a final appeal to an essential or "real" affiliation.

This position has made Stowe into something of a favorite target, in her time and in ours. In an 1852 article that appeared in the *Pennsylvania Free-*

man, the Philadelphian Robert Purvis encapsulated the responses of many northern free blacks when he wrote, in reference to Stowe, "Alas! . . . save us from our friends."[26] Along similar lines, scholars often cite the novel's conclusion as proof of Stowe's intractable racism. Such dismay is certainly comprehensible, insofar as this Liberian ending positions the United States as a white utopia secure in the belief that former slaves were happily and successfully Christianizing Africa. Nevertheless, the colonizationism evident at the end of *Uncle Tom's Cabin* is not simply Stowe's adherence to her own family's values (her father, Lyman Beecher, was a prominent advocate of colonization, and her sister Catharine Beecher supported the cause as well), nor should it be read exclusively as a retreat from the novel's progressive emancipatory politics. It is possible to read the ending instead as Stowe's pointed, if troubling, attempt to undermine the logic of the proslavery "family" and its figuring of perpetual black dependency and white supervision. The accusations leveled at Stowe as a result of the novel's conclusion testify to the hazards of this project: her own effort at interracial benevolence—publishing this book as a spur to end slavery—embroiled her in the very complications she was trying to write her way out of.

The novel's Liberian solution, in which a regenerated Topsy teaches the children of what Stowe calls "her own country" while a self-sufficient and newly educated George Harris goes to Liberia as "a teacher of Christianity," constitutes one of Stowe's many literary interventions into the question of how to prioritize benevolent responsibility.[27] By choosing Africa as the site of their good works, Topsy and the Harris family assert the primacy of racial affiliation over both regional and national considerations. In the process, they defy the proslavery faction's claim that slaves were naturally dependent on their masters and could never attain economic independence, much less benevolent agency.[28] Moreover, the former slaves' move to Liberia also allows them to distance themselves, at least geographically, from ties of gratitude and obligation toward the white benefactors who aided their escape. Their emigration serves as evidence that they have thrown off all dependence on white aid, a theme reinforced by the self-asserting rhetoric George Harris uses to justify his decision. That rhetoric, significantly, aligns him more closely with the era's black nationalists and emigrationists than with white colonizationists, who tended to emphasize whites' roles in preparing and guiding the emigrants.[29] Given that interracial responsibility as articulated in the antebellum United States often rested on reified structures of superiority and inferiority, it makes sense that Stowe, in the context of an antislavery project, might test out a theory that establishes interracial benevolence as a temporary measure, a means to its own elimination.

Still, this resolution is difficult to interpret. In some sense, Stowe minimizes the otherness of slaves and former slaves by remaking them into benevolent agents on a familiar, white-sanctioned model. But at the same time, her plan reinforces racial separation, ultimately providing for the benevolent, both black and white, objects of aid who belong to their own racial group and who therefore seem more like themselves. That is, black emigrants would serve Africans, while Anglo-Americans, in a postemigration United States, are left to serve the needy whites within its borders. (Or so colonizationists typically theorized; they tended to ignore the United States' nonblack and non-Anglo racial groups.) By eliminating or minimizing racial difference within benevolent relations—and, what was more important, within nations—Stowe's plan reestablishes the conventional notions of affiliation that so often initiated and compelled benevolent projects. But the inferiority of the helped remains intact here, insofar as African Americans' Christianizing and civilizing mission in Liberia retains the hierarchies of American benevolence. The helped, in this schema, are definitionally "benighted," "degraded," and inferior to the helpers. So rather than truly departing from the structures of interracial benevolence, Stowe's intraracial model replicates its terms but grants African Americans (abroad) access to positions of control and authority within it.

Such retrenchment notwithstanding, Stowe's interest in colonization's potential to promote racial solidarity or affinity should not be dismissed out of hand or reduced to its most conservative elements. In his boldly revisionist article "Racial Essentialism and Family Values in *Uncle Tom's Cabin*," Arthur Riss argues that Stowe's Liberian conclusion is less an example of white racist wish fulfillment than a logical extension of an emancipatory politics based on racial identity. According to Riss, Stowe defines legitimate families exclusively by "the bond of biology" and, by extension, the bond of a common racial identity, which invalidates proslavery notions of the family as a group whose relations are based not on literal "blood" ties, but on participation in a domestic economy structured around mutual obligations.[30] Stowe's much-maligned racial essentialism, Riss astutely argues, is therefore integral to rather than in conflict with her progressive politics. And since for Stowe "national solidarity is simply the extension of loving one's family," the utopic nation must be racially homogeneous, and Topsy must leave those Ophelia calls " 'our folks' for *her folks*."[31] Riss's rethinking of Stowe's essentialism, however, elides the complications that certain characters' mixed racial identities introduce. He writes that George Harris's letter at the end of *Uncle Tom's Cabin* (in which he justifies his decision to emigrate) "makes clear that, according to Stowe, an individual's communal identity is not generated by culture or by choice but by race. Nature is nation, and a nation is just a large family."[32] This argument, though applicable to Topsy's emigration, fails to account for George Harris's more ambiguous racial positioning. Riss here reproduces the logic of the one-drop rule by designating "all" or monolithically black any character with some African forebears, despite the fact that Stowe's novel dwells at length on the differences between mixed-race people and "pure" Africans and, in particular, on the conflict within George Harris between disparate though still essential racial characteristics. The novel situates him somewhere between "black" and "white." Although U.S. law and custom define him as black, Stowe writes that he and his family are light enough to "mingle in the circles of the whites" without detection (*UTC,* 374). As George's letter insists, he *chooses* to annul his "blood" ties to whites and to declare allegiance to his mother's race. Racial identification, for Stowe's biracial characters, is to some extent an act of volition, one that in George's case derives more from moral and affectional considerations than from some sense of his "true" African essence. He acknowledges, after all, that the "hot and hasty Saxon" will persist within him even after his emigration (*UTC,* 376).

Love and benevolence, rather than ancestry per se, determine George Harris's priorities: the love he has felt for and received from his mother translates into loyalty and benevolence toward others of her race, while his abhorrence of white Americans' moral choices (including his father's) forestalls the love that, for Stowe, is a prerequisite for effective benevolence toward them.[33] George is not simply choosing racial allegiance over other possible allegiances, as Oliver Wendell Holmes or white colonizationists might expect or insist; he is choosing his race and, ultimately, his nationality based in part on considerations of love and moral responsibility. Within the fictive world of *Uncle Tom's Cabin,* racial identity is certainly a factor in benevolent choice, as Topsy's move to Africa demonstrates. But the converse is also true: benevolence is a factor in racial allegiance, at least for those characters, like George Harris, who could conceivably adopt either of two racial identities. These doubled choices dramatize what was true of the broader culture as well—that benevolent identities and racial identities were mutually dependent and in some sense mutually constitutive. Just as notions of race informed benevolent acts, so did benevolence inform how a race was defined, in terms of its religiosity, its potential for self-reliance, or its guilt load, to name only the most salient features.

Dred and the Proslavery Family

Stowe's *Dred,* published four years after *Uncle Tom's Cabin,* offers a substantially different outcome for its fugitives. The novel's conclusion marks a departure from the racial separatism of the earlier text's resolution: none of *Dred*'s surviving characters leaves North America, though several settle in Canada, and all retain close interracial ties. Instead of privileging racially defined "blood" families, Stowe here champions non-kin, interracial families and communities that, while radically unlike the plantation family of proslavery rhetoric, nevertheless involve ongoing benevolent relations across racial lines.[34] Both novels engage proslavery perspectives, depicting enlightened slaveholders and the mildest of servitude on picturesque upper-South plantations, but then demonstrate the instability of such scenes, how financial and familial collapse can plunge the once-protected slave into the institution's worst horrors: separation from family, overwork, sexual exploitation, and brutal violence. But while Stowe's earlier rejection of the perpetual black dependence figured in proslavery ideology involved segregating her surviving characters, her strategy in *Dred* is to retain a kind of interracial "family" even as she re-configures the logics of affiliation and responsibility that undergird it.

In the pages that follow, I read *Dred* against proslavery novels that represent the idealized plantation family Stowe sought to undermine. While the proslavery ideology of the family was promulgated in a variety of texts, including polemical tracts and printed sermons, the novels are especially relevant because they employ strategies similar to Stowe's: heavy use of dialect and quotidian detail, a mix of comic and tragic tones, and the creation of both appealing and despicable characters who engage readers' emotions. Like Stowe's novels, these texts construct entire fictive worlds where the validity of a particular set of beliefs is borne out. Further, most 1850s proslavery novels were written in response to *Uncle Tom's Cabin* and so intervene in a cultural conversation that directly involved Stowe. Reading *Dred* in conjunction with these texts enables an examination of the next phase of this dialectic. Though largely excluded from the literary canon, proslavery novels contributed in important ways to the discourse of benevolent citizenship and to the nation's emerging politics of affiliation.

More than twenty "anti-Uncle Tom" novels appeared between the publication of *Uncle Tom's Cabin* and the beginning of the Civil War, many but by no means all by southerners, and many published in northern cities, primarily Philadelphia and New York.[35] The precise nature of Stowe's engagement with these texts is difficult to gauge. She clearly knew *The Cabin and the Parlor* (1852), published under the pseudonym J. Thornton Randolph, because she quoted it in *A Key to Uncle Tom's Cabin* as an example of the proslavery faction's false claim that slave families were rarely separated. But whether Stowe bought or borrowed or read these books from cover to cover is less relevant than is her general awareness of the ideologies they expressed. She had lived for years in Cincinnati, a border city and fairly significant publishing hub, where she surely heard a great deal of argumentation on all sides of the slavery question. More direct evidence can be found in her novels, whose characters echo the proslavery and antiabolitionist views in circulation at midcentury. And, crucially, Stowe was aware of herself as a target of proslavery attacks on northern meddling and misperception, of which these novels were widely distributed examples. In an 1853 letter to the North Carolina-born abolitionist Daniel R. Goodloe, she acknowledged that southerners "regarded [her] with so much bitterness as their accuser at the bar of the world."[36] In keeping with this awareness, she went to enormous lengths to respond to proslavery critiques of *Uncle Tom's Cabin,* most notably by publishing *A Key to Uncle Tom's Cabin* as proof of her novel's truth value but also by including in *Dred* some defensive footnotes and three authenticating appendixes, as if she might forestall future attacks before they could be formulated.

Like Stowe's fictions, proslavery novels from the 1850s concern themselves with pedagogy and its failures: abolitionist interlopers teach slaves incorrect ideas about the North and its promise of freedom, while harsh experience teaches those foolish enough to run away that, in fact, there is no place like home. Most relevant to my discussion of Stowe's antislavery novels, however, is these proslavery texts' articulations and defenses of a particular theory of the family—one characterized by mutual obligations and responsibilities, by white benevolence on the one hand and black gratitude and dependence on the other.[37] An anecdote related in the preface to Caroline Lee Hentz's 1854 novel *The Planter's Northern Bride* hyperbolizes these sentiments. In speaking of her long-dead master and mistress, a "negro woman" declares: " 'I loved my master and mistress like my own soul. . . . Oh! they were so good—so kind. All on [sic] us black folks would 'ave laid down our lives for 'em at any minute.' " When asked if she "did not sigh to be free," the woman responds with an unequivocal *no*, asserting that she loved her master and mistress better than she had her own mother and father, and that she loved her owners' children more than her own.[38] The bonds of this relationship, Hentz wishes to claim, are stronger even than "blood."

This benign view of slavery dominates proslavery fiction. Occasionally, the novels present some sort of injustice, such as the separation of families or ill treatment of slaves, but then insist that such instances are extraordinarily rare. Mary Eastman's *Aunt Phillis's Cabin* (1852), for example, includes a vignette about a slave woman whose children are sold away from her. The individual responsible for the sale, one white character asserts, "was held in utter abhorrence in the neighborhood" following "this wicked act," which violated both community standards and the principles of self-interest. "It is the interest of a master," Eastman's white patriarch claims, "to make his slaves happy, even were he not actuated by better motives."[39] In John W. Page's *Uncle Robin, in His Cabin in Virginia, and Tom without One in Boston* (1853), the evildoer is a hypocritical antislavery northerner who, when he acquires slaves upon his marriage to a Virginia woman, sells them to the highest bidder without regard to the disruption of family ties.[40] Such instances displace the cruelties of slavery onto a range of outsiders—northerners and other miscreants—who misunderstand and violate the patriarchal ideal.

With the plantation family thus established as a salutary and beloved institution, many of these novels derive their dramatic force from the threat posed to it by abolitionist agitation.[41] The genre's abolitionist characters, except for the few who experience a conversion to proslavery views, inevitably threaten the happiness of others. Sometimes malicious, sometimes lascivious, and sometimes merely misguided, these troublemakers tempt slaves to betray their plantation "families" in exchange for a life of destitution and struggle in the North or of mistrust and vilification in the South should they be caught and returned "home." In some cases, abolitionists' manipulations are held to be explicitly self-serving; for example, an unfortunate runaway in *Aunt Phillis's Cabin* becomes a domestic servant to a family of antislavery hypocrites, who overwork her and pay her less than they do their white servants, claiming that she "ought to be willing to work cheaper for Abolitionists, for they are [her] friends."[42] The antislavery movement, this novel suggests, is a thinly disguised plan for procuring cheap labor.

Integral to the proslavery ideology these novels express is the notion of a regional solidarity that crosses even as it reifies divisions of class and race. Northern interlopers, the novels insist, simply do not understand the slaves' needs or protect the slaves' interests in the way that fellow southerners, especially those of the master class, do. The frontispiece to *The Cabin and the Parlor* makes plain this ideal of interclass and interracial allegiance. Here the southern slaveholder Walworth, a model of gentlemanly (and fatherly or brotherly) behavior, saves a runaway slave named Cora and her child from a mob of lower-class northern whites. This illustration and the plot trajectory it represents pit humane southerners, black and white, against the violence of the urban North and its uncontrolled, unsupervised, and largely immigrant working class. (To antebellum readers, the coarse, almost animalistic features of Cora's attackers would have signaled their Irish ancestry.) This terrified fugitive's salvation demonstrates the superiority of the southern patriarchal ideal, with its vertically structured alliances across race and social class, over the horizontal, class-based allegiances and racial antipathies of the North. Cora eventually learns this lesson and, aided by another benevolent southerner, returns to Virginia. Readers encounter here a sort of underground railroad in reverse, putting to right a world made chaotic by misguided abolitionists.

Stowe undermines this notion of intraregional benevolence and solidarity in *Dred* by depicting a contentious and violent South. Rather than the northern urban mob of *The Cabin and the Parlor,* Stowe creates southern mobs that threaten the safety, liberty, and free speech of all. These bands of lower-class whites and their more prosperous instigators assault an outspoken antislavery minister, burn Edward and Anne Clayton's plantation school, and murder fugitive slaves, in the process undermining any notion of southern social cohesion. To differentiate her novel as much as possible from those of her proslavery contemporaries, Stowe makes Tom Gordon, her chief villain, the antithesis of proslavery rhetoric's benevolent southern gentleman. He is, as his sexual threats and general licentiousness make clear, more likely to rape a runaway slave than to rescue her.

Stowe also goes to great lengths in *Dred* to refute the claim, prominent in proslavery novels, that slaves run away out of selfishness and ingratitude. Harry Gordon, the well-educated mulatto who, through much of the novel, manages the Gordon plantation, flees only after Nina, his beloved mistress and half-sister, has died and her brother Tom has taken over. In fact, prior to that point, Harry has spent his own money, set aside to purchase his and his wife's freedom, in order to keep the plantation out of debt and Nina in the luxury she has always enjoyed. Another character's departure from his owner's home represents an even more extreme example of a slave's selflessness and sense of responsibility: Tiff, a dark-skinned slave whose domestic skills and general effeminacy are played for comic effect, leaves only when the mistress he loves has died and the white children he cares for are threatened by their new step-

WALWORTH RESCUES CORA FROM THE MOB.

10. Frontispiece to *The Cabin and the Parlor; or, Slaves and Masters.* Courtesy, American Antiquarian Society.

mother and her associates. Unlike Susan, Mary Eastman's character from *Aunt Phillis's Cabin,* who leaves her mistress's sick baby unattended in a Boston hotel room when she is "seduced off by the Abolitionists," Tiff escapes with his dead mistress's imperiled children in tow and puts their safety and comfort ahead of his own throughout the ordeal.[43] Proslavery novelists like Eastman asserted that, by running away, slaves ruined the interracial bond of love, duty, and responsibility that characterized these novels' idyllic plantation families. Stowe, by contrast, depicts characters who escape from the corruptions that slavery and its economic and moral consequences *introduce* into families.

The Gordons, on whom Stowe focuses much of her narrative, embody many of those corruptions. They contradict the proslavery ideal in that their slaves, rather than flourishing under whites' benign rule, must manage their irresponsible owners' financial affairs and to some extent their spiritual training.[44] Moreover, instead of presenting an ideal of non-kin affiliation between masters and slaves, Stowe makes the plantation's most trusted slave (Harry Gordon) the half-brother of his mistress (Nina), who remains unaware of their relationship despite his eerie resemblance to their dead father. In Stowe's portrayal, the plantation family is a disordered institution in which individuals own and exploit their "blood" relations, sometimes without even knowing it. This is no setting for the exercise of true benevolence, as the Gordon family's eventual disintegration makes clear.

Until late in the novel, it looks as though *Dred* will end, like *Uncle Tom's Cabin,* with racial separatism and resegregation as an antidote to proslavery notions of white-to-black benevolence. The crucial movement in this direction occurs when Harry, released by Nina's death from his bond of loyalty to the Gordon plantation and gravely threatened by Tom Gordon's acquisition of power, joins a maroon community in the Great Dismal Swamp. There Harry falls under the influence of Dred, a black revolutionary and mystic, and resolves the racial ambivalence that has tortured him throughout the novel by declaring allegiance to his mother's race. Although in some sense this is George Harris's story rewritten to include a more credible threat of antiwhite aggression, Stowe ultimately backs away from the violent potential of black solidarity. Dred, in response to the slave Milly's pacifist urgings and in the absence of a clear signal from God to proceed, agrees to delay his long-planned attack on the white plantations. Stowe then kills him off at the hands of Tom Gordon and his cohort before a later assault can be launched. The remaining fugitives, following the advice of Edward Clayton (the novel's exemplar of mature white benevolence), flee to the North rather than carry out the attack without their leader.

This choice marks Stowe's retreat from the racial separatism inherent in Harry's move to the swamp and Dred's insurrectionary plans. The escaping fugitives accept assistance from both whites and blacks, and go on to establish a number of sites of interracial cooperation and benevolent exchange. Harry Gordon has escaped the self-destructive loyalty he once felt toward his white sister but maintains a link to Edward Clayton. Clayton and his sister Anne, for their part, accomplish in Canada what hostile whites prevented in the southern United States and prove, in the process, that blacks' elevation can benefit whites as well. Their school for former slaves proceeds uninterrupted, its excellence eventually attracting the children of the area's white settlers, while "the value of the improvements which Clayton and his tenants have made has nearly doubled the price of real estate in the vicinity" (*D*, 2: 331). Clayton, Stowe's revision of the character of George Shelby, is a new and improved version of the recuperated southerner; he engages in long-term benevolent relations with his former slaves, with whom he works to build a single, integrated community. A hint of the old benevolent hierarchies persists, though, in that Clayton's former slaves, however industrious and successful they become in Canada, nevertheless remain his "tenants."

Transforming Parenthood

The most intriguing of these interracial benevolent sites are the alternative families formed by the escaped slaves Milly and Tiff. When they first arrive in New York, Milly, Tiff, and their dependents (Milly's grandson and Tiff's white foster children) "hire a humble tenement together; and she, finding employment as a pastry-cook in a confectioner's establishment, was able to provide a very comfortable support, while Tiff presided in the housekeeping department" (*D*, 2: 329–30). This gender-crossing cooperative household lasts a couple of years, until Tiff's children inherit money from a distant relative, a "maiden aunt" who had "quarrelled . . . with all her other relatives" (*D*, 2: 330). *Dred*'s final chapter relates Clayton's visits, years later, to their separate households. Tiff and his by now well-educated charges own "a little Gothic cottage" in a village near Boston, where Tiff continues to fuss over domestic details. (While Clayton serves as the children's legal guardian, Tiff remains in all daily respects their parent.) Milly, whose grandson is now an employee of "the anti-slavery office," has become a foster parent as well. She lives "in a neat little tenement" in New York City, "surrounded by about a dozen children, among whom were blacks, whites, and foreigners" (*D*, 2: 333). Caring for them, Milly says, helps to ease the pain of having lost her own children to slave traders. In her benevolent project, she "make[s] no distinctions of color" and adds that "white chil'en, when they 'haves themselves, is jest as good as black, and I loves 'em jest as well" (*D*, 2: 334).[45]

Stowe's portrayal of these households asserts the possibility, even the desirability, of establishing interracial though technically non-kin families within the borders of the United States. In *Uncle Tom's Cabin*, common racial identity comes to stand in for literal kinship; the two become, in fact, all but indistinguishable, as the emergent mother-daughter relationship between Cassy and Emmeline demonstrates. *Dred* adopts this model to a point: the maroon community in the swamp becomes like a family in part because of common racial identity, though the presence of common enemies proves equally significant. But by the end of the novel, the salience of "blood," in terms of both familial and racial kinship, has faded. Harry and his wife Lisette end up together, but readers encounter none of the earlier novel's reunions of extended families separated by slavery. The only miraculous reunion is Tiff's with his foster children, following a shipwreck in which he is given up for lost. Milly's and Tiff's families also invert proslavery rhetoric's familial ideal, making a former slave the wise head of household and placing under his or her care white dependents. The interracial Gordon family—non-kin and benevolent in theory but neither in fact—has been replaced by these alternative, volitional arrangements. If we accept the argument that antebellum Americans conceived of familial and national structures as analogous, then *Dred*'s conclusion can be read as Stowe's attempt to envision a cooperative interracial United States, in which African Americans occupy a variety of positions within households and within benevolent relations.

By making slaves and former slaves into foster parents, Stowe works to uncouple benevolent agency from high social status. Benevolence here is not the sole province of educated white ladies and well-heeled merchants but is instead open to, indeed required of, a variety of social actors. Nevertheless, as we ought to expect, there are limits to Stowe's social restructuring in *Dred*. For one thing, the caretaking roles that these figures assume very much resemble the work they did as slaves, and while it matters that their participation in these households is volitional, the similarities are striking: they still perform unpaid domestic labor for the benefit of whites (and in Milly's case, other blacks and "foreigners," the third term in Stowe's racial schema). Moreover, the whites these characters aid are children and adolescents rather than adults, whose dependence on a former slave might seem more alarming to Stowe's white readership. And *Dred*'s conclusion recontains the threat of interracial sex that underlies much of the novel's plot. Stowe articulates that threat in earlier chapters through Tom Gordon's attempts to make a slave his concubine and through Nina's behavior toward Harry Gordon, which includes more flirtation than their siblinghood and owner-slave relationship can comfortably accommodate.[46] But by constructing *Dred*'s final interracial families around self-sacrificing black parents—feminine or feminized—and needy white children, Stowe forecloses the possibilities of interracial pairings, which would make these alternative families into "blood" families after all. She even provides for Edward Clayton an acceptable Anglo-American mate, Nina Gordon's school friend Livy Ray, reassuring readers that he will not end up marrying one of the black members of his community. Thus Stowe concludes this integrationist novel with a careful disavowal of "amalgamation," the most radical revision of American families that Stowe and her contemporaries could imagine.

Stowe constructs these new families so cautiously because they anatomize the future of the nation, an entity that had come to seem quite fragile by the mid-1850s. In *Uncle Tom's Cabin,* she offers former slaves membership in a separate-but-equal parallel nation, which they would consolidate and raise up in the eyes of the world through their benevolent acts. But in *Dred* she holds out the hope of a single, reformed United States. In keeping with the era's diffuse theories of a connection between the health and legitimacy of the nation and the benevolence of its citizens, Stowe's novel suggests that these former slaves are true Americans *because* they do good. That is, benevolence, rather than race or nativity or freeborn status, is the mark and guarantor of legitimate membership in the nation, which Stowe figures as a Christian utopia in the making. Here, as elsewhere in antebellum culture, the language of benevolence is the language of national identity.

Good Citizenship

The charitable works-in-progress with which Stowe's antislavery novels conclude have their unlikely analogue in the final chapter of Hawthorne's *Scarlet Letter*, a text whose canonical status has rested in part on its supposed distance from the earnest social reformations of novels like Stowe's. Yet Hester Prynne's way of life following her return to New England sounds a great deal like one of Stowe's inventions. Hester, the narrator intones, "had no selfish ends, nor lived in any measure for her own profit and enjoyment." Instead, she "comforted and counselled" others, in particular the troubled women of the community, assuring them that "in Heaven's own time, a new truth would be revealed, in order to establish the whole relation between man and woman on a surer ground of mutual happiness."[47] While awaiting this utopia, Hester devotes her life to easing the pain of others.

Brook Thomas has argued that Hester's return marks a critical shift in the novel's representation of "good citizenship."[48] Instead of offering "absolute obedience" to the state, the John Winthrop-inspired model of political subjection with which the narrative begins, Hester engages in benevolent acts that "extend the parameters of good citizenship to an interpersonal realm concerned with affairs of the heart." She participates, Thomas argues further, in the creation of "an independent civil society" characterized not by individual striving or assertion but by its members' investment in what Hawthorne's contemporaries would have understood as benevolent relations.[49] Stowe's narratives attempt similar reconfigurations, suggesting that a government willing to enact the Fugitive Slave Law forfeits its claim on the obedience of its citizens. In place of that submission to state authority, Stowe's exemplary characters devote their lives to interpersonal benevolence under the higher authority of God. Given that, as Marianne Noble has claimed, Stowe privileges "the intersubjective nature of human identity" alongside selfhood's "bodily dimension," it makes sense that her conception of citizenship would be routed through a daily practice of caretaking among fellow citizens rather than through the abstraction and individuation characteristic of conventional political theory.[50]

But the African American foster parents Stowe presents at the conclusion of *Dred* participate in the creation of a civic myth rather different from Hester Prynne's good citizenship. For one thing, while Hawthorne has Hester wait until she has finished raising Pearl to settle into her civic role, thus separating the commitment to one's family from broader social obligations, Stowe makes the raising of children integral to her characters' benevolent projects, a move that, in keeping with the long-standing ideology of republican motherhood, posits good parenthood as a form of good citizenship. More crucially, Stowe's model operates not within an extradomestic civil society as typically conceived but rather within the domestic made civil—that is, within domestic settings that, like civil society, are porous, volitional, and heterogeneous. That Stowe' domestic sites are also interracial, interfamilial, and, in Milly's case, interregional—she takes in poor northern children—demonstrates an alternative vision of national life, one that supersedes the culture's usual lines of affiliation and priority. The evolution of Stowe's thinking after the composition of *Uncle Tom's Cabin* is clearest here, as the earlier novel's evacuative logic gives way to a more inclusive American nation/home. But this revision has limitations as well, as a range of texts by antebellum African Americans, treated in chapter 6, will show. They register a desire for overt political power and economic access that Stowe's new domesticity, however compelling, does not supply.

CHAPTER SIX

"Save Us from Our Friends"
Free African Americans and the Culture of Benevolence

We are not humbly begging the white man to "elevate us." He cannot do it. We have emanated from the same high origin, and are equally clothed with the divine image as he is.

"Our Elevation," *National Reformer* (December 1839)

The August 1838 issue of the *Mirror of Liberty,* edited by the African American activist David Ruggles, included an anecdote illustrating the treachery of whites who supported Liberian colonization and celebrating the ingenuity of their free black opponents. A group of colonizationists, dubbed "pseudo philanthropists" in the report, secured permission to meet in an African American church in Middletown, Connecticut, by "lull[ing]" the church's officers "to sleep" with their "serene [siren?] song." When Mrs. Beman, the wife of the minister (probably the abolitionist Jehiel C. Beman) in whose absence the agreement was made, found her objections ignored, she chose another course of action: "At length, the hour appointed [for the meeting] . . . arrived . . . when the [Colonization Society] agent, the doctors, the lawyers, and esquires, the Rev.'s, and the D.D.'s went to hold forth in glorification speeches. But lo! And behold! The door was shut, and the key in Mrs. Beman's pocket!"[1] Finding themselves without a venue, the colonizationists soon dispersed, cursing the church and its congregation.

The article then closed with a quatrain deriding those whites who

Ask our lives to stake
In "Afric's clime" to roam,
They disclose their friendship like a *snake!*
By biting us at *home.*[2]

The proximity of *friendship* and *home* in these lines underscores the linkage I have argued for throughout this book between the language of benevolence and the terms of national membership. Here, colonizationists' insistence that they were African Americans' truest friends stood in contrast to this author's rejection of the argument that black Americans' proper home was Liberia, a rejection endorsed by the vast majority of free blacks in the United States and Canada, even those who supported other emigration plans.[3] This account of Mrs. Beman's sabotage belies the attributions of passivity and lack of resourcefulness on which much colonizationist rhetoric rested, demonstrating instead the force and creativity of African Americans' resistance to (certain forms of) white benevolence.

The *Mirror of Liberty*'s representation of this act was part of a lively, often rancorous conversation among free African Americans about the theory and practice of benevolence. Although their contributions were less voluminous and less reliably archived than those of their Anglo contemporaries, African Americans were thoughtful critics of and participants in the era's culture of benevolence, employing a range of rhetorical strategies. Some expressed gratitude overtly for white aid but more subtly reminded readers that justice would better serve black people's interests than charity; others pointed to the hypocrisies of white benevolence; and still others proposed a kind of charitable separatism—practices of intraracial aid that circumvented and surpassed the efforts of Anglo-Americans. Most registered a desire to embrace some form of benevolence as an ideal, even as they rejected its infantilizing or coercive elements. And while only a portion of these gestures responded directly to whites' projects and publications or invited whites' responses, nearly all alluded to the dominant Anglo-American culture. Just as white benevolence and its attendant discourses were shaped by the presence of African Americans, so too did whites' acts, perceptions, and attributions inflect blacks' representations of doing good.

Two interrelated themes suffused those conversations: the question of national membership and the question of the free black person's responsibility to aid slaves and fugitives. The first arose most obviously in the context of the era's hotly debated emigrationist proposals. Should black Americans fight for equality and civil rights within the United States, or would their energies be better spent in establishing separate settlements in Canada, the Caribbean, western North America, Central or South America, or Africa? Should such territories, especially those in Canada, be considered permanent homes or temporary refuges? And what of England, a nation that seemed, to many who visited, to be far more welcoming than the United States, North or South? Where, in short, should African Americans invest their desires for full citizenship? When arguing for or against staying or leaving, African American authors repeatedly invoked their responsibility to those still (or more recently) enslaved—how and where might they, through act and example, best effect the emancipation of those they often referred to as their "brethren"? In the process, the texts that this chapter engages, including material published in Canada and England by U.S.-born authors, challenged the forms of benevolent racism that were gaining currency in the antebellum period, all the while demonstrating the extent to which African

Americans' gratitude, anger, and desire for autonomy were in tension and in conversation.[4]

The fugitive slave, activist, and author William Wells Brown explored themes critical to this racialized discourse of benevolence. As John Ernest has argued with regard to his best-known work, the 1853 novel *Clotel,* Brown reveals the United States' "national disunity—not the meaninglessness of the national text but rather its meaningful incoherence."[5] And so he does with the national debate over benevolence, rewriting its key elements in modes ranging from earnest evocation to ironic critique. Two of these representations bear exploring at length: an encounter related in Brown's 1853 and 1855 travel narratives between himself and a destitute fugitive slave in London and a scene in his 1858 play *The Escape* involving northern beggars and the abolitionist who ignores their pleas. While Brown's accounts of his experience in London foreground genuine need and admirable self-sacrifice, *The Escape* suggests that benevolence is thoroughly bankrupt, as it provides only bleak comic relief before the aggressive work of self-emancipation can be staged.

This shift, from the earnestness of the travel narratives to the cynicism of the 1858 play, dovetails with some of our dominant historical narratives about the 1850s: as the ugly decade got uglier, as moral suasion lost ideological ground, as the antislavery movement proceeded inexorably toward John Brown's raid, William Wells Brown lost faith in benevolence and invested instead in violent resistance. But such a narrative reduces the complexity of Brown's writings and of the broader conversations in which he participated. For one thing, Brown expressed discomfort with certain manifestations of benevolence elsewhere in his early 1850s writings and represented benevolence favorably in some later texts. Moreover, some of his writings allow for the joining of benevolence and violence, against the neat distinction drawn above.[6] As Robert Levine has claimed, Brown was a master of literary pastiche; his texts blend disparate genres and tones, combining the new and the reprinted, the original and the borrowed.[7] This chaotic method argues against any overarching change of ideology, at least one discernibly represented. Instead, I advance a synchronic argument, one that takes into account the embeddedness of benevolent discourse in broader debates over African American capacity and, more pointedly, over the terms of national inclusion.

Like many of his contemporaries, Brown seems most uncomfortable with benevolence when it involves outright supplication and most invested in it when the African American figures he represents are in a position to help others as well as to be helped. Enslaved persons have no such mobility, as the memoir he published with *Clotel* suggests. In fact, his desire to escape from slavery is there aligned with a desire for benevolent agency. He "could not do anything for [his enslaved mother and siblings] if he remained in slavery; consequently he resolved, and consecrated the resolve with a prayer, that he would start [i.e., escape] on the first opportunity."[8] In this instance, benevolent masculinity—for Brown, the ability to protect and aid weaker family members—is figured not simply as a perquisite of freedom but as a reason to seek it. Although some of Brown's enslaved characters become the objects of white benevolence, he tends not to dwell on such relations. For example, in the chapter from *Clotel* titled "The Liberator," Georgiana Carlton and her husband engage in a conventional version of interracial benevolence when they initiate the gradual emancipation of their slaves. But even here Brown emphasizes the slaves' industriousness, demonstrating their readiness for the opportunity to improve their own lives. More often in his texts well-meaning whites aid those who have already freed themselves, as when Wells Brown feeds and clothes the fugitive narrator in Brown's memoirs, then sends him on his way.

The Escape, despite a similar encounter between helpful Quakers and grateful fugitives, does more to displace the benevolent tropes that dominated much antislavery literature. The beggars Brown presents near the end of the play serve as foils for his self-helping fugitives, as he ridicules benevolence and privileges a discourse of rights, self-possession, and necessary violence. This disavowal makes sense; it would have been politically awkward for Brown to foreground interracial benevolence as an emancipatory strategy in the late 1850s, when African Americans were becoming increasingly vocal about the failures of white abolitionism and the necessity of black self-help. But in the context of freedom, benevolence—both across and within racial categories—can be ushered back in. In Brown's travel narratives, benevolence emerges as integral to the formation of the free citizen. Unlike the colonizationists, who offered black Americans a citizenship elsewhere, negotiated through the benevolence of missionary work and through the violence and self-denial of settlement, Brown's free black citizen is constructed abroad specifically in order to return to the United States. His narrative persona's commitment to aiding a more destitute fellow fugitive on the streets of London not only prefigures Brown's own repatriation, but it also references the activist imperative so many free African Americans expressed with regard to those still or recently enslaved. Benevolence here takes the form of a rededication to activism on U.S. soil, itself made possible by the white Englishwoman who purchases Brown's freedom, allowing his safe return.

Brown's citizenship is not the static, guaranteed status of those the nation had always included—the white propertied men who could vote, hold office, and serve on juries—but rather an assertion against antebellum law and practice that rests on the moral authority conferred by his principled return. If he shunts benevolence aside as the fugitive crosses the border into Canada, its tropes and its vocabulary too freighted with suggestions of black dependence, he nevertheless resurrects it for the fugitive abroad, most critically as that figure reenters the United States in order to join those he calls his "colored fellow-citizens."[9] Whereas Stowe's version of benevolent citizenship for African Americans is negotiated through an interracial and intergenerational domestic caretaking, Brown articulates a horizontal, fraternal vision of racial solidarity and citizenship, linking benevolent responsibility to violence in what he calls "this moral warfare" against slavery and racial injustice.[10] In doing so, he lays claim to an "imagined fraternity" of activist citizens analogous to, but crucially distinct from, the structures that, as Dana Nelson has persuasively argued, characterized white male citizenship in the early republic and antebellum periods.[11]

"We Would Rather Die at Home"

In the face of legalized slavery and slave-hunting, residency restrictions, disfranchisement, and limited access to education, employment, and legal protection, African Americans could hardly have considered themselves full citizens of the United States or of any particular state in the Union. Yet black authors frequently used the term *citizen* to describe themselves and the communities they addressed. Myriad announcements and convention reports addressed the "colored citizens" of the United States or of a particular state or city, while a notice that appeared in *Frederick Douglass's Paper* referred to "citizens of both colors" (presumably "black" and "white") who prevented a group of fugitive slaves from being apprehended as they boarded a steamer bound for Canada.[12] Like William Wells Brown's, these usages connoted struggle, promise, and possibility—a studied rejection of African American subordination—rather than an already achieved status. Some authors, in fact, made explicit this paradoxical invocation of and argument for national membership. A piece that appeared in Samuel Cornish's newspaper the *Colored American* in 1841, for example, repeatedly addressed readers as "fellow citizens" but also asserted "let our motto be, Agitate, Agitate . . . until victory is obtained, and we stand disenthralled, a free and independent people, in the enjoyment of all the rights, privileges, and immunities of American citizens."[13] Thus the term *citizen* was used to compel activism toward its own literal realization.

Not all free black authors put stock in that trajectory, however, especially once the Compromise of 1850 had renewed and intensified northern complicity with slavery. Martin Delany, for example, in his speech "Political Destiny of the Colored Race on the American Continent," delivered at an emigrationist convention in 1854, delineated what Glenn Hendler has called Delany's "alienation from citizenship."[14] Delany here studiously avoided the term *citizen,* instead referring to African Americans as his "FELLOW-COUNTRYMEN." Conscious of his auditors' expectations, he stated that "we have not addressed you as *citizens*—a term desired and ever cherished by us—because such you have never been." Eschewing also the term *freemen,* Delany explained his reasoning: "Our oppressors are ever gratified at our manifest satisfaction, especially when that satisfaction is founded upon false premises; an assumption on our part, of the enjoyment of rights and privileges which never have been conceded, and which, according to the present system of the United States policy, we never can enjoy."[15] The use of such terms, Delany argued, suggested a dangerous complacency rather than the call to struggle I have identified elsewhere.

Interestingly, Delany used *citizen* to refer to himself two years earlier in *The Condition, Elevation, Emigration, and Destiny of the Colored People of the United States* (1852), dedicating the book to "THE AMERICAN PEOPLE, NORTH AND SOUTH. BY THEIR MOST DEVOUT, AND PATRIOTIC FELLOW-CITIZEN, THE AUTHOR."[16] Given that Delany published the work himself, we have to assume that this usage was his decision rather than the imposition of an editor or publisher. I call attention to it not to illustrate or critique Delany's already well-known variability but to suggest the degree to which the notion of black U.S. citizenship was wedded to specific lines of argumentation. In "Political Destiny," Delany's disavowal of citizenship was integral to his argument that black Americans must seek elsewhere what they were denied on U.S. soil. But in *Condition,* several chapters of which argued for African Americans' right to U.S. citizenship, his invocation of the term accorded with a pointed rejection of colonizationists' claims that black Americans ought to "return" to Africa. For Delany, the figure of the black U.S. citizen receded in the face of the separatist, nationalist options he frequently explored, including in the final chapters of *Condition,* but emerged vis-à-vis those Anglo-Americans who sought his or her expulsion.[17]

This alignment of the term *citizen* with anticolonizationist and, sometimes, antiemigrationist positions extended well beyond Delany's writings. Bruce Dorsey points out that free black activists linked colonization to Anglo-Americans' contemporaneous efforts to deny them suffrage and other political rights, against which array they defended their related claims to manhood and citizenship. "The first black national convention in 1830," Dorsey writes, "lodged their attack against colonization 'as citizens and men,' reminding their audience that 'many of our fathers, and some of us, have fought and bled for the liberty, independence, and peace which you now enjoy.'"[18] An 1852 piece that appeared in *Frederick Douglass's Paper* adopted a milder though no less gendered tone: "*Brethren, stay where you are, so long as you can stay. Stay here and worthily discharge the duties of honest men, and of good citizens. Stay here, not menacingly,* for we are feeble, and our enemies are strong. God in His providence has left us no means of defense but *truth, justice, humanity,* and *religion.*"[19] The benevolence of the black U.S. citizen, this quotation suggests, is both a defense against white prejudice and a vindication of blacks' worthiness in the face of the dominant culture's ongoing derision.

Alongside such attempts to endow those who remained in the United States with moral authority, African American commentators presented the humanitarian claims of colonization's supporters as a false benevolence. Certainly, some granted colonizationists their professed good intentions. The 1831 *Constitution of the American Society of Free Persons of Colour,* for instance, affirmed the "sincerity of many friends who are engaged in that cause" but asserted that black Americans' "habits, manners, and customs are the same in common with other Americans," and therefore they would reject any move to Africa. Samuel Cornish and Theodore Wright, in an 1840 tract addressed to colonizationists, wrote that "we say not a word against your sincerity, when you profess to have in view only the promotion of our happiness—however fully we may be convinced, that you have mistaken the channel in which your beneficence should be made to flow." And *Frederick Douglass's Paper,* which published innumerable condemnations of colonizationists, conceded at one point that some of them were "honest" and humane, though it maintained that such an admission did not "abate" one's "abhorrence of the . . . scheme."[20] More commonly, though, black authors asserted the hypocrisy of colonizationists' claims to benevolence. Delany called the colonization movement "misanthropic in its pretended sympathies," while an 1852 article in *Frederick Douglass's Paper* insisted that the "seeming benevolence" of the movement's national organization, the American Colonization Society (ACS), was in fact "animated and controlled by a deep-seated and malignant prejudice."[21] Almost two decades earlier, Maria Stewart suggested that "if the colonizationists are real friends to Africa, let them expend the money which they collect, in erecting a college to educate her injured sons in this land of gospel light and liberty."[22] Among the many indictments of colonization's supporters, one stands out as especially incisive. "If we must be sacrificed to their philanthropy," declared a report from the First Annual Convention of the People of Colour" (1831), "we would rather die at home."[23]

Trying Friends

With few exceptions, free African Americans were adamant in their opposition to Liberian colonization. Responses to the efforts of white abolitionists, meanwhile, were more ambivalent, ranging from effusive expressions of gratitude to critiques of the movement's blind spots and shortcomings. Especially instructive is the contrast between these mixed responses and the fantasies of black gratitude and deference that some antislavery whites indulged. Elizabeth Margaret Chandler's poem "The Enfranchised Slaves to Their Benefactress" provides an apt, if extreme, example of the latter. Ventriloquizing the freed slave, Chandler writes:

Oh, blessings on thee, lady! We could lie
Down at thy feet, in our deep gratitude,
And give ourselves to die,
So thou could'st be made happier by our blood;
Yet life has never seem'd so dear as now,
That we may lift a free, unbranded brow.[24]

White abolition's cherished hierarchies, so evident here, would encounter significant resistance in the writings of African Americans.

Certainly, black authors sometimes expressed unalloyed gratitude toward whites engaged in antislavery activism. One tract, for example, called the abolitionist editors of the *Genius of Universal Emancipation* and the *Liberator* "our tried friends, and fearless . . . promoters of our best interests, . . . [who are] entitled to a prominent place in our affections."[25] But appreciation was often tempered by critique and redirection. An 1837 article titled "Difficulties of Abolition" insisted that "the colored man who does not hold the person, the character and the doings, of American Abolitionists in the highest estimation, is unworthy [of] the form he wears." But after asserting that abolitionists are "emphatically, our best friends," the author added that "they have much to investigate, and much to learn." The article then urged black Americans to invest themselves in "guiding the holy zeal, and rightly applying the benevolent efforts of our abolition friends."[26] Along similar lines, the Board of Managers of the American Moral Reform Society praised white-run antislavery periodicals and organizations, but added that "the 'colored people' have not been idle spectators to this grand and interesting scene. They have approved it by their lips—by the expressions of their primary assemblies—their labors—their means—and their prayers."[27] Frederick Douglass, a veteran of power struggles with white abolitionists, exemplified this uneasy collaboration in his responses to *Uncle Tom's Cabin.* As Robert Levine has shown, Douglass strongly disagreed with Stowe's advocacy of Liberian colonization at the end of her novel, but he nevertheless chose to promote the book in his paper. In response to Martin Delany, who questioned the legitimacy of Stowe's interracial benevolence, Douglass wrote that "to scornfully reject all aid from our white friends, and to denounce them as unworthy of our confidence, looks high and mighty enough on paper; but unless the back ground is filled up with facts demonstrating our independence and self-sustaining power, of what use is such display of self-consequence?"[28] For Douglass, white benevolence was welcome so long as it was useful—that is, so long as black self-reliance was not yet completely in place.

Even if, as Douglass suggested, Delany's attitude toward Stowe was both maladaptive and reductive, Delany's broader criticism of white abolitionists bears consideration. In *The Condition, Elevation, Emigration, and Destiny of the Colored People of the United States,* Delany took abolitionists to task for their failure to aid northern free blacks. "It was expected," he wrote, "that Anti-Slavery, according to its professions, would extend to colored persons . . . those advantages nowhere else to be obtained among white men. That colored boys would get situations in their shops and stores, and every other advantage tending to elevate them as far as possible, would be extended to them." But, Delany pointed out, such opportunities rarely materialized: "Instead of realising what we had hoped for, we find ourselves occupying the very same position in relation to our Anti-Slavery friends, as we do in relation to the pro-slavery part of the community—a mere secondary, underling position." Any deviation from this pattern, he added, came not by "established anti-slavery custom or right" but "by mere sufferance."[29] Mary Ann Shadd Cary, the U.S.-born editor of the Canadian paper the *Provincial Freeman,* pointed out a similar hypocrisy, remarking in her article "The Humbug of Reform" that abolitionists were primarily concerned with their own "interests as white *freemen*" and, in particular, with maintaining their superior positions.[30] White abolitionists, both authors suggested, were overly invested in the notion of black Americans as faraway victims in need of rescue and, consequently, resisted seeing them as potential equals, coworkers, and neighbors.

Hierarchies and Alliances

Colonization and abolition drew a great deal of commentary in the black press, no doubt because they spoke so centrally to African Americans' most significant concerns. But these movements existed within a matrix of interracial benevolent projects, including orphanages that served "colored" children and other efforts geared toward, in the lexicon of the era, the "elevation" and "improvement" of black Americans. A salient characteristic of nearly all such projects, and what African American authors critiqued most vigorously, was their hierarchical structure—the habit of excluding black people from decision-making roles, essentially enforcing their status as helped rather than helper, and the tendency to represent and treat black people as "degraded" beings. While a few whites resisted such structures and others regretted them—as one English abolitionist put it, "we humiliate while we relieve"[31]—some defended them as strategic. In response to those who called the ACS the "disparager of the free blacks," one commentator wrote that

> all benevolent operations must proceed upon the supposition that there is
> want to be alleviated, or ignorance to be enlightened, or degradation to be
> pitied; and the vigor with which such operations are sustained by the benevolent will be proportioned, not so much to the degree of this want, ignorance and degradation, as to their thorough and perfect exposure.[32]

In other words, the best way to help free African Americans was to represent them as negatively as possible.

The hierarchies of antebellum benevolence, usually expressed more subtly than in the above quotation, elicited a range of responses from African American commentators. Writing against a widespread investment, among black and white Americans, in the goal of black improvement, some took issue with the very language of elevation and degradation on which much benevolent discourse relied. The author and physician James McCune Smith, writing in the August 1859 issue of the *Anglo-African Magazine,* asked whether "the standard occupied by the whites [were] really elevated above that occupied by the black population?" He concluded that the question of elevation was indeterminate, a matter of opinion or perspective, and argued that a more appropriate register of progress was the presence (or absence) of harmonious and just interactions between the races.[33] More common was the strategy of pairing a rejection of white paternalism with an assertion of (or a call for) black strength and autonomy. Samuel Cornish and Theodore Wright, for instance, wrote that "the body of the colored people of this country who are free, are not *minors;* . . . as a class, they deem themselves reasonably well qualified, on the score of intelligence, to judge what will most promote [their happiness]."[34] The "Prefatory Remarks" that accompanied the *Proceedings of the National Emigration Convention of Colored People* (1854) put the matter more pointedly: "We are frequently asked by the impatient white American enquirer: 'What is it you black people want? What would the negro race desire at our hands more than we have done?' Our reply is, that we *ask nothing at your hands,* nor desire anything of *your giving.*"[35] Rejecting traditional forms of supplication, many black Americans asked instead for the removal of oppressive social and political structures. As one *National Reformer* author put the matter, "all we ask of them is, that they take their 'feet from of [*sic*] our necks.' "[36]

Many African American authors, however, sought a balance between asserting a current or achievable black independence and cultivating or at least not alienating benevolent whites. These commentators worked in a collaborative mode, engaging with white activists in an attempt to reshape their projects. One strategy was to seek greater black representation in the formation and execution of benevolent plans. When a group of white abolitionists—including Arthur Tappan and William Lloyd Garrison—proposed founding "a College" for free blacks "on the Manual Labour System," the First Annual Convention of the People of Colour, held in Philadelphia in 1831, resolved to support the effort but also made it clear that a majority of "the Trustees of the contemplated Institution" should "be coloured persons."[37] An 1839 article in the *Colored American* called for a general habit of consultation: "The time has come, in which all philanthropists, who have the interests of our people at heart, and who are willing to devise and prosecute measures for their improvement and elevation, should have a judicious and intelligent committee of *our* brethren, to consult on all occasions, where our interests are involved."[38] African Americans, this author insisted, were better judges of who among them merited aid, especially in the form of educational opportunities, than whites could possibly be.

Those working in this collaborative mode repeatedly insisted on the limitations of white benevolence. An 1838 article titled "Moral Work for Colored Men," written under the pseudonym "Augustine," claimed that "our moral elevation is a work in which we may be *assisted,* and in which we *need* much assistance, in which much assistance is *owed* to us, but which never can be done for us. We must become alive to its importance on our own part, and acquaint ourselves of its true nature."[39] And an 1854 piece in the *Provincial Freeman* used the colonizationist moment in *Uncle Tom's Cabin* to make a similar point: "Let black men learn from this, and ten thousand like cases, the great lesson that the vindication of their rights and liberties, *must be done mainly by themselves.* That however gratefully accepting the assistance of friends, *so far as it goes,* the work, under God, is their own."[40] These pronouncements carried a double valence. Appearing in periodicals edited by black activists, with a significant black readership, they functioned as calls to action, reminders to black Americans and Canadians that the elevation of the race was primarily their responsibility. But they also, at least obliquely, addressed well-meaning whites, reminding them that their benevolent projects could never be blacks' sole salvation.

Elevating the Race

Benevolent projects within free African American communities took a number of forms, including mutual aid arrangements, educational initiatives, short-term poverty relief, moral reform, abolitionist agitation, and participation in vigilance committees that sought to protect fugitive slaves and prevent kidnappings. While commentators argued, as Joanne Pope Melish has noted, over whether free black activists should focus their energies on ending slavery or improving their own communities, to a great extent African Americans and their allies perceived the two projects to be mutually dependent. Southern slavery, Melish writes, was often cited as "the real source of northern 'prejudice,' " while poverty, dependence, and vice among free blacks were thought to undermine the abolitionist cause.[41] In that sense, the benevolent work that African Americans advocated referenced slavery, whether or not the immediate recipients of aid were or had ever been enslaved. "Free people of color," to use the language of the era, found themselves living under tremendous scrutiny. Their successes served as proof that emancipation would do no harm to the republic, while their perceived shortcomings were used to argue for the necessity of maintaining slavery or encouraging colonization. Thus black Americans called attention to their own benevolent work in order to prove the worthiness of "the race" and its preparation for the challenges of freedom, even as they exhorted one another to improve themselves for the sake of those still enslaved.[42]

Americans across a range of ideological commitments conceived of the free person of color and the slave as linked beings, each of whose success or failure would affect the other. Along these lines, the constitution of the Philadelphia Association for the Moral and Mental Improvement of the People of Color urged free African Americans to "educate your children; cultivate your own mind; be industrious and economical, and acquire property and influence. These will speak volumes in behalf of the liberty of the slave."[43] Among African Americans, debates over emigration entered in as well. On the one hand, those who advocated remaining in the United States argued that to leave would be tantamount to abandoning one's benevolent responsibility toward the slave. Emigrationists, on the other hand, claimed that by creating separate communities (as refuge, as proof of black self-reliance), free blacks could succeed in "redeeming ourselves as a race," as Martin Delany put it. "Let us apply, first," he wrote elsewhere, "the lever to ourselves; and the force that elevates us to the position of manhood's considerations and honors, will cleft the manacle of every slave in the land."[44]

In addition to their particular burdens and concerns, however, African Americans to some extent shared the preoccupations of their white contemporaries. Like any number of Anglo-American activists, black authors chided readers for their selfishness and insufficient commitment to charitable projects. "Are not too many of us," one author asked, "satisfied with taking care of No. ONE?"[45] And in keeping with a widespread belief in the benevolent power of print, black editors framed their offerings as contributions to the social and moral improvement of their readers. Samuel Cornish was explicit on this score, declaring that his paper, the *Colored American,* was "elevating the moral standard, refining the taste, concentrating the means, directing the energies and giving tone to the character of Colored Americans." Supporting the paper was also a benevolent act. "We look to our brethren," Cornish wrote, "—both white and colored—who have the MEANS—to assist us liberally—to subscribe for as many COPIES as you can afford, and let us send such of them as you may not want, yourselves, where they are much needed. They will do good, and GOD will reward you for your benevolence."[46]

Like their Anglo-American counterparts, African Americans worried that deception, especially in the act of begging, might taint benevolent exchange. The *Colored American* reprinted in 1839 a notice cautioning readers against the "perfidious conduct, under the cloak of religion and humanity" of "a man of color" named Israel Lewis, who had claimed during the previous nine years to collect money for Canada's Wilberforce Settlement but who had been accused of pocketing most of it.[47] And in 1855, the *Provincial Freeman* reprinted an article warning readers to "look out for a rascal," a man who represented himself as a freed slave seeking funds to buy his family's freedom but who was instead a "vile imposter." Several months later, the paper warned that "many young men, too lazy to work, and too coward [*sic*] to steal . . . are perambulating the Western States, soliciting, pretending to buy a wife—to buy a sister—to buy children—some to re-build houses said to have been burned; some to get money to obtain an education; and others, to go to Africa,—when really, not one in ten is honestly engaged." The last line of the article retreated somewhat, assuring readers that a "Mr. Fulton," who was "trying to buy a mother," was not one of these deceivers.[48]

Within this discourse of suspicion, broad cultural anxieties became intertwined with African Americans' and Afro-Canadians' specific circumstances. That is, the suspicion recorded above derived in part from concerns that whites shared—whether limited charitable funds were going to deserving candidates, whether the benevolent could trust their own judgment—but it was also inflected by African Americans' precarious positioning vis-à-vis the dominant culture. How would deceptive black supplicants reflect on the character of the race as a whole? Would the actions of such deceivers undermine others' legitimate fundraising efforts? Would invented tales of suffering, once discovered, negate the testimonials of those who had actually been enslaved or otherwise abused? These concerns were well founded, given how eager white Americans were to credit stories of black trickery and to disbelieve accounts of cruelty against slaves.

A more general discomfort with supplication animated the rhetoric of certain commentators who hoped to prove the self-sufficiency of the race. An extended conflict that played out among black leaders in Canada is especially instructive on this score. On one side, activists such as Henry and Mary Bibb and Josiah Henson favored energetic appeals to white philanthropy for the support of fugitive slaves who settled in Canada.[49] These fugitives found themselves "in a strange land from necessity, uneducated, poverty stricken, without homes or any permanent means of self-support," Henry Bibb noted in an 1851 editorial. "However willing they may be to work," he continued, "they have no means to work with or land to work upon." Bibb advocated the distribution of Canadian land, purchased largely through white charity, by means of which fugitives would "become owners and tillers of the soil—and PRODUCE WHAT THEY CONSUME."[50] Thus he made the goal of eventual black self-reliance contingent on immediate aid, much of which, it seems, was to come from whites.

Bibb's efforts met with vehement opposition from such figures as Samuel Ringgold Ward and Mary Ann Shadd Cary, both affiliated with the *Provincial Freeman,* who advised Canada's free black residents and fugitives to eschew extended fundraising projects and to focus instead on achieving full acceptance and integration within Canadian society.[51] This faction decried a range of projects, especially those of the Refugee Home Society (RHS), the organization whose land distribution efforts Bibb supported. The report of "a meeting of the colored citizens of Windsor," for which Shadd Cary served as one of two secretaries, called into question the status of the RHS as "a benevolent institution," naming it instead "an exceedingly cunning land scheme." Deriding all such fundraising efforts as "begging," the report criticized their proponents for "holding us up before the world as a class of improvident, thriftless and imbecile paupers." This group resolved instead to "thank God for the impartial character and administration of the laws of this our adopted country," which allowed people of color "in common with other settlers, to appropriate the soil to our comfort and support." While endorsing the practice of "begging for gospel and educational purposes" (as did "Christians everywhere"), the group recommended that all other funds raised in their name be given "to aid those noble Abolitionists who have been dispoiled [*sic*] by the courts of the United States, for helping fugitives to a land of liberty."[52] Free people of color, this faction insisted, living under Canada's relatively just laws, were not especially or disproportionately abject—in fact, they were prepared to give something back to their erstwhile benefactors.[53]

Two related questions underlay these conflicts: To what extent would soliciting or even simply accepting white benevolence undermine blacks' dignity, reputation, and prospects for sociopolitical inclusion? And, more specifically, was immediate relief worth such long-term damage? Although Shadd Cary and her associates answered the latter with a resounding *no,* the degree to which they felt they had to elaborate their case—the many articles, resolutions, and editorials they launched against "begging"—suggests the extent to which these were open questions. William Wells Brown's disparate representations reveal a preoccupation with the same issues, as his texts finesse white benevolence without ever quite erasing it. The bonds of responsibility he represents between himself and a fugitive—and, by extension, between himself and oppressed black Americans in general—exact certain costs as well, though he is more sanguine about the compensations they offer.

Escaping Benevolence

The *Narrative of the Life and Escape of William Wells Brown* (1853) positions Brown squarely in the anti-"begging" camp. With regard to his travels in England, the memoir states that "most of the fugitive slaves, and in fact nearly all of the coloured men who have visited Great Britain from the United States, have come upon begging missions, either for some society or for themselves." "Mr. Brown," the text continues, "has been almost the only exception," a man whose "independence of feeling" requires that he "maintain himself and family by his own exertions—by his literary labours, and the honourable profession of a public lecturer." When, a few paragraphs later, the narrator relates an instance of English generosity, he is careful to frame it as a "spontaneous free will offering," which the donors, in a crucial reversal, "begged" Brown to accept "as a token of esteem, as well as an expression of their sympathy in the cause he advocates."[54] Such declarations, however self-serving, promoted the larger agenda of rescuing African Americans from the taint of dependence.

The Escape, which Brown published in 1858 but probably read in public the previous year, gives those projects dramatic form, emphasizing the resourcefulness (if not always the dignity) of his escaping slave characters and circumscribing the roles of well-intentioned whites.[55] The play's three protagonists—Glen and Melinda, a high-minded and well-spoken romantic pair, and Cato, the trickster figure who joins them on their journey northward—achieve freedom largely through their own exertions. Whites affiliated with the Underground Railroad offer them shelter, food, and transportation along the way, but the critical stages of their escape—leaving their master and crossing into Canada—are autonomous acts. More pointedly, the play's representative abolitionist, aptly named Mr. White, is a hypocritical and ultimately ridiculous figure whose advocacy of emancipation is made to seem, at best, beside the point.

As John Ernest has argued and as my foregoing discussion reinforces, Brown's swipes at white abolitionists in this text operated within an established network of critique.[56] In keeping with variously expressed reservations on the part of black authors about abolitionists' methods and motives, Brown sets up Mr. White's brief appearances in the play as demonstrations of the hollowness of his principles. He first appears in a tavern, where he delivers an impassioned antislavery speech before a hostile crowd of southerners, boasting of his origins in the "free State" of Massachusetts and insisting that "the worst act that a man can commit upon his fellow-man, is to make him a slave." In ludicrously flowery terms, he goes on to claim that slavery converts "a living soul . . . quivering with life and joy" into "a dead soul entombed in a living frame!" But a few moments later, fearing for his life when a more violent group arrives seeking runaway slaves, he begs the barkeeper to hide him in the cellar. The next time the audience encounters him, he has returned safely to the North, vowing never again to venture "south of Mason and Dixon's line."[57] For Mr. White, slavery's victims are best kept at a distance, from which he can contemplate their oppression without sharing their peril.

Mr. White's final appearance calls into question the legitimacy of benevolence more broadly conceived. While waiting for a ferry to take him across the Niagara River—the same ferry that the fugitive slaves are attempting to catch—Mr. White sketches the scenery, an activity that underscores his leisured disengagement from the surrounding dramas of flight and pursuit. At this point, he is approached by two men Brown calls "pedlars" but whose statements place them more in the category of beggars, as antebellum Americans typically understood the term. The first offers to sell Mr. White a cane and proceeds to declare his desperate need for patronage: "I've a wife and nine small children,—youngest is nursing, and the oldest only three years old. . . . I've had no breakfast to-day. My wife's got the rheumatics, and the children's got the measles. . . . I've a lame shoulder, and can't work." The second pedlar offers a similar if more concise pitch, drawing attention at first to the quality of his merchandise but quickly moving to an account of his troubles (a wife with "the fever and ague," a house "full of children, and they're all sick"). Mr. White responds peevishly to both, declaring that their interruptions have "spoiled a beautiful scene" with "nonsense."[58]

Brown's depiction of this encounter draws on the era's widely disseminated representations of trickster-beggars, who offer worthless goods for sale at high prices or who ask for alms outright, emphasizing their hunger, physical disability, and numerous sick dependents. Brown signals his characters' deceptiveness by having one of them claim nine children under the age of four—an impossibility barring polygamy or several multiple births—and then raise the number of children to thirteen in a later appeal. In antebellum print culture, representations of such deceivers were both comic and disruptive, making fun of gall and credulity but also calling into question the ability of donors to distinguish between genuine and deceptive claims. But Brown soon departs from the usual script by implying that Mr. White's dismissal of their pleas has nothing to do with questions of credibility, of worthy versus vicious poverty. Mr. White refuses to help these men because he does not want to be bothered. Here

Brown invokes an entirely different stereotype: the complacent, well-off citizen who wishes to avoid unsavory matters like poverty that might interfere with his pleasure. Need, as Mr. White puts it, spoils "a beautiful scene."

This episode, though it ostensibly involves free white men in the North, also engages the era's debates over slavery. Brown is playing at least two sides here. If these "pedlar"/beggars are meant to be lower-class whites, as their modes of speech would suggest, then this encounter accords with one strain of proslavery argumentation—that white abolitionists are so concerned with the plight of the slave and with the sins of the South that they ignore the destitution of members of their own race and region. But Brown undermines this triangulation even as he invokes it; the suffering of these beggars, after all, is not especially credible. So the proslavery argument collapses as the beggars' deceptions and obnoxious persistence are contrasted with the more credibly presented sufferings of the play's fugitive slaves, not to mention their more independent means of improving their lot.

The scene occurs near the end of Brown's play, just before Glen, Melinda, and Cato arrive, fight off their pursuers, and board the ferry to Canada. Although it does little to advance the plot, the encounter matters insofar as it counters the widespread cultural narratives of fugitive destitution that Shadd Cary and others railed against. In portraying this exchange, Brown displaces the shame of supplication onto white figures, in the process invoking and then comically devaluing certain hierarchical forms of benevolent exchange—forms so corrupted by hypocrisy that, as this representation would have it, they cannot serve urgent emancipatory purposes. Here, Brown's dismissal of benevolence accords with Ernest's claim that the play as a whole argues that "the revolution [i.e., the overthrow of U.S. slavery and racism] cannot be completed by abstract benevolence."[59] The play's resolution, however, does not stage a wholesale reeducation or retooling of white abolition. Granted, in the final scene Mr. White is converted to the principle of direct action when he joins the fugitives in their fight against the slavecatchers. But even here it is difficult to take him seriously. Though he proclaims "I'll fight for freedom," the stage directions indicate that he does so with his umbrella, held in both hands, as his weapon. His ridiculousness is compounded by the fact that Brown omits him from the play's descriptions of the characters' final outcomes: the slavecatchers are "knocked down" and the runaway slaves "jump into the boat," but Mr. White's fate goes unmentioned.[60] Whether or not Brown intended the erasure, this figure's final absence reinforces what the play has already made clear—that white abolition is a side note in the project of black emancipation.

Benevolence Abroad

In light of this layered dismissal, Brown's more earnest treatment of benevolence in his European travel narratives—in particular, his construction of himself as benevolent agent—warrants careful analysis. This is not to suggest that Brown presents himself as becoming benevolent only on leaving the United States. His autobiographies indicate otherwise, though there he typically appears, prior to his trip abroad, as trickster and benevolent figure by turns: his *Narrative of William W. Brown,* first published in 1847, recounts the decidedly unbenevolent act of duping another African American into taking a whipping meant for him but later frames his antislavery lecturing as devotion "to the cause of [his] enslaved countrymen."[61] Similarly, Brown's 1853 memoir includes an account of his shady business dealings as an amateur banker but also reprints a commendation from the Massachusetts Anti-Slavery Society: "For several years past, [Brown] has nobly consecrated his time and talents, at great personal hazard, and under the most adverse circumstances, to the uncompromising advocacy of the cause of his enslaved countrymen."[62] Nevertheless, Brown's benevolence abroad, if not new, is shaped and energized by his geographical and psychological distance from the threat of reenslavement. As he describes it, "For the first time in my life, I can say 'I am truly free.' My old master may make his appearance here, with the Constitution of the United States in his pocket, the Fugitive Slave Law in one hand and the chains in the other, and claim me as his property, but all will avail him nothing. I can here stand and look the tyrant in the face, and tell him that I am his equal!"[63] In Brown's representation, this experience of equality with those who would once have been his "superiors" enables new investments in benevolent agency.

Brown released two book-length accounts of his European travels. The first, published in London in 1852 while he was still living abroad, bore the rather generic title *Three Years in Europe; or, Places I Have Seen and People I Have Met* but announced its author's ties to American slavery through its cover illustration: a version of the abolitionist movement's image of a kneeling slave in chains. The book, as a material artifact, thus reiterates the conflict that animates its content, between the abjection of the fugitive and the privilege of the transatlantic traveler. Along with a self-deprecating preface (in which Brown attributes any errors or infelicities to his long enslavement and lack of formal schooling) and a brief "Memoir of the Author" written in the third person and attributed to the English abolitionist William Farmer, the book consists of twenty-three letters that relate, among many topics, Brown's impressions of various cities, palaces, and monuments, his encounters with Europeans and fellow Americans, and his thoughts on U.S. slavery.[64] After returning to the United States in 1854, Brown published a revised and expanded version of the book—without the cover illustration of the kneeling slave—under the more illuminating title *The American Fugitive in Europe: Sketches of Places and People Abroad.*[65] Brown's "Note to the American Edition" also strikes a more assertive tone than does his first preface; he informs readers that he has "found it advantageous to [his] purse" to publish the first edition and that, because it was reviewed favorably in British press, he has "been induced to offer it to the American public" (iv). Though the two editions are substantially similar, the second omits some material and includes several additional chapters. Most noticeably, where the English edition ends with a chapter titled "A Narrative of American Slavery" (a version of which appeared the following year in the last chapters of *Clotel*) and a tacked-on chapter relating an earlier segment of Brown's journey, placed here due to an error in the ordering of the manuscript, the American edition culminates in a lengthy account of the author's homecoming, once he is, against his title's pronouncement, no longer an American fugitive.

Before turning to the significance of that representation, I wish to examine an earlier chapter, number nine in both editions, which dramatizes the narrator's formation as a worthy citizen through the twinned acquisition of cultural capital and benevolent agency.[66] The chapter begins with a lengthy account of Brown's two-day visit to the British Museum, where he examines various antiquities, rare minerals, and portraits, and where he visits the "great library," which he presents as a retreat within which "men of different rank can meet" in a leveling anonymity: "No one inquires who the man is that is at his side, and each pursues in silence his own researches" (116). While Brown does not explicitly compare the library to U.S. cultural institutions, the contrast seems obvious, as does the Anglophilia inherent in his "admiration for the men whose energy has brought together [the museum's] vast and wonderful collection" (116). In this mode, Brown dutifully pursues self-culture, relying on his "guide-book" and lingering in the galleries until a museum officer or the setting sun reminds him that it is time to leave (114, 116–17).

This stamina is more fully explored in Brown's account of the night between his two museum visits. "Although fatigued by the day's exertions," he engages in edifying reading until two o'clock in the morning. "He who escapes from slavery at the age of twenty years," Brown explains, "without any education, . . . must read when others are asleep, if he would catch up with the rest of the world" (115). Knowledge here stands in for both loss and potential: Brown's ignorance, what keeps him up reading after hours, is the price of his twenty lost years, but it is a deficit that can be made up by exemplary effort. Knowledge, he insists, cannot be inherited, unlike property, which he mentions, or enslavement, which he does not; it is, therefore, a potential equalizer, like the masculine, democratic anonymity he attributes to the British Library. Anyone "who would be useful in his day and generation" must, he writes, "be up and doing" in the pursuit of knowledge (115). Brown's cultured tourism, these passages suggest, weds social usefulness to the energetic self-instruction that he claims flourishes in London, at a distance from the exclusions and threats of U.S. racial prejudice.

Brown's immediate "useful[ness]" is put to the test later in the chapter, when he encounters two strangers who solicit his aid. In order to frame these exchanges, Brown first summarizes the financial circumstances that render his subsequent donations extraordinary. Confident that his published autobiography will sell well enough to maintain him, he sends ten pounds to the United

States "for the support of [his] daughters, who are at school there" (117). He soon realizes, however, that he has miscalculated his own needs. Payment for his lodging is due, and his next stop, a public meeting in Worcester where he plans to sell more books, is ninety miles farther from London than he had thought. He finds himself, on a Monday morning, wandering the city with just over three shillings left, out of which he "was to get three dinners" (117). All is made worse by London's autumn weather, which on this day has served up a fog so dreary that what light there is "only serves as a medium for a series of optical illusions" (118). In this state, Brown is first approached by an English "beggar-boy" who "accosted [him] for a half-penny to buy bread" (119). The text notes only that he obliges the child, leaving aside the complications of race and class that such a scene might conjure—that is, of a fugitive from American slavery finding himself solicited as a donor rather than presumed to be a beggar. Immediately after, Brown writes, he encounters "a colored man" who "eyed [him] attentively . . . and seemed anxious to speak." Brown walks on at first but is unable "to resist the temptation to speak with him" and returns (119). The stranger tells of his escape from slavery in Maryland and his arrival in England, where he finds himself destitute, unable "to get employment" because his only work experience is "in the growing of tobacco" (119). Mixing sentiment and self-congratulation, Brown writes that he "was moved to tears" by the story and gives "this poor brother fugitive" half of his remaining money. At this point, Brown relates, the man "burst into tears," exclaiming " 'you are the first friend I have met in London' " (120).

Most immediately, Brown's representation of himself and another man crying together on the streets of London confirms the claim advanced by a number of recent scholars that nineteenth-century American men were far more invested in the culture of sentiment than has often been supposed: bathed in tears of friendship and renewal, these two communicate through the lingua franca of suffering.[67] But while the scene accords with myriad popular representations of sentimental identification between donor and object of aid, such a bond also defies certain of the rules and safeguards that structured conventional benevolence. Most egregiously, Brown does nothing to verify the stranger/supplicant's claim to destitution, allowing his feelings of sympathy to exclude the investigative rationality that charity experts urged. As Brown's history (as represented in his personal narratives) indicates, he was no stranger to deception, having practiced and observed it in many forms, as both a slave and a fugitive. Nevertheless, in contrast to his descriptions of the deceptive fog and the dim city, Brown chooses to accept the transparency of this supplicant. He allows the overwhelming power of sentimental identification, intensified by a (presumably) shared personal history of enslavement, to circumvent the "rational" responses of doubt, caution, and investigation. The pair's status as "brother fugitive[s]" opens up a space for credulity, prompting the donor's regret that he does not have sufficient means to place the other "beyond the reach of want" (120).[68]

This fraternal bond, however, is troubled by the terms and cultural resonances of benevolent exchange. The fact of occupying the position of donor demonstrates (or creates) a certain ascendancy, a distancing of helper from helped, even as the precise moment of exchange and the sympathetic extension that animates it work to unite the two figures. That the supplicant calls Brown his *friend*—in antebellum usage, the word could mean either benefactor or affectionate peer—underscores this dual movement. But even as Brown's donation makes possible a distancing of the benevolent self from the needy fugitive, it also presses for a recognition of the self *as* fugitive, rather than the aspirant to culture presented at the beginning of the chapter, or even the detached, casual donor who responds, moments earlier, to the English boy's plea. This is a moment of uncanny recognition, a "discovery," as Priscilla Wald has written, "that the unfamiliar is really familiar . . . but also that the familiar is unfamiliar."[69] Integral to that discovery is the moment's complex interplay between hierarchy and equivalence, a point to which I will return.

As Brown's subsequent account makes clear, this encounter also, for the moment, forces him to recognize himself as a supplicant.[70] Seemingly stunned by the emotional force of the meeting—and by the irrational behavior, in strict economic terms, that it has prompted—Brown then wanders "from street to street, with the hope that [he] might meet some one who would lend [him] money" (120). This admission is surprising, given Brown's much-vaunted distaste for begging; his use of *lend* rather than *give* hardly diminishes the embarrassment. Ultimately, though, he is rescued without having to beg. A clergyman's son arrives at Brown's hotel, to which he has returned "hungry and fatigued," and gives him money from the sale of some of his books (120, 121). Not only is the aid unsolicited, but it is money Brown has earned through his own writing, though he admits that the young man has sold the books "with more than ordinary zeal . . . for the cause of bleeding humanity" (121). So Brown's dignity and independence are restored soon enough, allowing his encounter with the fugitive to stand as a poignant moment of generosity, one that does no permanent violence to his developing identity as agent rather than object of benevolence. The shame of need is further delimited by its delayed telling. Brown admits in the chapter's final paragraph that he did not disclose to the man who rescued him how desperate his situation had become, relying instead on this published narrative to "discharg[e] in a trifling degree [his] debt of gratitude" (122). His beggar(ed) moment is broadcast only in retrospect, in the form of a memoir in which such exigencies have already been resolved. So while the chapter presents benevolent exchange in a positive, even idealized, light, it nevertheless bears the mark of Brown's discomfort, at least in face-to-face encounters, with any position other than that of agent.

The U.S. edition's final chapter evinces a similar ambivalence, underscoring Brown's refusal to play the kneeling slave from his first edition's cover illustration. After a single sentence describing Ellen Richardson's "redemption of [his] body from slavery," in effect granting him "the privilege of again returning to

[his] native country," Brown elaborates on the generosity of other English abolitionists (304). Most telling is his closing reference to John Bishop Estlin: "To Mr. Estlin I am indebted for many acts of kindness; and now that the broad Atlantic lies between us, and in all probability we shall never again meet on earth, it is with heartfelt gratitude and pleasure that I make this mention of him" (305). Only an ocean's distance can quell Brown's discomfort with a debt of gratitude.

Fugitives and Citizens

To an extent Brown's travel narratives mark his affiliation with what Paul Gilroy has termed the "black Atlantic," a diasporic configuration opposed to the notion that people of African descent in the West can be defined through allegiance to or placement within a single nation, though Brown seems more invested in the United States than in Africa as a site of origin.[71] In both editions he revels in his growing cosmopolitanism, noting in the second that after five years he "had begun to fancy [him]self an Englishman by habit, if not by birth" (303). When the fugitive tells of his desperate straits in London, Brown advises him to relocate not to the northern United States but to the West Indies, where Brown believes the man will be able to find agricultural work similar to what he had done as a slave.[72] And Brown's own trajectory after his London encounter is a continuation of his antislavery work—as well as his acculturating tourism—in England. But the United States remains a critical point of reference: Brown spends much of his time in England advocating, through lectures and in print, the abolition of U.S. slavery, an investment that comes across clearly in his travel narratives, and his act of aiding the fugitive in London recalls an elaborate discourse of responsibility toward the recently enslaved, whose primary locus was across the Atlantic. Moreover, U.S. residents were the first audiences for much of this writing. Most of the letters in the first edition, Brown's preface indicates, "were written for the private perusal of a few personal friends in America," and "some were contributed to *Frederick Douglass' Paper*" (iii). Most tellingly, the United States proves to be a magnetizing force for Brown himself; once he can return safely, he does so.[73]

The personal cost of that return is high, however, as the final chapter of *The American Fugitive in Europe* makes clear. After so many pages detailing his warm reception abroad, Brown focuses here on the trepidation, the "palpitating heart," he experiences at the thought of returning to his *"native land"*: "I seem still to hear the sound of the auctioneer's rough voice, as I stood on the block in the slave-market at St. Louis. I shall never forget the savage grin with which he welcomed a higher bid" (303, 304). But it is not only memories of enslavement that make life in the United States painful. When he arrives in Philadelphia, where "colorphobia is [even] more rampant . . . than in the pro-slavery, negro-hating city of New York," Brown is subjected to a representative indignity: he is barred from riding in an omnibus with his white traveling companions. "As soon as we touch the soil of America," he writes, "we can no longer ride in the same conveyance, no longer eat at the same table, or be regarded with equal justice, by our thin-skinned democracy" (312–13). Brown explains his decision to return in light of such insults: "I might have remained in a country where my manhood was never denied; I might have remained in ease in other climes; but what was ease and comfort abroad, while more than three millions of my countrymen were groaning in the prison-house of slavery in the Southern States?" (314). While his commitment to domestic struggle would waver in the early 1860s, when he briefly advocated Haitian emigration, here he dedicates himself to U.S.-based activism on behalf of the enslaved.

Brown's next move is to link such responsibility to righteous violence: "I came back to the land of my nativity, not to be a spectator, but a soldier . . . in this moral warfare against the most cruel system of oppression that ever blackened the character or hardened the heart of man" (314–15). This militant nationalism resembles the rhetoric of such figures as David Walker and Frederick Douglass who, as Lora Romero claims with regard to Douglass, "offered violence as a threshold for citizenship."[74] But violence alone is insufficient; it must be bound to a kind of benevolent fraternity, with Brown substituting the brother citizens of his homecoming for the brother fugitives of his London encounter. As this trajectory makes clear, Brown's embattled nationality, his citizenship of insistence, is inseparable from and comprehensible through his fraternal benevolence, a concept comprising both horizontal and hierarchical structures. That is, Brown and his "fellow-citizens" are united by their common racial ancestry and by a common if multivalent history of oppression, but some (the free, the literate, the well connected) are positioned to aid, educate, or elevate others (the enslaved, the ignorant, the isolated). In this regard, Brown's schema resembles long-standing structures of benevolent activism among free black Americans, who negotiated commonality and hierarchy in order to promote temperance and other forms of respectable conduct, as well as to rescue and resettle fugitives.[75] Echoed as well are the tenets of duty and sympathy that were central to Prince Hall freemasonry, a key element in the formation of black masculinity and community in the nineteenth century.[76]

The terms of Brown's dutiful return also mirror, at least superficially, the "hierarchized 'sameness'" that Dana Nelson has identified as structuring white men's fraternal bonds. But instead of fueling a tolerance for capitalist competition and an abhorrence of the "unmanaged sameness" of mobs and other threats—the outcomes Nelson cites for analogous white formations—Brown figures this contradiction as that which propels the "moral warfare" itself, with affectionate comradeship animated by dire need.[77] Brown's formulations intersect with, and depart from, the structures of national (white) manhood in other ways, as well. Nelson has argued that a pervasive, melancholic failure—a series of foreclosures—lies at the heart of national manhood's promised bonds. Melville's "brother captains," Amasa Delano and Benito Cereno, exemplify the workings of this failure. "Shadowed," Nelson writes, by an "otherness" that ever threatens retaliatory violence, their fraternal relations "can never be any more than symbolic and conditional enactments of the 'real' thing." They never share the "privileged spot" of warm, confidential brotherhood.[78] Brown's brother fugitives, by contrast, achieve (however briefly) on the streets of London the intense emotional connection that Melville's fictional captains keep missing. This success owes to an important difference in Brown's conception of what fraternity might mean—one that has much to do with how the figures within that imagined fraternity apprehend their relationship to benevolence.

Nelson identifies national manhood as a structure that understands itself to be benevolent. Within its "fraternal logic," she explains, individual white men are posited as able "to stand for the Good of the Whole," each representing and exemplifying an unquestioned collective good.[79] This formulation accords with my claims in the foregoing chapters that notions of benevolence and self-interest coalesced, each reinforcing the other, within the antebellum era's dominant culture(s). Brown's narrative, however, replaces such variously occluded instantiations of self-interest with a declared self-sacrifice. He does not have enough money to give away half, but he does so anyway. He is personally better off in England than in the United States, but still he returns. My point is not that Brown was some kind of secular saint, or that self-sacrifice, especially when so elaborately announced, can ever be free of self-interest. I am claiming, instead, that Brown's representations propose an alternative conception of national/fraternal manhood, one that mobilizes individual self-sacrifice in the interest of collective well-being. In doing so, that revised masculinity challenges the notion that atomized self-interest can stand in for the good of the whole, at least when that whole represents a marginalized and much-abused population. Like Frederick Douglass returning to the United States on a segregated passenger ship and Charlotte Forten returning to her chilly South Carolina classroom, Brown pursues benevolence at a significant personal cost.

Further, Brown's meditations on his benevolent efforts foreground the riskiness of this proposition. The very element that seems to make him the most uncomfortable—the slipperiness of benevolent categories, how easily one can move from agent to object and back again—is precisely what his formulation requires him to accept. The figure who aspires to fraternal benevolence must be open to the possibility of running out of money himself, of wandering around the metropolis looking for a kind face. And he must be willing to return to a place, in this case the antebellum North, where even the more sympathetic members of the dominant culture look on him as a social problem. Benevolent citizenship, for those who, like Brown, are positioned outside of privileged white fraternity, is challenging indeed.

Brown's brother fugitive, legible in the otherwise obscuring London fog, recalls the other figures of need in my preceding chapters: J. D. McKenzie's lurking black man, Child's "everlasting slave," Melville's penny-catching beggar, Forten's restless schoolchildren, and so on. While some of these have a ghostly quality, haunting the conscience of the benevolent speaker, more often antebellum authors represented the needy as alarmingly corporeal. They were sometimes frightening and unbidden, certainly, but far from otherworldly, as evidenced by the era's textual meditations on the bloodied back of the slave or the sunken eyes of the beggar. And though these figures prompted fantasies of removal or amelioration, of a benevolence so successful that it would consume or displace itself, more comfortable Americans were nevertheless arrested by the longevity of need. The biblical maxim that the poor would always be with us seemed to them all too apt.

However much such figures of need struck the benevolent as inconsistent with the nation's best hopes for itself, or with its rosiest representations of what it already was, their ubiquity demonstrated otherwise. Need, exclusion, and attendant forms of reproach were constitutive elements of the national cultural field. Indeed, just as the benevolent were never wholly united in their projects or their representations and never wholly secure in their status, the "helped" were never as silent or tractable as their most controlling benefactors wished. The free-born African Americans and former slaves who speak in this chapter, far from being the quiescent figures of desperation that much mainstream political and reformist discourse conjured, were instead quite energetically talking back, exceeding the categories as well as the regional and national borders set up to contain them. Their representations of sympathetic aid are crucial moments in the cultural history of Americans' good intentions, demonstrating the multiple and shifting roles, identities, and affiliations that antebellum benevolence offered.

The Afterlife of
Benevolent Citizenship

There is no great society which is not a caring society.

> GEORGE W. BUSH, quoted in
> the *New York Times* (21 May 2001)

I'm not sure a bad person can write a good book. If art doesn't make us better, then what on earth is it for?

> ALICE WALKER, quoted in *Ms. Magazine* (June 1982)

The foregoing chapters have defined the antebellum culture of benevolence as a contest over the forms and meanings of moral authority, at the core of which lay a conflict over the character of the nation as well as the "conditions and prospects," to use a common nineteenth-century locution, of its constituent racial groups. Although the bitter debate over slaveholding, among other historical phenomena, shaped and energized that culture, the notion of benevolent citizenship has had a significant afterlife in the contemporary United States, evident in such disparate sites as Hollywood films, presidential politics, the rationales for military interventions (e.g., the "humanitarian bombing" of Kosovo), and the formation and maintenance of literary canons. As my brief examination of this persistence shows, antebellum moral economies continue to inform our national self-fashioning.

At first glance, benevolence now appears to be out of style. Certainly the term is used far less often than in the nineteenth century, appearing primarily in the titles of long-standing mutual aid organizations like the Firemen's and Police Benevolent Associations. Apart from these narrow usages, *benevolence* has come to signify for many a misguided and coercive approach to social activism, one that reifies hierarchies and forestalls fundamental change. But such disavowal is not so distant from the antebellum conversations that this book has reconstructed, in which the suspicion of benevolence was integral to the culture of benevolence itself. Take, for example, Steven Spielberg's 1997 film *Amistad,* which recounts the mutiny, imprisonment, and eventual repatriation of a group of kidnapped and enslaved Africans.[1] Self-consciously rejecting dominant antebellum conceptions of interracial benevolence, the film replaces paternalistic white aid with images of African (and, by extension, African American) agency. In Spielberg's rendering, conventional benevolence is made to seem either sinister or ridiculous: Lewis Tappan, the evangelical Christian and antislavery activist, appears here as a cold strategist who would sacrifice human life for the good of his abstract cause, while the Anglo-Americans who gather to pray and sing in support of the Africans seem ludicrously ineffectual. One captive, through subtitles, asks "why do they look so miserable?" Kneeling outside the Connecticut prison where the Africans are held, these dour do-gooders evoke the captive's bewilderment and mild disdain but do nothing to improve his situation. The film also erases whites' efforts to educate the captives.[2] Rather, in a strange transmutation of the nineteenth century's faith in moral elevation by means of literacy instruction, one of Spielberg's Africans effectively Christianizes himself, deriving the basic tenets of the faith from the illustrations in a Bible that he has taken from one of his Anglo sympathizers. This paean to self-help even has catechism occurring independently.

The film's white heroes, meanwhile, come to the aid of the *Amistad* captives through avenues other than conventional benevolence. The young lawyer Roger Baldwin (played by Matthew McConaughey) starts out as a callow opportunist who sees the Africans only as disputed property. He awakens to an understanding of their humanity through his growing relationship with their leader, Cinque (Djimon Hounsou), whose stirring narrative of struggle serves as the film's dramatic core. Anthony Hopkins's cranky John Quincy Adams treads a similar path, from jaded defeatist to champion of equal rights and justice for the Africans. His speech before the Supreme Court focuses not on benevolence but on judicial independence, Cinque's heroism, and the wisdom of the founding fathers, whose relevance Cinque has taught him to appreciate. Baldwin's and Adams's efforts—among the few useful Anglo-American interventions presented in the film—are geared toward clearing legal obstacles to the Africans' freedom rather than toward improving their character or their habits. Such representations mirror a set of claims advanced in the antebellum black press that insisted on African Americans' ability to shape their destinies in the absence of legalized oppression. But Spielberg's *Amistad* is also an elaborate—to say nothing of expensive—benevolent gesture in its own right, one that owes much to antebellum forms of earnest didacticism. It teaches audiences to abhor slavery, to cherish human dignity, and to foster interracial cooperation with a clarity and affective intensity that Lydia Maria Child and her associates would have applauded. A nation riven by racial prejudice and misunderstanding, the film suggests, might be healed by right-minded (and overtly sentimental) instruction.

In the realm of contemporary politics and public policy, echoes of antebellum benevolence are more straightforward. Though current usage replaces *benevolence* with terms now deemed more congenial—humanitarianism, compassion, social responsibility—there are striking continuities from the nineteenth-century context to our own. A racialized discourse of self-help, much like the interventions analyzed in chapter 3, suffused the welfare reform initiatives of the 1990s, whose advocates posited a needy population debilitated by long-term material aid. Meanwhile, ongoing debates over failing inner-city schools resurrect the language of transformative pedagogy addressed in chapter 4, though that vocabulary is now largely secularized and imbued with a faith in standardized testing that nineteenth-century educators would have found most alien. Nowhere has the language of benevolence been more evident than in George W. Bush's 2000 presidential campaign, with its invocation of "compassionate conservatism" as a counter to charges that Republican party politics had become mean-spirited and dismissive of the poor. Compassionate conservatism, as campaign slogan and ideology, makes a bold claim for the compatibility of benevolence and self-interest, reassuring middle-class voters that care of the needy and fiscal restraint need not, after all, be at odds. Drawing on the work of Marvin Olasky and others, the Bush team put forward, both in the campaign and in early policy initiatives, the notion that a lean, efficient government could aid society's neediest members by fostering "faith-based" social service initiatives that would decrease the nation's reliance on government-sponsored welfare programs.[3] In a move that wedded nineteenth-century models of poor relief to an ongoing investment in proving the moral vigor of the United States, Bush offered religious benevolence as a cornerstone of public policy.

Such varied manifestations of benevolent citizenship have their analogue within literary studies in the search for authors who might serve as exemplars, figures we identify as transcending the prejudices of their time and place, as advocating the forms of inclusion or tolerance that resemble and seem to prefigure currently held beliefs. Wanting to be good people—*a good people*—and wanting our canonized authors to espouse good values, however contentious the attendant processes of definition may be, are interlocking forms of benevolent citizenship.[4] Literary figures are presented, especially to students, as representatives of the best that our national tradition has to offer, a superlative status that blends the aesthetic and the moral into a single inspiring icon. Antebellum authors occupy a prominent place in this schema; the project of reconstituting or recovering them as activists suffuses both scholarly interventions and pedagogical practices, belying the suspicion of moral earnestness that otherwise seems to prevail in the academy. Scholars' counterbalancing critiques operate within this matrix as well, excavating and analyzing these authors' shortcomings, their failure to live up to our ideals. Several of the figures on whom this book has focused have proven especially evocative of such claims and counterclaims. Perhaps most sensational has been the controversy over Herman Melville's private character—specifically, his treatment of his wife, Elizabeth Shaw Melville. Although the possibility of spousal abuse (emotional and perhaps physical) was raised in 1975, with the publication of previously unknown family letters, the matter took on new life following the appearance of Elizabeth Renker's provocatively titled article "Herman Melville, Wife Beating, and the Written Page" and her later book *Strike through the Mask.*[5] Renker notes the coded language in Elizabeth Melville's letters that might have signified literal battering (her reference to " 'ill treat[ment]' " and her resolution to face " 'whatever further trial may be before me' ") but admits that corroborating evidence is "largely anecdotal." She is on more solid ground in advancing the general claim that the Melvilles had a deeply conflicted and unhappy marriage, an assertion supported by ample evidence from family letters.[6] Ultimately, Renker's reconstruction of Herman Melville's unsavory domestic presence serves a larger argument about his relationship to his manuscripts and to the writing process, one that makes no attempt to undermine his position as an important author. Nevertheless, many read this inquiry into Melville's character as an attack on his canonical status, and some launched counterattacks against Renker herself.[7] To protect Melville's position as great writer, it seemed imperative to deny that he might have been a particularly bad husband.

Inquiries into the moral authority of antebellum authors have more often addressed their racial politics—in particular, their positions with regard to slavery and racial equality. At its most strident, the policing of authorial reputation in this context becomes a way of canonizing benevolent whiteness alongside the particular authors selected as its exemplars. But even more balanced claims betray a marked investment in the moral character of literary figures, as recent scholarship on Emerson and the antislavery movement shows. Against the charge that Emerson's endorsement of abolition was both tepid and relatively late, Len Gougeon and others have researched and foregrounded the antislavery elements of his life and writings, recuperating him as a socially engaged, principled figure rather than (or in addition to) the callous genius of "Self-Reliance."[8] More troubling than Emerson's tardy embrace of abolition has been Melville's ambivalent representation of slavery and rebellion in "Benito Cereno." Some scholars have made a forceful case for the story's abolitionist and antiracist sympathies, reading it as an anatomy of naïve white racism, the regime of which is ultimately overturned by the revelation of the brilliant strategy and targeted violence of the *San Dominick*'s pseudoslaves.[9] But for many readers, this reversal is undercut by the story's final reimposition of whites' legally sanctioned power: Melville's closing image of a silenced and decapitated African hardly makes an unequivocal abolitionist statement. Yet the *Heath Anthology,* widely assigned in American literature survey courses, includes Carolyn Karcher's long biographical introduction to Melville, which lays out her case for the author's antiracist commitments and which, no doubt, shapes students' readings of the subsequent selections. Within this frame, Melville is not only a great author but also a great critic of racial injustice, put in the service of a national pedagogy of benevolence.

This intersection of character and canonicity is by no means the exclusive province of white authors. Indeed, African American authors (and not only those from the nineteenth century) have been held to an especially high standard in this regard, expected to serve as role models for black students and as moral exemplars for all.[10] Frederick Douglass's legacy demonstrates some of the complications that these demands can engender. Douglass's canonization, his positioning as the representative black man of his generation, has been based not only on his rhetorical sophistication, which seems indisputable, but also on the more contestable ground of his politics. Specifically, Douglass's long-standing commitment to interracial cooperation, his rejection of various emigrationist plans, and his investment in the notion that Americans should strive to "transcend race" have made him an especially attractive figure for liberal, integrationist academics. As Robert Levine has argued persuasively, this appeal differentiates him from a figure like Martin Delany, whose reification as a black separatist has made him less palatable to those same canonizing figures and institutions.[11] Nevertheless, Douglass's personal life and his racial politics have provoked controversy among academics and other readers: Was this "representative black man" sufficiently immersed in African American culture, particularly in his later years when he married a white woman and enjoyed a level of material comfort that set him apart from many black Americans of his day? Was he adequately loyal to the black communities of his youth and adulthood? And was his public support of women's rights reinforced by ethical treatment of the women in his personal life and in his narratives?[12] Despite the authenticity that his direct experience of slavery granted and the activist credentials that his years of authorship and public agitation would seem to guarantee, Douglass has (at least for some readers) come to seem less heroic than his mainstream reputation would suggest.

That the antebellum culture of benevolence still resonates in literary studies is made most obvious in scholarly and pedagogical treatments of Harriet Beecher Stowe. Although Stowe's most widely read texts make her antislavery stance abundantly clear, her racial representations, as well as her short-lived advocacy of Liberian colonization, have set the stage for protracted moral and political controversies. Stowe's relatively recent canonization rested to a large extent on the claim that her texts espouse a progressive politics.[13] But the late 1980s and 1990s saw a backlash against certain of the ideological and racial projects in which she (and other sentimental authors) participated, in particular her representation of "pure" African quiescence in the character of Uncle Tom and her expulsion of the novel's more "vigorous" mixed-race characters from North America.[14] The critical conversation I am invoking is not as starkly divided as this sketch might suggest. Indeed, much of the scholarship highlighting Stowe's politics has attended closely to the ambivalence her antislavery fiction engenders. Nevertheless, it continues to matter how "good" Stowe's politics were, and not only because her most famous novel is so explicitly and passionately activist. Stowe has come to represent—within the academy and specifically within its classrooms—earnest, middle-class white activism. In the process, she has proven to be a troubling icon: both an honored foremother and a specter of good intentions gone awry.

This paradox is emblematic. More than any other literary figure, Stowe stands in for antebellum U.S. culture's racial antinomies, which compel our retrospective attention even as they continue to resonate within and beyond the academy.[15] The tensions that her work distills, though articulated and played out differently in the current context, have yet to be resolved. But if, as I am claiming, Stowe and her contemporaries are crucial to understanding the intersections of race, violence, and benevolence that have shaped U.S. culture and politics, we must develop scholarly and pedagogical practices that confront their moral ambiguity. Taking seriously the good intentions of historical actors who offend current standards of racial sensitivity (or, in Douglass's case, racial solidarity) offers such a method, a way of escaping the unproductive binary choice of recrimination or hagiography.

Despite its critical excavations, *The Grammar of Good Intentions* should not be read as a general condemnation of Americans' moral earnestness. Benevolent citizenship, however disturbing its manifestations, may yet prove useful, if the conversations it engenders can be made to acknowledge the subjectivity and agency of the needy and the power relations that structure well-intentioned acts. Such a reclamation requires close attention to the history of our national rhetorics of social responsibility. In particular, it compels us to examine the racialized constructions of human potential and human suffering that have persisted in U.S. culture and to identify and protest the subtle collapse of personal and group advantage into conceptions of the general good. I have offered such an inquiry here, one whose aim has been to disentangle sincerity from innocence. In the absence of that reassuring conflation, our goodwill may do less harm.

Notes

Introduction. Toward a Cultural History of Good Intentions

1. *Report of the Committee of Merchants for the Relief of Colored People, Suffering from the Late Riots in the City of New York* (New York: George A. Whitehorne, 1863), 36.

2. Ibid.

3. Qtd. in Deborah Pickman Clifford, *Crusader for Freedom: A Life of Lydia Maria Child* (Boston: Beacon, 1992), 260. Child included this assertion in a letter to Sarah Shaw (mother of Robert Gould Shaw, who led the Massachusetts Fifty-fourth regiment in the Civil War).

4. As I discuss in chapter 2, the overwhelming majority of white reformers and charity agents whose writings were published in the antebellum period were Anglo-American; therefore, in reference to such groups, I use the two designations interchangeably.

5. *An Address to the Executive Committee of Merchants for the Relief of Colored People,* included in *Report of the Committee of Merchants,* 34.

6. Harriet A. Jacobs, *Incidents in the Life of a Slave Girl,* ed. Jean Fagan Yellin (1861; Cambridge: Harvard University Press, 1987), 199, 201.

7. Historians concerned with the class dynamics of nineteenth-century benevolence have devoted a great deal of attention to the social control thesis, which holds that benevolent projects were primarily attempts on the part of middle-class and elite Americans to regulate the behavior of the poor and to defuse social unrest. For brief overviews, see John Stauffer, "Beyond Social Control: The Example of Gerrit Smith, Romantic Radical," *ATQ* 11 (1997): 233–37, and Gregory Eiselein, *Literature and Humanitarian Reform in the Civil War Era* (Bloomington: Indiana University Press, 1996), 11–13. See also Lois Banner, "Religious Benevolence as Social Control: A Critique of an Interpretation," *Journal of American History* 60 (1973): 23–41. Although social control arguments can seem simplistic, the best of them are grounded in nineteenth-century Americans' perceptions that they were engaged in much-needed projects of influence and uplift. The danger, to my mind, is that historical actors' efforts to reshape the needy in their own image are too often presumed to betray a fundamental disingenuousness.

8. "The politics of respectability," to borrow Evelyn Brooks Higginbotham's phrase, preoccupied free African Americans at least as much as did the related concept of benevolence (*Righteous Discontent: The Women's Movement in the Black Baptist Church, 1880–1920* [Cambridge: Harvard University Press, 1993], 186). See Eddie S. Glaude, *Exodus! Religion, Race, and Nation in Early Nineteenth-Century Black America* (Chicago: University of Chicago Press, 2000), 118–25, and Patrick Rael, *Black Identity and Black Protest in the Antebellum North* (Chapel Hill: University of North Carolina Press, 2002), 157–208.

9. Karen Sánchez-Eppler examines the complications of such appropriative rhetoric in *Touching Liberty: Abolition, Feminism, and the Politics of the Body* (Berkeley: University of California Press, 1993), 14–49.

10. Rosemarie Garland Thomson notes a similar confluence of benevolence and light/whiteness/elevation in Stowe's descriptions of Eva St. Clare (*Extraordinary Bodies: Figuring Physical Disability in American Culture and Literature* [New York: Columbia University Press, 1997], 90–91).

11. On this point I disagree with Christopher Castiglia, who represents benevolence as a ruse or stratagem of the (relatively) privileged. He writes, for example, that "the emergence of a white

national public from educational and religious discourse had the effect . . . of presenting white self-interest as liberal benevolence in ways that have made whiteness not only unmarked but, in its position on the moral high ground, unassailable" ("Pedagogical Discipline and the Creation of White Citizenship: John Witherspoon, Robert Finley, and the Colonization Society," *Early American Literature* 33 [1998]: 194). In my view, white self-interest does not masquerade as liberal benevolence so much as each element shapes and reinforces the other.

12. Toni Morrison, *Playing in the Dark: Whiteness and the Literary Imagination* (Cambridge: Harvard University Press, 1992), 6; see also 4–28.

13. David Roediger, *The Wages of Whiteness: Race and the Making of the American Working Class,* rev. ed. (London: Verso, 1999), 13.

14. On the qualities associated with Anglo ancestry, see Reginald Horsman, *Race and Manifest Destiny: The Origins of American Racial Anglo-Saxonism* (Cambridge: Harvard University Press, 1981).

15. *Twenty-First Report of the Board of Directors of the American Society for Meliorating the Condition of the Jews, Presented at Their Annual Meeting, May 7, 1844* (New York: American Society for Meliorating the Condition of the Jews, 1844), 29.

16. Jeremiah Evarts, *Cherokee Removal: The "William Penn" Essays and Other Writings,* ed. Francis Paul Prucha (Knoxville: University of Tennessee Press, 1981), 49; George B. Cheever, "An Article in the North American Review on the Removal of the Indians. The Letters of William Penn," *American Monthly Magazine* (Boston), January 1830, 704.

17. Frederick Douglass, "What to the Slave Is the Fourth of July? An Address Delivered in Rochester, New York, on 5 July 1852," in *Frederick Douglass Papers,* ser. 1, *Speeches, Debates, and Interviews,* vol. 2, *1847–54,* ed. John W. Blassingame et al. (New Haven: Yale University Press, 1982), 368, 367; Elizabeth Margaret Chandler, *The Poetical Works of Elizabeth Margaret Chandler: With a Memoir of Her Life and Character, by Benjamin Lundy* (Philadelphia: Lemuel Howell, 1836), 64.

18. Linda Kerber, *No Constitutional Right to Be Ladies: Women and the Obligations of Citizenship* (New York: Hill and Wang, 1998), xxi–xxiv.

19. Castiglia identifies an intriguing variation on benevolent citizenship in the rhetoric of white abolitionists like William Lloyd Garrison, who "enshrined [citizenship] as the highest goal black Americans could attain" but rejected conventional affiliation with the state for himself. His citizenship, Castiglia writes, was conceived as "a purely personal . . . phenomenon consistent both with the affective register of sympathy and his conscientious anti-institutionalism" ("Abolition's Racial Interiors and the Making of White Civic Depth," *American Literary History* 14 [2002]: 39).

20. Rogers Smith, *Civic Ideals: Conflicting Visions of Citizenship in U.S. History* (New Haven: Yale University Press, 1997), 14–15.

21. See especially Mary P. Ryan, *Cradle of the Middle Class: The Family in Oneida County, New York, 1790–1865* (Cambridge: Cambridge University Press, 1981); Nancy Hewitt, *Women's Activism and Social Change: Rochester, New York, 1822–1872* (Ithaca: Cornell University Press, 1984); Anne M. Boylan, "Women in Groups: An Analysis of Women's Benevolent Organizations in New York and Boston, 1797–1840," *Journal of American History* 71 (1984): 497–523; and Lori D. Ginzberg, *Women and the Work of Benevolence: Morality, Politics, and Class in the Nineteenth-Century United States* (New Haven: Yale University Press, 1990).

22. Matthew Frye Jacobson, *Whiteness of a Different Color: European Immigrants and the Alchemy of Race* (Cambridge: Harvard University Press, 1998), 28.

23. Railing against those who sought black male suffrage before woman suffrage, the author of a piece titled "Who Are Our Friends?" wrote: "What an insult to the women who have labored thirty years for the emancipation of the slave, now when he is their political equal, to propose to lift him above their heads" (*Revolution* [New York], 15 January 1868, 24). Benevolent credentials here compete with racial prejudice in the appeal for voting rights.

24. Along similar lines, Russ Castronovo has argued that "efforts to liberate freedom from context" and, I would add, citizenship from intersubjectivity, have worked to "eviscerate the possible plenitude of citizenship by making freedom the property of a disembodied and historically impoverished subject" (*Necro Citizenship: Death, Eroticism, and the Public Sphere in the Nineteenth-Century United States* [Durham, N.C.: Duke University Press, 2001], 27).

25. Paul Gutjahr notes that one of the American Bible Society's premises was that "the widest distribution of the Bible was the best way to insure religious and civil well-being" (*An American Bible: A History of the Good Book in the United States, 1777–1880* [Stanford: Stanford University Press, 1999], 19).

26. Charles I. Foster, *An Errand of Mercy: The Evangelical United Front, 1790–1837* (Chapel Hill: University of North Carolina Press, 1960); Paul Boyer, *Urban Masses and Moral Order in America: 1820–1920* (Cambridge: Harvard University Press, 1978), 85–86. On religion and antebellum reform, see Robert H. Abzug, *Cosmos Crumbling: American Reform and the Religious Imagination* (New York: Oxford University Press, 1994). Catholics used the language of benevolence as well, though a detailed treatment of their interventions lies beyond the scope of this study. See Eric C. Schneider, *In the Web of Class: Delinquents and Reformers in Boston, 1810s–1930s* (New York: New York University Press, 1992); Peter C. Holloran, *Boston's Wayward Children: Social Services for Homeless Children, 1830–1930* (Rutherford, N.J.: Fairleigh Dickinson University Press, 1989); and Thomas H. O'Connor, *Fitzpatrick's Boston, 1846–1866: John Bernard Fitzpatrick, Third Bishop of Boston* (Boston: Northeastern University Press, 1984).

27. David Morgan, *Protestants and Pictures: Religion, Visual Culture, and the Age of American Mass Production* (New York: Oxford University Press, 1999), 44.

28. Gayatri Spivak, *The Postcolonial Critic: Interviews, Strategies, Dialogues*, ed. Sarah Harasym (New York: Routledge, 1990), 160.

29. Boylan, "Women in Groups," 502.

30. Douglass, "Fourth of July," 377; Frederick Douglass, *My Bondage and My Freedom* (New York: Miller, Orton, and Mulligan, 1855), iii. Traces of Boylan's conservative-to-progressive schema appear in Caroline Healey Dall's criticism of "so-called benevolent societies," whose members, she claims, compete unfairly with poor women in the sewing trades. But Dall's use of the modifier "so-called" suggests an investment in a better benevolence, one that these organizations have failed to achieve (*"Woman's Right to Labor," or, Low Wages and Hard Work: In Three Lectures, Delivered in Boston, November, 1859* [Boston: Walker, Wise, 1860], 10).

31. Raymond Williams, *Keywords: A Vocabulary of Culture and Society* (New York: Oxford University Press, 1976), 15.

32. Henry L. Pinckney, *An Address Delivered before the Methodist Benevolent Society, at Their Anniversary Meeting, in the Methodist Protestant Church, in Wentworth-Street, on the 1st Monday in July, 1835* (Charleston, S.C.: E. J. Van Brunt, 1835), 3.

33. *Constitution of the Anti-Bell-Ringing Society* (Boston: Henry P. Lewis, 1839), 1; "Editor's Table," *Harper's New Monthly Magazine*, September 1853, 553.

34. Conrad Edick Wright, *The Transformation of Charity in Postrevolutionary New England* (Boston: Northeastern University Press, 1992), 7. For a late usage of this distinction, see Lorenzo White, *The Great Question; or, How Shall I Meet the Claims of God upon My Property*, in *Systematic Beneficence. Three Prize Essays. The Great Reform, by Abel Stevens. The Great Question, by Lorenzo White. Property Consecrated, by Benjamin St. James Fry* (New York: Carlton and Phillips, 1856). The term *beneficence* was less commonly used by midcentury.

35. Noah Webster, *An American Dictionary of the English Language* (New York: S. Converse, 1828), s.v. "benevolence."

36. Bruce Dorsey, *Reforming Men and Women: Gender in the Antebellum City* (Ithaca: Cornell University Press, 2002), 31.

37. John Brazer, *The Duty and Privilege of an Active Benevolence. Address, Delivered before the Seamen's Widow and Orphan Association, on Christmas Evening, 1835, in the Tabernacle Church, Salem, Mass.* (Salem: Essex Register Office, 1836), 6; italics in original.

38. Andrew P. Peabody, *Excuses for the Neglect of Benevolent Efforts Considered* (Boston: Charles Bowen, 1834), 4.

39. *The Friend. An Essay to Do Good: or, Relief from the Pressure. Addressed to the Wise, the Prudent, and the Liberal, among the Wealthy Classes of New-York* (New York: E. B. Clayton, 1837), 5.

40. *To the Christian Public. The Following is an Extract from a Sermon Delivered by Rev. Mr. Hutton, Colleague to Rev. Dr. Matthews, of New-York, on Occasion of Taking a Collection for Miss Misca* (New York[?]: n.p., 1836), 3, 1.

41. Ronald J. Zboray examines these phenomena in *A Fictive People: Antebellum Economic Development and the American Reading Public* (New York: Oxford University Press, 1993).

42. See David Paul Nord, *The Evangelical Origins of Mass Media in America, 1815–1835,* Journalism Monographs, no. 88 (Columbia, S.C.: Association for Education in Journalism and Mass Communication, 1984) and Gutjahr, *American Bible,* 9–37. On the American Tract Society's use of visual images, see Morgan, *Protestants and Pictures,* 43–120.

43. Lydia H. Sigourney, *The Girl's Reading-Book, in Prose and Poetry. For Schools,* 15th ed. (Newburgh, N.Y.: Proudfit and Banks, 1847), 62.

44. Hannah Townsend, *The Anti-Slavery Alphabet* (Philadelphia: Merrihew and Thompson, 1846), 4.

45. John Winthrop, *A Modell of Christian Charity,* in *Winthrop Papers,* vol. 2, *1623–1630* (Boston: Massachusetts Historical Society, 1931), 295.

46. David Cressy, for example, writes that "the colonists referred to themselves as 'the English.' . . . It was to England that they looked for their history, their cultural lifeline, and for many of their future expectations. It seems to me more appropriate to consider seventeenth-century New England as an outlier of the old country, as a detached English province, than as the seed-bed of a new nation" (*Coming Over: Migration and Communication between England and New England in the Seventeenth Century* [Cambridge: Cambridge University Press, 1987], viii).

47. Alexis de Tocqueville, *Democracy in America,* trans. George Lawrence, ed. J.P. Mayer and Max Lerner (New York: Harper and Row, 1966), 484; Charles Dickens, *American Notes and Pictures from Italy* (New York: Oxford University Press, 1997), 25 (*American Notes* was originally published in 1842 under the title *American Notes for General Circulation*). For comments on the cruelty of Americans, see Dickens's chapter on slavery in *American Notes* (228–43).

48. Qtd. in Joseph A. Conforti, *Jonathan Edwards, Religious Tradition, and American Culture* (Chapel Hill: University of North Carolina Press, 1995), 75.

49. Ibid., 76–78.

50. Joseph A. Conforti, *Samuel Hopkins and the New Divinity Movement: Calvinism, the Congregational Ministry, and Reform in New England between the Great Awakenings* (Grand Rapids, Mich.: Eerdmans, 1981), 117–18. See also Elizabeth Clark, " 'The Sacred Rights of the Weak': Pain, Sympathy, and the Culture of Individual Rights in Antebellum America," *Journal of American History* 82 (1995): 471–73. Antebellum commentators often asserted that humans should, in their charitable efforts, imitate God's benevolence toward human beings. See, for example, *The Benevolence of God,* whose anonymous author claims that God's love "ought to become a subject of *devout imitation*" ([New York: American Tract Society, n.d.], 9). According to the catalog of the Library Company of Philadelphia, this tract was published between 1833 and 1841.

51. Qtd. in John Saillant, "Slavery and Divine Providence in New England Calvinism: The New Divinity and a Black Protest, 1775–1805," *New England Quarterly* 68 (1995): 590.

52. Karen Halttunen, "Humanitarianism and the Pornography of Pain in Anglo-American Culture," *American Historical Review* 100 (1995): 303.

53. On the eighteenth-century backlash against sensibility, see ibid., 308–9, and Janet Todd, *Sensibility: An Introduction* (London: Methuen, 1986), 129–46.

54. Benevolent discourse has a demonstrably transatlantic history as well. Americans who took up benevolent themes often read, quoted from, and argued against English and continental authors; English and American antislavery organizations cooperated and communicated; and Europeans commented extensively on American benevolent structures. Transatlantic antagonisms developed as well, in that Americans often felt themselves judged by or in competition with the English, while proslavery southerners cited England's social welfare failures as evidence of its hypocrisy.

55. Of the 158 benevolent and reformist organizations listed in Charles Foster's appendix, 105 were founded between 1810 and 1829. Among these are such influential organizations as the American Sunday-School Union, the American Tract Society, and the American Board of Commissioners for Foreign Missions (*Errand of Mercy,* 275–79).

56. Sources on benevolent associations among free African Americans include Anne M. Boylan, "Benevolence and Antislavery Activity among African American Women in New York and

Boston, 1820–1840," in *The Abolitionist Sisterhood: Women's Political Culture in Antebellum America*, ed. Jean Fagan Yellin and John C. Van Horne (Ithaca: Cornell University Press, 1994), 119–37; Leonard P. Curry, *The Free Black in Urban America, 1800–1850: The Shadow of the Dream* (Chicago: University of Chicago Press, 1981), 196–215; Robert L. Harris, Jr., "Early Black Benevolent Societies, 1780–1830," *Massachusetts Review* 20 (1979): 603–25; James Oliver Horton and Lois E. Horton, *In Hope of Liberty: Culture, Community, and Protest among Northern Free Blacks, 1700–1860* (New York: Oxford University Press, 1997), 125–54; and Julie Winch, *Philadelphia's Black Elite: Activism, Accommodation, and the Struggle for Autonomy, 1787–1848* (Philadelphia: Temple University Press, 1988).

57. John Saillant, "Black, White, and 'The Charitable Blessed': Race and Philanthropy in the American Early Republic," *Essays on Philanthropy*, no. 8 (Indianapolis: Indiana University Center on Philanthropy, 1993), and "The Black Body Erotic and the Republican Body Politic, 1790–1820," in *Sentimental Men: Masculinity and the Politics of Affect in American Culture*, ed. Mary Chapman and Glenn Hendler (Berkeley: University of California Press, 1999), 89–111; Julie Ellison, *Cato's Tears and the Making of Anglo-American Emotion* (Chicago: University of Chicago Press, 1999), 67; Castiglia, "Pedagogical Discipline," 194. See also Saillant's "Slavery and Divine Providence." Julia Stern examines the dynamics and the limits of interracial sympathy in eighteenth-century fiction (*The Plight of Feeling: Sympathy and Dissent in the Early American Novel* [Chicago: University of Chicago Press, 1997], 22–26).

58. While I agree with Saidiya Hartman's claim that emancipation is "less the grand event of liberation than a point of transition between modes of servitude and racial subjection," I maintain that those transitions marked important shifts in Americans' conceptions of interracial benevolence (*Scenes of Subjection: Terror, Slavery, and Self-Making in Nineteenth-Century America* [New York: Oxford University Press, 1997], 6).

59. Marianne Noble, *The Masochistic Pleasures of Sentimental Literature* (Princeton: Princeton University Press, 2000), 66.

60. June Howard, "What Is Sentimentality?" *American Literary History* 11 (1999): 73.

61. Historians have paid a great deal more attention to American benevolence than have literature scholars. Exceptions include Eiselein, *Literature and Humanitarian Reform*, and a special issue of *ATQ* titled *Philanthropy in Nineteenth-Century America*, edited by Barbara J. Sáez (11 [1997]).

62. Adam Smith, *The Theory of Moral Sentiments* (1759; New York: Augustus M. Kelley, 1966), 3–4. For more detailed treatments of Smith and sentimentalism, see Lori Merish, *Sentimental Materialism: Gender, Commodity Culture, and Nineteenth-Century American Literature* (Durham, N.C.: Duke University Press, 2000), esp. 48–57, and Elizabeth Barnes, *States of Sympathy: Seduction and Democracy in the American Novel* (New York: Columbia University Press, 1997), 20–22, 33–36, 38–39.

63. Glenn Hendler, *Public Sentiments: Structures of Feeling in Nineteenth-Century American Literature* (Chapel Hill: University of North Carolina Press, 2001), 7–8.

64. I use *abjection* here and elsewhere to mean an extreme state of desperation or disadvantage, a definition with which antebellum Americans would have been familiar. See, for example, David Walker's claim that "we, (coloured people of these United States,) are the most degraded, wretched, and abject set of beings that ever lived since the world began" (*David Walker's Appeal to the Coloured Citizens of the World*, ed. Peter P. Hinks [1829; University Park: Pennsylvania State University Press, 2000], 3). I do not wish to engage the specific meaning of *abjection* within psychoanalytic criticism.

65. By this point, the use of a grid to organize space was well established in New York City. David Henkin points out that "in 1811 . . . a commission appointed by the state legislature to lay out new streets . . . established a uniform rectilinear grid for organizing all future development on the island" (*City Reading: Written Words and Public Spaces in Antebellum New York* [New York: Columbia University Press, 1998], 35).

66. Lydia Maria Child, *Letters from New-York* (New York: Charles S. Francis; Boston: James Munroe, 1843), 85.

67. Important reconsiderations of separate spheres include *No More Separate Spheres!* a special issue of *American Literature*, edited by Cathy N. Davidson (70 [1998]), and *America the Fem-*

inine, a special issue of *differences,* coedited by Philip Gould and Leonard Tennenhouse (11, no. 3 [1999]). On sentimentalism and masculinity, see especially Ellison, *Cato's Tears;* Chapman and Hendler, eds., *Sentimental Men;* and Mary Louise Kete, *Sentimental Collaborations: Mourning and Middle-Class Identity in Nineteenth-Century America* (Durham, N.C.: Duke University Press, 2000).

68. Dorsey's *Reforming Men and Women* provides an excellent analysis of gender within the culture of benevolence.

69. Jane Tompkins, *Sensational Designs: The Cultural Work of American Fiction, 1790–1860* (New York: Oxford University Press, 1985), 10–23.

70. Henry David Thoreau, *Walden,* ed. J. Lyndon Shanley (1854; Princeton: Princeton University Press, 1971), 74.

71. *Condition of the American Colored Population, and of the Colony at Liberia* (Boston: Peirce and Parker, 1833), 24.

72. This is not to say that the language of benevolence dominated all nineteenth century texts. For example, fears of insurrection and denials of black humanity, rather than a language of care-taking, animated much proslavery discourse.

73. Paul Lewis, " 'Lectures or a Little Charity': Poor Visits in Antebellum Literature and Culture," *New England Quarterly* 73 (2000): 265–66. This reading, while astute in its alignment of Thoreau's discussion with the conventions of charity writing, recapitulates academic authors' timeworn disdain for the antebellum culture of benevolence. Lewis remarks, for example, that Thoreau enters this home "as a finger-wagging messenger" (266).

74. Thoreau, *Walden,* 74, 205, 76, 74–79.

75. Like many studies of antebellum culture, mine draws heavily on works published in the Northeast, though I have included a number of texts by southerners (some published in the South, some not) as well as works published in what is now the Midwest.

76. For an elaboration of the latter position, see Marvin Olasky, *The Tragedy of American Compassion* (Washington, D.C.: Regnery Gateway, 1992).

Chapter 1. Benevolent Violence

1. Robert Montgomery Bird, *Nick of the Woods; or, The Jibbenainosay. A Tale of Kentucky,* ed. Curtis Dahl (New Haven: College and University Press Services, 1967), 234.

2. Ibid., 123.

3. Jeremiah Evarts, *Cherokee Removal: The "William Penn" Essays and Other Writings,* ed. Francis Paul Prucha (Knoxville: University of Tennessee Press, 1981), 96–97. George Cheever's response to Lewis Cass made a similar point. He wrote that, although Cass's arguments were phrased so that some would see "nothing but benevolence" in their "spirit," they in fact served only to promote the view that *"power makes right,* and that we may lawfully *do evil that good may come"* ("An Article in the North American Review on the Removal of the Indians. The Letters of William Penn," *American Monthly Magazine,* January 1830, 705–6).

4. Mary Hershberger's work on antiremoval activism is a case in point. Although she mentions both Isaac McCoy and Thomas McKenney, my representatives of "benevolent re-movalist" sentiment, she nevertheless argues that "the benevolent community" thoroughly opposed removal by 1830 ("Mobilizing Women, Anticipating Abolition: The Struggle against Indian Removal in the 1830s," *Journal of American History* 86 [1999]: 20). Antebellum America's "benevolent community" was far more complex and divisive than this formulation suggests.

5. According to Herman Viola, McKenney claimed, despite his military service, to have "re-mained a Quaker" as an adult, "in spirit if not in dress or demeanor" (*Thomas L. McKenney: Architect of America's Early Indian Policy, 1816–1830* [Chicago: Sage, 1974], 3).

6. Thomas L. McKenney to Jeremiah Evarts, 1 May 1829, rpt. in *Documents and Proceedings Relating to the Formation and Progress of a Board in the City of New York, for the Emigration, Preservation, and Improvement, of the Aborigines of America* (New York: Vanderpool and Cole, 1829), 19.

7. Hershberger notes that Georgia legislators, following Jackson's 1828 election, "forbade

Cherokee gold mining, nullified all Cherokee laws, and prohibited Indians from testifying against whites in court" ("Mobilizing Women," 21).

8. Susan Scheckel, *The Insistence of the Indian: Race and Nationalism in Nineteenth-Century American Culture* (Princeton: Princeton University Press, 1998), 4.

9. The Boston-based American Board of Commissioners for Foreign Missions initially opposed removal but, by 1833, was advising the Cherokees to emigrate. Some individual missionaries, however, continued to encourage natives' resistance. See William G. McLoughlin, *Cherokees and Missionaries, 1789–1839* (New Haven: Yale University Press, 1984), 299.

10. McCoy asserted that the government's sponsorship of removal simply "to make room for white settlements" was an "unjust policy" (*History of the Baptist Indian Missions,* ed. Robert F. Berkhofer, Jr. [1840; New York: Johnson Reprint, 1970], 326). According to George A. Schultz, support for removal was widespread, though hardly universal, among Baptists (*An Indian Canaan: Isaac McCoy and the Vision of an Indian State* [Norman: University of Oklahoma Press, 1972], 131). Hershberger, in contrast, argues that McCoy was something of an outlier among Baptists, at least those in the North ("Mobilizing Women," 30). Although McCoy ceased direct missionary work in 1824, turning his attention primarily to political lobbying, the Baptist Board did not officially dismiss him until 1842 ("Isaac McCoy," in *American National Biography,* ed. John A. Garraty and Mark C. Carnes [New York: Oxford University Press, 1999], 14: 931–32).

11. William Stanton, *The Leopard's Spots: Scientific Attitudes toward Race in America, 1815–59* (Chicago: University of Chicago Press, 1960), 1–44.

12. Matthew Frye Jacobson, *Whiteness of a Different Color: European Immigrants and the Alchemy of Race* (Cambridge: Harvard University Press, 1998), 31.

13. The rise of scientific racism in the early-nineteenth-century United States has been widely discussed. See, for example, Stanton, *Leopard's Spots;* Stephen Jay Gould, *The Mismeasure of Man* (New York: Norton, 1981); and Dana Nelson, *National Manhood: Capitalist Citizenship and the Imagined Fraternity of White Men* (Durham, N.C.: Duke University Press, 1998), 102–34. Reginald Horsman argues that "the scientific attack on the Indian as inferior and expendable . . . burgeoned from 1830 to 1850" (*Race and Manifest Destiny: The Origins of American Racial Anglo-Saxonism* [Cambridge: Harvard University Press, 1981], 191).

14. McCoy, *History of the Baptist Indian Missions,* 21.

15. The degree to which white missionaries influenced the management and content of the *Cherokee Phoenix* was a matter of some dispute. In response to the accusation that Samuel Worcester, a missionary sponsored by the American Board of Commissioners for Foreign Missions, was actually the editor, Boudinot replied that the paper "has never been, nor was it ever intended to be, under the influence of any Missionary or White man" (qtd. in Theda Perdue, ed., *Cherokee Editor: The Writings of Elias Boudinot* [Knoxville: University of Tennessee Press, 1983], 19).

16. I allude here to bell hooks's *Talking Back: Thinking Feminist, Thinking Black* (Boston: South End, 1989).

17. For analyses of McKenney's life and career, see Richard Drinnon, *Facing West: The Metaphysics of Indian-Hating and Empire-Building* (Minneapolis: University of Minnesota Press, 1980), 165–90, and Viola, *Thomas L. McKenney.*

18. See, for example, "Secretary of War Eaton on Cherokee Removal," in *Documents of United States Indian Policy,* ed. Francis Paul Prucha, 2d ed. (Lincoln: University of Nebraska Press, 1990), 44–47, and Andrew Jackson, "First Annual Message," in *A Compilation of the Messages and Papers of the Presidents, 1789–1897,* vol. 2, comp. James D. Richardson (Washington, D.C.: U.S. Government Printing Office, 1896), 456–59. Although Alabama was involved in similar conflicts over land and sovereignty, I focus primarily on Georgia because it figured more prominently in the national debates.

19. For a detailed discussion of the board's establishment and efforts, see Francis Paul Prucha, "Thomas L. McKenney and the New York Indian Board," *Mississippi Valley Historical Review* 48 (1962): 635–55. Episcopal and Presbyterian churchmen were involved in the organization as well (642).

20. Included in the pamphlet are McKenney's address to the board, several of his letters to board members, and a reprint of his earlier letter to Evarts, as well as the board's constitution and

some of its correspondence. According to Ronald Satz, the federal funds used to support this publication were "originally allocated for Indian education" (*American Indian Policy in the Jacksonian Era* [Lincoln: University of Nebraska Press, 1975], 16).

21. Lewis Cass published a lengthy and favorable review of the compilation, which became the occasion for advancing his own removalist arguments ("Removal of the Indians," *North American Review* [January 1830]: 62–121). See also George Cheever's response to Cass (cited in note 3). Prucha points out that the New York *Evening Post* also published McKenney's long letter to Evarts, included in the board's *Documents and Proceedings* ("Thomas L. McKenney," 648–49).

22. McKenney, "Address," in *Documents and Proceedings*, 38.

23. Ibid.

24. McKenney to Evarts, 1 May 1829, 13–14.

25. McKenney, "Address," 39–40.

26. McKenney to Evarts, 1 May 1829, 14.

27. McKenney, "Address," 41.

28. McKenney to Evarts, 1 May 1829, 13.

29. Ibid., 14.

30. Ibid., 17.

31. Qtd. in Prucha, "Thomas L. McKenney," 648. Lincoln, according to Prucha, was the "secretary of a Baptist missionary association in Boston" (648).

32. Philip Fisher asserts that "the killing of the Indians" is one of the "central hard facts of American history" (*Hard Facts: Setting and Form in the American Novel* [New York: Oxford University Press, 1985], 5).

33. Lewis Cass reiterated these guarantees: "There are two restraints upon ourselves, which we may safely adopt,—that no force should be used to divest them [the Indians] of any just interest they possess, and that they should be liberally remunerated for all they may cede. We cannot be wrong while we adhere to there [*sic*] rules" ("Removal of the Indians," 76).

34. *Memorial of the Indian Board for the Emigration, Preservation, and Improvement, of the Aborigines of America*, 21st Cong., 1st sess., 22 February 1830, H. Rept. 233, serial 200, 2. The board also wrote of its commitment to educating and Christianizing the Indians once they relocated in the West, for which it asked Congress to provide support (2–3), but it disbanded before any such projects could be carried out.

35. McKenney, "Address," 36, 37, 42.

36. McKenney to Evarts, 1 May 1829, 14.

37. Ibid., 18.

38. See Benedict Anderson, *Imagined Communities: Reflections on the Origin and Spread of Nationalism* (London: Verso, 1991). While McKenney's imagined community was not the entire nation, it did rely on a set of shared goals and allegiances, mediated through print, among individuals who in most cases did not literally know one another.

39. Michael Rogin makes a similar claim with respect to the rhetoric that the federal government used in its negotiations with the Seminoles in the 1820s (*Fathers and Children: Andrew Jackson and the Subjugation of the American Indian* [New York: Knopf, 1975], 199).

40. Not only did many eastern Anglo-Americans consider frontiersmen and settlers to be of "low character," but so did many Native Americans (which would seem to contradict McKenney's theory that the perception of their own inferiority was destroying native tribes). According to McLoughlin, Boudinot's editorials in the *Cherokee Phoenix* often expressed disdain for "uncivilized frontier ruffians" along with a host of other undesirables, including poor Irish immigrants and "'the wild savage Indians' of the West" (*Cherokees and Missionaries*, 131).

41. The removal debates also pitted North against South. Some of the strongest opponents of removal hailed from the northeastern states, especially New England, while those who stood to gain the most from it were southerners. Further, the removal debates pushed to the forefront the same questions of states' rights and charges of northern meddling that would play important roles in the slavery question. McKenney's attempt to rally New Yorkers' support for removal can be read as an attempt to defuse this interregional conflict.

42. McKenney had an inkling that further conflict would erupt in the West. Viola writes that

he "threw up his hands in exasperation" when white residents of Arkansas asked the government to move the Cherokees who had settled there in 1817 farther westward (*Thomas L. McKenney,* 217). In an 1828 letter, McKenney lamented: "I confess I had hope, nay I had no doubt of the final success of the policy which has been begun under such flattering auspices of sett'ling our unfortunate Indians in one last and good home. . . . But if those so far in the West, are not made to feel that there is something in our pledges, I shall *despair*" (qtd. ibid.).

43. Biographical sources on McCoy include McLoughlin, *Cherokees and Missionaries,* 267–79; Schultz, *Indian Canaan;* and Berkhofer's introduction to McCoy's *History of the Baptist Indian Missions* (v–xxvii).

44. Isaac McCoy, *Country for Indians West of the Mississippi,* 22nd Cong., 1st sess., 1832, H. Doc. 172.

45. Isaac McCoy, *Remarks on the Practicability of Indian Reform, Embracing Their Colonization; with an Appendix,* 2d ed. (New York: Gray and Bunce, 1829), 12–13; italics in original. I have used this edition rather than the first (Boston: Lincoln and Edmands, 1827) because it includes a more detailed description of the roles that McCoy hoped eastern Indian tribes might play in the West.

46. Ibid., 14.

47. McCoy, *History of the Baptist Indian Missions,* 265.

48. McCoy, *Address to Philanthropists in the United States Generally, and to Christians in Particular, on the Condition and Prospects of the American Indians* (1831), rpt. in *History of the Baptist Indian Missions,* 434; McCoy, *Remarks,* 14.

49. McCoy, *History of the Baptist Indian Missions,* 358. In the following paragraphs, quotations are cited parenthetically.

50. McCoy, *Remarks,* 41.

51. McCoy, *History of the Baptist Indian Missions,* 498.

52. Eric Lott, *Love and Theft: Blackface Minstrelsy and the American Working Class* (New York: Oxford University Press, 1993).

53. McCoy, *Country for Indians,* 10.

54. See Schultz, *Indian Canaan,* 188–94.

55. McCoy, *History of the Baptist Indian Missions,* 545.

56. Ibid., 344, 343.

57. Qtd. in Schultz, *Indian Canaan,* 199. McKenney also expressed faith in "the capacity of the Indian for the highest attainments of civilization" (qtd. in Drinnon, *Facing West,* 172).

58. McCoy, *Address,* 434–35.

59. McCoy, *History of the Baptist Indian Missions,* 40.

60. McCoy, *Country for Indians,* 10.

61. For all his civilizationist rhetoric, McCoy does occasionally express regret at the fading of "Indian ways." Of the western Osage nation, he writes: "In speech making, they exhibited more native eloquence, and acquitted themselves with much more credit, than our civilized and half civilized Indians. Ours had lost too much of native Indian character to appear to good advantage in an *Indian* council proper" (*History of the Baptist Missions,* 358).

62. McCoy, *Remarks,* 40. In this segment, McCoy referred to the "southern Indians" as a group, though in prior paragraphs he remarked specifically on the Cherokees' situation (40). An 1830 editorial published in the *Cherokee Phoenix* attested to the Cherokees' benevolent efforts, citing their establishment of "Missionary Societies, Tract Societies, Sunday School Societies, Benevolent Societies, Book Societies and Temperance Societies" (qtd. in Perdue, *Cherokee Editor,* 16–17). On Cherokees' benevolent efforts aimed at non-Cherokees, including their participation in the African colonization movement, see McLoughlin, *Cherokees and Missionaries,* 130–32.

63. McCoy, *History of the Baptist Indian Missions,* 265.

64. McLoughlin, *Cherokees and Missionaries,* 255.

65. On hybridity's liberatory or counterhegemonic potential, see Homi Bhabha, *The Location of Culture* (London: Routledge, 1995). For a more skeptical treatment of hybridity, see Samira Kawash, *Dislocating the Color Line: Identity, Hybridity, and Singularity in African-American Literature* (Stanford: Stanford University Press, 1997).

66. McCoy, *Remarks,* 40.

67. Ibid., 30. Not surprisingly, McKenney also advocated African colonization. See Drinnon, *Facing West,* 182–83.

68. On Liberia's administration and eventual independence, see P. J. Staudenraus, *The African Colonization Movement, 1816–1865* (New York: Columbia University Press, 1961), 59–68, 241, and Lamin Sanneh, *Abolitionists Abroad: American Blacks and the Making of Modern West Africa* (Cambridge: Harvard University Press, 1999), 182–237.

69. McCoy, *Address,* 432.

70. McCoy, *History of the Baptist Indian Missions,* 582.

71. See Schultz, *Indian Canaan,* 181.

72. In McKenney's defense, some evidence suggests that he disapproved of the level of violence that the Jackson administration proved willing to exert against native tribes. Prucha writes that the rift with Jackson, as McKenney describes it in his *Memoirs,* derived from his discomfort with the president's Indian policy. Prucha adds that other factors, including McKenney's support of Calhoun, Jackson's political rival, were probably in operation as well ("Thomas L. McKenney," 655). See also Viola, *Thomas L. McKenney,* 231–36. Earlier in his career, McKenney had opposed removal and, as Reginald Horsman has pointed out, he acknowledged after the fact "that Indian Removal had not created a haven for the Indians" (*Race and Manifest Destiny,* 206). His qualms are not apparent, however, in the Indian Board documents, nor do they invalidate his role, however brief, in promoting Jackson's removal plan.

73. Bhabha, *Location of Culture,* 86.

74. Priscilla Wald, *Constituting Americans: Cultural Anxiety and Narrative Form* (Durham, N.C.: Duke University Press, 1995), 28. The Cherokees' 1827 constitution took the U.S. Constitution as its model.

75. Toni Morrison, "Friday on the Potomac," introduction to *Race-ing Justice, En-gendering Power: Essays on Anita Hill, Clarence Thomas, and the Construction of Social Reality,* ed. Morrison (New York: Pantheon, 1992), xxv–xxvi.

76. Ibid., xxv.

77. Pratt, *Imperial Eyes: Travel Writing and Transculturation* (London: Routledge, 1992), 7; italics in original. According to Perdue, the *Cherokee Phoenix* had a significant number of Anglo-American subscribers (*Cherokee Editor,* 15–16).

78. Pratt, *Imperial Eyes,* 7.

79. Because the same arguments were still in circulation in 1828 and because the core issue had not been resolved, the newspaper's inclusion of these older documents does not seem especially odd.

80. "Correspondence between Commissioners on the Part of the United States, and the Council of the Cherokee Nation, in the Year 1823," *Cherokee Phoenix,* 18 June 1828, 1; "In General Council," *Cherokee Phoenix,* 18 June 1828, 2.

81. "In General Council," *Cherokee Phoenix,* 2 July 1828, 1–2; "New Echota: Wednesday, October 14, 1829" [editorial], *Cherokee Phoenix and Indians' Advocate,* 14 October 1829, 2; "Memorial of the Cherokees," *Cherokee Phoenix and Indians' Advocate,* 20 January 1830, 1.

82. "New Echota: Wednesday, October 14, 1829" [editorial], *Cherokee Phoenix and Indians' Advocate,* 14 October 1829, 2; "New Echota: Wednesday, November 11, 1829," *Cherokee Phoenix and Indians' Advocate,* 11 November 1829, 3.

83. Mary Young, "The Cherokee Nation: Mirror of the Republic," *American Quarterly* 33 (1981): 522–23.

Chapter 2. Misgivings

1. On Barnum and the culture of deceptive entertainment, see Benjamin Reiss, *The Showman and the Slave: Race, Death, and Memory in Barnum's America* (Cambridge: Harvard University Press, 2001), and James W. Cook, *The Arts of Deception: Playing with Fraud in the Age of Barnum* (Cambridge: Harvard University Press, 2001). The "sucker" quotation is attributed to Barnum in a number of texts, including *The Oxford Dictionary of Quotations* (5th ed., 1999) and Bartlett's *Familiar Quotations* (16th ed., 1992). For alternate explanations of the phrase's origins, see A. H. Saxon, *P. T. Barnum: The Legend and the Man* (New York: Columbia University Press,

1989), 334–37, and R. J. Brown, "P. T. Barnum Never Did Say 'There's a Sucker Born Every Minute,' " *History Buff's Home Page,* Newspaper Collectors Society of America, 4 January 2002. <http://www.historybuff.com/library/refbarnum.html>. Whatever the quotation's source, Barnum's fame as a deceiver makes him an appropriate figure to invoke here.

2. For example, Washington, D.C.'s black-run Union Benevolent Association, like its white-administered counterparts, focused on aiding "the deserving poor" ("The Address and Constitution of the Union Benevolent Association of the People of Color of the City of Washington," *National Reformer,* March 1839, 107). On the perception that black Americans relied too heavily on white benevolence, see "A Word to Our People," *Anglo-African Magazine,* September 1859, 295. For assertions of Jewish benevolence, see Hebrew Charitable Fund, *Report of the First Annual Dinner of the Hebrew Charitable Fund, of Philadelphia, Given at Sansom Street Hall, on Wednesday, Feb. 23, 1853* (Philadelphia: C. Sherman, 1853), and *Fifth Annual Report of the Association for the Relief of Jewish Widows and Orphans of New-Orleans: Together with the Anniversary Address by the Reverend Solomon Jacob* (New Orleans: Lathrop, 1860).

3. On the nineteenth century's economic instabilities, see Charles Sellers, *The Market Revolution: Jacksonian America, 1815–1846* (New York: Oxford University Press, 1991), esp. 103–201. My generalizations about "the benevolent" are based on a large body of scholarship. See especially Nancy Hewitt, *Women's Activism and Social Change: Rochester, New York, 1822–1872* (Ithaca: Cornell University Press, 1984); Paul Boyer, *Urban Masses and Moral Order in America, 1820–1920* (Cambridge: Harvard University Press, 1978); Lori D. Ginzberg, *Women and the Work of Benevolence: Morality, Politics, and Class in the Nineteenth-Century United States* (New Haven: Yale University Press, 1990); Steven Mintz, *Moralists and Modernizers: America's Pre–Civil War Reformers* (Baltimore: Johns Hopkins University Press, 1995), 50–116; and Mary P. Ryan, *Cradle of the Middle Class: The Family in Oneida County, New York, 1790–1865* (Cambridge: Cambridge University Press, 1981), 105–44, 210–18.

4. For a counterexample—a charity society report that includes a section explicitly addressed to nonwhite readers—see "Reply of the Chairman," in *Report of the Committee of Merchants for the Relief of Colored People, Suffering from the Late Riots in the City of New York* (New York: George A. Whitehorne, 1863), 35–37.

5. The Irish illustrate this instability nicely. As Reginald Horsman points out, "an Irishman might be described as a lazy, ragged, dirty Celt when he landed in New York, but if his children settled in California they might well be praised as part of the vanguard of the energetic Anglo-Saxon people poised for the plunge into Asia" (*Race and Manifest Destiny: The Origins of American Racial Anglo-Saxonism* [Cambridge: Harvard University Press, 1981], 4).

6. Some Irish American authors questioned the desirability of such absorption. The Catholic novelist Mrs. J. [Mary] Sadlier, for example, has one of her characters assert that it would be better to see Irish children "beggin' their bread" in their homeland than risking "the loss of their souls" in Protestant America. This speaker loses the argument—the Burke family persists in its plan to emigrate in search of economic opportunity—but the sentiment is registered nonetheless (*Willy Burke; or, The Irish Orphan in America* [Boston: Thomas B. Noonan, 1850], 8).

7. James Rees, "The Editor's Walk.—No. I," *The Philanthropist, or Sketches of City Life. A Monthly Periodical,* January 1855, 11.

8. Horsman, *Race and Manifest Destiny,* 4–5.

9. My examination of the antebellum discourse of suspicion is bolstered by Bruce Dorsey's claim that a general mistrust of and hostility toward the poor came to prominence among Philadelphians in the 1820s (*Reforming Men and Women: Gender in the Antebellum City* [Ithaca: Cornell University Press, 2002], 50–89).

10. See Boyer, *Urban Masses,* 96–107.

11. Baltimore Association for Improving the Condition of the Poor (AICP), *Annual Report, Constitution and By-Laws, and Visitor's Manual* (Baltimore: Office of the Association, 1851), 17; italics in original.

12. "Benevolence," *Jessie and Other Stories for Young People* (Boston: Otis Clapp, 1850), 36, 40.

13. Harvey Newcomb, *The Young Lady's Guide to the Harmonious Developement [sic] of Christian Character,* 3d ed. (Boston: James B. Dow, 1841), 215.

14. Boston Society for the Prevention of Pauperism, *Twenty-Fourth Annual Report, October, 1859* (Boston: John Wilson and Son, 1859), 15. On the relationship between pauperism and slavery, see Jonathan A. Glickstein, "Pressures from Below: Pauperism, Chattel Slavery, and the Ideological Construction of Free Market Labor Incentives in Antebellum America," *Radical History Review* 69 (1997): 114–59.

15. Boston Society for the Prevention of Pauperism, *Twenty-Fourth Annual Report*, 15.

16. "Caution," *Colonization Herald* (Philadelphia), July 1853, 147.

17. *First Report of the Association for the Care of Coloured Orphans, Embracing an Account of "the Shelter for Coloured Orphans," Instituted at Philadelphia, in the Year 1822* (Philadelphia: William Brown, 1836), 14.

18. Baltimore AICP, *Annual Report*, 18–19.

19. Newcomb, *Young Lady's Guide*, 215.

20. While normative female behavior differed substantially by class and race (enslaved and working-class women, for example, were expected to do manual labor, but privileged women were expected to avoid it), most antebellum Americans identified the economic support of women as, ultimately, a man's responsibility: the begging woman's father, brothers, husband, sons, employer, or owner ought to have kept her from destitution. Discussions of needy women in charity literature bear this out, often blaming poor women's situations on the shortcomings of these failed providers.

21. The English travel writer Frances Trollope, among others, remarked on Americans' opportunities for self-sufficiency: "It appears to me that the necessaries of life . . . are within the reach of every sober, industrious, and healthy man who chooses to have them" (*Domestic Manners of the Americans,* ed. Donald Smalley [1832; New York: Knopf, 1949], 116).

22. On the perils of the urban environment, see Karen Halttunen, *Confidence Men and Painted Women: A Study of Middle-Class Culture in America, 1830–1870* (New Haven: Yale University Press, 1982), 1–32.

23. David Rothman, *The Discovery of the Asylum: Social Order and Disorder in the New Republic* (Boston: Little, Brown, 1971), 3–29.

24. Glenn Hendler, *Public Sentiments: Structures of Feeling in Nineteenth-Century American Literature* (Chapel Hill: University of North Carolina Press, 2001), 123.

25. Qtd. in Robert W. Goodman, "A Study of Humanitarian Philanthropy in an American Urban Community: The History of Four Social Welfare Agencies in New York City, 1783–1905" (Ph.D. diss., Rutgers University, 1983), 311. On the prominence of home visiting, see Boyer, *Urban Masses,* 90–94, and Ginzberg, *Women and the Work of Benevolence,* 41.

26. Harryette Mullen, "Optic White: Blackness and the Production of Whiteness," *diacritics* 24, no. 2–3 (1994): 73.

27. Rees, "Editor's Walk.—No. I," 12.

28. Eliza Farrar, *The Adventures of Congo, in Search of His Master* (1823 [London]; Boston: Munroe and Francis, 1846). Farrar, an Englishwoman who eventually settled in the United States, makes her protagonist nominally free but otherwise espouses the benevolent paternalism so prominent in proslavery fiction. Congo, once separated from his beloved "master," searches frantically to find him or, if that proves impossible, to replace him. The story champions the dignity of such servitude over the shame of begging.

29. James Rees, "The Editor's Walk.—No. II," *The Philanthropist, or Sketches of City Life. A Monthly Periodical,* February 1855, 33.

30. Rosemarie Garland Thomson writes that "at least since the inception of English Poor Laws in 1388, the state and other institutions . . . have molded the political and cultural definition of what we now know as 'physical disability' in an effort to distinguish between genuine 'cripples' and malingerers" (*Extraordinary Bodies: Figuring Physical Disability in American Culture* [New York: Columbia University Press, 1997], 48–49). Because of the potential for deception, Americans were often more comfortable with the disabled who dwelled within asylums, not only because they were then out of public view but also because their disability was verified and their status as deserving thus guaranteed by the institution (which, of course, had to establish its own credibility). On benevolence and disability, see also Mary Klages, *Woeful Afflictions: Disability and Sentimentality in Victorian America* (Philadelphia: University of Pennsylvania Press, 1999).

31. The era's illustrations also marked trickster-beggars as Irish through stereotypical names and caricatured facial features (including low foreheads and apelike jaws and mouths).

32. Herman Melville, *Israel Potter: His Fifty Years of Exile*, vol. 8 of *The Writings of Herman Melville*, ed. Harrison Hayford et al. (Evanston and Chicago: Northwestern University Press and the Newberry Library, 1982), 165.

33. Burton J. Bledstein, *The Culture of Professionalism: The Middle Class and the Development of Higher Education in America* (New York: Norton, 1976), 89.

34. On the professionalization of charity work, see Ginzberg, *Women and the Work of Benevolence*, 61–66, 98–132.

35. See, for example, "The Beggar," in *Juvenile Poems* (Wendell, Mass.: J. Metcalf, 1830); "The Little Beggar Girl," in *Juvenile Poems; To Be Read and Learned* (Providence: Geo. P. Daniels, 1839); "Willy and the Beggar Girl," *The Rabbits,* Christmas Tree Tales, no. 1 (New York: John McLoughlin, n.d. [American Antiquarian Society lists 1854–58(?)]), 13–16; and *The Beggar's Petition* (Dayton: B. F. Ells, n.d. [American Antiquarian Society lists "not before 1835"(?)]).

36. William Logan Fisher, *Pauperism and Crime* (Philadelphia: published by the author, 1831).

37. Henry L. Pinckney, *An Address Delivered Before the Methodist Benevolent Society, at Their Anniversary Meeting, in the Methodist Protestant Church, in Wentworth-Street, on the 1st Monday in July, 1835* (Charleston, S.C.: E. J. Van Brunt, 1835), 15.

38. E[dwin] H[ubbell] Chapin, *Humanity in the City* (New York: De Witt and Davenport; Boston: Abel Tompkins, 1854), 69.

39. Cassandra Cleghorn treats periodical literature's rhetoric of suspicion in "Bartleby's Benefactors: Toward a Literary History of Charity" (Ph.D. diss., Yale University, 1995), 127–74.

40. One proslavery novel that expresses sympathy toward the Irish is J. Thornton Randolph [Charles Jacobs Peterson], *The Cabin and Parlor; or, Slaves and Masters* (Philadelphia: T. B. Peterson, 1852). John W. Page's *Uncle Robin, in his Cabin in Virginia, and Tom without One in Boston* (Richmond, Va.: J. W. Randolph, 1853) contrasts Irish laborers' filthy shanties with slaves' tidy and comfortable cabins, but the novel's anti-Catholicism undercuts any sympathy toward the Irish that this portrayal might conjure. The antislavery movement's emphasis on kindness toward those of African descent is especially evident in its juvenile literature. See the first volume (1836) of *The Slave's Friend*, a periodical published in New York City by the American Anti-Slavery Society. The intersections between antislavery movements and capitalism are debated at length in Thomas Bender, ed., *The Antislavery Debate: Capitalism and Abolitionism as a Problem in Historical Interpretation* (Berkeley: University of California Press, 1992).

41. Rees, "Editor's Walk.—No. I," 11. While the Irish in America eventually "became white," as Noel Ignatiev has argued, in part through their adoption of antiblack prejudice and their not-unrelated economic progress, in the antebellum period their extreme poverty and their Roman Catholicism made them particular objects of suspicion; see *How the Irish Became White* (New York: Routledge, 1995), esp. chaps. 4 and 5.

42. Sadlier, *Willy Burke,* 31.

43. Harriet Beecher Stowe, *A Key to Uncle Tom's Cabin; Presenting the Original Facts and Documents upon Which the Story is Founded, Together with Corroborative Statements Verifying the Truth of the Work* (Boston: Jewett, 1853), 183–84.

44. "Beware of Imposition," *National Aegis* (Worcester, Mass.), 30 October 1850.

45. Saidiya Hartman, *Scenes of Subjection: Terror, Slavery, and Self-Making in Nineteenth-Century America* (New York: Oxford University Press, 1997), 62–63.

46. Herman Melville, "Bartleby the Scrivener," in *The Piazza Tales and Other Prose Pieces, 1839–1860,* vol. 9 of *The Writings of Herman Melville,* ed. Harrison Hayford et al. (Evanston and Chicago: Northwestern University Press and the Newberry Library, 1987), 23.

47. Melville, "Bartleby the Scrivener," 35.

48. This talk of doubt and instability recurs in the scholarship on *The Confidence-Man,* whose narrative leaves readers unsure of whom to credit, whom to blame, and most centrally, whom to trust. John Bryant, for example, calls the novel "a comedy of doubt," while Geoffrey Sanborn asserts that, like "Benito Cereno" and *Pierre, The Confidence-Man* is "about the sources and consequences of uncertainty" (John Bryant, *Melville and Repose: The Rhetoric of Humor in the Amer-*

ican Renaissance [New York: Oxford University Press, 1993], 231; Geoffrey Sanborn, *The Sign of the Cannibal: Melville and the Making of a Postcolonial Reader* [Durham, N.C.: Duke University Press, 1998], 174).

49. Herman Melville, *The Confidence-Man: His Masquerade,* vol. 10 of *The Writings of Herman Melville,* ed. Harrison Hayford et al. (Evanston and Chicago: Northwestern University Press and the Newberry Library, 1984), 10. Subsequent citations appear parenthetically in the text, with the abbreviation *CM.* For a nineteenth-century account of a black hotel employee's participation in a similar penny-catching routine, see Eric Lott, *Love and Theft: Blackface Minstrelsy and the American Working Class* (New York: Oxford University Press, 1993), 18.

50. While abolitionists and slave narrators alluded to and, at times, discussed openly white men's sexual exploitation of female slaves, nineteenth-century sources tend to be silent with respect to the exploitation and rape of enslaved or otherwise vulnerable men. On Melville's veiled treatments of such exploitation, see Caleb Crain, "Lovers of Human Flesh: Homosexuality and Cannibalism in Melville's Novels," *American Literature* 66 (1994): 25–53.

51. The wooden-legged man says, specifically, "when you find me a virtuous jockey [evidently unlikely], I will find you a benevolent wise man" (*CM,* 15).

52. On the origins and various versions of these images, see Bernard F. Reilly Jr., "The Art of the Antislavery Movement," *Courage and Conscience: Black and White Abolitionists in Boston,* ed. Donald M. Jacobs (Bloomington: Indiana University Press, for the Boston Athenaeum, 1993), 54–55, and Jean Fagan Yellin, *Women and Sisters: The Antislavery Feminists in American Culture* (New Haven: Yale University Press, 1989), 5–6, 10–21. On images of kneeling slaves generally, especially those produced after the Civil War, see Kirk Savage, *Standing Soldiers, Kneeling Slaves: Race, War, and Monument in Nineteenth-Century America* (Princeton: Princeton University Press, 1997).

53. In his four-volume treatise *London Labour and the London Poor,* Henry Mayhew asserts that black beggars on the streets of London often displayed such images as part of their appeals for alms (vol. 4, *Those That Will Not Work, Comprising Prostitutes, Thieves, Swindlers and Beggars, by Several Contributors* [1861; New York: Dover, 1968], 425).

54. Such anxieties and their (possible) real-life analogues were not exclusive to the United States. *London Labour and the London Poor* claims that some whites who were "fortunate enough to possess a flattish or turned-up nose" were begging in blackface, claiming to be fugitive slaves who had escaped to England (ibid.).

55. Carolyn Karcher, *Shadow over the Promised Land: Slavery, Race, and Violence in Melville's America* (Baton Rouge: Louisiana State University Press, 1980), 220.

56. Michael Paul Rogin, *Subversive Genealogy: The Politics and Art of Herman Melville* (New York: Knopf, 1983), 220.

57. See Amy Robinson, "It Takes One to Know One: Passing and Communities of Common Interest," *Critical Inquiry* 20 (1994): 716.

58. Lott, *Love and Theft,* 20. Lott argues that the minstrel show's audiences became increasingly working class through the 1840s. Nevertheless, minstrelsy as a mode of representation remained prevalent in the culture at large. I am indebted to Robert Cantwell for the suggestion that the musicians' white identities were also a kind of performance, especially with respect to class affiliation.

59. My phrasing echoes Julie Ellison's discussion of the "embarrassed position" of white liberal guilt, though I have replaced that state with one of its analogues—white liberal doubt (*Cato's Tears and the Making of Anglo-American Emotion* [Chicago: University of Chicago Press, 1999], 172).

60. Karcher, *Shadow over the Promised Land,* 206.

61. Wai Chee Dimock, *Empire for Liberty: Melville and the Poetics of Individualism* (Princeton: Princeton University Press, 1989), 188. Because the confidence man's dupes make choices that at least appear to be free (that is, there appear to be alternatives), they command little sympathy. Melville, Dimock claims, thus replaces "the victim with the category of the 'contracting party' " (187; see also 204–7).

62. The most striking of these encounters occurs between the wooden-legged man and the

contentious Methodist, who nearly come to blows over the question of charity (*CM*, 14–16). The chapter's ever-shifting focus is forecast by Melville's headnote, which reads "In which a variety of characters appear" (*CM*, 10).

63. For example, the 1971 Norton Critical Edition of the novel, edited by Hershel Parker, promotes this interpretation through numerous leading footnotes.

64. All parenthetical references to "Benito Cereno" are to *The Piazza Tales*, vol. 9 of *The Writings of Herman Melville*, ed. Hayford et al., 46–117.

65. In the ensuing discussion, I follow a number of scholars who bring cultural phenomena of the antebellum period to bear on this text, even though Melville set the story in 1799 and used a narrative published in 1817 as his main source. Setting and sources notwithstanding, I read Melville's Delano as a man of the 1850s.

66. Delano at one point calls Babo "uncommonly intelligent" (*BC*, 90), but he does so in response to what he perceives as Babo's excellent service to his "master."

67. Eric Sundquist, for example, writes that "the stagecraft of Melville's tale theatricalizes slavery, exposing its supposedly 'natural' relations of mastery and racial supremacy as conventions of power" (*To Wake the Nations: Race in the Making of American Literature* [Cambridge: Harvard University Press, Belknap Press, 1993], 161).

68. In reference to Delano's tendency not to see evil in others, the narrator states that "whether, in view of what humanity is capable, such a trait implies, along with a benevolent heart, more than ordinary quickness and accuracy of intellectual perception, may be left to the wise to determine" (*BC*, 47).

69. Elizabeth B. Clark, " 'The Sacred Rights of the Weak': Pain, Sympathy, and the Culture of Individual Rights in Antebellum America," *Journal of American History* 82 (1995): 465, 467.

70. Gloria Horsley-Meacham argues that Melville's references to an admirable African past in "Benito Cereno" undercut the story's apparent antiblack paranoia ("Bull of the Nile: Symbol, History, and Racial Myth in 'Benito Cereno,' " *New England Quarterly* 64 [1991]: 225–42).

71. Karen Halttunen, "Humanitarianism and the Pornography of Pain in Anglo-American Culture," *American Historical Review* 100 (1995): 330 (both quotations). See also John Saillant, "The Black Body Erotic and the Republican Body Politic, 1790–1820," in *Sentimental Men: Masculinity and the Politics of Affect in American Culture*, ed. Mary Chapman and Glenn Hendler (Berkeley: University of California Press, 1999), 89–111.

72. Critics who have discussed the erotic elements of Delano's encounter on the *San Dominick* include Crain, "Homosexuality and Cannibalism," 44–45, and Karcher, *Shadow over the Promised Land*, 134.

73. As Marianne Noble points out, a number of critics "represent the masochistic position as one of self-empowerment through apparent repudiation of power" (*The Masochistic Pleasures of Sentimental Literature* [Princeton: Princeton University Press, 2000], 9). For Babo and his co-conspirators, this reversal becomes quite literal.

74. According to Halttunen, there is an eroticism in such lacunae: "In humanitarian reform literature, the self-conscious omission of certain material [that which was dubbed 'too horrid and indecent to mention' (328)] served primarily to highlight its prurient nature, by calling attention to the inescapable conviction that dreadful pain was obscene pain" ("Humanitarianism," 329).

75. Noble, *Masochistic Pleasures*, 108.

76. Peter Stallybrass and Allon White, *The Politics and Poetics of Transgression* (Ithaca: Cornell University Press, 1986), 5.

77. Robert S. Levine, *Conspiracy and Romance: Studies in Brockden Brown, Cooper, Hawthorne, and Melville* (Cambridge: Cambridge University Press, 1989), 223. Levine uses the term most immediately in relation to Delano but extends his discussion to antebellum relations of power more broadly conceived.

78. Ann Fabian, *The Unvarnished Truth: Personal Narratives in Nineteenth-Century America* (Berkeley: University of California Press, 2000), 11.

79. "The Boys We Want," *The Slave's Friend* 2, no. 4 (1837): 6–7.

80. Peggy Pascoe, *Relations of Rescue: The Search for Female Moral Authority in the American West, 1874–1939* (New York: Oxford University Press, 1990).

Chapter 3. The Racial Politics of Self-Reliance

1. Herman Melville, *The Confidence-Man: His Masquerade,* vol. 10 of *The Writings of Herman Melville,* ed. Harrison Hayford et al. (Evanston and Chicago: Northwestern University Press and the Newberry Library, 1984), 178, 179. Subsequent citations appear parenthetically in the text, with the abbreviation *CM.*

2. Ralph Waldo Emerson, "Self-Reliance," in *Essays: First Series,* vol. 2 of *The Collected Works of Ralph Waldo Emerson,* ed. Joseph Slater (Cambridge: Harvard University Press, Belknap Press, 1979), 30–31.

3. Bruce Dorsey, *Reforming Men and Women: Gender in the Antebellum City* (Ithaca: Cornell University Press, 2002), 74.

4. Emerson, "Self-Reliance," 30. In the following paragraphs, quotations are cited parenthetically.

5. Ralph Waldo Emerson, "Gifts," in *Essays: Second Series,* vol. 3 of *The Collected Works of Ralph Waldo Emerson,* ed. Joseph Slater (Cambridge: Harvard University Press, Belknap Press, 1983), 94.

6. Ralph Waldo Emerson, "An Address . . . on . . . the Emancipation of the Negroes in the British West Indies," in *Emerson's Antislavery Writings,* ed. Len Gougeon and Joel Myerson (New Haven: Yale University Press, 1995), 9, 18.

7. Ibid., 29, 31.

8. Emerson, "Self-Reliance," 29.

9. To be fair, Emerson expresses elsewhere a greater self-consciousness about such dependent relations, as in the following comment from "Man the Reformer" (1841): "I feel some shame before my wood-chopper, my ploughman, and my cook, for they have some sort of self-sufficiency, they can contrive without my aid to bring the day and year round, but I depend on them, and have not earned by use a right to my arms and feet" (*Nature, Addresses, and Lectures,* vol. 1 of *The Collected Works of Ralph Waldo Emerson,* ed. Alfred R. Ferguson [Cambridge: Harvard University Press, Belknap Press, 1971], 150).

10. Emerson, "Self-Reliance," 45.

11. Emerson, "Friendship," in *Essays: First Series,* 122, 123, 124.

12. Emerson, "Character," in *Essays: Second Series,* 64–65.

13. Emerson, "Friendship," 116.

14. Ibid., 121.

15. Ralph Waldo Emerson, "Fate," in *The Conduct of Life,* in *Ralph Waldo Emerson: Essays and Lectures,* ed. Joel Porte (New York: Library of America, 1983), 952.

16. Emerson, "Experience," in *Essays: Second Series,* 35; Emerson, "Fate," 958.

17. I allude here to David Robinson's *Apostle of Culture: Emerson as Preacher and Lecturer* (Philadelphia: University of Pennsylvania Press, 1982). On Emerson and hierarchy, see Julie Ellison, "The Gender of Transparency: Masculinity and the Conduct of Life," *American Literary History* 4 (1992): 584–606; David Leverenz, *Manhood and the American Renaissance* (Ithaca: Cornell University Press, 1989), 42–71; Michael Lopez, *Emerson and Power: Creative Antagonism in the Nineteenth Century* (De Kalb: Northern Illinois University Press, 1996); and Christopher Newfield, *The Emerson Effect: Individualism and Submission in America* (Chicago: University of Chicago Press, 1996).

18. Emerson, "Character," 56.

19. Emerson, "Manners," in *Essays: Second Series,* 76.

20. Ellison, "Gender of Transparency," 591. Christopher Newfield cites this observation as the point at which his reading intersects with hers (*Emerson Effect,* 223, n. 23). On Emerson's erotic friendships with men, see also Caleb Crain, *American Sympathy: Men, Friendship, and Literature in the New Nation* (New Haven: Yale University Press, 2001), 148–237.

21. Newfield, *Emerson Effect,* 125, 6, 125; Ellison, "Gender of Transparency," 597.

22. Emerson, "Friendship," 116, 118.

23. Emerson, "New England Reformers," in *Essays: Second Series,* 163.

24. Ellison, "Gender of Transparency," 597.

25. Frances Trollope, *Domestic Manners of the Americans*, ed. Donald Smalley (1832; New York: Knopf, 1949), 119–20.

26. Melville's own experiences in the 1850s, when he accepted—and had difficulty repaying—loans from friends and family, probably informed this representation. See Hershel Parker, *Herman Melville: A Biography*, vol. 2, 1851–91 (Baltimore: Johns Hopkins University Press, 2002), 6, 37, 122, 241, 255, 282, 286.

27. Scholarship on *The Confidence-Man*'s sources and allusions is usefully summarized in the "Historical Note" (*CM*, 276–94).

28. See, for example, Lee Rust Brown, *The Emerson Museum: Practical Romanticism and the Pursuit of the Whole* (Cambridge: Harvard University Press, 1997).

29. H. Clapp, Jr., "Self-Reliance," in *Liberty Chimes* (Providence: Ladies' Antislavery Society, 1845), 72.

30. Helen C. Knight, *Saw Up and Saw Down; or, the Fruits of Self-Reliance* (New York: American Female Guardian Society, 1852), 19, 20, 32.

31. *Gertrude Lee; or, the Northern Cousin* (Cincinnati: American Reform Tract and Book Society, 1856), 30, 26–27, 123.

32. Nancy Fraser and Linda Gordon, "A Genealogy of 'Dependency': Tracing a Keyword of the U.S. Welfare State," in Nancy Fraser, *Justice Interruptus: Critical Reflections on the "Postsocialist" Condition* (New York: Routledge, 1997), 142.

33. *The Mysteries and Miseries of Philadelphia, as Exhibited and Illustrated by a Late Presentment of the Grand Jury, and by a Sketch of the Condition of the Most Degraded Classes in the City* (Philadelphia: n.p., 1853), 7; Baltimore Association for Improving the Condition of the Poor (AICP), *Annual Report, Constitution and By-Laws, and Visitor's Manual* (Baltimore: Office of the Association, 1851), 3–4.

34. Baltimore AICP, *Annual Report*, 17.

35. Ibid., 17, 18.

36. Lydia H. Sigourney, *The Girl's Reading-Book, in Prose and Poetry: For Schools*, 15th ed. (Newburgh, N.Y.: Proudfit and Banks, 1847), 62.

37. *Little Book of Pleasure and Profit for Children* (Boston[?]: New England Sabbath School Union[?], 1842), 57.

38. Baltimore AICP, *Annual Report*, 4; "The Blind Beggar," in *Margaret*, no. 97 (New York: American Tract Society, n.d.), 7–9.

39. T. S. Arthur, "Uncle Ben's New-Year's Gift," in *Uncle Ben's New-Year's Gift, and Other Stories* (1852; Philadelphia: Lippincott, Grambo, 1854), 56.

40. Many of the destitute whites portrayed in juvenile fiction and charity literature have for some reason fallen from better-off positions, so benevolence is a matter of restoring them to a status they have previously occupied or to a "respectable" position above poverty but below their former (and perhaps extravagant) wealth.

41. Hosea Easton, *A Treatise on the Intellectual Character, and Civil and Political Condition of the Colored People of the U. States; and the Prejudice Exercised towards Them: With a Sermon on the Duty of the Church to Them* (Boston: Isaac Knapp, 1837), 43.

42. Qtd. in Leon F. Litwack, *North of Slavery: The Negro in the Free States, 1790–1860* (Chicago: University of Chicago Press, 1961), 207.

43. Theophilus Fiske, "Extracts from an Oration," *The National Crisis. An Antidote to Abolition Fanaticism, Treason and Sham Philanthropy*, 15 May 1860, 4; William Gilmore Simms, *Woodcraft; or, Hawks about the Dovecote: A Story of the South at the Close of the Revolution* (New York: Redfield, 1854), 509.

44. Jacob Abbott, *Congo; or, Jasper's Experience in Command* (New York: Harper and Brothers, 1857), 102, 149.

45. Ibid., 155–56, 160.

46. "Address to the People of the State of New York," *Pennsylvania Freeman*, 26 February 1852, 35.

47. William D[arrah] Kelley, *Address Delivered at the Colored Department of the House of Refuge* (Philadelphia: T. K. and P. G. Collins, 1850), 20; *Exposition of the Objects and Plans of*

the American Union for the Relief and Improvement of the Colored Race (Boston: Light and Horton, 1835), 11, 12; James Freeman Clarke, *Present Condition of the Free Colored People of the United States. By Rev. James Freeman Clarke. From the Christian Examiner for March* (New York: American Anti-Slavery Society, 1859), 26.

48. *Report of the Committee of Merchants for the Relief of Colored People, Suffering from the Late Riots in the City of New York* (New York: George A. Whitehorne, 1863).

49. Ibid., 4, 14, 17, 23. In opposition to the widely held view that receiving charity was inherently degrading, the *Report* asserted that even "unworthy" applicants for aid "may have been raised in their self-respect by the kind words and relief they received at our Central Depot" (4). That the committee conceived of its project as a temporary form of disaster relief rather than as ongoing charity may account for this difference.

50. Ibid., 12, 5.

51. Iver Bernstein affirms that New York's Republican elite (which included Merchants' Committee members) championed the free black population to some extent because of anti-Catholic and nativist sentiment (*The New York City Draft Riots: Their Significance for American Society and Politics in the Age of the Civil War* [New York: Oxford University Press, 1990], 160).

52. Although some colonizationists dispensed with benevolence altogether, arguing that free blacks should be sent to Africa because they posed a threat to the stability of southern slavery, the majority discussed the colonization of Africa in terms of what was best for black Americans and Africans.

53. Dorsey, *Reforming Men and Women*, 139–40.

54. Sarah J. Hale, *Liberia; or, Mr. Peyton's Experiments* (1853; Upper Saddle River, N.J.: Gregg, 1968), 127, 220. My remarks on Hale are adapted from my article, "Errand into Africa: Colonization and Nation Building in Sarah J. Hale's *Liberia*," *New England Quarterly* 68 (1995): 558–83.

55. Hale, *Liberia*, 128.

56. African Civilization Society, *Constitution of the African Civilization Society; Together with the Testimony of Forty Distinguished Citizens of New York and Brooklyn, to the Importance of the Objects Contemplated by Its Friends. Also, the Anniversary Address, Delivered by Rev. Joseph P. Thompson, D.D., at the Annual Meeting of the Society, May 19th, 1861* (New Haven: Thomas J. Stafford, 1861), 4.

57. Delany writes in his *Official Report of the Niger Valley Exploring Party* (1861) that "enlightened" African Americans, on emigrating to Africa, would aid the natives through "the establishment of social and industrial settlements among them, in order at once to introduce, in an effective manner, all the well-regulated pursuits of civilized life." The policy he proposes is, in short, "*Africa for the African race, and black men to rule them*" (*Search for a Place: Black Separatism and Africa, 1860*, by M. R. Delany and Robert Campbell [Ann Arbor: University of Michigan Press, 1969], 110, 121; italics in original).

58. Elizabeth Clark claims instead that "anecdotes of brutality helped foster arguments for the rights of the person in the context of relationships of authority and dependence" ("'The Sacred Rights of the Weak': Pain, Sympathy, and the Culture of Individual Rights in Antebellum America," *Journal of American History* 82 [1995]: 464). She concedes, though, that "repetitious images of slaves' degradation may have worked to set them apart as a class in the viewer's mind, to constitute difference rather than to obliterate it" (493). On Douglass's narrative, see Deborah E. McDowell, "In the First Place: Making Frederick Douglass and the Afro-American Narrative Tradition," in *Critical Essays on Frederick Douglass*, ed. William L. Andrews (Boston: G. K. Hall, 1991), 202.

59. Elizabeth McHenry, *Forgotten Readers: Recovering the Lost History of African American Literary Societies* (Durham, N.C.: Duke University Press, 2002), 50. On the transitory nature of these organizations, see ibid., 324, n. 33. Boylan's comment refers to mutual aid and other benevolent organizations formed by African Americans in New York and Boston ("Benevolence and Antislavery Activity among African American Women in New York and Boston, 1820–1840," in *The Abolitionist Sisterhood: Women's Political Culture in Antebellum America*, ed. Jean Fagan Yellin and John C. Van Horne [Ithaca: Cornell University Press, 1994], 121).

60. Robert L. Harris, Jr., "Early Black Benevolent Societies, 1780–1830," *Massachusetts Review* 20 (1979): 616–17. Harris briefly discusses African Americans' benevolent organizations in

slave states (617–19). On the cultivation of black leadership, see Julie Winch, *Philadelphia's Black Elite: Activism, Accommodation, and the Struggle for Autonomy, 1787–1848* (Philadelphia: Temple University Press, 1988), 6–7.

61. Bruce Dorsey's findings reinforce this point. African Americans in Philadelphia, he notes, "rarely blamed the poor for their poverty because they recognized that their neighbors were impoverished by racial and economic conditions beyond their control" (*Reforming Men and Women*, 64).

62. It was not only whites who made such claims, however. In an article titled "Africa to Be Christianized by Africans," an emigrant to Liberia asked "who are more capable to act as instruments to bring about this great change of morals [among Africans], than those who sprang from African stock?" (*Colonization Herald* [Philadelphia], July 1851, 52).

63. *Christian Education for the South* (Boston: n.p., 1865), 1, 2. The tone and word choice in this anonymous pamphlet strongly suggest white authorship. The piece consistently refers to African Americans, both free and enslaved, in the third person and includes disparaging remarks about their current level of attainment. Many black Americans also endorsed the notion of intraracial education, though they rejected this language of inadequacy.

64. "A Word to Our People," *Anglo-African Magazine*, September 1859, 294–95.

65. Clarke, *Present Condition*, 10, 14. Other commentators criticized black Americans who asked for money to redeem family members from slavery. An article from Philadelphia's *Colonization Herald* declared this an "unsafe" practice, in that the unaccustomed freedom and access to funds might destroy the supplicant's previous good habits, making him or her "unsteady, indolent, extravagant, and even dishonest" ("Purchasing Slaves for Emigration to Liberia," July 1855, 239).

66. Association of Friends, for the Free Instruction of Adult Colored Persons, *The Annual Report of the Board of Managers of the Association of Friends, for the Free Instruction of Adult Colored Persons* (Philadelphia: Joseph Rakestraw, 1858), 6.

67. Qtd. in Michael Meyer, introduction to *Frederick Douglass: The Narrative and Selected Writings* (New York: Modern Library, 1984), ix.

68. On Douglass's tendency to obscure personal debts, see Rafia Zafar, "Franklinian Douglass: The Afro-American as Representative Man," in *Frederick Douglass: New Literary and Historical Essays*, ed. Eric J. Sundquist (Cambridge: Cambridge University Press, 1990), 99–117.

69. See, for example, Leverenz, *Manhood and the American Renaissance*, 108–34; McDowell, "In the First Place"; Valerie Smith, *Self-Discovery and Authority in Afro-American Narrative* (Cambridge: Harvard University Press, 1987), 20–43; and Jenny Franchot, "The Punishment of Esther: Frederick Douglass and the Construction of the Feminine," in *Frederick Douglass: New Literary and Historical Essays*, 141–65.

70. Smith, *Self-Discovery*, 27; Waldo E. Martin, Jr., *The Mind of Frederick Douglass* (Chapel Hill: University of North Carolina Press, 1984), 262.

71. Martin, *Mind of Frederick Douglass*, 257; William L. Andrews, *To Tell a Free Story: The First Century of Afro-American Autobiography, 1760–1865* (Urbana: University of Illinois Press, 1986), 238; Robert S. Levine, *Martin Delany, Frederick Douglass, and the Politics of Representative Identity* (Chapel Hill: University of North Carolina Press), 131–32, 102.

72. Qtd. in Litwack, *North of Slavery*, 177. On Smith's land giveaway, see John Stauffer, *The Black Hearts of Men: Radical Abolitionists and the Transformation of Race* (Cambridge: Harvard University Press, 2002), 134–58.

73. Frederick Douglass, "We Ask Only for Our Rights: An Address Delivered in Troy, New York, on 4 September 1855," in *The Frederick Douglass Papers*, ser. 1, *Speeches, Debates, and Interviews*, vol. 3, 1855–63, ed. John W. Blassingame et al. (New Haven: Yale University Press, 1985), 93.

74. Qtd. in Martin, *Mind of Frederick Douglass*, 69.

75. See ibid., 66–68.

76. Frederick Douglass, "The Trials and Triumphs of Self-Made Men: An Address Delivered in Halifax, England, on 4 January 1860," in *Frederick Douglass Papers*, ser. 1, vol. 3, 300. According to the accompanying headnote, this was the "earliest surviving published text" of a speech that Douglass delivered many times in various forms (3: 289). Douglass tempered his individual-

ism here by admitting that there was no such thing as an entirely self-made man: "All," he conceded, "had begged, borrowed, or stolen from somebody or somewhere" (3:293).

77. Frederick Douglass to Henry C. Wright, 22 December 1846 [In Defense of Purchasing Freedom], in *Frederick Douglass: The Narrative and Selected Writings*, 239.

78. Frederick Douglass, *My Bondage and My Freedom*, ed. William L. Andrews (Urbana: University of Illinois Press, 1987), 239.

79. Ibid., 240.

80. Whites sometimes used this rhetoric as well, most often to make a case for a particular program of black elevation or improvement (e.g., abolition, colonization, vocational education); the proposal at hand, they claimed, would make slaves or otherwise "degraded" persons into men.

81. Qtd. in Bell I. Wiley, *Slaves No More: Letters from Liberia, 1833–1869* (Lexington: University Press of Kentucky, 1980), 262. In a (purportedly genuine) letter reprinted in the appendix to Hale's *Liberia*, one emigrant wrote that even if he were seventy years old, he would "come to Liberia and be a man, and no longer a nigger" (256).

82. "Preamble and Resolutions of the Anti-Colonization Believers in Syracuse," *Liberator*, 15 April 1853, 58. Such dueling masculinities were typical of the era. As Dorsey has noted, "competing languages of masculinity remained at the center of how northern black men interpreted colonization and emigration schemes" (*Reforming Men and Women*, 155).

83. Frederick Douglass, *Narrative*, vol. 1 of *The Frederick Douglass Papers*, ser. 2, *Autobiographical Writings*, ed. John W. Blassingame et al. (New Haven: Yale University Press, 1999), 50; Douglass, *My Bondage and My Freedom*, 151.

84. Here I disagree with Levine, who argues that the linkage of "Douglass's valorization of the 'manly' to dominant patriarchal models of power" is "anachronistic: in the face of unfathomable domination and degradation, Douglass in *Bondage* is celebrating the achievement of a self-mastery that promises to help him attain a fuller sense of his humanity" (*Martin Delany, Frederick Douglass*, 130).

85. Kevin K. Gaines, *Uplifting the Race: Black Leadership, Politics, and Culture in the Twentieth Century* (Chapel Hill: University of North Carolina Press, 1996), 130; Phillip Brian Harper, *Are We Not Men? Masculine Anxiety and the Problem of African-American Identity* (New York: Oxford University Press, 1996), x.

86. Hazel Carby, *Race Men* (Cambridge: Harvard University Press, 1998), 10.

87. Eddie S. Glaude ties these gender inequalities to a related cultural formation, the politics of respectability (*Exodus! Religion, Race, and Nation in Early Nineteenth-Century Black America* [Chicago: University of Chicago Press, 2000], 121).

Chapter 4. Pedagogies of Emancipation

1. Proslavery forces typically argued that slave literacy would bring bloody revolution rather than Christian salvation, especially after the discovery of the Denmark Vesey conspiracy in 1822, the publication of David Walker's *Appeal* in 1829, and Nat Turner's rebellion in 1831.

2. *Christian Education for the South* (Boston: n.p., 1865), 1.

3. Washington Association for the Education of Free Colored Youth, *Normal School for Colored Girls* (Washington, D.C.: n.p., 1856), 2.

4. Christopher Castiglia, "Pedagogical Discipline and the Creation of White Citizenship: John Witherspoon, Robert Finley, and the Colonization Society," *Early American Literature* 33 (1998): 197.

5. According to Joel Perlmann and Robert A. Margo, by 1860 "between 65 percent and 80 percent of teachers were women in the urban areas of every region"; rural areas varied more widely, with high percentages of female teachers in the Northeast and northern Midwest (e.g., 84 percent in New England) and relatively low percentages in the rural South (often below 33 percent) (*Women's Work? American Schoolteachers, 1650–1920* [Chicago: University of Chicago Press, 2001], 7–8).

6. Elizabeth McHenry, *Forgotten Readers: Recovering the Lost History of African American Literary Societies* (Durham, N.C.: Duke University Press, 2002); and Julie Winch, " 'You Have Talents—Only Cultivate Them': Philadelphia's Black Female Literary Societies and the

Abolitionist Crusade," in *The Abolitionist Sisterhood: Women's Political Culture in Antebellum America*, ed. Jean Fagan Yellin and John C. Van Horne (Ithaca: Cornell University Press, 1994), 101–18.

7. My thinking throughout this chapter has been informed by Sarah Robbins's work on mothering and literacy; I am grateful to her for allowing me to read two chapters of her book manuscript, titled "Managing Literacy, Mothering America, 1780–1920."

8. Lydia H. Sigourney, *The Girl's Reading-Book, in Prose and Poetry: For Schools,* 14th ed. (Newburgh, N.Y.: Proudfit and Banks, 1845), 62.

9. Isabelle Lehuu, *Carnival on the Page: Popular Print Media in Antebellum America* (Chapel Hill: University of North Carolina Press, 2000), 147.

10. *Walter Browning; or, The Slave's Protector* (Cincinnati: American Reform Tract and Book Society, 1856), vi.

11. Thomas G. Allen, *Report. To the President and Managers of the Philadelphia Society for Bettering the condition of the Poor* (Philadelphia: n.p., 1830), 2.

12. Susan Warner, *The Wide, Wide World* (1850; New York: A. L. Burt, n.d.), 31–38. For a trenchant analysis of the novel's uses of literacy, see Patricia Crain, *The Story of A: The Alphabetization of America from* The New England Primer *to* The Scarlet Letter (Stanford: Stanford University Press, 2000), 143–71.

13. Louisa May Alcott, *Little Women* (1868–69; New York: Penguin, 1989), 10.

14. Lucy Ellen Guernsey, *The Sign of the Cross; or, Edah Champlin* (New York: General Protestant Episcopal. S.S. Union and Church Book Society, 1856), 308.

15. *Acts Passed by the General Assembly of the State of North Carolina, at the Session of 1830–31* (Raleigh, N.C.: Lawrence and LeMay, 1831), 11.

16. Janet Duitsman Cornelius, *"When I Can Read My Title Clear": Literacy, Slavery, and Religion in the Antebellum South* (Columbia: University of South Carolina Press, 1991). Cornelius discusses the laws against teaching slaves to read on pp. 32–35.

17. On northern opposition to the education of African Americans, see Leon F. Litwack, *North of Slavery: The Negro in the Free States, 1790–1860* (Chicago: University of Chicago Press, 1961), 113–52.

18. See Philip S. Foner, "Prudence Crandall," in *Three Who Dared: Prudence Crandall, Margaret Douglass, Myrtilla Miner—Champions of Antebellum Black Education,* by Philip S. Foner and Josephine F. Pacheco (Westport, Conn.: Greenwood, 1984), 5–54.

19. Qtd. in *College for Colored Youth: An Account of the New-Haven City Meeting and Resolutions, with Recommendations of the College, and Strictures upon the Doings of New-Haven* (New York: Published by the Committee, 1831), 5.

20. George Lipsitz, *The Possessive Investment in Whiteness: How White People Profit from Identity Politics* (Philadelphia: Temple University Press, 1998), vii–viii.

21. Pennsylvania Society for Promoting the Abolition of Slavery, Board of Education, *Colored School Statistics* (Philadelphia: Moran, Sickels, 1853), 1.

22. *Statistics of the Colored People of Philadelphia. Taken by Benjamin C. Bacon, and Published by Order of the Board of Education of "The Pennsylvania Society for Promoting the Abolition of Slavery," etc.* (Philadelphia: T. Ellwood Chapman, 1856), 5. The report covers the year 1854.

23. Margaret Douglass, *Educational Laws of Virginia: The Personal Narrative of Mrs. Margaret Douglass, a Southern Woman, Who Was Imprisoned for One Month in the Common Jail of Norfolk, under the Laws of Virginia, for the Crime of Teaching Free Colored Children to Read* (Boston: Jewett, 1854), 4, 5.

24. Ibid., 4.

25. See, for example, *National Era,* 7 September 1854, 143, and *Frederick Douglass's Paper,* 8 September 1854 and 22 September 1854.

26. Douglass, *Educational Laws,* 10, 9. In the following paragraphs, quotations are cited parenthetically.

27. *Normal School for Colored Girls* (1856), 2.

28. Qtd. in Josephine F. Pacheco, "Myrtilla Miner," in *Three Who Dared,* 114. Seward represented Miner's home state of New York.

29. Qtd. ibid., 117.

30. Qtd. ibid., 114.

31. *The School for Colored Girls. Washington, D.C.* (Philadelphia: Merrihew and Thompson, 1854), 12.

32. Ibid., 5.

33. Ibid., 6.

34. *Normal School for Colored Girls* (1856), 2.

35. *School for Colored Girls* (1854), 4.

36. *Normal School for Colored Girls* (1856), 2.

37. *School for Colored Girls* (1854), 3–4.

38. Ibid., 4.

39. Ibid. (previous four quotations).

40. Ibid., 5.

41. From Miner's letter to E.D.E.N. Southworth, qtd. in Pacheco, "Myrtilla Miner," 117.

42. Lydia Maria Child, *The Freedmen's Book* (1865; New York: Arno, 1968), 270, iii. In the folowing paragraphs, quotations from this book are cited parenthetically.

43. Harriet Jacobs, *Incidents in the life of a Slave Girl,* ed. Jean Fagan Yellin (Cambridge: Harvard University Press, 1987), 36.

44. Child, *Freedmen's Book,* 97.

45. Ibid., 100.

46. Ibid., iii (both quotations). Carolyn Karcher's explanation of Child's publishing agreement with Ticknor and Fields resolves the apparent contradiction here. Child covered half of the cost of publishing the initial run of two thousand copies ($600 of a projected $1,200), planning to use money from subsequent sales to pay the balance and to pay for additional printing should the first run sell out. Karcher indicates that Child also planned to sell copies of the book to northern whites "at a competitive price" (*The First Woman in the Republic: A Cultural Biography of Lydia Maria Child* [Durham, N.C.: Duke University Press, 1994], 495).

47. Karcher presents evidence that former slaves preferred Child's book to *The Freedman's Third Reader,* a more conventional and Anglocentric primer published by the American Tract Society. The ATS text, however, had better financial backing and was ultimately more widely used (*First Woman,* 503–4).

48. Arthur Riss examines the nuances of legitimate and illegitimate possession in "Racial Essentialism and Family Values in *Uncle Tom's Cabin,*" *American Quarterly* 46 (1994): 531–34.

49. Harriet Beecher Stowe, *Uncle Tom's Cabin; or, Life among the Lowly,* ed. Elizabeth Ammons (1851–52; New York: Norton, 1994), xiii. Subsequent page citations appear parenthetically in the text, with the abbreviation *UTC.*

50. *The National Era,* 1 April 1852, 53. On Stowe's didacticism, see Sarah Robbins, "Gendering the History of the Antislavery Narrative: Juxtaposing *Uncle Tom's Cabin* and *Benito Cereno, Beloved* and *Middle Passage,*" *American Quarterly* 49 (1997): 531–73.

51. Harryette Mullen, "Runaway Tongue: Resistant Orality in *Uncle Tom's Cabin, Our Nig, Incidents in the Life of a Slave Girl,* and *Beloved,*" in *The Culture of Sentiment: Race, Gender, and Sentimentality in Nineteenth-Century America,* ed. Shirley Samuels (New York: Oxford University Press, 1992), 261.

52. Lynn Wardley offers Eva's "lock of hair" as an example of what she identifies as the novel's blending of "precious memento, sacred relic, and African fetish" ("Relic, Fetish, Femmage: The Aesthetics of Sentiment in the Work of Stowe," in *Culture of Sentiment,* 208).

53. Black literacy and white instruction were favorite themes among *Uncle Tom's Cabin's* illustrators. Jewett's 1853 illustrated edition, for example, features images of George Shelby teaching Tom, of Eva teaching Mammy, and of Tom reading the Bible to other slaves on Legree's plantation; Cassell's 1852 London edition includes George Cruikshank's image of Tom reading his Bible in front of a fireplace (Stowe, *Uncle Tom's Cabin; or, Life among the Lowly* [Boston: Jewett, 1853], 37, 332, 436; *Uncle Tom's Cabin* [London: Cassell, 1852], 302). Not all editions adhered to this emphasis, however; none of the eight engravings in Routledge's 1852 edition, for instance,

featured reading or literacy instruction (*Uncle Tom's Cabin; or, Negro Life in the Slave States of America* [London: G. Routledge; C.H. Clarke, 1852]).

54. My thanks to Sarah Robbins for helping me to clarify this point.

55. In at least one other version, the lake is replaced by a distant cottage, which weakens the reference to that specific revelatory moment (author's collection; date and origins unknown).

56. *Little Eva's First Book for Good Children* (Exeter, U.K.: Drayton and Sons, 1855[?]). On the cultural work of alphabet books, see Crain, *Story of A.*

57. *Little Eva: The Flower of the South* (New York: Phillip J. Cozans, 1855–1861[?]), 3, 5. The source of this approximate dating is the American Antiquarian Society's catalog.

58. Ibid., 5.

59. Gail Smith makes a similar argument with respect to Stowe's representations of reading and interpretation in *Dred* ("Reading with the Other: Hermeneutics and the Politics of Difference in Stowe's *Dred*," *American Literature* 69 [1997]: 289–313).

60. On the erotic Eva, see Hortense Spillers, "Changing the Letter: The Yokes, the Jokes of Discourse, or Mrs. Stowe, Mr. Reed," in *Slavery and the Literary Imagination,* ed. Deborah E. McDowell and Arnold Rampersad (Baltimore: Johns Hopkins University Press, 1989), 25–61; and P. Gabrielle Foreman, " 'This Promiscuous Housekeeping': Death, Transgression, and Homoeroticism in *Uncle Tom's Cabin,*" *Representations,* no. 43 (1993): 51–72. George Aiken's stage version of *Uncle Tom's Cabin* brings the reformed Ophelia into an economy of sexual desire, giving her a suitor when she returns to Vermont and joking about the possible sexual transgression underlying her parental relation to Topsy (*Uncle Tom's Cabin; or, Life among the Lowly. A Domestic Drama, in Six Acts* [New York: Samuel French, 1858(?)]). On Topsy's "intimate relation" to Ophelia, especially in Aiken's play, see Elizabeth Young, *Disarming the Nation: Women's Writing and the American Civil War* (Chicago: University of Chicago Press, 1999), 41.

61. Harriet Beecher Stowe, *A Key to Uncle Tom's Cabin; Presenting the Original Facts and Documents upon Which the Story Is Founded. Together with Corroborative Statements Verifying the Truth of the Work* (Boston: Jewett, 1853), 31.

62. Young, *Disarming the Nation,* 33.

63. Richard Brodhead, "Sparing the Rod: Discipline and Fiction in Antebellum America," in *Cultures of Letters: Scenes of Reading and Writing in Nineteenth-Century America* (Chicago: University of Chicago Press, 1993), 18, 19.

64. Ibid., 20.

65. Ibid., 41.

66. For more skeptical treatments of the link between literacy and freedom, see Valerie Smith, *Self-Discovery and Authority in Afro-American Narrative* (Cambridge: Harvard University Press, 1987), and Lindon Barrett, "African-American Slave Narratives: Literacy, the Body, Authority," *American Literary History* 7 (1995): 415–42.

67. Forten was not the only African American who took part in the Port Royal initiative. Nevertheless, as Brenda Stevenson points out, she was, "at the time she arrived, the first and only [African American teacher] stationed on St. Helena Island" (introduction to *The Journals of Charlotte Forten Grimké,* ed. Brenda Stevenson [New York: Oxford University Press, 1988], 38).

68. As Carla Peterson has argued, both the essay and the *Liberator* letters "are marked by . . . a retreat into the disembodied stance of the ethnographer who observes the culture of the (primitive) Other" (*"Doers of the Word": African-American Women Speakers and Writers in the North (1830–1880)* [New York: Oxford University Press, 1995], 193). Forten's journals offer evidence of her attraction to travel writing as a genre, which may help to explain her rhetorical choices. See, for example, her entries for 1–2 February 1857 (*Journals,* 188–89).

69. Charlotte Forten, "Life on the Sea Islands," *Atlantic Monthly,* May–June 1864, 587. Subsequent page citations appear parenthetically in the text.

70. Forten writes that "we cannot determine whether [the "shout"] has a religious character or not. Some of the people tell us that it has, others that it has not. But as the shouts of the grown people are always in connection with their religious meetings, it is probable that they are the barbarous expression of religion, handed down to them from their African ancestors, and destined to pass away under the influence of Christian teachings" (593–94).

71. Entries from June 1854, for example, include references to "our persecuted race" and "my oppressed and suffering people," in the context of a discussion of the fugitive slave Anthony Burns (Forten, *Journals,* 66–67). See Peterson, *"Doers of the Word,"* 192, and Lisa Long, "Charlotte Forten's Civil War Journals and the Quest for 'Genius, Beauty, and Deathless Fame,'" *Legacy* 16 (1999): 43. In light of these shifts, I question Long's claim that "Forten's trip to the South was clearly an effort to rediscover her racial identity, to work for and connect with her 'people'" (43).

72. Long has persuasively argued that Forten's class position was more complicated than is typically noted. While she was in many ways privileged, especially relative to her African American contemporaries, Forten nevertheless experienced "daily economic struggles" ("Charlotte Forten's Civil War Journals," 38).

73. II Kings 4:13. My interpretation of the phrase is indebted to the explanation offered in *II Kings: A New Translation with Introduction and Commentary by Mordechai Cogan and Hayim Tadmor,* vol. 11 of the *Anchor Bible* (New York: Doubleday, 1988), 57. Thanks to James Peterson for locating this source and related materials.

74. W. E. B. DuBois uses the same phrase in the autobiographical section of *Darkwater: Voices from within the Veil* (1920; New York: Schocken, 1969). In reference to his being sent from Massachusetts to a historically black college in the South (rather than to Harvard, "the goal of [his] dreams"), DuBois writes: "After a twinge, I felt a strange delight! I forgot, or did not thoroughly realize, the curious irony by which I was not looked upon as a real citizen of my birthtown, with a future and a career, and instead was being sent to a far land among strangers who were regarded as (and in truth were) 'mine own people'" (13).

75. Peterson notes that the *Atlantic* essay was "based largely on personal letters to Whittier," which in turn owed much to Forten's Port Royal diary entries (*"Doers of the Word,"* 193). Whether or not Forten knew in advance that Whittier would submit this piece to the magazine, she had reason to expect that he might publish material she sent him. She noted in a December 1862 journal entry, for example, that Whittier had, to her annoyance, sent one of her letters "to the 'Transcript.'" She continued, "He ought not to have done that. It was not worth it" (*Journals,* 422). An earlier entry indicates Forten's willingness to have a letter to William Lloyd Garrison published in the *Liberator* (*Journals,* 407).

76. Forten, *Journals,* 484.

77. Ibid., 289.

78. Ibid., 403.

79. Ibid.

80. Qtd. in Willie Lee Rose, *Rehearsal for Reconstruction: The Port Royal Experiment* (Indianapolis: Bobbs-Merrill, 1964), 161.

81. Ibid., 162.

82. The headnote accompanying the 12 December 1862 letter identifies the author as "a young colored lady of Philadelphia" and as the "grand-daughter of the late venerable James Forten" (199). A second letter simply identifies her by name (*Liberator,* 19 December 1862, 203). Because Forten was from such a well-known family, the inclusion of her surname likely identified her as African American for most readers of the *Liberator.*

83. "Letter from St. Helena's Island, Beaufort, S.C.," *Liberator,* 12 December 1862, 199.

84. Forten, *Journals,* 499.

85. "Interesting Letter from Miss Charlotte L. Forten: St. Helena's Island, Beaufort, S.C., Nov. 27, 1862," *Liberator,* 19 December 1862, 203.

86. According to Stevenson's chronology, Forten spent another seven months in South Carolina, returning to Philadelphia in May 1864 (Forten, *Journals,* xxxvii). Her direct engagement in the Port Royal project was ending just as the essay appeared.

87. Peterson, *"Doers of the Word,"* 192.

Chapter 5. Charity Begins at Home

1. Harriet Beecher Stowe, *Dred: A Tale of the Great Dismal Swamp,* 2 vols. (Boston: Phillips, Sampson, 1856), 1: iv. Subsequent citations appear parenthetically in the text, with the abbreviation *D.*

2. Amy Kaplan, "Manifest Domesticity," *American Literature* 70 (1998): 581–606; Lora Romero, *Home Fronts: Domesticity and Its Critics in the Antebellum United States* (Durham, N.C.: Duke University Press, 1997).

3. On Stowe's engagement with African American abolitionists, including Frederick Douglass, Sojourner Truth, and William C. Nell, see Robert S. Levine, *Martin Delany, Frederick Douglass, and the Politics of Representative Identity* (Chapel Hill: University of North Carolina Press, 1997), chaps. 2 and 4, and Robert Stepto, "Sharing the Thunder: The Literary Exchanges of Harriet Beecher Stowe, Henry Bibb, and Frederick Douglass," in *New Essays on* Uncle Tom's Cabin, ed. Eric Sundquist (New York: Cambridge University Press, 1986), 135–53.

4. Evan Radcliffe, "Revolutionary Writing, Moral Philosophy, and Universal Benevolence in the Eighteenth Century," *Journal of the History of Ideas* 54 (1993): 222.

5. Lysander Spooner, *Poverty: Its Illegal Causes, and Legal Cure. Part 1* (Boston: Bela Marsh, 1846), 45, 46. Spooner admits that "there is, of course, some sympathy between all men, for a common nature compels it; but it is not quick or strong between opposite classes, or strangers, as it is between similar classes and acquaintances" (45).

6. *The Kidnapped Clergyman; or, Experience the Best Teacher* (Boston: Dow and Jackson, 1839).

7. Baltimore Association for Improving the Condition of the Poor (AICP), *Annual Report, Constitution and By-Laws, and Visitor's Manual* (Baltimore: Office of the Association, 1851), 19; italics in original.

8. Frederick T. Frelinghuysen, *Address of Hon. F. T. Frelinghuysen, Senator from New Jersey* (Washington, D.C.: American Colonization Society, 1868), 4.

9. Oliver Wendell Holmes, *Oration Delivered before the New England Society, in the City of New York, by Oliver Wendell Holmes, M.D., at Their Semi-Centennial Anniversary, December 22, 1855* (New York: William C. Bryant, 1856), 42–43.

10. Alexander Crummell, "The Race Problem in America," in *Negro Social and Political Thought, 1850–1920*, ed. Howard Brotz (New York: Basic, 1966), 184; italics in original. Although this address is from relatively late (1888) in Crummell's career, it reflects his long-standing investment in racial allegiance.

11.. "Africa to Be Christianized by Africans," *Colonization Herald* (Philadelphia), July 1851, 52.

12. The official publication of the American Colonization Society printed the following account of relative survival rates from an expedition to Africa: "The colored persons who accompanied the expedition had not suffered at all in the same proportion as the whites; on the contrary, they had so far endured the trials of the African climate without any extraordinary loss, that of the whole number of deaths during the expedition, amounting to forty-eight, only three were reported of colored persons, and of these three, not one was occasioned by the 'river-fever' " ("Meeting of the African Civilization Society," *African Repository, and Colonial Journal* [Washington], November 1842, 356). Edward S. Morris's *Address to the Colored People of Pennsylvania* gave this argument an economic twist. Drawing on the suggestion that "there are large deposits of gold in Africa," he writes that, because "the climate" of Africa "is almost certainly fatal" to whites, "*the wealth of Africa is reserved exclusively for the colored race*" ([Philadelphia: Edward S. Morris, 1861], 25; italics in original).

13. William Aikman, *The Future of the Colored Race in America: Being an Article in the* Presbyterian Quarterly Review, *of July 1862* (New York: Anson D. F. Randolph, 1862), 34. Anglo-American participation in colonizationist efforts was generally conceived of as a short-term measure that would facilitate the success of black emigrants and missionaries; by these means, whites sought to discharge the "national debt" Americans owed "to Africa" (Frederick Freeman, *Africa's Redemption, the Salvation of Our Country* [New York: D. Fanshaw, 1852], 139).

14. Cornish is responding to a letter from William Whipper, which argues that benevolent and moral reform efforts should take no account of race (*Colored American*, 29 March 1838, cd-rom). This exchange was part of a larger debate among free African Americans over the salience of racial difference in reform efforts (see Patrick Rael, *Black Identity and Black Protest in the Antebellum North* [Chapel Hill: University of North Carolina Press, 2002], 49–51, and Eddie S. Glaude, *Exodus! Religion, Race, and Nation in Early Nineteenth-Century Black America* [Chicago: University of Chicago Press, 2000], 131–42).

15. "The Address and Constitution of the Union Benevolent Association of the People of Color of the City of Washington," *National Reformer*, March 1839, 107.

16. "The Influence of Early Education," *National Reformer*, January 1839, 82.

17. Ibid.

18. Gerrit Smith, *To the People of the County of Madison* (Peterboro, N.Y.: n.p., 1847). Elsewhere, Smith abandoned geographical priorities altogether, arguing that "an infinitely more important order of benevolence is, first, to labor for the total repudiation of the Heaven-forbidden idea of property in man" (qtd. in John Stauffer, *The Black Hearts of Men: Radical Abolitionists and the Transformation of Race* [Cambridge: Harvard University Press, 2002], 137).

19. Theophilus Fiske, "Extracts from an Oration," *The National Crisis. An Antidote to Abolition Fanaticism, Treason and Sham Philanthropy*, 15 May 1860, 4; "Lodging Places," ibid., 13. The gospels of Matthew and Luke both use the "mote" and "beam" expression as a figure for hypocrisy (see Luke 6: 41–42 and Matt. 7: 3–5). For images like those I have described, see "The Horrors of Slavery in Black and White," *Lantern*, 7 February 1852, 46, and *Slavery As It Exists in America. Slavery As It Exists in England* (Boston: J. Haven, 1850).

20. Emerson Bennett, *Ellen Norbury; or, the Adventures of an Orphan* (Philadelphia: T. B. Peterson, 1855), 12.

21. David Brown, *The Planter; or, Thirteen Years in the South. By a Northern Man* (Philadelphia: H. Hooker, 1853), 185.

22. "Missionary Hymn, for the South," *Voices of the True-Hearted* (Philadelphia: Merrihew and Thompson, 1846), 160; italics in original.

23. An old cataloging record at the American Antiquarian Society (AAS) identifies this undated lithograph as Reconstruction-era. However, Janice Simon, associate professor of art history at the University of Georgia and scholar in residence at the AAS (June–July 2000), determined that the image is almost certainly antebellum, based on the style in which the figures are drawn and the fashions depicted (personal conversation, 30 June 2000). In addition, the relatively youthful appearance of the (probable) Sumner figure suggests pre–Civil War origins. Sumner was in his fifties by the end of the war, and his 1865 portrait presents a much older-looking man.

24. I am grateful to my colleague Matthew Biberman for pointing to the significance of the man's occupied right hand. This representation is similar to late-twentieth-century attacks on affirmative action. Note, for example, Senator Jesse Helms's infamous "Hands" (1990) television advertisement, which shows a pair of hands (ostensibly belonging to a white man) crumpling what appears to be a rejection letter, while a voice intones, "you needed that job, but they had to give it to a minority." The video is available at http://www.pbs.org/30secondcandidate/text/timeline/years/1990.html (29 May 2002).

25. Philip Fisher, *Hard Facts: Setting and Form in the American Novel* (New York: Oxford University Press, 1987), 118; Elizabeth Barnes, *States of Sympathy: Seduction and Democracy in the American Novel* (New York: Columbia University Press, 1997), 92. While I admire Barnes's analysis of the novel's "affinitive politics," I am primarily interested in the instability of these extensions and the reinscription of difference at the novel's conclusion. See also Marianne Noble's exploration of the visceral and sadomasochistic elements of the novel's strategies of identification (*The Masochistic Pleasures of Sentimental Literature* [Princeton: Princeton University Press, 2000], 126–46).

26. Robert Purvis, "The Serpent of Colonization in 'Uncle Tom's Cabin,'" *Pennsylvania Freeman*, n.s., 29 April 1852, 70.

27. Harriet Beecher Stowe, *Uncle Tom's Cabin; or, Life among the Lowly*, ed. Elizabeth Ammons (1851–52; New York: Norton, 1994), 377, 376. Subsequent citations appear parenthetically in the text, with the abbreviation *UTC*.

28. As George Fredrickson has argued, "the South's fundamental conception of itself as a slaveholding society was unstable": paternalistic theories, which figured slaves as members of the "family," however dependent and inferior, were at odds with the view that slaves were "essentially subhuman" (*The Black Image in the White Mind: The Debate on Afro-American Character and Destiny, 1817–1914* [New York: Harper and Row, 1971], 58). Stowe engages with both theories in *Uncle Tom's Cabin*.

29. George Harris's apologia betrays Stowe's discomfort with the colonizationist arguments of

conservative whites. She eventually renounced colonization, in part as a result of readers' negative responses to the Liberian ending of *Uncle Tom's Cabin*. Leon Litwack writes that, in a note to the American and Foreign Anti-Slavery convention (whose black delegates had called the Liberian passage in *Uncle Tom's Cabin* an "evil influence"), Stowe "reaffirmed her opposition to the American Colonization Society, assured the delegates that she was not a colonizationist, and admitted that if she were to rewrite the book, Harris would not be sent to Liberia. At the same time, however, she called the African colony 'a fixed fact' and advised Negroes not to disregard completely this opportunity to construct an independent nation" (*North of Slavery: The Negro in the Free States, 1790–1860* [Chicago: University of Chicago Press, 1961], 255). On Stowe and colonization, see also Levine, *Martin Delany, Frederick Douglass,* 144–51, and Timothy Powell, *Ruthless Democracy: A Multicultural Interpretation of the American Renaissance* (Princeton: Princeton University Press, 2000), 106–32.

30. Riss, "Racial Essentialism," 532, 530. On proslavery notions of the family, see 526–29. Note, however, that racial and familial allegiances are not always identical for Stowe's characters. Tom's decision not to escape with Cassy and Emmeline because he feels called by God to minister to the other slaves on Legree's plantation involves choosing a benevolent allegiance to fellow slaves as a group over an opportunity to rejoin his own particular family in Kentucky.

31. Ibid., 534.

32. Ibid., 536.

33. While George Harris's discussion of Liberia focuses on the rights he will enjoy there and on the injustices that abound in the United States, his decision nevertheless entails an element of benevolent responsibility, evident in his assertion that he is going to teach Christianity in Liberia (despite his own struggles with faith).

34. Judie Newman notes that *Dred* pays more attention to politics and to the intransigence of proslavery southerners than does *Uncle Tom's Cabin* (introduction to *Dred: A Tale of the Great Dismal Swamp* [Halifax, U.K.: Ryburn, 1992], 9–25).

35. For a detailed discussion of the novels that responded to Stowe's, see Thomas F. Gossett, *"Uncle Tom's Cabin" and American Culture* (Dallas: Southern Methodist University Press, 1985), 221–38. See also Russ Castronovo's "Incidents in the Life of a White Woman: Economies of Race and Gender in the Antebellum Nation," *American Literary History* 10 (1998): 239–65.

36. Stowe goes on to assert her benevolence toward slaveholders, claiming that she could not "hope to be regarded as a friend [by Southerners] and must comfort [herself] with the simple pleasure of feeling friendly" (Stephen B. Weeks, "Anti-Slavery Sentiment in the South; With Unpublished Letters from John Stuart Mill and Mrs. Stowe," *Publications of the Southern History Association* 2, no. 2 [1898]: 124, 125).

37. Eugene Genovese discusses the proslavery ideologies of paternalism and gratitude at length in *Roll, Jordon, Roll: The World the Slaves Made* (1972; New York: Vintage, 1976), esp. in bk. 1, 1–158. See also Jennifer Fleischner, *Mastering Slavery: Memory, Family, and Identity in Women's Slave Narratives* (New York: New York University Press, 1996), 193.

38. Hentz, *The Planter's Northern Bride* (Philadelphia: T. B. Peterson, 1854), vii–viii.

39. Mary Eastman, *Aunt Phillis's Cabin; or, Southern Life as It Is* (Philadelphia: Lippincott, Grambo, 1852), 44. Eastman's preface includes a harsher view of the familial elements of slavery, invoking the biblical curse of Ham, whose act of "dishonoring" his "aged father" brought down "slavery as a curse on a portion of the human race" (12). Here slavery exacts appropriate submission to parental authority from the descendants of one who lacked such deference.

40. *Uncle Robin, in His Cabin in Virginia, and Tom without One in Boston* (Richmond: J. W. Randolph, 1853).

41. Not all proslavery novels were set on southern plantations. For example, Caroline Rush's *The North and South; or, Slavery and Its Contrasts. A Tale of Real Life* deals primarily with the sufferings of a white family in the urban North (Philadelphia: Crissy and Markley, 1852).

42. Eastman, *Aunt Phillis's Cabin,* 60.

43. Ibid., 57.

44. Milly spends a great deal of time evangelizing Nina Gordon, relating her own arduous conversion to Christianity and counseling Nina to place her trust in God (*D,* 1: 206–23, 165–67).

45. Stowe claims in a footnote that the circumstances she creates for Milly "are true of an old

colored woman in New York, known by the name of Aunt Katy, who in her youth was a slave, and who is said to have established among these destitute children the first Sunday-school in the city of New York" (*D*, 2: 334). Stowe is probably referring to Katy Ferguson, whose obituary asserted that "during her life she took forty-eight children,—twenty of them white—some from the almshouse, others from their parents, and brought them up, or kept them till she could find places for them" ("A True Woman," *Colonization Herald*, September 1854, 200).

46. This flirtation is most evident in the novel's opening scene, in which the narrator delays revealing Harry's identity as slave and sibling. His interactions with Nina recall the conversations in Jane Austen's *Emma* between the frivolous young heroine and the sensible, brotherly man she eventually marries.

47. Nathaniel Hawthorne, *The Scarlet Letter*, vol. 1 of *The Centenary Edition of the Works of Nathaniel Hawthorne*, ed. William Charvat and Roy Harvey Pearce (Columbus: Ohio State University Press, 1962), 263.

48. Brook Thomas, "Citizen Hester: *The Scarlet Letter* as Civic Myth," *American Literary History* 13 (2001): 196.

49. Ibid., 197, 199. While Thomas does not use the term *benevolence*, his notion of good citizenship accords with its nineteenth-century meanings.

50. Noble, *Masochistic Pleasures*, 131.

Chapter 6. "Save Us from Our Friends"

1. "Colonization in Middletown, Conn.," *Mirror of Liberty*, August 1838, 7.

2. Ibid.

3. In keeping with other scholars' practices, I use *colonization* to refer to the white-dominated movement to send free African Americans and former slaves to Liberia. *Emigration*, on the other hand, denotes a range of proposals that emerged among African Americans to form black colonies and, eventually, nations outside the United States. Some African Americans, of course, participated in colonizationist projects, just as some Anglo-Americans endorsed emigrationist proposals.

4. Because many of these texts appeared anonymously or were reprinted from other sources, it is impossible in every case to verify the author's racial identity. But even a white-authored text, if chosen or accepted by an African American editor, was in some sense a part of the era's African American print culture.

5. John Ernest, *Resistance and Reformation in Nineteenth-Century African-American Literature: Brown, Wilson, Jacobs, Delany, Douglass, and Harper* (Jackson: University Press of Mississippi, 1995), 34.

6. For an example of Brown's early mistrust of benevolence, see the disavowal of begging in *Narrative of the Life and Escape of William Wells Brown*, published with the 1853 edition of *Clotel* (*Clotel; or, The President's Daughter*, ed. Robert S. Levine [Boston: Bedford/St. Martin's, 2000], 74). William L. Andrews claims that Brown probably wrote this third-person memoir himself (*From Fugitive Slave to Free Man: The Autobiographies of William Wells Brown* [New York: Mentor, 1993], 4); Levine makes the same assertion in his edition of *Clotel* but without the qualifier (49). I accept their attribution, though I would add that, even if someone else penned it, Brown's decision to include the piece with *Clotel* implies an endorsement of its representations. For a late example of Brown's investment in benevolence, see *Clotelle; or, The Colored Heroine* (1867), in which Clotelle, passing as "a rebel lady," aids sick Union soldiers in a Confederate prison hospital (excerpt rpt. in Levine, ed., *Clotel*, 318–21).

7. Levine, ed., introduction to *Clotel*, 7.

8. *Life and Escape of William Wells Brown*, 60.

9. Brown, *The American Fugitive in Europe: Sketches of Places and People Abroad* (Boston: Jewett, 1855; New York: Negro Universities Press, 1969), 315.

10. Ibid. While the violence invoked here is largely rhetorical, Brown did support slaves' right to use violence against their oppressors (see Levine, ed., *Clotel*, 38, and William Edward Farrison, *William Wells Brown: Author and Reformer* [Chicago: University of Chicago Press, 1969], 292).

11. Dana D. Nelson, *National Manhood: Capitalist Citizenship and the Imagined Fraternity of White Men* (Durham, N.C.: Duke University Press, 1998).

12. See, for example, notices in the 8 January 1852 issue of *Frederick Douglass's Paper* announcing "A State Convention of the Colored Citizens of Ohio" and reporting on "a meeting of the colored citizens of Chicago" (cd-rom); "Sandbury, O., October 21," *Frederick Douglass's Paper,* 29 October 1852, cd-rom.

13. "An Appeal in Behalf of the Colored American," *Colored American,* 25 September 1841, cd-rom. For a counterexample, see Maria Stewart's "An Address Delivered at the African Masonic Hall, Boston, February 27, 1833," which avoids this double usage, reserving the term *citizen* to signify the state toward which African Americans ought to strive (*Pamphlets of Protest: An Anthology of Early African-American Protest Literature, 1790–1860,* ed. Richard Newman, Patrick Rael, and Phillip Lapsansky [New York: Routledge, 2001], 126).

14. Glenn Hendler, *Public Sentiments: Structures of Feeling in Nineteenth-Century American Literature* (Chapel Hill: University of North Carolina Press, 2001), 59.

15. Martin Delany, "Political Destiny of the Colored Race on the American Continent," in *Pamphlets of Protest,* ed. Newman et al., 227.

16. Martin Delany, *The Condition, Elevation, Emigration, and Destiny of the Colored People of the United States* (Philadelphia: published by the author, 1852; New York: Arno, 1968), 3.

17. Delany pursues a number of threads in *Condition,* arguing against colonization most forcefully in chapters 3, 6, and 7; making a case for the "claims of colored men as citizens of the United States" (49) in chapters 7 through 15; and turning to emigration (within the western hemisphere) in chapters 17 through 23.

18. Bruce Dorsey, "A Gendered History of African Colonization in the Antebellum United States," *Journal of Social History* 34 (2000): 87.

19. "The Colonization Scheme," *Frederick Douglass's Paper,* 22 January 1852, cd-rom.

20. *Constitution of the American Society of Free Persons of Colour, for Improving Their Condition in the United States; for Purchasing Lands; and for the Establishment of a Settlement in Upper Canada, also the Proceedings of the Convention, with Their Address to the Free Persons of Colour in the United States* (Philadelphia: J.W. Allen, 1831; Philadelphia: Rhistoric, 1969), 10; Samuel E. Cornish and Theodore S. Wright, *The Colonization Scheme Considered, in Its Rejection by the Colored People . . .* (Newark: Aaron Guest, 1840), 3; "Colonization against Caste," *Frederick Douglass's Paper,* 1 April 1853, cd-rom.

21. Delany, *Condition,* 32; "The Colonization Scheme," *Frederick Douglass's Paper,* 22 January 1852, cd-rom.

22. Stewart, "Address Delivered at the African Masonic Hall," 126.

23. *Minutes and Proceedings of the First Annual Convention of the People of Colour, Held by Adjournments in the City of Philadelphia, from the Sixth to the Eleventh of June, Inclusive, 1831* (Philadelphia: Published by Order of the Committee of Arrangements, 1831), 15.

24. Elizabeth Margaret Chandler, "The Enfranchised Slaves to Their Benefactress," in *The Poetical Works of Elizabeth Margaret Chandler: With a Memoir of Her Life and Character, by Benjamin Lundy* (Philadelphia: Lemuel Howell, 1836), 73.

25. *Minutes and Proceedings of the First Annual Convention of the People of Colour,* 11.

26. "Difficulties of Abolition," *Colored American,* 27 May 1837, 2. The author subsequently attacks abolitionist condescension, insisting that African Americans ought to be held to the same moral and intellectual standards as whites (2).

27. "Extract from the Report of the Board of Managers of the A.M. Reform Society," *National Reformer,* September 1839, 132.

28. Qtd. in Robert S. Levine, *Martin Delany, Frederick Douglass, and the Politics of Representative Identity* (Chapel Hill: University of North Carolina Press, 1997), 79.

29. Delany, *Condition,* 26, 27.

30. "The Humbug of Reform," *Provincial Freeman* (Canada), 27 May 1854, 2. The editors of *The Black Abolitionist Papers* attribute this unsigned article to Shadd Cary (vol. 2, *Canada, 1830–1865,* ed. C. Peter Ripley et al. [Chapel Hill: University of North Carolina Press, 1986], 285–88). According to Jane Rhodes, Mary Ann Shadd did not marry Thomas Cary until January

1856 (*Mary Ann Shadd Cary: The Black Press and Protest in the Nineteenth Century* [Blooming-ton: Indiana University Press, 1998], 112); nevertheless, in keeping with the practice of a number of scholars, Rhodes excepted, I refer to her as Shadd Cary throughout.

31. Qtd. in Leon F. Litwack, *North of Slavery: The Negro in the Free States, 1790–1860* (Chicago: University of Chicago Press, 1961), 219.

32. *Condition of the American Colored Population, and of the Colony at Liberia* (Boston: Peirce and Parker, 1833), 9.

33. James McCune Smith, "On the Fourteenth Query of Thomas Jefferson's Notes on Virginia," *Anglo-African Magazine,* August 1859, 225. The magazine has "M'Cune" rather than "McCune."

34. Cornish and Wright, *Colonization Scheme Considered,* 9–10.

35. National Emigration Convention of Colored People, *Proceedings of the National Emigration Convention of Colored People; Held at Cleveland, Ohio, on Thursday, Friday and Saturday, the 24th, 25th and 26th of August, 1854* (Pittsburgh: A. A. Anderson, 1854), 6. This piece goes on to suggest that "every black person" should keep a copy of this publication to give "in lieu of an argument, to his oppressor or wellwisher" (6).

36. "Our Elevation," 181.

37. *Minutes and Proceedings of the First Annual Convention of the People of Colour,* 7.

38. "Classical Education of Our Young Men," *Colored American,* 16 February 1839, cd-rom.

39. "Moral Work for Colored Men," *Colored American,* 10 February 1838, 18.

40. "George Harris," *Provincial Freeman,* 22 July 1854, 2.

41. Joanne Pope Melish, *Disowning Slavery: Gradual Emancipation and "Race" in New England, 1780–1860* (Ithaca: Cornell University Press, 1998), 261.

42. The 1855 report of a "committee of colored citizens of Philadelphia" asserted that black Philadelphians had formed "108 Mutual Beneficial Societies," which assisted 1385 families, "maintain[ing] a large portion of our poor under circumstances which would otherwise throw them upon public charity" (qtd. in Pennsylvania Society for Promoting the Abolition of Slavery, Board of Education, *Colored School Statistics* [Philadelphia: Moran, Sickels, 1853], 16).

43. "Constitution and By-Laws of the Philadelphia Association for the Moral and Mental Improvement of the People of Color," *Colored American,* 24 June 1837, 2.

44. Delany, "Political Destiny," 233; Delany, *Condition,* 206.

45. "Take Care of Number One!" *Colored American,* 27 January 1838, 10.

46. "Our Second Year," *Colored American,* 13 January 1838, 2; "Come Over and Help Us," *Colored American,* 25 March 1837, 3.

47. "Further Testimony against Israel Lewis," *Colored American,* 24 August 1839, cd-rom. On the implications of the Lewis case for African American notions of respectability, see Patrick Rael, *Black Identity and Black Protest in the Antebellum North* (Chapel Hill: University of North Carolina Press, 2002), 121–24. Rael notes that the antebellum black press paid a great deal of attention to cases of fraud, both within and beyond reform movements (138–46).

48. "Look out for a Rascal," *Provincial Freeman,* 29 September 1855, cd-rom; "Buying Slaves," ibid., 8 March 1856, cd-rom.

49. See introduction to *Black Abolitionist Papers,* 2: 31–32.

50. Henry Bibb, "Editorial by Henry Bibb, 18 June 1851," ibid., 2: 144.

51. Introduction to *Black Abolitionist Papers,* 2: 24; Dorsey, "A Gendered History of African Colonization," 95.

52. "No More Begging for Farms or Clothes for Fugitives in Canada," *Frederick Douglass's Paper,* 29 October 1852, cd-rom. The RHS was founded in 1851 by abolitionists in Michigan and combined forces in 1852 with the Fugitive Union Society, a black-run organization devoted to moral elevation. Although the RHS remained under the control of whites in Michigan, Henry and Mary Bibb, along with a white agent, took on local leadership roles (*Black Abolitionist Papers,* 2: 147).

53. Documents reprinted in *The Black Abolitionist Papers* indicate that not everyone was or claimed to be so convinced of Canada's commitment to racial equality. See "Dennis Hill to Egerton Ryerson, 22 November 1852" (2: 243–44), and "John W. Lewis to Frederick Douglass, 20 March 1855" (2: 310–15).

54. *Life and Escape of William Wells Brown,* in *Clotel,* ed. Levine, 74, 75–76.

55. John Ernest, introduction to *The Escape; or, A Leap for Freedom,* by William Wells Brown (Knoxville: University of Tennessee Press, 2001), x, xliii, n.7.

56. Ernest, introduction to *The Escape,* xxxvii–xlii.

57. Brown, *The Escape,* 35, 40.

58. Ibid., 46.

59. John Ernest, "The Reconstruction of Whiteness: William Wells Brown's *The Escape; or, A Leap for Freedom,*" *PMLA* 113 (1998): 1118.

60. Brown, *The Escape,* 47.

61. Brown, *Narrative of William W. Brown, A Fugitive Slave. Written by Himself,* 2d ed. (1848), in *From Fugitive Slave to Free Man,* ed. Andrews, 80.

62. *Life and Escape of William Wells Brown,* 72.

63. Brown, *Three Years in Europe; or, Places I Have Seen and People I Have Met* (London: Charles Gilpin, 1852), 9.

64. Brown's travel narratives fall into the category of "hybrid works" that, according to Sandra Gunning, "point to diverse cultural, economic, and religious alliances that complicate relations to America as home, to the world abroad, and especially to an African diaspora juxtaposed against and coalescing with other national dispersals enacted by western imperialism" ("Nancy Prince and the Politics of Mobility, Home and Diasporic (Mis)Identification," *American Quarterly* 53 [2001]: 62).

65. This edition bears an 1855 imprint, although Brown actually published it in December 1854 (Levine, ed., *Clotel,* 37). Citations appear parenthetically in the text.

66. Brown changed this chapter very little from the first to the second edition. I have chosen to quote from the U.S. edition (1855) because it clarifies a minor inconsistency from the first version and elaborates engagingly on the London fog.

67. See Mary Chapman and Glenn Hendler, eds., *Sentimental Men: Masculinity and the Politics of Affect in American Culture* (Berkeley: University of California Press, 1999).

68. Granted, Brown also gives money to the English beggar, but it is a much smaller amount and is given rather off-handedly, certainly without the emotional investment of this encounter. Also, he expresses no regret at being unable to raise the boy out of poverty entirely.

69. Priscilla Wald, *Constituting Americans: Cultural Anxiety and Narrative Form* (Durham, N.C.: Duke University Press, 1995), 7.

70. Brown waffles on exactly how much money he has. He claims to have spent his last "sixpence" on postage stamps but then says "the only vestige of money about me was a smooth farthing that a little girl had given to me . . . , saying, 'This is for the slaves'" (120). Why he would spend his last (or near-to-last) store of money on postage stamps is another question. These inconsistencies and lapses of logic underscore the fact that this is a construction rather than a (necessarily) reliable and exact account. In any case, my interest lies in Brown's self-presentation rather than in his literal adherence to the facts.

71. Paul Gilroy, *The Black Atlantic: Modernity and Double Consciousness* (Cambridge: Harvard University Press, 1993).

72. Brown made a general argument for the "propriety" of such emigration in a letter to the editor of the London *Times* (dated 3 July 1851) and encouraged "those [Englishmen] interested in the West India estates" to facilitate the project (reprinted under the title "Fugitive Slaves in England," *Frederick Douglass's Paper,* 24 July 1851, cd-rom).

73. According to Farrison, Brown sailed for Philadelphia in September 1854, after his freedom was purchased in July (*William Wells Brown,* 244, 241).

74. Lora Romero, *Home Fronts: Domesticity and Its Critics in the Antebellum United States* (Durham, N.C.: Duke University Press, 1997), 60.

75. Brown himself participated in several such projects, including the Underground Railroad and various antislavery and temperance initiatives.

76. Joanna Brooks discusses Prince Hall's emphasis on duty and sympathy in a pair of speeches he delivered and published in the 1790s ("Prince Hall, Freemasonry, and Genealogy," *African American Review* 34 [2000]: 213). On freemasonry and the construction of African American masculinity, see Maurice Wallace, *Constructing the Black Masculine: Iden-*

tity and Ideality in African American Men's Literature and Culture (Durham, N.C.: Duke University Press, 2002), 53–81. Both Brooks and Wallace list William Wells Brown as a freemason.

77. Nelson, *National Manhood,* 187.

78. Ibid., 200, 197.

79. Ibid., 203.

Epilogue. The Afterlife of Benevolent Citizenship

1. *Amistad,* dir. Steven Spielberg, DreamWorks, 1997.

2. Maggie Sale writes that "a number of 'young men connected with Yale College' engaged themselves in daily instruction with the Mendians [the Amistad captives], teaching them to read the English language and 'the plain and important truths of Christianity' " (*The Slumbering Volcano: American Slave Ship Revolts and the Production of Rebellious Masculinity* [Durham, N.C.: Duke University Press, 1997], 93).

3. Olasky, a member of the journalism faculty at the University of Texas at Austin, is the author of several books promoting faith-based social activism.

4. See Eric Cheyfitz's review essay "The Irresistibleness of Great Literature: Reconstructing Hawthorne's Politics," which examines the "linkages between processes of canonization and nationalization," using Hawthorne as a test case (*American Literary History* 6 [1994]: 540).

5. Elizabeth Renker, "Melville, Wife Beating, and the Written Page," *American Literature* 66 (1994): 123–50; *Strike through the Mask: Herman Melville and the Scene of Writing* (Baltimore: Johns Hopkins University Press, 1996). The implications of these letters were debated in a 1981 monograph, *The Endless, Winding Way in Melville: New Charts by Kring and Carey,* ed. Donald Yannella and Hershel Parker (Glassboro, N.J.: Melville Society, 1981), but the matter received little further attention until Renker's publications.

6. Renker, *Strike through the Mask,* 51, 50, 51.

7. For overviews of the controversy, see Robert S. Levine's review of *Strike through the Mask* (*Melville Society Extracts,* no. 110 [1997]: 22–24), and Philip Weiss's "Herman-Neutics" (*New York Times Magazine,* 15 December 1996; online version).

8. Len Gougeon's introduction details the debates over Emerson's commitment to abolition (*Virtue's Hero: Emerson, Antislavery, and Reform* [Athens: University of Georgia Press, 1990], 1–23). See also Robert D. Richardson, Jr., *Emerson: The Mind on Fire: A Biography* (Berkeley: University of California Press, 1995), esp. 395–99, 496–99; Albert J. von Frank, *The Trials of Anthony Burns: Freedom and Slavery in Emerson's Boston* (Cambridge: Harvard University Press, 1998); and *Emerson's Antislavery Writings,* ed. Len Gougeon and Joel Myerson (New Haven: Yale University Press, 1995).

9. See, for example, Carolyn Karcher, *Shadow over the Promised Land: Slavery, Race, and Violence in Melville's America* (Baton Rouge: Louisiana State University Press, 1980), 127–59.

10. Barbara Christian, among others, has examined a related phenomenon: the burden placed on African American authors to create in their texts "positive images" of the race ("Politically Incorrect Struggles/Syndromes," in *Defining Ourselves: Black Writers in the 90s,* ed. Elizabeth Nunez and Brenda M. Greene [New York: Peter Lang, 1999], 140).

11. Robert S. Levine, *Martin Delany, Frederick Douglass, and the Politics of Representative Identity* (Chapel Hill: University of North Carolina Press, 1997), 234, 3.

12. For a defense of Douglass against charges of excessive assimilation into white culture, see William S. McFeely, "Visible Man: Frederick Douglass for the 1990s," in *Liberating Sojourn: Frederick Douglass and Transatlantic Reform,* ed. Alan J. Rice and Martin Crawford (Athens: University of Georgia Press, 1999), 15–27. Appropriately, this essay appears under the heading "Douglass's Moral Legacy." My third chapter addresses the controversies over Douglass's treatment of women and his ties to African American communities.

13. Jane Tompkins, for example, finds in *Uncle Tom's Cabin* a revolutionary agenda calling for the emancipation of slaves and the cultural empowerment of women (*Sensational Designs: The Cultural Work of American Fiction, 1790–1860* [New York: Oxford University Press, 1985], 122–46). Lora Romero makes a more cautious argument for Stowe's progressivism. She

acknowledges that "*Uncle Tom's Cabin* does not fulfill its own fantasy of itself as radically liberatory across a range of race and class hierarchies" but goes on to assert that "the novel helped legitimate two historically momentous and politically progressive platforms: abolition and white middle-class women's intervention in putatively 'masculine' concerns" (*Home Fronts: Domesticity and Its Critics in the Antebellum United States* [Durham, N.C.: Duke University Press, 1997], 86).

14. Karen Sánchez-Eppler articulates many readers' dismay at Stowe's segregationist resolution, noting that "the utopian freedom [Stowe] constructs is predicated upon the absence of black bodies" (*Touching Liberty: Abolition, Feminism, and the Politics of the Body* [Berkeley: University of California Press, 1993], 48). For another trenchant analysis of sentimentalism's racial projects, see Laura Wexler, *Tender Violence: Domestic Visions in an Age of U.S. Imperialism* (Chapel Hill: University of North Carolina Press, 2000). Critiques of Stowe's racial representations, many by African Americans, of course preceded the recuperation of sentimentalism as well. Among the most famous of these is James Baldwin's "Everybody's Protest Novel" (1949), available in *James Baldwin: Collected Essays* (New York: Library of America, 1998), 11–18.

15. Robyn Wiegman, for example, writes that *Uncle Tom's Cabin* is the text "that most haunts" her book *American Anatomies*, on the linkages and "incommensurabilities" of race and gender in contemporary discourse (*American Anatomies: Theorizing Race and Gender* [Durham, N.C.: Duke University Press, 1995], 193, 195).

Index

ABOUT THE AUTHOR

Susan M. Ryan is assistant professor of English at the University of Louisville.

D0933661

THE DEBRETT SEASON

THE DEBRETT SEASON

*A Lighthearted Romp Through the
Social and Sporting Year*

Edited and compiled by
ADAM HELLIKER

DEBRETT'S PEERAGE LIMITED

Preface

It has been said many times that the traditional English Season died with the ending of debutantes' presentations at Court in 1958, and that the final nail in the coffin came with the last Queen Charlotte's Ball in 1977. Debrett believe that the Season is still alive and is, if anything, more popular than ever. It has certainly changed from the old pattern of a marriage market through which debs were launched into Society with the sole aim of finding a suitable husband; but the pattern of 'fashionable' people meeting at a series of sporting and social events during the spring and summer is still very strong. Events such as Ascot and Henley continue to prosper, as more and more people of widely differing backgrounds acquire the means to indulge in the pastimes once reserved for the well-connected.

It was with this in mind that Debrett began thinking of a general guide to the season, and with the upsurge in interest in British Society by those who are not natives of this land the idea became a positive must for a publishing house so dedicated to helping us all know about social mobility.

Until now there has been no single publication available which attempts to describe the history and importance of the English seasonal events and – often more important to those not in the know – how to get into these occasions. Methods of entrance to some of these events have, until quite recently, been kept as quiet as possible because they were considered the last bastions of the privileged classes – the only places left where friends could meet in a convivial atmosphere without being disturbed by the rabble.

Debrett would be the first to agree that the Season as it is today exists only with the support of the non-traditional members of Society – it is the successful businessmen and industrialists, not the aristocracy, who set the pace. The deb season may be unofficial without the Buck House presentations but it is still going strong, with the non-aristocratic members of the Elite highly represented. As Mrs Betty Kenward, the doyenne of Society, put it: 'There are more dances than ever, but the people are different. You see more industrialists, more people who have *made* money.'

Dates of the main social events in 1981

Badminton   9–12 April
University Boat Race   4 April
Grand National   4 April
Chelsea Flower Show   19–22 May
Royal Academy Summer Exhibition   16 May–9 August
Glyndebourne   27 May–11 August
Monaco Grand Prix   31 May
Lord's Test Match   1st week in June
Derby Day   3 June
Fourth of June at Eton   6 June
Royal Ascot   16–19 June
Wimbledon   22 June–4 July
Henley Regatta   2–5 July
Goodwood   28 July–1 August
Game Fair   30 July–1 August
Open Golf Championships   16–19 July
Cowes Week   1–9 August
Burghley Horse Trials   10–13 September
Edinburgh Festival   23 August–12 September
Beaujolais Noveau Race   15 November
Boat Show   7–17 January 1982
Cruft's   12–13 February 1982
Cheltenham Gold Cup   18 March 1982

Published by Debrett's Peerage Ltd.,
73/77 Britannia Road, London S.W.6

ISBN 0 905649 47 8

Designed by Jamie Hobson
Printed and bound in Great Britain by
The Garden City Press Limited, Letchworth,
Hertfordshire SG6 1JS

Contents

April

BADMINTON *by Adam Helliker*

The three-day event at Badminton, the home of the Duke of Beaufort, takes place early in April. This being the English spring it's not surprising that the outlook is distinctly green – green huskies, green wellies and green Range Rovers (not to mention the green complexions of those who are without these necessities).

Already you will see that, although this may appear to be a country spectator sport and dress should not be of the first importance, quite the reverse is true. The English unwritten rule strikes again. Take a tip from the Royal Family (who, after all, have done so much to promote this event) and find yourself some warm, thick, hairy tweeds, either a flat cap or headscarf, and woolly stockings. All these must be in the drabbest colours imaginable.

It should be noted as soon as possible that Badminton is curious among English seasonal occasions in that here the object of the exercise really is to watch the horses ard their riders. The trials consist of three disciplines – Dressage, Cross-country and Show-jumping. Points are deducted for errors and the horse and rider who have most points at the end of the event are the winners and receive the Whitbread Trophy. Whitbread and Co also add the curious sum of 4,000 sovereigns to be split among the owners of the top twelve horses.

9

Among the 100,000-or-so people who will be watching on Saturday, the popular Cross-country day, will be many who are really dedicated to the equestrian world. But even to those for whom horses are not the breath of life the Cross-country trial is the most exciting; among the thirty-four jumps are some of the trickiest and most dangerous ever devised. These include hedges, ditches, fallen trees, and a jump over a jetty into a real lake, then a leap out of the lake over a boathouse. One watches this one with the expectation of seeing at least one ducking. Among the fascinating names for the jumps are Huntsman's Grave, Vicar's Choice, and Lamb's Creep, and some of the obstacles are so massive that one can hardly believe that the horse, let alone the rider, can maintain its equilibrium.

The park around Badminton House, where all this takes place, belongs to the Duke of Beaufort, who was Master of the Horse for forty years and consequently was always in attendance when the Queen rode on occasions like the Trooping of the Colour. He is rare among modern-day Dukes in that he does not have to open his house to the public, but during the trials the beautiful grounds are trampled mercilessly by farmers, trainers, riders, and a multitude of horsey types. The Duke (know as 'Master') has his own pack of foxhounds and when the Royal children were young one of their treats was to be taken to feed the pack during Badminton week.

The Royal Family generally are fond of horses, the Queen having a very experienced eye which has enabled her to become a highly successful owner – she has thirty racehorses and has a stake in the Derby winner Troy. The Queen Mother encouraged her daughter's love of horses but her own interests lie principally with National Hunt racing. Princess Anne follows in her grandmother's footsteps and is a former European three-day event champion.

All this explains why you will see the Royal Family moving with absolute freedom at Badminton, taking their dogs for walks and chatting to people who share their equine interests. You may see a fleet of tatty Land Rovers which will be carrying various Royal personages and a whole host of Court officials overflowing from the back, or you may find yourself in the path of a blue or brown Range Rover driven by Prince Charles or Prince Andrew. If Princess Anne is at the wheel the best thing to do is to get out of the way fast because it's a certainty she will be going at speed and will not be prepared to stop for plebs. By contrast, last year Prince Charles took to riding about on one of the Duke's horses and was civil to everyone he met.

Sometimes it is difficult to follow the events because of the crowds, but nobody thinks it strange if the Queen is seen sitting on top of her Land Rover as this is one of the few sensible vantage points. For those who are not interested in seeing horses jump, fall and gallop, the secondary sport of the day is 'Spot the Royal Family'. For this the knowledgeable get up early and are present for the examination of horses on Sunday morning which takes place in the stables behind Badminton House; there the Queen and Prince Philip can be sure to be seen. Following the inspection the whole Royal party goes to the tiny village church, discarding their tweeds and wellies for more formal dress. Admission to the church is by ticket only, but for the dedicated Royal follower the service is relayed outside.

The Three-Day Event, being British, actually lasts for four days and starts with the dressage on Thursday and Friday. Here the splendid animals hop, step, and skip while their riders appear to be motionless. You have to be a keen eventer to know what's going on, but to help the amateur the British Horse Society issue a booklet telling you all that you need to know (if you can understand it). For instance, 'A horse should not be asked to walk on the bit at the early stages of his training'; 'All trot work is executed sitting unless otherwise indicated'. Apparently your horse will lose points if it grinds its teeth or swishes its tail, and it can't wear blinkers – difficult for a horse seeing plagues of flies and not being allowed to flick them away.

On the Sunday show-jumping takes place in the main

11

arena, which has seats around it, so the normally indispensable shooting sticks are not necessary. After lunch the Queen
and her party drive to the ring in two Land Rovers and watch
the event from the Royal Box. Towards the end of the afternoon the successful competitors receive their prizes from Her
Majesty, accompanied by much camera-clicking from the frequently noisy Press seas which are located embarrassingly
close to the Royal Box.

If you are trying to do Badminton in style then it really is
essential to wangle your way into one, preferably all, of the
parties that go on. There's the cocktail party at Badminton
House on Thursday, but probably more fun is the Badminton
Invitation Dance at Westonbirt School on Saturday night. If
you can't get yourself invited to this then there's always the
village hall disco at the same time, and there's a much greater
possibility of seeing bright young faces there.

Should you have had a private bet on the outcome of one of
the competitions and won don't think that just because the
setting is rural there's no place to spend your money immediately. Some of Britain's best-known shops are eager to tempt
you to spend in the tented 'village' that springs up in the
grounds each year, and should your fancy be for a £10,000
diamond tiara then surprisingly you'll find one among the 160
stands. Everything is available here, from oil paintings to
anoraks, toffee to wine, fur coats to popcorn, tractors to
oysters.

Somewhere in this array will be found the few select 'hospitality' marquees and, disregarding those that belong to certain car manufactures and gunsmiths, the best by far is the
Directors' Tent (where Prince Philip is a visitor) and the wes-
sex Yeomanry Tent. Entry to both of these is strictly controlled, but one of the next best is the Beaufort Hunt Club Tent –
the payment of a nominal sum will make you a member, give
you a nice blue badge, and gain you entry to their cosy little
bar. A very good idea is to join the British Horse Society
(membership costs about £9 a year) which entitles you
to a badge which gets you into the Society's members'

enclosure. Here things are slightly more peaceful and there's a nice long bar and a better choice of food than the hot dogs or cockles you'll find outside.

There are the several bars around the course but the place where the young fashionables hang out is a jolly place called The Yard of Ale in front of the main scoreboard. Here you can't move for the loud voices, huskies, and those green Wellingtons (and just to make quite sure you've got it right about these boots, they're the ones with craggy soles, straps at the top, and a 'Hunter' label. Every pair a walking advertisement for the manufacturer!)

How to get there: Badminton is 106 miles from London and by car you can get there by going straight down the M4, coming off at Exit 18. Then take the A46 to the B4040 and watch for signs. Trains go from Paddington Station to Swindon, but from then on it has to be by bus.

How to get in: Entrance charge for cars and all occupants is £7 for the cross-country day and £3 for the dressage and show-jumping days. A season ticket which gives entrance to all four days costs £11 and many who have these tickets arrive early to compete with each other for the front row position which gives the best view of a number of fences on cross-country day. Some even have their breakfast behind their cars. A grandstand seat is necessary to watch either the dressage or show-jumping heats and these cost between £2 and £5. For £5 you can book a Sunday seat in Row C to watch the show-jumping, which will give you a wonderful seat overlooking the Royal Box.

THE BOAT RACE *by Adam Helliker*

Sporting events always attract a strong local bias and in nothing is this more evident than in the Oxford and Cambridge Boat Race. Up and down the country the war of the rosettes is fought out with the enthusiasm which such an event can arouse only in the heart of the Englishman. The race

13

is seen on television by literally millions of 'fans' who cheer energetically from their armchairs, reassured by the smug knowledge that they've got a much better view of the race than those who are perched on the banks of the River Thames between Putney and Mortlake.

Be that as it may, we all know that it's being there that counts, regardless of who gets the best view. Just to hear oneself cheering for either Oxford or Cambridge is what it's all about – and everyone who's there will most definitely have decided which university they're supporting whether they went to Oxbridge or not. In the case of girl supporters it might even have been decided on whichever shade of blue they prefer to wear.

To be fair there are people to whom the outcome of the race matters an awful lot – such as the crews – not to mention their rowing forebears, many of whom litter the towpath and despite their age stamp up and down enthusiastically. It's these old buffers who complain the loudest when their team has lost, often making it known to whoever will listen that they would have put up a better show in *their* rowing days. These men can be ignored because one knows that if they were really keen they would have got a place on one of the fourteen launches which follow in the wake of the boats. Viewing from one of the launches is the most exciting way to see the race and, with the BBC launch on one side and the umpires on the other, you can shout your head off and be classed as an 'enthusiastic character'. Getting a place is quite simple – they can be booked through members of such patrio-tic institutions as the Victoria League, and, naturally, the United Oxford and Cambridge University Club.

The Boat Race is one of the last truly amateur events left to us, completely untouched by any hint of monetary reward. There are few written rules for the race, apart from the main one that it should be rowed over the odd distance of 4 miles and 374 yards along the Thames, and whether it takes place at all depends on an annual challenge issued by the losers of the previous year. Usually the challenge comes in the traditional pompous wording of the 19th century but in 1958 everyone felt so casual about it that the president of the Oxford boat simply sent Cambridge a telegram twenty-four hours before the appointed day saying: 'What about a race?' And one of Oxford's greatest ever strokes, Christopher Davidge (Eton and Trinity), forgot to post his challenge altogether.

In the old days the race was rowed at Henley. After much argument the course was moved to London (from Westminster to Putney) and after 1845 the gruelling course from Putney to Mortlake was chosen, with its nasty north-westerly wind and rough water. The double-S bends at Putney ensure that a wind which favours one crew at one point inevitably favours the other at another point, but the better crew still has time to establish its superiority. Much, therefore, depends on the toss of a coin for the choice of side and, in keeping with this traditional event, that coin is an 1829 gold sovereign struck in the year of the first race. For all the agonizing about sides the records show that it doesn't seem to matter that much.

Victorian prints and paintings of the race show that there was then a fairground atmosphere along the river and the towpath was crowded with sightseers, including horsewomen wearing black hats and riding habits, scarlet-coated guardsmen in bearskins, and urchins climbing posts for a better view. Altogether a colourful scene, unlike that of today. Now the most colourful thing among the ranks of duffle-coated and anorak-clad onlookers is the selection of college scarves, but even these are only worn for a specific purpose – to keep out the biting cold that so often prevails at this time of the year. There is no doubt that in times past it was a great day out for Londoners, but these days the city-dwellers grumble about the congestion the race brings. As with so many of Britain's social events probably the main people who are now the greatest supporters are foreigners. They're fascinated by the mystique of the Boat Race, even though they may not understand it completely, like the Italian newspaper which reported: 'The annual race between Butney and Mortlady took place yesterday. The former won.'

15

These days even the crew members aren't treated with the reverence they used to command. To 19th-century historians of the race the oarsmen were Olympian figures who were above all gentlemen amateurs – and highly virtuous with it. They posed dramatically for photographs against pretty ivy-covered walls, their moustaches bristling and their curly-brimmed bowlers worn absolutely straight. The epitome of this gentlemanly ideal must surely be the stroke of the Leander crew watching the 1852 race. When a passing launch swamped his boat and it began to sink, the cox begged, 'Give me your oar, sir, for I cannot swim'. The gallant stroke tossed him the oar, but then said, 'Nor can I'.

The only comment that can be made about today's oarsmen is that they seem to get bigger every year. This is particularly noticeable from the size of the shoes which are built in to each new boat, tailor-made yearly for the crew. For the crew members who like the pleasures of the flesh the race is really bad news; not only is their diet particularly rigorous but all contact with girlfriends is barred for the three weeks before the race. Oxford forbids all alcohol to its crews, but Cambridge kindly allows one pint of beer a day. No doubt this accounts for the riotous celebrations after the race, when the crews – whether they've won or not – let all hell loose and go berserk with beer, food and girls.

From the time of their selection the two crews live a hard monastic life. At Oxford the oarsmen are out for early morning exercise before the clock strikes 7.30 am, while at Cambridge the crew are running along the Backs. These are the men who have been selected from the trial eights picked in November and whittled down in January before a final trial in February.

Oxford had a head start psychologically, for it was an Oxford man. Charles Wordsworth (nephew of the poet William), who got the ball rolling – or rather the boats racing. Since then Cambridge has raced ahead and the score now stands at sixty-eight wins for Cambridge and fifty-seven for Oxford.

Teams struggling in the Oxford and Cambridge Boat Race

One of the remarkable features of the Boat Race is the high proportion of Old Etonians who've competed – out of the Blues awarded, which so far number just over 2,000, Etonians have taken around 600. Second on the list is Shrewsbury, with about 100 Blues to its name, so it's quite clear which school one is to choose if one's sons are to be supreme rowers. Out of the university colleges Magdalen (Oxford) gives the best chance of success, closely followed by Trinity (Cambridge).

How to get there: Travelling by car is pretty hopeless as the place gets clogged up and parking can be a nightmare, so the only alternatives are taxi, bus (to Putney Bridge) or train (to Putney station). The steamers and launches leave from Putney Pier.

Getting in: The race can be watched by anyone from the

river bank but this is unsatisfactory and you, of course, will want to be on one of the launches or steamers that follow the two main boats. One way is to join the Victoria League at 18 Northumberland Avenue, London, W.C.2, and then you can ask to be booked on a boat as a member. But there is a very useful name and telephone number for those who don't feel like joining this institution: Mr Alan Mays-Smith, of Beefeater House, Montford Close, London, S.E.11 (tel. 01-735 8131). He's the organizer of the race and if you're nice to him and pay a couple of pounds a place on one of the steamers will be yours.

THE GRAND NATIONAL *by Richard Pitman*

Even if you have never been to the Grand National, you can hardly fail to be reminded each year of its existence, unless, of course, you happen to be a stalactite polisher who lives at the scene of his work. For each year it fills the newspapers and is given a superb three-hour build-up on television. In 1980 it went out live to Australia for the first time. Many international doors are opened to the winning rider who, when doing the rounds of cocktail parties in American horse-racing circles, finds his hand being shaken from the elbow, whereas previously, when introduced as the British Champion Jockey, his hand was regarded as if it were an overripe banana!

Today the race is run over 4 miles and 856 yards with thirty huge obstacles to be negotiated en route. This is 856 yards longer and one fence more than the inaugural race in 1839 when William Lynn, a publican in the small village of Aintree, started the ball rolling. In that first year the race was run over natural terrain, most of which was ploughed land, with natural boundaries, including a huge stone wall and two vast ditches, to be negotiated.

We would all display our instinct for self-preservation if faced with a massage from sixteen $\frac{1}{2}$-ton horses travelling at speed and equipped with steel-shod shoes, and Captain Becher in 1839 was no different from the rest of us, throwing himself into the brook for safety, having fallen with his mount Conrad at the chasm which has retained his name to this day.

In 1975 Andy Turnell's instinct for self-preservation caused Paul Kellaway to test the famous bounce in that ancient turf. Paul, having judged his approach and take-off to perfection on Barona, leaned back to counterbalance the force of gravity, mentally praising his equine partner, together with a measure for himself, when, for no apparent reason, he found himself lying in the grass with the rest of the runners landing all around or, in several cases, on him. Spectators who had chosen to watch the race from this point saw exactly what had happened. Andy Turnell, who rides with as short a stirrup as most flat-race riders, in an effort to prevent his departure from April The Seventh's back, grabbed at the nearest thing within reach, which unfortunately happened to be Kellaway, and the pair plummeted to the ground holding hands like two lovers jumping to their deaths from a cliff top!

It is to see incidents such as this or, conversely, to watch the great Aintree jumpers like Crisp and Red Rum take the famous fence with contemptible ease that tempts people to forgo the preliminaries and the finish and watch the race from this point. From here the first five fences are head-on to viewers, so they can only see the silk crash-helmet covers bobbing above the tops of the jumps, with occasional flashes of colour as the field rises to clear a jump.

Other good places in the country from which to watch the race are on the high grass bank that runs parallel to the first five jumps or at the Canal Turn, two fences after Becher's. At this point the course takes a ninety-degree turn and the cleverest partnerships cross at an angle in order to save what is sometimes more ground than they eventually win by. Not all horses, however, respond to their riders wishes; some do just the opposite, which, in the years before an eight-foot-high fence was erected to guard the Leeds-Liverpool Canal, which runs only thirty yards beyond the jump, caused those horses which could not or would not turn sharply to the left

19

on landing to take a premature wash-down. To the layman thirty yards may sound a sufficient distance in which to correct any misunderstanding between horse and rider, but I can assure you that, when travelling at speeds of up to 35 mph it is eaten up with alarming rapidity!

Watching from the country should be done with a picnic and a battery radio as companions. For the rest the main grandstand area offers much more than just a lofty view: it is nice to see the horses before the race and to share in the excited air of anticipation during the parade. Then they're off and one waits breathlessly for the commentator to identify the fallers out in the country and to see the survivors tackle the mighty Chair fence which stands five feet three inches high, is four feet thick and is preceded by a six-foot-wide open ditch After jumping the water jump those still standing have another full circuit in front of them, bypassing the casualties of the early action, before tackling the 465-yard run-in from the last fence which has seen so many herculean struggles.

This race is so far removed from the normal that it can have lasting effects on faint-hearted horses; conversely, it brings out the best in others. The now legendary Red Rum ran in five consecutive Grand Nationals, negotiating 149 of the 150 fences without making a mistake, winning on three occasions and finishing second on the other two.

The Chair fence got its name from the iron chair, used by an assistant judge, beside and level with the top of the fence. Although it is no longer used, many jockeys have since ended up emulating the good judge when their mounts could jump neither high enough nor far enough to clear the obstacle; it also happens to be on the narrowest part of the course, thus giving it an optical illusion of even greater height.

Dress to keep out the weather which in April can often be wet and windy. The older gentry still wear bowler hats, while the trainers and jockeys sport brown trilbys, mostly perched at cocky angles.

The course has changed hands three times since the turn of the century and has been under threat of extinction on numerous occasions since 1945, with the bookmakers Ladbrokes coming to the rescue in 1975 by leasing the meeting for eight years. They paid £1,500,000 for the privilege and have now offered to buy the course when that lease runs out and then donate it to a Trust Foundation who will develop it as a recreational area, while the buyers continue running the Grand National meeting.

The County Stand is steeped in tradition and full of racing memorabilia, including the stuffed head of The Wild Man of Borneo, the winning horse in 1895, and the colours carried successfully by Lottery's rider in 1839. The cost in 1980 for this stand was £24, giving spectators a fine choice of dining and tea facilities, and a selection of champagne or wine bars, not to mention the chance to rub shoulders with the racing hierarchy. Either side of this stand are Tattersalls and the Silver Ring, neither of which boast enough catering facilities or comfort, and which cost £12 and £7, respectively. The Western Enclosure and the 'Cabbage Patch' cost £2.50 each, while the country viewing areas represent good value at £1. To get there by road, the M6 leads on to the M62 which in turn leads on to the M57, taking visitors to within a mile of the course. There is an excellent train service from London via Birmingham and coaches run from all major towns.

Having once witnessed the Grand National, you will agree that the race itself overrides discomfort, bad weather and empty pockets and, being a part of our heritage, must not be allowed to die.

OTHER EVENTS IN APRIL

Crown Jewel Ball, Dorchester Hotel, London
Berkeley Dress Show in aid of NSPCC, Berkeley Hotel, London
Royal Scottish Academy Summer Exhibition, Edinburgh.
Toyota International Dressage Championships, Goodwood, Sussex.
Rugby: John Player Cup Final, Twickenham.

Racing: Newmarket (Ladbroke Craven Stakes).
Racing: Ayr (William Hill Scottish Grand National).
Racing: Epsom Spring Meeting.
Inverness Highland Festival Week, Scotland.
Easter Parade, Battersea Park, London.
West of England Ladies' Kennel Society Show, Malvern, Worcestershire.
Weston Park Horse Trials, Shropshire.
Bach Festival, Oxford and London.
South Africa Club Dinner, Savoy Hotel, London.
Luncheon in aid of Leukaemia, Inter-Continental Hotel, London.
St George's Day Grand Banquet, in aid of John Groom's Association for the Disabled, St Bartholomew's Great Hall.
Racing: Sandown Park (Whitbread Gold Cup).
Racing: Longchamp (Poule d'Essai des Poulains).
Devizes to Westminster Canoe Race, Devizes, Wilts.
Football: FA Cup Final.
British Olympic Yachting Appeal Dinner, Savoy Hotel, London.
Royal Society of St George Dance, Savoy Hotel.
Rugby: Ulster Cup Final, Belfast, Northern Ireland.
Shakespeare's Birthday Celebrations and opening of Royal Shakespeare Company's season, Stratford-on-Avon.
Moffat Golf Week, Moffat, Scotland.
Royal Maundy Presentations, Westminster Abbey, London.
Racing: Newmarket (Spring Meeting).
International Youth Music Festival, Harrogate, Yorkshire.
Tattersall's Mixed July Sales, Newmarket, Suffolk.
Cannes International Film Festival, Cannes, France.

May

THE MONACO GRAND PRIX *by Maurice Hamilton*

Frankly, the Monaco Grand Prix is a bore. The race itself runs for about two hours and you would be well advised to spend that time preparing for the Gala Prize Giving in the evening. Don't worry about what actually happened in the race; ask the hall porter; he'll know. Usually there isn't much to say except that the favourite led from start to finish or so-and-so won because the favourite retired after sixty-nine laps.

The fact is that the race is incidental to four days of practice, Press receptions and parties on yachts. What other reason can there be for running modern cars with fat tyres on the same narrow streets used by Bugattis and the like with spindly wheels in 1929?

Overtaking at Monaco is not difficult, it's impossible. The cars of today are hemmed in by crash barriers and tight corners; their 180 mph potential muzzled to an 80 mph average on the two-mile track. Each year the drivers wring their hands in despair; each year the hoteliers rub theirs' with glee.

Regardless of the physical problems involved, the Monaco Grand Prix is there because it forms a useful niche on the social calendar. The trick is to visit the Cannes Film Festival, drift from jolly to jolly and murmur that you're really there for the Grand Prix – but isn't this fun all the same?

The following week you roll up at the Hotel de Paris, engage an ex-world champion or two in conversation and casually remark that noisy racing cars are all very well – but wasn't Cannes simply splendid this year?

Naturally, you will have booked in advance if you want the hotel of your choice. The Hotel de Paris has that aloof feel about it which comes with the name. Tables in the cocktail bar are reserved for rather sedate regulars and, if you are well known, the bottle of your fancy will carry a silver plaque bearing your name.

The Hermitage, an agreeable, rather more lively version of the Hotel de Paris, retains its splendid dignity after an expensive face-lift. This hotel is popular among the teams and trips smartly along without giving the impression that the residents in the lounge are about to pass away at the first rasp of a racing engine. Rooms are available for a minimum of five nights, a single costing approximately 450 francs per night, a double 650 francs.

The Loews Hotel is draped around a hairpin bend at the foot of a steep hill on the circuit and it won't be long before some desperate racer leaves his braking too late and arrives in the foyer. The Loews is the one hotel which could cope with such a contingency, its rather characterless American style and in-house casino seemingly designed for the fast-moving world of motor racing.

Each room is identical in decor and, once inside, the feeling that you could be anywhere in the world persists – at least until practice starts on Thursday.

With the exception of the Beach Plaza, all the best hotels overlook the circuit, but when cars hurtle past your bedside at 6 am you may question the wisdom of paying extra for a room with a view of the track.

Of course there are alternatives. Apartments are available at comparatively reasonable terms but choose carefully. A map may show the location to be three streets back from the circuit but what the map doesn't show is a vertical climb between the streets akin to the North Face of the Eiger. Monaco is built on a rock face and, since motorized transport is out the question while the circuit is in use, pedestrians seem

Ready for the off at the Monaco Grand Prix

to spend their time going up and down at a debilitating rate.

On the other hand, you may have friends living in the principality. In that case, approach with caution. Residents of Monte Carlo generally lead quiet, unassuming lives, receiving perhaps a handful of guests during 51 weeks of the year. Their patience stretches rather when friends 'just happen to be passing' during Grand Prix week. Balconies, usually the dusty domain of pot plants and a shabby deck-chair, become overcrowded with visitors; the incumbents become distraught and you are likely to be dispatched to buy more croissants just as the race is due to start.

Practice takes place all day Thursday and Saturday as well as for a few hours on Friday morning. The race starts at around 3 pm on Sunday. In between there is plenty of time to eat and drink and generally be seen in the right places. Monaco regulars escape the crowds by eating out of town. The Chevron d'Or in Eze and The Pirate at Roquebrune are worth a visit while the more adventurous drive into the mountains for excellent French cuisine without the scandalous Monaco prices.

Press receptions are, of course, both plentiful and free. Some are strictly monitored and, as a result, boring, while others simply require a fresh shirt and a brass neck to gain admission. The secret is not to appear over-enthusiastic, otherwise you will stand out among the herd of yawning Pressmen as they wait for the signal to scramble for the food.

Conversation will frequently cover the delay at Heathrow, the hotel charges, the weather, the flight home. Rarely will anyone mention work. That is reserved for the pit lane.

The pits and paddock are the 'Members' Enclosure' of motor racing. The members, however, are strictly limited to the teams, their sponsors, the Press and the trade personnel. Pit passes are not on sale to the public but they are available through the right contacts in either the Automobile Club or the teams.

Should you be fortunate enough to gain access to the pits then bear in mind the following: motor racing is a dangerous, hectic sport and those who are attempting to work in the middle of the Monaco razzmatazz will not take kindly to by-standers stepping on spanners or tripping over air-lines. Be prepared for fast-moving cars and four-letter words should you step out while waving to friends in the grandstands.

There are no privileged areas and, judging by their admission charges, the Monégasques consider the whole town to be one big Special Enclosure. If you want to see anything, grandstand seats are useful. If you want to hear anything afterwards, ear-plugs are essential. There's no joy in looking your best at the prize-giving when a battalion of bees appear to be attacking your ear-drums.

The weather can vary but dress is as relaxed as you care to make it. The prize-giving is strictly formal, however, and it's the one place where you can expect to see the drivers. The winning car is usually there and you may have the opportunity of talking to the man who led the procession on the last lap.

Don't ask him what speed he was doing. He won't know; racing cars do not have speedometers. Don't ask him if he was frightened; you'll be the umpteenth person to do so that weekend. Try to talk about anything other than motor racing.

Of course, if in doubt, you could always tell him how much you enjoyed Cannes.

How to get there: Regular flights to Nice. Take a taxi to Monte Carlo. Try to avoid having a car in Monaco at all costs.

Getting in: For admission tickets and grandstand seats, apply to:

Automobile Club de Monaco
23 bvd Albert 1er
Monaco
Tel: 30 32 20

Prices range from £20 to £50 per seat. Beware of forged tickets from Italy.

Page & Moy Ltd, 136 London Road, Leicester, are experienced and reliable organizers of all-in trips to Monaco.

THE ROYAL ACADEMY SUMMER EXHIBITION
by Gillian Darley

'So you want to go to the Royal Academy?' said my aged aunt, the more sophisticated one. (Graham Greene is not the only person with such an aunt, it turns out.)

'Well, of course it used to be a mysterious affair, as anything that's been running 213 years is bound to be. An invitation to the Private View came your way and you never quite knew how. It was one of those curious lists, one year you were there and the next not. Then you might get back again. It was as unpredictable as the summer, really. But the list you really aimed for was the one for the Annual Dinner – now that the Private View has lost its special glamour, it's the dinner that is the Big Event. They invite around 400 people, including the seventy Royal Academicians; I heard that 240 sat down this year. But you have to be important in your field, a Glenda Jackson or a chairman of ICI; so, my dear, I think you'd better set your sights on the Private View.'

'What has changed about the Private View then?'

'Since they set up the Friends of Royal Academy the guest list has got a bit longer. There are around 25,000 of them and so even with two days, things get a bit tight. £12.50, or £7 for you and I (you being under twenty-five, me being over sixty) and an invitation is yours. But let me give you a tip or two. First you have to decide why you are going. If it is just to spot the celebrities then you aren't going to have much luck – they'll have been to the dinner and if they are at the Private View then it'll be hard to pick them out of the crowd. Still, next year there might be a special view for buyers and for a small extra sum you'll be able to have a more exclusive preview. It means you'll see the works better and, who knows, you might spot that MP who always lobbies for the arts or the filmstar who paints. Anyway, let me give you a tip or two. Dress: well, anything goes, it seems, now. It all depends whether you want to look like an artist, a buyer, a visitor from the country or just someone "who doesn't know much about art but knows what they like." I couldn't tell you exactly what to wear to fit those images but I'd say satin, silk, tweed and cotton would about do, respectively.'

'You haven't mentioned what you *see* there,' I interrupted. My aunt *does* have a tendency to run on.

'I was getting to that. I want to finish the matter of dress first. Footwear is what you want to concentrate on. It's hard work, a long walk, and if you do want a break, the restaurant is downstairs, quite a way off. So make sure your feet are comfortably shod. The other thing is to remember to take your glasses. The Royal Academy follows the 17th-century habit of hanging its pictures in ranks up the wall (and its architectural models, oddly enough). You'll need your glasses for the catalogue as well. It's tiny and the lines are apt to get confused; when you're looking for No 27 "Man at the Underground Station", you get "Single Chrysanthemum" on that line instead. By the way, the catalogue has the names and addresses of all the exhibitors at the back. If you want to survive (and after all with your Friends' card you can always go again another day) concentrate on one category—say, the miniatures or sculpture. Work is generally grouped according to size and medium so you can walk round the rooms and stop when you see the kind of thing that interests you. Architecture and prints have their own sections too and there is always a small memorial exhibition to an academician who has died in the last year in one of the first galleries. So you can either be a bit particular and choosy, or you can take the gardening approach.'

'Gardening approach?' I asked. (I thought she'd got confused; she had always promised to take me to the Royal Horticultural Society Daffodil Show one year.)

'Look at the rooms as an experienced gardener looks at an herbaceous border – luxuriate in the general effect and look for the rare blooms. It's not that easy because the things you notice are generally the oddest, most garish, most daring (though life studies being what they are nowadays there's not much that can shock) but don't be taken in by the ones that

29

shout too hard at you. It's worth picking on an established artist or two, see if they're on form (the racing approach, this), and they sometimes get beaten by an outsider who just catches your eye.'

'So who are these artists?'

'Anyone can enter. You just buy an entry form. Twelve and a half thousand works were submitted last year, my friend on the Hanging Committee told me (though of course you can put in more than one), and of the 3,000 or so chosen only half get hung. So some people get disappointed early on and some get even more disappointed when they discover there just isn't room for them. The Hanging Committee (sounds rather final, I always think) is made up of the Royal Academy Council, which changes, as each member only stands for three years. Of course,' said my aunt brightly, 'there is another way of getting a special kind of invitation to the Royal Academy.'

'What's that?' I asked.

'Well, getting something accepted and hung. Then you can just stand there, smiling sweetly in front of your work, looking neither too smart nor to dishevelled, and hope for luck. I used to send my botanical woodcuts in and for several years they were on show.'

'But you know I don't draw or paint, sculpt or design buildings.'

'Rubbish, dear child,' she assumed her most matronly manner. 'You've done your share of linocuts and I remember that imaginative collage you once did at school. Anyone can have a go.'

I quickly got her off the subject.

Well, we went, and we saw much more than I'd expected. At the Private View there were so many people talking to each other in the middle of the room that it wasn't hard to progress round the edges. Just as we were limping out a loud voice hailed us. It was my other aunt, the unsophisticated one who lives in Kirkcudbrightshire. She wouldn't miss the Royal Academy for anything, she told us; she'd been there for three hours and was wearing a good pair of walking shoes and had a stick for good measure. The sophisticated one, whose shoes were quite elegant and who had, like me, found that an hour and a bit had been about enough for one day, shrugged and whispered to me. 'You see, there's no mystique; but it is fun, don't you think?' I had to agree.

How to get there: The Royal Academy is in Piccadilly, almost opposite Fortnum and Mason and next to the Burlington Arcade. When the Summer Show is on they fly a special flag over the entrance (a different one each year, designed by an Academician). It is only a short walk from Piccadilly Circus tube station and lots of buses pass the door. So will taxis, for a little more money.

Getting in: To become a Friend of the RA you pay £12.50 a year. There is a concession for teachers, museum staff, etc., who pay £10; for OAPs and those between sixteen and twenty-five it is £7. Otherwise you pay at the door and buy an ordinary ticket. The exhibition opens in late May/early June and runs until mid-August.

CHELSEA FLOWER SHOW *by Adam Helliker*

Members' day at the Chelsea Flower Show used to be quite an occasion and was looked upon as the only civilized way in which to see this magnificent display. Now, with membership of the Royal Horticultural Society standing at 68,000, it is just as much of a bunfight as when the show is open to the public. The plain fact is that anyone can get in on Members' day but those who do still seem to think they have performed a feat of tremendous prestige and importance.

Nothing, however, can detract from the breathtaking beauty of the show itself. Held at the end of May in the grounds of the Royal Hospital at Chelsea the scale of the show is simply amazing – the marquee alone covers $3\frac{1}{2}$ acres and takes twenty-four men over two weeks to erect, provided there are no gales.

The Royal Horticultural Society first organized what was then called a Great Spring Show in 1913 and every year since then, except during the two world wars, this charming and practical display of horticultural perfection has been held. The number of visitors to the show is expected to top a quarter of a million this year, with an increasing number of Americans being ferried over by their popular gardening clubs. These club tours take in several continental garden shows but it is generally agreed that we British do it best. (After all, it is an historical fact that it was a British monarch, Henry VIII, who first insisted on the perfection of a mown lawn, so as a nation we've been at it for quite some time.)

The importance of the show in the London social calendar has declined somewhat in the past few years, although it is still just as well to say you have been and to drop in a few unusual Latin names here and there. Mention of a Malus Tschonoskii at the next cocktail party may sound as if you're sneezing but is good enough proof that you took an interest in this year's tree display at Chelsea. Still on the social side, it is worth remembering that, unlike other nations who hold flower shows in their capitals, there is no pre-show ball at Chelsea, so don't be disappointed if a stiff ivory card doesn't plop through your letterbox.

The real target for those who are purely there for social reasons is the President's Tea Party which is held on Tuesday afternoon. Talk of sprigs and branches here is more likely to refer to family trees than the old poplar in the garden. Each person is announced at the entrance of the President's tent and received by Lord and Lady Aberconway who personally vet the guest list which last year consisted of a mixed bag of 370 ambassadors and mayors, and even a few gardeners. Tea and a choice of runny ice-cream or cakes (not, surprisingly, Chelsea buns) are provided by the caterers currently in vogue, Ring and Brymer. The size of the tent makes the whole affair a trifle uncomfortable but if it's warm you can wander into a small area outside where there are a few tables and chairs dotted about.

A moment's rest in the heat of The Flower Show

One can generally hear some hopeful complaining that she hasn't seen the Queen. But she, fortunate lady, will already have exercised the Monarch's prerogative of touring the show before the crowds are admitted. This she does on Monday evening, when, at 5 pm sharp, the motley crew of journalists who have been enjoying the Press day (and the free lunch) are ushered out by the police ready for the arrival of HM half an hour later.

She is escorted around a suddenly quiet marquee by Lord Aberconway, who afterwards whisks her off to the President's tent for tea. At five-minute intervals after the Queen's arrival come the other members of the Royal Family who want to see the show. The Queen Mother always takes an interest, if only to seize a new cutting for her Scottish castle where she has lovingly transformed the garden. Last year Princess Michael of Kent turned up, bringing with her an unexpected party of four high-spirited ladies. Princess Margaret, whose knowledge of palm trees is probably greater than that of primroses, is also a regular visitor and tends to linger longer than the other Royal ladies.

But we should remember that the purpose of the show is the flowers and everything that goes with them. This hardy annual of the social scene means a great deal of hard work, sometimes for years in advance, for the professional exhibitors. The pick of the most extensive orchid collection in the world is shown here by Rittenhauser and it is chastening to think these exotic flowers take seven years to develop to perfection. Likewise the beautiful hybrid tea roses that are bred by that jolly firm, Wheatcrofts.

Last year, for those who believe small is beautiful, the Chinese and Japanese showed for the first time an enormous range of that fascinating art Bonsai (the miniaturization of trees and shrubs). One could see a perfectly formed pine tree standing only eighteen inches high next to a delicate wistaria with lovely purple flowers just fifteen inches tall. At the other end of the scale were large and vulgar exotica from South Africa, dazzling in their garish colours against a background of sand and stone.

The most prominent tree nurseries of England are Hilliers of Winchester and some idea of the scale of their stand can be gained when one realizes that they bring up to Chelsea twelve huge lorry-loads of material for the background alone. This is in addition to 5,000 assorted trees, ranging from a pretty ornamental cherry to one-inch-high, three-year-old dwarf conifers. They claim that their Indian Horse Chestnut, a glory to behold, has been to the show so often it could walk there by itself. Even if it could, one wonders whether it would be able to find its way around the new one-way system that was introduced last year to avoid congestion in the marquee.

Well, you've ooohed and aahed over roses of every hue from white to darkest red, you've sniffed at the excitingly perfumed geraniums and the heady lilies, you've sworn to grow those lovely sweet peas in your own garden, and now your senses need a change. Wander outside and you can be transported back to Victorian times: a lovely gazebo and conservatory complete with reproduction cane furniture await you. Wander further and enjoy the sound of the 'must-be-heard' military brass band and do not miss the Chelsea Pensioners' stands where these proud old gentlemen in their scarlet tunics will offer you hand-painted mementoes. Proceeds from any sales they make are added to their pensions.

Many people will tell you that Chelsea is a 'dressy occasion', with most women bringing out their prettiest summer dresses and hats. But the old hands will remember not to wear a hat which will obscure someone else's view, and, given the English weather, the wise will carry a mackintosh and umbrella. Most of the men wear comfortable suits and traditional tweeds and last year wellies were much in evidence because of the dismal rain. Comfort is the keynote as there's plenty of walking to be done.

How to get there: Taking a taxi is really the best way of getting to the show, but if you decide you can't afford that and don't want the trouble of taking the car then the Underground is the next best choice. Take the Circle or District line to Sloane Square and then the No 11 bus to Chelsea Bridge Road. It is best for visitors travelling by car, taxi, or coach to alight at the Embankment entrance although there's a 'no parking' rule on the Embankment.

How to get in: To join the Royal Horticultural Society and thus get a Private View ticket for the show it is now no longer even necessary to apply for membership by writing in advance of the show dates. Anyone who wishes to join can do so by enrolling at special kiosks at the entrances off Royal Hospital Road and on the Embankment on all of the show dates. A subscription of £16 gains entrance to all the Society's meetings and shows and includes two tickets for the Private View. Although the Private View tickets are transferable they may be used only once. A subscription of £10 gives a member most of the Society's members' privileges but only one Private View ticket.

GLYNDEBOURNE *by Jane Slade*

The Christies' country house in Sussex became unique when John and Audrey Christie added their own private opera house to it in 1934. It is not uncommon for a family to turn a second garage into a playroom for the children but to build an opera house for one's wife because she 'does a bit of the operatic stuff' is quite amazing.

GFO (Glyndebourne Festival Opera) presents five operas each season which lasts from June until August. Each performance starts at 5 pm and the interval lasts a full seventy-five minutes. It is this feature, oddly enough, which distinguishes Glyndebourne from any other opera house and makes it the social occasion it is.

It is strange to see the dainty damsels sweep into the auditorium at the beginning of the opera full of fancy furbelows, only to thrust themselves through the exit at the end of the first half ready to dive for the best place on the lawn for supper. It is up to these athletic women to emerge first while their husbands get submerged under a harem of equally energetic females all aiming for the same destination.

Should you arrive in a Rolls or private helicopter then you must dine on tables and chairs, and drink out of silver wine goblets. Those who arrive by train usually have to manage with a rug and paper plates. British Rail passengers must ensure everything is neatly packed to prevent the humiliation of serving squashed sandwiches.

The other alternative, and probably the wisest, is to dine in one of the Wallop Dining Halls. Wallop is the family name of the Earls of Portsmouth and Lady Rosamond Wallop was John Christie's mother.

An essential discipline at the dining table is a severe restriction on the quantity of wine drunk, particularly if you are prone to dozing after a few glasses. It is not an uncommon sight to see some of the audience in the second half sunk well down in their seats snoring in quiet contentment. But it is a shame to over-indulge in the interval and miss the second half

36

The Interval at last!

of the performance since Glyndebourne is first and foremost a serious opera house which is promoting fresh operatic talent as well as providing a platform for established stars. From the theatre's inception there has been a constantly high standard of singing and beautifully detailed sets of the highest quality. Two years ago David Hockney designed a set for *The Magic Flute* which encouraged as many people to go and admire the artwork and scenery as the opera itself. Glyndebourne has something to offer everyone.

The stage at Glyndebourne is wider than Milan's La Scala or London's Covent Garden, although paradoxically Glyndebourne's opera house is renowned for its original intimacy (it seats 800 people) and the fact that you can see the stage no matter where you sit. Glyndebourne also has the unique feature of keeping the orchestra out of sight – underneath the stage. This rules out any chance of them drowning the singers and also demonstrates excellent use of space.

Glyndebourne is synonymous with Mozart, since light opera suits the theatre best, but Strauss, Verdi, Debussy and Tchaikovsky have recently nosed their way more frequently into the programme.

It might be prudent to mention here that the so-called birds which are known to hover in the ceiling and sometimes on the stage are actually bats. They don't bite and are just another characteristic of Glyndebourne that the audience has to get used to. They provide a useful distraction for the uninformed and unappreciative opera-goer who can leap in when asked about a certain aria at a later date, 'Oh, *that* was the part I missed – it must have been when the bat came through the ceiling.' The bats made their first stage appearance in the first season's *The Marriage of Figaro* and John Christie forbade anyone to interfere with them, so they stayed to enjoy the operas free of charge.

It can be awkward deciding what to wear to Glyndebourne. Hats are not advised since they are likely to incur the wrath of the person sitting behind but no matter what the fashion long dresses predominate. A warm shawl or lurex jacket are advisable stand-bys since the English weather is as temperamental as the opera singers themselves.

Glyndebourne has been the Christie family home for seven centuries. It is hallmarked on every opera lover's calendar as a 'must' each year, regardless of the price – and you do have to pay. Last year tickets were around £13 each without dinner and next year you will be expected to pay considerably more. It also qualifies as a social function because of its breath-taking setting and unique atmosphere. After all, in what other international opera house can you play a round of croquet during the interval, walk the dog and stretch yourself out on the magnificent lawn to watch the cattle grazing and dragonflies hovering over the lake?

How to get there: Glyndebourne is in East Sussex and is 52 miles from London. The traditional way to travel is by train, from Victoria to the tiny station of Glynde where special coaches ferry the opera-lovers to Glyndebourne. By car, which isn't so exciting, the opera house can be reached by following the A23 to Purley, the A22 to Halland, turning right on to the B2192, and then it's a matter of watching for signs.

Getting in: Bookings are always heavy so it's as well to make reservations well in advance towards the beginning of the year. Postal bookings are accepted by enclosing a stamped addressed envelope to the Box Office Manager, Glyndebourne, near Lewes, East Sussex. Personal callers can obtain tickets at the opera house itself or from Ibbs and Tillett Ticket Office, 122/124 Wigmore Street, London, W.1 (tel. 01-935 1010). Any other enquiries are admirably fielded by the Glyndebourne Information Office (tel. 0273 812321).

THE LORD'S TEST *by Brian O'Hanlon*

Cricket's annual Durbar is the five-day Test Match at Lord's, home of the Marylebone Cricket Club, the noble game's headquarters and Alma Mater. This is the occasion when the old order has a chance to reassert itself – from the spectating side of the boundary ropes anyway – over the unionized, uni-class player and administrator who runs the show today. For almost a week in June Lord Hawke's ghost bestrides the Pavilion, the Warner Stand, the Cricket Museum, the plethora of private boxes, even, one hopes, the elbow-benders in front of the Tavern.

It was Lord Hawke who prayed that no professional 'shall ever captain England'. His prayers remained answered through two world wars, indeed for fifty years, until Len Hutton became the first paid servant of the game to skipper an England side in the mid-50s. He was knighted for his impertinence. Until not-so-many years ago there were 'Gentlemen', who were amateurs, and 'Players', who were professionals. You could tell which was which by watching them take the field and seeing from which gate they emerged. The scoreboard was also a great help. The Gentlemen, as good officers, had their initials paraded *before* their names. They were addressed as 'Mister' on the field by the hired help, as well as sirred. The Professionals were referred to by their surnames, with never more than two permitted initials to follow. For instance, you could tell Ted Dexter was a toff. They called him 'Lord Edward', and he had an Adam's apple. It wasn't just how he cracked a half volley to the rails, it was the manner – imperious, arrogant, with perfect symmetry of movement. The public schools supplied England's batsmen; the pits supplied the bowlers. Trueman, F. S., was archetypal of the genre. A beetle-browed quickie with hate in every pounding stride up to the delivery crease, whose accent was reckoned to be broader in St John's Wood than in Bradford, Trueman was the essence of the Yorkshire professional. Indeed, when the Great Man took his 300th test wicket he made sure he did so in the Lord's Test and was rewarded by a cluster of photographers at his dressing-room bath-side. Trueman, F. S., obliged with a spate of regional rhetoric which delighted the quality newspaper readership at the nation's breakfast tables the following morning.

That is all in the past, as is the midweek Eton/Harrow fixture, with its beautifully dressed ladies parading around between the innings, on the arms of their top-hatted escorts.

Today big cricket is choked with sponsorship, a steady diet of pot-hunting from May to September, with many aspects of the Sunday John Player League having more in common with the soccer terraces than with the finer points of the ancient game which for over 250 years was held to be all that was purest in a sporting contest. Perhaps the occasion overcomes the times, because at the Lord's Test there is ample opportunity to sit back and reflect, as the upper reaches of the pavilion break out into a rash of the 'blood & sick' – the red and yellow tie of MCC membership.

There are two ways to enjoy the Lord's Test in a civilized fashion. The first is to go as a member's guest into the Warner

The Test Match at Lord's

Stand and Bar; the second to be invited to a member's private box for a lunch of cold chicken, salmon and champagne. The boxes are balloted for by members each year. How much a man pays depends upon whether he wishes to use it for his own personal pleasure, or whether he is acting as a social catalyst for his firm. There is an air of a Cambridge May Ball about them: people visit from one to another, and, as the day wears on, all pretence of interest in what is happening out there in the centre of the field is gradually given up. Lord's is all about diversions. The boxes overlook the beer-drinking horde in front of the ugly NAAFI-type canteen shutters of the new Tavern, and there are numerous exchanges between the elevated and the lumpen-proletariat:

'Hey, mate! That's right. You! Who played at Lord's in the morning and Wembley in the afternoon?'

' 'Um, don't know, actually.'

'The Band of the Grenadier Guards, yer berk!'

At other times the mood is gratuitiously subservient.

'Come on! Chuck us down a chicken wing. Just *one*. Come on! Don't be so bleedin' mean! Ah! Mutt & Jeff, eh? All right.

41

Be like that. That bit of salmon'll probably give you a heart attack, and it'll serve you ———— well right!'

You may take it that the gentleman endorsing his view in your direction, with two raised fingers, is not a boy scout.

Saturday is the best day to go with an MCC member into the Warner Stand – a sort of halfway-house between the hedonistic life of the private-box and the ascetic vigil of the pavilion, which is out of bounds to you, as a non-member, on Test Match days. Perhaps you will want to call again, when you *are* allowed in as a guest, to see the sparrow killed in flight by a six and now preserved in the museum behind the pavilion, together with the urn containing the Ashes, W.G's bat, and a host of memorabilia from the game's Golden Age in the years leading up to the Great War. Lord's is full of surprises. They even have a Real Tennis court next to the museum. The pavilion is the inner sanctum, hung with portraits of venerable gentlemen with full sets of whiskers, or else the brilliantined centre parting of the between-the-wars years. Its main area is the Long Room, where members sit on the equally long table, or else on rows of tennis-umpires' seats, graded for varying height, so that all can see out of the Victorian windows. The pavilion is also the most intimidating place on God's earth for the batsman who has failed. He returns amid total silence, his spikes grating on the highly polished linoleum, steadfastly ignored, as he wends his way through the gamut and up aloft to the dressing-room he so recently left.

MCC membership costs £26.50, plus your first year's sub for the same amount. There is, in theory, a ten-year waiting list which no amount of sucking-up will allow of queue-jumping. It is here that the Old Boy Network still performs miracles, as most members one meets have certainly not had to wait that long themselves. Members usually bring their own sandwiches, since Lord's catering is of the 'light buffet' (i.e. cheese roll) variety. The more dedicated types spend whole summers of retirement sitting inside the pavilion behind the bowler's arm, insulated from opprobrium by picture windows of safety glass. Somewhere there is a 1930s Bateman original: 'The member who got up in the middle of an over from the pavilion end . . .' Those outside sit like statues, half-eaten fishpaste sandwich frozen in mid-bite. Off the Long Room is the Members' bar, in the corner of which is a colour television set. During play members sit around it, with their backs to the game, in order to get a better idea of what's happening, in close-up, on the field outside! To your right you will see the crowd below the Warner Stand turn and face it when a wicket falls. That has nothing to do with the beatification of the late Sir Pelham, or, indeed, with Islam. The Press box is at the back of that stand and it also has a large television set for people to watch the immediate-action replays.

Knowing types can always guess what time of day it is by the volume of noise emanating from the Tavern. Not quite as ribald, perhaps, as the notorious hill at Sydney, but full of good-natured unsolicited advice, and with its own favourites. Geoff Boycott is one. Greg Chappell is not. Yet, like the stands, it settles down with the bowler's run-up. There are usually more people who have played the game in earnest to be found here than in the pavilion.

There is a Direct Entry qualification, of course, for MCC membership, given to those who have actually played for them, but the bulk of the 'blood & sick' is to be found in the middle-aged, better-off, who wear the tie as a social 'gong', and whose own playing days were with the Old Bumbledonians' 2nd XI, scratching about in the lower half of the batting order. People such as the aforementioned Mr Dexter and Trueman, F. S., don't need to wear the yellow & red. Notwithstanding all that, Lord's is still a very tie-conscious place. A colleague recalls taking a guest there some seasons ago when the late Lord Portarlington was ensconced on one of the high stools in the pavilion. Not a man to be ignored, he demanded of the wide-eyed guest: 'D'ye know what tie I'm wearing?'

'Well, no.'

'I Zingari.'

'Oh, 'um. I Old Parkhurstians.'

'Parkhurst, *Parkhurst!*' snorted His Lordship. 'We know Eton and Harrow, and, of course, Winchester, although *they* don't play here, but who the hell are you?'

The tie rule has been relaxed, albeit unofficially. You will see members nowadays wearing open-necked shirts in the pavilion, but seldom on Test Match days. Jackets are permitted to be taken off, as well, but only in very hot weather, with the secretary's tacit approval. Shirts *never*, although some bearded wonder from the London School of Comics started the shirtless fad amongst the paying public some years ago and got himself in all the newspapers.

Because of the liquid aspect of Test Match watching Lord's has some very well-appointed members' loos. The major one in the pavilion itself has 'Out' and 'Not Out' doors; that in the Warner Stand, urinal stalls at right angles to the field of play, enabling people to continue watching through the day's relieving moments.

Ladies are never allowed in the pavilion at Lord's, with the exception of Her Majesty the Queen, but they are, if accompanied, in the Warner Stand. Those who one sees on the public terraces tend to bring their knitting and read women's magazines, or else are going through the lionizing stage with a new cricket-mad boyfriend.

Perhaps the most vintage piece of English eccentricity is to be found in the crowd leaving at close of play who rush to buy an evening newspaper – to read what has been happening . . . at Lord's.

How to get there. Underground (Jubilee line) to St John's Wood. Buses 2, 2b, 13, 113 pass the gates in Wellington Road, N.W.6. A 74 comes to the St John's Wood roundabout in Prince Albert Road.

Getting in. £7.75 Grandstand, £7.50 Grandstand Balcony, Mount Stand and G Stand £6.30. Ground admission £3.50. Car parking (very limited) £2.50. Public tickets already sold out for Friday and Saturday of the 1981 Test.

OTHER EVENTS IN MAY

Royal Caledonian Ball, Grosvenor House Hotel, London.
Game Conservancy Ball, Dorchester Hotel, London.
International Gathering – Scotland 1981, Edinburgh.
Sherborne Castle Horse Trials, Sherborne, Dorset.
Bath Festival, Avon.
Castaways Club Annual Dinner, Hyde Park Hotel, London.
National Society for Mentally Handicapped Children Ball, Inter-Continental Hotel, London.
The World Red Cross Day Gastronomic Dinner, Inter-Continental Hotel.
Racing: Newmarket (1,000 and 2,000 Guineas).
Racing: Longchamp (Poule D'Essai des Pouliches and Prix Ganay).
Commonwealth Development Corporation Dinner Dance, Hyde Park Hotel.
Floral Luncheon, Savoy Hotel, London.
Election of Sheriffs, Guildhall, London.
May Morning Carols at Magdalene College, Oxford.
American Women's Club Golden Eagle Ball, Savoy Hotel, London.
Spring Ball, Grosvenor House Hotel, London.
Dublin Spring Show, Ireland.
Oxford and Cambridge University Sports, White City, London.
Chatsworth Angling Fair, Chatsworth, Derbyshire.
Royal Windsor Horse Show, Royal Windsor Horse Trials.
Stock Exchange Walk, Westminster (start).
The Rose Ball, Grosvenor House Hotel, London.
The Shikar Club Dinner, Savoy Hotel, London.
The Derby Club Dinner, Savoy Hotel, London
Racing: Chester Summer Meeting (Chester Vase and Ladbroke Cup).
Racing: York (Mecca-Dante Stakes, Yorkshire Cup).
Show-jumping at Hickstead, Sussex (Everest Double Glazing International).

Amberley Horse Show and Country Fair, Cirencester Park, Gloucestershire.

Royal Bath and West Show, Shepton Mallet, Somerset.

Chichester Festival Theatre Season opens, Chichester, Sussex.

The Walker Golf Cup, Muirfield, Scotland.

Lytham Trophy, Royal Lytham and St Anne's Golf Club.

Photo World Exhibition, Olympia, London.

Rugby: League Cup Final, Wembley, London.

Polo Season opens, Guards Polo Club, Windsor Great Park.

Devon County Show, Exeter.

May Eights Week, Oxford University.

Ragley Hall Horse Trials, Warwickshire.

Lavinia, Duchess of Norfolk's XI v. West Indies, Arundel Castle, Sussex.

Martini International Golf Championships, Wentworth, Surrey.

Beaufort Hunt Farmers Ball, Badminton, Gloucestershire.

British Driving Society First Official Meet, Windsor.

Show-jumping at Hickstead (Lambert & Butler Nations Cup).

Football: Football Association Cup Final, Wembley, London.

Racing: Longchamp (Prix Lupin and Prix Saint-Alary).

The Golden Horseshoe Ride, Exmoor, Devon.

Suffolk County Show, Ipswich.

Shropshire and West Midlands Show, Shrewsbury.

Bramham Three-Day Event, Wetherby, Yorkshire.

Brabazon Trophy, Little Aston Golf Club.

Ice Skating Championships, Wembley, London.

Saffron Walden Festival, Essex.

Charlwood Festival, Charlwood, Surrey.

Perth Festival of Arts, Perth, Tayside, Scotland.

St Mark's Fair, Abingdon, Oxfordshire.

Stirling Festival, Stirling, Scotland.

Blessing the Sea Ceremony, Hastings, Sussex.

Riverside Studios Spring Bank Holiday Festival, Hammersmith, London.

Philips' Night of Athletics England Match, Crystal Palace, London.

Southern Counties Craft Market, Farnham, Surrey.

English Schools National Race Walk.

Benson & Hedges Annual Fishing Festival, Enniskillen, Ireland.

Scottish Kennel Club Show, Ingliston.

British Jousting Centre Tournaments, Chilham Castle, Kent.

Commemoration of Murder of King Henry VI, Tower of London.

Cricket: One-day matches.

Tattersall's Mixed Spring Sales, Newmarket, Suffolk.

Racing: Kempton Park (Victor Wild Handicap).

Racing: Sandown Park (Brigadier Gerard Stakes).

The boats leaving the brocas for Surley Hall

June

THE FOURTH OF JUNE *by Charles Mosley*

The Fourth of June celebrations at Eton started in the late 18th century as a gala in honour of George III's birthday. This monarch and Henry VI, Eton's founder, share the honour of being the two English sovereigns who have been to the greatest extent benefactors to the school. Interestingly, both were insane.

As with most great English institutions, it is impossible to say when at any given moment the Fourth of June started. Like the leader of the Conservative Party in the good old days, it just 'evolved'. (He, too, was usually an old Etonion, after all.) After George III's death, it is alleged that the fact that his successor's birthday fell in the holidays led to the retention of the Fourth as a celebration day. 'Prinny's' general unpopularity may have been a contributing factor, and in any case schoolboys are natural conservatives.

There used to be two great features of the Fourth of June: the fireworks display and the procession of boats. The former, although held within living memory, is now one with the Montem and Election Saturday as regards Etoniana – of antiquarian interest only. None the less, they were a pretty sight, as fireworks usually are. They were held across the river from Eton, near Fellows' Eyot, the audience sitting on the Buckinghamshire bank. There were tasteful set-piece renderings of the College's armorial device and the sovereign. The end of the entertainment was heralded by multiple-bursting rockets which were greeted with shouts of 'one', 'two', 'three' according to the number of detonations.

Although the fireworks met Mr Andrew Faulds', MP, ideas of propriety in being thoroughly supervised, it was perhaps thought that the audience, sitting on a damp grass, might suffer colds in the head or rheumatism. Or conceivably local old age pensioners, who, Mr Faulds claimed some years ago, are frightened to venture out on Guy Fawkes' Night, successfully lobbied the Provost and Fellows. Whatever the reason, the squibs, catherine wheels, volcanic showers, golden rain and roman candles are seen no more.

The procession of boats is a different matter. The boats in question are stirringly named. The chief one is the *Monarch*, now thought to be the only ten-oared boat of its kind in the world, though in Gladstone's day (1827), as the future prime minister noted in a letter of that date, there were two ten-oars that raced against each other. Arthur Hallam, Gladstone's great school chum and the subject of Tennyson's *In Memoriam*, mentioned the two ten-oars at about the same time. In a letter to *The Field* in 1924 a correspondent claimed of the *Monarch* that 'The ten-oar was a subtle compliment to royalty, for the King's Barge, which is still in commission, and has carried their present Majesties at the Henley Regatta, is fitted for ten oars.'

The other boats have the conventional number of oars (eight) and are: *Dreadnought*, *Victory*, *Thetis*, *Hibernia*, *Defiance*, *Britannia*, *Alexandra*, *St George* and *Prince of Wales*. From the earliest days of the 19th century it was the fashion to take names from Nelson's navy.

Until recently there were two processions of boats, one before and one after sunset. In the 19th century the crews used to row upstream some way and be given a sumptuous supper, including wines and syllabubs. In these degenerate times there is only one procession, in daylight hours, and apparently the crews are subjected to some sort of breathalyser test before being sent out on to the water. Although this is pussyfooting with a vengeance, it must be remembered that as the boats drift gently downstream past the spectators, each crew member stands up until all nine (including the cox) are vertical. It is quite difficult to keep the boat from turning turtle even when sober and it only needs one crew member with less than perfect equilibrium to spill all nine people into the Thames. In any case, rowing men, tall and muscular, are not blessed with low centres of gravity. Not so long ago a further hazard was provided by a certain triple-barrelled baronet, as bold and bad as any villain of Victorian melodrama, who donned a frogman's outfit, swam underwater and rocked the occasional boat while the helpless crew were standing up. So much for *esprit de corps*.

There is a special costume which the boats (i.e. the boys in the boats) wear, and which looks like a surrealist's design for Henley. The oars (i.e. the boys who pull them) are kitted out in dark blue jackets of mess uniform cut, a striped shirt and a straw hat bearing the name of the boat. There is usually a good deal of foliage attached to the costumes so that as the bosky craft glide along the water it seems that Birnam wood has come a good deal closer than Dunsinane. Perhaps, to extend the speculation of the *Field* correspondent, it is a subtle compliment to HM the Queen Mother, who of course hails from Glamis Castle. The coxes are dressed as 19th-century admirals, captains and lieutenants – epaulettes, cocked hats and all. In the early years of the last century, before the standardization of the costumes, the crew of the *Monarch* once or twice appeared as galley slaves chained to the oars. It sounds like a scene from *Quo Vadis*.

The above glories excepted, and they are now mostly vestigial emasculations of the past, the Fourth of June is more or less like any other school open day. There is an all-day cricket match between the XI and the Eton Ramblers, who have a pleasant club tie. There is an 'ephemeral', as the yearly magazines are called, which, appearing for one day only under a different name each time, are none the less curiously alike in their devotion to literary experiment in preference to hard news. There are the obligatory picnic hampers containing champagne and lobster salad and strawberries and cream. For the curious, there is an exhibition at the Art Schools by schoolboys from the same stable that produced Burne-Jones. There is often the churning of fine grass to mud by a thousand Rolls-Royces.

To get there, simply point your Hispano-Suiza or whatever in a westerly direction (assuming you are starting from London; if from elsewhere, simply go first to London). You can tell whether you are going in a westerly direction or not because, provided you start in the morning, the sun should be behind you. After midday, of course, it will be in your chauffeur's eyes, so it would be more considerate to him to start in the morning. About twenty miles along the M4 you will notice a large castle on the left. At this point you have a choice of whether to get stuck in the traffic jams leading from the Slough East, Slough West or Slough Central motorway exits. The RAC or local police should have put up helpful signs directing you to the site of the festivities so that more detailed instructions would be otiose.

An alternative method of arrival would be to make use of the quaint railway system linking London and Windsor. Main line Station: Waterloo (as in Battle of, Eton, playing fields of, won on — a simple mnemonic). The electrified line will take you the twenty-five miles in well under the hour, and from Windsor and Eton Riverside Station you bear right out of the station and over the bridge spanning the river. This is in fact the best way of approaching Eton, provided the womenfolk of your party are not too footsore, because the bridge is now closed to motor traffic so that Eton High Street is as tranquil as in George III's day.

There is only one further point to add: because the school output quota of Latin proses and quadratic equations is sacrosanct, nothing must be allowed to interrupt it. Therefore the Fourth of June nowadays is invariably celebrated on a Saturday, and a simple calculation will show that the Fourth of June falls on a Saturday, on average, once every seven years. Hence the communications to be seen in the Court Circular of *The Times* in April and May every year, sounding like a presumptuous tampering with the calendar worthy of the French Revolution: 'Eton College – The Fourth of June will take place on Saturday the 7th of June.' Watch that space.

THE DERBY *by Adam Helliker*

In times past the Derby was a national outing, with Parliament adjourning for the three days of the Epsom meeting. Now it's still the nearest thing we have to a national picnic and provides another opportunity to hear a multitude of champagne corks popping. It's a fact that top racing and champagne go hand in hand. The precedent at Epsom was created when Moët et Chandon's agent owned a winning horse in 1908 and he served free champers to everyone there.

The sound of the corks being drawn vies on Derby Day with the noise of the tipsters and their certainties, the calls of the bookmakers, and that pleasant sound of laughter which hangs over all the excitement and anticipation of enjoyment. The eyes of the nation are fixed on this one race; most of the country is interested in the result and many have their one annual flutter on it. Crowds flock in their thousands to see the race for themselves and to enjoy the thrill of actually being there. The Derby attracts the rich, the poor and the middling, the gamblers, the horsey set, the drinkers and the holiday-makers.

Because the Downs are open, it is truly a wonder to see the care taken by the public to keep the famous course clear and in condition. Everything is on trust, which is even more amazing when one realizes that it is also the time and venue for the traditional annual reunion of gypsies. Against the lush emerald green of the the turf the hundreds of vans make quite a spectacle, though not so colourful as when they were of the horse-drawn and hand-painted variety. The gypsies mix with those other 'royalties', the Pearly King and Queens, covered in thousands of pearl buttons, with enormous feather hats. It is fatal to refuse to buy a sprig of so-called lucky white heather from one of the gypsy women, for she will surely utter a curse and you'll back a loser.

Loud and colourful as this aspect of the Derby scene may be, it all makes way for the sight most people are hoping to see – the Queen driving down the course to the accompaniment of the band of the Welsh Guards (with whom the Clerk of the Course has a connection). This is another event marked high in the Royal calendar and the Queen will be hoping, as many others will be, that hers is the winning horse.

Short of being on HM's guest list, the best way to see the Derby is to join the Epsom Race Club, which has about 1,000 members paying a subscription of £40 a year, plus £25 for each of the two permitted guests. As at Ascot, morning dress or national costume is required for the club enclosure or the old Prince's Stand. Last year the comedian Max Bygraves had the cheek to turn up in a black jacket, check trousers, grey trilby and a red shoulder bag, and was taken aback to be refused entry. Luckily for him, a friend living near the racecourse came to the rescue and lent him a morning coat, which although far too big, was at least the right colour. In the same year the septuagenarian scholar, Raphael de Sola, arrived in a chocolate-coloured suit and topper, looking very much like a walnut whip. For women the Derby meeting is not so dressy as Ascot, but if they want a jolly good excuse to try out a new outfit it's best done on the day of the Oaks. To be fair, on Derby day it's the horses, for once, that really matter and not the female fashions.

The next most patrician way of seeing the Derby is from the vantage of a private box, high up in the Grandstand, from where you can see the Post Office Tower fifteen miles to the north on a reasonably clear day. Morning dress for the box inhabitants is not compulsory although many feel they have to wear tails as a gesture of some sort. Nowadays a box costs around £700 and they're let annually to individuals and companies, more often than not for the purpose of business entertainment. Only the large corporations can afford to dispense

Celebrations after The Derby

hospitality in the old-fashioned way, with lobster and lashings of booze the order of the day in the lunch rooms attached to the boxes. There is a preponderance of elderly gentlemen superannuated by their firms, who still seem to expect the deference they knew at the height of their careers. As with all these things there's a hangers-on priority list for the best out of the 196 boxes, the most points going to the Home Secretary's box. (United Racecourses, the owners of the course, give him a free one every year.)

A little further down the scale you can buy a Grandstand

ticket for only £10, giving access to the paddock for a look at the horses, a glimpse of the famous, and probably sore feet, as going between the stand and the paddock involves a good deal of walking. There are no dress requirements here other than those of public decency. This was liberally interpreted in the heatwave of 1976 when some women racegoers came in brief bikinis.

For the *hoi polloi*, entrance to the Downs is free and a totally different atmosphere prevails. There's a gentle haze of cooking smoke from the dozens of hot-dog stands and hamburger carts, and a whiff of the sea from the jellied-eel stalls. All this is backed by the fruity sound of the Wurlitzer organs at the funfair, where people are only too happy to pay for a sickmaking ride on the Big Wheel after a surfeit of beer and whelks. More up-to-date entertainment is offered in the form of topless go-go dancers who perform in a series of buses. The bus companies do pretty well out of the Derby: about 300 open-topped double-deckers are hired by groups as diverse as the secretarial staff of *Horse and Hound* and under-employed Leyland workers. The buses are lined along the course and provide a rollicking way of enjoying the day, eating and drinking whatever one likes and wearing whatever one cares. (Anyone who wears a topper in a bus deserves to lose it – and does.) From the salmon in the boxes to the picnics in the car parks feasting is all part of a scene which hasn't changed since Charles Dickens recorded the flatulent daze left by too much indulgence at the Derby in 1851.

Transport to Epsom is as varied as the dress and ranges from the picturesque to the practical. Dozens of extra trains are run, tremendous road jams build up, and a heliport has been opened (last year over 200 helicopters dropped delighted passengers). One day someone is bound to suggest parachuting in (complete with topper) but until that happens it's still possible to take to the old ways of travelling in a horse-drawn waggonette, although this sort of thing appeals more to the trendy young.

The fervour of this Blue Riband of the turf even affects the

Stock Exchange, whose staid gentlemen desert their posts to join the crowds, bringing about a marked decline in business. In America Wall Street stopped business in 1881 when an American colt won. That horse's American owner was an exception because in those days the winning owners were usually members of the aristocracy; today they're just rich. In fact this is the richest race in the world. Although other races in Kentucky, Germany and Australia have been named after it this is the race after which the winning horse will be valued in millions. Every owner dreams of saddling a Derby winner, not only for the money but for the prestige. Stud fees for the winner are colossal and it's too bad if it doesn't live to fulfil its duties, as happened to the 1921 winner, Humourist, who died after the race from a haemorrhaged lung, and the 1961 favourite, Angers, which had to be destroyed on the course. Lester Piggott, eight times a winning Derby jockey, has described the horseshoe-shaped course as the greatest test of horse and rider in the game, because of the varied contours of the ground. It's such a fast course that very few of the thousands watching ever get a really good look at the horses flashing by on the switchback ride.

The Derby began with a wager back in 1779. The twenty-one-year-old 12th Earl of Derby leased a house at Epsom called the Oaks and during his stay he and his friends decided to institute a new race for three-year-old fillies (previous races had always been for four-year-olds) to be run over $1\frac{1}{2}$ miles. He named it the Oaks and a similar race was introduced the next year for colts; a toss of the coin determined that this race should be called the Derby. It could have been called the Bunbury, after Sir Charles Bunbury, Chief Steward of the Jockey Club, who lost the toss.) As Lord Rosebery said: 'A roistering party at a country house founded two races and named them greatly after their host and his house, the Derby and the Oaks. Seldom has a carouse had a more permanent effect.'

The Derby hasn't always had a happy history. In 1913 a suffragette, trying to attract attention to her cause, sought to seize the bridle of King George V's horse as it neared Tattenham Corner. Neither the horse nor the jockey were injured but the sad and misguided Miss Davison died from her injuries a few days later.

How to get there: Only sixteen miles from the centre of London, the racecourse on Epsom Downs can be reached by five main approach roads for those going by car. There are always dreadful jams on Derby day so early arrival is vital – the gates open at 10 am. Railway passengers have the choice of three stations, Epsom Town, Tattenham Corner and Epsom Downs, all of which are within one mile of the course (and there's a special bus service from the Town station on racedays). The fifteen-minute trip by helicopter from the London Heliport – a journey that will give you fascinating views of all the motorists stuck in the race traffic – can be booked through Hascome Aviation Services of Bishop's Stortford. They also run choppers from Sandown Park Racecourse in Esher to the centre of the Epsom course, and they even provide cars to take racegoers to the Grandstand.

Getting in: As has been described, the best way of going to the Derby is as a member of the Epsom Race Club, but if you can't manage that then Grandstand tickets can be bought on arrival or booked through Keith Prowse Ltd. For £6 you can get into the Silver Ring or Rosebery Stand, where the dress is more informal and the betting more knowledgeable. Seats in the best part of the Grandstand known as the Anglesey Enclosure may be booked in advance for £21 each (or a four-day badge costs £30). Car parking spaces can be reserved and cost from £7 for the best to £1 for the ones farthest away.

ROYAL ASCOT by Adam Helliker

The very mention of the words Royal Ascot conjures up a picture of elegance, tradition and chic, for these are the only words to describe this highlight of the Season. It also happens to be one of the world's greatest race meetings.

The Queen, whom one might call the star performer of the whole show, gives a house party at Windsor Castle during Ascot week and is fond of asking her guests to join in an early-morning gallop along the course. Later on each day, their thirst for hard exercise quenched, she, Prince Philip and their guests head a procession of open landaus along the straight mile – a formal tradition in total contrast to their earlier ride.

The highly-polished landaus are drawn by Windsor Greys accompanied by outriders in scarlet coats and gold-laced top hats. To add to the colourful scene the bewigged postilions wear purple, red and gold. The Queen Mother and Princess Margaret head a list of the other Royalties who follow Her Majesty into the Royal Box, which is situated high above the course near the finishing post and is always ablaze with flowers. The most noticeable feature in the comfortable two-storey suite, with its bamboo chairs and panelled walls, is a magnificent Lalique horse's head on a pedestal. The Royal nosh, which is light and delicate to suit HM's tiny appetite, is always sent over from the Castle.

In the few weeks before the Royal Ascot meeting the main London branches of Moss Bros are packed to overflowing with gentlemen of all shapes and sizes squeezing themselves into the morning dress that is required for the Royal Enclosure. Likewise dressmakers and milliners are rushed off their feet trying to produce pretty, often outrageous, creations for those women who wish to attract the attention of Press photographers.

The 7,000 people who crowd the Royal Enclosure are required to dress according to the rules of Her Majesty's Representative, the Marquess of Abergavenny. These are that women should wear day dresses with hats and gentleman morning or service dress. Both rules are enough to ensure that everyone looks their best and tries to outdo each other.

But there are some who have made a reputation for themselves by going over the top in the dress stakes, notably Mrs Gertrude Shilling, mother of one-time shirtmaker Mr David

Shilling. Her hats have been so incredibly bizarre that some years she has found it almost impossible to walk. And, speaking of walking, another great spectacle at Ascot is to see beautifully dressed women in high heels rooted to the spot when it rains and their shoes become embedded in the muddy grass. The custom is to save expensive shoes by carrying them and walking barefoot.

However lightly the Royal guests may lunch, others at Ascot seem to feel that they must generate the energy needed to stroll between the enclosure and the paddock with vast quantities of luxurious food washed down with the inevitable champagne. Taking one's own supply of champers is always a wise move as last year one of the bars actually ran out – and Ascot-goers without champagne are like deep-sea divers without oxygen. There are 280 private boxes, each with its own dining-room and at lunchtime (before the Queen drives past at 2 pm) these are filled with guests knocking back lobster and salmon mayonnaise, followed by strawberries and cream. There are also half a dozen restaurants but many enclosure patrons would rather be seen lunching from large hampers in the car parks than frequenting these establishments. Surprisingly, eating in the car parks can be quite acceptable, particularly if the car is right (and after all a Rolls can be hired by the week, although chauffeurs are not so easy to come by during the Ascot races).

Eating at Ascot used to be a lot easier when there was a selection of club tents dotted about, but now the only one remaining belongs to White's, London's most exclusive club which has a six-year waiting list. Unfortunately for those who would like to wangle their way in, the tent's entrance is guarded by the same porters who staff the club's St James's Street premises; they can recognize each member at a glance. The only way to get in is as the guest of a member, although the number of guests is limited and even then lunch has to be served in three sittings (rather like a holiday camp, but White's tent is not so large, only seating 120 at a time). If you really can't get in there for lunch then a box will have to do but

Arrival of the illustrious visitors at Royal Ascot

remember that last year the Ascot Authority was charging £1,670 for a 'Grade A' box.

Although this is a race meeting at which the standard of racing is of the highest, some of the racegoers make it quite clear that they would rather be watching horses playing other games at nearby Smith's Lawn, where the Guards' Polo Club is located and where special Ascot Week tournament matches are played each afternoon. Last year that great polo player Prince Charles made his exit from the racecourse even before the second race, which is named after him, had been run. The noise of the military band behind the main grandstand covered the roar of his Aston Martin very nicely.

For those who do take their racing seriously Ascot provides a really good race on each of its four days: on Tuesday there's the Ascot Stakes, on Wednesday there's the Royal Hunt Cup, on the Thursday it's the Gold Cup and on Friday there's the King's Stand Stakes. For the fashion-conscious Gold Cup Day is the most important, also known as Ladies' Day. This is the day when women go in their best outfits and is usually the day when most attend. On the Wednesday women wear their second best and on the other two days they do the best they can.

Traditionally Ascot is the time for lavish house parties, often held in houses rented for the week at phenomenal charges. The cost of temporary but very necessary domestic staff has made this a very expensive pastime which with the march of Socialism will soon be impossible. One of the most extravagant party-givers was the late Sir Charles Clore whose eve-of-Ascot dances for 700 close friends were loud but enjoyable.

The first races at Ascot were run in August 1711, on the instructions of Queen Anne. She was accustomed to being driven in a carriage across the grass of Ascot Common, being far too fat actually to ride a horse, and one day she observed that it would make a good place for horse racing. So at a cost of only £574 the turf was enclosed and a new course was born.

After her death interest in racing lapsed as George I was indifferent to the sport, but luckily later on in the century the Duke of Cumberland (son of George II) made a determined effort to re-establish the course, which was not easy as other courses were already well established and the roads to lonely Ascot were swarming with highwaymen. In those days too there were plenty of distractions from the racing as the event attracted booths for cockfighting, wrestling and boxing, not to mention plenty of pickpockets and confidence men to trap the unwary. But the King and his friends, who looked on from two magnificent marquees, could always rest assured that if things got out of hand the cavalry would gallop from Windsor to quell the crowds with their sabres.

One notable horse to have raced at Ascot was called Baronet and George III, when congratulating the Prince of Wales on the horse's victory, was reputed to have said of his £17,000 winnings: 'I made fourteen baronets last week but I get nothing by them. Your single Baronet is worth all mine put together.' As King George IV, the Prince of Wales was to entertain some of the most glittering members of society at Ascot; to ensure their comfort John Nash was commissioned to design a Royal Box.

Another monarch to enjoy the view from this splendid box was William IV. He made his own bit of Ascot history by setting up a court of summary justice to deal with a disgruntled chap who had lobbed a brick at him and dented his hat. This established a tradition which only died out four years ago whereby a senior magistrate on the course dished out immediate justice to wrongdoers and criminals. The crowd took their own vengence on one fellow who welshed on a bet. They cut off his pigtail, slit his breeches and, after ducking him in the pond, led him up the course with a rope round his neck. Nowadays any trouble is looked after by eighty uniformed policemen and forty-five plain-clothes detectives (some of whom look rather awkward in top hats) who mingle with the crowds.

Queen Victoria in her youth found herself being booed as she rode up the course after she had accused her Maid of Honour, the unmarried Lady Flora Hastings, of being pregnant. It was later discovered that Lady Flora had an incurable cancer and outraged society women felt strongly enough about the Queen's insult to vent their feelings in public. But Victoria soon regained her popularity and she went to Ascot every year until 1860. A year later Prince Albert died and she forswore all public pleasures.

Fortunately, her son, the Prince of Wales, had a wide circle of raffish friends who all loved the turf. The widowed Victoria, who was impossibly stern towards her son, once wrote and complained to him about his visits to Ascot. She advised him to confine his visits to Tuesday and Thursday and not to go on all four days. For once dear Bertie defied his mother by replying that as he was past twenty-eight and had considerable knowledge of the world and society he could be relied upon to use his own discretion. Later on, in his short reign as Edward VII, Ascot reached spectacular heights of fashion with dresses similar to the ones worn in the memorable show

My Fair Lady. Even after Edward's death, only a month before the race meeting, the pageant continued with society attending in the most elegant mourning ever seen.

So many records have been made at Ascot it is difficult to know which to mention. Probably the most famous partnership to date is that of Steve Donoghue and Brown Jack, a famous gelding with the eccentric habit of having a nap in his box immediately before a race. From 1929 this pair won the Alexandra Stakes for six consecutive years and now a statuette of the horse by Sir Alfred Munnings stands by the jockeys' weighing-room on the Friday, the day of the Alexandra Stakes. Of recent Royal wins the most spectacular was in 1954 when the Queen's horse, Aureole, squeezed home in the Hardwicke Stakes in a photofinish – no mean feat for a horse that had an eye injury and was ridden by Eph Smith who was partly deaf.

How to get there: British Rail operate a frequent service of trains from Waterloo, Guildford and Reading to Ascot station which is within ten minutes' walk of the course. This is probably the best way to travel as the journey takes only 40 minutes when the trains are running fast and it also allows one to be a bit more liberal with the champagne glass. By car from London the best route is along the M4, coming off at the Slough Central interchange and following the Windsor Relief Road (A355) and the A332 through Windsor Great Park. From the West proceed via the M4 to the Winnersh interchange (Junction 10) along the A329 to the junction with the A332, turning left towards Bracknell and Ascot. For the Royal meeting an early start is advisable and a reserved car parking ticket is a great asset. These can be purchased from January onwards at a cost of £10 for the best spaces down to £2 for the ones farthest away. The Number One West Car Enclosure is reserved for Royal Enclosure applicants and is divided into numbered berths which are booked in advance.

Getting in: Anyone can get into the course's Grandstand, Silver Ring, and Heath by simply paying £7, £2 and 50p, respectively, but it is the Royal Enclosure which should be aimed for and to gain entrance there is a special procedure. The list of applicants to the enclosure is open from January and those wishing to get in should apply for vouchers in writing to Her Majesty's Representative at the Ascot Office, St James's Palace, S.W.1, by not later than the end of April. Each application should only include members of one family and must state full names. Young people aged between sixteen and twenty-five may apply for a special voucher exchangeable at reduced rates, but those under sixteen are not admitted to the enclosure except on the Friday when their badges cost £2 each.

Those applying for vouchers for the first time will be sent an ominous-looking form which requires the signature of a sponsor who has been granted vouchers for the enclosure on at least four occasions in recent years or is of high enough birth to be known personally to the Marquess of Abergavenny. Visitors from overseas should apply for their vouchers to their Ambassador or High Commissioner in London.

Vouchers are sent four weeks before the meeting and they may then be exchanged for either a badge costing £36 and valid for all four days or a daily badge which costs £14.50 for each day. The young people's vouchers are exchanged for badges at half price – £18 for the lot or £7 for a day.

WIMBLEDON *by Adam Helliker*

Anyone for tennis? Sunny skies, sunburned faces, the crisp thwack of tennis balls on the most famous grass courts in the world – this is Wimbledon fortnight in most people's eyes. More likely it will consist of a vista of umbrellas and huge tarpaulins covering the courts.

So one's first preparation for Wimbledon should be to take a book and a crossword puzzle to occupy one's time while huddled in a mackintosh waiting for the skies to clear. Of course it has been known for this annual tennis spectacular to be held in a heatwave, in which case the itinerant street vendors descend with sunglasses, 1920s-style eyeshades and, more recently, those peculiar nose-protectors which make people look very silly indeed. The weather really counts at Wimbledon because if it does rain there's not much to do except queue for Scotch eggs and pictures of Bjorn Borg. But if the sun shines then everyone's happy, including the St John Ambulance Brigade who can busy themselves attending to those who keel over in the heat.

The complex inside the ivy-covered walls at Wimbledon, which includes fifteen grass courts and ten hard courts, is the headquarters of the All-England Lawn Tennis and Croquet Club. This is, in fact, a tiny club with an exclusive membership of 375, but visitors to the championships last year numbered 350,000, all of whom, it seems, want to get into the hallowed centre court where there are seats for only 11,700.

This is where the ticket touts come in – either discreet advertisers in *The Times* or the chaps in the car parks who sidle up to innocent-looking tennis fans. Both have the same ambition – to make a killing by charging something approaching a 700 per cent premium for centre court tickets. But the men on the spot don't mind those who try to bargain with them and it's worth remembering that their prices are highest a couple of hours before play and drop sharply as two o'clock looms.

For those who don't fancy taking chances with the scalpers there are other ways of getting a seat on the centre court. The county tennis clubs receive about 2,400 seats a day, which isn't a large ration when one considers how many active club members there are; but the Wimbledon authorities decided long ago that non-players and possible players ought to be able to enjoy watching as well as the converted. More and more travel agencies are trying to get their hands on seats for overseas customers who now regard Wimbledon even more highly than Shakespeare's birthplace. For the keen and hardy it used to be possible to queue for unreserved seats sold at the gates on the last three days, but last year this custom ended after complaints about the noise from nearby residents.

If the championships really mean an awful lot to you then

An early battle at Wimbledon

there's a very faint possibility that you may be able to buy a debenture seat, but be prepared to pay a lot of money. Most of the 1,740 debenture seats are held by rich uncles who really like the game, or companies whose managing directors bought them with the aim of entertaining clients. The companies also have the run of the eighty-four private marquees at the far end of the ground. Here firms like the Chase Manhatton Bank and Hertz Cars pay a reputed £10,000 each for the privilege of letting their favourite customers trample on the artificial grass spread on the floor and nick all the drinks.

Before taking your dearly-purchased seat in the centre court it's wise to do a quick recce of the buffets and the loos, bearing in mind that most spectators stay for up to six hours. It's no use being able to pinpoint the bank or the Post Office if your bladder is reminding you of over-indulgence in liquid pleasures. Eating at Wimbledon can't be said to be one of the major pleasures of the event: the main offerings seem to be meat pies, hamburgers and hot-dogs, with the odd tired lettuce leaf. Lots of provincial ladies up for the day indulge in the extravagance of buying the traditional strawberries and cream, and extravagance is the operative word with the cost

67

last year at 75p for about five indifferent and tasteless straw-berries. Actually, if you have to eat something – and you do – it's best to do it on the lawn near the Church Road gates before the start, where you can wave to people you think you know. On the continent the food is done considerably better at tennis championships – at the Foro Italico in Rome they offer cold stuffed aubergines and chicken, and the German tour-naments have real culinary surprises. But at Wimbledon the hallmark of the ordinary spectator is a humble thermos flask and a packet of soggy sandwiches.

The glorious grounds at Wimbledon were laid out in Church Road back in 1922 and the centre court was first grassed with virgin seaside turf. Unhappily the live shrimps therein didn't enhance the quality of tennis and the turf itself, while being lovely to look at, was too velvety and slow for tournament play. Today it's the fastest, hardest and truest court in the world and the play is restricted entirely to the midsummer matches, except for one doubles contest by a quartet of women club members to play the grass in, stamp it down and get rid of some of the sap. As soon as the last trophies are presented the court is reseeded; and it's reseeded a second time the following spring. Constant attention assures an immaculate surface, protected by a large tarpaulin weighing over four tons.

The atmosphere at the centre court is so overwhelming it has frequently induced stage fright in players, notably Vir-ginia Wade, who, although a magnificent player, loses time after time at Wimbledon. Dress for the players used to be very formal – cream flannels and long-sleeved shirts for the men and discreet and unremarkable white dresses for women. Very slow progress led to both sexes wearing shorter gar-ments below the belt and cool shirts. Then designer Teddy Tinling burst on the scene and introduced female frilly knick-ers worn beneath brief and provocative dresses. These pan-ties are still with us but they now look more like baby pants – and perhaps they are, given the ever-decreasing age of some of the players.

In the last few years the dress rules have been relaxed to permit touches of colour on a white background. Initially this meant some of the women wearing Tinling creations with embroidered dresses, still with the emphasis on femininity. Now the clothes are much more practical, but some of the geometric designs have an eye-searing effect when one is following the ball from left to right and right to left during a long volley.

In the Royal Box the dress is always correct, as one would expect. Tennis at Wimbledon has enjoyed Royal patronage for some time: King George V donated the massive silver cup that is presented to the men's singles winner every year, and his son, the Duke of York, played in a doubles match in the 1926 championships. The Kent family have been the staunchest Royal supporters of them all, holding the club presidency for forty-five years. Favoured guests join them in the Royal Box, which has a chintzy room at the back where sandwiches are served from a large round table. There are the pink-painted Royal loos, with matching tiles and tissues, which are guarded from the plebs by the club secretary's wife.

Apart from such attractions as the Royal loos, the All-England Club's village at Wimbledon also contains a bookstall, a couple of sweet shops, a museum, six first-aid posts, a Post Office (where letters posted get the bonus of a special tournament postmark) and an information desk staffed by jolly WRVS women. These women are part of a massive workforce, which includes eighty-five ball boys, 190 blue-blazered umpires and linesmen and an army of ground cleaners who used to be university students; many have long since graduated but still come back for the jamboree. Then there are the administrators, the club committee that begins arranging the next championships as soon as the last player has flown home. Before Christmas new tickets must be printed because by January requests for seats are already pouring in, not only from Britain but from the fifty other nations whose players will possibly compete. The whole well-oiled machine swings into action again, with foreign and out-of-town players checking into West End hotels, London hostesses sending out invitations to cocktail parties, and caterers at a top hotel planning the annual Wimbledon Ball.

How to get there: Wimbledon is only seven miles from the centre of London and therefore within easy driving distance, although taking a car means queuing for a car park and parking will cost at least £2 for those that don't hold debenture tickets. By rail Wimbledon can be reached direct from Waterloo or Blackfriars station and by underground on the District line.

Getting in: Apart from the various methods already mentioned one way to get a centre court or No 1 court ticket is to try your luck in the public ballot. For this you have to write to the Secretary of the All-England Club between 1 October and 31 December for an application form (but they won't reply unless you enclose a stamped addressed envelope). More than a quarter of a million spectators see matches by getting tickets this way and the authorities have evolved another charming way to make seats available to people willing to risk going out to the courts on the off-chance. Ticket-holders who must leave early drop their tickets into specially-provided boxes and these are then re-sold at only 20p each. So thousands see first-class tennis they would otherwise have missed and the proceeds from this little custom go to the National Playing Fields Association. Even if both these methods fail you can still enjoy the general atmosphere by paying just £2 at the gate (if you don't mind queueing for them to open at noon) and then you can wander round all the outside courts and use the standing room for the show courts. After 5 pm admission is reduced to £1.

OXBRIDGE MAY BALLS *by Adam Helliker and Jane Slade*

Oxford and Cambridge abandon their intellectual image once a year to indulge in a high society fling at which élitist groups shake the dust from their white ties and

70

cummerbunds to cultivate that *je ne sais quoi* required for a college May Ball. Paradoxically these occasions take place in June and apart from the sheer fun of the things they're valuable to students as a respite after the exams.

Those colleges with the most prestige, romantic flavour, enthusiasm and above all cash, deck their halls with boughs of fairy lights and punctuate their lawns with marquees to give their undergraduates a chance to drown their loved ones, or potential loved ones, in a whirlpool of wine, music and romance. The professional can always be distinguished from the amateur because he's accustomed to taking a different partner to each of the various balls during May Week, by the end of which the long summer vacation comes as a well-earned rest.

Providing the Oxbridge student has worked hard during the term, mummy and daddy may fork out the £60 necessary for a double ticket. If he's had to save up the money himself it will have been a case of starvation on baked beans and coffee or a loan from a friendly inmate or an even friendlier bank manager. Those less affluent among the student community can often be spotted on the night of the ball either astride a college wall attempting illegal entry or pleading with a policeman half-way across a river, their shabby dinner jackets splattered with mud from either the Cam or the Isis.

If you have the misfortune to be of lowly birth or unable to purchase a ticket there are still several options left open: (1) Do not go at all. (2) Wait outside bemoaning your fate until the gates are opened to you. (3) Find other ways of getting in free of charge – and here are some methods which have won the seal of success over the years.

One girl last year hadn't got a ticket and was desperate to join those on the other side of the college wall who she could hear having a wonderful time. Having made two attempts to scramble over the wall, each time being escorted away by a policeman because a rose bush happened to get in the way, she decided to play the jilted girlfriend. She walked up to the porter and explained that her boyfriend had abandoned her

71

and was now probably whooping it up with some other young thing and she just had to go and see for herself who it was. The porter was remarkably sympathetic and eventually escorted her into the ball, saying over and over again that he hoped she would be all right.

Of course this method is exclusive to women; it's up to the men either to pose as members of a rock band or, in the case of Cambridge balls, to tie plastic bags round their legs before attempting the great wade across the river. A pogo stick is a useful piece of equipment for overcoming the next hurdle – the college wall. Great care must be taken once access has been gained and any ropes or parachutes must either be buried or hidden behind a shrubbery, for if anyone discovers you're an 'illegal immigrant' the exit will appear long before you had planned.

Presuming that you've done things correctly and are not an illegal immigrant, one of the vital things to remember is not to arrive until at least midnight, for at 4 am the night is still considered young. The wine may not be gushing forth so freely at this hour but the bands will play on until dawn, after which a full breakfast is served.

One could argue that the cost of entry to these revered functions is a trifle extravagant for the young, but it must be said that you do get what you pay for. It costs a lot to get a well-known band to play, almost as much as it does to have good wine flowing from every available source, but the price deters very few and the tickets disappear within a week. The general public can only attend if they're quick and affluent enough; the unlucky ones will make every attempt to get in even if it means posing as a plumber for those champagne corks that refuse to budge. It's the enthusiasm of these immigrants that makes the aid of the local bobbies essential. The college porters also make every effort to eject any undesirable intending to deprave or corrupt the proceedings for which the crested thoroughbreds have paid their money.

It's usual to make up a party for the ball and dine handsomely beforehand to whet the appetite for what's coming

Waiting for the music to begin at a May Ball

later in the evening. Parents, son and girlfriend is not always the ideal combination for a foursome but there are methods of escape available to each party should the need arise.

At the ball itself the marquees are varied according to musical taste, ranging from a full orchestra to a heavy blast of drums and twang emanating from an apparently pulsating blob that has been known to move gradually across the lawn throughout the night. It's in the tent where the 'named' band has been playing that shoes, shawls, and sometimes a lot more get shoved under tables only to emerge much later draped somewhere about their owners, who can be seen wincing as they walk into the daylight.

One way to communicate to friends and relatives that you had a truly smashing time at the ball is to send them a photograph. The up-and-coming David Baileys of this country reserve a decorative archway in the college and trap any pair of starry-eyed lovers who happen to be passing beneath it. A beaming smile with heads together is a favourite pose, or a loving clutch with empty wine glasses pushed into the fore-ground.

Punting in May Ball clothing is an art apart and demands a certain amount of rehearsal. It's not uncommon to see a gentleman gallantly standing at one end of the punt with his kneecaps revealed beneath his rolled-up trousers while his ladylove, tear-stained with mascara, performs a *grande toilette* on her new dress in an attempt to dislodge the mud from the layers of lace. The romanticism of the occasion can be recap-tured, however, during the dawn firework display. Many of the fireworks resemble the results of failed chemical experi-ments but, nonetheless, they coax the masses from the mar-quees to stand in loving embrace against the colourful skyline.

At a certain hour, usually about 4 or 5 am, the gates are opened to anyone who has waited long enough to get in without a ticket, although they may be crushed by those worshippers of Bacchus who have over-indulged and decide to leave now the evening has tailed off. At this time in the proceedings all the newcomer will find are a few half-glasses of wine and some dwindling bars of music persistently pumped out by a few remaining hardy musicians. At 6 am diehards radiate towards the exits, searching for lost shoes and jewellery on the way, as a whisper from the streets beckons them to their beds. It's a curious sight to see the cobbled alleyways dense with tired persons meandering home, some still in perfect condition, others with their bow ties somewhere around their middle, partially supported by their female counterparts.

How to get there: Driving can be a problem if you've got to face a long haul back the next day, when you will still be very tired and probably still over the limit, so the best way is by train. The journey takes just over an hour by Inter-City from

Paddington to Oxford and about the same from Liverpool Street to Cambridge. If you think you will need a bed for what's left of the night you should book well in advance at one of the hotels in the area, preferably one at walking distance from the college.

Getting in: Obtaining tickets is difficult if you haven't a contact at either University, but a letter addressed to the Ball Committee chairman at a particular college should guarantee you consideration if you write early.

OTHER EVENTS IN JUNE

Benenden Ball, Hyde Park Hotel, London.
British Amateur Golf Championships, St Andrews, Scotland.
Fine Art and Antiques Fair, Olympia, London.
The Summer Ball, Inter-Continental Hotel, London.
Order of the Garter Ceremony, Windsor Castle, Berkshire.
Final of Queen's Cup, Guards Polo Club, Windsor Great Park.
May Bumps, College Rowing Races, Cambridge University.
Royal Western/Observer Single-Handed Transatlantic Race, Plymouth.
Silver Clef Ball, Inter-Continental Hotel, London.
Cirencester Park Polo Club Dance, Cirencester Park, Gloucestershire.
Trooping the Colour – Queen's Official Birthday Parade, London.
Embassy Grand Prix Power Boat Racing, Bristol, Avon.
Racing: Chantilly (Prix du Jockey Club and Prix de Diane).
Racing: Auteuil (Grand Steeple Chase de Paris).
Racing: Longchamp (Grand Prix de Paris, Prix d'Ispahan).
Three Counties Show, Malvern, Warwickshire.
Royal Highland Show, Ingliston, Scotland.
Golf: Remy Martin Amateur Tournament, Royal Portrush, Ireland.
International TT Motorcycle Races, Douglas, Isle of Man.

Royal Island Yacht Race, Isle of Wight (from Cowes).
British Driving Society Annual Show, Smith's Lawn,
  Windsor, Berkshire.
Royal Norfolk Show, Norwich.
Racing: Newcastle.
Beating the Retreat, Whitehall, London.
Dickens Festival, Broadstairs, Kent.
Montrose Festival, Scotland.
The Royal Show, Stoneleigh, Warwickshire.
Stour Festival of Music and Painting, Wye, Kent.
Mystery Plays, York Cathedral, York.
Midsummer Druid Festival, Stonehenge, Wiltshire.
British Grand Prix Waterski Championships, Brighton,
  Sussex.
Summer Festival of the Arts, Reading, Berkshire.
East Coast Boat Show, Ipswich, Suffolk.
Oxford v. Cambridge Universities Polo Tournament,
  Kirtlington.
Hallé Proms, Manchester, Lancashire.
Grass Tennis Championships, Queen's Club, London.
South of England Show, Ardingly, West Sussex.
Grosvenor House Antiques Fair, Park Lane, London.
Burns Festival, South-West Scotland.
Cricket: Prudential World Cup Final, Lords.
The Knollys Rose Ceremony, Mansion House, London.
Cricket: Test Matches.
Polo: Ascot Week Tournament, Guards Polo Club. Windsor,
  Berkshire.
Racing: Sandown Park (Trafalgar's Day).
Le Mans 24-Hour Race, Le Mans, France.

July

HENLEY ROYAL REGATTA *by Adam Helliker*

The important thing to remember about Henley Royal Regatta is that it serves two purposes: *you* may be there because you're a hearty rowing type with secret dreams of winning the Diamond Sculls, but for many of the 50,000 people present the important business of the day, or rather the four days, will be in the form of Pimms and strawberries.

It is *de rigueur* for any respectable gentleman (and of course you are one because you're in the Stewards' Enclosure) to sport a blazer – not just any old blazer but a dazzling striped one. The regatta provides an excuse for men to blossom forth in some of the most outrageous club gear ever seen outside an Edwardian music hall. Whether you freeze or roast, depending on the vagaries of the English weather, under no circumstances will you loosen your collar or take off your blazer. The rules for dress are strictly observed – gentlemen may wear blazers so gaudy as to stop an elephant in full-charge but they must also wear a tie or cravat at all times. Actually this rule has once been broken in the 141 years the regatta's been established: in the heatwave of 1976 the regatta chairman gave the word that jackets could be shed, but do not presume this has created a precedent.

Men, previously thought to be hatless, will suddenly sally forth in shamelessly nostalgic headgear – mostly straw boaters girded with ribbons of their old school. You may be alarmed at seeing a fellow wearing pink socks, a pink tie and pink schoolboy cap that is usually too small. Although he may have a matching complexion which suggests an imminent stroke, he is in fact a member of Leander, the exclusive club for old Oxford and Cambridge rowing blues and those who have done well in their rowing careers.

The lady accompanying you will, if she is wise, have taken a tip from the late Sir Cecil Beaton's stage productions – dresses to be worn long, lavish and languorous, with shady hats and, of course, gloves. Princess Alexandra, when she was last there as a guest, was heard to describe the style for ladies as 'gay formal' (using the word gay in its proper sense). Although many have tried, women wearing trousers will not be admitted to the Stewards' Enclosure.

The Henley course is 1 mile and 570 yards long, but the only bit that matters is the seventy-five feet of lawn by the finishing post that is the Stewards' Enclosure. This still purports to be exclusive. Princess Grace's father, John Kelly, was prevented from rowing because the stewards regarded him as an Irish bricklayer: he was a multi-millionaire builder. At one time the stewards forbade a king to enter the enclosure simply because he had drunk too much champagne.

One of the most impressive things about Henley is that it's all temporary, unlike Lords and Wimbledon where there are permanent stands. The whole caboodle of boathouses, offices and loos is erected only for the regattta. The only full-time asset is the river, which is what inspired the originators of what's now the world's most famous regatta, back in 1839. At a public meeting in Henley Town Hall Mr Williams-Freeman proposed 'the establishing of an annual regatta under judicious and respectable management which would not only be productive of the most beneficial results to the town, but from its peculliar attractions would also be a source of amusement and gratification to the neighbourhood and the public in general'.

But within a year Oxford dons were condemning the public regatta as vulgar, and refusing to allow their undergraduates

Cheering the teams on at Henley

to take part. Those who defied their ruling were not permitted to stand for Fellowships, nor given references for Holy Orders. Oarsmen anxious to enjoy their rowing as well as keeping in with the college authorities had to row under assumed names, and some even went so far as to wear false beards.

Despite this, Prince Albert's visit in 1851 was enough to give Henley its royal title, and his son, the future Edward VII, continued the royal favour by attending in 1887. Unfortunately our present Queen seems to prefer horses to water and, unlike other events during the Season, she is not likely to be seen there.

Besides the written rules of Henley about dress there are plenty of unwritten ones to trip the socially unaware, so tread carefully. Never, never, get in the way of an irate gentleman riding a bicycle on the towpath – he is important, being the coach of a crew, and he will be engaged in bellowing instructions to his men through a megaphone. And do remember that only certain types of food and drink are considered palatable here. Mr Fortnum and Mr Mason will be delighted to prepare a special Henley hamper, which will contain caviar, foie gras, strawberries and, of course, champagne. It is champagne and Pimms that keep Henley afloat and in the Stewards' Enclosure these two tastes are properly catered for by separate bars. If your natural inclination is for beer and sandwiches you are provided for outside in the Enclosure or you take your picnic and watch the boats for free on the river bank.

Whatever you decide it's certainly no longer worth wandering into the town because its pubs are dry apart from the normal opening times, thanks to a mean judgment made last year which halted the 'open all day' rule during the regatta on the grounds that it caused rowdy behaviour.

In the last three years a veritable village of hospitality tents has sprung up at Henley for such firms as De Beers and B.P. to entertain favoured clients; well worth wangling an entry for the free drinks and eats.

If you want to hang around on the Saturday evening there's a firework display which can be viewed free from the Regatta Enclosure and at which people enthusiasticallly cheer and peep their car or boat horns. Afterwards many who live near give private dinner parties but if you haven't been invited the two best places to dine are the Compleat Angler at Marlow and the French Horn at Sonning.

Do remember that the right side of the boat is called the stroke side and the left is the bow side. This is important when you are cheering you favourite crew. You can't just shout 'Hooray' or 'Come on that boat', but screaming 'Jesus' won't be taken as profanity. The knowledgeable will realize you are sticking up for Jesus College. Possibly you may yell, 'Emma, Emma'. This is not to be taken as a cry for your latest girlfriend, but as sounds of encouragement for the Emmanuel College crew.

It has been said by some Americans that Henley is the USA's premier regatta and American crews are always the first to complete the racing entry forms. The fact that the

Nottinghamshire International has been held a week before Henley has made it well worth while for American oarsmen to come to Britain, and last year they accounted for half the overseas entries. In spite of all this Henley still doesn't have an Olympic standard course. Competitors race on moving water, instead of on still, and the Thames is only wide enough for two boats. It is entirely possible for the river to be widened because the Regatta authorities own 120 acres of land on both sides, but it is unlikely that such a step will ever be taken, simply because Henley is essentially English.

Mind you, that is not to say that the authorities are completely hidebound in their outlook – facilities generally have been improved for the 2,000 or so oarsmen who take part and the 14,000 who crowd the Steward's Enclosure. New booms have been made which stretch nearly to the start, and at a cost of nearly £17,000 for the timber alone. This will ensure there is less disarray from the wash.

1981 will see the most remarkable change of all, since for the very first time ladies will be competing in the races, but only after they have taken part in some exhibition events to see if they really are acceptable. This change is guaranteed to upset the same traditionalists who were horrified when in 1976 the ultra-conservative Leander actually served port on the rocks because of the heatwave. It has even been whispered that some cads are using plastic boats for speed these days. What is Henley coming to?

How to get there: To get to Henley from London, simply follow the M4 motorway, but be prepared on the day for slower going once you join the A423 near Maidenhead. The distance from London is thirty-six miles. Trains to Henley run from Paddington station, and coaches from Victoria Coach Station.

Getting in: Payment of £2 will gain entrance to the Regatta Enclosure, which corresponds roughly to the Tattersalls area on a racecourse. For the Stewards' Enclosure entry is more difficult – the 4,500 members pay £25 a year which entitles

81

them to a metal badge for entry on each day and to bring guests. Anyone can apply to join but you must be proposed and seconded by a member, although the secretary, Mr Richard Goddard, can help with this by suggesting the names of members who are in your area. Members are entitled to three guests, who will each have to pay £10 for their badges. With the help of Mr Goddard overseas visitors can quite easily get into the enclosure as a guest even if they don't know a member. One word of warning – despite the fact that the regatta never advertises, it is becoming more and more popular, and as there is a limit on the number of members' guests who can be admitted to the Stewards' Enclosure, it is well worth making an early start – last year on the Saturday (the 'Social' day) all guests' badges were sold out by 12 noon.

GOODWOOD *by Bryn Frank*

I was so sick of those ladies at Royal Ascot ('cheeks of porcelain and voices of tin' as sportswriter Frank Keating put it) who seem more interested in what Arabella did for her holidays than the racing that I decided it was time to give Ascot a miss.

'If you want to spend twenty quid on a nice day out,' said a friend of mine, 'you ought to take a gander at Goodwood instead. *Hoi polloi* keep their distance on Trundle Hill (the poor sods have a lovely view of the Downs but don't see much of the racing) and the champers is a bit cheaper. There's no military bandstand but they do have a four-piece Trinidadian steel band – very broadminded they are, down in Sussex.'

'Twenty quid,' I said. 'It seems a bit steep.'

'Not as steep as Trundle Hill,' he replied, 'but you don't want to do Goodwood on the cheap, do you? It'll cost about £12 to get into the best enclosure, where you get the best view of the finish *and*, by the way, the best view of any race, which is from the old Richmond stand. Then you'll want some of their excellent seafood and champagne, and naturally a few bets.'

I brightened a little, mentally several pounds ahead even after an orgy of Bollinger and Pacific prawns. After all, hadn't I once been sworn at by a bookie while collecting on a nine to two favourite in the last race at Newmarket, on an afternoon when every winning horse but one had been the favourite?

'Don't they have the best position of any racecourse in the country?' I said, warming to it. 'And isn't the new stand that the Queen opened on the first day of the 1980 July meeting so well planned that it takes all the hassle out of Tote betting and getting to the paddock and then back to see the race in time?'

He nodded enthusiastically.

'You're on,' I said. 'Which day shall we go?'

'Oh, I'm not going,' he said. 'I'll be in the betting shop. I can't stand all that stuff.'

He was right about Trundle Hill, which I dutifully climbed, but on the morning of one of the days of the meeting, not to watch the racing. It's *very* smart to climb Trundle, and if the view of the Downs and the point where the mile and a quarter and mile and a half races start is spectacular from the Lennox Level of the new grandstand, it is multi-screen spectacular from Trundle Hill. (I don't know what it's like for jockeys out there in such a bucolic setting, but I wouldn't be too surprised to hear on the loudspeakers, 'The start of the 2.35 has been delayed on account of Willie Carson, Pat Eddery and Joe Mercer having stopped off for a champagne picnic.')

You won't be into your first Pimms – which are, incidentally, even in the upper echelons of the club-enclosure end of the new £3.6 million grandstand, served in those stubby half-pint glasses that in every pub in New Cross or Bermondsey are familiarly known as 'jugs' – before some unoriginal punter tells you that 'Goodwood is really just a garden party with racing thrown in'. Well, it's corny, but there's a certain amount of truth in it.

If it's a garden party it's a country garden party, not a Chelsea or a Virginia Water one. Be smart but informal. (Not even stable lads and girls parading their charges round the paddock, you will notice, wear the jeans that are *de rigueur* at

83

Kempton and Catterick.) Wear straw panamas (men and women) and not Florida cocktails. Certainly not top hats. I saw two men wearing morning dress and toppers. One spent the afternoon in a dark upper corner of the Richmond Stand, shunned by his fellow men; the other borrowed a sports jacket and hurried to the Daimler he had hired for the day from Guy Salmon to change. Shirtsleeves are fine if it's hot, and if it's good enough for Lavinia, Duchess of Norfolk, to turn up in her Ford Escort then you can leave the Porsche at home. Even the Earl of March, who after all does own the place, comes in his homely two-seater Triumph Dolomite.

It's not a mind-your-p's-and-q's sort of place. There are plenty of both, but the places where you pee are roomy and efficient, and the queues, except when you are waiting to collect your winnings from the bookie or the Tote and the weigh-in is delayed, move fast. Unlike Royal Ascot, where in the Royal Enclosure many people will think it rather cute if you don't know what an each-way double is, at Goodwood it's considered more *infra dig* not to know that Lester Piggott could have been champion jockey every single year between 1970 and 1980 if he had preferred to race in England rather than abroad, where the money is, than not knowing how to address a marchioness if you happen to be standing next to one in the bar.

It's generally a knowledgeable crowd, so when, after the penultimate race of the 1980 July meeting, it was announced that Piggott had won the Ritz Trophy for riding more winners at the meeting than any other jockey *and* for the third year running, the lack of response from the assembled masses was probably due to the fact that people already knew rather than that they didn't care.

Don't worry then, about social niceties, even in the best enclosure. Nobody will turn a neatly coiffed hair if you munch one of the course caterers' jumbo hot-dogs in the Richmond stand. (*The Art of Coarse Catering* has not yet appeared, but it should. At most racecourses you're supposed to be grateful, not that it's done well but that it's done at all. At Goodwood,

Glorious Goodwood at a distance

it's done well.) And if you order a light ale in the Lennox Level
people will charitably assume you're having a bad day and
that you're saving your cash in order to get out of trouble at
the last. What *is* bad form is to have a good win and buy just
half a bottle of champagne.

I did hear one winner in the champagne bar say, 'Good
God. If they're going to charge £20 for a bottle of bubbly they
might at least chill the glasses for you,' a point of view I share.
Actually, eavesdropping is part of any race meeting, but
especially, on account of the unique social mix, of an upmarket one. Thus: 'They say you should never get involved with a
jockey, Miranda. You never know what they're up to.' Or:
'They say Lester's worth about three million. That's about
5,000 dollars an ounce.' Or, as somebody looked reproach-
fully at the Elisabeth Frink horse in its commanding position
at the west end of the new stand, 'I should have backed that. I
couldn't have done any worse.'

If the sun shines – and it always does in your memory even if it doesn't in reality – people are noticeably reluctant to tear themselves away from Goodwood. Champagne parties go on long after the last race has finished, and one couple, *in flagrante delicto* in the Press Stand, had to be uncoupled by officials as late as six in the evening.

Lily Langtry loved Goodwood because, as she said, 'It was a heavenly relief after the rush and fatigue of a London season.' There are, however, few signs of fatigue among the dukes and duchesses you will rub racecards with, even though most of them will have been up half the night at one or several of the house parties that take place all over Sussex during the July meeting.

Goodwood is one of the very few occasions when aristocracy and proletariat let their hair down together. Parsimony is a dead cert giveaway. So if you are going to lose your shirt make sure it's a hand-made one from Turnbull and Asser.

How to get there: Driving to Goodwood from London can be quite pleasant; after the A3 you can choose the route through Petworth (A285) or through Midhurst (A286). Access to the racecourse is generally quite easy with good car-parking facilities – spaces can be booked in advance but they're quite pricey with reserved spaces for the No 5 car park costing £20. Other spaces in less prestigious parks cost from £2 upwards. Trains leave from Victoria and go straight to Chichester but from then on it has to be by bus. Helicopters can land at Goodwood Airfield and passengers can be driven the two miles to the course by taxi.

Getting in: Annual membership of the Richmond Enclosure costs £15 but on top of that there is a charge for badges – £40 for an annual one or £12.50 for a daily badge to the July meeting. For those aged between thirteen and twenty-one the subscription is still £15 but badges are only £6. The membership is closed shortly before the July meeting and enquiries should be made to the Membership Secretary, Goodwood Racecourse, Chichester, Sussex. Entrance to the

Grandstand and Paddock is open to all and costs £6.50, with the Public Enclosure costing only £2.

THE GAME FAIR *by James Hughes-Onslow*

The Game Fair happens at the end of July for a reason that is not entirely satisfactory for the field sports community: there is not much killing to be done at this time of the year. Within a couple of weeks it's the Glorious Twelfth of August, the opening of the grouse shooting season, when the guns will be blazing away again, as they will continue to do right through the winter. This is not to say that sporting folk have nothing better to do in the summer – game conservancy is an all-year-round job, they never tire of telling you – but it's about the last chance they have of getting together without disrupting something frightfully important. So, while the rest of us are going abroad in search of that last glimpse of sun that has eluded the British Isles, there is an ever-growing band of eccentrics putting on their tweed plus-fours and dreaming of rain-swept moors. Needless to say the Game Fair is usually very hot, making these people look redder, dustier, sweatier and more crazed than ever.

This might suggest that this uniquely British occasion is a minority interest and an anachronism. The truth is that it has attracted record crowds almost every year since it was started in 1958, except when it has been held in the remoter parts of the country, namely Scotland. At Bowood in Wiltshire in 1979, the last one to be held in the South of England, they had 113,000 visitors. This year, at Stowe in Buckinghamshire, they are expecting even more.

It is, of course, a gigantic open-air booze-up. But it is also a very serious trade fair demonstrating the highly commercial and technical skills of game management. For gamekeepers, international gun-dealers and other interested parties, it is an annual reunion. Some also go for the chance to see a stately home, and its park, in action for a change, with authentic pheasants, trout and gun-dogs instead of the lions, giraffes

87

and porpoises favoured by the box-office-conscious landed gentry these days.

Each year experienced observers from country magazines like *The Field* and *Country Life* try to analyse Game Fair attendances and they nearly always come up with words like 'inexplicable' or 'puzzling'. 'Why is it,' asked *Country Life* in its report on Woburn in 1977, 'that thousands of sportsmen and sportswomen more used to the peace of the moor or the tranquillity of the riverside brave enormous traffic jams and even larger crowds to see an almost exact repeat of what they saw at last year's fair?' One theory is that these people are city-dwelling trendies heavily disguised and determined to do their ecological bit. Occasionally, more deer-stalker hats are seen, or fewer red setters, but even the experts are happy to confess that they really have no idea who the Game Fair is designed for. It has just grown mysteriously of its own accord.

Certainly the organizers, the Country Landowners Association, were taken by surprise in 1958. Instead of 2,000, as they had expected, 8,500 people turned up. And that was before fishing, said to be Britain's most popular participant sport (with a greater following even than darts and football), was included in the programme. It may be that your particular interest is much more esoteric. If you want an electronic bleeping ferret locator or a new breed of red-legged partridge, go to Stowe. You will be wasting your time trying to find such things anywhere else. You may learn one or two fascinating things you never thought you'd want to know: how a Mrs Seymour makes pictures with single strands of silk, how the Duke of Bedford saved Père David deer from extinction (at Woburn), Maureen Foster's home-made fudge recipe, or how Harry Stanley can pluck a pigeon in forty-six seconds (you too can compete). There is often a delightful lack of accuracy in the clay pigeon shooting, archery and fly-casting competitions which suggests that the participants are trying these things for the first time. One of the puzzles of the Game Fair is that these apparently peaceful country people are so fiercely competitive.

If you do have a serious interest, it would be as well to seek it out without being distracted by too many side issues. Those who try to see everything usually end up completely exhausted. Gun-dog handlers always seem to be a splendidly single-minded fraternity. This is probably because only a fool would offer himself to the scrutiny of the judges with an untrained mongrel. In any case the conditions at the Game Fair are far more difficult than any normal circumstances. Wilson Stephens, a former editor of *The Field* and now a leading judge of gun-dogs, once wrote that the main problems in the working tests at the Game Fair are, 'Will the wind be off the spectators? Will the day be so hot that dogs will be slow and listless? Not everybody will realize the effects, on a dog's scent discrimination, of effluvia from the cosmetics and tobacco of 5,000 or so sun-warmed watchers crowded round the upwind half of the arena.'

Not just hot dogs, but hot-dogs – frankfurters – picnic lunches, food tents, dog food stalls, all kinds of game, including quite possibly Big Game when the site happens to be one of our stately safari parks, are picked up by the sensitive noses of the dogs. There were an estimated 30,000 dogs of various kinds at the Bowood Game Fair. If you think that upsets the dogs, consider the unfortunate pheasants in pens on the World Pheasant Association stand. 'An excellent display,' wrote *Country Life* a couple of years ago, 'ranging from the rare white-eared pheasant from China to the colourful but common Lady Amherst.'

Stowe is only the third place in England to have been chosen a second time as a site for the Game Fair – the last one at Stowe was in 1971 – so the organizers evidently believe it has the formula for success. As you drive up the long avenue from the town to the park you may care to observe the Corinthian arch designed by Thomas Pitt, Lord Camelford, and the trees saved by Eton College who bought the avenue and presented it to Stowe when it became a public school in 1923.

If you want to go by train or bus, good luck to you. The traditional way to get to such events is in a Range Rover with a couple of retrievers breathing down your neck. The Country Landowners Association has tried to arrange facilities for coaches and train connections at previous Game fairs but there has never been any demand for them. Last year, for the Welbeck Game Fair, travellers were advised to take a train to Worksop and get a taxi. My own advice, based on experience, not having a car, is to go to some such place and, wearing suitably daft attire and an air of authority, wave down the first motorist who looks like a gamekeeper. He *will be* a gamekeeper.

As I said at the beginning, this peculiarly British institution is an enigma. I met one well-satisfied customer who had spent the entire day finding out ways of making a split-cane fishing rod. Another had found a gadget, a white disc with nobs on, to remind his loader where his grouse had fallen. Perhaps you will find what you are looking for, or something quite different but equally useful. Otherwise there are the bars. You may find that your own bank has set up a pavilion to distribute the hard stuff free. Take advantage of it. Otherwise try Sotheby's, Christie's, Cluttons' or Knight Frank and Rutley's. These people make packets of money out of you and me. That's why they're there.

How to get there: Stowe is about fifty miles from London and by car can be reached via the M40, the A418 to Aylesbury, and the A413 to Buckingham. For railway passengers trains leave from Euston and arrive at Bletchley or Milton Keynes, but as both of these stations are some way from Stowe the rest of the journey has to be made by either bus or taxi.

Getting in: The gates of the fair open at 9.30 am and close at 6 pm. For adults the cost of admission is £3 on the Thursday and Friday, and £2 on the Saturday (rates for children are £1 and 50p, respectively). A car park pass costs £2.

THE BRITISH OPEN GOLF CHAMPIONSHIP
by Peter Dobereiner

The British weakness for turning great sporting occasions into a ritual is evident at the Open Golf Championship in July, but it is not nearly so obvious as the formal dress and behaviour of Ascot or the fancy dress of Henley. Golf is the subtlest of games and it takes a practiced eye to detect and savour the subtleties of the spectating game.

The first problem is accommodation. The Open alternates between England and Scotland, on a rota of courses which changes from time to time. If you are to have a pick of hotels or rented houses you need to know where the Open is to be played in three years' time, before it has been publicly announced. The only way to obtain this information is through intimate friendship with a member of the champion-ship committee of the Royal and Ancient Golf Club of St Andrews, who run the event. Naturally, they book up all the best places before announcing where the Open is to be held so, unless you can force an indiscretion out of a committee man, and they spend a long apprenticeship building up a tolerance to alcohol before they are even considered for the job, your only hope is to wheedle one of the rooms out of the R and A. To qualify for such consideration you must either have won the Open three times in the past, or possibly the Amateur championship four times back in the days when it amounted to a row of beans.

The opportunities for living in comfort during Open week, without involving yourself in a fifty-mile drive each day, are therefore limited. The most popular plan is to make up a house party and hire a cottage for the week. Cottagers who live near championship courses are alert to the financial opportunities of letting their premises and when the Open goes to somewhere such as Carnoustie the entire population moves out to the Costa del Sol. They spend the week sunning themselves in five-star luxury and return when the golf is over, having turned a tidy profit on the deal.

91

Getting in to the Open is no problem. Privilege tickets (car parking often less than a mile's walk across a muddy field from the course, special dining-tent, access to the best seats in the grandstands) are on sale early in the year, at discount prices for the early birds, and the special badge carries a certain cachet. However, one badge is not enough. The idea is to accumulate a whole cluster of them, and this can only be done through personal contact and influence, so that you can drink in the R and A tent and also penetrate into the club house. This last privilege is important if only to avoid the horrendous portable loos which have permanent queues of spectators in various stages of impatience.

The Open is a vast festival of golf, as well as a championship, and companies erect lavish tented premises to entertain their important guests. Entry to these hospitality centres is by private invitation so it is not a bad idea to let it be known about the place that you are head of a purchasing commission from the Middle East with unlimited oil revenues at your disposal. There is also a flourishing black market in hospitality centre invitations and if you keep your eyes open you can observe seedy characters swapping one Westminster Bank invitation for a permit to the local council's private marquee.

Of course, your enjoyment of the Open and your success at spectatormanship will depend greatly on your choice of costume, a matter of infinite subtlety. The main thing is to avoid anything which smacks of the golf course. The Open is thronged with hordes of fanatical amateur golfers, zealots who play off six handicap and who dress like competitiors, in spiked golf shoes, trousers of unlikely hue and sweaters with club motifs on the breast. They drink beer in the public refreshment tents, eat what appear to be hockey pucks but which research reveals to be mutton pies, and above all they tramp round and round the course.

It is a curious social phenomenon that this stamp of spectator can only watch golf while dressed for golf. Anthropologists would probably classify them as a sub-species of the cannibals of Fiji who used to eat Welsh missionaries in the

A bustle of activity on the green

hope of acquiring a talent for rugby football by a process of osmosis. These golf-watchers seek to play like Jack Nicklaus by dressing in his clothes.

Of course, you will never actually set foot on the course because that is not the correct way to watch the Open. The aim must be to spend the championship comfortably seated in front of a television set, sipping free drinks and making knowledgable comments such as, 'Beats me how that feller Watson gets it round with that left-hand grip'.

That desirable state of affairs will depend on your dress. A popular ensemble is a well-cut tweed jacket, cavalry twill trousers, old but hand-made brogues and a club tie, preferably with a tiny tweed cap of the type favoured by Captain Mark Phillips. The mistake most people make in selecting this costume is that the clothes are too new and/or pressed. If you must go for the English-country-gent look then you should sleep in your outfit, preferably under a hedge, for a month before the Open to get the true golfing flavour into your dress. No matter how diligently they get their tailors to follow the patterns from back numbers of *Country Life*, Americans always make the mistake of being too neat. That knife-edge crease is a dead give-away.

The one item of dress which sets the tone of your ensemble is the tie. For preference it should be the navy R and A tie in the very old narrow style, tied with a tiny knot and almost black with stains of the club's own brand of whisky. All doors open to such a badge of status.

Naturally there are dangers in wearing an R and A tie at the championship. The club is fairly lax about admitting overseas members but this is done on the strict, if unofficial, understanding that the member will stay in the jungles of Borneo, or wherever, and not cause any embarrassment by setting foot in the club or at one of the club's functions. Anyone who actually intends to use the club is vetted with the thoroughness of a Papal commission investigating the credentials of a new saint. Perhaps that is a slightly unfortunate metaphor since the club is full of scoundrels of all kinds, but they are the right kind of scoundrel.

The next best tie is, oddly enough, the garishly striped MCC tie whose design, as a matter of completely incidental intelligence, is an exact reproduction of a popular Polynesian penis wrapper. After that you descend through the better connected golf clubs, with the ties of the Honourable Company of Edinburgh Golfers being on a par with that of Royal St George's of Sandwich. The Oxford and Cambridge Golfing Society's tie carries a certain social wallop, since it means that once upon a time you were good enough at golf to win your blue. The Savage Club tie is useless at a championship, although White's might get the odd nod of recognition.

Any blazer with a club emblem is a mark of the outsider and must be avoided. This is a fairly recent development. Twenty years ago a blazer with the badge of, say, the Royal Burgess Club on the pocket might have branded you as no worse than a social-climbing twerp, but the golf equipment manufacturers started issuing their sales representatives with fancy blazers, complete with curious designs on the pocket, and since then any blazer is liable to stamp you with the stigma of commerce.

The safest dress for the Open is a stalking jacket, old and shabby but undeniably of Jermyn Street origins. This will mark you as a man of substance, with strong sporting instincts; and it is not a bad idea to put a piece of smoked salmon in the pocket and hang the garment in the airing cupboard for a week to let the flavour permeate the fibres.

When you go to the Open you should put a small walkie-talkie in the breast pocket. Of course, in your case it will have to be a tape recorder disguised as a walkie-talkie, a simple technical adjustment which any competent electronics engineer can arrange. With a hidden switch in your trouser pocket you can thus arrange at propitious moments for a voice to issue from your gadget saying: 'Could you give us a word of advice, George?' You then take the instrument from your pocket and rasp at it: 'This is George, what's the problem?' Your next recording is muffled as you hold the thing to your ear and you impress everyone when you snap at it: 'Slap a two-stroke penalty on him and tell him not to be a buffoon.' By this simple device you have established to the assembled company that while you are not actually engaged in the hurly-burly of administering the championship, you are a man so respected in the game of golf that your word is law.

One other item of advance planning for the really serious golf spectator is to discover the surname of the greenkeeper and the nickname of the club secretary. Armed with that information you gain enormous kudos by dropping casual remarks such as: 'Logan's done his usual sound job getting the old place into shape but Paddy's going out of his mind with all those *women* invading the club house.' This last one is a particularly useful ploy if you have failed to acquire a club house badge, because you can add: 'I'm keeping well away from the place all this week; it's absolute bedlam. I've been practically living in the Bollinger tent.'

It is safest to avoid all conversation involving golf, although there will be times when this is unavoidable. A few phrases are handy, such as 'It will be a different story if the wind blows' and 'Golf is a completely different game on links' should see you safely through the week. If you are forced to talk about individual golfers the rule among the *cognoscenti* is that previous champions are referred to only by their first names – Jack, Tom, Lee, etc. – while golfers who have not won an Open are called by their surnames – Coles, O'Connor or Lyle.

Alternatively, if you are really interested in watching the Open championship, then the sensible thing is to stay at home and switch on the television. If you are sensitive to the traditions of the game and to its finer points you can always turn the sound down and eliminate the inanities of the commentators.

GARDEN PARTIES *by James Hughes-Onslow*

Sixty-two thousand pieces of crockery are provided by the caterers for each of the Queen's Buckingham Palace garden parties in July, surely the biggest tea party in the world. Joe Lyons and Co estimate that the 9,000 guests will use about six items – cups, saucers, plates and glasses – each and they like to have a few thousand to spare to cope with the vagaries of British weather, which can be unpredictable even in the gardens of Buckingham Palace. On a cold, wet day the guests may consume half a dozen cups of tea and as many cakes between 3.30 and 6 pm as they shelter in the tents. On a hot day it will be glasses of iced lemon or orange and a walk around the garden.

In the good old days when strawberries were on the menu the munching was strictly limited to the time the Queen spent mingling with her guests, from four o'clock when, with the precision of a cuckoo clock, she and her family came out of her french window, until six o'clock when they all went back inside. These days there are no strawberries but Britannia waives the rules and tea is served from 3.30. The idea was to take the pressure off Joe Lyons who had to be prepared for a tremendous rush as soon as the regimental brass band struck up the National Anthem, signalling the Queen's appearance. It also relieves garden-party goers of a hideous dilemma: whether to see the Queen or eat strawberries. The new plan, specially sanctioned by the Lord Chamberlain, has not been entirely satisfactory for Joe Lyons, however. Those people who know the ropes make straight for the tea-tent at 3.30; they stare at the Queen and the Royal Family as they progress through the crowd from the Palace to their special tent between four and five o'clock. While the Queen is having her tea a second tea rush starts. With two rushes instead of one, despite the lack of strawberries, garden party guests are now thought to be greedier and thirstier than ever.

When Queen Victoria started holding garden parties in 1865 they were private social occasions for her friends and courtiers. Somehow Her Majesty's Chief Minister managed to gatecrash this exclusive circle and it was only a matter of time before the entire Cabinet and all the Ambassadors at the Court of St James had got their feet in the door. If Queen Victoria could see the way things have developed, especially since the present Queen came to the throne in 1952, she would probably think it had all got completely out of hand.

Twelve thousand white invitation cards inscribed 'The Lord Chamberlain is commanded by Her Majesty to invite . . . 'are sent out for each of the three Buckingham Palace garden parties in July. (There is also a Scottish one at Holyrood in Edinburgh and occasionally an extra one in London, last year for instance, to mark the Queen Mother's 80th birthday.) Three-quarters of those invited actually attend, a remarkable success rate for a midweek tea party, when you consider that it is the holiday season, that most people have to travel great distances to be there and are probably not in the prime of life anyway, and that a good proportion of the local dignitaries invited may be politically opposed to such fripperies.

'Once you've seen one,' a Tory councillor from Wolverhampton told me last year, 'you've seen the lot.' Yet there he was, a second time, reserving a table, some chairs and a plateful of cakes while his wife and daughter went off for a glimpse of Prince Charles. However blasé you may be, an invitation from the Lord Chamberlain's office seems a difficult one to turn down. 'I'm only here so that I can tell the kids what it's like,' is a good line which covers a multitude of activities, like pressing your nose against the windows to see what's inside the palace, or taking cuttings of the royal shrubs, which would not usually be thought acceptable behaviour at a tea party.

Simply standing around and staring at the Queen, trying to eavesdrop on her conversation and slowing her progress to the tea-tent, which seem to be the principal objectives on these occasions, must sound pretty odd to the kids back in Wolverhampton. It must look pretty odd to the Queen for that matter: does she think her subjects always carry on like this? 'We think it's all perfectly understandable,' a palace spokesperson explains. 'After all for most people it's their only chance to see the Queen.'

As for actually meeting the Queen or other members of the Royal Family, 95 per cent of introductions are said to be totally haphazard. A select few, whom the Queen has specially asked to meet, are told to be near the french window in question at around four o'clock. And of course there are the VIPs specially invited to the Queen's tea-tent. To be one of the haphazard 95 per cent you have to catch the eye of a roving equerry who, if he likes the cut of your jib, will probably add your name to a list on the back of an envelope. It's no good trying to catch the eye of a member of the Royal Family: in the hands of the courtiers they do as they're told.

How do you get yourself invited in the first place? This is a question you will be tempted to ask every time you see a friend at a garden party, if the friend doesn't ask you the same question first. The biggest tea party in the world is not the most exclusive affair, very much the contrary to judge by the police signs warning motorists to avoid the Buckingham Palace area on the days in question, but if you are excluded there is no easy way you can get in. You may have to become a member of your local Save the Children Fund, an MP, clergyman, county councillor, diplomat, influential businessman, peer of the realm or wife or unmarried daughter of any of these. Why, in this age of women's liberation and women Prime Ministers, only unmarried daughters and not unmarried sons? This has been the form since 1958 when debutantes stopped being presented to the Queen. Instead of being introduced to high society at the annual Queen Charlotte's Ball they are asked to accompany their parents to a garden party where, apart from Prince Charles, the most eligible bachelors they will see are Edward Heath and Norman St John-Stevas. Clearly this policy is a failure because most of the unmarried daughters you see on these occasions have often seen more garden parties than hot dinners but Buckingham Palace is not worried about this situation: 'Unmarried sons will just have to make it on their own,' they say sternly. Illustrating this point to me at a garden party last year, the hawk-eyed social editor of *The Tatler* was greatly puzzled to find Lord and Lady Hawke, who have seven daughters, accompanied by only one of their brood.

'Where are all your other daughters?' asked *The Tatler*.

'All of them married,' came the reply. So none of them will see the inside of the palace again until their husbands have 'made it on their own'.

If you have to pull strings to get yourself admitted your best bet is probably to attach yourself to one of those organizations which are asked to send a list of names to the Lord Chamberlain's office. Given a batch of, say, forty invitations they can choose whether to give them to forty individuals, twenty couples or perhaps fifteen couples with unmarried daughters. Speaking for myself I have been to garden parties only as a hack attached to a Fleet Street newspaper. But, however you get in, the mere fact that you have been inside Buckingham Palace clearly impresses some people. 'Where have you been? Buckingham Palace? Well done,' said a passer-by, seeing me discarding my tails in the Mall car park afterwards.

There are seven members of the Royal Family you will not meet, at least not if the ever-protective flunkies in the household have anything to do with it. They are the corgis. Usually the dogs (most of them are long-haired half-dachshunds, known as dorgis, the oldest fourteen-year-old corgi being the great-grandmother of some of them) are given the run of the garden in the afternoons, but not during garden parties. While the Queen is being led by the Lord Chamberlain to her tea-tent, the dogs appear from another french window and are taken by a footman in a red coat to a secluded spot behind the trees where they can be exercised in secret. It's not that they're fierce, I'm assured by the footman, who still boasts two sets of fingers. If anything they're too friendly and inclined to get lost in the crowd. There is also the danger, not officially mentioned, that they might attract more attention than their mistress. Wouldn't this be rather a good thing if it reduced the Queen's burden of tedious introductions and at the same time made these curious events less formal? The real problem is that dorgis are not the best observers of protocol and there's nothing that annoys the courtiers, who organize these things, more than that. (An alternative attraction might be feeding time for the flamingoes, with special prawns, I understand, to keep them pink.) The caterers, too, like things to be in order. When the Queen finishes her tea (to a round of applause) and goes back inside the palace the band plays the National Anthem again. 'All the food off the tables,' barks an officious little white-haired man from Joe Lyons. 'No more service after the Queen,' and he quickly removes all the bowls of gladioli.

OTHER EVENTS IN JULY

Eton v. Harrow Cricket Match, Lord's, London.
British Grand Prix, Silverstone, near Towcester, Northamptonshire.
Berkeley Square Ball, London.

Belgrave Square Fair, London.
Golf: Ladies' British Open, Wentworth, Surrey.
Hurlingham Club Ball, London.
Racing: Sandown Park (Coral Eclipse Stakes).
Racing: Newmarket July Meeting.
Canada Club Dinner, Savoy Hotel, London.
American Fourth of July Ball, Inter-Continental Hotel, London.
Aldeburgh Festival, Aldeburgh, Suffolk.
Royal Tournament, Earl's Court, London.
Racing: Ascot (King George VI and Queen Elizabeth Diamond Stakes).
Imperial Polo Tournament, Guards Polo Club, Windsor Great Park.
Battle of Flowers, Jersey, Channel Islands.
Solent to Cherbourg Yacht Race, Cowes, Isle of Wight.
New Forest Show, Brockenhurst, Hampshire.
Cricket: Benson and Hedges Cup Final, Lords, London.
All-England Lawn Tennis Club Champions' Dinner, Savoy Hotel, London.
Show-jumping: Lambert & Butler International, Hickstead, Sussex.
Great Yorkshire Show, Harrogate, Yorkshire.
Royal International Horse Show, Wembley, London.
Swan Upping, Temple Stairs to Henley.
Royal Welsh Show, Builth Wells, Powys.
Royal Garden Party, Holyroodhouse, Edinburgh, Scotland.
Cricket: Test Matches.
Polo: Final of Gold Cup, Cowdray Park, Sussex.
Polo: Goodwood Week Tournament, Cowdray Park, Sussex.
Royal Garden Parties, Buckingham Palace, London.
International Air Tattoo, RAF Greenham Common, Newbury, Berkshire.
Moffat Gala Week, Moffat, Scotland.
Royal Isle of Wight Agricultural Show, Northwood, Isle of Wight.
Haslemere Festival, Haslemere, Surrey.

101

Windsor Dog Society Show Championships, Windsor, Berkshire.

East of England Show, Peterborough, Cambridgeshire.

Tennis: Davis Cup.

National Rifle Association's meeting at Bisley.

King's Cup Air Race.

National Archery Championships.

Royal Solent Yacht Club Regatta, Yarmouth, Isle of Wight.

National Rowing Championships, National Watersports Centre, Nottingham.

Morpeth Regatta, Morpeth, Northumberland.

World Wine Fair, Bristol, Avon.

Scottish Driving Trials, Kelso.

Festival of the City of London, the City.

Oxford International Film Festival, Oxford.

National Waterski Championships, Southend, Essex.

Menai Strait Regatta Fortnight, Royal Anglesey Yacht Club, Gwynedd.

British Croquet Association's Open Championships, Hurlingham Club.

Pernod Waterski Championships, Tayside, Scotland.

Cheltenham International Festival of Music, Cheltenham, Gloucestershire.

Southern Cathedrals Festival, Winchester, Hampshire.

Cumberland Agricultural Show.

South of Scotland Lawn Tennis Championships, Moffat, Scotland.

Harrogate International Festival, Harrogate, Yorkshire.

International Folklore Festival, Sidmouth, Devon.

Peel Viking Festival, Isle of Man.

Lammas Fair, Exeter, Devon.

Cambridge Festival, Cambridgeshire.

Summer Fair, Hintlesham.

Bexhill-on-Sea Festival of Music, Sussex.

King's Week Festival, Canterbury, Kent.

August

POLO *by John Lloyd*

Polo lasts for and encompasses the whole of the English Social Season. It provides one with the horses of Ascot and Goodwood, the mobility of the 'trots' at Cowes, the drama of Glyndebourne, the elegance of Henley, the social mixture of Wimbledon and as many 'Palace People' as you would see at the average Royal Garden Party.

All this is offered at a fraction of the cost of other events at centres throughout the country during most weekends from late April to September. There are some twenty Polo Clubs scattered over the British Isles from Devon to Perth, the main ones being in the South of England. Cirencester Park, Cowdray Park, The Guards and Ham are the most popular and the places where one is most likely to be seen by those by whom one most wants to be seen.

The various clubs are all happy meeting places for 'all sorts and conditions of men' and regularly during the season aristocrats and commoners alike thrill to the joy of watching this fastest and most exciting of games. The newcomer to the game need not be daunted so long as he remembers that a polo match is a relatively informal affair and that he has a part to play in the proceedings.

Weekend matches do not begin until mid-afternoon so there is ample time to arrive and enjoy a good picnic lunch beforehand. The clubs charge a modest entrance fee for each

103

car and its occupants and this entitles the early visitor to park directly on the sidelines of the field of play – a definite bonus when it is raining.

As with most English events, there is a strict separation between 'Public' and 'Members' sides of the pitch but, as will be seen, the usefulness of the plebeian visitors breaks down even this barrier. Should you attain membership status or be fortunate enough to be invited as a guest you are advised that at all times *badges will be worn*. This is not as bad as it sounds as, not only does it proclaim to the world that you *belong*, but also, bearing as it does the title and name of the wearer, it enables you to know who it is you are so fascinated by and of what oriental state he is prince.

Meals are provided in the rather grandly labelled Club Pavilions. These prefabricated huts do have a certain ambience, and the Guards is the most splendid, but a picnic is preferred. Oceans of cling-film, fish-paste sandwiches, stewed tea drunk from plastic cups may just pass unnoticed on the Public side but on the Members' side it is best to assume an elegant air and get cook to pack something in a hamper.

It goes without saying that Pimms and champagne are the accepted drinks on the polo field. Be it said, though, that Heidsieck and Abel Lepitre are the best champagne houses to support. Monsieur Jean Marc Charles Heidsieck sponsors the Warwickshire Cup at Cirencester, one of the best social events of the season, and the son of the Chairman of the Hurlingham Polo Association ships Abel Lepitre and gives away the odd magnum to match winners at Cowdray. The Guards Polo Club has recently made a major contribution in this field by having their own smart Label (their capital) put on a cheap but drinkable white Bergerac and red Vin de Table. Shipped by Haynes Hanson and Clark of London, the production of one of these bottles attracts admiring glances at any polo picnic but particularly when produced at one of the other clubs.

Dress at polo matches is varied. Especially popular these

Enjoying the spectacle of a polo match

days is a range of clothing introduced by Julian Hipwood, our top English player, and Sam Simmonds from the Malta Polo Club. This range has been designed for both player and spectator and is being worn by all the Top Polo People, so is an absolute must. Sam sells the stuff from a rather smart horse box which moves from ground to ground. It is advisable to wear such informal gear only if you really *belong*, however; but do wear Hipwood labels elsewhere. It will certainly impress your friends. Blazer and flannels or dark suits are safest wear for men at the Guards, and for the ladies anything really does go. Short summer dresses are always acceptable and trousers will do; Cirencester and Cowdray tend to be less formal and more tweedy. Ham and the smaller clubs are something else again and seem to be 'come as you are' sort of places with the accent on the stable look.

At all cost you should wear shoes suitable for 'treading in'. This bizarre custom is one of a number of strange things with which the spectator has to come to grips. All barriers come down at half-time and between games when all who take their polo seriously troop on to the field of play to 'tread the divots'. This helps to keep the ground in good condition and also provides the opportunity for much social intercourse. If you really want to show the stuff of which you are made you will head for the cut-up areas in front of the goal posts. The area around the Royal Box does tend to get rather well trodden and in any case there will be plenty of time to see Them during the prizegiving.

Treading the divots is only one of the mysteries awaiting the newcomer. Initiation into the delights of the game is certainly helped by the first-rate commentaries which are broadcast during all the matches at the big clubs. All is usually made clear as the game progresses and the reasons why one team begins half a goal ahead or why teams change ends every time a goal is scored are usually explained.

There are lots of pitfalls for the unwary so it is wise to creep silently around taking everything in if you are not yet a Polo Person. There is much that is different and is found nowhere else. For example, Sergeant Lasbrey's hoarse cry of 'Get mounted!' can take the unwary spectator by surprise as he passes the pony lines at Windsor. He should not worry though; this is only an instruction from the stable manager to the players. On the subject of mounts something should perhaps be said. Just as everyone knows that on the hunting field red is called pink – only now it isn't – so everyone thinks they know that a horse in polo is called a pony. This does still apply, but Real Polo People, now that the peasants have got the hang of it, have begun to call their mounts horses. It seems good that you should know this.

If, having once been to a polo match, you feel that you would like to play, there are a number of courses open to you. Should you not be young enough to attend Millfield School or join the Pony Club – whose Championships held at Cowdray in August are a delight – then much the best thing is to join a good regiment. The Household Brigade provides cheap polo along with a commission. Sea-going types can join the Royal Naval Equestrian Association, but water polo is another game altogether and opportunities for the sport are somewhat limited at sea. Service polo can be difficult, as NATO exercises tend to be rather serious affairs and leave to play in the 'Captains and Subalterns' match is not so readily granted these days.

More expensive but open to all, are two polo schools; Hugh Dawnay's at Waterford in Eire and New Zealander Peter Grace's at Windsor. Both offer a comprehensive training programme and hire out horses for games. If you would rather just read about it the best all-round introduction to the game is still the late Earl Mountbatten of Burma's book *An Introduction to Polo*, which he wrote under the pseudonym of 'Marco'. More reading matter is provided in a regular spread in *Horse and Hound*, an occasional piece in *The Times* and in a regular fortnightly magazine, *The Polo Times*. This latter publication is backed by a German, Christian Heppe, and gives current news of the polo scene throughout the world.

Foreigners, as visitors from overseas are unequivocally called, play an important part in English polo. Many of the best players are foreign and they like to come over here to play. Those rich enough pay their own way, others come as professionals to be hired by the highest bidder. It is a touchy subject and few questions should be asked. It might be worth getting to know one or two foreigners, however, as playing polo in the Argentine while all your friends are wintering in England can be a very rewarding pastime.

The Social Season being what it is, you might be limited in the time that you can spend on polo. If this is the case you should try to fit in at least one of the big High Goal matches. Polo Balls and cocktail parties are added incentives and tend to coincide with the major tournaments.

The first official High Goal tournament of the season is played at the Guards Club and more often than not Her Majesty the Queen presents the cup to the winners. Soon after this the Club organizes a series of tournaments to coincide with Ascot Week. Conveniently timed to begin some time after the last race the polo provides a relaxed end to each day. During the latter half of June Cirencester Park Club run their Warwickshire Cup tournament. Cowdray Park's top tournament, for the Cowdray Park Gold Cup, is the most prestigious in English polo and takes place in July. Their Challenge Cup is played for during Goodwood Week. August tends to be a quiet month because many of our Top Polo People slip off to Deauville. There is no doubt that that is *the* place to be during August and if you want to know what the label 'exclusive' means, then go.

International Polo Day takes place each year at the end of July at Windsor. It is the one event that is guaranteed to bring together everyone who is anyone in polo. Two English teams play two foreign sides and in between each game there is a great deal of razzamatazz. HRH The Prince of Wales usually plays for England II and the party held afterwards at the Horswells is always worth going to.

Prince Charles has said about his favourite sport, 'I cannot help feeling that there are few team games in existence to rival polo for sheer excitement, speed and fascination.' If such a recommendation can come from so high a source you will do well to attend some polo matches this season. Many exciting sights, sounds and smells will impress themselves upon your senses; you will meet a rich variety of people and a feast of sport and fine afternoon's entertainment can always be expected.

The Hurlingham Polo Association, Pephurst Farm, Loxwood, Billingshurst, Sussex RH14 0RW (tel Loxwood (0403) 752738).

Clubs
Cirencester Park Polo Club, Cirencester Park, Cirencester, Gloucestershire (tel Cirencester 3225).
President: The Earl Bathurst.

Cowdray Park Polo Club, Cowdray Park, Midhurst, Sussex (tel 073081 3257).
President: The Viscount Cowdray.

108

The Guards Polo Club, Windsor Great Park, Englefield
   Green, Egham, Surrey (tel 0784 34212).
President HRH Prince Philip, Duke of Edinburgh.

Ham Polo Club, Richmond Park Surrey (tel 01 948 3627).
President: W. H. D. Riley-Smith, Esq.

Getting in:
All clubs have a public admission charge, between £1 and £3,
for a car and all its occupants. Membership offers free entrance to polo for the entire season for the member, his car and
a guest. Additional guests can be introduced at the appropriate day member charges. Prospective members should
apply to the Club Secretaries. There is usually a small joining
fee and an annual subscription of between £10 and £40.

Read all about it
The Polo Times, The Manor House, Houghton, Stockbridge,
   Hampshire (tel 07947 854).
Editor: Colin Cross.

COWES WEEK *by Maldwin Drummond*

Cowes is a peculiar place. Half the town looks towards the
sea and half tries to forget all about it. The *Memorials of the
Royal Yacht Squadron* records early views of this yachtsmen's
mecca:

   'Nothing like its aspect was ever seen out of a box of Dutch
   toys. From the sea it looks like a heap of superior dog-
   kennels, which have been rolled down from the hill on
   which it lies and brought up full on the edge of the water.'

Of the social scene it was written:

   'It is no longer a small party who come down to live seafar-
   ingly with their lovers and bretheren, but a large crowd,
   mostly of new people, who flit in and out of the little town

with one object of showing dresses, seeing the latest beauties and keeping clear of the hated sea.'

The houses still tumble down the hill, some look more and more like dog kennels and there certainly are a lot of new people about, but most of them now revel in the water.

There used to be two forts at the entrance of the Medina River, built by Henry VIII in 1539. These two 'cowes' give the port its name. West Cowes Castle, the one remaining, became the home of the Royal Yacht Squadron on 16 May 1857. Not everyone approved of the alterations to the building that followed. A correspondent of the *Isle of Wight Observer* wrote:

'Some have compared the front (of the Castle) to a monastery, and the rear of the building to a nobleman's mews, while others have declared it, from its irregular appearance, to resemble a disciplinary establishment.'

The Yacht Club, as it was first called, was founded on the glorious first of June 1815, in a coffee house in St James's Street. Later, members adopted the Medina Hotel in East Cowes as their headquarters and later still the Gloucester, now the Gloster, near the Castle.

The Royal Yacht Squadron was given sole right to wear the white ensign in 1842. The 'national utility' of the Club was recognized because of members' contribution to naval architecture. Lord Yarborough with his *Falcon*, Lord Vernon's *Harlequin* and the Duke of Portland's *Pantaloon* made significant contributions to the design of Royal Navy vessels. Lord Belfast, too, improved the 'coffin' or ten-gun brig, with the advances seen in his yacht *Waterwitch*.

The Club was difficult to join and on one occasion the black ball had strange results. In the latter half of the last century, members had rejected the owner of a 150-ton, black-hulled, 15-gun schooner. The would-be member was known as 'The Pirate'. The evening following the election this beautiful yacht anchored on the Squdron line and demanded an apology of

The picnic on board at Cowes

one particular member, Sir Percy Shelley. 'The Pirate' was convinced that this gentleman was responsible for his downfall and said that if he did not obtain an apology on his own quarterdeck he would open fire on the Castle. Sir Percy's first inclination was a blank refusal but he was reminded by his dining companion, the legendary Arctic sailor Sir Allen Young, of the inconvenience of a bombardment during dinner. He, therefore, sent a note and 'The Pirate', seemingly satisfied, dipped his ensign and sailed away.

Next door to the Squadron is Castle Rock, the Royal Corinthian Yacht Club's headquarters. Rosa Lewis of the Cavendish Hotel in Jermyn Street lived there and gave balls in the little annexe at the bottom of her garden, sometimes to the discomfort of the wives of the members next door.

The Royal London Yacht Club's elegant building on the Parade is a reminder of the old look of Cowes before the monstrous block of flats marred the front before the last war.

The Royal London was founded in 1838, while the Corinthian, whose mother club still flourishes at Burnham and was founded in 1872, came to the Island in 1948.

The majority of Island sailors belong to the Island Sailing Club and this is really the heart of nautical Cowes. The Club started in 1889 and now has 3,500 members. The clubhouse looks like a three-tiered cake, climbing upwards, searching for a broader view of the sea, while its utilitarian jetty stretches out into the harbour, keen on deeper water.

Salt-stained faces and clothes designed for wet wind or sparkling sun give way, as the observer wanders westward, to yachting suits or white flannels as the Castle battlements and the Squadron lawn come into view. Even today the white linen summer cap-covers can be seen there, looking so much better than their new plastic imitators, a down-turn started, regrettably, by the Royal Navy after the war. Back in fashion are the small, cloth-peaked and narrow-brimmed caps of the 1890s. Brown shoes are worn with blue suits by members of the Squadron by Royal example.

Those visiting Cowes in their yachts or members of other

yacht clubs momentarily on the beach may become temporary members of Cowes clubs by contacting the Secretary or with the help of a member. During Cowes Week the Squadron issues a card disc to be worn by guests to the Castle, coloured according to sex.

The Squadron Ball brings many to the Castle on the Monday of Cowes Week and the battlements are again crowded for the fireworks, traditionally held on the Friday. It is difficult to struggle along the front that evening of 'The Week'.

The little town, the marinas and 'the Roads' are full of purpose during 'The Week', that is the first week in August, even if it occasionally starts in the end of July. The yachts look more determined and their owners and crews seem to have reason to be ashore as they march between Groves & Gutteridge and Pacall Atkey for shackles and sea water soap or on to the clubs for refreshment and more unlikely tales of the sea.

After 'The Week' the tide goes out and Cowes is left bereft of 'the new people' and a little sad at their going.

How to get there

The best way to arrive is on your own boat. To take a car to the Island in high summer without booking is more difficult than entry to the Royal Yacht Squadron.

British Rail Seaspeed Hovercraft and the Red Funnel Hydrofoil take twenty minutes from Southampton. The latter is quieter and more comfortable. Booking is essential at peak times.

For those who have more time, Red Funnel also run a car ferry which takes foot passengers as well; the voyage takes forty minutes.

Car ferries run from Lymington to Yarmouth in the west and from Portsmouth to Fishbourne in the east. Bookings are accepted from October onward for the following year and July and August Saturday places are usually all gone by January. Mid-week reservations are easier but the car space should be reserved two or three weeks before sailing. It may be

113

important to return too, so that space must be remembered as well.

THE GLORIOUS TWELFTH *by Douglas Sutherland*

It would be ingenuous in the extreme to imagine that the twelfth of August is by tradition described as 'glorious' on account of the weather, which frequently falls short of being anything of the sort.

Nor is it termed 'glorious' in anticipation of a holocaust of blood-letting on the Scottish moors. All too frequently, particularly in recent years, the amount of blood shed has been minimal, unless one takes into account the odd long shot at a beater or two.

It is called glorious because it marks the end of the London Season, an event looked forward to by most gentlemen of my acquaintance, and in particular those burdened with a debutante daughter, with all the excited anticipation of the end of a particularly wearying term at school.

Of all the events in the social calendar the opening of the grouse shooting is perhaps the most prestigious. The one-upmanship starts on the departure platforms of Euston or King's Cross. Gentlemen, already got up in tweeds and deerstalkers, are to be seen being towed in the direction of the first-class sleepers by a couple of salivating labradors, followed by a twittering of female camp followers and a clutch of perspiring railway porters wheeling barrowloads of cabin trunks, gun cases and all the other equipment necessary to destroy life on the misty hillsides.

The porters, equipped with the numbered ticket of the sleeping compartment, push their way purposefully forward, while the tweedy passengers gather round the lists on the carriage doors, not to locate their own cabins but to ascertain the names of their fellow travellers. A Duke or an Earl as a next-door neighbour, even for a few brief hours, can set the most blasé of young ladies all aquiver.

Of course not all the migrants to the north for the grouse

114

Waiting for the Glorious Twelfth

shooting are of the type described. Just as there are horses for courses so there are shooting guests for shooting hosts. It all depends who owns the moors to which they are invited.

On some moors, far from being a sort of *fête-champêtre*, with the accent on the fête, conditions are positively spartan. The guns are not driven in cushioned luxury to their butts to while away their time in idle chat while awaiting the arrival of the driven birds. Instead they are required to walk in disciplined line abreast, a soggy packet of ham sandwiches in one pocket for consumption during a brief midday break. Woe betide the impetuous who press on too enthusiastically or the slow-coaches who fall behind. A head keeper worth his salt can outdo any sergeant-major when it comes to maintaining order: 'You are overwalking the birds, number three, blast your bloody eyes', followed by a belated 'Sir', is a mild reproof. Generally it is only the hardiest of ladies who volunteer as walking guns, most of them preferring to remain at home at the castle helping to arrange the flowers.

The other type of shoot is a different matter altogether. These take place on moors rented by the very rich and, one sometimes feels, rather more pride is taken in showing the size of the host's bank balance than in the number of birds in the bag. Still, we Scots, with our reputation for being a grasping lot, should be the last to complain.

The shoot *de luxe* is a pretty dazzling affair. Guests are driven to the edge of the moor in smart limousines and then transported up the line of butts in a variety of vehicles from Range Rovers to Snowcats, depending on the roughness of the terrain. Up to a couple of dozen beaters (at £6–8 a day) will have already been out on the moor, blanking in the birds from the remoter parts of the moor in preparation for the first drive of the day. A loud blast on a whistle is the signal for the guns to stop whatever they are doing, like chatting up the assorted females who will have ventured forth to witness, or even participate in, the *battue*, and to pay attention to what is going on.

I defy anyone, least of all myself, not to feel the adrenalin flow faster at the first sight of the tiny figures of the distant beaters advancing with flags waving and to hear the faint cries of 'forward' as a pack of grouse is flushed and set on course for the guns. It takes an experienced gun to spot the birds while they are still far off. To those who have dined unwisely the night before they seem indistinguishable from liver spots before the bloodshot eye. Then with extraordinary suddenness they flash into focus, whirr overhead and are gone. Any word beginning with 'B' is admissible as the first two empty cartridge cases of the day are ejected while the birds cackle merrily on their way.

After each drive there is the ritual of the pick-up. Some guns, in which category I include myself, get almost as much pleasure from the performance of their own dogs in retrieving a difficult bird as in having executed the bird in the first place.

A note here for the inexperienced. Never try to explain why the number of birds picked up behind your butt is rather fewer than behind your neighbour's. 'Didn't come right for me', 'Got a fly in my eye', and so on only draws attention to your deficiencies. Remember, too, that the most disliked man on the hill is the man who boasts of his score.

The highlight of the day for many is when stumps are drawn for luncheon. None of your soggy sandwiches at the grander shoots. In the shooting hut the table will be laid out with the sort of spread which would do many a Hunt Ball Committee credit. More tweedy ladies arrive, the bag is laid out for inspection and success or failure is toasted impartially. Then it is back to the business in hand and if the birds seem a little larger and not to fly so fast after luncheon you will have your host's hospitality to thank for your sharpened reflexes. On the other hand, if quite the opposite is the case, you have only yourself to blame.

One of the pleasures of grouse shooting is, of course, the *après-shoot*. After a day's pheasant shooting the guests tend to linger only long enough for a couple of drinks before departing to their own homes with their hard-earned brace of birds.

To be asked as a guest for the grouse shooting is generally also to be asked to make up a house party. Even the coldest day on the hill for the most meagre of returns can seem, in retrospect, pleasurable from the depth of a hot bath with a large whisky and soda to hand, your evening clothes laid out and a decent dinner to look forward to.

That many moors are now syndicated, bringing together comparative strangers, has not altogether destroyed the house party spirit. Like shipboard romances, friendships are readily formed in the forcing-frame of *après-shoot* hospitality and, tell it not in Gath, when tycoon meets tycoon on the heathery hillsides, the seal has been set on many an important deal.

Perhaps, however, it is among the grouse themselves that the new commercial element is most approved. Distracted as they are by thoughts of stocks and shares, mergers and take-overs, the aim is perhaps not so deadly as in the days when it was the Scottish lairds who ruled the roost.

As the last shot echoes round the hills, the call of the grouse, 'cum-bak, cum-bak' may indeed be more sincere than of yore.

OTHER EVENTS IN AUGUST

Sovereign's Parade at Royal Military College, Sandhurst, Berkshire.
Champagne Reception, Royal Thames Yacht Club, Cowes, Isle of Wight.
Royal Yacht Squadron Ball, Cowes, Isle of Wight.
Arab Horse Show, Ascot Paddocks, Berkshire.
British Field Sports Society Country Fair, Stoneleigh, Warwickshire.
Racing: Deauville Season (Prix Morny, Grand Prix de Deauville).
Racing: Redcar (William Hill Gold Cup).
Royal London Yacht Club Ball, Cowes, Isle of Wight.
Dublin Horse Show, Ireland.
Edinburgh Highland Games, Meadowbank, Scotland.
Cricket Week, Canterbury, Kent.
British Music Fair, Olympia, London.
Midland Bank Championship Horse Trials, Locko Park, Derbyshire.
Show-jumping: Lambert and Butler Jumping Derby, Hickstead, Sussex.
Cricket: Test Matches and One-Day Matches.
Racing: York (Benson & Hedges Gold Cup, Gimcrack Stakes).
Racing: Goodwood (Waterford Mile).
Football: European Cup Final.
Cardiff Searchlight Tattoo, Cardiff, Wales.
Cockermouth Agricultural Show, Cumbria.

Edinburgh Military Tattoo, Edinburgh Castle, Scotland.
Venetian Festival, Hythe, Kent.
Pineapple Ball, Stowe School, Buckinghamshire.
Greater London Show, Clapham Common.
National Pony Show, Malvern, Worcestershire.
Royal Manx Agricultural Show, Douglas, Isle of Man.
Gieves New Forest Polo Tournament, Rhinefield, Hampshire.
Wilton Horse Trials, Salisbury, Wiltshire.
Cricket: MCC v. Scotland, Lord's, London.
Benson & Hedges International Open Golf Championships.
Victoria Fair, Belton Park, Grantham, Lincolnshire.
Racing: Epsom (Moet and Chandon Silver Magnum).
Racing: Sandown Park (Variety Club Day).
London Festival Ballet, Royal Festival Hall.
Arabian Horse Performance Show, Wilton, Salisbury, Wiltshire.
Hayward Annual Exhibition, South Bank, London.
Port of Dartmouth Royal Regatta, Dartmouth, Devon.
Ould Lammas Fair, County Antrim, Northern Ireland.
Doggett's Coat and Badge Race, London Bridge.
Scottish National Sheepdog Trials, Glamis Castle, Scotland.
Three Choirs Festival, Worcester Cathedral, Worcestershire.
Royal National Eisteddfod of Wales, Machynlleth, Powys.
Old English Games, Grasmere, Cumbria.
Highland Games, Edinburgh, Scotland.
Serpentine Regatta, London.
British Driving Society Second Official Meet, Osberton, Nottinghamshire.
Show-jumping: National Schools, Riding Clubs & Pony Clubs Championships, Hickstead, Sussex.
National Gundog Association Show, Malvern, Worcestershire.
English National Sheepdog Trials, Tackley, Oxfordshire.
Ponies of Britain Show, Peterborough, Cambridgeshire.
Argyllshire Highland Gathering, Oban, Strathclyde.
Water Game, Bourton-on-the-Water, Gloucestershire.

Aldeburgh Olde Marine Regatta and Carnival, Aldeburgh, Suffolk.
West Highland Yachting Week, Tobermory, Argyll.
Ramsey Regatta, Isle of Man.
Plymouth Navy Days, Plymouth, Devon.

September

THE EDINBURGH FESTIVAL AND FRINGE
by Adam Helliker

For three weeks in the autumn visitors to the City of Edinburgh have the opportunity to taste, and in some cases positively guzzle their way through, a cultural feast unrivalled anywhere else in the world. No other festival packs in such a diversity and quantity of high-standard performances, and Edinburgh Festival patrons often require a long holiday afterwards to recover from a particularly unpleasant complaint known as 'culture saturation'.

The festival is truly international, with over 170 performances from twenty countries last year, including opera, dance, drama, orchestral concerts, chamber concerts, recitals by individual artists, and art exhibitions. Never, ever, has a visitor to Scotland's capital during this time been heard to moan that there's nothing to do, because not only is the Festival proper staged at Edinburgh but at the same time there's an international film festival, a television festival, and for the patriotic there's a military tattoo, set against the splendid background of a floodlit Edinburgh Castle.

The icing on the rich fruit cake of the Festival is the Fringe, which is actually quite separate from the main event but has grown from a few unofficial shows twenty-five years ago into a massive attraction of its own. The Fringe is Edinburgh's biggest game of cultural hide and seek, where the name of the

121

game is to spot the successes and avoid the excesses, no easy task when the fringe programme lists nearly 400 happenings.

The official festival is a mixture of visiting star orchestras, ballets and soloists, whereas the fringe is a voluntary but vast constellation of mime groups, musicals, revues, one-man shows and poetry recitals. Many come straight from college and university dramatic societies and are very good; others are simply awful. There are something like 5,000 fringe performances crammed into the three weeks, so it's up to the skill of the individual to pick out what will be the hits.

Starting in the middle of August, the bemused citizens of Edinburgh know they are about to be put through their annual endurance test with the arrival at Waverley Station of lots of flustered travellers with musical instrument cases or unwieldy theatrical hampers. The festival officially kicks itself off in rather a heavy way with a service in St Giles Cathedral. It is a traditional opening to what is going to be a frenetic few weeks, and is attended by the Lord Provost of Edinburgh and all the local dignitaries. After the service there's a cavalcade with marching bands that passes along Princes Street (which, in case you didn't know, is the city's main street and houses the most elegant shops). Flags mounted on tall flagstaffs are unfurled along the length of the street to show that the festival has really begun. For the visitors then it's back to the hotel room to pick out from the book-size souvenir programme which performances they will patronize.

The performances are given in Edinburgh's numerous theatres and halls – opera usually in the King's Theatre, drama in the Lyceum Theatre, concerts generally in the Usher Hall or the Freemasons' Hall, or, farther afield, in the Leith Town Hall. The international nature of the programme is illustrated in no better department than in opera. In one year the Bavarian State Opera of Munich presented Mozart's *Cosi Fan Tutte* and Richard Strauss's *Intermezzo*, the first performance of this opera in Great Britain, while the English Opera Group put on the uncommonly English work by Britten, *Albert Herring*, and the Holland Opera Group presented

122

Mozart's *Don Giovanni* and Haydn's *Le Pescatrici*. Several orchestras are always engaged for the Festival, with plenty of world-famous conductors, and on the literary side there is the series of 'Poets in Public' where acclaimed poets are made to read their own work. Lump all this in with the numerous choral concerts and recitals (which last year ranged from Ravi Shankar with his sitar to Gillian Weir on the organ) and you've got a veritable feast of highbrow entertainment.

More than half the Festival visitors are foreign and, together with the British patrons, they're reckoned to pour about £20 million into the economy of Edinburgh during the Festival. Naturally the Scots, being the good and thrifty people they are, have engineered a whole industry to catch a share of this booty before the city burghers swallow it all. Visitors are tempted by displays of imitation Celtic pewter, hand-carved love spoons, clan tee-shirts, Bannockburn fire screens and teddy bears with tartan bow ties.

All this ensures that the usually dour face of the Scotsman carries a beaming grin as he mentally reviews his bank balance. However awful the 'souvenirs' are, you're supposed to feel better about them because they are authentically produced in Scotland. (If you really must go hunting for such things, then try in the part of the Royal Mile called Canongate, where at least there are a few original gift shops.) Even the custodians of the museums manage a sickly smile, for the Scottish Tourist Board lists fifty-five 'further explorations', ranging from the Fire Station Museum to the St Cuthbert Co-operative Society Coachbuilders' Museum, if you can stomach such heady delights.

When you're sated with culture, or deafened by the din of some of the more *outré* offerings, there are twenty-two golf courses within the city limits. Even if one's not a golfer it's easy enough to walk around the course with a purposeful look, breathe deeply of the fresh air, and if you're lucky, find a lost ball. And there is always the all-year ski slope. Just imagine the cachet of breaking a leg skiing at the Edinburgh Festival.

Going back to the fringe, one is inevitably reminded of Peter Cook and Dudley Moore and their show *Beyond the Fringe*, which went on from the Festival to a very successful London run. No doubt this thought is uppermost in the minds of the producers of some of the most peculiar and bizzare offerings ever to sink without trace when Edinburgh is over. Luckily these offbeat shows only risk their own money, as all the authorities do is point them in the direction of available halls, and all thereafter depends entirely on the group's own initiative (which is probably why half of them forget vital items like programmes).

Whatever the triumph or despair, most of the entertainers and their audiences will find consolation at the Fringe Club. This is a beehive of a place on several floors, with super nosh, lashings of liquor and an obliging message (*not* massage) system, as well as being a wonderful place to make friends and dance until 2 am. Anyone can become a member and it's well worth while because it's the one place where you can reliably find out who's doing well, what's going on and which shows are really worth seeing. The other club worth belonging to at Festival time is the Festival Club at 54 George Street, which, although more traditional, has been known to let its hair down in the evenings for a discotheque. It was in this building that Sir Walter Scott disclosed that he was the author of the Waverley Novels and here you are more likely to see the artists from the Festival proper.

Accommodation at Festival time seems quite plentiful and it's really a waste of time to book anything more than bed and breakfast because if you're doing the Festival properly you'll hardly ever be there. For those who want to stay in a Scottish Versailles, the five-star Gleneagles Hotel is an hour's drive away, with hotel cars available to drive guests to Edinburgh and back. On the other hand remember that Scottish Presbyterian priggishness still prevails and in Edinburgh you won't fare very well if you seek a meal after 10.30 pm (with the notable exceptions of Dario's Italian restaurant, Henderson's Salad Table, Cosmo's and Flappers).

A big must is comfortable shoes, as Edinburgh is built on very steep hills and the local chiropodists reckon to make a fortune at Festival time. It's all part of the illness generally called Festivalitis – the symptoms being glazed eyes, sore feet and overwhelming exhaustion.

For a bit of peace and quiet there's no better place than the Royal Scottish Academy summer exhibition, but only if you time it just right because at certain times the queues are as bad as those back in London for the more fashionable Royal Academy exhibition. The Academy usually features just one artist or school – a couple of years ago it was an absolutely stunning display of works by Degas. Other galleries which have comfortable seats as well as something to look at include the National Gallery, the Scottish Arts Council Gallery, and the Scottish National Portrait Gallery. One of the other attractions that also runs at the same time as the festival is the Film Festival, where over 100 films get their première. Film buffs can grab the opportunity to meet some of the great directors and join in enthusiastic conversations after the screenings, but the increasing number of Third World films being shown here could possibly be avoided.

For tourists there's the Military Tattoo on the esplanade of Edinburgh Castle, where every night massed bands of the Scottish regiments march relentlessly up and down bathed in light. Even if one's opinion of bagpipes is that they sound like the anguish of a dying calf, the spectacle of all those swinging kilts and highland dancers will bring a rush of blood to the head, although one's rear end will long have been numbed by the spartan seating arrangements.

The same type of people who find pleasure in being seen at Glyndebourne were the ones that Mr Rudolf Bing and Mr Harvey Wood (of the British Council) had vaguely in mind when they suggested to the then Lord Provost the idea of an arts festival in Edinburgh. That was three decades ago and it's come a long way since then, both as an aesthetic event and as a fun, artistic event. Some say the festival has become less fashionable now that Lord Harewood, the Queen's cousin, is no longer the Director, but those sort of comments should be ignored while the rest of us go up to Edinburgh to have a jolly good time.

The parties that are worth going to are the Film Festival party, held at the Royal Commonwealth Pool; the Festival Times party at the Fringe Club on the opening day of the Festival, and the gathering hosted by Scottish Television. After-show drinks at the Lord Provost's are reckoned to be very boring and more the thing for the dedicated socialite is the Lanark Ball at Biggar, which is the first ball of the Scottish Season and is usually held half-way through festival time.

How to get there: A car is invaluable for getting around Edinburgh from one performance to another, otherwise it's a case of relying on buses and taxis, both of which can be most unsatisfactory at this time of year. The only drawback with a car is the long journey up there, when it's quite possible to fall asleep unless you break the journey. A good answer to the problem is to put the car on a train – there's nothing quite like the feeling one gets when you know you've made a trip to Edinburgh but miraculously the car's fuel gauge is still registering full. From London the trains leave at King's Cross Station. By car the distance is 378 miles from London and it's possible to take the A1 all the way.

Getting in: With planning and booking, getting to see the productions you want to see is no problem, although it can be expensive (grand circle seats for the Cologne Opera last year were £15 each, but most seat prices hover around the £5 mark). For entrance to the small amount of cocktail parties given at festival time it's necessary to cultivate either the festival director, John Drummond, the publicity director, Iain Crawford, or one of the twenty-three members of the festival society's council.

BURGHLEY HORSE TRIALS *by Jane Holderness-Roddam*

The Burghley Three-Day event, traditionally held in early

September, could be described as Eventing's Autumn Classic. Close followers of this increasingly popular sport know that shortly after Badminton the Spring Horse Trials season closes and that the Autumn one starts at the end of July with Burghley as the ultimate goal.

The horses have usually been given a break during the summer before being prepared for this event. with most of the top riders in Horse Trials competing, Burghley is considered the ideal start for future international prospects and many young riders aim to catch the selectors' eye here for possible inclusion on short lists for international competitions.

The beautiful park and magnificent architecture of Burghley House make an impressive backdrop to a competition undoubtedly considered second in prestige only to Badminton. Burghley can probably claim to have had more foreign riders round its courses than any other international event and certainly has staged more championships, having held two World Championships, three European championships and one Junior European Championship since it first started in 1961.

For the competitors the event starts on the Wednesday with a briefing on the event and a somewhat hilarious conducted tour of the course in vehicles for the roads and tracks sections, the steeplechase and cross-country sections being walked. In the evening the first of the three veterinary inspections takes place when every horse is trotted up before the Ground Jury and must be passed sound and fit to start the competition.

Thursday morning heralds the first of the two days of dressage. Those new to the sport will find it confusing that a Three-Day Event actually takes four days! This is because it is impossible to judge all the tests on the one day and so this phase is split into two, competitors doing dressage on Thursdy having Friday off and vice versa, unless they are riding two horses. No competitor is now allowed to ride more than two horses in a three-day event.

On Thursday evening competitors, officials, judges and all in any way involved in the event are invited to a cocktail party in the house. Whether this does in fact have any bearing on the dressage, scores usually being lower on the Friday, is always a matter for conjecture!

Spectators who have decided to take a long weekend arrive on Thursday or Friday and spend hours browsing through the trade stands, when not watching the riders, elegantly dressed in top hats and tail coats, often vainly struggling to control their mounts to perform a ten-minute dressage test to demonstrate obedience when fit. The movements include half pass (moving sideways), rein back (moving backwards) extension and collection at the walk, trot, canter and counter canter (cantering on the opposite leg to the direction in which the horse is travelling). Don't let the side down by announcing to everyone that the horse is on the wrong leg during this movement as it is in fact performing one of the more difficult parts of the test!!

The trade stands vary from wrought ironwork to picture galleries, wines and food to joke shops, antiques to clothes. It's all there, as is the historic town of Stamford a mile away, and of course Burghley House and its treasures. The Marquess of Exeter, its owner, an Olympic Gold Medallist Hurdler, may be spotted in a car with an AAA number plate, a sign of his association with the Amateur Athletics Association (not Alcoholics Anonymous Association, as one spectator thought), or accompanying any visiting member of Royalty, in which case Range Rovers are usually out in force.

To avoid the crowds on Saturday, many walk the course on the dressage days and get a better view of the fences and decide where the best vantage points will be once the competition starts. The Trout Hatchery is the place to see the action if you are the sadistic type who enjoys watching riders getting submerged! Knowledge of where the bars are obviously helps towards ensuring a perfect day. Anyone who is anyone will have ensured they are members, as the Members' Marquee is 'the place' for meeting if you are not otherwise to be found studying the somewhat complicated scoring on the giant scoreboard opposite the Members.

Cross-country day is the highlight of the event, attracting crowds in excess of 100,000. The seasoned campaigners wear country casuals with a definite emphasis on the quilted look, and if it's wet (or even if it isn't) wellington boots – green being the predominant colour.

The idea is to arrive in plenty of time (allow plenty for queues getting in), to have a huge picnic with friends before the excitement begins, or to walk the course first to work up an appetite, if your picnic merits this. The picnic is important. Champagne and strawberries are out. They are not Burghley. All wines, *pâté*, liver sausage, quiches, raspberries, cheese, sloe gin, brandy and ginger, Pimms are all very Burghley. Rugs on the ground, boots of cars and chairs are the usual props; tables are rarely resorted to.

As the speed and endurance phase usually starts at midday with the first horse setting off on phase A (roads and tracks) many spectators go up and watch the early competitors round the steeplechase, phase B, which is held round the golf course (also the site of the caravan park where hundreds of enthusiasts camp during the event). The competitors then take approximately forty minutes on phase C (roads and tracks) before returning to 'the box' where everything happens horsewise during the competition – starting, finishing, weighing, etc. (All competitors must carry a minimum weight of 11 st 11 lb.) At this stage the second veterinary inspection takes place to ensure the horses are fit to continue to the cross-country phase. After a compulsory halt during which the horses are refreshed and rested, the riders can often be seen engrossed in the closed circuit television, watching how the course is riding, or sitting rather quietly, looking somewhat pea-green as they battle with nerves before tackling the most demanding and exciting part of the whole competition.

After the thrills of cross-country day, the final day comes as a bit of an anti-climax. Having passed another vet's inspection in the morning all those still in the competition jump a show-jumping course designed to prove that the horse is still active and supple after his exertions on the previous day. After

129

lunch competitors parade and then jump in reverse order of merit with the overnight leader jumping last. When the scores are close the suspense is almost unbearable as one jumping mistake can cost several places.

The knowledgeable can reminisce in the grandstands of some of the great wins: Princess Anne becoming European Champion and being presented with that coveted Raleigh Trophy by the Queen; the British Team winning the European Championships in 1977 with Lucinda Prior-Palmer winning her second European individual title; and some will remember the very first Burghley won by the great Merely-a-Monarch and Aneli Drummond-Hay.

The Burghley Horse Trials are due to be held in 1981 from 10–13 September.

How to get there

Burghley Horse Trials are just off the A1 one mile from the centre of Stamford, Lincolnshire. It will be well signed from all directions.

Getting in:

Car passes, season or daily, can be bought prior to the event or at the gate: £2.50 daily; £12 season. £17.50 (£20 after the end of August) entitles members to extra guest badges at reduced rates, car pass for all days and free admission for occupants; admittance to any grandstand except West on Thursday and Friday; all stands on Saturday. Caravan Park for use by Burghley Members, including full membership, £35.

Any enquiries about membership can be made to the Horse Trials office at Stamford (tel 0780 52131).

OTHER EVENTS IN SEPTEMBER

Royal Highland Gathering, Braemar, Grampian, Scotland.
Buckinghamshire County Show, Bucks.
Golf: Hennessy Cognac Cup, Sunningdale, Berkshire.

Wylye Three-Day Event, Wiltshire.

Great Autumn Flower Show, Vincent Square, Westminister, London.

Chelsea Open Air Art Exhibition, Royal Avenue, London.

Skye Balls.

Lochaber Gathering.

World Carriage Driving Championships, Smith's Lawn, Windsor, Berkshire.

Horseman's Sunday, Hyde Park Crescent, London.

Benson & Hedges Music Festival. The Maltings, Snape, Suffolk.

Burlington House Fair, Royal Academy of Arts, Piccadilly, London.

Racing: Doncaster (Laurent Perrier Champagne Stakes, St Leger).

Racing: Longchamp (Prix Vermeille).

Election of Lord Mayor, Guildhall, London.

Cricket: Gillette Cup Final, Lords, London.

Battle of Britain Day, Biggin Hill.

CBI Annual Conference, Brighton, Sussex.

Last Night of the Proms, Albert Hall, London.

Northern Meeting Ball.

Angus Forfar Ball.

Battle of Britain Ball, Grosvenor House Hotel, London.

Racing: Ayr (Ladbroke Ayr Gold Cup).

Racing: Newbury (Mill Reef Stakes).

St Giles Fair, Oxford.

Chatsworth Country Fair, Chatsworth Park, Derbyshire.

Tin Pan Alley Ball, Hilton Hotel, Park Lane, London.

Richmond Dog Show Society Championships, Ascot, Berkshire.

British Hard Court Tennis Championships, Bournemouth, Hampshire.

European Championship Polo Tournament, Smith's Lawn, Windsor.

Loweswater Agricultural Show, Cumbria.

National Surfing Championships, Bude, Cornwall.

Offshore Power Boat Race, Isle of Wight.

Beaufort Hunt Club Party, Bath Racecourse, Avon.

Windsor Festival of Arts and Music, Windsor, Berkshire.

Labour Party Conference, Brighton, Sussex.

Liberal Party Conference, Harrogate, Yorkshire.

Racing: Kempton Park (September Stakes).

Final of the Polo Magazine Tournament, Ham, London.

Racing: Newmarket.

Racing: Ascot Heath.

Westmorland County Show, Cumbria.

Southampton Boat Show, Mayflower Park, Southampton, Hampshire.

Aberdeen Angus Show, Perth, Scotland.

Northern Antiques Fair, Harrogate, Yorkshire.

Sheriff's Ride, Lichfield, Staffordshire.

Highland Games, Aboyne, Scotland.

Tattersall's October Sales (Yearlings), Newmarket, Suffolk.

October

CHARITY BALLS *by Peter Townend*

Charity Balls are not confined to any particular season and take place at any time of the year except August and September, when prospective ticket-buyers are presumed to be on holiday, and January, when they may well have spent all their spare money on Christmas activities. In recent years of inflation and squeeze there are many fewer than there were twenty years ago and the survivors are for the most part well-established and in aid of well-known charities. People who at one time would not have questioned the relief of Peruvian flood victims or Tibetan refugees now want some idea where their money is going, so those who plan new charity occasions must tread warily.

In direct opposition to this trend it is surprising that Queen Charlotte's Ball, probably the best know and certainly the most talked- and written-about charity ball, labelled for decades the Harlots' Hop, was abandoned in 1976. Founded by Margherita Lady Howard de Walden as a function exclusively for debutantes and always held on the first Tuesday in May, it was only intended to be an extra item of the 'Season' but when the Queen discontinued the Buckingham Palace presentation parties in 1958 it became the focal point of the debutantes' year and in the 60s filled Grosvenor House to capacity, usually with a waiting list. But then the Press turned sour on the debutantes and it became fashionable not to want

133

to go to the ball; the numbers dwindled and the organizers decided that it was the end, even though Queen Charlotte's Maternity Hospital had benefited considerably in the past. Each year gatecrashers created a problem and some new prank to terrorize the guests had to be accepted stoically – white mice, a snake, streakers (female) and finally a smoke bomb which damaged the ceiling of the Grosvenor House Great Room all contributing to the demise.

Since 1977 the Rose Ball has become the main ball of the year. It is in aid of Alexandra Rose Day and has been held for seventy years, also in May, but appealing to older age groups. Now, with the addition of the displaced debutantes, an attendance of 1,400 was clocked up last year (plus a waiting list) and £30,000 was raised.

Second on the list must be the Royal Caledonian Ball, now in its 132nd year, in aid of the Royal Caledonian Schools and other Scottish charities, which is the big night of the year for Scots north or south of the Border, although it now has two rivals in the Foolish Hooley in spring and the St Andrews Ball in the autumn – Scottish dancing is very popular nowadays. Strict regulations decree that dress must, if not Scottish, be full evening dress, white tie and tails, no one in dinner jacket being admitted even if they have paid for their ticket. Unlike the Rose Ball, where the £17.50 tickets include dinner, the Caledonian is entirely an after-dinner affair continuing into the very wee hours. Princess Alexandra, as President of Alexandra Rose Day, has attended the ball once in the last few years but Princess Margaret appears almost every year at the Caledonian Ball.

Junior in years to these but a money-spinner nevertheless is the Westminster Ball held at the beginning of December under the joint chairmanship of Mrs Leonard Pearl and Mr Adrian McAlpine, who have cleverly arranged that each year a different charity will benefit, thereby involving different sets of people and not always pumping the same pockets.

Also becoming a hardy annual is the Crown Jewel Ball in aid of Spina Bifida, organized by Mrs Una-Mary Parker and

Raising money in style at a Charity Ball

usually including a fashion display. The Red Cross Ball, the Lifeboat and Mermaid Ball, the Ambassadorial Ball (in aid of the United Nations Association) and, more recently, the Berkeley Square Ball also come round each year, as does the Winter Ball in aid of Conservative Party marginal seats. Most local Conservative Associations, especially in Greater London, have an annual fund-raising dance but the Winter Ball usually produces the Prime Minister/Leader of the Party plus a lot of top Conservative brass. For Americanophiles there is the George Washington Birthday Ball in the spring and the British-American Ball in winter in aid of the English-Speaking Union.

On the younger side the biggest sell-out of all is the Feathers Dance in December for twelve- to sixteen-year-olds in aid of the Feathers Youth Clubs. Held at the Lyceum Ballroom (this year at the Hammersmith Palais) it always has a waiting list of hundreds and applications should be made by September. The NSPCC also cater largely for the young. Their

Pied Piper Ball which was held every year in the summer fell by the wayside but was successfully replaced by the Blue Bird Ball in January for young teenagers and the Cinderella Ball for slightly older ones in December. The Blizzard Ball in January in aid of the Greater London Fund for the Blind is another must for this category.

Attendance at charity balls is not cheap and although tickets are in the region of £20–25 that is only the beginning. Drink is not included – the hotel gets the money from this, not the charity: you are expected to buy tombola tickets and raffle tickets and you may have transport on top of all this. Dress is invariably black tie for men and long dress for ladies – apart from the Caledonian Ball, white ties are never seen now – but at the balls for the young anything seems to go and the heat of modern dancing soon brings the ties off.

The keenest charity ball-goers are the rich ambitious-to-get-on-in-society types (there still are such people even in these egalitarian days) who hope eventually to buy their way into the more exclusive private parties. To encourage the young many balls sell after-dinner tickets at less than half-price. This can be disastrous, as some drink rather than eat beforehand and arrive in riotous mood, drawing flocks of gatecrashers in their wake.

Eating, drinking, dancing (both to a band and a discotheque) and socializing might be thought to be enough, but some enterprising organizers try to arrange a cabaret. This must be someone able to hold an already wayward audience – the cast of *Hair* silenced all comers by sheer weight of noise but Frankie Vaughan, Julie Felix and even Dame Edna Everage have had their troubles from those eager to barrack. Moreover, in these mercenary days few artists are able to give their services free, so the form now is to have a star celebrity to draw the raffle prize. With twenty or more prizes and tickets bought by anyone from the Chairman to her daily this can be a long and tedious diversion, particularly after an indifferent dinner. Menus are obviously chosen to involve the minimum of expense and a Chairman enterprising enough to depart from the inevitable fish mousse, a chicken which has seen better days, frozen peas and bombe surprise has to balance her budget carefully. Choice of food must depend on the size of the ball and the hotel itself.

The most popular venues for charity balls seem to be Grosvenor House, the Dorchester, Hilton and Savoy, and the newer Inter-Continental and Inn on the Park, not so much the Hyde Park. The Ritz and the Connaught do not have the facilities and Claridge's and the Berkeley seem to prefer private parties. A City or legal hall can occasionally be acquired but for a teenage romp the Café Royal or Whitbread's Brewery off Moorgate cannot be bettered.

How to get there: It's advisable not to risk travelling to any ball by train or underground – the sight of evening dress might well provoke an attack from the groups of punks, skinheads, mods and other unlikeables who patronize these forms of transport at night. Arriving by your own car has its difficulties too – parking is a hazard and driving means watching the amount of drinking you can do in an evening, so the best way is to arrive and leave by taxi.

Getting in: Providing you've got the money and the right dress there are really no restrictions on who can get into any of the charity balls, but, as has been said, some are more popular than others and it's a good idea to make an early application with a cheque. Applications should be made to the chairman of the various organizing committees – the dates of the balls and the addresses for tickets are advertised in either *The Times, Telegraph, Tatler,* or *Harpers and Queen*.

PHEASANT SHOOTING *by Anthony Burghersh*

October the first has all the possibilities of being the most insignificant day of the year unless the Court Circular announces it to be the wedding day of the Heir to the Throne. However, since spring, weather permitting, hundreds of enthusiastic sportsmen and gamekeepers will have been preparing for October the first. Guns will have been lightly oiled and supplies of cartridges will have been replenished, shooting schools will have had full bookings and dogs and their masters will have watched Barbara Woodhouse enthusiastically. The gamekeepers will have complained about the power strike that robbed the young pheasant chicks of the warmth from the overhead lamps and it will more than likely have rained during Royal Ascot, not only drowning Mr Shilling's latest creation, but also several young birds who failed to find protection under the wing of their mothers. The stoats, weasels and foxes will have been on their annual rampage to feed their young, leaving trails of destruction that would make the tribesmen of Tripura seem like choirboys. As for the surviving pheasants, they will have suffered all the vagaries of the English weather before facing the final insult on October the first, when they will be out of the woods over a line of tweed-encrusted gentlemen armed with twelve-bores of varying ages who will try to shoot them.

A day's shooting starts with a huge breakfast, ideally yards of very crisply fried streaky bacon and lashings of scrambled eggs carefully floating on immaculately executed triangles of lightly buttered toast, if for no other reason than that it helps to keep out the cold. Tardiness is totally unacceptable, the early-morning drive through the countryside must be quick if you are to arrive in good time. Also it affords the time upon arrival to accept the 'pipe-opener' that is invariably offered and to meet the other guns.

The meeting place is a conglomerate of parked estate cars, slightly bloodstained gun-slips and dogs, gallivanting around sniffing other dogs between cocking their legs against the tyres of the parked cars. The host, suitably attired, will pass around the bottle and invite guests to draw a peg from the well-used leather pouch he is carrying and inform the guests that they will be 'moving two after each drive'.

Once each gun is fully acquainted with his position he will glance nervously at the other guests, especially the Italian armed with the over-and-under and wearing a suede pork-

Pheasant shooting at Sandringham

pie hat. The sighs of relief from those not standing next him are almost audible. Everyone climbs into the fleet of four-wheel-drive vehicles to set off for the first drive where the head keeper will be waiting. With the modesty reserved for keepers, he will doff his cap, tug his forelock and generally mumble about the wealth of birds that will be seen today. His beaters, recruited from the nearby pubs, will be lined up on the far side of the covert waiting for his instructions.

The host will take each gun to his allotted peg and wish him luck and good sport before blowing his whistle or a horn to inform the beaters that everyone is ready and the drive can begin. The guns will have positioned their cartridge bags at a strategic angle so that they can reload quickly and placed their labradors or spaniels in a good position for marking the fallen birds.

The beaters move slowly through the wood tapping at the undergrowth, driving the pheasants forward to the flushing points where they will strut around before flying towards the guns. Pheasants climb and accelerate with great ease for a

139

large bird and once airborne are electric with colour and grace. However, they are short-lived on October the first. The guns raise their weapons with a well-practised swing and unleash a hail of hot lead into the sky. A fine cock bird, its head thrown back, its wings collapsed, begins its slow spiral to the hard ground which it hits with a flurry of feathers. A dog sits up, eyes glued to the settling feathers and ears alert to any instruction. Another falls, and another, until the line of beaters appear in front of the wood.

The first drive is over and there is a fine bag which deserves a celebratory drink. The King's Ginger Liqueur or home-made sloe gin or cherry brandy is passed around in silver cups and the conversation wrestles between the fine right and left that one gun shot, or that very high hen. One or two of the more unashamed try between guffaws of laughter to translate 'Stops and beaters, oft unseen, lurk behind some leafy screen' into Italian, while the host supervises the picking-up and the logistics of moving on to the next drive.

After the third drive a very large lunch is prepared and women make an appearance. It is rare for women to be seen in the morning with the guns; they tend to prefer to lie in or do the shopping, but are encouraged to help prepare the lunch to which little attention is paid. Drinking is an integral part of shooting and fine clarets do not go unappreciated during lunch; there is no question of the next drive starting until the port decanter has passed round the table at least four times.

The keepers and beaters are huddled in a barn supping on a pint of the local ale or some cider and munching on sandwiches that have travelled well within their silver paper cocoons. Their conversation is invariably about the ability of certain guns to shoot well, or more than likely the inability of others. The head keeper will have counted up the bag so far and supervised the pairing off of the cocks and hens to be tied together with short strands of orange binder twine. His tip at the end of the day will depend on the amount of birds killed and the two big drives after lunch are going to put the new colour television almost within his reach.

The two drives of the afternoon are everything the keeper expected, and the guns are shooting well, with one exception, but Italian enthusiasm is hard to beat and the bag rises dramatically. The birds had flown high and fast and everyone at the end of the day complimented the keeper for the fine display of birds he had put on. The politely doffed cap while accepting a brace of ten pound notes is accompanied by the compliment of how well the gun had shot. Everyone is happy.

A day's shooting is the ultimate thank you. However, I would not suggest that anyone who can shoot but is not fortunate enough to own a suitable establishment should spend the rest of the year being nice to those who have. The shoots in this country are very private and, though times have changed dramatically, money is the greatest provider. So unless you are a natural wit, clean killer and fine 'fella', it would probably be best to start saving and buy a gun in a syndicate which will cost a small fortune but give you many days of extreme excitement, good company and sport.

NIGHTCLUBS *by Nicholas Monson*

When, on its opening night, a distinguished Society lady was asked her opinion of Regine's, she replied, 'It'll never succeed. It's too far out of London.'

The *cognoscenti* deem only two clubs worth serious consideration – Annabel's in Mayfair and Tramp in Jermyn Street. Annabel's is the grandest. Ninety per cent of its membership belongs to the *ancien régime*. The other ten qualifies by owning large chunks of Venezuela and mysterious holding companies in the Bahamas.

Of all clubs only Annabel's does not have to suck up conspicuously to oillionaires for patronage. Indeed one hardly notices the yashmak'd invaders, but perhaps that is because of the discreet emerald lighting.

The food in Annabel's is excellent and for its quality not expensive. There is even a news and financial ticker-tape machine in the Gents, thoughtfully provided for all the big-bottomed businessmen from the city. It stimulates the adrenalin flow knowing how many thousands you have made or lost in between boogies.

When you walk in the man whose name you volubly drop is 'Louis'. Louis is the powerful and influential Maitre d – second only in importance to 'Mark'. Mark Birley owns the club and vets you for membership; unless you feature in Debretts or own large chunks of South America, you do not stand much chance of getting in.

Tramp is more racy. Every night it is packed with the new aristocracy – hairdressers, photographers and Rod Stewart lookalikes. The women, mostly models, tend to be very beautiful and have disconcertingly long legs which stretch somewhere up to their armpits. Though still very trendy, its members are beginning to age. These glamorosi Peter Pans do not carry their wrinkles as gracefully as their counterparts in Annabel's. Still it is always intriguing to meet fifty-five-year-old lead guitarists.

As most of its members think Cordon Bleu is a foreign port, the food you are served in Tramp is strictly grub, though, when you are casually rubbing elbows with Britt Ekland, I, for one, am happy chomping polystyrene.

If you want membership of Tramp, the person you suck up to is called, believe it or not, and frankly I don't, Johnny Gold. Impress Johnny with your gossip-column snippets. If you do not have any, pretend you are a famous foreign hairdresser. Tramp say their membership is booked up for the next two years. Do not believe a word of it. It is only to keep out pushy undesirables, i.e. non-hairdressers.

Wedgies is a two-tiered affair in the King's Road which specializes in gossip-column roués for greeters. The top tier consists of the dining-room and a bar with backgammon table. Of late the bar has been dominated by plotting Iranian monarchists. A drink on this small strip of carpet is always educational.

Downstairs the bar is filled with implausible wide-boys,

overtanned actresses and sour young socialites. The dancing at Wedgies is very good. It is especially fun manoeuvring through the dense clouds of carbon dioxide that billow up from hidden pipes.

Further down the road is Raffles. Raffles is probably the straightest club in London, consisting of guardsmen, city brokers and Sloane Rangers. In this age of Future Shock jigging around in a decor resembling grandpa's library is strangely reassuring.

A club that is not is Bennetts across the river in Battersea. Beneath the stomping high heels on the perspex disco floor swim tropical piranha fish. Dancing for the nervous at Bennetts consists of a delicate tiptoe on the outer edges. The one thing to be said for Bennetts is they do try hard. They have so far spent just under £1 million on refurbishing.

Since its marmalade-topped namesake parted these shores (she has promised to return) Regine's has been rechristened The Garden, sensibly emphasizing its greatest asset, but unfortunately for its owner, the silver-headed Ram, people spend more time inside a club than out.

The Garden has yet to find a homogeneous atmosphere. Still, a disjointed atmosphere is better than the heavy-handed French chauvinism of Regine. It is too pricey but, just for the flamingoes, The Garden is worth a visit. It remains though, as one journalist put it, 'where the middle-aged meet the Middle East'.

Dial 9 is one of London's most underestimated clubs. Smart bitchy people sneer when you mention it, saying they never knew it still existed. Their absence from this upmarket, Marble Arch dive is quite one of its most attractive features. Owned by Michael Caine and David Niven Junior, it has an eclectic membership. Leon, the French manager, boasts that some of the most beautiful women in London come to the club. This is true, but they wear the sort of wistful expressions that suggest they wish the same could be said for the men.

Three factors combine to make Dial 9 a really good club. The waiters are exceedingly polite, it is comfortable, and the music is not monotonous disco but highly danceable boogie. Entrepreneurs take note.

Legends is a nightclub to go to late in the week when it's full, otherwise it's depressing. Its decor is a cross between a milk bar and a space ship. Presumably the designer meant the pink tablecloths, relentless mirrors, brittle lighting and portraits of Holywood has-beens to transmogrify into some zingy futuristic ambience. But without a comforting crush of revellers Legends has all the inviting warmth of a Bergman psychiatric ward. The clientele seem to be Old Etonians, goons from the music industry, and gawping shopgirls who hope to be picked up by a lead guitarist. It does, however, have a hospitable greeter called Trevor who defies the theory that gays are never gay.

Nightclub details
ANNABEL'S, 40 Berkeley Square, W1. Membership £100 pa.
BENNETTS, 5–13 Battersea High Street, SW11. £80 pa.
DIAL 9, 34 Great Cumberland Place, W1. £75 pa.
THE GARDEN, Kensington High Street. £150 pa.
LEGENDS, 79 Old Burlington Street, W1. Pay at the door
RAFFLES, 287 Kings Road. £75 pa
TRAMP, 40 Jermyn Street. £50 pa
WEDGIES, Kings Road. £100 pa.

OTHER EVENTS IN OCTOBER

Horse of the Year Show, Wembley Stadium, London.
Cheltenham Festival of Literature, Gloucestershire.
Women of the Year Luncheon, Savoy Hotel, London.
English Bach Festival, South Bank, London.
Wigton Horse Sales, Cumbria.
Racing: Newmarket (William Hill Middle Park Stakes).
Scottish Boat Show, Troon, Strathclyde.
Opening of the Law Courts, London.
Lords v. Commons Bridge Tournament, London.
Racing: Longchamp (Grand Criterium).

International Motor Show, National Exhibition Centre, Birmingham.
London Fashion Exhibition, Olympia.
Oyster Festival, Colchester, Essex.
Conservative Party Conference, Blackpool.
Horse of the Year Ball, Hilton Hotel, London.
Trafalgar Day Celebrations, London.
Chatsworth Horse Trials, Chatsworth Park, Derbyshire.
London Welsh Rugby Football Club Dinner, Savoy Hotel, London.
Anglo-Danish Society Dinner Dance, Savoy Hotel, London.
Racing: Longchamp (Prix de l'Arc de Triomphe).
Commonwealth Games Preview, Brisbane, Australia.
Tattersall's Houghton Sales (Yearlings), Newmarket, Suffolk.
Multiple Sclerosis Society Luncheon, Savoy Hotel, London.
South Africa Club Dinner, Savoy Hotel, London.
Frankfurt Book Fair, Germany.
Racing: Newmarket (Dewhurst Stakes, Cesarewitch.)
Racing: Longchamp (Prix Royal Oak).
English Open All-Round Clay Pigeon Shooting Championships, Melton Mowbray, Leicestershire.
Clandon Park Horse Trials, Surrey.
Great Missenden Horse Trials, Buckinghamshire.
British Sand Yacht Championships, Lytham St Anne's, Lancashire.
Osberton Three-Day Event, Nottinghamshire.
Mop Fairs at Stratford-on-Avon, Cirencester and Tewkesbury, Warwick and Abingdon.
Stroud Festival, Gloucestershire.
Wexford Opera Festival.
Steeplechasing at (among other venues): Ludlow, Wincanton, Chepstow, Perth, Cheltenham, Ayr, Plumpton, Market Rasen, Newbury, Ascot, Southwell, Sandown Park.
Racing: Kempton Park (Charisma Gold Cup).
Nottingham Goose Fair, Nottinghamshire.

Racing: Sandown Park.
Children's Dancing Matinee in aid of the League of Pity,
Theatre Royal, Drury Lane, London.

November

FOXHUNTING *by Michael Clayton*

Despite its associations with ducal grandeur, foxhunting is easily the most democratic and accessible of all field sports.

Its greatest literary figure, Jorrocks, was an unabashed Cockney grocer, and when sallying forth to sample the joys of the Chase you should recall his famous remark: ' 'appy is 'e wot 'unts to please himself, and not to h'astonish others.'

The portly sporting gent created by Robert Surtees also declared that: ' 'unting is an expensive amusement or not, jest as folks choose to make it.'

Both statements are still relevant. People pay a lot for blood hunters and contribute hefty subscriptions to hunt in foxhunting's capital, which is *not* near London but in the Shires – in Leicestershire. Indeed the nearer you hunt to London the more likely you are to be described as hunting 'in the provinces'.

Yet the vast majority of hunting folk continue to follow hounds sublimely unaware, and usually uncaring, about such niceties of definition. They are secure in the knowledge that *their* hounds are the best in the world.

For the majority there is a vast range of Hunts: little packs in Wales or the West Country, and parts of the North, where the subscriptions are minimal, rubber boots are often the order of the day and anyone seen jumping a fence would be the object of wonder, if not ridicule. Here, venery – the science of hunting the fox with hounds – is all.

Then there is a considerable variety of splendid two-day-a-week provincial packs with hunting countries which can be anything from superb to simply dreadful, all characterized by the loyalty and enthusiasm of their subscribers and other followers. What is the difference? It is all part of the apparent mystery of foxhunting which baffles or even annoys the uninitiated. Yet it is basically all quite simple.

The very language of foxhunting can so easily puzzle or deter the newcomer. Cubbing or cubhunting? Pink, red or scarlet coats? Ah, the joy of getting the right terms tripping off the tongue at the meet; oh, the misery of calling foxhounds 'doggies' or referring to a hunting horn as a 'trumpet'.

Believe me, many a long and happy hunting career has survived such initial setbacks. Indeed the jargon of hunting has often been the subject of some wit from within the sport. For example, a lady Master of Foxhounds is a Master not a Mistress – it has been explained that the definition of a Mistress is 'somewhere between a Master and a mattress'.

The foxhunting season starts with cubhunting (*not* cubbing) as early as mid-August in some West Country moorland areas, but usually in September elsewhere because it cannot begin until the harvest is completed.

Cubhunting starts very early in the morning, perhaps 6.30 am when hounds first go out, and hounds meet progressively later as the weeks draw nearer to the official start of the season proper – 1 November; at 11 am until the end of the season, in March or April.

The early start of cubhunting is due to the better scenting conditions which prevail in the mornings in the autumn when temperatures are often high later in the day. It is quite easy to appear to talk knowledgeably about a 'good scent' and a 'bad scent' because the most experienced, and truthful, foxhunters will confess that no one has really discovered the secret of what weather or temperature produces it. Basically, however, scent tends to be better when it is a beastly cold, wet day – and this is why a certain streak of masochism is essential in the dedicated foxhunter. It is all the more ironic that the poor chap is more likely to be accused of the very reverse by those dreadful fellows known as 'the Anti's'.

During cubhunting only the huntsman and his official helpers, the whippers-in, wear red coats and black velvet caps. Frequently the huntsman is a full-time professional who supervises the Kennels as well as controlling the hounds in the hunting field. Alternatively one of the Joint Masters acts as huntsman himself, and has professional whippers-in to aid him.

So when someone says he is 'going hunting' he really means he is going to follow hounds as a spectator, whether on horseback or on foot or in a heated Mini-Minor with his terrier and a packet of pork pies. Only the huntsman is actually hunting the fox, and his biggest obstacle is all too often the enthusiasm of his followers. To put it bluntly, they can easily get in the way.

During cubhunting the mounted followers, known as the field, wear informal dress called picturesquely 'ratcatcher': bowler hats, tweed coats, fawn breeches, black or brown boots without tops.

Once again hunting's language misleads us: the fox is not a furry little cub at this stage, it is a young adult and to the inexperienced impossible to differentiate from a more mature fox. The aim is to cull the fox population by putting hounds into coverts (don't sound the 't') where the foxes live.

Most foxes run from the covert and escape unharmed; a few are caught and immediately killed by hounds within the covert. It is the age-old way of 'entering' or teaching the young hounds to hunt the fox with their older brothers and sisters (doghounds and bitches to you; and by the way, they are *always* hounds, not dogs).

In October cubhunting speeds up, with hounds being allowed to run more frequently in the open. It can be especially exciting (in hunting language this means 'dangerous') for the mounted field. Ditches are usually blind ('overgrown') and some foolish young horses may put their front feet into such a ditch on landing, with spectacular results.

149

Everyone will be most interested and concerned if the horse is hurt; the rider's condition will not evince much interest unless he actually has to be carried off the hunting field, which can be something of a nuisance to other people. Foxhunting *is* guaranteed as one of the remaining risk sports. Even on a bicycle you need to keep your wits about you if you linger in a gateway at the wrong moment.

Some of the bravest riders are at an age when their contemporaries are tottering into geriatric wards. I have been astonished to see foxhunters over eighty return to the Chase after horrific falls involving nasty fractures which they will later recall with much relish at the covert-side.

From 1 November everyone dons full rig, and this *is* a bit complicated for the raw recruit. Gentlemen, which means anyone who is not a farmer or a vet (and both categories benefit from the distinction, as I shall explain), wear top hats and black or red coats, white breeches, black boots with tan or white tops, spurs, white gloves, and carry hunting whips with lashes attached. Hunting coats are *not* 'pink' (this was merely the name of a tailor, not the colour) and whips are not 'crops'- both gentlemen and ladies wear hunting ties *not* 'stocks'. You may practise tying these for hours in front of a mirror, with the aid of a diagram from Moss Bros.

Ladies should wear bowler hats, dark blue or black coats, white breeches, black boots, spurs and white gloves. In many Hunts they are nowadays allowed to wear black velvet caps instead of bowlers, and most look much better for it.

Farmers and veterinary surgeons are allowed to wear black velvet caps with black coats, drab-coloured breeches, and black boots; an exceedingly comfortable and practical outfit, secretly envied by some condemned to top hats for life (known as silk hats, but only obtainable nowadays in brushed nylon at horrendously increasing prices, and they need expensive repairs after a crunching fall).

The subscribers each contribute a lump sum per season towards the cost of the Hunt; the Master or Joint Masters pay considerably more, and devote much time to running the

Taking a spill in the Hunting field

Hunt; visitors on horses pay a 'cap' for one day's sport, collected at the meet by the Hunt Secretary (usually in a little satchel, not a cap).

Nearly everyone says they simply can't afford it, but hunting prospers as never before. There are more than 200 packs of foxhounds in Britain, and despite soaring costs most are bulging with subscribers. Hunts have to exert some limits on mounted fields in the interests of their hosts, the landowners and farmers, who remain wonderfully co-operative in allowing hounds and their followers to pursue the fox. For this reason your foxhunting cousin may suddenly appear at the meet at the height of season shorn of his red finery; he wears a bowler hat and hacking jacket and carries bundles of string on his saddle. It is his turn to be an official 'gate-shutter', scurrying at the back of the field to ensure that gates are shut to keep in farm stock when the riders have passed.

It is all part of the Hunt's debt to the farmer and landowner. The real crimes out hunting are: (a) allowing your horse to kick a hound; (b) riding over a newly sown field; (c) letting stock out of fields; (d) anything else the Field Master can think of. He has a marvellous time working off any latent aggression by bossing the mounted field about as much as he likes. Those Masters with lurid vocal resources may not always be liked, but are treated with respect. Their ultimate sanction is to send an offender home forthwith; this is yet another peril of the hunting field, and adds still more spice to a situation which may be precarious enough at the best of times.

The greatest sanction of all is for the Master to take hounds home immediately if his followers really misbehave. This works remarkably well, but in practice is very rarely employed; yet it is quite a useful threat on a dull day.

Foxhunting is not really a team sport, but there is a genuine cameraderie of the Chase; its followers do not ride horses to win prizes or renown. They do enjoy it enormously, and for a variety of reasons: the thrill of riding across the countryside, the excitement of a hunt, and for some the pleasures of understanding intimately what hounds and huntsman are actually doing. Always there is the thrill of the unknown because no two hunting days are alike. There is no guarantee of finding a fox; the weather can never be relied upon; and there is that dratted complication, scent.

Where to see foxhunting at its most colourful? A drive up the M1 takes you to Leicestershire, the home of the Quorn, Belvoir and Cottesmore. Each hunts four days a week in the season, with large mounted fields. (Most fixtures are published in *Horse and Hound*.) They already have large, regular car followings on the roads, most of them members of the enormously enthusiastic Supporters' Clubs, which hold social functions throughout the year to raise money for the Hunts.

Take a pair of binoculars, a one-inch map, a flask and sandwiches, and with patience you may see a great deal of hunting from the roads, especially in the Shires where the broad sweep of the fields provide fabulous views.

You may see those marvellous professional huntsmen Michael Farrin of the Quorn, Jim Webster of the Belvoir, and

Peter Wright of the Cottesmore, blowing their horns as their hounds leave coverts on the lines of their foxes. It is one of the most exciting moments in a run. The Field Master eventually allows the mounted field to follow; they surge across the grass, and tackle the fences in the wake of hounds. They may run half a mile or many miles.

Do resist the temptation to rush ahead of hounds in your car in the lanes and roads adjoining the line of the hunt. You may all too easily head the fox back towards the hounds, probably causing his instant demise, and almost certainly disrupting the run.

In Gloucestershire one of the great sights of sporting England may be witnessed: the Duke of Beaufort, born in 1900, and still at the head of the family Hunt. He hunted hounds personally for forty-seven years, and remains in office as Master since he succeeded his father, the 9th Duke, in 1924. The 10th Duke is foxhunting's figurehead (indeed his car number plate is MFH 1); he is revered and admired throughout foxhunting as a huntsman, hound breeder and horseman.

The Beaufort Hunt subscribers wear distinctive blue coats with buff facings, the family tradition, and the huntsman and whippers-in wear green coats, the family livery. This mounted field is an impressive spectacle indeed, and includes a number of ladies riding side-saddle.

Their neighbouring pack, the Berkeley, sport yellow coats for the Hunt staff, a link with the family livery of the Earls of Berkeley. In the 18th century the family hunted country stretching from the Severn to Charing Cross in London.

For something completely different go to the Lake District, where you can see foxhunting with hounds but no horses. The Fell hounds sweep like gulls across the steep slopes above the famous lakes; their followers perch on hillsides or scan the fells with binoculars from the valleys. There is a dedication and fierce local loyalty here that is not exceeded elsewhere. In the spring these Fell packs go on special 'lamb patrols' to hunt foxes reported to be worrying the newly born offspring in the lakeland flocks.

153

The dangers to wildlife are pollution, destruction of the countryside by building, and sheer ignorance. Foxhunting plays a vital part in encouraging the preservation of those coverts, the little woodlands and copses, which accommodate so many birds and beasts as well as foxes.

The fox excapes the horn and the sweet cry of hounds completely unscathed, or he is killed instantly if hounds catch him – a much better end than traps, poisons and guns can offer. So you may follow hounds with a clear conscience, and a sense of exploration. Once you have become a foxhunter, on your feet, on wheels, or even on a horse, the countryside will acquire dimensions of pleasure you had never dreamed existed.

To quote that 19th-century grocer again: 'The 'oss loves the 'ound and I loves both . . . Believe me, my beloved hearers, if a man's inclined for the Chase, he'll ride almost anything, or walk sooner than stay at 'ome.'

BEAUJOLAIS NOUVEAU *by Allan Hall*

It is significant that last summer, when it had already emerged that the 1980 vintage of Beaujolais – and of every other wine in Europe, if it comes to that – might be troublesome, several producers of Nouveau had already got together to postpone the release date of the new wine. Such a decision would normally be taken as late as possible: changing the day, normally 15 November, is much resented by the French – they regard it as on a par with tampering with the Constitution of the Republic. But the British needed to know so that their Beaujolais Nouveau Rally could be properly planned, and the French producers were not prepared to offend us. The British, it has emerged, are the most faithful, passionate and copious consumers of Beaujolais Nouveau in the world.

The Beaujolais Nouveau Rally wasn't much of a social event before the uproarious British turned it into a circus. Before the Rolls-Royces and noisy sports cars joined in, there were just a few French lorry drivers competing with each other to get the wine to Paris so that it would be on Chez Gilbert's breakfast tables before it hit Chez Albert's.

In the very beginning it was entirely a local custom to bottle a bit of the new wine in November, when it had completed its fermentations, and distribute it to the vineyard workers as a promise of the wine still maturing in cask until the following spring. You can't keep that sort of thing secret, of course, and gradually Beaujolais Nouveau spread – a relative, no doubt, would secure a few bottles for the family in Lyons and eventually it was seen that the wine was too good to give away: much better to sell it.

Well before there was an export market, the sale in France, most particularly to big industrial centres where your average Jacques needs a good glass of red wine (probably pursuing a pastis) to get him on to the morning production line, was already subject to governmental regulation. It had to be. Obviously some unscrupulous producer or dealer who didn't care whether the wine was ready would rush it off to be first on the market. Now there is a release date, and of course as soon as you have somebody shouting 'They're Off!' you have a race on your hands, and as soon as you have a race on your hands you have the British muscling in for a piece of the action.

It started with a few Beaujolais-fanciers in the wine trade like Peter Reynier and the Hon Ralph Mansfield. Then Ralph Mansfield and I turned it into a competition. I think it was at this time that Clement Freud and the restaurateur Joseph Berkmann struck a bet on who could get the wine back first. Two such stalwart citizens would in no way transgress speed restrictions merely to win a wager, but they both had Beaujolais Nouveau for breakfast. Who hit London first seems never to have been resolved; nor do I know if money ever finally changed hands. However, Berkmann was to ring me later suggesting a properly organized event and the race was on.

The fact that this was illegal – racing on the public highway

155

– was curiously overlooked for three years until Scotland Yard stepped in, in the nicest possible way. It was no longer to be a race, but a rally. My interview at the Yard, in which the alternative of a life sentence was made plain, was brief. A rally it would become. The deal was sealed over a rather pleasant home-made wine produced by one of the coppers (elderberry, I think) and the rally has just gone on growing ever since to become today's exuberant cavalcade of cars of all shapes and sizes, usually led by Victor Barclay's Rolls and any number of Aston Martins. Freud, for all his playboy image, is a dedicated constituency man and doesn't have time for this sort of frolic any more, while Berkmann is too busy shipping Nouveau by the container load (he has the Duboeuf agency).

Most of the entrants these days seem to be hoteliers and wine-bar proprietors and their Beaujolais-swilling friends with money to spend on what has become an important date in the sporting calendar. To do it properly you need four days – one day going down, staying overnight so that you are rested for the drive back the following night, the day-long binge when you get the booze back to Britain and a fourth day to recover – and the cost will be anything between £250 (if you are being careful) and £500 which will take in lunch down the road at Paul Bocuse.

If you are determined to win the trophy for the lowest mileage then you will recce the run through Paris. The *peripherique* is fast but adds miles to the journey. It is surprising how straight a line you can, with planning, describe through the heart of Paris, but you do need to rehearse it and you need to be sure the cunning French are not, while your back is turned in Beaujolais, going to confound you with road-work diversions.

Even the route from the coast through South London is critical if you are seriously trying to win. I speak with authority since I navigated an Aston Martin back home to win in 1979. The fact that the adjudicators were close friends of mine had absolutely nothing to do with it.

Serious drinkers despise the Beaujolais Nouveau Rally in

156

Harvesting the Beaujolais ready for the tables of London

much the same way that serious tauromachs write off the running of the bulls in Pamplona, but these are people who do not smile much. Certainly Beaujolais Nouveau is not at its best drunk on the pavement at ten o'clock in the morning after an all-night dash from the vineyard to Hyde Park Corner. I usually leave mine for a fortnight, storing it outside so that it is just the right temperature for drinking in December. I rarely have any left by the New Year, by which time I am already looking forward to the Beaujolais the producer still has in cask, perfecting itself for drinking in the spring.

But all that said, that first swig at the end of a 500-mile journey is the best. He who can't get any fun out of a glass of wine should stop drinking.

WEEKENDING *by Tom Hartman*

Weekends in the country can easily be divided into two categories: the relaxing and the unrelaxing. A relaxing weekend (and it should be said at once that the Mitfordesque

157

foible of referring to a weekend as a 'Friday to Monday' is now *passé* to the point of being affected) is one spent with old friends to the rhythm of whose life one has become totally attuned and who know one's likes as well as one knows their dislikes. One knows what time to leave London; one knows that it will be boring but not catastrophic if one is stuck in a traffic jam on the M4 for two hours; one knows that there will be as much as one wants to drink when one arrives; one knows what time to go to bed, what time to get up, which of the household chores to offer to help with, what to tip the servants – if there are any – and when it is time for one to leave. So one has nothing to worry about – except, of course, whether one's house is being burgled in one's absence, whether one's next-door neighbour will remember to feed the cat, water the plants, remove the papers and the milk from the front doorstep, and whether the car will break down on the way home. Apart from such minor anxieties one can leave it to one's hostess to knit up the ravelled sleeve of one's cares, and look on with detached amusement when she makes a fool of herself declaring the village fête open on Saturday afternoon.

The unrelaxing weekend is a very different matter and presents innumerable pitfalls for the unwary. Let us assume that you have been asked to stay by people you don't really know, perhaps for a Hunt Ball, in a part of the country with which you are not familiar and the directions you have been given are sketchy to say the least: 'If you get to a pub called The Bar Sinister you've gone too far'. If you've got any sense, leave plenty of time, go to The Bar Sinister, have a couple of strong drinks, buy one for the landlord and find out all you can about your host and hostess *before* asking for directions to your ultimate destination. If you have not already done so, this is a good opportunity to take on board your emergency rations. Old Khayyam made his supplication to 'Thou who didst with pitfall and with gin Beset the road I was to wander in'. Of pitfalls we know there will be plenty, but one can't always count on the gin; so emergency supplies are *de rigueur*. These, however, must be handled with discretion.

One never knows that some ferret-nosed housemaid or valet may not be lurking in the wings waiting to pounce on one's luggage and unpack it; and it is very embarrassing to find half-bottles of gin or whisky staring accusingly at one from the bathroom shelf when one goes up to change for dinner. It is, therefore, essential to have a briefcase capacious enough to accommodate one's reserve rations. A housemaid who opens your briefcase will have more on her conscience than you need have on yours.

Having one's suitcases whisked away and their contents analysed by judges far more criticial than any Customs Officer is in itself an unnerving experience. What seemed to you quite clean in the sooty light of a London dawn frequently fails to pass muster in the clear evening air of Snowdonia and when you come to change for dinner you may well find that everything you possess has been whisked away to be washed and ironed. There are two ways to counter this one-upmanservantship ploy; one is to lock your suitcase and, if challenged, say boldly, 'The key won't come off my keyring, Cooper, but don't worry; I'll look after myself.' The other is to put an old shirt in a fresh laundry wrapper.

It is a good idea to aim to arrive at about seven o'clock. This gives you time for a couple of drinks before changing and, assuming that your hosts dine at a civilized hour, time for a bath, an appraisal of the situation with your wife/girl-friend/mistress or whatever, a measure of Dutch courage from the emergency supplies while changing, and, if you are lucky, a couple more downstairs before dinner.

If a Hunt Ball or local dance is the *raison-d'être* of the weekend events thereafter will be taken out of your hands and out of the scope of this article – so we will skip to the coffee and, one hopes, the brandy. A good hostess makes it quite clear what time she expects one to go to bed and what routine one is expected to observe in the morning. If she fails to do so, she is obviously a happy-go-lucky type and one can be fairly certain that it is safe to lie in in the morning. One's host is a trickier problem as he is likely to want to stay up later than his wife and consume large quantities of whisky with his guests, an indulgence possibly forbidden him during the week. He is, in my view, a bad host who expects you to stay up half the night with him watching a Test Match relayed by satellite from Australia when it is quite clear that you couldn't tell the difference between Botham, Borg and Ballesteros.

In Edwardian days the weekend shooting party was merely a polite front for the more clandestine sporting activities which took place after the guests had retired to each other's rooms, and a hostess was judged by the skill with which she allocated the bedrooms. A good hostess would know who was currently pairing off with whom and would arrange things so that corridor traffic was kept to a minimum. Nevertheless a certain amount of *va-et-vient* was inevitable, as Hilaire Belloc reminds us:

There will be bridge and booze till after three,
And after that a few of them will grope
About the corridors in *robes-de-nuit*,
Pyjamas or some other kind of dope.

Today such activities are regarded with a degree of tolerance which renders any advice superfluous. But perhaps it should be said in passing that it is inadvisable to try and play 'Hump the Hostess' on one's first visit.

Saturday morning is the Salisbury Plain of the country weekend – a seemingly interminable expanse in which the natives are occupied with their daily chores but in which the visitor wanders without purpose. It is a good idea to keep out of the way and use the time as an alibi for one's briefcase – it is a splendid opportunity to reply to all those letters which are now lying unanswered under the emergency rations.

More often than not a preprandial inspection of the garden will be part of the agenda. Unless you are a plantsman of some assurance it is better to confine your remarks during this ritual to such commonplaces as 'What a dazzling show of colour!' or, indeed, simply to asking the names of the plants. Your

The beginning of another weekend

hostess will be delighted to show off her knowledge, but if she gets her Viburnum Carlesii mixed up with her Carlcephalum it is advisable not to tell her. And when she refers to 'J. C. Williams' or 'Nelly Moser' try not to let on that you thought she was talking about her gardener or an Australian opera singer: she will in fact be talking about her favourite camellia and clematis.

Well-run country houses do not have people to lunch on Saturday. Midday drinking, except in *nouveau riche* households, is minimal, as some energetic form of entertainment is likely to have been laid on for the afternoon. This may be a point-to-point or local Horse Show, or an excursion to some place of historical, architectural or even ornithological interest. Such expeditions are likely to involve walking the last few miles, so it makes sense not to get boozed up at lunchtime. It is a good idea to take a pair of Wellington boots with you, although in most country houses there always seem to be at

161

least fifteen or twenty ill-matched boots in the passage leading to the downstairs loo.

Saturday evening is the time when you are put on display.
Rigged out in long dresses and velvet smoking jackets, you
assemble in the drawing-room to await the arrival of Colonel
Buffy ffoulkes-Horses and his memsahib. Their entrance is
heralded by a curious explosion of guffaws and titters which
take the place of conventional greetings. Conversation at this
stage should be restricted to polite banalities; in any case the
temptation to turn to Mrs ffoulkes-Horses and say, 'Were you
truly wafted in from Paradise?' is likely to be resistable. Only
when all are safely arranged round the dining-room table
should you allow your brilliance free rein. But even now you
have a wobbly tightrope along which to walk. Colonel
ffoulkes-Horses may be a narrow-minded old country bump-
kin but it is not polite to say so, even by inference, so nothing
too literary or too theatrical, nothing politically or theologi-
cally controversial. It is really safest to fall back on your fund
of anecdotage and just hope for the best that you sing sweetly
enough for your supper.

When the ffoulkes-Horses finally depart there is likely to be
a post-mortem before you are allowed to go to bed. Your host
and hostess will say how ghastly they were: 'Can't *think* why
we asked them.' 'Nonsense,' you reply hypocritically,
'they're really very sweet.'

Sunday morning is made easier, if one is not a totally
uncivilized distance from London, by the arrival of the Sunday papers, the study of which helps to fill in the yawning gap
after breakfast, mercifully shortened by God's providence
and church at 11 am. Those who do not normally go to church
need no longer have any fear of being caught on the wrong
knee; the liturgical variations now on offer in the Church of
England allow for an almost limitless margin of error.

Then its back to the house for the thirst after righteousness,
which is definitely allowed on Sundays; but bear in mind that
you may well have to discuss the sermon with the vicar over
luncheon.

You should by now have weighed up your hostess sufficiently accurately to know at what time you are expected to
leave. If, when you come back from church, you notice that
the Visitors' Book is already open on the hall table you can
safely assume that prompt departure after lunch is indicated.

Do you make your own bed? Do you offer to help with the
washing-up? How much do you tip the servants? Well, as Sir
Thomas Browne said, these things are not beyond all conjecture, but, in truth, they must be left to your own judgement. It
does no harm to make your bed, nor to help with the
washing-up, and over-tipping only spoils it for others, never
for you.

Sing sweetly for your supper, tip well, and the chances are
that you'll be asked again, as long as you remember to write
your bread-and-butter letter, and don't do as one American
did and hand it to your hostess as you are saying goodbye.

OTHER EVENTS IN NOVEMBER

**London to Brighton Veteran Car Run (Hyde Park to Brighton
    Sea Front).**
Men of the Year Luncheon, Savoy Hotel, London.
St Andrew's Ball, Grosvenor House Hotel, London.
St Andrew's Day, Eton College.
Lord Mayor's Procession and Show, City of London.
Lord Mayor's Banquet, City of London.
State Opening of Parliament, London.
Poppy Day Rag, Cambridge.
British Bobsleigh Championships, Winterberg.
Canada Club Dinner, Savoy Hotel, London.
Sports Aid Foundation Dinner, Savoy Hotel, London
Racing: Doncaster (William Hill November Handicap).
Racing: Newbury (Hennessy Cognac Gold Cup).
Festival of Remembrance, London.
Guy Fawkes Celebrations, Rye and Lewes, Sussex.
Daily Mail International Ski Show, Olympia, London.
Vision Charity Ball, Hilton Hotel, London.

Working Breeds Association of Scotland Dog Show.
  Ingliston.
Christmas Horse Show, Stoneleigh, Warwickshire.
City of Westminster Chamber of Commerce Ball,
  Inter-Continental Hotel.
Lombard RAC Rally, Bath, Avon.
Racing: Cheltenham (Mackeson Gold Cup).
Racing: Ascot (Buchanan Whisky Gold Cup).
British Fur Fashion Exhibition, Olympia, London.
NSPCC Christmas Bazar, Claridge's London.
RNLI Ball, Hilton Hotel, London.
Buccleuch Hunt Ball.
Steeplechasing at (among other venues): Wetherby,
  Worcester, Lingfield Park, Uttoxeter, Hexham,
  Wolverhampton, Catterick Bridge, Folkestone, Haydock
  Park, Sedgefield.

December

CHRISTMAS SHOPPING *by Sheila Black*

The ideal time to start Christmas shopping is during the January sales, but if you are too broke or too busy there are still bargains to be had at the July sales – bargains of the kind that gifts ought to be, making the gift look much more expensive than it actually was.

Always embarrass the recipient if possible. A single Wedgewood dish or a glass paperweight can have any or no price tag – only experts really know what they cost. The thing is to buy from the right places. Whether the Wedgwood plate comes from Fortnums or Debenhams it costs the same but it's the box, the wrapper and the telltale signs of Fortnums you are after, rather than the plate itself. The paperweight should naturally come from Spink of St James's because their paperweight buyer is *the* expert on the subject; but don't buy the antiques, only the modern ones come within a reasonable price range.

When Christmas comes, don't forget to buy your own daily bread, household needs or special wants at Fortnums, Harrods, Harvey Nichols or the local equivalent of same if you are low on monogrammed or logo'd paper for the things you bought at Tesco or the special jar of pickled peaches from Marks and Spencer.

Always be seen slipping obtrusively in and out of side doors. It is terribly *déclassé* to enter Fortnums from Piccadilly or Harrods from the Brompton Road (which is the correct address of that emporium, although it pays the Post Office a special fee to be labelled 'Knightsbridge' when it's not there at all). Enter Fortnums from Jermyn Street and Harrods by the Number Five entrance in Hans Crescent. Have your parcels sent there by the relevant assistant and collect them all in one massive armful when you leave, lingering as long as possible in order to be seen loaded down with what may well be mainly your own personal wants. Try to make a coffee date with your most gossipy friend and leave with him/her so that everyone gets told about how you did all your shopping at Harrods or the like.

Upstage in every possible way. To a movie buff give a blue movie (short ones at fifty feet come relatively inexpensive), and to the boaster about his/her video-cassette TV recorder one of the cheaper cassettes now in the softish/hardish porn collections, especially if he/she talks of having kept the Nureyev or Beecham tapes. You might enjoy buying blue tapes since, at many a Soho joint, you can actually watch the tape, for a small price, before buying it. You then emerge with 'Confessions of a Girl Guide' and an air of sacrifical innocence, having made the trip solely in the cause of giving A or B exactly what they want (or need?).

Upstage also by using the catalogue system of buying, Make it something from 'The Millionaire's Toyshop' catalogue (60 Fulham Road, London SW3). It lurks behind a very chic shop called Occasions and from it you can choose your own TV satellite that beams up to 23,000 miles. Looking like a giant wok (Chinese circular cooking dish), it can pick up programmes from all of Europe, even from India (if you're less than 23,000 miles away and you wanted to). You are pirating, of course, and you never know what's on around the world because there isn't a World TV Times but it does give a marvellous chance to hurl out initials like STR (Satellite TV Receiver), SDA (ditto Dish Antenna) and LNA (low noise amplifier). On second thoughts, £18,000 is a lot of money to spend on someone else, so keep it and ask them all round for

Just before the Christmas crush

drinks just after Christmas, refusing to tell anyone who gave it to you while you give them some title fight from Madison Square Gardens.

You might, from Millionaire's Toyshop, get the giant TV screen converter which gives you a sixty-two-inch screen (around £3,500) or you could, for one-tenth of that, buy the world's smallest colour TV set with a seven-inch screen. Very cheaply, at around £40, you can buy a magnifier to clip on to it or any other smallish screen, a 'water-filled' thing that really blows up your picture.

Throw away the formbooks and buy a Horserace Computer Analyser (the HCA, of course), a calculator that throws up each horse's form and usually displeases because it produces short-odds winners, though many a man is walking around shirtless because he is invariably attracted to long-odds horses. Try a jogging-on-the-spot machine to save mixing with the *hoi polloi* in the park. Preset the pace, wait for the bleeper to tell when you reach it and finally use the underfoot massager, a built-in bamboo pole, to ease you while a Pulsetach gives the bad news of what the exercise has done to your heart.

167

Ego-trippers might appreciate a sterling silver razor from Occasions for around £32. These can always be sold when the price of silver soars or kept as heirlooms for descendants who will either never shave or use a miniaturized microchip electronic shaver. While on the subject, please, please never buy anything electric. It must be electronic or, for the real traditionalists, good old-fashioned electro-mechanical or hand-operated. Electric is out.

For ladies, who rarely shave, even in these days of equal opportunity, there are make-up mirrors, portable, but framed with tiny bulbs à la star's dressing-room, either gold- or silver-plated, if you must, but much, much more stylish in handbag-size and tortoiseshell, only £14.95 (but do buy lots of spare batteries). After that, an excellent briefcase that's also a fitted handbag is rather prosaic but the price is not and neither is the appearance. The best I've seen, this one (Occasions again).

Lalique is very much in, whether as perfume bottles or sprays of flowers. Humorous china started with those walking cups and teapots (never buy them straight now but only the peg-legged Long John Silver types). They go further now with dying swans over the handle, or bunnies on ashtrays, surrounded by the message, 'You're no bunny until some bunny loves you', which must be given to Dean Martin addicts (I know he's out, but some of us still exist).

The ultimate doodle is The Nurd, a spongy shape with vaguely-etched features that sits smugly on the table until picked up and punched, pulled, twisted or bashed into tortuous shapes, after which he very slowly finds his original, almost urbane shape with its enigmatic smile. Humidifiers have gone sculptural and kinetic, moving as the water drips from one sculptured platform to another. Made to many designs in copper that turns artistically green at the watering points, signed by the designer and maker, these are art and health (and beauty?) combined at around £400.

For just under £20 there is the instant wine cooler, a box into which you place ice cubes on a miniature radiator that chills a bottle in sixty seconds. Take it to someone who has a cellarful of champagne that he never serves because he always forgets to put a bottle on ice. Make him show it off several times. Hurts him, but how can he refuse to use your gift? With luck, you and yours can drink £20 worth of good champagne before having to rush away.

At Palace Bathrooms, where bathrooms cost from around £3,000, table and standard lamps are gleaming brass cobras poised to strike, with bulbs beneath the spread hoods. £1,000 will buy you one of these and several thousands more a dining-table supported by brother cobras. The indoors equivalent of the superior garden gnome is the indoor fountain-cum-pot-plant-holder, a tall craggy fountain of realistic glass-fibre rockery down which water falls into a pool in which a gilded mermaid sits curvaceously. Safe on carpets (a special base and non-drip systems) the Aqua Serena fountain has a hidden secret, a little stone which makes or breaks contact so that the water can be switched off for conversation or on again for seduction. The late Lord Beaverbrook, I am reminded, had a giant crucifix on a little mound outside his dining-room window. When conversation ebbed away from him and he ceased to be the centre of attraction, he would press a little floor-button and the crucifix would burst into light – a real conversation-stopper. I mean, you can't say things like, 'I say, old man, that's a jolly nice cross you have out there', can you? But you could admire the fountain and the plants or get your guests to admire yours – all for a little more than £300 (dawn chorus tape is about £60 extra).

The best Christmas presents are intimate. Wives and mistresses might redress their beds, being thus practical and pretty all at once (husbands and lovers might also take the hint and redress beds for these ladies). The Fabric Shop on Chelsea Green can reproduce any of its curtain and furnishing fabrics in a crease-resistant polyester for sheets, pillowcases and bedspreads so that she and he can nest in spring flowers and lie amid hosts of daffodils or a cloud of butterflies.

Alas, we do not all come from Dallas and we have to shop

rather more cheaply. Cheap is good, and you can make a virtue of it, refusing to embarrass giftees by running it up yourself. Your own pickles, chutneys, jams and jellies should have pretty labels, delightful names and gingham or flowered tops – try using the *Country Housewife's Handbook* for recipes for things like High Dumpsie Dearie Jam (a mixture of summer fruits from the glut seasons of August and September made into a single jam). Use large and showy jars or merely save the ones you had for instant coffee or pickled onions and fill with your own colourful mixtures. Mint jelly is a great gift, one that few people ever get and ideal for gardeners who want to cut back the mint (make cooking apple jelly but add masses of chopped mint at the final stirring). Give garden produce to town dwellers whose balconies yield only the odd, very odd, geranium.

Fishermen should get their spoils smoked and give some smoked salmon or trout for Christmas – ditto game which then keeps for ages. Children might make scented, coloured candles from those rubbery moulds which abound in handicraft shops, phallic to see but ideal as presents. Clever children will offer a gift in kind, a gift of work around the house or garden, the kind of thing they never do if asked. They might clear snow or leaves or relay the paving or something of that kind. The gift in kind is highly appreciated and all too frequently produces some kind of welcome gratuity which makes the giver very happy indeed (and the giftee not too miserable).

Teenagers always want clothes or money (for clothes). The best way is to try giving both. A trip to a local market will often yield some relatively cheap gear that does for their parties while the expensive stuff is worn for casual affairs (casual outings, sorry). The fact that money has to be given as well is just one of those things, alas. Aprons are always right, short for him, long, hostess-style, for her. Make them of scraps left over from furnishings or dressmaking but always monogram them (paint if you must).

Quite seriously, the nicest gift is the Christmas Stocking.

Pack it through the year (oh, cut the top of the tights off first, please) and wrap each tiny little thing separately. For old people who rarely reach the shops, a pair of tights, a drum of pepper, a packet of salt, another of tea, some brown sugar lumps, that sort of thing. For girls, eye shadow, lipstick (but check the colours), tights, ballpoint pens and suchlike. For boys, more difficult but usually OK with tapes, batteries (for cassette player or calculators), ballpoint pens, especially those with nudes in the stems, cards, dice and suchlike. For him, extras for his fishing, shooting or shaving, or even gardening or DIY equipment. For her, tights, face cream, hand cream, perfume, etc. The stocking holds large as well as small items, stretching like crazy. It can take all of an hour or more to unwrap every little thing in it, an hour of mystery, surprise and delight, an hour that spells out how long and how lovingly the shopping was done. An hour to treasure, an hour of thoughtfulness. What could be nicer and what, above all, could be more easily tailored to one's pocket since stockings hold everything from trinkets to diamonds?

FIRST NIGHTS AND FOOTLIGHTS *by Sheridan Morley*

First Nights, in case you hadn't noticed, are not what they were. A look at the prewar, or even immediately postwar, diaries of Cecil Beaton, Harold Nicolson, Chips Channon or even the redoubtable Jennifer herself will indicate that there was a time when a First Night was the theatrical equivalent of a Henley Regatta, that's to say an event for which a large number of people are gathered who have no actual interest in what they are watching but are merely there to be seen by a large number of other people who also have no discernible interest in the event itself.

A First Night thus fulfilled the function of a modern charity auction, but with the added thrill that a number of actors', directors' and playwrights' livelihoods could be favourably or adversely affected by the outcome. Stalls and Dress Circle seating plans were arranged by managers with all the care of

171

Berkshire hostesses giving dinner parties in Ascot Week: critics were not encouraged to cluster, backers were spread through the auditorium so that they might infect others with their nervous enthusiasm, and the stage boxes were only to be occupied by the most avid and vociferous admirers of the leading lady, or, better yet, those in the direct employ of her current patron.

Nor was this an exclusively West End arrangement; on Broadway, too, the First Night used to be an all-or-nothing, make-or-break occasion on which it was decided whether a show would run for two years or merely stagger through until Saturday. First Nights were frequently more dramatic front-of-house than on stage: it was on a First Night, remember (of *An Ideal Husband*, 1895), that the Marquess of Queensberry left his celebrated vegetable bouquet at the stage door for Oscar Wilde.

The social decline of First Nights, a blessing incidentally for actors and others directly involved in opening a production, since there is now a fighting chance that their work will be taken more seriously than the boats at Henley, dates from about the beginning of the 1960s and can be traced to a number of causes. When actors began appearing on stage in jeans and sweatshirts, audiences began to feel pretty daft dressing up in tuxedos to watch them; when the economics of touring a show pre-London became impossible, previews were introduced to allow actors to work a play in before showing it to critics. It is now legal to play up to fourteen previews before opening a show; so a First Night may often be in reality a Fifteenth Night, and with the decline of the old star system has gone the old habit of pavement gawping.

Many of the best shows in town now come out of the subsidized companies, whose repertoire systems also militate against the old idea of a première, and cliffhanging 'will it run?' questions therefore become equally irrelevant. Though there is, I believe, in continued existence a Gallery First Nighters' Club, which exists principally to allow its members to occupy the Gallery and (all too occasionally) shout their

Friends meet at a First Night

views after the final curtain, the idea of anyone being a First Nighter is about as up-to-date as the idea of someone still being a J. Arthur Rank Starlet.

Nor do I much regret any of this; by and large it means that First Night audiences now consist of dedicated theatregoers rather than gossip-column fodder, and that a play or even a musical will therefore get a better hearing and a more adult response. At up to £10 a ticket, nobody goes to a theatre just to be seen, not when you have to double that for your friend's ticket and then think about the parking and the dinner and the babysitter.

True, you'll still find friends of the cast, uneasy financial investors and professional critics scattered through the stalls; but they'll be there for financial, personal or theatrical reasons, not simply because there was a blank page in the diary between Cowes and Goodwood.

In that sense First Night audiences have at last grown up; they tend now to be professionals rather than amateurs, and though you will still hear the occasional braying giggle or horsey laugh in the stalls bar of certain of our more old-fashioned playhouses (the Theatre Royal, Haymarket, comes instantly to mind, perhaps because it is just about the last theatre in town where you can still be sure of seeing a black tie or two on opening nights) you can now be reasonably certain that the play is going to get a decent hearing instead of being regarded, as once it was, as a tiresome interruption of the intervals.

I do not in any sense regret the passing of the old First Nights. Indeed one of the reasons I stay far away from opera and ballet in general, and Covent Garden in particular, is that large numbers of people in dinner jackets always make me feel I have strayed into a convention of headwaiters instead of a theatre; though in my more mindlessly nostalgic moments I do occasionally regret the passing of the really great conversations that it was occasionally possible to overhear as one left the theatre.

I shall always cherish the memory of leaving a particularly long and terrible *Hamlet* opening night behind two ladies one of whom turned to her friend as we reached the pavement and said, 'Well, dear, all I hope now is that the dog has not been sick in the car,' perhaps because that seemed the best possible review of what we had just witnessed.

Then there was a memorable *Antony and Cleopatra* on which the final curtain descended to a stage encumbered with the dead bodies of the two principal characters. 'Do you know,' a lady in Row B shouted to her friend above the applause, 'that the very same thing happened to Mildred?'

Those of us who occasionally moonlight as narrators of the stage show *Side By Side By Sondheim* have been building up our own dossier of great overheard audience remarks. Ned Sherrin swears that on his first night there were two Americans in front, one of whom turned to the other just before the interval and boomed audibly, 'Great show, this. But it lacks something.' 'Yeah,' said his companion, 'I wonder what it could be?' 'Well,' said the first one, 'I think it could be tap dancing.'

I myself still cherish the lady who turned to her friend five and a half hours into the National Theatre's gala opening performance of *Tamburlaine* and said, 'Now that is more of a play than a show,' and Peter Bull swears that at a matinee of *Waiting For Godot* a woman turned to her friend and said, 'Yesterday my flat was burgled and now this'!

Another friend recalls a particularly lengthy *Hedda Gabler* which the management, for reasons best known to themselves, decided to open at a 2 pm matinee rather than the more conventional First Night. The last act eventually drew to a close and my friend was leaving behind a couple one of whom turned to the other as they reached the foyer and said, 'My God, look! It's still daylight.'

It is in the hope of collecting such great overheard conversations as these that some of us still lurk around foyers on First Nights. If that also happens to appeal to you, remember that a First Night costs no more than any other night, and that tickets are often easier to come by since there will have been as yet no reviews to encourage queues at the box-office. Failing all else, hang around on the pavement outside and then slip into the stalls with the returning audience after the interval; it is, alas, all too likely that you will find an empty seat, and it shouldn't take you too long to work out the plot, especially if it's yet another revival of *Oklahoma!*

OTHER EVENTS IN DECEMBER

Royal Smithfield Show, Earls Court, London.
Cresta Ball, Savoy Hotel, London.
KIDS Birthday Ball, Inter-Continental Hotel, London.
Red Cross Ball, Hilton Hotel, London.
International Show-jumping Championships, Olympia, London.
NSPCC Cinderella Ball, Dorchester Hotel, London.

Racing: Kempton Park (King George VI Chase).
Feathers Dance in aid of Feathers Youth Clubs, London.
Westminster Ball, Hilton Hotel, London.
British Utility Breeds Association Dog Show, Stafford.
Cambridge Blues' Hawks Club Dinner, Savoy Hotel,
   London.
Limelight Ball, Savoy Hotel, London.
Closing the Gates of Derry, Londonderry, Northern Ireland.
Sportsmans Aid Society Ball, Grosvenor House Hotel,
   London.
Racing: Cheltenham (Massey Ferguson Gold Cup).
Tattersall's December Sales (Mixed), Newmarket, Suffolk.
RNLI Mermaid Ball, Hilton Hotel, London.
Carol Festival, Broadstairs, Kent.
Festival of Nine Lessons, King's College Chapel,
   Cambridge.
Mumming Play, Andover, Hampshire.
Mumming Play, Marshfield, Avon.
New Year's Eve Celebrations at St Paul's and Trafalgar
   Square, London.
Hogmanay Celebrations in Scotland.
Torchlight Procession, Comrie, Perthshire, Scotland.
Swinging the Fireballs Ceremony, Stonehaven, Scotland.

January

EATING OUT IN LONDON *by Viscount Newport*

Do you eat to live or live to eat? If your answer is the latter, where better to indulge yourself than in the varied cuisines of London in the chilly months of January.

London eating has changed vastly in the postwar years, the stiffness of starched white collars giving way to greater infor-mality and soggy public-school-type vegetables making way for Italian 'al den+e' (although it must be said that these vegetables can still be found at Simpsons in the Strand, where one can look at them and sing 'Memories were made of these'!)

Hotels and clubs still cater for many people and very fine food can be found at the Connaught, the Savoy, the Berkeley, the Dorchester, and the Chelsea Room at the Carlton Tower. There are also many fine traditional restaurants such as L'Ecu de France or one that has undergone a remarkable recent revival, Le Boulestin, founded by that pioneer of television cooking, Marcel Boulestin. However, in this piece I will look at some of the newer, fresher and more informal restaurants which have opened in recent years.

Top of almost everyone's list must come Ma Cuisine where Guy Mouilleron and his Japanese assistants produce wonder-ful French food most beautifully presented. Alas, the restaur-ant only seats thirty which means that an evening reservation has to be made long in advance, but lunch is more accessible.

177

Robert Carrier is probably the best known chef, cooking writer and gastronomic raconteur of recent years. He is also the owner of a delightful restaurant called Carrier's in Camden Passage, Islington. There, within the confines of a fixed-price menu, he puts on many of his famous dishes in a lovely ambience which makes one think of summer in the middle of winter.

While Carrier has been the single most important influence, the Roux brothers, Albert and Michel, have been a double influence. Starting from Le Gavroche, an excellent but quite pricey restaurant in Lower Sloane Street, they have spread their tentacles to create a chain of establishments, all of them totally individual. There's Le Poulbot in the City, L'Interlude in Covent Garden, and finally Tante Claire, the latest recipient of two stars in the Guide Michelin, situated in Royal Hospital Road, Chelsea. Do have an elastic chain on your wallet as it's easy to spend a lot of money, although you really won't regret one penny.

London has always been a cosmopolitan city, attracting people from all over the globe and here one can eat the food of the world without the trouble of travel. The two most popular ethnic groups of restaurants are Chinese and Italian. Many people consider the variety and subtlety of Chinese cuisine superior to the French and the choice in London runs from the real Chinatown in Soho where Dumpling Inn, Lee Mo Fook, and Lido reign supreme, to the smart Mr Chows and Chelsea Rendezvous where the service is by Italian waiters. What would Marco Polo have thought?

Eating Chinese food can have its problems. I once sent back a most indifferent meal and was immediately confronted by a six-foot, sixteen-stone, completely bald Chinese chef looking rather like Oddjob's big brother, standing with a meat cleaver in his hand. He appeared to be somewhat displeased and was making dire threats in Cantonese, the first being that I should leave and not darken the doorsteps of his restaurant again. Chinese food is seldom tedious but it should normally be a little less exciting than that.

Table d'hote at the Trocadero

Alexander Shihwarg (Shura to his friends) has created some marvellous Chinese restaurants, all of which offer interesting and well-cooked food in pleasant surroundings. A favourite of mine for about ten years now has been the Golden Duck in Chelsea's Hollywood Road. Recently Shura, with Patrick Lichfield, has opened Tai Pan which has rapidly become one of the 'in' restaurants.

Another recent addition to the scene is Kenneth Lo's Memories of China. This internationally famous authority on Chinese food has opened his first restaurant in Ebury Street, where in plain but pleasant surroundings he serves wonderful food, with recipes culled from his many visits to grand and to simple eating places in his native China.

People tend to be rather suspicious of Indian food and do funny things like checking that all their pets are at home before going out for an Indian meal, or inviting a vet along to accompany them. But there's no need for any fear and trying any of the following four restaurants will prove to you that all Indian food is not hot curry and you don't need an asbestos-lined mouth to enjoy it.

Firstly, two informal and reasonably priced places in Westbourne Grove, which, although they've only been going for about three years, have established themselves as happy eating places with a lack of the usual characteristics of Indian restaurants. They are Khan's and the Khyber. Secondly, if you really want the finest food from the Indian sub-continent, go to Shezan or Salloos, where the dishes are in fact Pakistani, but the English, of course, call them Indian. These are both elegant restaurants with very fine cuisine.

HOTEL RESTAURANTS
Connaught Hotel, Carlos Place, W1 (tel 01-492 0668).
Savoy Hotel, The Strand, WC2 (tel 01-836 4343).
Berkeley Hotel, Wilton Place, SW1 (tel 01-235 6000).
Dorchester Hotel, Park Lane, W1 (tel 01-629 8888).
Carlton Towers Hotel, 2 Cadogan Place, SW1
  (tel 01-235 5411).

FAMOUS OLD RESTAURANTS
Scotts, 20 Mount Street, W1 (tel 01-629 5248).
Le Boulestin, 25 Southampton Street, WC2 (tel 01-836 7061).
Simpsons, 100 The Strand, WC2 (tel 01-836 9112).

NEWER, EXCITING RESTAURANTS
Ma Cuisine, 113 Walton Street, SW3 (tel 01-584 7585).
Carrier's, 2 Camden Passage, N1 (tel 01-226 5353).
Le Gavroche, 61 Lower Sloane Street, SW1 (tel 01-730 2820).
Le Poulbot, 45 Cheapside, EC2 (tel 01-236 4379).
L'Interlude de Tabaillaud, 8 Bow Street, WC2
   (tel 01-379 6473).
La Tante Claire, 68 Royal Hospital Road, SW3
   (tel 01-352 6045).

CHINESE RESTAURANTS
Dumpling Inn, 15a Gerrard Street, W1 (tel 01-437 2567).
Lee Ho Fook, 15 Gerrard Street, W1 (tel 01-734 8929).
Lido, 41 Gerrard Street, W1 (tel 01-437 4431).
Mr Chow's, 151 Knightsbridge, SW1 (tel 01-589 7347).
Chelsea Rendezvous, 4 Sydney Street, SW3 (tel 01-352 9519).
The Golden Duck, 6 Hollywood Road, SW10
   (tel 01-352 3500).
Tai Pan, 8 Egerton Garden Mews, SW3 (tel 01-584 2499).
Kenneth Lo's Memories of China, 67 Ebury Street, SW1
   (tel 01-730 7734).

INDIAN RESTAURANTS
Khan's Tandoori Restaurant, 13/15 Westbourne Grove, W2
   (tel 01-727 5420).
Khyber, 56 Westbourne Grove, W2 (tel 01-727 4385).
Shezan, 16/22 Cheval Place, SW7 (tel 01-589 7918).
Salloos, 62 Kinnerton Street, SW1 (tel 01-235 4444).

THE BOAT SHOW *by Adam Helliker and John Fenn*

If there's one thing about the British that amuses their envious friends, annoys and vastly exasperates their enemies, but is totally taken for granted by themselves, it's their bland refusal to accept defeat (however much they're eyeball to eyeball with it), or submit to the inevitable. They made Hitler bite the carpet in apoplectic fury when they couldn't see that they'd lost the war at Dunkirk. To them it was a passing annoyance to be brushed aside with a stiff upper lip, even something of a victory. They obstinately defend their last wicket in test matches with the scoreboard remorselessly proclaiming that they need 250 to avoid an innings defeat. They happily sally forth to the seaside on a bank holiday totally ignoring the weather forecaster who has forcibly warned, completely justifiably as it always turns out, that the heavens will open that day all day.

And in January, when the frosty days are short, gloomy, cold and boring, they don't do the obvious and sensible thing, submit to winter's numbing touch and crouch round the fireside clutching a warming drink with a totally blank mind. Oh dear no, not the British. They tell themselves that summer's just around the corner, their blood stirs. They get that old sea-dog feeling. They fancy the heady tang of ropes and canvas is in the air. The diesel fumes from the juggernauts are metamorphosed into the jolly aroma of a marine engine. Their minds dwell on inviting stretches of sunlit water with cool drinks and even cooler bikini-clad shipmates. And they go off through the snow and fog to the Boat Show to put it all together.

It's a fascinating, and slightly awesome, experience to see these present-day descendants of Drake and Raleigh, Hawkins and Nelson striding down the splendid centre aisle at Earls Court, sniffing the air appreciatively while the gleaming and exotic craft lift their varnished prows on either side like some deferential guard of honour and the seagulls' cries screech defiance to winter over the public address system.

A new purchase from the Boat Show

Who but the British could have a successful Boat Show in the middle of London in the depth of winter? The London International Boat Show, now in its 27th year, proves us again to be just a little different. Apart from the bizarre timing and location, they fill up a near-Olympic-size swimming pool with 2 million gallons of water to make an artificial harbour and float boats on it. Approaching 300,000 visitors pass through the turnstiles of Earls Court during the ten-day Exhibition.

The Boat Show, arriving soon after the close of the enforced festive season, comes like a breath of fresh air for those waiting for the next event on the social calendar. And, as with so many seasonal happenings, a certain amount of fashion creeps in. On the first, and higher-priced, days Savile Row-dressed gentlemen and elegantly clad ladies grace the aisles. White-gloved commissionaires, standing militarily at the gangways of fashionable yachts, dutifully usher the prospective customers to the poop-deck interview room where the business of buying a £½ million yacht can be discussed in befitting surroundings.

On Opening Day one can nod with satisfaction, not to say *approval*, at the acceptable gaggle of VIPs jostling very politely for the best camera angles on the jetty-staged Opening Ceremony. All is then hushed for the nautical fashion spectacular – not, as one might expect, sea-boats and oilskins, but bikini-clad maidens and their counterparts dressed in the more exotic and revealing nautical fashions. But, after all, going boating is a bit of a dream, so why shouldn't the fashions reflect such ideas? And under the imitation sun this year was a paradise-type Carribean island. Gentlemen with furled umbrellas and pin-striped suits delight in observing the shapely lines, even occasionally those of the craft on show.

Around the pool on balconies and specially constructed elevated areas finance houses, banks and other institutions offer hospitality to the would-be client, old friend, passing acquaintance or anybody else who can talk their way in on the pretext perhaps of wanting to borrow a cool million or so to refurbish father's yacht, or to buy something larger to accommodate an ever-expanding family.

But not all parts of the Show are quite like this. There is an area called the Casbah on the first floor. Here row upon row of exhibitors, mainly concerned with the gadgets and knick-knacks that go on boats, establish a warm feeling of goodwill among the visitors. This is always an extremely popular area. Here, particularly at weekends, the pseudo-sailor, in heavy Guernsey sweater, binoculars round his neck, fights his way through the aisles to observe some treasured piece of equipment.

The corridors of power adjacent to the area of the Marine Artists Exhibition are the setting for much of the social activity. Guided by the velvet-gloved iron hand of the Chief Executive, Tom Webb, and aided by the Honorary Chairman of the National Boat Shows and President of the Ship and Boat Builders National Federation, the guest lists are prepared for the much-coveted Directors' Luncheons. On the Opening Day, when the distinguished guest has performed the Opening Ceremony, the beige-clad doors on the first floor slam closed for pre-lunch drinks and the fine fare that is to follow. Usually it is a male affair but this tradition was broken when the Right Honourable leader of HM Government, when in Opposition, accepted the challenge to open the Show.

The lucky invitees to this and the rest of the Directors' Luncheons are chosen with great care. Not a yellow wellie, oilskin or seaman's sweater in sight on these occasions. Dress, while not stipulated, is understood and there is no record of anyone being black-balled from the sacred Directors' Luncheon because of their attire.

Conversation is about the intricacies of hull design, the setting of sails or the power that an engine can develop, and those who are fortunate enough to attend these occasions no doubt leave with a slight nautical roll.

One really should go to the London Boat Show in January. Everybody with a hint of salt water in their veins and the right cut to their jib will be there. The entertainment flows freely and they're all determined to meet summer half-way.

How to get there: The exhibition centre at Earls Court is easily accessible by taxi, underground or chauffeur-driven car. Should you decide to take your own vehicle there is limited parking at the discretion of National Car Parks Ltd, and in sidestreets unknown to traffic wardens.

Getting in: Hopping aboard is really quite easy. The first two days usually have an entrance fee of about £4 and after that it's £2.20 with a reduction for children.

OTHER EVENTS IN JANUARY

West London Antiques Fair, Kensington.
Racing: Ascot (Lambert & Butler Premier Chase).
Maple Leaf Ball, Hilton Hotel, Park Lane.

Blizzard Ball, Hilton Hotel, Park Lane.
Winter Ball, Grosvenor House Hotel, Park Lane.
Rugby: Scotland v. Wales, Murrayfield.
King Charles I Commemoration, London.
Burns Night Celebrations, Ayr, Scotland.
Annual Slipper Fair, Norbeck Castle, Blackpool.
County Athletics Union Cross Country Championships, Leicester.
International Road Race (Ras Uladn), Newry, Ireland.
Rugby: Wales v. England, Cardiff.
Scottish Universities Track & Field Event Championships.
Racing: Kempton Park (Lanzarote Hurdle).
Racing: Sandown Park (Mildmay Cazalet Memorial Chase).
Braniff Indoor Tennis Championships.
Blue Bird Ball, London.
London Shop Sales at (among others): Gucci, Loewe, Harrods, Conran, Swan and Edgar, Heal's, Liberty, Selfridges, Simpson's, Burberrys.
Cresta Run, St Moritz.
Monte Carlo Rally.
Lauterbrunnen Skiing, Wengen.

February

SKIING *by Mark Lines*

The Departure Hall of Gatwick Airport at 8 am on a Saturday morning in February is not most people's idea of a Society event but that is what it has become. Not only do the upper crust now buy their sausages in packages but also their holidays in the Alps. For some reason types who would never contemplate going on a package tour to the Mediterranean in the summer are quite happy to do so in the winter. Everybody's doing it. When the Dukes of Kent and Gloucester went to Méribel last season they took their families on packages; aristocrats by the dozen, Members of Parliament by the score, landowners in flocks and Captains of Industry by the drove all happily get frisked by the security guards and then sit on a charter flight with their knees around their ears as they are winged towards the hills.

A few people, it is true, either own their own property or, more likely, know friends off whom they can sponge a cheap holiday. Prince Charles is a case in point. He is an enthusiastic (although still rather agriculturally styled) skier who has in the recent past managed to cadge holidays off chums in Isola and Davos. Since the lifting of exchange control regulations he may, like many of his mother's subjects, find that he too can afford to buy his own place in the snow.

Prince Charles is also out of the ordinary, fashionwise, in his choice of resorts, while his cousins have all the right ideas.

Davos and Isola really are not places where an up-and-coming monarch ought to be seen! In fairness it is not always easy to follow the changing tide of fashion and no two people can agree on which resorts are worth visiting. Go to any ski bore's dinner party and you are bound to hear it:

'Zermatt? Huh! Vowed never to go back there. Never in my life spent so much time walking from place to place.'

'Well, I can't imagine what you see in the Trois Vallées. Completely flat – just miles and miles of nursery slopes.'

At a stroke two of the world's top ten resorts have been written off. Worse, sometimes the prejudices are passed down the line like family heirlooms. Tell a Moore-Brabazon or a Curzon that there are any towns in the Alps other than St Moritz and they will laugh at you.

Only a few of the very old resorts have lived with the changing fashions. Alpbach, Lenzerheide, Arosa, Wengen, Murren and Grindelwald – sunk without trace, all of them. Davos still hosts the annual Lords v. Commons race but, as in all other matters, the Lords haven't yet heard the news that things are changing and the Commons follow the Lords' example slavishly in the hope of things to come! Don't be misled by the reports in the gossip columns of the popular newspapers which describe the antics of film stars and pop singers in Gstaad. It is a dull town which is far too expensive and no place for a gentleman. St Anton, Lech and Zermatt still attract quite a number of smart people who are particularly keen skiers because they offer some of the most difficult slopes in the Alps but sadly none of them could really claim to be fashionable any more.

St Moritz, of the old resorts, is different. St Moritz will always be St Moritz and it will always have a strong following of the best sort. The skiing, by the standards of the 1980s, is pretty unexciting but it does have style. Even in the mountain huts the waiters wear dinner jackets. Surprisingly it is not as expensive as you might expect.

Above all St Moritz still has the Cresta run. This is now dominated, in racing terms, by talented foreigners, but it still allows a quorum of incompetent Englishmen to ride so as to retain the original British aristocratic charm of the club. It is a bit like being back at school where you can be awarded your 'colours' for trying hard rather than being good at the sport. Sir Dudley Cunliffe-Owen was awarded his and was described by the then President of the Club as 'by no means a great Cresta rider but his bravery on the course is second to none'.

In general it is the more modern resorts in the western part of the Alps which have become the most popular for the smart set. In particular Val d'Isère, Méribel and Verbier have developed magnetic powers over the Society Skiers. To be really fashionable you need to be familiar with all of these three resorts. You must know that Dick's Bar is run by Dick Yates-Smith in Val d'Isère; the Rhododendron is not a flowering shrub in the gardens at Kew but one of the best mountain restaurants in Méribel; The Farm is not where cows live but the most popular discotheque in Verbier. Furthermore, any self-respecting ski buff will casually refer to the fact that he is to be staying in one of Chalets Tom Hall, Hewson or Tomkins and expect you to know that these are the smartest English-owned chalets in Méribel, while Chalets Abel, McReady, Warburg and Mackworth-Young are the equivalents in Verbier.

For simple social desirability Méribel, at present, beats all comers. Last season the Kents and Gloucesters stayed there; half the village is owned by the Duchess of Bedford and you can't get near the ski lifts for tripping over minor European Royals. It has been suggested that the place has been tainted by the presence of Show Biz in the form of Brigitte Bardot who is rumoured to own a chalet there but luckily no one has ever seen her. Shopping in the supermarket is a bit like standing in the queue for the Bride's Book at Peter Jones. You know simply *everyone* there. The only difference is that the Méribel supermarket usually has what you want in stock.

There is really only one resort in the Alps to which a visit would be pure social suicide – Sauze d'Oulx. This is varyingly known as the Blackpool or the Benidorm of the Alps. If someone describes something as being Sauze they are using the skiing adjective for Super Grotty!

In the old days *après-ski* was a major feature of life in a ski resort. Immediately after skiing everyone would meet in a tea-shop where they ate delicious gooey cakes and drank gluhwein. Often there was an Alpine band and one could clomp around the dance floor wearing your ski-boots indulging in the famous *'thé dansant'*. After dinner in your hotel you went with the group to a nightclub and settled down to the serious business of a little holiday romance. All this has now changed. Tea-shops are all but dead and most skiers in one of the most fashionable resorts will only go dancing once or twice during their holiday. The reasons are twofold. Not many people will now stay in hotels but prefer to organize a private party taking the whole of a chalet or apartment. They can have a riot in their own place and the bother of going to a sweaty discotheque has lost its appeal. Furthermore, holiday romances are far more easily conducted in the 1980s and stealthy kisses in the nightclub are a rather archaic means of showing a girl your affections!

In the French resorts *après-ski* is either dead or bizarre. In Méribel the only thing to do after 5 pm is to go to the many cocktail parties which the British throw in their chalets. It's the furry boots and anoraks, not the conversation, which reminds you that you are in the Alps and not Chelsea. In Val d'Isère the done thing is to go swimming in the nude in the Fitness Centre swimming pool which is in full view of L'Aventura Bar. From the bar this is disappointingly innocent because the water is completely covered by a million ping pong balls to keep the heat in. From the main room of the Fitness Centre, however, the view through the large underwater windows is different.

If it is easy to know what not to wear in the swimming pools of Val d'Isère the same cannot be said of one's choice of clothing on the slopes. First decide upon the image to be put across on the holiday and then buy accordingly. Beware of looking devastating in the latest and most expensive ski suit if you can't ski. You will soon be found out and made to look a fool.

Natty Harrys who can ski and who want to look their best can pay anything up to £300 for the best French or American *haute couture*. An extraordinarily large number of people will buy three or four such suits for a one-week holiday and then buy another three or four the following year so as not to get left behind in the fashion race. This is the skier's equivalent of changing your Rolls-Royce just because the ashtrays need emptying.

The traditionalists would never dream of buying modern ski kit despite the fact that it's infinitely warmer and more practical than the stuff which was being produced twenty years ago. They will sit tut-tutting in a mountain restaurant wearing their inevitable parkah and stretchy trousers with a loop to go under the foot which holds the creases in. There will be a lot of talk of 'things not being what they were' and 'when we were young there were not even lifts; one had to walk up the hills on skins'. You will see these types wearing their clothes which should have been sent to the V & A years ago but you won't see them walking up hills on skins. Hypocrites!

Young country gents and their wives and girl friends are often too frightened of not being recognized as such to wear proper ski clothes. They will stick to the trusty Huskys and Barbours in their effort to make everyone realize that they are the 'right sort'. On a clear day in Méribel you can even occasionally see a few pairs of green wellies.

The smartest thing of all is to wear just a pair of jeans and a jumper. This is only really available to good skiers for the simple reason that you only produce enough body heat to keep you warm if you are skiing fast. Beginners would soon die of exposure if they tried this trick.

Whatever you do, avoid just one thing. On no account wear an oily anorak with stripes down the arms and a Ford Rally Team badge. Very Sauze.

Some people squeeze themselves into the very hugging variety of ski pants which are similar to modern nylon riding breeches. They look fine if your bottom has the same finely chiselled lines as Lucinda Prior-Palmer's but dreadful if the creases caused by your sagging bum are reminiscent of two little smiling faces peeping out from under the anorak. The best thing to do if you cast a much wider shadow than Twiggy's is to wear the padded variety of ski-suit called Salopettes which are of similar design to an eiderdown. They are terrifically warm and are the best disguisers available as they make everybody look fat!

Generally it is not necessary to look particularly alluring on the slopes in order to have a win in the Romance Stakes. Something to do with the high altitude makes all runners start at odds on. Despite this you must do the thing properly and fall for the right person. Local ski instructors used to be acceptable but not now. If you see them in the summer when they revert to their peasant-farmer rôle they are not quite so attractive. Shovelling manure does not do much for the sex appeal. American and Australian ski bums are, however, quite different. You need a rich father to be able to afford to do no work for a whole season and the dirtiest and least well-dressed ski freak can probably offer an excellent cheap summer holiday in his parents' New England mansion. Chalet girls are the time-honoured philander for male skiers. So much so that one chalet party operator reports an average of fifteen per cent of its girls getting married to customers after each season.

If it is *de rigeur* to misbehave after lights out it is also, in this day and age, OK to behave quite appallingly on the slopes. It is really a question of when in Verbier do as the Romans. There is no point in going apoplectic at the back of a lift queue for three-quarters of an hour; when you get to the Pearly Gates you are awarded no points for having let others past. You can adopt one of three methods of barging: you can engage the people whom you wish to pass in charming conversation and they will hardly notice you as you sidle past;

you can keep looking straight ahead and simply ski to the front of the queue hoping that everyone will think you are an official of the ski school with priority; you can put your head down and push. The last is much the most fun but when dealing with Germans for goodness sake do not mention who won the war.

TOUR OPERATORS TO USE
Hotel Holidays:
    Inghams, 329 Putney Bridge Road, London SW15 2PL (tel 01 788 6145).
Chalet Parties and Self Catering:
    Bladon Lines, 1 Broomhouse Road, London SW6 3QU (tel 01 731 4228).
    John Morgan, 35 Albemarle Street, London W1X 3FB (tel 01 499 1911).
    Supertravel, 22 Hans Place, London SW1X 0EP (tel 01 584 5060).
Cheap Flights to the Alps:
    All the above.
    Falcon, 260a Fulham Road, London SW10 9EL (tel 01 351 2191).
Helicopter Skiing in the Bugaboos:
    David Brooksbank, 12 Orange Street, London WC2H 7ED (tel 01 839 2941).
Non-package holidays:
    Made to Measure Holidays, 236A Upper Richmond Road West, London SW14 (tel 01 876 7405).

Where to buy the kit:
Alpine Sports, 309 Brompton Road, London SW3. Also 10–12 Holborn, London EC1.
Pindisports, 15 Brompton Arcade, London SW3. Also 14 Holborn, London EC1.
Sun and Snow, 229 Brompton Road, London SW3.

CRUFT'S DOG SHOW *by Fernand Auberjonois*

Once a year, every year since 1891 except in wartime, tens of thousands of Britons have been going to the dogs and enjoying the experience.

Cruft's Dog Show, the Wimbledon of the dog world, is held in February, long before the official Season begins. It is professional rather than social, and yet it attracts an élite in the top dogs of England, Scotland, Wales and Ireland. The process of selection is rigid. Owners matter less than their prize exhibits. They dress as they please, but their dogs' outfits must be perfect and the animals' behaviour exemplary.

Over the two days of the show in the vast exhibition halls of Earls Court no less than 9,000 dogs representing 144 breeds come to be judged, graded, rewarded or consoled. Their bark is infinitely better than their bite since biters would be banished from the arena without right of appeal. The din is overwhelming. The 118 judges are very much aware of their powers. The contestants display infinite patience, more so than their masters, who fuss and fret with brush, comb and talcum powder at the ready.

We are not absolutely accurate when we say that dress doesn't matter. Cruft's means tweeds. The tweedier the better, say the exhibitors. They come, in most cases, from the countryside. They look like outdoor types.

For three decades or more Cruft's has been sponsored by the Kennel Club whose membership until 1979 was restricted to men, this despite the fact that so many dog breeders are women. As far as Cruft's entries are concerned there is little evidence of sex discrimination. In 1980, of the fifty-nine participants in the obedience championships thirty-one were dogs and twenty-eight bitches. Their performance must be of exceptionally high standard. The tests get harder year by year as the Kennel Club intensifies its crusade on behalf of the well-behaved dog, the answer to growing anti-dog publicity in urban areas.

Cruft's Dog Show fills the whole of Earls Court's ground

Vying for the honour at Crufts

floor and upper level. The entries are divided into six groups: Utility, Working, Toy, Hounds, Gundogs and Terriers. Finally, the six group winners appear before the supreme judge. For the past twenty years the same man has selected the Best in Show, the top dog among top dogs.

As a rule show dogs can only take part if they have a recorded pedigree. The exception to the rule is for entries in the obedience tests. The selection of the Supreme Champion increases the popularity of a given breed, so much so that pet shop owners cannot satisfy the demand for the latest model and there are waiting lists for litters.

There is no business like dog show business, and no trade like the dog trade. In the case of the British Isles, however, it is a one-way trade. Foreign dogs would have to spend six months in quarantine if they were sent over to compete at Cruft's.

Exports are booming. According to Kennel Club statistics the countries buying most dogs from Britain in 1979 were, in order, France, the United States, Italy, West Germany, the Netherlands, Canada, Australia, Switzerland, Belgium and Spain. The most popular breeds on the exporters' list were, again in order, Yorkshire Terriers, Old English Sheepdogs,

Toy Poodles, Labrador Retrievers, German Shepherds, Pekingese, West Highland White Terriers, Cocker Spaniels, Miniature Poodles and Golden Retrievers.

At Cruft's, foreign buyers are catered for and made to feel at home in the Overseas Lounge where officials from the Kennel Club and the Ministry of Agriculture, Fisheries and Food help them fill in forms and obtain veterinary certificates before taking dogs away.

Cruft's is named after its founder, Charles Cruft, the son of a jeweller who preferred dogs to diamonds. In 1876 he joined a firm specializing in the manufacture of *dog cakes*, an American invention, the by-product of ship's biscuits. Cruft proved to be an excellent salesman and peddled his meal pellets to big country estates in England and to dog breeders in France. In 1891 he organized his first dog show at the Royal Agricucultural College. These were Victorian times when exhibitions were all the rage and dog shows were profitable ventures, which is no longer the case nowadays.

Charles Cruft died in 1938. His widow tried to carry on for a while, but ten years later the Kennel Club took over the sponsorship and organization of the world-famous beauty contest for top dogs.

There had been dog shows in England before Cruft's exhibition. The first recorded one goes back to June 1859. The venue was the Town Hall at Newcastle upon Tyne. The sixty entries were either pointers or setters.

Early Kennel Club literature stresses the need for a system of distinctive nomenclature for dogs. All dogs seemed to be named Spots, Bobs, or Bangs. The Kennel Club imposed surnames and middle names for candidates to the Stud Book. It acquired a monopoly in ancestry research. Today no one disputes the Club's rules and regulations, which have been adopted by overseas clubs.

Historians note that at the end of the 19th century 'the character of dog-showing had so improved that about half of the exhibitors were women, and members of the Royal Family were showing dogs regularly. His Royal Highness the Prince of Wales was a staunch supporter of the movement to prevent the cropping of dogs' ears, and from 9 April 1898 such dogs have been ineligible for competition under Club rules.'

Today, in Britain, some 4,000 dog shows of all types are held every year, but Cruft's remains the supreme test of dog purity. This doesn't mean that commercialism has no place in the show ring. The catalogue of Cruft's contains many a page in praise of 'concentrated crunchy nutrition', of 'kennel journals', of 'Cruft's Official Souvenirs, T-shirts, Teatowels, Key-rings, Pens, Aprons, Paperweights and Royal Portraits'. It advertises 'Munch Bars', 'Liver Goodies' and a whole range of disinfectants, the 'answer to odour problems'.

So Cruft's is the high point in a dog's season. It is the democratic way to the top for dogs of good breeding. No question of refusing entry on racial or religious grounds. And the working dog is not excluded. The Personality Parade, a popular feature of the show, gives top billing to 'Her Majesty's Prison Service Dogs'. Who said that dogs were snobs?

How to get there: By underground Earls Court can be reached on the Piccadilly and District lines. For car drivers Cruft's rather snootily point out that parking is limited and suggest public transport – buses No 31 and 74.

Getting in: The cost of admission for adults is £3 but only £1 for 'senior citizens' and children under fourteen years old. For exhibitors there are free passes. No dogs other than those for exhibition are admitted. The show is open until 8 pm at night but Cruft's say that at 6 pm many exhibitors remove their dogs so going too late is a bad idea.

SALMON FISHING *by Douglas Sutherland*

Of all the fish, flesh or fowl, edible or inedible, whose destruction is considered a worthy ambition by the upper echelons of society, the salmon has the least respite from pursuit.

197

The close season for salmon varies from river to river but, generally speaking, it must seem to the salmon that after the season is closed, they scarcely have time to get Christmas over with before it opens up again.

It would be unreasonable to expect the salmon, sporting chap tho' he undoubtedly is, to co-operate with his pursuers through virtually eleven months of the year. This explains why certain times of the year are better for salmon fishing than others. During the hot summer months, for example, the waters of the most majestic of our salmon rivers are apt to fall so low as to make fishing them about as profitable as casting a fly in one's bath.

Come the autumn, conditions improve. Indeed they may improve to such an extent that the salmon become positively suicidal and even the most inexpert fisherman may have something to boast about. On the other hand, he may not. Fishing, for salmon in particular, is an unpredictable business.

There can be no doubt, however, that among the real aficionados of the sport it is the capture of a fresh-run spring salmon which presents the greatest challenge and the most coveted reward. It is in the end of January and through February that *salmo ferox* sorts out the men from the boys. It is then that the heavily muffled figure of the true fisherman can be seen, wading up to his middle in a rushing torrent, the better to come to terms with his adversary. This particular species of *homo sapiens*, observed at closer quarters, may be seen to have an icicle forming on the end of his nose.

There are, of course, aspects of salmon fishing which make it more attractive to the less intrepid devotees of the sport. It is a poor beat indeed which does not boast a cosy fishing hut, and, in some instances, the accommodation is positively luxurious. So, too, is the hospitality provided. One host of my acquaintance insists that any guest who has taken an over-long break from his duties on the river bank be required to take a breathalyser test before being allowed to resume thrashing the water. 'It is so tiresome having to spend time gaffing them after they have fallen in', he explains.

'Tell me,' she inquired, 'do you ever catch anything?'

It would be wrong to assume, however, that this is only a sport for the sort of chap who would think little of climbing Mount Everest before breakfast. Quite the contrary. Some of the keenest and most expert anglers are members of what is sometimes described as the weaker sex. This is a matter of considerable irritation to the average male fisherman who is apt to mutter something about sheer bloody luck when some pretty little thing struggles into the fishing hut with a fish almost larger than herself slung over her shoulder. I should add that the record salmon caught in these islands was caught on the Tay by a woman as far back as 1921, when she beat the record held by another woman, who happened to be my aunt.

Salmon rivers, particularly in Scotland, differ widely in character. In the far north there are the short 'spate' rivers like the Brora or the Carron, some scarcely a dozen miles from source to sea. These are particularly popular with the more sociable of both sexes, as to be invited to fish is usually to be invited to join a house party when the jollifications can more than compensate for any lack of co-operation from the fish.

Another increasingly fashionable river is the picturesque, fast-flowing River Spey in Morayshire. Farther south are the more majestic Aberdeenshire rivers like the Dee, the Don and the Deveron. Balmoral, of course, stands on the Dee which is a great favourite with the Royal family.

Further south still, in Perthshire, the Tay is regarded by some as the finest of all salmon rivers. Others do not hold it in such high regard, not on account of the quality of the sport but because the finest beats between its broad banks are fished from a boat where all a fisherman has to do is sit and read the *Financial Times* while the ghillie strives to manoeuvre his bait over the fish.

Then of course there is the Tweed, noted both for the sport it provides and for the number of blue-blooded owners of its coveted stretches.

He would be a chauvinistic Scot indeed who failed to acknowledge that the adjacent lands of England, Wales and

Ireland boast many fine rivers. Each have their own advocates and each year convivial parties gather to pay their homage to King Salmon.

Just as there are a multitude of rivers whose appeal varies according to the eye of the beholder, so there are a great variety of schools of thought when it comes to the common problem of how best to persuade the wily salmon to give battle.

This is no place to discuss the rival merits of the minnow, the shrimp or the sand eel as an infallible lure, nor to take sides in the controversy which has raged since time immemorial between the dyed-in-the-wool fly fisherman and the determined bait caster. Suffice it to say that these are matters in which it behoves the unwary to tread delicately. Generally speaking the fly fisherman considers himself a cut above the rest but many a happy social occasion has become less than harmonious because someone has dared to dispute the claim.

Never argue with the man who makes extravagant claims for the one that got away. Just accept that they are *always* the largest ones. Nor is it socially acceptable to put on airs should you happen to be the one who lands the most fish. I have a delightful American cousin who is a fine fisherman and a finer squelcher.

On one memorable occassion when he had had a blank day, he was greeted by two fellow fishermen, each of whom had two or three smallish fish.

'I guess where I come from, folks,' he remarked gravely, 'we throw back anything under thirty pounds.'

Another American, faced with the hazards of river bank etiquette, found himself badly false-footed. A dour Scottish ghillie had attended him all through a fruitless day of cold and driving rain. The American had frequent recourse to his hip flask without extending the customary hospitality to his attendant.

At the end of the day he tried vainly to light his cigar with a box of damp matches.

201

'Is there no dry place I can strike a goddam match?' he complained.

'Ye could try the back of my throat,' replied the ghillie.

The camaraderie of the river bank is a very real part of the pleasure. It has been so since the days when to reach the northern rivers from the metropolis meant a gruelling journey of several days by stage coach and remains so when a chap can leave his office in the City at midday and be into a salmon on the Tay by teatime.

As for the *creme de la creme* among fishermen, show me the man who will brave the elements from dawn to dusk in a February snowstorm. Come to think of it, what the hell has a chap to do when it is too hard for hunting anyway?

OTHER EVENTS IN FEBRUARY

British Open Curling Championships, Falkirk, Scotland.
Racing: Whitbread Day at Ascot Racecourse.
Aberdeen Angus Show and Cattle Sale, Perth, Scotland.
Chinese New Year and Dragon Dance, Gerrard Street, London.
Rugby: Scotland v. Wales, Cardiff.
Ulster Motor Show, Balmoral, Belfast.
Rugby: Wales v. Ireland, Cardiff.
Scottish National Cross Country Championships, Falkirk.
George Washington Birthday Ball, Grosvenor House Hotel, London.
Guards Club Annual Dinner.
South Dorset Hunt Ball, Bovington.
Rugby: England v. Scotland, Twickenham.
Racing: Sandown Park (Freshfield Holidays Chase).
Racing: Kempton Park (Tote Pattern Chase).

March

DOWN ON THE HEALTH FARM *by Deirdre Vine*

The day your mirror stops being your best friend is probably the time to head for a health farm. That's the day when it inimically catches you out. You notice the malicious lines etched around the jowls; inky shadows underline eyes that have seen too many late nightclubs, and fleshy insults cling to what once passed as alluring assets.

It's a shock comparable only to an insouciant stranger guessing your age with alarming accuracy.

You curse your carelessness (wasn't getting fat/old/haggard something which always happened to *other* people?) and realize that drastic counteraction is called for if the aftereffects of life's glee and gloom are to be erased from mind and body. The time has come to leap from your piranha-pool life and flop into the jacuzzi.

But humankind, especially the excessively avoirdupois kind, often find it hard to confront too much reality. Bearing up to the overweight burden and discarding it, or breaking with a destructive lifestyle, even temporarily, needs sympathy, support, patience and perseverance. All these you can purchase from experts at a health farm, in a gift-wrapped package labelled 'positive health'.

Health farms are arguably among the most popular social institutions to have emerged since the war: rural, remote-seeming, strangely egalitarian retreats, where you can

203

unwind, grow thinner, fatter, more supple, sleek or younger-looking and *healthier*, in an albeit abstemious country-house-party atmosphere.

Embedded still in the minds of some of the uninitiated might be the notion that health farms are simply catering for sado-masochists – a sort of Spartan, punitive mix of boarding-school and prison, blending strict discipline with starvation. Not so.

Admittedly, decades ago fanatical folk pilgrimed to health hydros for a thorough cleansing – for what the Germans call *entschlackungskur*, being, roughly translated, a defurring of your clogged-up pipes, and fasting featured heavily in the ritual.

Nowadays, though, you're more likely to be pampered rather than tortured into shape.

Champneys, founded in 1925, was England's original health resort, but the ninety or so guests are considerably more coddled than they were in the early days when patients had to commit themselves to a minimum purgation period of three weeks. You won't find any rough treatment today at this former Rothschild home set in a 170-acre estate high in the Chilterns. Instead, the approach at the 'new' Champneys is pragmatic, appropriate to dealing with health hazards of the 80s (the effects of stress, lack of exercise, booze, cigarettes and the eating of deliciously evil foods) and a form of sensible preventive medicine is offered. 'At Champneys,' I am told, 'you get a medically supervised, controlled environment where you can simply learn how to live healthily – without disrupting your life style too much.' Translated, treatment like this means you succumb to massage, steam and sauna baths, the solarium and sensible eating. Although guests with specific health or weight problems are advised to stay for a few weeks an average visit to relax, tone up and learn healthy living habits at a health farm would be one week.

On arrival at Champneys the health of every guest is assessed by a doctor and the diet is chosen by the Resident Dietician, determining whether you join the fruit, soup and salad

All action down at the Health Farm

set in the Light Diet Room or more exotic munchers in the 'proper' dining-room. There, towards the end of their stay, well-behaved weight losers gradually come to terms with normal menus again. To my amazement, for those not on diets wine is served with dinner.

Exercise, as well as diet, is emphasized at Champneys: swimming in the heated indoor pool with aquajet, yoga, bicycles for hire, gymnastics, volley ball, riding, croquet – the list goes on and on. In fact recreation facilities are so abundant that lots of people go to Champneys for a holiday, and the wide range of indoor activities (pottery, painting, music, dancing, chess, backgammon, lectures, even learning a language) makes it an ideal spot to hibernate.

The cost, as at most health farms, varies according to the type of accommodation you prefer – a very comfortable room or an unashamedly luxurious suite – and includes many (but by no means all) of the treatments, consultations, accommodation, food, exercises and activities. Expect to fork out at least £250–300 a week.

Three main motives lure inmates to Champneys – the need to slim, relax or train. Footballers, pulchritudinous starlets, plentitudinous tycoons, a smattering of Middle-Eastern businessmen, tired execs and convalescents are among visitors you regularly find there.

Add the adjacent 700 acres of National Trust protected countryside to the 47 acres of Hampshire belonging to Grayshott Hall and you can see why assorted MPs, diplomats, and the Duke and Duchess of Bedford have been known to come and hide or de-toxify there. The Hall itself is a carefully reconstructed Victorian home with some fifty new rooms added since Alfred, Lord Tennyson stayed there a century ago. Though not providing so many extra-cure-icular activities as glossy Champneys, you can always hop off for a spot of trout fishing at nearby Waggoner's Wells, and there's a fine billiard and snooker room. No chance of your getting pickled at Grayshott Hall as alcohol is strictly forbidden.

Equally impressive is Shrubland Hall Health Clinic which for years has ambushed aristos and their acolytes in pursuit of rest and peace. Built in 1740 on one of the highest points in Suffolk, the hall has been thoroughly modernized and equipped with treatment rooms. Nevertheless it defiantly remains a very grand country house with much of the original furniture and paintings preserved. Smaller than most health farms, it accommodates only forty people and, as well as general treatments, offers sinister-sounding 'manipulative therapies' and 'colonic irrigation' sessions for patients demanding them. A word of warning: cooked meals are not provided and, even if you're not there to lose weight, you must accept a raw food diet. Sybarites a little weary of stoic jogs, gym and squash and preferring a softer treatment should head for Stobo Castle in Peebleshire, the newest and most northerly mecca for improving well-being, taking only a maximum of twenty-six people with a ratio of one member of staff per guest. Ambience is more like a holiday than an enforced rest.

Stobo is exceptionally strong on beauty therapy (being under the direction of Gayner Winyard, past Chairman of the Society of Health and Beauty therapists) and jaded jet set waifs can receive all the pampering they crave. Joan Collins, Miss World, Lulu, Peter Gabriel come here. Though, as dashing young Stephen Winyard (ladies feel better the moment he smiles a welcome at the portals) explained, they do get a tremendous cross-section of types. A duchess was there one week with a Scottish lady lavatory cleaner occupying the room above.

The régime is definitely less strict than most, with protein-rich low calorie delicacies like grouse or fresh trout popping up in the banqueting hall.

Bountiful buffets are a speciality at the Savoy-group-owned Forest Mere in Hampshire. As you approach the splendid manor house overlooking the placid mere which gives the place it's name, you feel you've been tossed into a time warp into which Merrie England may well still be tucked, uncompromisingly British but far from stuffy. Celebrities, an ex-governor of an African State or two, the odd Royal have all crossed it's rather genteel threshold. But alcohol is un-equivocally out, as Victoria Principal, star of TV's *Dallas*, discovered when, after an attempted champagne-coup, she was courteously expelled.

You can imagine a no more therapeutic setting: rhododendrons blob the sweeping lawn with mauve; ducks waddle idly towards the lake, and the whole wonderful wooded vista is surmounted by Hampshire's evergreen hillocks.

For the unfortunate few who can't take time off for a week's retreat there are alternatives. At Brighton's luxury, sea-fronted Metropole, for a budget sum of around £35 including VAT, you can buy a 'healthy weekend'. There you submit to all the comforts of a four star hotel as well as benefiting from the amenities of its immaculate health hydro, run by Ron Jacobs, a wizard masseur who's been rubbing tensions from the backs of the famous for fifteen years.

Sometimes a bit of polishing can be a way of improving your image, and if you can't get to the sun, all you need do is nip into London's luxurious Uvasun Centre. Without fear of burning or shrivelling up, an hour's bask produces a bronzed gleam comparable to a day in the Caribbean sun. Donald Sutherland, Susan Hampshire and others who are too busy or impatient to cultivate a tan on a beach are among the habituées.

A final word of warning: if you do head down to the health farm, beware. Like all life's luxuries, once you've acquired the taste the habit may be hard to kick.

ADDRESSES

A list of health farms can be obtained from the English Tourist Board, 4 Grosvenor Gardens, London SW1 0DU. Individual details from:

Champneys, Tring, Hertfordshire (tel Berkhamsted 3351).

Forest Mere, Liphook, Hants (tel Liphook 2051).

Grayshott Hall Health Centre, Grayshott, Nr Hindhead, Surrey (tel Hindhead 4331).

Shrubland Hall Health Clinic, Coddenham, Suffolk (tel Ipswich 830404).

Stobo Castle, Stobo, Peebleshire, Scotland (tel Stobo 249).

Metropole Health Club, Metropole Hotel, Brighton, Sussex (tel Brighton 775432).

Uvasun Centre, 25 Albemarle Street, London W1 (tel 01 491 4309).

THE CHELTENHAM NATIONAL HUNT MEETING
by George Hill

Lions and tigers, firework parties and public breakfasts and, on the Monarch's birthday, or something equally important like the first day of the races, Mr Van Ambergh's 'stupendous elephant swimming in Pittville Lake' – such were the temptations that once drew the multitudes to Cheltenham.

Now all it takes is three days of racing in the middle of March to make the handsome Regency spa the centre of the first big social event of the year – the National Hunt Festival, the premier jumping meeting in the British racing calendar.

Quieter now is the famed Pittville Pump Room which made Cheltenham a social magnet in the mid-19th century after the Duke of Wellington cured himself of a liver disorder with 'the waters', the only drinkable natural alkaline waters in the country.

Visit the town during Festival week, however, and you may be forgiven for thinking that half the population of England, and the entire population of Ireland, has descended around you. For although Cheltenham celebrates more festivals than any other town in Britain, to most people, and certainly the Irish, the March event is the jewel in the crown.

No Royal Ascot formality of dress or social exclusivity operates here. All you need is insulation from the bracing blasts sweeping down from Cleeve Hill, a sharp ear to decipher the congested tapestry of accents from every level of British life compressed with traditional good humour into a relatively restricted area, and a determination to keep your head and your money about you while all around you will be losing theirs.

Cheltenham is the perfect antidote to Sir Abe Bailey's famous comment: 'I do not say that all those who go racing are rogues and vagabonds, but I do say that all rogues and vagabonds seem to go racing.' Indeed, Harriett, Lady Ashburton's equally well-known observation is much more apposite: 'If I were to begin life again, I would go to the turf to get friends. They seem to me to be the only people who really hold together. I don't know why; it may be that each knows something that might hang the other, but the effect is delightful and most peculiar.'

The old Cheltenham image of crusty retired army officers and magisterial matrons with which the town was so long associated now seems to have faded away, to be replaced with a sunnier, busier and more open atmosphere; and perhaps we have the benign influence of the good-humoured Irish racing army to thank for that.

'The Irish are boisterous and there are always so many of them. But they are charming and so much fun, despite the problems that their enthusiasm sometimes brings,' says David Dodd, general manager of the famous Queen's Hotel, as important a centre of racing activity as the racecourse itself.

The Queen's must figure high on anyone's agenda for the week, because, although you are unlikely to find yourself a room there – 'We're usually fully booked by the end of race week for the following year,' says Dodd – a visit to its famous bar any evening after racing is something every racegoer ought to do once.

For the price of a drink you will rub shoulders with owners, trainers, gamblers and celebrities of all kinds and, if you look extra carefully, a contingent of special branch police officers whose job it is to mingle at all times as unobtrusively as possible.

The security is necessary because at the Queen's Hotel you will not only be in close proximity to an intense concentration of large sums of money, but you are also likely to get a glimpse of the famous trophies that go with the meeting's two top races, the Gold Cup and the Champion Hurdle.

It is not unknown for a celebrating owner to have one of the glittering prizes paraded proudly for all to admire and the hotel often faces the responsibility of a cup's safe custody.

Such celebrations bring the town to life every night and the effort to share in or witness them is well worth while. Some require more seeing through than others, of course, as poor David Dodd and the weary staff at the Queen's Hotel will confirm. 'Last year,' says Dodd, 'we finally thought we'd got them all off to bed by about 4 am on Gold Cup eve. I was just completing my rounds when I discovered a party of our Irish friends playing pitch-and-toss in the foyer.

A quick eavesdrop suggested that confrontation might not

A quiet glass after The Cup

be the wisest policy, so I tiptoed to the lights, switched them off and left them in darkness. They carried on playing.'

The success rate of the Irish at Cheltenham is phenomenal. Trainers big and small, from plush yards run on sophisticated lines to remote farms in unknown backwaters, spend most of the year preparing to keep it that way. All their compatriots are aware of that fact, so, armed to the teeth every year with old form books and new punts, they proceed to jam every flight and ferry to give Cheltenham a bigger accommodation problem than the rest of the year put together.

Angela Rowlands, Cheltenham's Tourist Information Officer, expects to place upwards of 3,000 people alone just walking in off the street with casual enquiries.

'How we fit them in I never know. Advance bookings normally cover all the hotels and even most of the guest houses. But we have lists of every possible accommodation and, by juggling with cancellations and a miracle or two, we somehow get by.'

The racecourse now boasts a spectacular new grandstand, which was opened in March 1979. Before its advent, a useful requirement for the Festival was a period of intensive rugby or wrestling tuition in order to cover any distance in excess of 10 yards in something less than a yard or so a minute.

Life at the first meeting up on Cleeve Hill in 1819, when the Duke of Gloucester presented the prizes for flat racing, couldn't have been much less uncomfortable, despite the exposure to the spectacular winds that later drove the course to be re-sited on safer ground.

Now the visitor can make the most of the excellent racing in relatively civilized comfort and take maximum advantage of the efforts of Letheby and Christopher, caterers to Cheltenham for fifty-four years. The sophisticated offerings they make available for the lucky élite in the private boxes are not far removed from the 10,000 lunches they serve in the delightful Prestbury Suite, where if you wish you can book in advance for lunch or tea.

March might not seem to be the perfect time for them to have available ten tons of ice, but with over 5,000 bottles of wine and champagne to chill perhaps it's understandable. Another 13,000 lb of meat, 5,000 lb of vegetables and 80 gallons of double cream, all dealt with by over 1,200 staff, demands an operation that few will give a thought to but all ought to be grateful for.

Five bars are available in the Members' stand, for which a reduced badge can be bought covering all three days, which also gives access to the Members' lawn and all steppings on the front of the new stand.

Entrance on all three days is £15 per day for the Members' enclosure (£40 for a three-day badge); £8 (£10 on Gold Cup day) for Tattersalls (access to grandstand and paddock but not to the Members' enclosure); course enclosure £3 (£4 on Gold Cup day). Public car park is £2 per day.

Cheltenham is situated off the A40, eight miles north-east of Gloucester and the course, well sign-posted, is one mile north of the town on the road to Evesham.

The Tourist Information Office is located on the tree-lined Promenade, as is the Queen's Hotel, in the centre of the town.

The Hotel de la Bere, complete with country club, is another popular venue for regular visitor; the Golden Valley and Lilleybrook Hotels are others with high reputations.

Whether you leave, as the talented and ebullient Irish trainer Mick O'Toole recently did, with a record £55,000 Tote Jackpot in your pocket or simply with the experience behind you of a unique British social occasion, you will carry the memory of it all with you for a long time.

DETAILS:

Tourist Information Office, Promenade, Cheltenham (tel 0242 22878).

Cheltenham Racecourse, Prestbury Park, Cheltenham (tel 0242 513014).

Racecourse luncheon or tea reservations (tel 0242 41150).

Queen's Hotel, Promenade, Cheltenham (tel 0242 514724).

Hotel de la Bere, Southam, Cheltenham (tel 0242 37771).

Golden Valley Hotel, Gloucester Road, Cheltenham (tel 0242 32691).

Lilleybrook Hotel, Cirencester Road, Charlton Kings, Cheltenham (tel 0242 25861).

WEDDINGS *by Neil Mackwood*

Weddings are nobody's favourite form of entertainment. Above all they are a duty, things to be attended to please someone else. The aftermath of weddings, such as the familiar dry champagne-mouth and morose feeling of anti-climax, makes one swear that one will never attend another. But one does.

And yet this absurd ceremony is 'the most important day in the life of' the courageous couple who have decided to go

213

through the long walk up the aisle. According to the Statistical Office more people are doing it every year. The pill and countless devices like it, endless advice from feminist columnists and the divorce figures do not seem to deter the young and idealistic from swearing allegiance, until death do them part, under the eyes of some stained-glass God.

Some couples later confess that they went through with the charade to satisfy their parents, or a stuffy but rich aunt who would have boycotted anything other than a full Church service; the more honest ones admit to feelings of tradition and pomp.

Weddings are enormously useful to some people, as they are ideal vehicles for the social show-off. The opportunities are endless. The best of everything can be produced, the most expensive tent hired, liveried staff on hand, quantities of vintage champagne, distinguished guests in abundance and with a bit of luck a pretty bride on display in antique family veil and a dress which has had the seamstress up all night.

The hallmark of a successful wedding is one where all the stresses are hidden from the guests and the appearance given is that it has hardly been planned at all. Any hostess marrying off her daughter will be anxious to preserve her reputation and do things as they should be done – which is where the dilemma starts. How do you put on a do which is lavish yet tasteful, extravagant but not showy? Should the tent be lined? Certainly. The champagne vintage? Certainly. A toastmaster employed? Definitely. Flowers in abundance? Absolutely. Liveried staff? That's kitsch. There is such a thing as instinctive good taste but only a few of the few really have it, just as only a few men really like women – but that is another problem.

Royal Ascot and upper class weddings seem to have much in common, apart from the obvious fact that the men dress up in the everyday dress of our Victorian forebears and the women climb into the new dress that they have demanded from their husbands for the occasion. At both occasions the social kiss will be fully employed, and after all that smooching

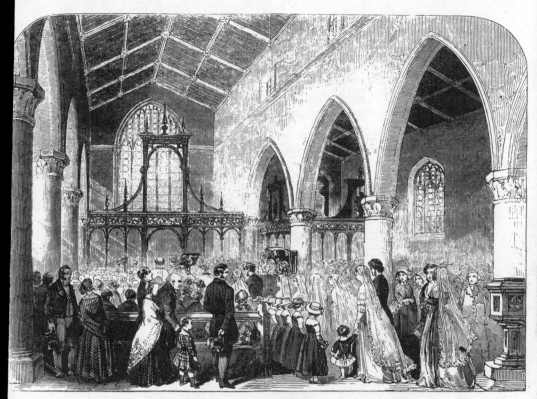

A Society wedding

in the line-up I have always thought what an unhygienic proposition the bride must be.

Of course quite another type of wedding exists and it is not a question of rich and poor or taste versus the conspicuous lack of it. Weddings are as good an indicator of class as lichens are at indicating pollution. Even an Icelandic cod fisherman would notice the difference between a wedding where morning dress is the order and another where the blue suit is ubiquitous. Emotion is generally in short supply at upper-class weddings, probably because they got over separations (mothers from sons – fathers from daughters) when the children were packed off to prep school at the age of seven or eight. But blue suit weddings often overflow with emotion and tears – 'Doesn't our Doreen look lovely?'; 'They make a lovely couple' – and talk of babies will be in the air. The parents will genuinely feel they are losing a daughter or a son whereas the uppers will be turning their thoughts to the deal struck. Either young Camilla will have done well, because young Tom is heir to a considerable fortune or a title, or will have caused concern by marrying out of the social group. Everyone knows that love is all very well – but love alone?

England being England, everything from the hired transport to the confetti is class-ridden. An abundance of Cortinas swathed in shiny silver ribbon with Jim and Pat written across the windscreen, behind which a pair of mini-football-boots swings from the mirror, is evidence of a working man's wedding. The middle-middles overdo it by hiring one too many antique Rolls-Royces and having more than one photographer to record the happy day. The really smart have taken to video-taping their receptions so that they have a living, moving record of the auspicious day. Some nobs rather like involving the horse at weddings; the rich usually provide a helicopter; the middles make do with a Rolls or limo, and the others: well, it's back to the Cortinas. The patrons of the Ford Motor Co are also inclined to throw rice or confetti with rather too large horseshoes in among the blow-away bits of pink raffia. Guests at such weddings also favour large red roses or carnations for buttonholes, despite the absence of the necessary incisions in their blue suits.

Wealth has a definite advantage when choosing a smart place to hold the reception. One's club, the better class hotel or garden wins out over the local WMC or village hall. And it is only the rich who can afford to hire a choir like those of the Brompton Oratory, St Peter's, Eaton Square or Winchester Cathedral. Getting together the right assemblage of ecclesiastics is a bonus. How often one has read among the wedding reports in the paper, 'The bride wore a veil of Honiton lace, carried a bouquet of stephanotis and was attended by the Hon Hugo Maltravers and Lucinda fforde-Abbots, the bridegroom's cousins . . . The Bishop of Salisbury, the bride's uncle, officiated, assisted by the Rev Jeremy Child-Okeford, the bridegroom's brother.' Of course we are all equal in the eyes of God; it's just that some are more equal than others.

There is no better time for one-upmanship than at weddings. The presence of Royalty in one's wedding snaps can hardly be topped, especially if you have the Earl of Lichfield or Tony Snowdon taking them.

To whatever socio-economic class one belongs (or one thinks one belongs) the end product, as far as marriage is concerned, is the same. A lifetime spent together, as the dour Robert Louis Stevenson reminded us, is a battle 'not a bed of roses'! The urbanized Anglo-Saxon Protestant and his fellow Christians have done everything to desymbolize the wedding service. That matches life in the Egalitarian Eighties. No stamping on glasses for us, no public witnessing of the consummation, no fertility rites or pinning money on to the bride.

No, it has come down to a bearable three-quarters-of-an-hour church service followed by the secular delights of the champagne and sausage rolls or whatever. Bernard Shaw had his own theory as to why so many couples go through the hoop: 'Marriage is popular because it combines the maximum of temptation with the maximum of opportunity.'

He could just be right, and, come springtime, when the sap begins to rise, the announcement pages in the *Daily Telegraph* and *The Times* will once again fill with names of young hopefuls, blissfully unaware of the obstacle race which they will have to undergo before climbing into the marriage bed.

OTHER EVENTS IN MARCH

Horse and Hound Ball, Grosvenor House Hotel, London.
Highland Ball, Claridge's, London.
Pitlochry Festival Theatre Season opens, Pitlochry, Scotland.
Daily Mail Ideal Home Exhibition, Earls Court, London.
St David's Day Dinner, Savoy Hotel, London.

Chalfont Dinner, Savoy Hotel, London.
Edinburgh Folk Festival.
Rugby: Scotland v. Ireland, Edinburgh.
National Stamp Exhibition, New Horticultural Hall,
 London.
BUPA Doctor of the Year Luncheon, Savoy Hotel, London.
Racing: Sandown Park (Horse and Hound Grand Military
 Gold Cup).
Racing: Doncaster (William Hill Lincoln Handicap).
Isle of Wight Music Festival.
English Cross Country Union Championships, Parliament
 Hill.
Dungannon Music Festival, County Tyrone, Ireland.
Racing: Ulster Harp National, Downpatrick, County Down,
 Ireland.
Camden Festival, Camden, London.
Scottish National Road Relay Championships, Strathclyde
 Park.
International Spring Fair, National Exhibition Centre,
 Birmingham.
Chelsea Antiques Fair, Old Town Hall, Chelsea.
Observer Festival of Theatre, Oxford.
Pytchley Hunt Point-to-Point, Gildborough.
Taunton Vale Hunts Point-to-Point, Ilminster, Somerset.
Tideway Head of River Race, Putney to Mortlake.
Institute of Directors Annual Convention, Albert Hall,
 London.
International Food and Drink Exhibition, Olympia, London.
Rugby: England v. France, Twickenham.
Rugby: England v. Wales, Cardiff.
British Open Single Barrel Clay Pigeon Shooting
 Championships, Notts.
Sunningdale Foursomes Golf, Sunningdale, Berkshire.
Kipling Cotes Derby, Humberside.
National Heavy Horse Show, Peterborough,
 Cambridgeshire.
Racing: Sandown Park (Royal Artillery Meeting).

Beautfort Hunt Point-to-Point, Badminton, Gloucestershire.
Boat and Leisure Show, National Exhibition Centre,
  Birmingham.
Dole Ceremony, Tichborne,
All England Badminton Championships, Wembley,
  London.

The Perfect Hostess

by Rose Henniker Heaton

First published in 1931, this charming book of rhyming rules is a nostalgic look at that bygone era when the perfect wife always thought men knew best and the perfect host met his guests at the station with chauffeur, footmen and Rolls-Royce. Illustrated with delightful period line drawings, *The Perfect Hostess* covers everything from simple rules for simple servants to little comforts for the bachelor's room. Filled with menus for every occasion, this is the perfect gift for any hostess.

£3.95

Debrett's Peerage Limited
73-77 Britannia Road
London SW6 2JR

MARIE CURIE
1867–1934

The Marie Curie Memorial Foundation

A unique independent organisation dedicated to the welfare of those with cancer, supported by voluntary contributions, interest-free loans and bequests. This worthy cause needs your help - to the extent of nearly £5 million annually simply to maintain, for those in need, its vital humanitarian services.

These include, within the United Kingdom, eleven residential Nursing Homes, nationwide Home Nurses, Welfare Needs in kind, an Enquiry and Advice Bureau together with specialised Research Laboratories contributing to the understanding of the cancer problem. Will you please help?

If you require further details or wish now to respond to this appeal, or perhaps interest others, please write to the Secretary at:-

THE MARIE CURIE MEMORIAL FOUNDATION
124 Sloane Street, LONDON SW1X 9BP
Tel: 01-730 9157

PATRON: Her Majesty Queen Elizabeth The Queen Mother

No genuine call for help remains unanswered

January brings the boats,
Feb, Crufts champions' glossy coats,
March at Cheltenham breaks the punter,
April's eventing tests the hunter,
May brings RA crowds (a menace),
June brings balls (both May and tennis),
July sees Lord's, for Eton v. Harrow,
August, Cowes - and you're soaked to the marrow,
September for Gatherings (especially Braemar's),
October, the Motor Show's Japanese cars,
November for Wall games, treason and plot,
December for presents that cost you a lot.

MORAL:
IF YOU GO TO ALL THESE,
BOTH TO SEE AND BE SEEN,
YOU *MUST* BE A READER OF
HARPERS & QUEEN!